The Holocaust

THE HOLOCAUST:
THEORETICAL READINGS

Edited by
Neil Levi and Michael Rothberg

EDINBURGH UNIVERSITY PRESS

© Introductions, selection and editorial
materials, Neil Levi and Michael Rothberg,
2003

Edinburgh University Press Ltd
22 George Square, Edinburgh

Typeset in Sabon and Gill Sans
by Bibliocraft Ltd, Dundee, and
printed and bound in Great Britain by
Cromwell Press Ltd, Trowbridge

A CIP record for this book is available from
the British Library

ISBN 0 7486 1654 3 (hardback)
ISBN 0 7486 1655 1 (paperback)

The right of the contributors to be
identified as authors of this work has been
asserted in accordance with the Copyright,
Designs and Patents Act 1988.

CONTENTS

Acknowledgements   xi

Publisher's Acknowledgements   xiii

About this book   xix

General Introduction   1

PART I: **THEORY AND EXPERIENCE**

Introduction   25

1   *The Drowned and the Saved*
    Primo Levi   29

2   'Resentments'
    Jean Améry   36

3   *Days and Memory*
    Charlotte Delbo   45

4   'The Camps'
    Ruth Kluger   50

PART II: **HISTORICIZING THE HOLOCAUST?**

Introduction   59

5   'On the Public Use of History'
    Jürgen Habermas   63

6   'The "Final Solution": On the Unease in Historical
    Interpretation'
    Saul Friedlander   69

7   'Historical Understanding and Counterrationality:
    The Judenrat as Epistemological Vantage'
    Dan Diner   75

8   'The Uniqueness and Normality of the Holocaust'
    Zygmunt Bauman   82

9 'The European Imagination in the Age of Total War'
   Omer Bartov   89

10 *The Origins of the Nazi Genocide*
    Henry Friedlander   96

PART III: NAZI CULTURE, FASCISM, AND ANTISEMITISM

Introduction   103

11 'The Rhetoric of Hitler's "Battle"'
    Kenneth Burke   107

12 'The Psychological Structure of Fascism'
    Georges Bataille   113

13 'Elements of Anti-Semitism'
    Max Horkheimer and Theodor W. Adorno   121

14 'The Fiction of the Political'
    Philippe Lacoue-Labarthe   127

15 'Anti-Semitism and National Socialism'
    Moishe Postone   132

16 'Ordinary Men'
    Christopher Browning   140

PART IV: RACE, GENDER, AND GENOCIDE

Introduction   147

17 'Floods, Bodies, History'
    Klaus Theweleit   151

18 'Racism and Sexism in Nazi Germany'
    Gisela Bock   160

19 'The Unethical and the Unspeakable:
    Women and the Holocaust'
    Joan Ringelheim   169

20 'Women and the Holocaust:
    Analyzing Gender Difference'
    Pascale Rachel Bos   178

PART V: PSYCHOANALYSIS, TRAUMA, AND MEMORY

Introduction   189

21 'Trauma and Experience'
    Cathy Caruth   192

22 'Trauma, Absence, Loss'
    Dominick LaCapra   199

23   'Trauma and Transference'
     Saul Friedlander   206

24   'History Beyond the Pleasure Principle:
     Some Thoughts on the Representation
     of Trauma'
     Eric L. Santner   214

25   'Bearing Witness or the Vicissitudes of Listening'
     Dori Laub   221

PART VI: **QUESTIONS OF RELIGION, ETHICS, AND JUSTICE**

     Introduction   229

26   'Thinking the Tremendum'
     Arthur A. Cohen   233

27   'To Mend the World'
     Emil L. Fackenheim   237

28   'Ethics and Spirit'
     Emmanuel Levinas   241

29   *Eichmann in Jerusalem*
     Hannah Arendt   246

30   'What is a Camp?'
     Giorgio Agamben   252

31   *The Differend*
     Jean-François Lyotard   257

32   'New Political Theology – Out of Holocaust
     and Liberation'
     Gillian Rose   263

PART VII: **LITERATURE AND CULTURE AFTER AUSCHWITZ**

     Introduction   273

33   'Theses on the Philosophy of History'
     Walter Benjamin   277

34   'Cultural Criticism and Society'
     Theodor W. Adorno   280

35   'Meditations on Metaphysics'
     Theodor W. Adorno   282

36   'Writing and the Holocaust'
     Irving Howe   288

37 'Non-Philosophical Amazement – Writing in
    Amazement: Benjamin's Position in the
    Aftermath of the Holocaust'
    Sigrid Weigel   291

38 *The Writing of the Disaster*
    Maurice Blanchot   299

39 'Shibboleth'
    Jacques Derrida   306

40 'Language and Culture after the Holocaust'
    Geoffrey H. Hartman   313

41 'Representing Auschwitz'
    Sidra DeKoven Ezrahi   318

PART VIII: MODES OF NARRATION

Introduction   325

42 'The Moral Space of Figurative Discourse'
    Berel Lang   329

43 'Writing the Holocaust'
    James E. Young   335

44 'The Modernist Event'
    Hayden White   339

45 'Against Foreshadowing'
    Michael André Bernstein   346

46 'Deep Memory: The Buried Self'
    Lawrence L. Langer   354

47 'The Return of the Voice:
    Claude Lanzmann's *Shoah*'
    Shoshana Felman   360

PART IX: RETHINKING VISUAL CULTURE

Introduction   371

48 *Reflections of Nazism*
    Saul Friedlander   375

49 'Holocaust'
    Jean Baudrillard   380

50 'Anselm Kiefer: the Terror of History,
    the Temptation of Myth'
    Andreas Huyssen   383

51 'The Aesthetic Transformation of the Image
    of the Unimaginable: Notes on Claude
    Lanzmann's *Shoah*'
    Gertrud Koch   389

52 'In Plain Sight'
    Lilliane Weissberg   396

PART X: LATECOMERS: NEGATIVE SYMBIOSIS,
            POSTMEMORY, AND COUNTERMEMORY

Introduction   407

53 'Memory Shot Through with Holes'
    Henri Raczymow   410

54 'Mourning and Postmemory'
    Marianne Hirsch   416

55 'Negative Symbiosis:
    Germans and Jews after Auschwitz'
    Dan Diner   423

56 'The Countermonument: Memory Against
    Itself in Germany'
    James E. Young   431

PART XI: UNIQUENESS, COMPARISON, AND THE
            POLITICS OF MEMORY

Introduction   441

57 'Two Kinds of Uniqueness:
    The Universal Aspects of the Holocaust'
    Alan Milchman and Alan Rosenberg   444

58 'What Was the Holocaust?'
    Yehuda Bauer   451

59 *The Black Atlantic*
    Paul Gilroy   455

60 'Thinking about Genocide'
    Mahmood Mamdani   461

61 'Dare to Compare: Americanizing the Holocaust'
    Lilian Friedberg   468

62 *The Holocaust in American Life*
    Peter Novick   474

Index   481

ACKNOWLEDGEMENTS

Our first thanks must go to our editor, Jackie Jones. Without her insight and enthusiasm this volume would not have been possible. We are deeply grateful to James Dale for his remarkable efforts to secure reprint permissions and his patient care in overseeing the latter stages of the manuscript's production. Carol Macdonald of Edinburgh University Press provided much needed logistical advice and assistance.

We are indebted to Bryan Cheyette, Geoffrey Hartman, and Dominick LaCapra for their valuable feedback and support, and also wish to express our gratitude to our able research assistants Ausra Paulauskiene and Kate Scherler, as well as to the participants in the Jewish Studies Workshop at the University of Illinois, who helped bring final shape to the collection, and to Jennifer Uleman, for her sensitive reading of the general introduction. Work on this book was facilitated by support from the University of Illinois Research Board and a Drew University summer research grant. Ryan Saylor and Dan Tracy compiled the index.

As always, Beth Drenning and Yasemin Yildiz offered illuminating advice, detailed commentary, general moral support, and much more.

PUBLISHER'S ACKNOWLEDGEMENTS

Grateful acknowledgement is made to the following sources for permission to reproduce material previously published elsewhere. Every effort has been made to trace the copyright holders, but if any have been inadvertently overlooked, the publisher will be pleased to make the necessary arrangements at the first opportunity.

Reprinted with permission of Simon & Schuster Adult Publishing Group from *The Drowned and the Saved* by Primo Levi. Translated by Raymond Rosenthal. English translation © 1988 by Simon & Schuster, Inc.

Améry, Jean (1980), 'Resentments', in J. Améry, *At the Mind's Limits: Contemplations by a Survivor on Auschwitz and its Realities*, trans. S. Rosenfeld and S. P. Rosenfeld, by permission of Indiana University Press and Granta Books.

Delbo, Charlotte, *Days and Memory*, trans. with a preface by R. Lamont, Evanston: Northwestern University Press, 2001. © 1990 Rosette Lamont. Originally published in French as *La Mémoire et les jours*. © 1985 Berg international éditeurs, Paris. Reprinted by permission of Northwestern University Press.

From *Still Alive: A Holocaust Girlhood Remembered*, © 2001 by Ruth Kluger, by permission of the Feminist Press at the City University of New York, www.feministpress.org and by permission of Bloomsbury Press in the UK.

Habermas, Jürgen (1989), 'On the Public Use of History', *The New Conservatism: Cultural Criticism and the Historians' Debate*, ed. and trans. by Shierry Weber Nicholsen, MIT Press. © 1989 Massachusetts Institute of Technology. © Suhrkamp Verlag Frankfurt am Main 1987.

Memory, History, and the Extermination of the Jews of Europe, by Saul Friedlander. © 1993 by Saul Friedlander. Reprinted by permission of Georges Borchardt, Inc.

Diner, Dan, 'Historical Understanding and Counterrationality: The Judenrat as Epistemological Vantage', *Beyond the Conceivable: Studies on Germany, Nazism, and the Holocaust.* © 2000 by The Regents of University of California.

Reprinted from Zygmunt Bauman: *Modernity and the Holocaust.* © 1989 by Zygmunt Bauman. Used by permission of the publisher, Cornell University Press, and also by permission of Blackwell Publishing Ltd.

From *Murder in our Midst: The Holocaust, Industrial Killing and Representation* by Omer Bartov, © 1996 by Oxford University Press, Inc. Used by permission of Oxford University Press, Inc.

From *The Origins of Nazi Genocide: From Euthanasia to the Final Solution* by Henry Friedlander. © 1995 by the University of North Carolina Press. Used by permission of the publisher.

Burke, Kenneth, *The Philosophy of Literary Form*, 3rd edn rev., University of California Press. © 1974 The Regents of the University of California.

Bataille, Georges, 'The Psychological Structure of Fascism', trans. Carl R. Lovitt, *New German Critique* 16 (Winter 1979), pp. 137–59 reprinted by permission of Telos Press Ltd.

Dialectic of Enlightenment by Max Horkheimer and Theodor W. Adorno. English translation © 1972 by Herder and Herder. Reprinted by permission of The Continuum International Publishing Company.

Lacoue-Labarthe, Philippe, *Heidegger, Art and Politics: the Fiction of the Political*, trans. by Chris Turner. Basil Blackwell, 1990. Reproduced by permission of Blackwell Publishing.

Postone, Moishe, 'Anti-Semitism and National Socialism: Notes on the German Reaction to "Holocaust"', *New German Critique*, 19 (Winter 1980, pp. 97–115). Reproduced by permissions of *New German Critique*.

Browning, Christopher R., *Ordinary Men: Reserve Police Battalion 101 and the Final Solution in Poland.* © 1992, 1998 by Christopher Browning. Reprinted by permission of HarperCollins Publishers Inc.

Theweleit, Klaus, 'Floods, Bodies, History', *Male Fantasies, 1. Women, Floods, Bodies, History*, University of Minnesota Press. Originally published in Germany as *Männerphantasien*, Volume 1. *Frauen, Fluten, Körper, Geschichte.* © 1977 by Verlag Roter Stern. English translation © 1987 by the University of Minnesota. Reprinted in the UK by permission of Blackwell Publishing.

Bock, Gisela, 'Racism and Sexism in Nazi Germany: Motherhood, Compulsory Sterilization, and the State', from Renate Bridenthal, Atina Grossman and Marion Kaplan (eds), *When Biology Became Destiny: Women in Weimar and Nazi Germany*, New York: Monthly Review Press, 1984. Reproduced by permission of Monthly Review Press.

Ringelheim, Joan Miriam (1984), 'The Unethical and Unspeakable: Women and the Holocaust', *Simon Wiesenthal Center Annual*, vol. 1. Reproduced by permission of the Simon Wiesenthal Center.

Pascale Rachel Bos, 'Women and the Holocaust: Analyzing Gender Difference'. Reprinted from *Experience and Expression: Women and the Holocaust* by Elizabeth Baer and Myrna Goldenberg (eds), 2003 with the permission of the Wayne State University Press. © Wayne State University Press.

Caruth, Cathy, (ed.), *Trauma: Explorations of Memory*, pp. 3–12. © 1995 by The Johns Hopkins University Press. Reprinted with permission of The Johns Hopkins University Press.

LaCapra, Dominick, *Critical Inquiry*, Summer, University of Chicago Press. © 1999 by The University of Chicago.

Reprinted by permission of the publisher from 'History Beyond the Pleasure Principle' by Eric L. Santer in *Probing the Limits of Representation: Nazism and the 'Final Solution'*, edited by Saul Friedlander, pp. 143–53, Cambridge, MA: Harvard University Press, © 1992 by the President and Fellows of Harvard College.

© 1992 by Routledge, Chapman and Hall, Inc. from Laub, Dori, 'Bearing Witness or the Vicissitudes of Listening', *Testimony: Crises of Witnessing in Literature, Psychoanalysis, and History* edited by S. Felman and D. Laub. Reproduced by permission of Routledge, Inc., part of the Taylor and Francis Group.

The Tremendum: A Theological Interpretation of the Holocaust by Arthur A. Cohen. © 1981 by the author. Reprinted by permission of The Continuum International Publishing Company.

To Mend the World: Foundations of Post-Holocaust Thought, by Emil L. Fackenheim. © 1982, 1989, 1994 by Emil L. Fackenheim. Reprinted by permission of Georges Borchardt, Inc., for the author.

Levinas, Emmanuel. *Difficult Freedom: Essays on Judaism*. pp. 6–10, 296. © 1990. Reprinted with permission of The Johns Hopkins University Press. © 1990 The Athlone Press. Reproduced with permission of Continuum International Publishing Group Ltd. French edition: © Editions Albin Michel 1963 and 1976.

"Epilogue", from *Eichmann in Jerusalem* by Hannah Arendt, © 1963, 1964 by Hannah Arendt. Used by permission of Viking Penguin, a division of Penguin Group (USA) Inc.

Agamben, Giorgio, 'What is a Camp?', *Means without End: Notes on Politics*, trans. Vincenzo Binetti and Cesare Casarino, University of Minnesota Press. Originally published in Italy as *Mezzi senza fine*. © 1996 Bollati Boringhieri editore s.r.l. English translation © 2000 by the Regents of the University of Minnesota.

Lyotard, Jean-François, *The Differend: Phrases in Dispute*, trans. Georges Van Den Abbeele, University of Minnesota Press. Originally published in France as *Le Différend* © 1983 by Les Éditions de Minuit. English translation © 1988 by the University of Minnesota.

Rose, Gillian, 'New Jerusalem Old Athens: The Holy Middle', *The Broken Middle: Out of Our Ancient Society*. Blackwell Publishers. Reproduced by permission of Blackwell Publishing.

Excerpts from 'Theses on the Philosophy of History' from in *Illuminations* by Walter Benjamin, © 1955 by Suhrkamp Verlag, Frankfurt a.M., English translation by Harry Zohn © 1968 and renewed 1996 by Harcourt, Inc., reprinted by permission of Harcourt, Inc. This essay will be included in a forthcoming volume of the *Selected Writings of Walter Benjamin* to be published by Harvard University Press.

Adorno, Theodor W., 'Cultural Criticism and Society', *Prisms*, trans. S. and S. Weber, Cambridge, MA: The MIT Press. © Theodor W Adorno, 1967.

Negative Dialectics by Theodor W. Adorno. English language translation © 1973 by The Continuum Publishing Company. Reprinted by permission of The Continuum International Publishing Company.

Howe, Irving, 'Writing and the Holocaust'. Reprinted by permission of *The New Republic*, © 1986, The New Republic, LLC.

Body- and image-space: Re-reading Walter Benjamin, by Sigrid Weigel, trans. G. Paul with R. McNicholl and J. Gaines, London and New York: Routledge, 1996. Reproduced by permission of the publishers.

Blanchot, Maurice, *The Writing of the Disaster*, trans. Ann Smock, Lincoln and London: University of Nebraska Press, 1995. Reproduced with the permission of University of Nebraska Press.

Derrida, Jacques, 'Shibboleth,' trans. Joshua Wilner, in Geoffrey Hartman and Sanford Budick (eds), *Midrash and Literature*, Yale University Press. © 1986 by Yale University.

Hartman, Geoffrey, 'Literature and Culture After the Holocaust', in *The Fateful Question of Culture*, New York: Columbia University Press. Reprinted by permission of the publisher.

Ezrahi, Sidra DeKoven, 'Representing Auschwitz,' *History and Memory* 7.2. Reprinted by permission of Indiana University Press.

Lang, Berel, *Act and Idea in the Nazi Genocide*, The University of Chicago Press, 1990,. Reprinted by permission of the author.

Young, James E., *Writing and Rewriting the Holocaust: Narrative and the Consequences of Interpretation*, Indiana University Press, 1990. Reprinted by permission of Indiana University Press.

White, Hayden. *Figural Realism: Studies in the Mimesis Effect*. pp. 66–72, 74, 79–82, 187, 189, 190. © 1999 The Johns Hopkins University Press. Reprinted with the permission of The Johns Hopkins University Press.

Bernstein, Michael André, *Foregone Conclusions: Against Apocalyptic History*. © 1994 by The Regents of the University of California.

Langer, Lawrence L., *Holocaust Testimonies: The Ruins of Memory*, Yale University Press. © 1991 by Yale University.

© 1992 by Routledge, Chapman and Hall, Inc. from Felman, Shoshana, 'The Return of the Voice: Claude Lanzmann's *Shoah*', *Testimony: Crises of*

Witnessing in Literature, Psychoanalysis, and History, edited by Shoshana Felman and Dori Laub. Reproduced by permission of Routledge, Inc., part of the Taylor and Francis Group.

Friedlander, Saul, *Reflections of Nazism: An Essay on Kitsch and Death*, reproduced by permission of the author.

Baudrillard, Jean, 'Holocaust', *Simulacra and Simulation*, trans. Sheila Faria Glaser, University of Michigan Press. English translation © by The University of Michigan 1994. Originally published in French by Editions Galilée 1981.

Andreas Huyssen, 'Anselm Kiefer: The Terror of History, The Temptation of Myth', *October*, 48 (Spring, 1989), pp. 25–45. © 1989 by October Magazine, Ltd. and the Massachusetts Institute of Technology.

Gertrud Koch (translated by Jamie Owen Daniel and Miriam Hansen), 'The Aesthetic Transformation of the Image of the Unimaginable: Notes on Claude Lanzmann's Shoah', *October*, 48 (Spring, 1989), pp. 15–24. © 1989 by October Magazine, Ltd. and the Massachusetts Institute of Technology.

Weissberg, Liliane, 'In Plain Sight', *Visual Culture and the Holocaust*, in ed. Barbie Zelizer. © 2001 by Rutgers, the State University Press. Reprinted by permission of Rutgers University Press.

Raczymow, Henri, 'Memory Shot Through with Holes', in *Yale French Studies 85, Discourses of Jewish Identity in Twentieth-Century France*, ed. and trans. A. Astro, Yale University Press.

Reprinted by permission of the publisher from *Family Frames: Photography, Narrative, and Postmemory* by Marianne Hirsch, pp. 22–3, 25, 31–4, 36–40, Cambridge, MA: Harvard University Press, © 1997 by the President and Fellows of Harvard College.

From *Reworking the Past* by Peter Baldwin. © 1990 by Peter Baldwin. Reprinted by permission of Beacon Press, Boston.

Young, James E., 'The Countermonument: Memory against Itself in Germany', in J. E. Young, *The Texture of Memory: Holocaust Memorials and Meaning*, New Yale University Press. © 1993 by Yale University.

Milchman, Alan and Alan Rosenberg, 'Two Kinds of Uniqueness: The Universal Aspects of the Holocaust', in R. Millen (ed.), *New Perspectives on the Holocaust: A Guide for Teachers and Scholars*, New York University Press, 1996. Reproduced by permission of the publisher.

Bauer, Yehuda, *Rethinking the Holocaust*, Yale University Press. © 2001 by Yale University.

Reprinted by permission of the publisher from *The Black Atlantic* by Paul Gilroy, pp. 20 56, 213–17, 248–51, Cambridge, MA: Harvard University Press, © 1993 by Paul Gilroy.

Mamdani, Mahmood; *When Victims Become Killers*. © 2001 by Princeton University Press. Reprinted by permission of Princeton University Press.

Friedberg, Lilian, 'Dare to Compare: Americanizing the Holocaust', *The American Indian Quarterly*, 24:3. Reprinted by permission of Indiana University Press.

PUBLISHER'S ACKNOWLEDGEMENTS

ABOUT THIS BOOK

The Holocaust: Theoretical Readings has been designed with a number of different readers in mind. The volume will introduce those who are new to study of the Holocaust to some of the fundamental concerns, challenges, and debates provoked by the Nazi genocide over the course of several decades. At the same time, readers who are already acquainted with the major issues that have emerged from study of the Holocaust will find the most important theoretical reflections on the Nazi genocide collected in one source for the first time.

Although the entries can of course be read in any order, we recommend looking over the general and section introductions first in order to get a sense of how the reader has been organized and why particular selections have been included. The general introduction maps out the field of Holocaust studies in an overarching way; it also offers a brief account of the emergence of scholarly and public interest in the Holocaust and some preliminary thoughts on the theoretical challenges posed by the events. Section introductions delve further into particular areas of concern and provide necessary context for the individual selections and themes. Each section also contains a selected bibliography of further readings in Holocaust studies as well as suggestions for companion readings in other areas of literary and cultural theory. These section introductions are meant to construct bridges for dialogue between Holocaust studies and other realms of contemporary intellectual engagement.

The Holocaust: Theoretical Readings is also designed for course use. We can imagine several different types of courses being built around this reader. It provides a basic outline and sufficient readings for a semester-long course on the theoretical implications of, and intellectual debates surrounding, the Nazi genocide. The reader could also be used as one of the main texts for an inter-disciplinary course in Holocaust studies. That is, it could be combined with a literary anthology like Lawrence Langer's *Art from the Ashes*, a collection of documents, such as Lucy Dawidowicz's *A Holocaust Reader*, or a historical reader, such as Omer Bartov's *The Holocaust: Origins, Implementation, Aftermath*, in order to provide a varied and comprehensive approach to the Holocaust. Finally, it could serve as one of the main texts for a course in literary theory or cultural studies. Instructors could either integrate the question of the Holocaust's theoretical implications into a course in twentieth-century or contemporary theory; or they could put the Holocaust at the center of the course and supplement it with the works of general theory mentioned in the intro-ductions and bibliographies.

In editing this volume, we have been acutely aware of the difficulties of col-lecting a comprehensive set of readings for a field that is already characterized by a vast range and profound depth of contributions and that continues to grow exponentially. Due to limitations on space, we have had to leave out the work of many important scholars, have had to leave aside further favorite contributions by some scholars who are included, and have, in most cases, had to make excerpts from entries that we would have preferred to leave intact. It is a tes-timony to the vibrancy and significance of the field of Holocaust studies that even as large a collection as this one can only cover a selection of the most important works. We urge readers to follow our suggestions for further reading.

GENERAL INTRODUCTION: THEORY AND THE HOLOCAUST

Neil Levi and Michael Rothberg

I

At the end of an essay on the role Jewish ghetto councils unwittingly played in the deportation of Jews to the Nazi death camps, historian Dan Diner claims that 'Auschwitz must be *thought* before it can be written about historically.'[1] Diner's conclusion may seem surprising coming from an historian, since it appears to subordinate concrete historical engagement with the events of the Holocaust to abstract reflection upon them. Yet his claim emerges out of an attempt to provide an historical explanation of those events – and out of a direct encounter with the limits of such explanation. Because the dilemmas the Nazis created for the inhabitants of Eastern Europe's ghettos cannot be understood through reference to any familiar notion of rationality, the historian must posit the existence of an unprecedented form of reason – which Diner calls 'counter-rationality' – before being able to write the history of Nazi terror. It is this encounter with the limits of conventional historical understanding that leads to Diner's call to 'think' Auschwitz.

It is worth noting that Diner says that Auschwitz *must* be thought, not that it *can* be thought. The imperative to rework conventional categories of understanding in the face of their limits comes with no promise of success. Diner's form of engagement with the Holocaust – simultaneously examining specific historical events and revising the conceptual vocabulary available for understanding them – exemplifies what we value and have searched for in the work collected here. *The Holocaust: Theoretical Readings* explores the extent to which recent theory in the humanities and social sciences can help us think about a series of events – the Holocaust – that seems to defy all attempts at comprehension. At the same time, it suggests that deep engagement with those events can, and indeed ought to, impinge on the practice of theory. There is much to be gained by bringing study of the Holocaust into conversation with developments in literary, cultural, and social theory. On the one hand, the very extremity of the Holocaust can teach us a lesson in theoretical modesty. Like the contemplation of other limit cases, study of the Holocaust often illuminates the places where understanding breaks down and forces us to reconceive ideals and phenomena we thought we understood, such as experience, memory, poetry, and justice. On the other hand, even after Auschwitz, theory can play an important role by demystifying received ideas and common sense. Indeed, without many of the insights of twentieth-century thought, our understanding of the Holocaust would risk becoming rigid and would be plagued with simplifications and stereotypes.

Yet the conjunction between theory and the Holocaust cannot be taken for granted. In particular, the varieties of poststructuralist theory, which have been dominant in the Anglo-American academy for the past few decades, have seemed to raise a number of difficult questions for many Holocaust scholars.[2] How can the abstract speculations of theory be brought together with the brute facts of genocide? Isn't theorizing in the wake of catastrophe more an evasion of than a response to the crisis posed by the Holocaust? Many scholars demand respect, even piety, towards the Holocaust and the Nazis' victims, while some theorists are preoccupied with transgression, play, and *jouissance*. Historians of the Holocaust understandably insist upon the distinction between fiction and reality; theory, especially poststructuralism, questions our ability to know a reality existing independently of our representations of it. For writers such as Deborah Lipstadt, this 'relativism' actively aligns poststructuralism with Holocaust denial.[3] Seen from this perspective, there is a wide gap between the kinds of questions usually broached by theory and those habitually and necessarily addressed by Holocaust studies. Additionally, some may point to the problem of the intellectual heritage of theory, especially in the French form that dominated American understandings of the term in the 1980s: poststructuralism and American deconstruction are unimaginable without the influence of Martin Heidegger, Paul de Man, and Maurice Blanchot – each of whom, in one way or another, either endorsed the Nazi party or produced writings complicit with antisemitic currents of the pre-Holocaust period.

While it is important to recognize the divergences between the practice of theory and the study of the Holocaust, the cost of failing to bring one of the landmark events of the twentieth century into dialogue with important dimensions of that century's intellectual history would be great. How can we hope to understand the Nazi genocide without employing at least some of the intellectual tools that have been shaped and reshaped by theorists over the last half century? And what would theory be if it remained silent before the most extreme historical developments of its time? Despite resistance from both sides, much work has already been done to connect the concerns of theory with those of Holocaust studies. This can be glimpsed not only by surveying the number of contemporary thinkers who have written in the direct shadow of the events, but also by seeking out the conceptual categories that are shared by a broad range of theorists and a broad range of Holocaust scholars. A dialogue between theory and the Holocaust has been going on for decades – in the academic writings of professional philosophers, historians, and critics, as well as in the more personal documents of survivors of the camps.[4] Despite the existence of this ongoing dialogue, no anthology has yet brought together the diversity of writings that could be characterized as attempts to theorize (after) the Holocaust.[5] Our book hopes to remedy this absence by making accessible an interdisciplinary array of writings that have engaged theoretically with the implications of the Nazi genocide.

This volume represents an attempt to describe what we see as an already existing field of theoretical investigation that is not always recognized as such; but in calling for this field to be recognized, and mapping out what seem to us to be its major preoccupations, we are, of course, also trying actively to construct it. In what follows we want briefly to chart some of the salient historical moments in the popular consciousness of the Holocaust and in theoretical reflection upon the events and their ramifications. Rather than present a continuous and complete narrative of Holocaust consciousness, we want to point out how the emergence of Holocaust consciousness has had effects on theory and how theoretical debate has had an impact on scholarly and public understanding of the Nazi genocide. In the next section, we begin by clarifying what we mean by the Holocaust and by theory and why we find it valuable to think about each with reference to the other. In the remainder of the introduction we proceed to consider three large areas in which theory after the Holocaust has been elaborated: ethics and history, aesthetics and culture, and the politics of memory.

II

We understand the Holocaust as the systematic genocide of approximately six million European Jews by the Nazis and their allies.[6] Given the scale and extent of the Nazi destruction, it is useful to think of the Holocaust not as a single event, but rather as a series of events. The genocidal events took place during World War II, but were not a part of the war. They were rather the product of an extremist, antisemitic worldview that attempted to actualize a 'utopian' vision of racial purity, even at the expense of the war effort. While the Nazis did not succeed in murdering all the Jews under their dominion, they had a clearly articulated intention to do so. They also came close to wiping out a millennium of European Jewish culture, especially in the central and eastern parts of the continent. The Jews were certainly not the Nazis' only victims; nor is the Holocaust the only modern genocide. Yet the Jews occupied a central position in Nazi ideology that can be differentiated – albeit carefully and with a simultaneous sense of connectedness – from that of other victim groups, such as Roma (gypsies), the handicapped, Poles, homosexuals, political opponents, and myriad others (all of whom also stand in very particular relationships to Nazi ideology).

The amount of research and writing about the Holocaust is mind-boggling; despite a slow start in the early postwar years and the many famous warnings about these events' incomprehensibility, scholarship on the Nazi genocide is impressive both in its extensive details and in the overall picture that it presents of the events and their implications.[7] Yet understanding of the Holocaust is fractured along a number of axes. There is little correspondence or communication between the ground-breaking archival work of historians on the events of the genocide and the more speculative investigations of philosophers, literary critics, and some psychoanalysts. Neither historians nor other humanists are, in turn, necessarily conversant with the findings of social scientific researchers (and vice versa). These fractures are particularly in evidence whenever Holocaust studies conferences attempt to bring together scholars of different disciplinary orientations – misunderstanding, if not outright bafflement, often reigns.[8]

A parallel heterogeneity can be found today in the world of theory. In the 1970s and 1980s deconstruction and Lacanian psychoanalysis set the standard for what counted as sophisticated thought. Today, strands as diverse as queer theory, transnational feminism, cultural studies of science and technology, and postcolonial studies uneasily coexist with a variety of other approaches. Many of these approaches share assumptions and overlapping methodologies, and yet, despite the stature and influence of scholars such as Judith Butler, Gayatri Spivak, and Slavoj Žižek, there is no current sense of a single dominant school or figure.

In a situation of such plurality, how can we get a hold on what theory means in general and what it might mean for study of the Holocaust? A recent attempt at definition may be illuminating. In *Literary Theory: A Very Short Introduction* Jonathan Culler offers the following four glosses on the concept of theory:

> Theory is interdisciplinary – discourse with effects outside an original discipline ... Theory is analytical and speculative – an attempt to work out what is involved in what we call sex or language or writing or meaning or the subject ... Theory is a critique of common sense, of concepts taken as natural ... Theory is reflexive, thinking about thinking, enquiry into the categories we use in making sense of things, in literature and other discursive practices.[9]

Missing from Culler's useful definition is the notion of history. For theory to be interdisciplinary means for it to change as disciplines change, for it to critique common sense means for it to change as common sense changes – and for theory to be reflexive means for it necessarily to be self-altering, as the limits and failings of previous theoretical categories are discovered. We also want to suggest that theory is what Edward Said, speaking of literary criticism, called 'worldly' activity.[10] It responds to events in the world and shapes the way these events are understood and remembered; it is not produced by neutral, detached observers writing from outside of history and politics, but by people who can never entirely extricate themselves from currents and preoccupations in popular awareness.

Now it would be perverse to suggest that one could substitute 'the Holocaust' for the word 'theory' in Culler's definitions and generate useful, true statements. But it could be said that the challenge of theory to common sense and to the categories we use in making sense of things is also, albeit in a different way, the challenge presented by the Holocaust. Indeed, in *Negative Dialectics*, Theodor W. Adorno asserts that in the wake of the Holocaust 'if thinking is to be true ... it must also be thinking against itself.'[11] In addition, the briefest survey of scholarly research on the Holocaust shows a remarkable interdisciplinarity, including work in history, political science, sociology, philosophy, literary and film studies, art history, psychology, and theology. Furthermore, there is considerable overlap in the phenomena that interest both writers on the Holocaust and theorists working in non-Holocaust contexts. Both groups are concerned with questions of history and memory, 'race' and identity, experience and representation, ethics and politics, justice and trauma, uniqueness (specificity) and comparison – to name just a few of the concepts this book explores.

In this volume we want to generate an expanded understanding of what we mean when we talk about theory. Amongst the authors whose works on the Holocaust we consider theoretical we include alongside the iconic, principally French, names of theory – Jacques Derrida, Jean-François Lyotard, Jean Baudrillard – the names of German philosophers, American literary critics, English sociologists, Israeli and German historians, and German-Jewish film scholars, among others – as well, crucially, as some of the most important witnesses of the concentration camp universe itself: Primo Levi, Charlotte Delbo, Jean Améry, and Ruth Kluger. The lives of many of the century's foremost theorists were deeply affected by the experience of the Second World War and the Holocaust. One thinks of those who survived labor camps, like Emmanuel Levinas, or lived in hiding, like Saul Friedlander, or in Vichy-ruled Algeria, like Derrida, or those who left Germany for American exile, as did Adorno and Hannah Arendt, or for England as part of a *Kindertransport*, like Geoffrey Hartman – not to mention those non-Jews whose lives were indelibly marked by the experience. What all of these writers and thinkers share at the broadest level is a determination to *reflect* upon the Holocaust and its implications for our understanding of history, ethics, representation, and memory, both despite and because of the event's reputed unthinkability.

What exactly has made the Holocaust such a frequent, if troubling, reference point in contemporary theoretical reflection? Certainly, the number of victims and the extent of cultural destruction have challenged understanding. More than any one feature, however, we would identify a nexus of defining characteristics with which thought has had to grapple: the totalizing nature of the

Nazis' exterminationist designs; the 'rational' means they employed to actualize them; the abject and inexpressible suffering of the victims that resulted from those means and left survivors traumatized; and the crucial cultural and mythic place of the Jews in 'Christian' Europe. Because at least some of these elements obviously characterize other histories of extreme violence as well, the very features that constitute the specificity of the Nazi genocide can also serve as the basis for bringing post-Holocaust theory into the more general critical conversations about race, gender, colonialism, and power (among other topics) that have defined postwar intellectual life. We believe strongly in the importance of posing comparative questions and in linking diverse histories, as is evidenced by several sections of this reader that include reflections by and on non-Jewish victims of the Nazis and on other modern histories. However, we also believe that it is important that such comparative questions be posed on the basis of a specific understanding of the different histories at issue. One of the goals of collecting these reflections is to promote dialogue between different theoretical traditions, especially those that entail a critical perspective on modern rationality and on European cultures.

III

The events of the Holocaust took years to be perceived as distinctive and significant. And the significance of the events has changed over time, as has knowledge of what happened, and why. There is now broad consensus amongst scholars that public awareness of the Holocaust was low in the first decade and a half after the end of World War Two, an interval that many think of as a kind of 'latency period' but which might also be thought of in terms of what Marxist cultural theory describes as the inevitable 'cultural lag' between the emergence of the new and the development of a vocabulary – be it conceptual or artistic – to describe it. The lack of a widespread consciousness of the murder of European Jews as a distinctive and unprecedented event should not, however, be confused with silence. The fate of European Jews attracted attention in a variety of different forms: in the Nuremberg Trials as part of a larger prosecution of crimes against humanity; in numerous survivor testimonies, which, however, confronted an often unreceptive audience; in Adorno's essays on culture and society, where he famously pronounced the writing of poetry after Auschwitz 'barbaric'; and in the popular success of Anne Frank's diary, which has continued to serve as a point of identification with Holocaust victimhood for generations to come.

The birth of something like broad, public Holocaust consciousness in the Western world, however, can be dated relatively precisely to 1961 and the trial of Adolf Eichmann, who headed the Gestapo's office for Jewish affairs. Eichmann had been tracked down and kidnapped by Israeli intelligence, and his trial in Israel attracted worldwide attention. Not only was a major trial broadcast internationally on television and radio for the first time, but the occasion also marked the first time the Nazi genocide of Jews was presented to an international public as a singular event distinguishable from the broader context of German wartime atrocity.[12] Amongst those covering the Eichmann trial was political theorist Hannah Arendt, a German-Jewish émigré, and author of the pathbreaking *The Origins of Totalitarianism*. Her report on the trial, *Eichmann in Jerusalem*, first appeared as a series of articles in *The New Yorker* magazine in February and March 1963. Arendt's work aroused a heated and often acrimonious debate that continues to this day on issues ranging from the appropriate tone in which to write about the Holocaust, to the degree of complicity of the Jewish councils whom the Nazis had administer the ghettos (Arendt's judgment was harsh), to the distinctive nature of Nazi evil, which Arendt provocatively labeled 'banal.'

Besides the enigmatic figure of Eichmann, perhaps most striking in the trial itself was the public testimony of surviving victims of Nazi atrocity. For the first time, non-victims proved willing to confront the voices and stories of the victims. In his account of Holocaust memory in Israel, Tom Segev relates one particularly dramatic moment when the survivor Yehiel De-Nur collapsed on the witness stand (3–4). De-Nur's collapse, together with the many other eyewitness testimonies that made up a large part of the trial, ushered in an era in which personal accounts of the events would begin to shape the historical memory of the Holocaust and eventually the theoretical discourse of literary and cultural studies.

Given the centrality these accounts have assumed for attempts to understand the Holocaust, the first chapter of this anthology presents a series of reflections on the experience of the Shoah by some of its most preeminent memoirists: Jean Améry, Charlotte Delbo, Ruth Kluger, and Primo Levi. The works of Levi, Améry, and Delbo in particular have crucially determined the shape of conceptual work in the study of the Holocaust. One thinks, for example, of Levi's concept of the 'gray zone' to describe the moral-spiritual quagmire into which the Nazis dragged their victims, Améry's account of the enduring effects of torture upon his sense of self and of time, and Delbo's distinction between external and deep memory of the experience of the camps. A limit-event such as the Holocaust unavoidably raises questions of authenticity, subjectivity, and epistemological standpoint. For this reason, these texts might also be read productively in conjunction with recent theoretical work on 'experience,' one of the most hotly debated and intellectually and politically consequent topics in recent decades.[13]

In addition to fostering public consciousness and bringing the voices of victims to the fore, the Eichmann trial raised two other issues that are central to this volume: the nature of Nazism and antisemitism, and the status of ethics and justice after the Shoah. In 'Antisemitism, Nazi Culture, and Fascism,' we include selections from some of the most provocative approaches to understanding this complex of murderous hatred and totalitarian organization. Most of these insightful, sometimes disturbing, entries ask more or less the same question: how could the masses be mobilized, and be so obviously ecstatically excited by, a movement and a leader whose goals and demands of them were so clearly in conflict with not only their own best interests but also, it would seem, universal moral precepts?

Whereas for the most part the materials in this anthology are drawn from the post-Eichmann period, valuable efforts to understand and explain antisemitism and Nazism pre-date the Second World War. Striking in the work of these early theorists of Nazism is the emphasis on its intense affective power, which they interpret as originating in premodern rites and rituals. Thus Georges Bataille refers to primitivist notions of taboo and transgression to explain the attraction of fascism, and Kenneth Burke focuses on how Hitler refunctioned religious structures in order to exploit their accompanying fervent belief and preparedness for self-sacrifice for political ends.

Accounts of Nazi antisemitism often echo this sense that Nazism draws its affective force from an appeal to the distant past: Horkheimer and Adorno go back to the origins of religion and the supposedly intolerable demands of the Jewish prohibition on idol worship; Philippe Lacoue-Labarthe's speculative explanation of Nazi racism hinges on how various German thinkers and ideologues chose to understand ancient Greek myth. The crucial element in both selections, however, as in the work of Moishe Postone, is the Nazi perception of 'the Jew' as undermining the systems of representation by which meaning and pleasure are derived from the world.

Despite the many serious (and to our minds valid) critiques it has received, the success and scandal of Daniel Jonah Goldhagen's *Hitler's Willing Executioners* (1996), which attributed the Holocaust to a particularly German tradition of 'eliminationist antisemitism,' could be seen to indicate a widespread sense that Nazism and antisemitism are phenomena that remain to be adequately explained. Influential accounts of the Nazi genocide such as Arendt's and that of historian Christopher Browning's *Ordinary Men* give far less weight to antisemitism itself as a sufficient explanation than to such factors (of varying importance for each) as the nature of the totalitarian state, which leaves its murderous agents no room for independent judgment; the pressure to conform in a peer group that is the recipient of orders to kill from such a state; and the tendency of modernity in general to distance agents from their actions, and thus from moral responsibility for them. A striking absence in Browning's important work, however, is a consideration of the status of masculinity in the psychological makeup of his 'ordinary men,' an omission that is all the more glaring when one considers the centrality it holds in an earlier, and still widely-referenced, work, which we excerpt here, on the psyche of perpetrators: Klaus Theweleit's mammoth *Male Fantasies*. Indeed, scholarship in Holocaust studies has increasingly gravitated in the last decade toward a consideration of gender issues – a fact that also indicates how work in the field has become more open to newer theoretical perspectives.

The Holocaust offers something of a limit- or test-case for feminist scholarship because it raises questions about the scope of gender as an analytic category. Is the Holocaust not a case in which one identity category – in this case 'race' – outweighs all others? Such has been the argument of traditional Holocaust scholars, many of whom continue to insist that consideration of gender issues can only cloud the essentials of our understanding of genocide. And yet a crime that aims to eliminate a 'race' is necessarily attuned to questions of biological, including sexual, difference. Even if the central category of the Nazi genocide of Jews was a pseudo-scientific 'racial' category, the Nazis sometimes targeted men and women in different ways, and men and women experienced and responded to their fates in relationship to already given gender roles, as Pascale Bos remarks in her entry. Because feminist theory of the last decades has pursued an ambitious research agenda attentive to the intersection of identity categories, including especially the intersection of gender with 'race' and ethnicity, feminist theory is in an excellent position to contribute new insights into the Holocaust. Indeed, various recent essays, monographs, and collections by scholars including Marion Kaplan, Sara Horowitz, Gisela Bock, Joan Ringelheim, Dalia Ofer and Lenore Weitzman, and Carol Rittner and John Roth, among others, demonstrate that this contribution is already well under- way and needs only to be continued and more fully integrated into the main- stream of understanding of the Shoah.[14] As the recent use of mass rape as an instrument of genocidal violence in Bosnia indicates – and as the successful prosecution of these atrocities as crimes against humanity for the first time confirms – a deeper and more complex understanding of the relationship of gender and genocide, as of sexuality and 'race,' is not simply of historical interest.

The reappearance in the last decade of 'ethnic cleansing' and genocide in Europe and Africa, as well as many nations' attempts to come to terms with recent crimes against humanity in their own histories, has also made the interrogation of ethics and justice in the face of extremity all the more relevant. The issues of ethics and justice discussed in the wake of the Shoah partly emerge from such inevitable questions as: how could people have done this, or have let this happen, and how can we prevent it from happening again? Inevitably, however, these questions open up more tangled inquiries. The moral repulsion most of us feel when confronted with images or stories of the catastrophe would seem to distinguish us from 'them,' the perpetrators, whom we imagine to have a different ethical makeup. Indeed, the sense of this constitutive difference is precisely what produces a distinctive cognitive 'unease' in the face of the Holocaust for historians like Saul Friedlander. Yet sources such as Browning's *Ordinary Men* and even SS leader Heinrich Himmler's notorious October 4, 1943 speech at Posen, suggest that many perpetrators too felt such horror, and still managed to commit genocide. The questions then become: what lacunae in conventional morality made it possible for the perpetrators to think that, despite their repulsion, they were acting morally? And what allowed bystanders to believe they had no obliga- tion to help or resist? In *Modernity and the Holocaust* Zygmunt Bauman suggests that '[t]he most frightening news brought about the Holocaust and by what we learned of its perpetrators was not the likelihood that 'this' could be done to us, but the idea that we could do it.'[15]

In other words, if accounts of the culture of Nazism wish to know how that movement managed to anaesthetize the consciences of its followers in the face of obvious wrong, theoretical inquiry into the implications of the Shoah for moral thought has been more radical, asking how the premises and categories of the Western ethico-political tradition might have failed or been complicit in the face of man-made mass death. Are the death camps the culmination of this tradition, a sort of fulfillment of the Enlightenment dream of universal reason in which the desire for universality demands the elimination of all that is not identical with this universal model, as Horkheimer and Adorno claim? Or do the camps rather, as Jürgen Habermas and others have argued, signify precisely the *failure* to properly understand and implement the Enlightenment project? Much of the theoretical work represented in this anthology is more easily aligned with Horkheimer and Adorno than with Habermas. This line of thought sees the Nazi genocide as the rage of homogeneity at difference: ethics after Auschwitz must therefore find ways to protect and even cultivate that difference.

One might see the entire project of the Jewish philosopher Emmanuel Levinas, to place ethics at the center of philosophy, as committed to this task. Levinas's influential inquiry into the subject's responsibility toward the other takes his thought in a religious direction: not only is Levinas's writing rich with religious terminology, but Levinas also identifies one of the central concepts of his philosophy – the infinite nature of the other's ethical demands of me – with the divine. Yet if for Levinas post-Holocaust philosophy seems to lead toward God, post-Holocaust theology in the Jewish and Christian traditions has, instead, consisted precisely of an ongoing crisis about the nature of God and religious belief: how could God have allowed such evil and suffering? How can religious faith be sustained in its wake? In post-Holocaust theology too there is an initial delay or lag, with major responses to the events beginning to appear in the late 1950s and early 1960s; here too, the Eichmann trial and, perhaps more significantly for Jewish religious thinkers, the 1967 Arab-Israeli war catalyze a more intensive engagement with the nature of the events. The clear risk theology runs in confronting the Holocaust is that of reducing Auschwitz to the longstanding problem of theodicy (how to maintain a belief in divine omnipotence and benevolence in view of the existence of evil). Yet while well-known Jewish thinkers such as Richard Rubenstein pose traditional questions about evil and its consequences for religious faith, others, such as Emil L. Fackenheim, Arthur A. Cohen, and Irving Greenberg insist on exposing their religious belief to alteration and even possible outright rejection in the light of historical events. Fackenheim takes the radical step of proposing a supplement to the 613 commandments handed down to Moses on Mt. Sinai and calls for a 614th commandment, according to which Jews must not allow Hitler any posthumous victories – which for Fackenheim means forbidding the destruction of the Jewish faith. Meanwhile, Christian thinkers such as A. Roy Eckhardt and Franklin Littell have explored the complicity of their own faith's historical tenets with the Nazi genocide.[16]

Philosophical research outside of the theological tradition has recently witnessed a resurgence of interest in the ethical implications of the camps. In his recent reflections on Primo Levi's writings, *Remnants of Auschwitz*, the Italian philosopher Giorgio Agamben reasserts the notion that the Holocaust presents a crisis for moral philosophy in the West: 'almost none of the ethical principles our age believed it could recognize as valid have stood the decisive test,' namely, that of coming to terms with Auschwitz.[17] The figure central to Agamben's meditations on an ethics that *could* pass that test is the exhausted, malnourished *Muselmann*, the concentration camp inmate no longer capable of thought or self-preserving action – and thus not considered by fellow inmates as either quite alive or even quite human. Agamben regards the *Muselmann* as 'an absolutely new phenomenon' (51), in the face of which we need to reconceive our notion of the 'human being.' An ethics that accounted for the *Muselmann* would, according to Agamben, not only teach us about the limits of such conventional ethical notions as dignity and respect, but also provide insight into the paradoxical nature of testimony, since for Agamben, following Levi, the *Muselmann* is simultaneously the absolute witness – the one who has experienced the limit in the camps – and yet, because of his physical state, the one incapable of speaking about what he has seen.

Agamben clearly continues a certain post-Holocaust ethical tradition insofar as he reads a figure of alterity – here, the 'outsiders' within the concentrationary universe – as the site of ethical truth. The present volume also, however, presents powerful reconsiderations of such models of post-Holocaust ethics. Thus Gillian Rose, inspired by Hegel, critiques the socially regressive nostalgia Levinas and Bauman display for an ethics free of the laws and social institutions central to modern society; elsewhere, Alain Badiou has issued a stinging attack on the very idea of premising ethics on notions such as otherness or alterity.[18]

Those closer to the events of the Holocaust have not only (or primarily) been concerned with the elaboration of a philosophical ethics, but have also been concerned with politico-legal questions of justice and judgment. Arendt devoted the last part of *Eichmann in Jerusalem* to the question of how such excessive, unprecedented crimes could be judged by conventional law – from what standpoint could one judge, or conceive of a punishment, for a crime against humanity? And both Améry and Levi devoted important essays to issues of justice and judgment. Améry sailed against what he felt to be the prevailing moral wind of the 1960s, which he saw as dominated by notions of forgiveness and the healing power of time. He insisted instead on the moral relevance of his 'resentments' and expressed the wish for a punishment that would annul what had happened to him and 'nail the criminal to his deed.' Améry clearly had no trouble judging the situation he had lived through, and claimed to be 'captive of the moral truth of the conflict.' In *The Drowned and the Saved* Levi suggests a more cautious attitude to judgment in his exploration of the gray zone, a zone of moral complexity and 'contamination' by the Nazis from which, as one who was saved, he did not necessarily exempt himself. When considering the *Sonderkommando* – Jewish death camp inmates forced to shepherd victims into the gas chambers – Levi requests 'that judgment of them be suspended.' Levi and Améry were, of course, addressing different moral issues – Levi the collaborating victim, Améry the unrepentant perpetrator – and that difference suggests some of the divergent ethical challenges posed by experiences of atrocity.

IV

Because the perpetrators of the Nazi genocide came from Germany, a nation renowned for its 'poets and thinkers,' the events and aftermath of the Holocaust have also led theorists to inquire into the value of aesthetics and culture 'after Auschwitz.' No philosopher, and no phrase, is more closely associated with this line of inquiry than Theodor W. Adorno and his provocative and frequently misunderstood dictum from 'Cultural Criticism and Society' that 'to write poetry after Auschwitz is barbaric.' Adorno's thought is in part inspired by German-Jewish thinker Walter Benjamin's well-known claim that '[t]here is no document of civilization which is not at the same time a document of barbarism.' What initially concerned Adorno, then, was less the impropriety of any given artistic response to the Holocaust than how culture in general and poetry in particular failed to recognize their own implication in the 'sinister' forces of total social integration that made the barbarism of Auschwitz possible in the first place. Those who write in Adorno's wake have often shifted the terms of the problem from one of the status of culture in late capitalist society to one of how language and writing can register and commemorate what has been called 'the disaster' (Blanchot) and problematized as 'the unrepeatable' (Derrida).

Such reflections on representation and catastrophe have historically had a high cultural, even specifically high modernist bias: both Adorno and Derrida, for example, see the work of Samuel Beckett and Paul Celan as central to the question of post-Holocaust literature. Yet public consciousness and memory of the Holocaust have in important ways emerged in response to popular forms, in particular film and television. In an earlier period, the Anne Frank diaries, as well as their various theatrical and cinematic incarnations, were a touchstone for popular understanding of the Holocaust. But one might argue that 'Hollywood' (in the broadest sense) has done most to shape the popular imagination of these events. One defining moment was the broadcast of the 1978 television mini-series *Holocaust*, the story of the German-Jewish Weiss family, which resonated powerfully with audiences both in the United States and elsewhere, and secured the worldwide predominance of the term 'Holocaust,' already dominant in English in the 1960s, to refer to the Nazi genocide. The series raised anew for intellectuals questions that had initially emerged in relation to literature: could one represent these events at all? If they were to be represented aesthetically, which forms were appropriate? What did it mean to present systematic, bureaucratic murder in the form of a melodrama that allowed one to identify with individual victims?

The mini-series was also an enormous success in West Germany, where it apparently allowed Germans to identify with the victims of their parents' and grandparents' crimes for the first time, as Andreas Huyssen argues. The success of *Holocaust* also put into crisis the tendency of the German left to 'relegate the Holocaust to the periphery of historical events' and to privilege artistic representations of the Holocaust in the modernist tradition.[19] This debate was reawakened in the 1990s by endless comparisons of *Schindler's List*, a Hollywood blockbuster, and *Shoah*, an austere nine and a half hour French film, in terms of culture industry and avant-garde paradigms.

The debates around *Holocaust*, *Shoah*, and *Schindler's List* (represented in the volume by Koch's essay) tend to be predicated on, or struggle against, notions like 'unrepresentability' and the ethics and codes that should govern the aesthetic presentation of extraordinary suffering. Jean Baudrillard's typically hyperbolic 'Holocaust' presents an unsettling twist on these debates, arguing that the cool medium of television produces forgetting, which 'is part of the extermination.' For the most part, however, these discussions take for granted the existence of a more or less unbridgeable distance between the events and their representation. Yet of at least equal importance in the theorization of culture after the Holocaust has been the recurring concern with the *diminution* of distance between now and then, us and them. Seminal essays such as Susan Sontag's 1974 'Fascinating Fascism' and Saul Friedlander's *Reflections of Nazism*, originally published in 1982, do not so much focus on the propriety of representations of the Holocaust as inquire into the seductiveness of imagery associated with that most improper of objects, Nazism itself. Both texts link what Friedlander calls the 'new discourse on Nazism' that emerged in the late 1960s with two distinctive cultural preoccupations, namely, an aesthetic turn towards kitsch, which we would now recognize as the sign of a certain postmodern sensibility, and the eroticization of death. Both Sontag and Friedlander also share an unease about the ways in which Nazi transgressions are neutralized or forgotten in the interests of aesthetic and erotic investments. For Sontag, however, the fascination with fascism is the product of a culture that could not be more different from the reality of Nazi Germany: 'The fad for Nazi regalia ... indicates a response to an oppressive freedom of choice in sex (and other matters).'[20] For Friedlander, on the other hand, the new discourse on Nazism – exemplified, amongst other places, in the films of Rainer Werner Fassbinder and Hans-Jürgen Syberberg – can be shown, when their aesthetic effects are subject to critical analysis, to reveal 'previously unsuspected aspects' of the past. The disclosure of these aspects – 'structures of the imagination' – in turn puts 'us on the track of the psychological hold of Nazism itself,' a hold which, according to Friedlander, continues to this day.

Questions of narrative form have provided another focal point for scholars interested in the ways in which the boundaries between past and present are blurred in representations of the Holocaust. The work of Hayden White has been influential here. Yet White's 1973 *Metahistory*, which argues that historical narratives inevitably conform to the laws of one of several literary genres, also left White vulnerable to charges of relativism, and to serious critique from scholars unconvinced that the Holocaust could be narrated, as White's argument seemed to imply, in any genre at all, including comedy (a debate that has recently been revived by the film *Life is Beautiful*). Nevertheless, the dialogue about cultural cognition he opened up between historiography and studies of fictional narrative has proven immensely important for theory's engagement with Holocaust studies. For example, Eric Santner formulates his notion of 'narrative fetishism' in an analysis of both the German Historians' Debate [*Historikerstreit*] and the narrative perspective of Edgar Reitz's German miniseries *Heimat*.[21] The desire to tell a sympathetic story of German suffering and sacrifice leads both historical revisionists and Reitz to marginalize Jewish suffering. According to Santner, they thereby share a drive to repress the traumatic knowledge of Nazi crimes, even as the trauma of those crimes constitutes the initial impetus behind their narratives. While such fetishistic narratives offer a sense of 'intactness' and a renewal of 'narrative pleasure' in remembering a previously distressing past, in fact, Santner argues, without an appropriate working through of the kind described by Freud in *Beyond the Pleasure Principle*, 'the loss will continue to represent a past that refuses to go away.'

In *Foregone Conclusions: Against Apocalyptic History*, Michael André Bernstein takes similar advantage of the kinds of questions opened up by White's research. Treating historical, journalistic, and novelistic work with equal seriousness, he demonstrates the disturbing prevalence of what he labels 'backshadowing' in narratives about pre-war European Jewry. Despite the widespread acknowledgement of the unprecedentedness, and therefore unforeseeability of the Holocaust, backshadowing narratives turn hindsight into inevitability. Along with the sense of inevitability comes a more or less explicit criticism of the Nazis' victims 'blindness' to their fates, 'as though they too should have known what was to come.' Drawing on the theories of Mikhail Bakhtin, Bernstein suggests 'sideshadowing' as a narrative and ethical alternative. With sideshadowing, narratives make explicit the contingency of events, how they might have unfolded otherwise. If there is a way in which Bernstein's work circles back to high modernist aesthetics (his central exhibit of a sideshadowing narrative is Robert Musil's monumental *The Man Without Qualities*), post-war texts like Philip Roth's *The Counterlife* and Jaroslaw M. Rymkiewicz's *The Final Station: Umschlagplatz* (another Bernstein favorite), not to mention contemporary popular film's interest in sideshadowing, demonstrate that the notion is not inherently modernist or even 'high cultural.'

One of the most interesting cultural forms that has emerged in the aftermath of the Holocaust and that has become central to discussions of ethics, aesthetics, and memory is the genre of testimony (whether written, oral, or videotaped). Indeed, one of the more improbable effects of the *Holocaust* mini-series was as a catalyst for what became Yale University's Fortunoff Video Archive for Holocaust Testimonies, a massive project of videotaping and archiving the accounts of survivors of and witnesses to the Holocaust that began in 1979 as a local initiative. According to critic and co-founder Geoffrey Hartman, the initiative was meant in part to provide a corrective to the mini-series, which 'struck the [Holocaust] survivors as a sanitized and distorted version of what they had suffered.'[22] This project has provided a source of primary materials that in subsequent years would change the way the Holocaust and the nature of witnessing in general are understood. But its importance goes well beyond its documentary value. Because testimony does not fit easily into the categories of high or low culture and because it does not conform to the received patterns of literary and autobiographical narration, as critics including Lawrence Langer have argued, testimony helps to open up a new space of knowledge at the intersection of life history and collective historical experience. The emergence of the genre of testimony therefore stands as an instance of how, because of the very sense of a prohibition on received aesthetic forms in the wake of the Holocaust, culture after Auschwitz has in fact been compelled to innovate formally.

V

Over the course of the same decades in which confrontation with the history of the Holocaust led to new thinking about ethics and justice as well as culture and representation, memory itself came into focus as a topic of historical and theoretical urgency. The culture of memory, which Andreas Huyssen has described as a global phenomenon emerging in response to changes in the perception of time and space wrought by the new media, raises a series of questions for what has now become known as Holocaust studies.[23] Beyond issues pertaining to the 'accuracy' and 'authenticity' of memory, which continue to trouble historians but which are of less interest to us as *theoretical* problems, the key questions emerging out of the culture of memory concern the political and economic uses to which the past can and will be put.

While concern with a culture of memory implies a particular focus on questions of collective remembrance and identity, the effects of this culture can be felt in subjective and intimate realms as well. Indeed, memory serves as a charged locus for thinking about the intersection of the individual and collective axes of social life. The recent fascination with traumatic memory, in both popular and academic realms, comes to mind as one example of a phenomenon that links collective, historical experiences – such as war and genocide – with the psychic suffering of individuals. The reasons for the dramatic rise of trauma as a theoretical category are complex – and certainly not immune to skeptical critique, as for instance in recent work by Patricia Yaeger, Mark Seltzer, and Ruth Leys.[24] Yet the psychoanalytically inflected writings of such critics as Cathy Caruth, Eric Santner, and Dominick LaCapra cannot be rejected as a simple trend. Rather, they represent, in part, an attempt on the part of theorists influenced by poststructuralism to come to terms with urgent ethical concerns posed by the catastrophes of the twentieth century and by the belated recognition of various degrees of intellectual complicity in those catastrophes – in particular, the very different complicities of such figures as Martin Heidegger and Paul de Man. A prime example of this form of critique can be found in Santner's analysis of the treatment of mourning and loss in deconstruction in general and de Man in particular as almost exclusively linguistic and structural and as unable to acknowledge 'anything at all to do with human grief, pain, or survival, with the community of human subjects and their particular, concrete stories and histories.'[25] Caruth's important theorization of trauma via a reading of Freud's *Moses and Monotheism* and *Beyond the Pleasure Principle* can be understood as an attempt to reconcile the deconstructive resistance to reference with the demand for referentiality in the face of suffering. Santner and Caruth, as well as LaCapra, continue to work in a theoretical register, with a vocabulary that draws on poststructuralism and psychoanalysis, even as they break with or modify the ideas that prevailed in American deconstruction of the 1980s. Their work thus exemplifies how the Holocaust can present a challenge to (one version of) theory and simultaneously force us to modify an excessively reified and oversimplified notion of just what 'theory' is.

Reflection on traumatic memory has also played a role in recent attempts to think about the status of generations and other collectivities. Dan Diner's provocative notion of 'negative symbiosis' points to the way that the Nazi genocide has, ironically, forged divergent postwar Jewish and German identities around the common negative core of Auschwitz. Even if there never was a 'German-Jewish symbiosis' – that is, a shared, commonly produced culture – before the war, there now exists a shared collective identity produced 'virtually' by memory of the disaster. The sense that identities have been constructed in relationship to genocide holds not only for some members of the most obvious groups – the victims, the perpetrators, and the bystanders – but also for the second and third generations of the Holocaust's aftermath. Marianne Hirsch has coined the term 'postmemory' to refer to the way that individuals may be haunted by events that they never experienced, but which have been passed down, often in attenuated or even 'unconscious' forms, by parents and grandparents. There is currently much debate about the status of the 'transgenerational transmission' of trauma, but regardless of what one thinks about it as a psychic reality, there can be no doubt that the relationship of the generations of the aftermath to the events of the Holocaust has produced useful theoretical concepts as well as important, aesthetically innovative works by Art Spiegelman, Henri Raczymow, and others. The notions of 'remembering the unknown'

(Nadine Fresco) and 'memory shot through with holes' (Raczymow), as well as negative symbiosis and postmemory, provide important theoretical resources for thinking through the status of historical consciousness from within a postmodern condition that has been famously diagnosed as anti-historical. Such concepts might be helpful not only for thinking about the status of Holocaust memory, but also for other experiences of and responses to historical trauma, as the novels of Toni Morrison concerning slavery and its aftermath amply demonstrate.

As reflection on the Holocaust has become increasingly central to public culture in Europe and North America and has increasingly turned on rubrics such as memory that are themselves subject to intensive interdisciplinary and cross-cultural investigation, questions about the relationship between the Nazi genocide and other historical traumas have become inevitable. For many years debate has raged over the alleged 'uniqueness' of the Holocaust, and many people – including scholars, survivors, and members of the Jewish community at large – continue to object to attempts to think comparatively about this genocide. It seems clear to us, however, that uniqueness and comparison necessarily go together and that the singular and unprecedented features of the Shoah emerge most clearly in relation to other histories – a position articulated here by Alan Milchman and Alan Rosenberg. Discourses that seek to segregate the genocide of Jews from either other Nazi crimes or other examples of extreme political violence risk not only moral coarseness but a coarsening of conceptual categories and ultimately a distortion of the inter-connected nature of historical processes. The evaluation of comparative his-tories must take place on a case by case basis, with attention to levels of abstraction and particularity. It makes a difference whether the point of the comparison is to put forth a large-scale critique of modernity from the perspective of its underside – as in the work of Paul Gilroy – or to rescue certain traumatic histories from oblivion, as in the case of scholars of the Nazi extermination of the Roma, the Armenian genocide, or the devastation of the indigenous Americas. These equally pressing projects require and produce different conceptual tools – but they can all benefit from work in Holocaust studies, just as Holocaust scholars can benefit from the kinds of questions raised by these projects.

Of course an openness in principle to questions of comparison does not imply an acceptance of all discourses in which the Holocaust, as history or metaphor, may circulate. The *Historikerstreit* of the mid-1980s stands as a warning about how the act of comparison itself is not innocent or neutral; the attempt by conservative historians in the German Federal Republic to relativize Nazi crimes through comparison to Stalinist terror demonstrated how the will to comparison can sometimes serve to screen a less historically justified will to forgetting, a desire for absolution from history's responsibilities. Whatever their questionable role in the *Historikerstreit*, the relativizers (some of whom are in fact important historians who have made significant contributions to our knowledge of the Nazi past) should be distinguished from their less seemly cousins, Holocaust deniers, who, in the meantime, continue to propagate their apologetic, antisemitic agendas. The deniers, however, remain a small and marginal group. Focusing too much on them not only grants them more attention than is their due, but also tends to distract from more pressing and difficult questions about why the Holocaust has come to occupy such a central place in North Atlantic culture.

As the volatility of the uniqueness debates demonstrates, the problem of comparison leads directly back to the larger issue of the politics of memory. The question posed by the politics of memory can be put like this: what is at stake for the present and future in discourses on the past? Such a question is also necessarily one that Holocaust scholars must pose about their own endeavors. After Bosnia and Rwanda, the legitimation provided by the phrase 'never again' rings particularly hollow. Several recent works have addressed this matter sharply. Peter Novick's *The Holocaust in American Life*, Norman Finkelstein's *The Holocaust Industry*, and Tim Cole's *Selling the Holocaust* appeared so nearly simultaneously that they seem to constitute a peculiar cultural moment in themselves – a moment, it should be added, that has not passed. While these works are of wildly varying quality, they share a general concern about the ways that the Nazi genocide has come to be commodified and instrumentalized in the service of Jewish, especially Jewish-American, identity formation and in the service of the state of Israel's often oppressive policies vis-à-vis the Palestinians.[26] Such concerns are entirely legitimate, even if we have serious criticisms of each book. We find that Novick downplays the extent to which the Holocaust does pose important questions to postwar America, that Finkelstein exaggerates the degree to which various kinds of response to the genocide serve venal interests, and that Cole misses the ways that commodification is unavoidable and can produce legitimate and necessary forms of knowledge. Nevertheless, a self-reflexive attention to the 'political-economy' of Holocaust memory now needs to be factored into post-Holocaust theory.

Approaching the global culture of memory through attention to the discourses of the aftermath of the Holocaust – trauma studies, generational discourse, comparative historiography, ideological critique – provides a specific angle of access for a seemingly universal problem. Whether memory is authentic or virtual, instrumentalized or beyond subjective control, what is clear today is that memory matters: it has political effects and ought to have theoretical implications. Memory may serve as a site of what Wendy Brown somewhat disparagingly calls 'wounded attachments' – a locus for the constitution of identity through *ressentiment* and a fixation on injury – or it may serve as a bridge between radically different experiences of oppression, and thus may contribute to new possibilities for reconciliation with justice (as ideally in the 'truth commissions' that have emerged in Latin America and South Africa).[27] Attention to Holocaust memory shows that scenarios of both resentment and justice, as well as a diversity of other responses, are possible and, therefore, that critics and theorists need to bring a conceptual flexibility to investigation of the aftermath of traumatic events.

VI

In the course of this introduction we have not been able to address all of the questions raised by the entries we have selected, not to mention the wider array of interrogations of the history, memory, and representation of the Nazi genocide over several decades and in dozens of different intellectual traditions. We have mapped out some significant sites where Holocaust studies intersects with versions of contemporary theory – for instance, in the questioning of traditional notions of mimesis or of overlapping identity categories such as gender and race. We are also cognizant that Holocaust studies and contemporary theory have arrived at similar questions for different historical reasons, and that theory has been marked as much by the end of empire and by feminist and anti-racist struggles as by confrontation with the legacy of the Nazi genocide. Nevertheless, we remain convinced that an explicit and open exchange between Holocaust scholars and practitioners of theory and cultural studies will be mutually beneficial. Such a belief derives not from naïve optimism or sentimentality, but from a fundamental commitment to the idea that thought and historicity, theory and events, are part of the same universe. Their interaction can be ignored only at our own peril.

As Holocaust studies becomes institutionalized – both within and outside the university – it must remain responsive to the paradoxical status of knowledge of the Nazi genocide. On the one hand, with a few notable exceptions, such as the still debated date of Hitler's decision to proceed with the 'Final Solution,' it is possible to establish an accurate chronology of the major events of the Holocaust. On the other hand, all of the questions raised by the writings collected here about the meaning and implications of the events remain open; this openness suggests that we cannot 'know' the Holocaust once and for all. Attending to this paradox does not entail sacrificing an orientation toward the Holocaust's specificity and slipping into historical relativism. Yet the very fact that the Holocaust has penetrated into global consciousness – for example, through the powerful testimony of survivors and the enormous success of such films as *Schindler's List* and *Life is Beautiful* – ensures that it will accrue diverse and sometimes contradictory meanings, will intersect with non-European and non-Jewish histories, and will be reframed in other intellectual traditions – as in fact has happened all along.[28] If study of the Holocaust remains separate from other intellectual currents, it risks insularity. If theoretical reflection relegates the Nazi genocide to the margins of concern (as it often has), theory's exploration of the politics and history of culture will be damaged at its very heart.

NOTES

1. Diner's essay, 'Historical Understanding and Counterrationality' can be found in Part II of this anthology. Throughout this introduction we will provide full citations only for those works that are not included in this book.

2. Despite the important theoretical work on the Holocaust documented in this collection some scholars (even some we include here) remain suspicious of theory. For instance, in a thoughtful review essay, the eminent literary critic Lawrence Langer writes about recent work in Holocaust studies, 'When the language of criticism skirts the ugly facts of history instead of searching for a way to include them in the process of theory formation, an audience can easily lose a sense of the human (and inhuman) ordeals that generated the need for theory in the first place' ('Recent Studies on Memory and Representation,' *Holocaust and Genocide Studies* 16.1 [2002]: 82). Paradoxically, Langer's work frequently draws on such practitioners of high theory as Jean-François Lyotard and Maurice Blanchot.

3. See Deborah Lipstadt, *Denying the Holocaust* (New York: Free Press, 1993), 18. We believe Lipstadt is mistaken.

4. Often, the gap between 'objective' scholarship and 'subjective' memory is difficult to isolate. As historians Saul Friedlander and Dominick LaCapra have been at pains to point out, especially when it comes to traumatic events such as the Shoah, personal investments – in the form of unmastered emotions or psychoanalytic 'transference' – mark even the most seemingly distanced, 'objective' history writing. Conversely, as we hope to illustrate through the inclusion of selections from survivor testimonies in our reader, ostensibly 'personal' writings often contain an intellectual, even theoretical, dimension.

5. Despite the lack of a comprehensive anthology, there are some excellent collections that have emerged out of conferences. We have found especially helpful: Saul Friedlander, ed. *Probing the Limits of Representation: Nazism and the 'Final Solution'* (Cambridge, MA: Harvard University Press, 1992); Bryan Cheyette and Laura Marcus, eds. *Modernity, Culture, and 'the Jew'* (Cambridge, UK: Polity Press, 1998); Alvin Rosenfeld, ed. *Thinking About the Holocaust* (Bloomington, IN: Indiana University Press, 1997); Lawrence Kritzman, ed. *Auschwitz and After* (New York: Routledge, 1995).

6. A note on terminology: in our introductions to this volume we will alternate between several different ways of referring to the events at issue in order to signal that no single word captures their significance unproblematically. While Holocaust has become the accepted and most well known term in the English-speaking world (if not throughout the world), it is not without its problems. Derived from the Greek translation of the Bible, 'Holocaust' refers to a 'burnt offering.' The word's sacrificial connotation imports an inappropriate suggestion that there was a meaning or logic to the murder of the Jews. Other frequently used alternatives include *Shoah* – a Hebrew word meaning destruction, with a suggestion of natural disaster, whose use has become widespread because of Claude Lanzmann's film of that name – and 'Nazi genocide,' which has both the virtues and disadvantages of having a more neutral tone. *Churban*, also meaning destruction, has been popular among Yiddish speakers; it taps into a long history of Jewish response to catastrophe, but tends to assimilate the genocide to previous, incommensurable disasters, such as the destruction of the Temples in Jerusalem. 'Final Solution' [*Endlösung*] was the Nazis' own term for their attempt to exterminate the Jews of Europe, and should only be used with this origin in mind. For further discussion of terminological issues, see Zev Garver and Bruce Zuckerman, 'Why do We Call the Holocaust 'The Holocaust'? An Inquiry into the Psychology of Labels,' *Modern Judaism* 9.2 (1989): 197–211; and James Young, *Writing and Rewriting the Holocaust: Narrative and the Consequences of Interpretation* (Bloomington, IN: Indiana University Press, 1988).

7. For non-specialists who want to get some sense of the current state of research, especially on the history of the Holocaust, we recommend Omer Bartov, ed. *The Holocaust: Origins, Implementation, Aftermath* (New York: Routledge, 2000). Michael Marrus's *The Holocaust in History* (New York: Penguin, 1987) remains a useful account of historiographical debates. Saul Friedlander's *Nazi Germany and the Jews, Vol. 1: The Years of Persecution, 1933–1939* (New York: HarperCollins, 1997) and Marion Kaplan's *Between Dignity and Despair: Jewish Life in Nazi Germany* (New York: Oxford University Press, 1998) provide gripping accounts of everyday life in the pre-Holocaust Nazi period. To get a broad sense of the Nazi regime's genocidal policies, see Michael Burleigh and Wolfgang Wippermann, *The Racial State: Germany, 1933–1945* (New York: Cambridge University Press, 1991). The classic account of the mechanics of the genocide is Raul Hilberg, *The Destruction of the European Jews* (New York: Holmes and Meier, 1985).

8. For an account of the fracturing of understanding in Holocaust studies, see Michael Rothberg, *Traumatic Realism: The Demands of Holocaust Representation* (Minneapolis, MN: University of Minnesota Press, 2000), esp. 1–15.

9. Jonathan Culler, *Literary Theory: A Very Short Introduction* (New York: Oxford University Press, 1997), 14.

10. See Edward W. Said, *The World, the Text, the Critic* (Cambridge, MA: Harvard University Press, 1983). In *Critical Social Theory* (Cambridge, MA: Blackwell, 1995), Craig Calhoun provides an excellent introduction to the more historicized and politicized branches of theory – especially, but not exclusively, those deriving from the Frankfurt School of critical theory.

11. Theodor W. Adorno, *Negative Dialectics*, tr. E. B. Ashton (New York: Continuum, 1973), 365.

12. For accounts of the public impact of the Eichmann trial, see Peter Novick, *The Holocaust in American Life* (New York: Houghton Mifflin, 1999); Tom Segev, *The Seventh Million: The Israelis and the Holocaust*, tr. Haim Watzman (New York: Hill and Wang, 1993); and Jeffrey Shandler, 'The Man in the Glass Box: Watching the Eichmann Trial on American Television,' in Barbie Zelizer, ed. *Visual Culture and the Holocaust* (New Brunswick, NJ: Rutgers University Press, 2001), 91–110.

13. See the introduction to section I for references to these debates.

14. For bibliographical information, see the introduction to section IV.

15. Zygmunt Bauman, *Modernity and the Holocaust* (Ithaca: Cornell University Press, 1989), 152. Bauman's italics.

16. For an extensive survey and selection of theological responses to the Holocaust to which this paragraph is indebted, see Michael L. Morgan, *A Holocaust Reader: Responses to the Nazi Extermination* (New York: Oxford University Press, 2001).

17. Giorgio Agamben, *Remnants of Auschwitz: The Witness and the Archive*, tr. Daniel Heller-Roazen (New York: Zone Books, 1999), 13.

18. For Rose, see section VI; for Badiou, see his *Ethics: An Essay on the Understanding of Evil*, tr. Peter Hallward (New York: Verso, 2001).

19. Andreas Huyssen, *After the Great Divide* (Bloomington, IN: Indiana University Press, 1986), 95.

20. Susan Sontag, 'Fascinating Fascism,' *Under the Sign of Saturn* (New York: Farrar, Straus, and Giroux, 1980), 104.

21. The *Historikerstreit* was a debate among German intellectuals in the mid-1980s about the place of the Holocaust in German history and its relationship to other political crimes, such as those of Stalin. See below and, especially, the introduction to Section II for more on this important debate.

22. Geoffrey H. Hartman, *The Longest Shadow: In the Aftermath of the Holocaust* (Bloomington: Indiana UP, 1996), 21.

23. See Andreas Huyssen, 'Pasts Present: Media, Politics, Amnesia,' in Arjun Appadurai, ed., *Globalization*, (Durham, NC: Duke University Press, 2001), 57–77.

24. See the introduction to section V for references.

25. Eric Santner, *Stranded Objects: Mourning, Memory, and Film in Postwar Germany* (Ithaca, NY: Cornell University Press, 1990), 27. See also LaCapra's related distinction between structural and historical trauma in *History and Memory after Auschwitz* (Ithaca, NY: Cornell University Press, 1998) and in his entry in section V.

26. See also Slavoj Žižek's provocative, and we believe exaggerated, claims that '*the 'objective' ideologico-political content of the depoliticization of the Holocaust, of its elevation into the abyssal absolute Evil, is the political pact of aggressive Zionists and Western Rightist anti-Semites at the expense of* today's *radical political possibilities.*' Slavoj Žižek, *Did Someboday Say Totalitarianism?* (NY: Verso, 2001), 68.

27. On 'wounded attachments,' see Wendy Brown, *States of Injury* (Princeton: Princeton University Press, 1995).

28. For an approach to the globalization of Holocaust memory, see Daniel Levy and Natan Sznaider, 'Memory Unbound: The Holocaust and the Formation of Cosmopolitan Memory,' *European Journal of Social Theory* 5.1 (2002): 87–106. For an exploration of how to chart the intersection of histories without sacrificing specificity, see Michael Rothberg, 'W. E. B. Du Bois in Warsaw: Holocaust Memory and the Color Line, 1949–1952,' *The Yale Journal of Criticism* 14.1 (2001): 169–89.

PART I
THEORY AND EXPERIENCE

THEORY AND EXPERIENCE:
INTRODUCTION

A crucial starting place for any consideration of the implications of the Nazi genocide and camp system is the writings of first-hand witnesses. While some historians remain skeptical about the historical accuracy of victims' testimony, most scholars now agree on the human value of oral and written testimonies. Whatever the problems of memory and point of view that such documents exhibit, they offer an unparalleled access to the unfolding of the Holocaust and to the subjective experience of catastrophe. We would go even farther and assert that some survivor testimony engages in precisely the kind of self-reflexive, critical meditation that we call theory. The writings of Primo Levi, Jean Améry, Charlotte Delbo, and Ruth Kluger do not only convey powerfully the experience of atrocity but also provide models for intellectual engagement with extremity and categories for theoretical reflection on traumatic events and their aftermath. The authors we have selected by no means exhaust the richness of survivor writings, and could be supplemented by other well-known figures, such as Elie Wiesel, Jorge Semprun, and Ida Fink. Many who experienced the Nazi assault first hand have also made more conventional scholarly contributions, including the historian Saul Friedlander and the psychoanalyst Dori Laub, who appear elsewhere in this reader.

We open this part with the preface to *The Drowned and the Saved*, the great last work of Primo Levi, the Jewish-Italian chemist and author, who survived Auschwitz and went on to become one of its most renowned chroniclers. Writing forty years after the liberation of the camps, Levi's concern is with the problems of transmitting knowledge of the Nazi system. Taking account of both the Nazis' design of what David Rousset called the 'concentrationary universe' and more universal problems of memory and perspective (not unlike those that trouble historians), Levi paints a dark picture of the possibilities for future understanding of the Holocaust. But despite Levi's doubts, his own discourse sheds significant light on the phenomenon of the 'lagers' or camps. He simultaneously captures their historical singularity and their internal complexity, and he hints at the moral ambiguity that the camps instantiated and that he famously named the 'gray zone' in another of his last essays.

Jean Améry, an Austrian survivor categorized as Jewish by the Nuremberg Laws despite his complete lack of Jewish cultural or religious identification, writes in a deliberately strident tone diametrically opposed to Levi's dispassionate discourse. For Améry, who fled to Belgium after the Nazi annexation of his homeland, and returned there after the war, it is precisely the subjective experience of the victim that holds the moral truth of the events. If Levi emphasizes the complexity and moral grayness of the camp world, Améry paints a starkly binary portrait that opposes the victim both to the perpetrator and to his non-victimized contemporaries. In 'Resentments,' his reflections on psychology, ethics, and law produce significant insights not only into those domains of knowledge, but also into our understanding of time and corporeality, two central concerns of contemporary theory.

The writings of Charlotte Delbo have already served as the spur for theoretical and critical practice, as Lawrence Langer's *Holocaust Testimonies* demonstrates. Langer draws in particular on Delbo's distinction between 'deep' and 'external' memory in his consideration of the dynamics of oral testimony. Delbo's reflections on memory, taken from her last work *Days and Memory*, provide insight into what it means to 'survive' extremity and complement Améry's considerations of time and the body. They also provide a useful way to think about testimonial writings, not least her own masterpiece, *Auschwitz and After*. Delbo, who was a non-Jewish participant in the communist-led French Resistance before being deported to Auschwitz and Ravensbrück, also writes movingly of the bitter disappointment that many survivors experienced upon return, and in particular upon their discovery of those other camps that made up the Gulag. Bringing together the two very different camp systems of the Nazis and the Soviets, Delbo raises questions about historical comparison and the politics of memory that will return in our final part.

Ruth Kluger is also concerned with comparison and the politics of memory. In this selection from her recent memoir *Still Alive*, Kluger reflects on the contemporary fascination with memorializing historical events. Writing in a voice that, like Améry's, is confrontational and provocative, Kluger challenges platitudes about the preservation of the sites of Nazi terror and asks critical questions about the value of 'a worldwide museum culture of the Shoah.' Kluger, who in her adolescence was deported from Vienna to Theresienstadt and Auschwitz, before later emigrating to the United States, also prompts us to reflect on whether there is in fact anything to learn from the camps. Even if her skepticism is warranted, her own writings simultaneously conjure the ghosts of the past and provide conceptual tools (like her notion of the 'timescape') for their understanding.

The writings of survivors of the Holocaust are often emotionally overwhelming, and indeed part of their theoretical interest lies in the way they demand consideration of affect alongside understanding. Besides illuminating aspects of the Nazi genocide, these selections also include reflection on various matters of concern to a range of contemporary theorists, including the relationships between memory and history, time and justice, and violence and the body. In addition, the very relationship between theory and experience, foregrounded by all of these selections, has itself been at the center of theoretical debate in recent years, especially in feminist and minority studies. From Joan Scott's influential critique of 'experience' as the basis of writing alternative histories to the attempts by Satya Mohanty and the contributors to *Reclaiming Identity* to reinstate experience as an essential epistemological category, the links between subject position, knowledge, and political critique have been passionately contested. Levi, Améry, Delbo, and Kluger do not speak with one voice on these matters, but they clearly suggest that there is much to be gained by a full and open exchange between theory and survivor testimony.

OTHER WORKS IN HOLOCAUST STUDIES

Des Pres, Terrence (1976) *The Survivor: An Anatomy of Life in The Death Camps*. New York: Oxford University Press.

Greenspan, Henry (1998) *On Listening to Holocaust Survivors: Recounting and Life History*. Westport, CT: Praeger.

Langer, Lawrence (1991) *Holocaust Testimonies: The Ruins of Memory*. New Haven, CT: Yale University Press.

Rousset, David (1947) *The Other Kingdom*, trans. Ramon Guthrie. New York: Reynal & Hitchcock.

Semprun, Jorge (1997) *Literature or Life*, trans. Linda Coverdale. New York: Viking.

Weissman, Gary (1998) 'Lawrence Langer and "The Holocaust Experience,"' in Stephen Feinstein, Karen Schierman, and Marcia Sachs Littell (eds), *Confronting the Holocaust: A Mandate for the 21st Century – Part Two*. Lanham, MD: University Press of America.

OTHER RELEVANT THEORETICAL STUDIES

De Lauretis, Teresa (1984) 'Semiotics and Experience,' in T. de Lauretis, *Alice Doesn't: Feminism, Semiotics, Cinema*. Bloomington, IN: Indiana University Press.

Haraway, Donna (1991) 'Situated Knowledge,' in D. Haraway, *Simians, Cyborgs, and Women*. New York: Routledge.

Mohanty, Satya P. (1997) *Literary Theory and the Claims of History*. Ithaca, NY: Cornell University Press.

Moya, Paula M. L. and Michael R. Hames-Garcia (eds), (2000) *Reclaiming Identity: Realist Theory and the Predicament of Postmodernism*. Berkeley, CA: University of California Press.

Scott, Joan (1992) , '"Experience,"' in J. Butler and J. Scott (eds), *Feminists Theorize the Political*. New York: Routledge, pp. 22–40.

I

THE DROWNED AND THE SAVED

Primo Levi

The first news about the Nazi annihilation camps began to spread in the crucial year of 1942. They were vague pieces of information, yet in agreement with each other: they delineated a massacre of such vast proportions, of such extreme cruelty and such intricate motivation that the public was inclined to reject them because of their very enormity. It is significant that the culprits themselves foresaw this rejection well in advance: many survivors (among others, Simon Wiesenthal in the last pages of *The Murderers Are Among Us*) remember that the SS militiamen enjoyed cynically admonishing the prisoners:

> However this war may end, we have won the war against you; none of you will be left to bear witness, but even if someone were to survive, the world will not believe him. There will perhaps be suspicions, discussions, research by historians, but there will be no certainties, because we will destroy the evidence together with you. And even if some proof should remain and some of you survive, people will say that the events you describe are too monstrous to be believed: they will say that they are the exaggerations of Allied propaganda and will believe us, who will deny everything, and not you. We will be the ones to dictate the history of the Lagers.

Strangely enough, this same thought ('even if we were to tell it, we would not be believed') arose in the form of nocturnal dreams produced by the prisoners'

From Primo Levi (1989) 'Preface', *The Drowned and the Saved*, trans. R. Rosenthal. New York: Vintage International.

despair. Almost all the survivors, orally or in their written memoirs, remember a dream which frequently recurred during the nights of imprisonment, varied in its detail but uniform in its substance: they had returned home and with passion and relief were describing their past sufferings, addressing themselves to a loved one, and were not believed, indeed were not even listened to. In the most typical (and cruelest) form, the interlocutor turned and left in silence. This is a theme to which we shall return, but at this point it is important to emphasize how both parties, victims and oppressors, had a keen awareness of the enormity and therefore the noncredibility of what took place in the Lagers – and, we may add here, not only in the Lagers, but in the ghettos, in the rear areas of the Eastern front, in the police stations, and in the asylums for the mentally handicapped.

Fortunately, things did not go as the victims feared and the Nazis hoped. Even the most perfect of organizations has its flaws, and Hitler's Germany, especially during the last months before the collapse, was far from being a perfect machine. Much material evidence of the mass exterminations was suppressed, or a more or less dextrous attempt was made to suppress it: in the autumn of 1944 the Nazis blew up the gas chambers and crematoria at Auschwitz, but the ruins are still there, and despite the contortions of epigones it is difficult to justify their function by having recourse to fanciful hypotheses. The Warsaw ghetto, after the famous insurrection in the spring of 1943, was razed to the ground, but thanks to the superhuman concern of a number of fighter-historians (historians of themselves!), in the rubble, often many meters deep, or smuggled beyond the wall, other historians would later rediscover the testimony of how the ghetto lived and died day by day. All the archives in the Lagers were burned during the final days of the war, truly an irremediable loss, so that even today there is discussion as to whether the victims were four, six, or eight million – although one still talks of millions. Before the Nazis had recourse to the gigantic multiple crematoria, the innumerable corpses of the victims, deliberately killed or worn down by hardship and illness, could have constituted evidence and somehow had to be made to disappear. The first solution, macabre to the point of making one hesitate to speak of it, had been simply to pile up the bodies, hundreds of thousands of bodies, in huge common graves, and this was done, in particular at Treblinka and other minor Lagers, and in the wake of the German army in Russia. This was a temporary solution decided upon with bestial insouciance when the German armies were winning on all fronts and final victory appeared certain: they would decide afterward what should be done, and in any case the victor is the master even of truth, can manipulate it as he pleases. Somehow the common graves would be justified, or made to disappear, or attributed to the Soviets (who, for that matter, proved at Katyn not to be lagging too far behind). But after Stalingrad there were second thoughts: best to erase everything immediately. The prisoners themselves were forced to exhume those pitiful remains and burn them on pyres in the open, as if so unusual an operation of such proportions could go completely unnoticed.

The SS command posts and the security services then took the greatest care to ensure that no witness survived. This is the meaning (it would be difficult to excogitate another) of the murderous and apparently insane transfers with which the history of the Nazi camps came to an end during the first months of 1945: the survivors of Maidanek to Auschwitz, those of Auschwitz to Buchenwald and Mauthausen, those of Buchenwald to Bergen-Belsen, the women of Ravensbrück to Schwerin. In short, everyone had to be snatched away from liberation, deported again to the heart of a Germany that was being invaded from the west and east. It did not matter that they might die along the way; what really mattered was that they should not tell their story. In fact, after having functioned as centers of political terror, then as death factories, and subsequently (or simultaneously) as immense, ever renewed reservoirs of slave labor, the Lagers had become dangerous for a moribund Germany because they contained the secret of the Lagers themselves, the greatest crime in the history of humanity. The army of ghosts that still vegetated in them was composed of *Geheimnisträger*, the bearers of secrets who must be disposed of; the extermination plants, also very eloquent, having been destroyed, had to be moved to the interior, it was decided, in the absurd hope of still being able to lock those ghosts up in Lagers less threatened by the advancing fronts and to exploit their final ability to work, and in the other, less absurd hope that the torment of those Biblical marches would reduce their number. And in fact their number was appallingly reduced, yet some nevertheless had the luck or the strength to survive and remained to bear witness.

Less well known and less studied is the fact that many bearers of secrets were also on the other side, although many knew little and few knew everything. No one will ever be able to establish with precision how many, in the Nazi apparatus, could *not not know* about the frightful atrocities being committed, how many knew something but were in a position to pretend that they did not know, and, further, how many had the possibility of knowing everything but chose the more prudent path of keeping their eyes and ears (and above all their mouths) well shut. Whatever the case, since one cannot suppose that the majority of Germans lightheartedly accepted the slaughter, it is certain that the failure to divulge the truth about the Lagers represents one of the major collective crimes of the German people and the most obvious demonstration of the cowardice to which Hitlerian terror had reduced them: a cowardice which became an integral part of mores and so profound as to prevent husbands from telling their wives, parents their children. Without this cowardice the greatest excesses would not have been carried out, and Europe and the world would be different today.

Without a doubt those who knew the horrible truth because they were (or had been) responsible had compelling reasons to remain silent; but inasmuch as they were depositories of the secret, even by keeping silent they could not always be sure of remaining alive, witness the case of Stangl and the other Treblinka butchers, who after the insurrection there and the dismantling of that Lager were transferred to one of the most dangerous Partisan areas.

Willed ignorance and fear also led many potential 'civilian' witnesses of the infamies of the Lagers to remain silent. Especially during the last years of the war, the Lagers constituted an extensive and complex system which profoundly compenetrated the daily life of the country; one has with good reason spoken of the *univers concentrationnaire*, but it was not a closed universe. Small and large industrial companies, agricultural combines, agencies, and arms factories drew profits from the practically free labor supplied by the camps. Some exploited the prisoners pitilessly, accepting the inhuman (and also stupid) principle of the SS according to which one prisoner was worth another, and if the work killed him he could immediately be replaced; others, a few, cautiously tried to alleviate their sufferings. Still other industries – or perhaps the same ones – made money by supplying the Lagers themselves: lumber, building materials, cloth for the prisoners' striped uniforms, dehydrated vegetables for the soup, etc. The crematoria ovens themselves were designed, built, assembled, and tested by a German company, Topf of Wiesbaden (it was still in operation in 1975, building crematoria for civilian use, and had not considered the advisability of changing its name). It is hard to believe that the personnel of these companies did not realize the significance of the quality or quantity of the merchandise and installations being commissioned by the SS command units. The same can be, and has been, said with regard to the supplies of the poison employed in the gas chambers at Auschwitz: the product, substantially hydrocyanic acid, had already been used for many years for pest control in the holds of boats, but the abrupt increase in orders beginning with 1942 could scarcely go unnoticed. It must have aroused doubts, and certainly did, but they were stifled by fear, the desire for profit, the blindness and willed stupidity that we have mentioned, and in some cases (probably few) by fanatical Nazi obedience.

It is natural and obvious that the most substantial material for the reconstruction of truth about the camps is the memories of the survivors. Beyond the pity and indignation these recollections provoke, they should also be read with a critical eye. For knowledge of the Lagers, the Lagers themselves were not always a good observation post: in the inhuman conditions to which they were subjected, the prisoners could barely acquire an overall vision of their universe. The prisoners, above all those who did not understand German, might not even know where in Europe their Lager was situated, having arrived after a slaughterous and tortuous journey in sealed boxcars. They did not know about the existence of other Lagers, even those only a few kilometers away. They did not know for whom they worked. They did not understand the significance of certain sudden changes in conditions, or of the mass transfers. Surrounded by death, the deportee was often in no position to evaluate the extent of the slaughter unfolding before his eyes. The companion who worked beside him today was gone by the morrow: he might be in the hut next door, or erased from the world; there was no way to know. In short, the prisoner felt overwhelmed by a massive edifice of violence and menace but could not form for himself a representation of it because his eyes were fixed to the ground by every single minute's needs.

This deficiency conditioned the oral or written testimonies of the 'normal' prisoners, those not privileged, who represented the core of the camps and who escaped death only by a combination of improbable events. They were the majority in the Lager, but an exiguous minority among the survivors: among them, those who during their imprisonment enjoyed some sort of privilege are much more numerous. At a distance of years one can today definitely affirm that the history of the Lagers has been written almost exclusively by those who, like myself, never fathomed them to the bottom. Those who did so did not return, or their capacity for observation was paralyzed by suffering and incomprehension.

On the other hand, the 'privileged' witnesses could avail themselves of a certainly better observatory, if only because it was higher up and hence took in a more extensive horizon; but it was to a greater or lesser degree also falsified by the privilege itself. The discussion concerning privilege (not only in the Lager) is delicate, and I shall try to go into it later with the greatest possible objectivity. Here I will only mention the fact that the privileged par excellence, that is, those who acquired privilege for themselves by becoming subservient to the camp authority, did not bear witness at all, for obvious reasons, or left incomplete or distorted or totally false testimony. Therefore the best historians of the Lagers emerged from among the very few who had the ability and luck to attain a privileged observatory without bowing to compromises, and the skill to tell what they saw, suffered, and did with the humility of a good chronicler, that is, taking into account the complexity of the Lager phenomenon and the variety of human destinies being played out in it. It was in the logic of things that these historians should almost all be political prisoners: because the Lagers were a political phenomenon; because the political prisoners, much more than the Jews and the criminals (as we know, the three principal categories of prisoners), disposed of a cultural background which allowed them to interpret the events they saw; and because, precisely inasmuch as they were ex-combatants or antifascist combatants even now, they realized that testimony was an act of war against fascism; because they had easier access to statistical data; and lastly, because often, besides holding important positions in the Lager, they were members of the secret defense organization. At least during the final years, their living conditions were tolerable, which permitted them, for example, to write and preserve notes, an unthinkable luxury for the Jews and a possibility of no interest to the criminals.

For all the reasons touched on here, the truth about the Lagers has come to light down a long road and through a narrow door, and many aspects of the *univers concentrationnaire* have yet to be explored in depth. By now more than forty years have passed since the liberation of the Nazi Lagers; this considerable interval has, for the purposes of clarification, led to conflicting results, which I will try to enumerate.

In the first place, there has been the decanting, a desirable and normal process, thanks to which historical events acquire their chiaroscuro and perspective only some decades after their conclusion. At the end of World War II, quantitative data on the Nazi deportations and massacres, in the Lagers and elsewhere, had not been acquired, nor was it easy to understand their import and specificity. For only a few years now has one begun to understand that the Nazi slaughter was dreadfully 'exemplary' and that, if nothing worse happens in the coming years, it will be remembered as the central event, the scourge, of this century.

By contrast, the passage of time has as a consequence other historically negative results. The greater part of the witnesses, for the defense and the prosecution, have by now disappeared, and those who remain, and who (overcoming their remorse or, alternately, their wounds) still agree to testify, have ever more blurred and stylized memories, often, unbeknownst to them, influenced by information gained from later readings or the stories of others. In some cases, naturally, the lack of memory is simulated, but the many years that have gone by make it credible. Also, the 'I don't know' or 'I did not know' spoken today by many Germans no longer shocks us, as it did or should have when events were recent.

Of another or further stylization we are ourselves responsible, we survivors, or, more precisely, those among us who have decided to live our condition as survivors in the simplest and least critical way. This does not mean that ceremonies and celebrations, monuments and flags are always and everywhere to be deplored. A certain dose of rhetoric is perhaps indispensable for the memory to persist. That sepulchres, 'the urns of the strong,' kindle souls to perform lofty deeds, or at least preserve the memory of accomplished deeds, was true in Foscolo's time and is still true today; but one must beware of over-simplifications. Every victim is to be mourned, and every survivor is to be helped and pitied, but not all their acts should be set forth as examples. The inside of the Lager was an intricate and stratified microcosm; the 'gray zone' of which I shall speak later, that of the prisoners who in some measure, perhaps with good intentions, collaborated with the authority, was not negligible. Indeed, it constituted a phenomenon of fundamental importance for the historian, the psychologist, and the sociologist. There is not a prisoner who does not remember this and who does not remember his amazement at the time: the first threats, the first insults, the first blows came not from the SS but from other prisoners, from 'colleagues,' from those mysterious personages who nevertheless wore the same striped tunic that they, the new arrivals, had just put on. This book means to contribute to the clarification of some aspects of the Lager phenomenon which still appear obscure. It also sets itself a more ambitious goal, to try to answer the most urgent question, the question which torments all those who have happened to read our accounts: How much of the concentration camp world is dead and will not return, like slavery and the dueling code? How much is back or is coming back? What can each of us do so that in this world pregnant with threats at least this threat will be nullified?

I did not intend, nor would I have been able, to do a historian's work, that is, exhaustively examine the sources. I have almost exclusively confined myself to the National Socialist Lagers because I had direct experience only of these; I also have had copious indirect experience of them, through books read, stories listened to, and encounters with the readers of my first two books. Besides, up to the moment of this writing, and notwithstanding the horror of Hiroshima and Nagasaki, the shame of the Gulags, the useless and bloody Vietnam War, the Cambodian self-genocide, the *desaparecidos* of Argentina, and the many atrocious and stupid wars we have seen since, the Nazi concentration camp system still remains a *unicum*, both in its extent and its quality. At no other place or time has one seen a phenomenon so unexpected and so complex: never have so many human lives been extinguished in so short a time, and with so lucid a combination of technological ingenuity, fanaticism, and cruelty. No one wants to absolve the Spanish conquistadors of the massacres perpetrated in the Americas throughout the sixteenth century. It seems they brought about the death of at least sixty million Indios; but they acted on their own, without or against the directives of their government, and they diluted their misdeeds – not very 'planned' to tell the truth – over an arc of more than one hundred years, and they were also helped by the epidemics that they inadvertently brought with them. And, finally, have we not tried to dispose of them by declaring that they were 'things of another time'?

2

'RESENTMENTS'

Jean Améry

[...]

I speak as a victim and examine my resentments. That is no amusing enterprise, either for the reader or for me, and perhaps I would do well to excuse myself at the start for the lack of tact that will unfortunately be displayed. Tact is something good and important – plain, acquired tact in everyday behavior, as well as tact of mind and heart. But no matter how important it may be, it is not suited for the radical analysis that together we are striving for here, and so I will have to disregard it – at the risk of cutting a poor figure. It may be that many of us victims have lost the feeling for tact altogether. Emigration, Resistance, prison, torture, concentration camp – all that is no excuse for rejecting tact and is not intended to be one. But it is a sufficient causal explanation. Let us begin then: without tact, with just that much literary decorum as my effort to be honest and the theme itself force upon me.

My task would be easier if I wanted to shift the problem into the area of political polemics. Then I could cite the books of Kempner, Reitlinger, and Hannah Arendt and, without any further intellectual effort, come to a rather obvious conclusion. It would follow that resentments persist in the victims because on the West German public scene personalities who were allied with the torturers continue to play a role, because in spite of the extension of the Statute of Limitations for major war crimes the criminals have a good chance to attain a

From Jean Améry (1980) 'Resentments' in *At the Mind's Limits: Contemplations by a Survivor on Auschwitz and Its Realities*, trans. S. Rosenfeld and S. P. Rosenfeld. Bloomington and Indianapolis, IN: Indiana University Press.

venerable old age and triumphantly to outlive us. Their activity during their days of glory guarantees it. But what would be gained by such a polemic? Practically nothing. The cause of justice has been pleaded in our name by honorable Germans, better, more vigorously than we ourselves could do it. But I am not at all concerned with a justice that in this particular historical instance could only be hypothetical anyway. What matters to me is the description of the subjective state of the victim. What I can contribute is the analysis of the resentments, gained from introspection. My personal task is to justify a psychic condition that has been condemned by moralists and psychologists alike. The former regard it as a taint, the latter as a kind of sickness. I must acknowledge it, bear the social taint, and first accept the sickness as an integrating part of my personality and then legitimize it. A less rewarding business of confession cannot be imagined, and in addition it will subject my readers to an unusual test of patience.

Resentments as the existential dominant of people like myself are the result of a long personal and historical development. They were by no means evident on the day when I left the last of my concentration camps, Bergen-Belsen, and returned home to Brussels, which was really not my home. We, the resurrected, all looked approximately the way the photos from those days in April and May 1945, now stored in archives, show us: skeletons that had been revived with Anglo-American canned corned beef, toothless ghosts with shaven heads, just about useful enough to give testimony quickly and then to clear out to where they really belonged. But we were 'heroes,' namely to the extent to which we could believe the banners that were stretched over our streets and which read: Gloire aux Prisonniers Politiques! Except that the banners quickly faded, and the pretty social workers and Red Cross nurses, who had turned up in the first days with American cigarettes, tired of their efforts. Still, for quite some time there lasted what was for me a totally unprecedented social and moral status, and it elated me to the extreme: being what I was – a surviving Resistance fighter, Jew, victim of persecution by a universally hated regime – there was mutual understanding between me and the rest of the world. Those who had tortured me and turned me into a bug, as dark powers had once done to the protagonist of Kafka's *The Metamorphosis*, were themselves an abomination to the victorious camp. Not only National Socialism, *Germany* was the object of a general feeling that before our eyes crystallized from hate into contempt. Never again would this land 'endanger world peace,' as they said in those days. Let it live, but no more than that. As the potato field of Europe, let it serve this continent with its diligence, but with nothing other than that. There was much talk about the collective guilt of the Germans. It would be an outright distortion of the truth if I did not confess here without any concealment that this was fine with me. It seemed to me as if I had experienced their atrocities as collective ones. I had been just as afraid of the simple private in his field-gray uniform as of the brown-clad Nazi official with his swastika armband. I also could not rid myself of the sight of the Germans on a small passenger platform where, from the cattle cars of our deportation train, the corpses had been unloaded and piled up; not on a single one of their stony faces was I able to detect an expression of abhorrence. Let collective crime and collective guilt balance each other and produce the equilibrium of world morality. *Vae victis castigatisque.*

There was no reason, hardly a real possibility, for resentments to form. Certainly, I wanted no part of any compassion with a people that for me was laden with collective guilt, and it was rather indifferently that I helped some Quakerly inspired persons to load a truck that was bringing used children's clothes to impoverished Germany. [. . .] For the first time in my life I was in tune with the public opinion that resounded around me. I felt just fine in the entirely unaccustomed role of conformist. For me the potato-field and war-ruins Germany was a lost area of the globe. I avoided speaking its, my language and chose a pseudonym with a Romance ring. Which way the international political winds were blowing, that, of course, I didn't know. For while I fancied myself as the conqueror of those who yesterday had tortured me, the real victors were all set to work out plans for the losers that had nothing, but absolutely nothing more to do with potato fields. At the very moment when I was imagining that through the fate I had suffered I had finally caught up with world opinion, the latter was about to transcend itself. I thought that I was right in the middle of contemporary reality and was already thrown back onto an illusion.

I had my first doubts in 1948, while passing through Germany on a train. I chanced upon a page from the American occupation forces newspaper and skimmed a letter to the editor, in which the anonymous writer said to the GIs: 'Just don't act so big around here. Germany will become great and powerful again. Hit the road, you crooks.' The letter writer [. . .] had as little idea at that time as I myself that this Germany was, in fact, destined to celebrate a most grandiose resurrection of might, not in opposition to the khaki-clad transatlantic soldiers but with them. I was puzzled only that there actually was such a letter writer and because I heard a German voice that sounded different from the way I believed it was obliged to sound for a long time to come: remorseful. In the following years there was less and less talk of remorse. First the pariah Germany was accepted into the community of nations, after that it was courted, finally it had to be dispassionately reckoned with in the power game.

Under these circumstances – circumstances of an unprecedented economic, industrial, and military rise – one cannot reasonably demand of someone that he go on tearing his hair and beating his breast. The Germans saw themselves absolutely as victims, since, after all, they had been compelled to survive not only the winter battles of Leningrad and Stalingrad, not only the bombardments of their cities, not only the judgment of Nuremberg, but also the dismemberment of their country. Thus, as can all too easily be understood, they were not inclined to do more than to take the past of the Third Reich and, in their own way, to 'overcome' it, as one said back then. In those days, at the same time as the Germans were conquering the world markets for their industrial products and were busy at home – not without a certain equanimity – with overcoming, our resentments increased; or perhaps I must restrain myself and say only that *my* resentments increased.

I witnessed how Germany's politicians, only a few of whom, if I was properly informed, had distinguished themselves in the resistance movement, speedily and enthusiastically sought to affiliate with Europe. Effortlessly, they joined the new Europe to the other one that between 1940 and 1944 Hitler had already successfully begun to reorder according to his own plan. Suddenly there was good reason for resentments. It was not at all necessary that in German towns Jewish cemeteries and monuments for resistance fighters be desecrated. Conversations like the one I had in 1958 with a South German businessman over breakfast in the hotel were enough. Not without first politely inquiring whether I was an Israelite, the man tried to convince me that there was no longer any race hatred in his country. The German people bear no grudge against the Jewish people, he said. As proof he cited his government's magnanimous policy of reparations, which was, incidentally, well appreciated by the young state of Israel. In the presence of this man, whose mind was so at ease, I felt miserable: Shylock, demanding his pound of flesh. *Vae victoribus!* Those of us who had believed that the victory of 1945, even if only in small part, had been ours too, were forced to relinquish it. The Germans no longer had any hard feelings toward the resistance fighters and Jews. How could these still demand atonement? Jewish-born men of the same stamp as a Gabriel Marcel showed themselves most eager to reassure their German contemporaries and fellow human beings. Only totally obstinate, morally condemnable hate, already censured by history, they said, clings to a past that was clearly nothing other than an operational mishap of German history and in which the broad masses of the German people had no part.

But to my own distress, I belonged to that disapproving minority with its hard feelings. Stubbornly, I held against Germany its twelve years under Hitler. I bore this grudge into the industrial paradise of the new Europe and into the majestic halls of the West. I 'stuck out,' as I once had in the camp because of poor posture at roll call; I attracted the disapproving attention no less of my former fellows in battle and suffering, who were now gushing over about reconciliation, than of my enemies, who had just been converted to tolerance. I preserved my resentments. And since I neither can nor want to get rid of them, I must live with them and am obliged to clarify them for those against whom they are directed.

There seems to be general agreement that the final say on resentments is that of Friedrich Nietzsche, in whose *Genealogy of Morals* we read: '... resentment defines such creatures who are denied genuine reaction, that of the deed, and who compensate for it through an imaginary revenge. ... The resentful person is neither sincere, nor naïve, nor honest and forthright with himself. His soul squints; his mind loves hiding places and back doors; everything concealed gives him the feeling that it is his world, his security, his balm. ...' Thus spake the man who dreamed of the synthesis of the brute with the superman. He must be answered by those who witnessed the union of the brute with the subhuman; they were present as victims when a certain humankind joyously celebrated a festival of cruelty, as Nietzsche himself has expressed it – in anticipation of a few modern anthropological theories.

But am I attempting this rejoinder in full command of my mental powers? Mistrustingly, I examine myself. It could be that I am sick, for after observing us victims, objective scientific method, in its lovely detachment, has already come up with the concept of the 'concentration camp syndrome.' I read in a recently published book about 'Delayed Psychic Effects After Political Persecution' that all of us are not only physically but also mentally damaged. The character traits that make up our personality are distorted. Nervous restlessness, hostile withdrawal into one's own self are the typical signs of our sickness. It is said that we are 'warped'. That causes me to recall fleetingly the way my arms were twisted high behind my back when they tortured me. But it also sets me the task of defining anew our warped state, namely as a form of the human condition that morally as well as historically is of a higher order than that of healthy straightness. Thus I must delimit our resentments on two sides and shield them against two explications: that of Nietzsche, who morally condemned resentment, and that of modern psychology, which is able to picture it only as a disturbing conflict.

Vigilance is imperative. Seductive, consoling self-pity could entice. But one can believe me when I say that for me this is no problem. In the jails and camps of the Third Reich all of us scorned rather than pitied ourselves because of our helplessness and all-encompassing weakness. The temptation to reject ourselves has survived within us, as well as the immunity to self-pity. We don't believe in tears.

In pondering this question, it did not escape me that resentment is not only an unnatural but also a logically inconsistent condition. It nails every one of us onto the cross of his ruined past. Absurdly, it demands that the irreversible be turned around, that the event be undone. Resentment blocks the exit to the genuine human dimension, the future. I know that the time-sense of the person trapped in resentment is twisted around, dis-ordered, if you wish, for it desires two impossible things: regression into the past and nullification of what happened. [...] For this reason the man of resentment cannot join in the unisonous peace chorus all around him, which cheerfully proposes: not backward let us look but forward, to a better, common future!

To the very same degree that for me a fresh, calm look toward the future is too difficult, my persecutors of yesterday manage to find it too easy. Lame-winged as I am after exile, life in hiding, and torture, I can't keep up with the lofty ethical flights that a man like the French publicist André Neher propounds to us victims. We victims of persecution, the high-soaring man says, ought to internalize our past suffering and bear it in emotional asceticism, as our torturers should do with their guilt. But I must confess: I lack the desire, the talent, and the conviction for something like that. It is impossible for me to accept a parallelism that would have my path run beside that of the fellows who flogged me with a horsewhip. I do not want to become the accomplice of my torturers; rather, I demand that the latter negate themselves and in the negation coordinate with me. The piles of corpses that lie between them and me cannot be removed in the process of internalization, so it seems to me, but, on the contrary, through actualization, or, more strongly stated, by actively settling the unresolved conflict in the field of historical practice.

[...] I know, somebody will object that what I am presenting is a barbaric, primitive lust for revenge, which I have merely disguised in nice, or not-so-nice, at any rate, in highbrow terms, but which has fortunately been overcome by progressive morality. Self-confessed man of resentments that I am, I supposedly live in the bloody illusion that I can be compensated for my suffering through the freedom granted me by society to inflict injury in return. The horsewhip lacerated me; for that reason, even if I do not dare demand that the now defenseless thug be surrendered up to my own whip-swinging hand, I want at least the vile satisfaction of knowing that my enemy is behind bars. Thereupon I would fancy that the contradiction of my madly twisted time-sense were resolved.

[...] When I stand by my resentments, when I admit that in deliberating our problem I am 'biased,' I still know that I am the captive of the *moral truth* of the conflict. It seems logically senseless to me to demand objectivity in the controversy with my torturers, with those who helped them, and with the others, who merely stood by silently. The atrocity as atrocity has no objective character. Mass murder, torture, injury of every kind are objectively nothing but chains of physical events, describable in the formalized language of the natural sciences. They are facts within a physical system, not deeds within a moral system. The crimes of National Socialism had no moral quality for the doer, who always trusted in the norm system of his Führer and his Reich. The monster, who is not chained by his conscience to his deed, sees it from his viewpoint only as an objectification of his will, not as a moral event. The Flemish SS-man Wajs, who – inspired by his German masters – beat me on the head with a shovel handle whenever I didn't work fast enough, felt the tool to be an extension of his hand and the blows to be emanations of his psycho-physical dynamics. Only I possessed, and still possess, the moral truth of the blows that even today roar in my skull, and for that reason I am more entitled to judge, not only more than the culprit but also more than society – which thinks only about its continued existence. The social body is occupied merely with safeguarding itself and could not care less about a life that has been damaged. At the very best, it looks forward, so that such things don't happen again. But my resentments are there in order that the crime become a moral reality for the criminal, in order that he be swept into the truth of his atrocity.

SS-man Wajs from Antwerp, a repeated murderer and an especially adroit torturer, paid with his life. What more can my foul thirst for revenge demand?

But if I have searched my mind properly, it is not a matter of revenge, nor one of atonement. The experience of persecution was, at the very bottom, that of an extreme *loneliness*. At stake for me is the release from the abandonment that has persisted from that time until today. When SS-man Wajs stood before the firing squad, he experienced the moral truth of his crimes. At that moment, he was with *me* – and I was no longer alone with the shovel handle. I would like to believe that at the instant of his execution he wanted exactly as much as I to turn back time, to undo what had been done. When they led him to the place of execution, the antiman had once again become a fellow man. If everything had taken place only between SS-man Wajs and me, and if an entire inverted pyramid of SS men, SS helpers, officials, Kapos, and medal-bedecked generals had not weighed on me, I would have died calmly and appeased along with my fellow man with the Death's Head insignia. At least that is the way it seems to me now.

But Wajs from Antwerp was only one of a multitude. The inverted pyramid is still driving me with its point into the ground. Thus the special kind of resentments, of which neither Nietzsche nor Max Scheler (who wrote on the subject in 1912) was able to have any notion. Thus also my scant inclination to be conciliatory – more precisely, my conviction that loudly proclaimed readiness for reconciliation by Nazi victims can only be either insanity and indifference to life or the masochistic conversion of a suppressed *genuine* demand for revenge. Whoever submerges his individuality in society and is able to comprehend himself only as a function of the social, that is, the insensitive and indifferent person, really does forgive. He calmly allows what happened to remain what it was. As the popular saying goes, he lets time heal his wounds. His time-sense is not dis-ordered, that is to say, it has not moved out of the biological and social sphere into the moral sphere. As a deindividualized, interchangeable part of the social mechanism he lives with it consentingly, and when he forgives, his behavior is analogous to the social reaction to crime, as the French trial lawyer Maurice Garçon described it in connection with the debate on the Statute of Limitations. 'Already the child,' so the *maître* instructs us, 'who is reproached for a past lack of obedience, answers: but that's already past. This already-being-long-past appears to the child in the most natural way as an excuse. And we, too, regard the remoteness through time as the principle of the Statute of Limitations. A crime causes disquiet in society; but as soon as public consciousness loses the memory of the crime, the disquiet also disappears. The punishment that is temporally far removed from the crime, becomes senseless.' This is correct to the point of being a platitudinous revelation – to the extent that we are dealing with society, or with the individual who incorporates himself morally into society and dissolves in its consensus. It has no relevance whatsoever for the person who perceives himself to be morally unique.

And thus, with the help of a trick, I have placed my mean irreconcilability in the shining light of morals and morality. Without a doubt, I will be reproached for this, and I must reply, since I am aware from the start that the overwhelming majority of the world's nonvictims will hardly accept my justification. But it doesn't matter. In two decades of contemplating what happened to me, I believe to have recognized that a forgiving and forgetting induced by social pressure is immoral. Whoever lazily and cheaply forgives, subjugates himself to the social and biological time-sense, which is also called the 'natural' one. Natural consciousness of time actually is rooted in the physiological process of wound-healing and became part of the social conception of reality. But precisely for this reason it is not only extramoral, but also *anti*moral in character. Man has the right and the privilege to declare himself to be in disagreement with every natural occurrence, including the biological healing that time brings about. What happened, happened. This sentence is just as true as it is hostile to morals and intellect. The moral power to resist contains the protest, the revolt against reality, which is rational only as long as it is moral. The moral person demands annulment of time – in the particular case under question, by nailing the criminal to his deed. Thereby, and through a moral turning-back of the clock, the latter can join his victim as a fellow human being.

[...]

In order to clarify and simplify what I mean, I need only return to the conviction already expressed that the unresolved conflict between victims and slaughterers must be externalized and actualized, if both the overpowered and those who overpowered them are to succeed in mastering the past, a past that, despite its extreme oppositeness, they still have in common. Externalization and actualization: most certainly, they cannot consist in a revenge dealt out in proportion to what was suffered. I cannot prove it, but I am certain that there is no victim who would even have considered hanging the man Bogner, of the Auschwitz trial, in the Bogner swing. Even less would any sane person among us ever venture the morally impossible thought that four to six million Germans should be forcibly taken away to their death. Nowhere else could the *jus talionis* make less historic and moral sense than in this instance. It can be a matter neither of revenge on the one side nor of a problematic atonement, which has only theological meaning and therefore is not relevant for me, on the other. Of course, it cannot be a matter of settlement by force, which is historically unthinkable anyhow. What then is it a matter of – since I have spoken expressly of a settlement in the field of historical practice?

Well then, the problem could be settled by permitting resentment to remain alive in the one camp and, aroused by it, self-mistrust in the other. Goaded solely by the spurs of our resentment – and not in the least by a conciliatoriness that, subjectively, is almost always dubious and, objectively, hostile to history – the German people would remain sensitive to the fact that they cannot allow a piece of their national history to be neutralized by time, but must integrate it. If I remember rightly, it was Hans Magnus Enzensberger who once wrote that Auschwitz is Germany's past, present, and future. But unfortunately he is not what counts, for he and his moral peers are not the people. But if, in the midst of the world's silence, our resentment holds its finger raised, then Germany, as a whole and also in its future generations, would retain the knowledge that it was not Germans who did away with the dominion of baseness. It would then, as I sometimes hope, learn to comprehend its past acquiescence in the Third Reich as the total negation not only of the world that it plagued with war and death but also of its own better origins; it would no longer repress or hush up the twelve years that for us others really were a thousand, but claim them as its realized negation of the world and its self, as its own negative possession. On the field of history there would occur what I hypothetically described earlier for the limited, individual circle: two groups of people, the overpowered and those who overpowered them, would be joined in the desire that time be turned back and, with it, that history become moral. If this demand were raised by the German people, who as a matter of fact have been victorious and already rehabilitated by time, it would have tremendous weight, enough so that by this alone it would already be fulfilled. The German revolution would be made good, Hitler disowned. And in the end Germans would really achieve what the people once did not have the might or the will to do, and what later, in the political power game, no longer appeared to be a vital necessity: the eradication of the ignominy.

How this shall come about in actual practice, every German may picture for himself. This writer is not a German and it is not for him to give advice to this people. At best, he is able to imagine vaguely a national community that would reject everything, but absolutely everything, that it accomplished in the days of its own deepest degradation, and what here and there may appear to be as harmless as the Autobahns. Remaining within his exclusively literary frame of reference, Thomas Mann once expressed this in a letter: 'It may be superstition,' he wrote to Walter von Molo, 'but in my eyes the books that could be printed in Germany between 1933 and 1945 are less than worthless and one ought not to touch them. An odor of blood and disgrace clings to them; they should all be reduced to pulp.' The spiritual reduction to pulp by the German people, not only of the books, but of everything that was carried out in those twelve years, would be the negation of the negation: a highly positive, a redeeming act. Only through it would our resentment be subjectively pacified and have become objectively unnecessary.

[...]

3

DAYS AND MEMORY

Charlotte Delbo

Explaining the inexplicable. There comes to mind the image of a snake shedding its old skin, emerging from beneath it in a fresh, glistening one. In Auschwitz I took leave of my skin – it had a bad smell, that skin – worn from all the blows it had received, and found myself in another, beautiful and clean, although with me the molting was not as rapid as the snake's. Along with the old skin went the visible traces of Auschwitz: the leaden stare out of sunken eyes, the tottering gait, the frightened gestures. With the new skin returned the gestures belonging to an earlier life: the using of a toothbrush, of toilet paper, of a handkerchief, of a knife and fork, eating food calmly, saying hello to people upon entering a room, closing the door, standing up straight, speaking, later on smiling with my lips and, still later, smiling both at once with my lips and my eyes. Rediscovering odors, flavors, the smell of rain. In Birkenau, rain heightened the odor of diarrhea. It is the most fetid odor I know. In Birkenau, the rain came down upon the camp, upon us, laden with soot from the crematoriums, and with the odor of burning flesh. We were steeped in it.

It took a few years for the new skin to fully form, to consolidate.

Rid of its old skin, it's still the same snake. I'm the same too, apparently. However . . .

How does one rid oneself of something buried far within: memory and the skin of memory. It clings to me yet. Memory's skin has hardened, it allows

From Charlotte Delbo (1990) *Days and Memory*, trans. R. Lamont. Evanston: Northwestern University Press, 2001.

nothing to filter out of what it retains, and I have no control over it. I don't feel it anymore.

In the camp one could never pretend, never take refuge in the imagination. I remember Yvonne Picart, a morning when we were carrying bricks from a wrecker's depot. We carried two bricks at a time, from one pile to another pile. We were walking side by side, our bricks hugged to our chests, bricks we had pried from a pile covered with ice, scraping our hands. Those bricks were heavy, and got heavier as the day wore on. Our hands were blue from cold, our lips cracked. Yvonne said to me: 'Why can't I imagine I'm on the Boulevard Saint-Michel, walking to class with an armful of books?' and she propped the two bricks inside her forearm, holding them as students do books. 'It's impossible. One can't imagine either being somebody else or being somewhere else.'

I too, I often tried to imagine I was somewhere else. I tried to visualize myself as someone else, as when in a theatrical role you become another person. It didn't work.

In Auschwitz reality was so overwhelming, the suffering, the fatigue, the cold so extreme, that we had no energy left for this type of pretending. When I would recite a poem, when I would tell the comrades beside me what a novel or a play was about while we went on digging in the muck of the swamp, it was to keep myself alive, to preserve my memory, to remain me, to make sure of it. Never did that succeed in nullifying the moment I was living through, not for an instant. To think, to remember was a great victory over the horror, but it never lessened it. Reality was right there, killing. There was no possible getting away from it.

How did I manage to extricate myself from it when I returned? What did I do so as to be alive today? People often ask me that question, to which I continue to look for an answer, and still find none.

Auschwitz is so deeply etched in my memory that I cannot forget one moment of it. – So you are living with Auschwitz? – No, I live next to it. Auschwitz is there, unalterable, precise, but enveloped in the skin of memory, an impermeable skin that isolates it from my present self. Unlike the snake's skin, the skin of memory does not renew itself. Oh, it may harden further ... Alas, I often fear lest it grow thin, crack, and the camp get hold of me again. Thinking about it makes me tremble with apprehension. They claim the dying see their whole life pass before their eyes ...

In this underlying memory sensations remain intact. No doubt, I am very fortunate in not recognizing myself in the self that was in Auschwitz. To return from there was so improbable that it seems to me I was never there at all. Unlike those whose life came to a halt as they crossed the threshold of return, who since that time survive as ghosts, I feel that the one who was in the camp is not me, is not the person who is here, facing you. No, it is all too incredible. And everything that happened to that other, the Auschwitz one, now has no bearing upon me, does not concern me, so separate from one another are this deep-lying memory and ordinary memory. I live within a twofold being. The Auschwitz double doesn't bother me, doesn't interfere with my life. As though it weren't I at all. Without this split I would not have been able to revive.

The skin enfolding the memory of Auschwitz is tough. Even so it gives way at times, revealing all it contains. Over dreams the conscious will has no power. And in those dreams I see myself, yes, my own self such as I know I was: hardly able to stand on my feet, my throat tight, my heart beating wildly, frozen to the marrow, filthy, skin and bones; the suffering I feel is so unbearable, so identical to the pain endured there, that I feel it physically, I feel it throughout my whole body which becomes a mass of suffering; and I feel death fasten on me, I feel that I am dying. Luckily, in my agony I cry out. My cry wakes me and I emerge from the nightmare, drained. It takes days for everything to get back to normal, for everything to get shoved back inside memory, and for the skin of memory to mend again. I become myself again, the person you know, who can talk to you about Auschwitz without exhibiting or registering any anxiety or emotion.

Because when I talk to you about Auschwitz, it is not from deep memory my words issue. They come from external memory, if I may put it that way, from intellectual memory, the memory connected with thinking processes. Deep memory preserves sensations, physical imprints. It is the memory of the senses. For it isn't words that are swollen with emotional charge. Otherwise, someone who has been tortured by thirst for weeks on end could never again say 'I'm thirsty. How about a cup of tea.' This word has also split in two. *Thirst* has turned back into a word for commonplace use. But if I dream of the thirst I suffered in Birkenau, I once again see the person I was, haggard, halfway crazed, near to collapse; I physically feel that real thirst and it is an atrocious nightmare. If, however, you'd like me to talk to you about it . . .

This is why I say today that while knowing perfectly well that it corresponds to the facts, I no longer know if it is real.

[. . .]

When we emerged from the camps, run down to the point of stupor, we had not even the strength to feel joy. Just to rest, to sleep, sleep our fill. Never, it seemed to us, would our tiredness go away. Nor our sadness. Upon us lay the weight of all those who were not returning. A few thousand survivors as against millions of dead, a sum of suffering that will never be reckoned, by anyone.

We, though, we were going home and life would resume. We still didn't have a very clear understanding of it. All the things we had planned to do, all our dreams of how it would be afterward faded into a mist of unreality. Our preoccupations did not extend beyond the immediate: slaking our thirst, sleeping, eating, not hearing the siren anymore, not commanding our bodies to keep upright, to keep walking; ceasing that exhausting supervision of our every gesture, ceasing to be eternally on the alert; letting go, relaxing. That is, not having to worry about everything. For my part, I felt that, no longer stiffened by my efforts of will, my limbs were going slack, my backbone was melting.

47

In the confused state we were all in, certain things did however stand out clearly: the guards' watch towers were collapsing, barbed wire enclosures were toppling, the camps were being swept away by a cleansing whirlwind: victory. Grass would sprout on the mustering grounds. The enormous sores that had disfigured vast stretches of territory would be effaced by vegetation, covered by earth's natural mantle. Victory had been costly, but it was here at last, glowing. Freedom had been won. Our dead, our millions of dead, our suffering, our humiliation would be inscribed in history. We were coming back. We had a tale to tell.

We'd tell it later on. For the moment the thing to do was get our strength back, get our bearings, get back into the mainstream of life, into our former life or a new one: marry, have children, work, embark on studies or take them up again, return to an old job or switch to another to make a fresh start. Slowly our thinking began to revive. You had to reconstruct your personality, so to speak. That is, you had to resume possession of yourself, collecting the scattered pieces which reappeared all of a sudden or else came back to light little by little, pieces you had believed lost and that you had now to stick back together, as you did so erasing the scars left by the camp. And so once home again, each of us was seen to go his own way; those who had been inseparable companions now sometimes went for years without seeing one another. Each was too much taken up with all the problems he was beset by, unforeseen difficulties very often of the most prosaic sort. No, it wasn't self-centeredness, self-absorption. Europe was picking up the wreckage, criminals were being brought to justice and sentenced; history had no further need of us. The next generation would grow up in freedom.

Everyone wanted life to be pleasant and nice again, wanted the comforts of old habits, illusions, beliefs, dreams.

When the raw reality was revealed about the country which, since 1917, had represented the hope of the world's disinherited, when the truth about things in the Soviet Union finally burst into the open, many refused to believe it: it meant relinquishing their faith, the very purpose of their lives, the reason for which some had taken such great risks and had been deported.

A lofty, clear voice rose up then, so high and clear that it drowned out those which earlier had whispered the same truth: there are concentration camps in the USSR. Such was the ring of sincerity in this voice, such was its truthfulness that it was impossible to impugn its testimony, impossible to ignore it. From one end to the other of a land as vast as a continent stretched an archipelago of leprous islands, evil places with watch towers and barbed wire, camps enclosing men, women, adolescents, even children, millions of people.

Following his, other voices arose – just as clear, just as true. In the camps where the regime was the harshest deportees in striped prison garb like ours were being worked to death. They were being marched in columns five abreast, to the commands of dehumanized brutes, just as we had been marched in the Nazi camps. From east to west they extended, and into the far north – and in that country north means the Arctic Circle. For half a century, the living dead had been mining gold in the Kolyma region, the very gold out of which Lenin declared that urinals should be fashioned. Supreme derision. The balance sheet was frightful. Millions of dead, whole ethnic groups wiped out of existence, republics expunged from official maps.

We victims of a bloodthirsty madman, we who thought that this bloodthirsty madman's downfall meant the end of the concentration-camp system – here then is the truth we must live with now: camps still exist. An unbearable truth.

To tear down our barbed wire called for the combined effort of the most powerful nations, it required their armies, the mobilization of all their industrial might, and the resistance of subjugated peoples. But for the military victory we would all have perished.

We, caged behind our barbed wire, we were able to count on Hitler's eventual defeat. For us it was a certainty. Hope gave us the strength to hang on. We did not know for how long we would have to endure – victory sometimes seemed so far off that we feared we would no longer be alive to see it – as alas turned out to be true for most of us –; but our certainty remained. Hitler will be crushed, we'll pull through.

What then of the prisoners in Siberian camps, condemned for years and years? How do they hang on? What hope gives them the strength to fight to survive until a liberation which keeps receding all the time? Who'll get them out of there? Who will tear down the watch towers and the wire? When, thanks to what circumstances, will the concentration-camp system – this shame we associated only with Nazism – be abolished? No one will wage a war for their sake, there is no sign of the political system collapsing, our protests are ineffectual.

The frozen songs of the Kolyma freeze our hearts.

Comrades, O my comrades, we who swore not to forget our dead, what can we do for these forgotten souls? Some of them are yet alive. Some of them continue to hope.

4

'THE CAMPS'

Ruth Kluger

[...]

Today, more than half a century after the liberation of the camps, Germany is dotted with their carefully tended, unlovely remains: tourist attractions like the ruins of medieval castles. The same people who gather at noon in front of Munich's municipal hall to watch the pretty wooden figures emerge from the bell tower to do their jousting and dancing will take the bus to Dachau in the afternoon, somberly follow a guide, and pay obeisance to the old remains of Hitler's first concentration camp. If you are in the least interested in German literature, you'll want to travel to Weimar, Goethe's town, and once you are there, you feel obligated to trudge up the steep hill of nearby Buchenwald in a show of awe and consternation. The camps are part of a worldwide museum culture of the Shoah, nowhere more evident than in Germany, where every sensitive citizen, not to mention every politician who wants to display his ethical credentials, feels the need to take pictures at these shrines or, even better, have his picture taken.

Yet to what purpose? Of course one is glad that the Germans, who had been in denial for so long that we thought they would never face themselves in the mirror of their past, finally did face up, and once they started, did so with the proverbial German thoroughness. And yet I feel something is missing. In the eighties I happened to spend time at the University of Göttingen, and one afternoon I invited a colleague's class to visit me at home. As I listened to two

From Ruth Kluger (2001) 'The Camps', in *Still Alive: A Holocaust Girlhood Remembered*. New York: Feminist Press at the City University of New York.

likable first-semester graduate students who were talking animatedly about Auschwitz, it dawned on me that they were using the name not as shorthand for the Holocaust in general, as has become customary, but concretely, for a place they seemed to know well. I questioned them without letting on that I had a previous acquaintance with the camp, and learned that they had done their alternative national service, their *Zivildienst*, there. Instead of serving in the military, they had whitewashed the fences at Auschwitz. I associate Tom Sawyer and his friends with whitewashed fences, and I wondered aloud whether this cheerful activity made any sense in an extermination camp. My doubts astonished them in turn. Preservation was a form of restitution, they argued. Not that they liked the tourists (all those Americans!), and they were less than enthusiastic about the noisy schoolchildren with their know-it-all teachers. Nevertheless, the site of suffering has to be preserved.

And I ask myself: Why?

Drunken August, the darling of Viennese legend, spent a besotted night in a ditch full of dead bodies and awoke with only a hangover. He staggered out of the ditch, left it behind him, and continued to play his bagpipe. We are different. We don't get off so cheaply; the ghosts cling to us. Do we expect that our unsolved questions will be answered if we hang on to what's left: the place, the stones, the ashes? We don't honor the dead with these unattractive remnants of past crimes; we collect and keep them for the satisfaction of our own necrophilic desires. Violated taboos, such as child murder and mass murder, turn their victims into spirits, whom we offer a kind of home that they may haunt at will. Perhaps we are afraid they may leave the camps, and so we insist that their deaths were unique and must not be compared to any other losses or atrocities. Never again shall there be such a crime.

The same thing doesn't happen twice anyway. Every event, like every human being and even every dog, is unique. We would be condemned to be isolated monads if we didn't compare and generalize, for comparisons are the bridges from one unique life to another. In our hearts we all know that some aspects of the Shoah have been repeated elsewhere, today and yesterday, and will return in new guise tomorrow; and the camps, too, were only imitations (unique imitations, to be sure) of what had occurred the day before yesterday.

In today's Hiroshima, a busy industrial city, there is a memorial site to the great catastrophe which ushered in the atomic age. It is a park with flowers and temples, where Japanese children, in their English school uniforms, seem to have a thoroughly good time. The Japanese are as frustrated in coping with past horror as we are, because they, too, can think only of the mantra 'Never again.' It's easier to recognize this helplessness in a strange city. The children, with their history teachers in tow, hang origami toys, cranes, and other symbolic paper objects, on various bushes and trees dedicated to the goddess of peace, and then they romp about the park, screeching and chasing each other. There is the soothing sound of water, so typical of the aesthetics of Japanese landscaping, and tape-recorded messages with humanistic content are released at regular intervals. In the very midst of these efforts to propitiate and tranquilize the visitor, there is *the* monument, the ugliest ruin in the world: the building, we remember, wasn't hit by a bomb in the usual way; the bomb exploded above the building and disfigured it through heat, so that it looks as unnatural as a human face which has been ravaged by fire.

During a discussion with some youngsters in Germany I am asked (as if it was a genuine question and not an accusation) whether I don't think that the Jews have turned into Nazis in their dealings with the Arabs, and haven't the Americans always acted like Nazis in their dealings with the Indians? When it gets that aggressive and simple, I just sputter. Or I sit in the student cafeteria with some advanced Ph.D. candidates, and one reports how in Jerusalem he made the acquaintance of an old Hungarian Jew who was a survivor of Auschwitz, and yet this man cursed the Arabs and held them all in contempt. How can someone who comes from Auschwitz talk like that? the German asks. I get into the act and argue, perhaps more hotly than need be. What did he expect? Auschwitz was no instructional institution, like the University of Göttingen, which he attends. You learned nothing there, and least of all humanity and tolerance. Absolutely nothing good came out of the concentration camps, I hear myself saying, with my voice rising, and he expects catharsis, purgation, the sort of thing you go to the theater for? They were the most useless, pointless establishments imaginable. That is the one thing to remember about them if you know nothing else. No one agrees, and no one contradicts me. Who wants to get into an argument with the old bag who's got that number on her arm? Germany's young intellectuals bow their heads over their soup plates and eat what's in front of them. Now I have silenced them, and that wasn't my intention. There is always a wall between the generations, but here the wall is barbed wire. Old, rusty barbed wire.

And yet they could easily have objected. Don't I often insist that I learned something in the camps about what happens to us in extreme situations, which was good to know later on and was usable precisely because I don't reject all comparisons? And don't I resent those who would deny me this knowledge and those who assume, without further inquiry, that we all lost our minds and morals there?

In the late sixties, when I was teaching in Cleveland, a young Jewish political scientist, engaged to a German woman, said to my face, without flinching: 'I know what you survivors had to do to stay alive.' I didn't know what we had had to do, but I knew what he wanted to say. He wanted to say, 'You walked over dead bodies.' Should I have answered, 'But I was only twelve'? Or said, 'But I am a good girl, always have been'? Both answers implicate the others, my fellow prisoners. Or I could have said, 'Where do you get off talking like that?' and gotten angry. I said nothing, went home to my children, and was depressed. For in reality the cause of survival was almost pure chance.

So we few survivors are either the best or the worst. And yet, as Bertolt Brecht was fond of saying, the truth is concrete, meaning specific. The role that prison plays in the life of an ex-prisoner cannot be deduced from some shaky psychological rule, for it is different for each one of us, depending on what went before, on what came afterwards, and on what happened to each during his or her time in the camps. Though the Shoah involved millions of people, it was a unique experience for each of them.

The museum culture of the camp sites has been formed by the vagaries and neuroses of our unsorted, collective memory. It is based on a profound super-stition, that is, on the belief that the ghosts can be met and kept in their place, where the living ceased to breathe. Or rather, not a profound, but a shallow superstition. A visitor who feels moved, even if it is only the kind of feeling that a haunted house conveys, will be proud of these stirrings of humanity. And so the visitor monitors his reactions, examines his emotions, admires his own sensi-bility, or in other words, turns sentimental. For sentimentality involves turning away from an ostensible object and towards the subjective observer, that is, towards oneself. It means looking into a mirror instead of reality.

In contrast, a German psychiatrist of my generation, who is a good friend, tells me that right after the war she organized a group of other children and took them on an excursion to a nearby concentration camp. The camp was deserted, but the traces of the prisoners could still be seen: rusty objects, bits of clothing, and of course, the living quarters. It had been quickly abandoned after the liberation and had not been revisited. My friend says that there she got a whiff of the Shoah, and it wasn't a Shoah museum. Years later the teachers would shepherd their flocks to the same place, and if possible, steer their reactions along the right channels. But when my friend was there with her group, everything was still fresh; the blood had been shed but hadn't congealed yet. I imagine these children, open-mouthed, giggling with embarrassment, as they held up a tin spoon or stroked a straw mattress. They must have enjoyed the innocently guilty feeling of having pulled one over on the adults, having lifted a curtain and discovered a Bluebeard type of secret, led and seduced by a plucky fellow student.

Or there is Claude Lanzmann, director of the unforgettable documentary *Shoah*, pursuing his tortured search for what happened where, his obsession with place the guiding principle of his film. 'Was it three steps to the right or to the left of here?' he asks the natives. 'In this or that spot?' 'When were these trees planted? Were they part of the old site?' It's a fetish with him, I think, watching him on screen in the dark theater, half of me admiring him while the other half feels ahead of him. You need the places, I tell his image; I need only the names of the places. Yet what is the difference? We are entangled in the same web, only in different meshes.

I once visited Dachau with some Americans who had asked me to come along. It was a clean and proper place, and it would have taken more imagination than your average John or Jane Doe possesses to visualize the camp as it was forty years earlier. Today a fresh wind blows across the central square where the infamous roll calls took place, and the simple barracks of stone and wood suggest a youth hostel more easily than a setting for tortured lives. Surely some visitors secretly figure they can remember times when they have been worse off than the prisoners of this orderly German camp. The missing ingredients are the odor of fear emanating from human bodies, the concentrated aggression, the reduced minds. I didn't see the ghosts of the so-called *Muselmänner* (Muslims) who dragged themselves zombielike through the long, evil hours, having lost the energy and the will to live. Sure, the signs and the documentation and the films help us to understand. But the concentration camp as a memorial site? Landscape, seascape – there should be a word like *timescape* to indicate the nature of a place in time, that is, at a certain time, neither before nor after. Lanzmann's greatness, on the other hand, depends on his belief that place captures time and can display its victims like flies caught in amber.

It's all right to believe in ghosts, but you have to know to whom you are praying. One of my two Tom Sawyers is a good Christian and found plenty of opportunity for prayer in Auschwitz One – the core of the sprawling death facility – but he definitely didn't know the difference between the Good Lord and a ghost. For the former is personified serenity and holds all creation in the balance of his imagined hands, whereas the fence in need of refurbishing stood at best in limbo, the realm of the unredeemed. So it is only fitting that on this site a religious war has been raging, Jews against nuns, our victims against your victims. Church dignitaries have a say, but there is no dignity here for the living or the dead. A stalking ground for ghosts, not God's acre.

These two students, who took an unintentional yet voluntary interest in my childhood, refused stubbornly to admit the difference between Poles and Jews and to include Polish anti-Semitism in their meditations on good and evil. The Poles had been invaded and mistreated, so they must be good. How else are we to tell victims from victimizers? The camp sites hide as much as they communicate. At Auschwitz the Jewish victims have been so coopted into the Polish losses that my two Tom Sawyers couldn't handle the difference. They believed everything, even the worst, of their own grandfathers, they had unkind thoughts about the Allies, but they couldn't cope with criticism of the victims. That is, they were convinced that the grandparent generation was still in denial, and that the Allies hadn't liberated the concentration camps soon enough, although they could have, or at least bombed the rails that led to the camps. But they categorically refused to believe that the Poles weren't all that averse to getting rid of their Jews. They both energetically rejected my objection to tossing Christian and Jewish Poles into the same kettle, although I pointed out that it was mainly the Jews who went to the gas chambers, and the murdered children had all been Jewish and Gypsy children. I was amazed how sure they were, these thoughtful and excellent specimens of what is best in the new Germany. And yet I hadn't even voiced my nastiest suspicion, about the hard currency which Jewish pilgrims, especially the American variety, bring to Poland and which has presumably made the Auschwitz museum into a lucrative venture for nearby Cracow. But I admit that I am more hard-boiled than I want others to be.

It won't do to pretend that we can evoke the physical reality of the camps as they were when they functioned. Nevertheless, I want my timescapes. Evocations of places at a time that has passed. I first wanted to call this book *Stations* and tie my diverse memories to the names I connect with them. (It seemed a modest title, until Catholic friends reminded me of the stations of the cross. Cultural differences: I hadn't even thought of it. Once it was pointed out, I was appalled at the unintended hubris.) Now I ask myself, why place names, when I am a woman who has never lived anywhere for long? These are not the names of present or former homes; they are more like the piers of bridges that were blown up, only we can't be quite sure of what these bridges connected. Perhaps nothing with nothing. But if so, we have our work cut out for us, as we look out from the old piers. Because if we don't find the bridges, we'll either have to invent them or content ourselves with living in the no-man's-land between past and present. We start with what is left: the names of the places.

Remembering is a branch of witchcraft; its tool is incantation. I often say, as if it were a joke – but it's true – that instead of God I believe in ghosts. To conjure up the dead you have to dangle the bait of the present before them, the flesh of the living, to coax them out of their inertia. You have to grate and scrape the old roots with tools from the shelves of ancient kitchens. Use your best wooden spoons with the longest handles to whisk into the broth of our fathers the herbs our daughters have grown in their gardens. If I succeed, together with my readers – and perhaps a few men will join us in the kitchen – we could exchange magic formulas like favorite recipes and season to taste the marinade which the old stories and histories offer us, in as much comfort as our witches' kitchen provides. It won't get too cozy, don't worry: where we stir our cauldron, there will be cold and hot currents from half-open windows, unhinged doors, and earthquake-prone walls.

PART II
HISTORICIZING THE HOLOCAUST?

HISTORICIZING THE HOLOCAUST?: INTRODUCTION

For some thinkers, Elie Wiesel and Claude Lanzmann among them, the event of the Holocaust has taken on a kind of sacred significance. For the most part, however, the question of the Holocaust's historicization is not quite so metaphysical. The debates that fall under this rubric concern, rather, the nature of historical explanation. To inquire into the historicization of the Holocaust can mean asking where and when historical accounts of the events should begin, considering to which other historical events the Holocaust can be related, or reflecting upon the limits that traditional modes of historical understanding face when addressing the Nazi genocide.

Questions of how to explain the Holocaust assumed a different shape, however, in the mid-1980s, when a group of conservative and reactionary historians in Germany began to call for a 'historicization' of the Nazi past. These historians put forward a cluster of suggestions that included overcoming the 'block' that consciousness of Nazi crimes presented to a confident sense of German national traditions and identity; recognizing that these crimes, committed during a brief span of German history, belonged in and to the past; explaining the Nazi genocide as largely an imitation of and reaction to Soviet crimes, and therefore neither unique nor uniquely German; and constructing historical narratives that paralleled German suffering on the eastern front with that of the Jews in the camps. The resultant dispute, which unfolded in the nation's leading newspapers, came to be known as the *Historikerstreit* or German Historians' Debate. It reveals how important historiographical questions can be for broader public and national consciousness, particularly in Germany. The German philosopher Jürgen Habermas took a strong critical stand against the conservative positions. In the essay presented here, Habermas reflects on the changing nature of historical memory as generations age, and insists on the importance of future generations of Germans remembering Auschwitz, for the sake of Jews living in Germany and as a matter of national self-respect. German political and cultural traditions, says Habermas, contributed to an unprecedented 'injury to the substance of human solidarity.' The Nazi past therefore needs to be recalled to educate a more critical, suspicious attitude toward those traditions.

The essays by the historians Saul Friedlander and Dan Diner also reflect obliquely on issues raised by the German Historians' Debate. Of more direct concern for both, however, are the limits historical methodology and understanding encounter when addressing the Holocaust. Friedlander focuses on the subjective feeling of incomprehension confessed by many historians of the Holocaust, especially Jewish ones. Central to Friedlander's sense of this 'unease,' which he wishes to locate in the nature of the events themselves, is the psychology of the perpetrators. Friedlander argues that the accounts that Nazis like SS leader Heinrich Himmler give of their actions show the Nazis to be ideologically distinct from the perpetrators of other political genocides of the century. The Nazi desire for and ecstasy in mass-scale killing cannot but vitiate all attempts at empathetic understanding.

German-Jewish historian Dan Diner is interested in the question of the rationality that he sees as the basis of all historical understanding. The Nazis determination to exterminate European Jewry even at the expense of their own war effort presents an obvious problem to this model: to see all forms of Nazi action *except* an economically counterproductive genocide as implicitly 'rational' is problematic, if not offensive; to see them as 'irrational' explains nothing. Diner proposes that Nazi action be examined from the perspective of its Jewish victims, in particular, the *Judenräte* – the Jewish councils who ran the ghettos and were charged to make decisions about who would be allowed to work and who would be sent to the camps. The councils negotiated on the assumption that the Nazis were rational – specifically, that they would not want to exterminate a productive labor source while at war. The Nazis utilized this assumption to facilitate the killing process, with which the councils found themselves unsuspectingly cooperating. It is the Jewish experience of participating in their own destruction while acting according to the logic of self-preservation that Diner terms *counterrational*. It is in reflecting on the Jewish experience of Nazi counterrationality, and on the Nazis' own counterrationality, that Diner says we encounter the limits of historical understanding. But it is only at this limit point that we can begin to 'think the Nazis' via what he calls negative historical cognition.

The remaining entries in this part, by Omer Bartov, Zygmunt Bauman, and Henry Friedlander, display less anxiety about historical understanding, and instead situate the Holocaust within significantly different narratives of modern European history. The Israeli-American historian Bartov puts Auschwitz at the conclusion of a narrative of increasingly large-scale, and eventually industrialized, killing in France and Germany. Offering an interesting contrast to later chapters in this book that address representation and the imagination's limits, Bartov emphasizes that the deathscapes of the world wars were precisely the products of the human imagination. Historical images of Hell, the progressive development of the concept of total national mobilization, and, most of all, the terror and incomprehension inspired by the mass mechanical slaughter of World War I all played their part in realizing the hell on earth of the death camps.

The sociologist Bauman sees the Holocaust as an ever-present possibility within the complex of large-scale social phenomena he labels 'modernity.' The specifically modern aspects of the Holocaust emerge out of a utopian vision of socially engineered societies, a vision served by peculiarly modern institutional structures: rational planning, efficient scientific management, and (not least for Bauman) a large administrative apparatus that distances individuals from the outcomes of their actions, and therefore also from a sense of responsibility for them. Whereas the conservative German historians of the *Historikerstreit* protested a national consciousness they thought excessively preoccupied with Auschwitz, Bauman believes that knowledge of Auschwitz has not changed modern consciousness, especially modern moral consciousness, nearly enough.

Like Bauman, Henry Friedlander understands systematic mass extermination as a byproduct of Nazi racist utopianism. Operating with an understanding of genocide as the systematic murder of certain biologically defined groups, Friedlander breaks with scholarly consensus, refusing to separate the case of the Jews from those of other groups selected by the Nazis for the same fate, namely the Gypsies and the handicapped. He thereby raises issues about context and comparison that are taken up in more detail in the last part of this volume.

OTHER WORKS IN HOLOCAUST STUDIES

Baldwin, Peter (ed.) (1990) *Reworking the Past: Hitler, the Holocaust, and the Historians' Debate*. Boston, MA: Beacon Press.

LaCapra, Dominick (1998) *History and Memory after Auschwitz*. Ithaca, NY: Cornell University Press.

Forever in the Shadow of Hitler? The Dispute About the Germans' Understanding of History, Original Documents of the Historikerstreit, The Controversy Concerning the Singularity of the Holocaust (1993), trans. James Knowlton and Truett Cates. Atlantic Highlands, NJ: Humanities Press.

Maier, Charles S. (1988) *The Unmasterable Past: History, Holocaust, and German National Identity*. Cambridge, MA: Harvard University Press.

Mayer, Arno J. (1989), *Why Did the Heavens Not Darken?: The 'Final Solution' in History*. New York: Pantheon Books.

RELEVANT THEORETICAL STUDIES

Chakrabarty, Dipesh (2000) *Provincializing Europe: Postcolonial Thought and Historical Difference*. Princeton, NJ: Princeton University Press.

Foucault, Michel (1977) 'Nietzsche, Genealogy, History,' *Language, Counter-memory, Practice*. ed. D. B. Bouchard. New York: Basil Blackwell.

Jameson, Fredric (1981) *The Political Unconscious: Narrative as a Socially Symbolic Act*. Ithaca, NY: Cornell University Press.

Koselleck, Reinhardt (1985) *Futures Past: On the Semantics of Historical Time*, trans. Keith Tribe. Cambridge, MA: MIT Press.

Nietzsche, Friedrich [1874] (1983) 'On the Uses and Disadvantages of History for Life,' *Untimely Meditations*, trans. R. J. Hollingdale. New York: Cambridge University Press.

Scott, Joan W. (1988) *Gender and the Politics of History*. New York: Columbia University Press.

Trouillot, Michel-Rolph (1995) *Silencing the Past: Power and the Production of History*. Boston: Beacon Press.

White, Hayden (1973) *Metahistory: the Historical Imagination in Nineteenth-Century Europe*. Baltimore, MD: Johns Hopkins University Press.

Young, Robert (1990) *White Mythologies: History Writing and the West*. New York: Routledge.

5

'ON THE PUBLIC USE OF HISTORY'

Jürgen Habermas

[...]

Today the grandchildren of those who at the close of World War II were too young to be able to experience personal guilt are already growing up. Memory, however, has not become correspondingly distantiated. Contemporary history remains fixated on the period between 1933 and 1945. It does not move beyond the horizon of its own life-history; it remains tied up in sensitivities and reactions that, while spread over a broad spectrum depending on age and political stance, still always have the same point of departure: the images of that unloading ramp at Auschwitz. This traumatic refusal to pass away of a moral imperfect past tense that has been burned into our national history entered the consciousness of the general population only in the 1980s, with the fiftieth anniversary of January 30, 1933 [the Nazi seizure of power], and the fortieth anniversaries of July 20, 1944 [the German officers' attempt to assassinate Hitler], and May 8, 1945 [when Germany surrendered]. And yet barriers that held up even yesterday are now breaking down.

[...]

[...] Mortality intervenes even in a life that has been damaged. Compared with the situation forty years ago, when Karl Jaspers wrote his famous treatise *The Question of Guilt*, our situation has changed fundamentally. At that time the issue was the distinction between the personal guilt of the perpetrators and the

From Jürgen Habermas (1989) 'On the Public Use of History', in *The New Conservatism: Cultural Criticism and the Historians*, ed. and trans. Shierry Weber Nicholsen. Cambridge, MA: MIT Press.

collective liability of those who – however understandable the reasons for it may have been – failed to do anything. This distinction no longer fits the problem of later generations, who cannot be blamed for their parents' and grandparents' failure to act. Is there still a problem of joint liability for them?

JASPERS'S QUESTIONS TODAY

As before, there is the simple fact that subsequent generations also grew up within a form of life in which *that* was possible. Our own life is linked to the life context in which Auschwitz was possible not by contingent circumstances but intrinsically. Our form of life is connected with that of our parents and grandparents through a web of familial, local, political, and intellectual traditions that is difficult to disentangle – that is, through a historical milieu that made us what and who we are today. None of us can escape this milieu, because our identities, both as individuals and as Germans, are indissolubly interwoven with it. This holds true from mimicry and physical gestures to language and into the capillary ramifications of one's intellectual stance. As though when teaching at universities outside Germany I could ever disclaim a mentality in which the traces of a very German intellectual dynamic from Kant to Marx and Max Weber are inscribed. We have to stand by our traditions, then, if we do not want to disavow ourselves. [...] But what follows from this existential connection between traditions and forms of life that have been poisoned by unspeakable crimes? At one time a whole civilized population, proud of its constitutional state and its humanistic culture, could be made liable for these crimes – in Jaspers's sense of a collective joint liability. Does something of this liability carry over to the next generation and the one after that as well? There are two reasons, I believe, why we should answer this question affirmatively.

First, there is the obligation incumbent upon us in Germany – even if no one else were to feel it any longer – to keep alive, without distortion and not only in an intellectual form, the memory of the sufferings of those who were murdered by German hands. It is especially these dead who have a claim to the weak anamnestic power of a solidarity that later generations can continue to practice only in the medium of a remembrance that is repeatedly renewed, often desperate, and continually on one's mind. If we were to brush aside this Benjaminian legacy, our fellow Jewish citizens and the sons, daughters, and grandchildren of all those who were murdered would feel themselves unable to breathe in our country. This has political implications as well. In any case I do not see how the relationship of the Federal Republic to Israel, for instance, could be 'normalized' in the foreseeable future. For many, of course, the 'indebted memory' is only in the title, while the text itself denounces public manifestations of a corresponding feeling as rituals of false subordination and gestures of feigned humility. It amazes me that these gentlemen cannot even distinguish – if we are to use Christian terminology – between humility and atonement.

The current debate, however, concerns not an indebted memory but the more narcissistic question of the attitude we are to take – for our own sakes – toward our own traditions. If we do not resolve this question without illusions, remembrance of the victims will also become a farce. Until now, the Federal Republic's officially proclaimed self-understanding has had a clear and simple answer. [...] After Auschwitz our national self-consciousness can be derived only from the better traditions in our history, a history that is not unexamined but instead appropriated critically. The context of our national life, which once permitted incomparable injury to the substance of human solidarity, can be continued and further developed only in the light of the traditions that stand up to the scrutiny of a gaze educated by the moral catastrophe, a gaze that is, in a word, suspicious. Otherwise we cannot respect ourselves and cannot expect respect from others.

Until now the official self-understanding of the Federal Republic has been based on this premise. This consensus has now been terminated by the Right. For there is concern about the result: An appropriation of tradition that takes a critical view does not in fact promote naive trust in the morality of conditions to which one is merely habituated; it does not facilitate identification with unexamined models. [...] The more we can regard the National Socialist period calmly as the filter through which cultural substance that is adopted voluntarily and with awareness must pass, the less that period will block our path like a locked door.

Dregger and those who share his convictions are now opposing this continuity in the self-understanding of the Federal Republic. In my understanding, their discomfort stems from three sources.

THREE SOURCES OF DISCOMFORT

First, neoconservative-derived interpretations of the situation play a role. According to those interpretations, a moralistic defense against the recent past is blocking the view of a thousand-year history prior to 1933. Without the memory of this national history, which has come under a 'thought ban,' a positive self-image cannot be created. Without a collective identity, the forces of social integration decline. The lamented 'loss of history' is even said to contribute to the weakness of the political system's legitimation and to threaten this country's domestic peace and international predictability. This is used to justify the compensatory 'creation of meaning' through which historiography is to provide for those uprooted by the process of modernization. But an appropriation of national history for purposes of facilitating identification requires that the status of the negatively cathected Nazi period be relativized; for these purposes it is no longer sufficient to shunt this period aside; its significance must be leveled off.

Second, there is a deeper motivation for a revisionism that wants to make the past harmless, a motivation that is completely independent of functionalist considerations [...]. Since I am not a social psychologist, I can only make some conjectures about it. Edith Jacobson once gave a very penetrating exposition of the psychoanalytic insight that the developing child has to gradually learn to connect his experiences with a loving and permissive mother with experiences derived from contact with a withholding and withdrawing mother. Obviously the process in which we learn to synthesize the initially competing images of the good and bad parents into complex images of *the same* person is a long and painful one. The weak ego acquires its strength only through nonselective interaction with an ambivalent environment. In adults the need to defuse the corresponding cognitive dissonances is still alive. It is all the more understandable the more the extremes diverge: as, for example, in the contrast between the positive experiential impressions of one's own father or brother and problematizing information provided us by abstract reports on the actions and entanglements of persons close to us. Thus it is by no means the morally insensitive who feel compelled to free the collective fate in which those closest to them were involved from the stigma of unusual moral obligations.

The third motivation lies at still another level – the struggle to reclaim encumbered traditions. As long as the appropriating gaze is directed toward ambivalences that are disclosed to later generations by virtue of their knowledge of the later course of history rather than through their own efforts, even what was exemplary cannot escape the retroactive force of a corrupted effective history. After 1945 we read Carl Schmitt and Heidegger and Hans Freyer, and even Ernst Jünger differently than before 1933. This is often hard to bear, especially for my generation, who – after the war, in the long latency period up to the end of the 1950s – were under the intellectual sway of prominent figures of this sort. This may, incidentally, explain the persistent efforts at rehabilitation so earnestly expended – and not only in the *Frankfurter Allgemeine Zeitung* – on the legacy of the Young Conservatives.

Forty years later, then, the debate that Jaspers in his time managed, albeit with difficulty, to settle has broken out again in another form. Can one become the legal successor to the German Reich and continue the traditions of German culture without taking on historical liability for the form of life in which Auschwitz was possible? Is there any way to bear the liability for the context in which such crimes originated, a context with which one's own existence is historically interwoven, other than through remembrance, practiced in solidarity, of what cannot be made good, other than through a reflexive, scrutinizing attitude toward one's own identity-forming traditions? Can we not say in general that the less internal communality a collective context of life has preserved, the more it has maintained itself externally, through the usurpation and destruction of life that is alien to it, the greater is the burden of reconciliation imposed on the griefwork and the critical self-examination of subsequent generations? And does not this very thesis forbid us to use leveling comparisons to play down the fact that no one can take our place in the liability required of us? This is the question of the uniqueness of the Nazi crimes. What can be going on in the mind of a historian who would claim that I had 'invented' this question?

The debate about the correct answer to this question is conducted from the first-person point of view. This arena, in which none of us can be nonparticipants, should not be confused with discussion among scientists and scholars who have to take the observational perspective of a third person in their work. The political culture of the Federal Republic is, of course, affected by the comparative work of historical scholars and others engaged in the *Geisteswissenschaften*, but the results of scholarly work reach the public flow of the appropriation of tradition, with the corresponding return to the perspective of the participant, only by way of mediators and the mass media. It is only here, in the public sphere, that comparisons can be used to settle damages. Prissy indignation about an ostensible conflation of politics and scholarship puts the issue on a false basis. [...]. It is not a question of Popper versus Adorno, not a question of scholarly theoretical debates or of value freedom – it is a question of the public use of history.

FROM COMPARISONS COMES AN OFFSETTING OF CLAIMS

In the academic discipline of history if I assess it correctly as an outsider, three primary positions on the Nazi period have been developed: one describes it from the perspective of the theory of totalitarianism, one focuses on the person and worldview of Hitler, and one is directed toward structures of power and authority or the social system. To be sure, one position will be more suitable than another for externally derived purposes of relativizing and leveling. But even the view that focuses on Hitler's person and his delusions about race works as a revisionism that renders the past harmless and relieves the conservative elites in particular of their burden only when it is presented in the corresponding perspective and in a certain tone of voice. The same is true of the comparison between Nazi crimes and Bolshevist extermination operations, even of the abstruse thesis that the Gulag Archipelago was more of 'an original' than Auschwitz. Only when a daily newspaper publishes a corresponding article can the question of the uniqueness of the Nazi crimes assume the significance for us, who appropriate traditions from the perspective of participants, that makes it so explosive in this context. In the public sphere, in connection with political education, museums, and the teaching of history, the question of the apologetic production of images of history is a directly political one. Are we to undertake macabre reckonings of damages with the help of historical comparisons in order to evade our liability for the collective risks of the Germans? Joachim Fest, an editor of the *Frankfurter Allgemeine Zeitung*, complains (in the issue of August 29, 1986) about the lack of sensitivity 'with which professors at their desks set about deciding who the victims were.' This sentence, the worst in a bad article, can only reflect back on Fest himself. Why does he give an official air, in public, to the kind of reckoning of damages that until now has been current only in radical right-wing circles?

That certainly has nothing to do with forbidding scholars to discuss certain questions. If the dispute that began with the rejoinders of Eberhard Jackel, Jürgen Kocka (in the *Frankfurter Rundschau* of September 23, 1986), and Hans Mommsen (in the *Blätter für deutsche und internationale Politik*, October

1986) had taken place in an academic journal, I could not have been offended by it – I would not even have seen it. Of course the mere publication of Nolte's article by the *Frankfurter Allgemeine Zeitung* is not a sin, as [the historian] Thomas Nipperdey says mockingly, but it does mark a watershed in the political culture and self-understanding of the Federal Republic. The article was seen as indicating this by other countries as well.

Fest does not defuse this turning point by making Auschwitz's moral significance for us dependent on one's partiality to more pessimistic or more optimistic interpretations of history. The practical conclusions suggested by pessimistic interpretations of history differ depending on whether one holds the wickedness of human nature accountable for the constants of disaster or conceives them as socially produced – Gehlen versus Adorno. Nor are so-called optimistic interpretations of history always focused on the 'new man'; we all know that American culture is incomprehensible without its meliorism. Finally, there are intuitions less one-sided than these. If historical progress consists of diminishing, eliminating, or preventing the suffering of a vulnerable creature, and if historical experience teaches us that progress finally achieved is followed only by new disasters, then we may certainly suppose that a balance of tolerability can be maintained only if we do our utmost for the sake of whatever progress is possible.

[. . .]

6

'THE "FINAL SOLUTION": ON THE UNEASE IN HISTORICAL INTERPRETATION'

Saul Friedlander

[...]

Most interpreters try to avoid the problem posed by the psychology of total extermination by concentrating exclusively on specific ideological motives (i.e., theories about the role of the Jew in society and history) or on institutional dynamics. There is no way of denying the importance of both the radical antisemitic theme and competitive internal politics, as well as the dynamics of bureaucracy in giving general interpretations of the 'Final Solution.' But an independent psychological residue seems to defy the historian. The psychological dimension, whenever recognized, is usually reduced to a vague reference to the 'banality of evil.' My hypothesis, in this first part, is that for some historians this particular dimension remains a kind of riddle subsumed under other explanatory categories, but which accompanies any discussion about the 'why' and not the 'how' of the 'Final Solution.' Here I shall try to distinguish between various elements of this psychological dimension in order to better circumscribe what could well be the sense of its irreducible core.

Let me intentionally choose one of the most notorious documents of the 'Final Solution' in order to direct our questions to a text familiar to anybody dealing with this subject: the Himmler speech given in Posen on October 4, 1943, before an assembly of high-ranking SS officers:

From Saul Friedlander (1993) 'The "Final Solution": On the Unease in Historical Interpretation', in *Memory, History, and the Extermination of the Jews of Europe*. Bloomington, IN: Indiana University Press.

> Most of you know what it means when 100 corpses are lying side by side, when 500 lie there or 1,000. Having borne that and nevertheless – some exceptional human weaknesses aside – having remained decent [*anständig geblieben zu sein*] has hardened us. ... All in all, we may say that we have accomplished the most difficult task out of love for our people. And we have not sustained any damage to our inner self, our soul and our character [*und wir haben keinen Schaden in unserem Inneren, in unserer Seele, in unserem Charakter daran genommen*].

The horror and uncanniness (understood here in the sense of the German word *Unheimlichkeit*) of these lines lies at first glance in what for the reader may appear as a fundamental dissonance between explicit commitment to breaking the most fundamental of human taboos, i.e., wiping from the face of the earth each and every member of a specific human group (eleven million people, according to Heydrich's calculation at the Wannsee Conference) and the declaration that this difficult task was being accomplished satisfactorily, without any moral damage. This sense of inversion of all values is reinforced by the mention, later in the speech, of those rare weaknesses which have to be ruthlessly extirpated, such as stealing cigarettes, watches, and money from the victims.

However, the source of the strangeness is not limited to this dissonance. It is augmented by a further key sentence of that part of the speech: 'This [the extermination of the Jews of Europe] is the most glorious page in our history, one not written and which shall never be written.' Himmler thereby conveys that he and the whole assembly are well aware of some total transgression which future generations will not understand, even as a necessary means toward a 'justifiable' end.

In a later speech, Himmler comes back to the extermination of women and children, which he states is imperative in order to prevent the rise of future avengers. In this context, he restates the necessity of carrying the secret of this extermination to the grave. One could object that the vow of secrecy belongs precisely to the forging and existence of an elite and is, almost by itself, the distinctive sign of an elite. This may indeed be so, except for the fact that for religious movements, as well as for modern political religions, the mass killing of enemies of the faith or the party belongs to the well-publicized campaigns of these entities [...]. Such killings are always linked to the most explicit aims propagandized with pride by such institutions or movements, and they are presented as almost self-understood in terms of ideological necessity and ultimate generally recognized aims.

Himmler's vow of secrecy for all time seems to indicate that there is no higher comprehensible argument which could 'justify' such an annihilation in the eyes of posterity. This may well indicate that Himmler himself had some doubts about the ideological foundations of these actions and that his arguments about the 'love of the Fatherland' and about 'destroying the people that wanted to destroy us' have to be considered, in part at least, as rhetoric.

There can be little doubt about the centrality of the anti-Jewish obsession in Hitler's worldview, as well as about elements of antisemitic motivation at various levels of the Party and the population, but the overwhelming centrality of this factor is not apparent in the case of Himmler and his Posen audience. The core motivation may well be more decisively attributed to a series of elements which I shall mention further on, among which are the 'Führer-Bindung' and the 'Rausch.'[1]

There lies one aspect of the difference between the Nazi 'project' and the Stalinist one. Whatever the magnitude of the crimes committed by Stalin, they were committed, at least on their face, in the name of a universal ideal; or, more precisely, the universal ideal was maintained as explanation, most probably in the eyes of the perpetrators themselves. The Nazi extermination of the Jews, if we take seriously Himmler's vow of future secrecy, appears as an aim which cannot be explained by 'higher, commonly understandable' ends. Thus, the singularity of the Nazi project seems to lie not only in the act, but also in the language and the self-perception of the perpetrators.

From this viewpoint, then, the exterminations perpetrated by the Nazis are not an 'inversion of all values' (as would be the case if human beings were worked to death or killed for a very specific political aim), but represent an amorality beyond all categories of evil. Human beings are no longer instruments; they have entirely lost their humanness.

Before probing further, we should ask whether the contemporaries who were not involved as perpetrators in the extermination process understood its nature, on the basis of their knowledge of the events.

Various recent studies dealing with the 'terrible secret' stress in diverse ways the simultaneity of considerable knowledge of the facts and of a no less massive inability or refusal to transform these facts into integrated understanding.[2] Clearly, each group had its own reasons for not internalizing what, in great part, could be known or was known. One cannot compare the reasons of the victims with those of surrounding German society, but one common denominator appears nonetheless: the 'Final Solution' was, in a way, 'unthinkable.'

A comparison with Stalinist Russia will, again, put this type of contemporary incomprehension into clearer perspective. It seems that the victims of Stalinism who were not committed Bolsheviks faced no impossibility in understanding the all-pervasive terror that descended on their country: They grasped the significance of the Lubianka, of the Siberian camps, of the starvation and the shootings; they may have considered all of it in terms of Bolshevik terror in general, but none of the more detailed accounts of these events [...] raise the issue of some kind of paralysis of comprehension.

This type of argument should not be misunderstood as an exoneration of the 'bystanders,' whoever they were. The widespread knowledge of monstrous crimes perpetrated against the Jews and the almost general indifference that accompanied them is a sufficient indictment; an understanding of the full scope of the 'Final Solution' is not a necessary precondition for all the questions later raised about European society; about the behavior of the Allies, the Neutrals, and the Churches; about that of German society in particular.

In terms of the incomprehension of contemporaries, that of the victims stands out in its incommensurably tragic dimension. It is impossible to elaborate here on the oft-described mechanisms of 'denial' in the face of a reality which, at some stage, was only too obvious. But, as is known, 'denial' was not the only element involved. What misled the immense majority of European Jews was the compelling belief, as far as Nazi behavior was concerned, in some elements of 'instrumental rationality' (some rational link between utilitarian aims, such as producing clothing or shoes for the Wehrmacht in the ghetto workshops, and appropriate means, such as keeping the able-bodied Jewish working force alive). The fate of the Jews was sealed in any case; the reason for their extermination they could in no way comprehend.

The main question about interpretation, however, must be addressed to those who acquired full knowledge of the events after the end of the war. The life span of many of the present-day readers of Himmler's speech still overlaps in part with his. On the basis of the assumption of sharing a common humanity and even a common historical experience, and thus basically common perceptions of human existence in society, we try to overcome the feeling of strangeness and horror and try to find the point of psychological identity. We try to identify our own thinking with that of Himmler's world by an understanding stemming from the postulate of these psychological common denominators. By doing so we assume the validity of the notion of the 'banality of evil,' as it supposedly allows us to grasp the mind-set we are probing: the 'banality of evil' suggests that we all do share the same common propensities eventually leading to ultimate criminality. We will not even attempt to analyze the conceptual fuzziness of the 'banality of evil.'[3] On a more concrete level, by accepting this notion, we disregard several major elements which we will try to circumscribe more precisely in the following section.

A closer analysis of Himmler's speech can lead us to a more precise delimitation of the areas of incomprehension. One could argue that the extirpation of blemishes such as the stealing of the victims' cigarettes, etc., belongs to a well-known category: military or monastic discipline as far as minute details of behavior are concerned, such as is found in elite military groups and religious orders of various kinds. One could argue, moreover, that the elimination of potential avengers by exterminating the women and children can be reduced to the logic of 'instrumental rationality.' Thus, if we accept the thesis that Himmler and his generals were driven not by an overriding anti-Jewish ideological obsession (in contradistinction with Hitler), we are faced with the 'Führer-Bindung' as part of the explanation and some imponderables which indeed seem to escape us, included in the overall notion of 'Rausch.'

I have mentioned in the previous pages that the word 'strangeness' or 'uncanniness' was used as the equivalent of the German *Unheimlichkeit*. It manifestly brings to mind Freud's famous essay 'On the Uncanny.' Freud quotes a 1906 article by Jentsch which relates the feeling of the uncanny to the impossibility of distinguishing the animate from the inanimate; in his essay Freud denies, on several occasions, that Jentsch's indications are in any way plausible.[4] We will allude further on to Freud's interpretation, but, at a first stage, Jentsch's intuition appears of relevance. Let me repeat Jentsch's position as summarized by Freud himself:

> [Jentsch] believes that a particularly favorable condition for awakening uncanny sensations is created when there is intellectual uncertainty whether an object is alive or not and when an inanimate object becomes too much like an animate one.[5]

When we consider again the text of Himmler's speech, or in more general terms, the mass extermination actions of the various perpetrators and particularly of the higher bureaucracy of death, we cannot but admit, on the one hand, the human ordinariness of the perpetrators and notice, on the other hand, the 'mechanical,' nonhuman aspect of their actions. In a sense, we are confronted with some kind of uncertainty as defined by Jentsch, except that we are not dealing with automata approaching the semblance of life, but with human beings of the most ordinary kind approaching the state of automata, by eliminating any feelings of humaneness and of moral sense in relation to groups other than their own. Our sense of *Unheimlichkeit* is indeed triggered by this deep uncertainty as to the 'true nature' of the perpetrators, except, as I mentioned, as far as their own group is concerned. This is the point of inception of 'Rausch.'

Could one of the components of 'Rausch' be the effect of a growing elation stemming from repetition, from the ever-larger numbers of the killed others: 'Most of you know what it means when 100 corpses are lying side by side, when 500 lie there or 1000.' This repetition (and here indeed we are back, in part, at Freud's interpretation) adds to the sense of *Unheimlichkeit*, at least for the outside observer; there, the perpetrators do not appear anymore as bureaucratic automata, but rather as beings seized by a compelling lust for killing on an immense scale, driven by some kind of extraordinary elation in repeating the killing of ever-huger masses of people (notwithstanding Himmler's words about the difficulty of this duty). Suffice it to remember the pride of numbers sensed in the Einsatzgruppen reports, the pride of numbers in Rudolf Höss's autobiography; suffice it to remember Eichmann's interview with Sassen: he would jump with glee into his grave knowing that over five million Jews had been exterminated; elation created by the staggering dimension of the killing, by the endless rows of victims.[6] The elation created by the staggering number of victims ties in with the mystical Führer-Bond: the greater the number of the Jews exterminated, the better the Führer's will has been fulfilled.

However, precisely at this point – the elation created by the dimensions of the killing – our understanding remains blocked at the level of self-awareness, and

73

this after the events and because of these events. As the British philosopher Alan Montefiore put it very aptly:

> The unimaginable belongs to that part of my darkest imagination – or, at least, that imagination which, whether it be mine or not, I may have to recognize within me – to which my whole conscious, 'normally' sensitive being refuses the very right of existence.[7]

Thus, the greater the moral sensitivity, the stricter the repression will be of a subject deemed too threatening to both the individual and society. The historian can analyze the phenomenon from the 'outside,' but, *in this case, his unease cannot but stem from the noncongruence between intellectual probing and the blocking of intuitive comprehension.*

[...]

The most elementary question remains open: How will all this be affected by the passage of time? Will distance from the events allow for the construction of meaningful patterns of interpretation? [...]

Paradoxically, the 'Final Solution,' as a result of its apparent historical exceptionality, could well be inaccessible to all attempts at a significant representation and interpretation. Thus, notwithstanding all efforts at the creation of meaning, it could remain fundamentally irrelevant for the history of humanity and the understanding of the 'human condition.' [...]

NOTES

1. I would translate these terms as 'the Bond to the Führer' and 'elation.'
2. See, essentially, Walter Laqueur, *The Terrible Secret* (Boston, 1980), but also Hans Mommsen, 'Was haben die Deutschen vom Völkermord an den Juden gewusst?' in Walter H. Pehle, ed., *Der Judenpogrom 1938. Von der 'Reichskristallnacht' zum Völkermord* (Frankfurt/Main, 1988). [...]
3. For an analysis of this fuzziness, see Nathan Rotenstreich, 'Can Evil Be Banal?' *The Philosophical Forum* XVI/1–2 (1984–85).
4. Stanley Cavell, 'The Uncanniness of the Ordinary,' in *In Quest of the Ordinary. Lines of Skepticism and Romanticism* (Chicago, 1988), p. 155.
5. Sigmund Freud, 'The "Uncanny",' *Collected Papers* 4 (New York, 1959), p. 385.
6. For further analysis, we would need a new category equivalent to Kant's category of the sublime, but specifically meant to capture inexpressible horror. In *Reflections of Nazism* (New York, 1984), I tried to describe one of the elements of the 'Rausch' as the exaltation stemming from visions of utter destruction.
7. Alan Montefiore, 'The Moral Philosopher's View of the Holocaust,' in Marcel Marcus, ed., *European Judaism* (London, 1977), pp. 13–22.

7

'HISTORICAL UNDERSTANDING AND COUNTERRATIONALITY: THE JUDENRAT AS EPISTEMOLOGICAL VANTAGE'

Dan Diner

The difficulty inherent in describing Nazism – or, more precisely, in representing the mass extermination in historiographical terms – reflects the basic unimaginability of the event itself. Such an observation would be trivial if this problem of describability and representation did not have a powerful epistemic dimension: one directly bound up with the entire question of understanding Nazism. Moreover, the remarkable debate between Martin Broszat and Saul Friedländer on the historization of the Nazi era has underscored just how narrow the boundaries indeed are of a descriptive mode aimed at achieving historiographical understanding, *Verstehen:*[1] a considerable theoretical and analytic effort is necessary before any effort to historicize Nazism can begin.

[...]

Despite all assertions to the contrary – namely, that what faces them is an incomprehensible set of events – historians approach Nazism and the mass extermination [...] as accessible to a process of *Verstehen* guided by rational principles. Such an assumption is manifest, for example, when historians note an extreme disparity between ends and means, between the necessities of the conduct of war and the mass extermination: a disparity that dissolves a relation generally assumed to be socially operative. The assumption informs treatment of the Nazis' ideologically motivated aims: by dint of their inaccessibility to the

From Dan Diner (2000) 'Historical Understanding and Counterrationality: The Judenrat as Epistemological Vantage', in *Beyond the Conceivable: Studies on Germany, Nazism, and the Holocaust*. Berkeley, CA: University of California Press.

judgmental standards of the rational personality, those aims are classified as 'irrational.' They are hence *disqualified* as incomprehensible – to be sure, according to those very standards.

And yet, this commonly advanced postulate of 'irrationality' is deeply questionable. It raises two historiographical problems that, in their epistemological resonance, merit some scrutiny. To begin, the postulate serves as an impediment to analysis, blocking, by its very nature, any approach *oriented* toward a 'rational' comprehension (*Verstehen*) of a process of pure destruction that remains past understanding. At the same time, and just as problematically, the postulate is in turn predicated on a highly particularistic vantage – that of a specific collective experience. For it amounts to an assertion that Nazi German conduct was not in keeping with a 'rational' pursuit of Germany's *own* interests, that Nazi behavior caused intolerable injury and harm to the collective whose leadership it commandeered and whose fate it had been presumptuous enough to try to control.

The particularism becomes evident if we attempt to view the Nazi anti-Jewish campaign from the perspective of its victims. From such a perspective, the notion of the mass extermination's 'irrationality' emerges as something akin to a mocking euphemism within the total context of Nazi anti-Jewish policy – as if we might classify measures such as mass expulsion, graded below the critical threshold of the Final Solution and evaluated in its terms, as being 'rational' by contrast. It is the case that almost by default, owing to the sheer mass and horror of the extermination, all Nazi measures anterior to that event would, in the eyes of the victims, seem to claim the attribute of rationality. Indeed, such attribution might well be regarded as itself reflecting a specific experiential vantage: that of the Jewish victims. And in turn, this vantage emerges from a dimension of historical consciousness addressing a familiar complex of anti-Semitic traditions – the old, in their own way virulent forms of anti-Jewish enmity. To the extent that the Nazi measures *before* the Einsatz squads and gas chambers can be understood as familiar phenomena – as a sort of historical repetition – these measures, in their relative calculability and familiarity, may thus well have appeared reassuringly 'rational' to the desperate victims of impending collective murder.

[...]

Articulated within the context of 'decision theory' – an assessment of the character of the social relations at work in processes of intersubjective communication – George Shackle's argument that 'rationality means something only for the outside observer' has clear meaning: it is impossible to determine the rational content of a given action from the internal perspective of an actor.[2] The argument points, for a start, to the impossibility of a credible evaluation of the 'rational' content of Nazi actions being offered by the Nazis themselves. In this regard, we need only note that however problematic the 'irrationality' thesis for Nazism and the Holocaust may be, ascribing 'rationality' to actions on the grounds of their accordance with Nazism's own criteria and objectives is all the more problematic. Shackle's argument thus also points, albeit less directly, to the possibility of such evaluation emerging from the perspective of the Nazis' victims – that is, within an 'outside' framework supplied by historians struggling toward a reconstructive *Verstehen*. For within such a framework, the perceptions and forms of behavior of the victims, reflecting the existential urgency of their predicament, can serve to some extent as a practical vantage point – an epistemological grounding. It is from such a vantage that the Nazi system, and its annihilative purpose, emerges as neither rational nor irrational, but rather *counterrational*.

As Isaiah Trunk first stressed, within the ghetto, confined in a condition characterized by seeming, albeit specious, self-determination, the Jews were able to contemplate options for action – hence to reflect on their predicament. They were allowed just enough social normality, and just enough semblance of political autonomy, to retain an illusion of their capacity to further their own long-term survival. Within what thus amounts to a *boundary locus* – trapped between total subjugation and a modicum of self-organization – the victims were nonetheless furnished with socially viable time: a period between the sentence of collective death and postponement of the execution, hence time to assess their relation with the executioner. In this respect, the situation of Jews in Eastern European ghettos differed fundamentally from that of individuals in *death camps*. There the victims possessed virtually no options for action or volition – no alternatives, however aporetic. And by virtue of the presumption of such alternatives – in the interests of survival both for others who had entrusted themselves to their care and for themselves – the Jewish councils struggled to anticipate Nazi actions, and to exert a moderating influence on them: to *think* the Nazis.

We can move toward a deeper understanding of the counterrational nature of Nazi policies with some closer consideration of the concept of labor within the ghettos.[3] Three different meanings of labor are in fact involved here. First of all, there is labor in its immediate role as a *practical activity*, aimed at survival and based on material reproduction. As a result of ghettoization, the Jews had been torn, of course, from a social context that had previously functioned to guarantee material existence. [...] Expropriation measures, loss of jobs, and resulting pauperization meant that the only potential work was in the framework of domination and servitude: work offered by the Nazis themselves. In addition to the role of work as the only value that Jews could exchange for food, it had a meaning and function bound up with the role of the Jewish councils: as we noted, it provided the Germans with Jewish labor for production in an organized manner. This second role meant, for the Jews, a 'rationalizing' of the Nazis – a rendering of their arbitrary and unpredictable behavior more transparent and amenable to calculation. Such an apparently viable option presumed, in turn, certain skills and a social context with some complexity. In this manner, work became both a means of rationalization and a medium for *social communication:* for 'civilizing' the Germans through the obligations and ties the work relation engendered. The Jewish survival strategy thus involved an assumption preshaped by social forms of exchange – an assumption of reciprocity on the part of one's deadly enemies for behavior demonstrated toward them. To this extent, the councils acted in accordance with the following, socially self-evident stipulation: an organization of human cooperative endeavor and a self-rationalizing structure of interreferential behavior modes are possible only if they make use of an external fact.[4] And work was such an external, self-objectifying fact.

A third role of labor for the ghetto's Jews was linked to Nazi use of Jewish trust in the exchange act as a trap – the shift of an offer of labor at the ghetto's own initiative to a demand for labor by the Nazis themselves. As a result of knowledge, or at least premonition, of the ultimately annihilatory aims of deportation, the Jewish councils no longer tried simply to 'rationalize' the Nazis in a communicative context; rather, they now used the value-creating function of human work as a means of postponing the death sentence. For in light of the war effort, it was of obvious benefit to the Nazis to give priority to the practical exploitation of Jewish labor over the ideologically motivated desire for Jewish death.

Proceeding on the basis of rationally structured forms of everyday social behavior, the strategy of 'rescue through labor' pursued by the Jewish councils thus appeared well founded, at least to some degree. The economicizing veneer to the Jewish labor, visible for all to see, suggested to the Jews that an economic relation was now predominant: hence that a social process was now operative with a certain rough normality. The very form of work demanded from the Jews – productivity and efficiency – suggested such a process.[5] It generated a blinding effect, masking the extermination project from its intended victims. [...]

The Jewish councils' presumption – all signals to the contrary – of utilitarian motives on the part of the Nazis was tied to a more broadly operative civilizing logic: that of *homo oeconomicus.* Ultimately, their reliance on rationality had its source within this logic.[6] But the operational system of *homo oeconomicus* does not simply aim to maximize utility and minimize costs; rather, it proceeds on the supposition that acting subjects are indeed reasonable. *Homo oeconomicus* transposes the maxims of reason of economic life to the sphere of social action in general.[7] [...] Every decision-making process meant to be rational relies on calculations of utility, since no human activity assumes greater rationality than the effort to engage in gainful pursuits. When individuals facing a decision receive contrafactual input, they give greater credence to information that appears in keeping with the utilitarian character of economy as a form of social intercourse.

In other words, the only information they allow into consciousness is information pointing to alternatives relevant for action. When, for example, skilled Jewish workers in Czestochowa received word about the deportation of similarly qualified workers in Warsaw, they failed to draw any conclusions from this about their own fate. Owing to its absolutely negative valence, news concerning the industrial annihilation was blocked out and the principle of rationality, materialized in the form of labor, preserved. Here it is useful to once more recall Uriel Tal's terse formulation of the Jewish councils' strategy of survival: 'I act economically, ergo I exist.' Given the situation of the councils, this strategy constituted a plausible effort to draw conclusions from the means – namely, labor – about the ends – namely, the production of value. In this way, the councils fell victim to a fundamental, yet necessary, misperception, since for the Nazis the form of labor did not possess any *systemic* meaning.

[...]

In retrospect, faced with the Nazi intention to destroy the Jews, the Jewish councils tried to defend themselves through forms of thought and action unsuitable in their indebtedness to criteria of rationality. Labor, as the materialized form of communicative social rationality, was not isolated in this context but rather interlinked with a key strategic fact that concerned the councils: protraction, forestalling, the struggle for 'time.'

Where for the Jewish councils, labor thus represented a form of concretized rationality, first oriented toward presumably utilitarian motives on the part of the Germans, later functioning as a psychological denial filter to block out the ever more obvious hopelessness of the ghetto dwellers' plight, the category of *time* here represents, in contrast, a strategic element to which everything else is subordinate. As we saw, the councils tried to gain more time, or to protract the period of 'borrowed time,' by expending their sole asset: the physical labor at their disposal. In the early phase, the councils hoped that through time gained, some miracle might happen; later they harbored, as indicated, illusory hopes that the front would soon be approaching or that, for whatever reason, there would be some saving shift in German policy. Yet the struggle to gain time by labor was bound up with a further factor: *terror*, as a reversal of the formal ethical proportionality of ends and means. The strategy aimed at gaining time forced the councils to make decisions in keeping with the logic of utilitarian considerations. However, the originally rational aspect of that forestalling logic – warding off the worst by means of the lesser evil – successively shifted and then reversed.

We now arrive at the ultimate consequence of the process of forced self-selection that the Jewish councils themselves implemented: the program of participatory self-destruction by means of self-preservation. Because the Nazis continued to control time – owing, for example, to the fact that the front was not approaching with the expected rapidity – the process of weighing options, using an ethics of ends and means, turned back on itself. The small numbers of those consigned to death as a result of the self-selection had, in the course of events, long since become multitudes. The upshot was that the councils, bereft of any alternative, directed the Nazi-engendered reversal of all values – the ethics of ends and means and the associated assumptions of rationality – against themselves, and against the Jewish communities entrusted to their care.

This absolutely radical value reversal does not only inform the specificity of Jewish historical experience; it also represents, more generally, a historical negation of the basic faith in the civilizing power of rational judgment per se. Under this analytic light the logic of the mass extermination no longer appears *irrational* but takes on decidedly *counterrational* significance – one experienced existentially by the Jewish councils. The Nazis' counter-rationality is the key, in turn, to identifying the deep-seated problem facing historiography of the Holocaust, the problem tied to the basic, rational links between *explanans* and *explanandum:* guided by a desire to understand inherently attached to rational epistemological premises, historians tend, intuitively or self-consciously, to read such premises into the structures of Nazi behavior – structures that nevertheless can hardly be seen as rational when measured by the imperatives of Nazi self-preservation. As suggested, the ensuing frustration can lead to a retreat – in some cases, into evocations of incomprehensibility, or of impenetrability to rational scrutiny.

For historians, awareness of the Jewish councils' situation can offer an epistemological alternative to such impenetrability. To begin on a practical level: that situation relates to a number of precious *proleptic* historical insights – insights emerging from the need to anticipate Nazi behavior by penetrating as 'participant players' into the Nazi bureaucratic administrative apparatus. In a double sense, the strategy of trying to influence this apparatus by offering support to various factional interests more concerned, apparently, with the exploitation of Jewish ghetto labor than with immediate annihilation makes the Judenrat an epistemologically relevant indicator for assessing the adequacy of a given theoretical methodological approach. Hence perceptions taking the Judenrat as point of departure reveal just how closely the structuralist explanatory paradigm for Nazism, with its stress on the chaos of conflicting authorities and power, indeed adheres to an underlying reality. Furthermore, the practical failure of Judenrat strategy reflects a salient fact: despite such chaos, the plan of the Nazis to destroy the Jews was highly successful.

On a more theoretical level, reconstruction of the councils' situation demonstrates that if 'rationality' was ever involved in the Nazi enterprise, it was a very fractured rationality – one embedded in the overriding logic of the mass-exterminatory project. Posing its own problem for the process of rational, historical *Verstehen*, the reality of the Nazi project makes its logic of bureaucratic administrative action inherently impossible to follow: it demolishes such rationality, as the object of *Verstehen*. In this manner, the endeavor to describe Nazism and the Final Solution requires what we can term a *negative historical cognition* because historians must accept a cancellation of basic principles of rationality before venturing on their enterprise. Auschwitz must be *thought* before it can be written about historically.

NOTES

1. See Martin Broszat and Saul Friedländer, 'A Controversy about the Historicization of National Socialism,' *YVS* 19 (1988): 1–47.
2. George I. S. Shackle, 'Time and Thought,' *British Journal for the Philosophy of Science* 9 (1958–59): 290.
3. See Yisrael Gutman, 'The Concept of Labor in Judenrat Policy,' in *Patterns of Jewish Leadership in Nazi Europe 1933–45*, ed. Yisrael Gutman and Cynthia J. Haft (Jerusalem, 1979), 151–80.
4. See Arnold Gehlen, 'Probleme einer soziologischen Handlungslehre,' in *Soziologie und Leben: Die soziologische Dimension der Fachwissenschaften*, ed. Frank Altheim et al. (Tübingen, 1952), 33.
5. See F. H. Knight, *The Ethics of Competition and Other Essays*, 2d ed. (Salem, N.H., 1955), 74: 'Efficiency is a value category.'
6. See Otto von Zwiedineck-Südenhorst, 'Der Begriff homo oeconomicus und sein Lehrwert,' *Jahrbücher für Nationalökonomie und Statistik* 140 (1934): 521.
7. See Karl Acham, 'Über einige Rationalitätskonzeptionen in den Sozialwissenschaften,' in *Rationalität: Philosophische Beiträge*, ed. Herbert Schnädelbach (Frankfurt am Main, 1984), 34. See also G. Hartfiel, *Wirtschaftliche und soziale Rationalität: Untersuchungen zum Menschenbild in Ökonomie und Soziologie* (Stuttgart, 1968).

8

'THE UNIQUENESS AND NORMALITY OF THE HOLOCAUST'

Zygmunt Bauman

[...]

'Wouldn't you be happier if I had been able to show you that all the perpetrators were crazy?' asks the great historian of the Holocaust, Raul Hilberg. Yet this is precisely what he is *unable* to show. The truth he does show brings no comfort. It is unlikely to make anybody happy. 'They were educated men of their time. That is the crux of the question whenever we ponder the meaning of Western Civilization after Auschwitz. Our evolution has outpaced our understanding; we can no longer assume that we have a full grasp of the workings of our social institutions, bureaucratic structures, or technology.'[1]

This is certainly bad news for philosophers, sociologists, theologians and all the other learned men and women who are professionally concerned with understanding and explaining. Hilberg's conclusions mean that they have not done their job well; they cannot explain what has happened and why, and they cannot help us to understand it. This charge is bad enough as far as the scientists go (it is bound to make the scholars restless, and may even send them, as they say, back to the drawing board), but in itself it is not a cause for public alarm. There have been, after all, many other important events in the past that we feel we do not fully understand. Sometimes this makes us angry; most of the time, however, we do not feel particularly perturbed. After all – so we console ourselves – these past events are matters of *academic interest*.

From Zygmunt Bauman (1989) 'The Uniqueness and Normality of the Holocaust', in *Modernity and the Holocaust*. Ithaca, NY: Cornell University Press.

But are they? It is not the Holocaust which we find difficult to grasp in all its monstrosity. *It is our Western Civilization which the occurrence of the Holocaust has made all but incomprehensible* – and this at a time when we thought we had come to terms with it and seen through its innermost drives and even through its prospects, and at a time of its world-wide, unprecedented cultural expansion. If Hilberg is right, and our most crucial social institutions elude our mental and practical grasp, then it is not just the professional academics who ought to be worried. True, the Holocaust occurred almost half a century ago. True, its immediate results are fast receding into the past. The generation that experienced it at first hand has almost died out. But – and this is an awesome, sinister 'but' – these once-familiar features of our civilization, which the Holocaust had made mysterious again, are still very much part of our life. They have not gone away. Neither has, therefore, the *possibility* of the Holocaust.

[...]

First, ideational processes that by their own inner logic may lead to genocidal projects, and the technical resources that permit implementation of such projects, not only have been proved fully compatible with modern civilization, but have been conditioned, created and supplied by it. The Holocaust did not just, mysteriously, avoid clash with the social norms and institutions of modernity. It was these norms and institutions that made the Holocaust feasible. Without modern civilization and its most central essential achievements, there would be no Holocaust.

Second, all those intricate networks of checks and balances, barriers and hurdles which the civilizing process has erected and which, as we hope and trust, would defend us from violence and constrain all overambitious and unscrupulous powers, have been proven ineffective. When it came to mass murder, the victims found themselves alone. Not only had they been fooled by an apparently peaceful and humane, legalistic and orderly society – their sense of security became a most powerful factor of their downfall.

To put it bluntly, there are reasons to be worried because we know now that *we live in a type of society that made the Holocaust possible, and that contained nothing which could stop the Holocaust from happening.*

[...]

No doubt the Holocaust was another episode in the long series of attempted mass murders and the not much shorter series of accomplished ones. It also bore features that it did not share with any of the past cases of genocide. It is these features which deserve special attention. They had a distinct modern flavour. Their presence suggests that modernity contributed to the Holocaust more directly than through its own weakness and ineptitude. It suggests that the role of modern civilization in the incidence and the perpetration of the Holocaust was active, not passive. It suggests that the Holocaust was as much a product, as it was a failure, of modern civilization. Like everything else done in the modern – rational, planned, scientifically informed, expert, efficiently managed, co-ordinated – way, the Holocaust left behind and put to shame all its alleged pre-modern equivalents, exposing them as primitive, wasteful and ineffective by comparison. Like everything else in our modern society, the Holocaust was an accomplishment in every respect superior, if measured by the standards that this society has preached and institutionalized. It towers high above the past genocidal episodes in the same way as the modern industrial plant towers above the craftsman's cottage workshop, or the modern industrial farm, with its tractors, combines and pesticides, towers above the peasant farmstead with its horse, hoe and hand-weeding.

On 9 November 1938 an event took place in Germany which went down in history under the name of *Kristallnacht*. Jewish businesses, seats of worship, and homes were attacked by an unruly, though officially encouraged and surreptitiously controlled, mob; they were broken down, set on fire, vandalized. About one hundred persons lost their lives. *Kristallnacht* was the only large-scale pogrom that occurred on the streets of German towns throughout the duration of the Holocaust. It was also the one episode of the Holocaust that followed the established, centuries-old tradition of anti-Jewish mob violence. It did not differ much from past pogroms; it hardly stood out from the long line of crowd violence stretching from ancient time, through the Middle Ages and up to the almost contemporary, but still largely pre-modern, Russia, Poland or Rumania. Were the Nazis' treatment of the Jews composed only of *Kristall-nächte* and suchlike events, it would hardly add anything but an extra paragraph, a chapter at best, to the multi-volume chronicle of emotions running amok, of lynching mobs, of soldiers looting and raping their way through the conquered towns. This was not, however, to be.

This was not to be for a simple reason: one could neither conceive of, nor make, mass murder on the Holocaust scale of no matter how many *Kristallnächte*.

> Consider the numbers. The German state annihilated approximately six million Jews. At the rate of 100 per day this would have required nearly 200 years. Mob violence rests on the wrong psychological basis, on violent emotion. People can be manipulated into fury, but fury cannot be maintained for 200 years. Emotions, and their biological basis, have a natural time course; lust, even blood lust, is eventually sated. Further, emotions are notoriously fickle, can be turned. A lynch mob is unreliable, it can sometimes be moved by sympathy – say by a child's suffering. To eradicate a 'race' it is essential to kill the children.
>
> Thorough, comprehensive, exhaustive murder required the replacement of the mob with a bureaucracy, the replacement of shared rage with obedi-ence to authority. The requisite bureaucracy would be effective whether manned by extreme or tepid anti-Semites, considerably broadening the

pool of potential recruits; it would govern the actions of its members not by arousing passions but by organizing routines; it would only make distinctions it was designed to make, not those its members might be moved to make, say, between children and adults, scholar and thief, innocent and guilty; it would be responsive to the will of the ultimate authority through a hierarchy of responsibility – whatever that will might be.[2]

Rage and fury are pitiably primitive and inefficient as tools of mass annihilation. They normally peter out before the job is done. One cannot build grand designs on them. Certainly not such designs as reach beyond momentary effects like a wave of terror, the breakdown of an old order, clearing the ground for a new rule. Ghengis Khan and Peter the Hermit did not need modern technology and modern, scientific methods of management and co-ordination. Stalin or Hitler did. It is the adventurers and dilletantes like Ghengis Khan and Peter the Hermit that our modern, rational society has discredited and, arguably, put paid to. It is the practitioners of cool, thorough and systematic genocide like Stalin and Hitler for whom the modern, rational society paved the way.

Most conspicuously, the modern cases of genocide stand out for their sheer scale. On no other occasion but during Hitler's and Stalin's rule were so many people murdered in such a short time. This is not, however, the only novelty, perhaps not even a primary one – merely a by-product of other, more seminal features. Contemporary mass murder is distinguished by a virtual absence of all spontaneity on the one hand, and the prominence of rational, carefully calculated design on the other. It is marked by an almost complete elimination of contingency and chance, and independence from group emotions and personal motives. It is set apart by the merely sham or marginal – disguising or decorative – role of ideological mobilization. But first and foremost, it stands out by its purpose.

Murderous motives in general, and motives for mass murder in particular, have been many and varied. They range from pure, cold-blooded calculation of competitive gain, to equally pure, disinterested hatred or heterophobia. Most communal strifes and genocidal campaigns against aborigines lie comfortably within this range. If accompanied by an ideology, the latter does not go much further than a simple 'us or them' vision of the world, and a precept 'There is no room for both of us', or 'The only good injun is a dead injun'. The adversary is expected to follow mirror-image principles only if allowed to. Most genocidal ideologies rest on a devious symmetry of assumed intentions and actions.

Truly modern genocide is different. *Modern genocide is genocide with a purpose.* Getting rid of the adversary is not an end in itself. It is a means to an end: a necessity that stems from the ultimate objective, a step that one has to take if one wants ever to reach the end of the road. *The end itself is a grand vision of a better, and radically different, society.* Modern genocide is an element of social engineering, meant to bring about a social order conforming to the design of the perfect society.

To the initiators and the managers of modern genocide, society is a subject of planning and conscious design. One can and should do more about the society than change one or several of its many details, improve it here or there, cure some of its troublesome ailments. One can and should set oneself goals more ambitious and radical: one can and should remake the society, force it to conform to an overall, scientifically conceived plan. One can create a society that is objectively better than the one 'merely existing' – that is, existing without conscious intervention. Invariably, there is an aesthetic dimension to the design: the ideal world about to be built conforms to the standards of superior beauty. Once built, it will be richly satisfying, like a perfect work of art; it will be a world which, in Alberti's immortal words, no adding, diminishing or altering could improve.

This is a gardener's vision, projected upon a world-size screen. The thoughts, feelings, dreams and drives of the designers of the perfect world are familiar to every gardener worth his name, though perhaps on a somewhat smaller scale. Some gardeners hate the weeds that spoil their design – that ugliness in the midst of beauty, litter in the midst of serene order. Some others are quite unemotional about them: just a problem to be solved, an extra job to be done. Not that it makes a difference to the weeds; both gardeners exterminate them. If asked or given a chance to pause and ponder, both would agree; weeds must die not so much because of what they are, as because of what the beautiful, orderly garden ought to be.

Modern culture is a garden culture. It defines itself as the design for an ideal life and a perfect arrangement of human conditions. It constructs its own identity out of distrust of nature. In fact, it defines itself and nature, and the distinction between them, through its endemic distrust of spontaneity and its longing for a better, and necessarily artificial, order. Apart from the overall plan, the artificial *order* of the garden needs tools and raw materials. It also needs defence – against the unrelenting danger of what is, obviously, a disorder. The order, first conceived of as a design, determines what is a tool, what is a raw material, what is useless, what is irrelevant, what is harmful, what is a weed or a pest. It classifies all elements of the universe by their relation to itself. This relation is the only meaning it grants them and tolerates – and the only justification of the gardener's actions, as differentiated as the relations themselves. From the point of view of the design all actions are instrumental, while all the objects of action are either facilities or hindrances.

Modern genocide, like modern culture in general, is a gardener's job. It is just one of the many chores that people who treat society as a garden need to undertake. If garden design defines its weeds, there are weeds wherever there is a garden. And weeds are to be exterminated. Weeding out is a creative, not a destructive activity. It does not differ in kind from other activities which combine in the construction and sustenance of the perfect garden. All visions of society-as-garden define parts of the social habitat as human weeds. Like all other weeds, they must be segregated, contained, prevented from spreading, removed and kept outside the society boundaries; if all these means prove insufficient, they must be killed.

Stalin's and Hitler's victims were not killed in order to capture and colonize the territory they occupied. Often they were killed in a dull, mechanical fashion with no human emotions – hatred included – to enliven it. They were killed because they did not fit, for one reason or another, the scheme of a perfect society. Their killing was not the work of destruction, but creation. They were eliminated, so that an objectively better human world – more efficient, more moral, more beautiful – could be established. A Communist world. Or a racially pure, Aryan world. In both cases, a harmonious world, conflict-free, docile in the hands of their rulers, orderly, controlled. People tainted with ineradicable blight of their past or origin could not be fitted into such an unblemished, healthy and shining world. Like weeds, their nature could not be changed. They could not be improved or re-educated. They had to be eliminated for reasons of genetic or ideational heredity – of a natural mechanism, resilient and immune to cultural processing.

The two most notorious and extreme cases of modern genocide did not betray the spirit of modernity. They did not deviously depart from the main track of the civilizing process. They were the most consistent, uninhibited expressions of that spirit. They attempted to reach the most ambitious aims of the civilizing process most other processes stop short of, not necessarily for the lack of good will. They showed what the rationalizing, designing, controlling dreams and efforts of modern civilization are able to accomplish if not mitigated, curbed or counteracted.

These dreams and efforts have been with us for a long time. They spawned the vast and powerful arsenal of technology and managerial skills. They gave birth to institutions which serve the sole purpose of instrumentalizing human behaviour to such an extent that any aim may be pursued with efficiency and vigour, with or without ideological dedication or moral approval on the part of the pursuers. They legitimize the rulers' monopoly on ends and the confinement of the ruled to the role of means. They define most actions as means, and means as subordination – to the ultimate end, to those who set it, to supreme will, to supra-individual knowledge.

Emphatically, this does not mean that we all live daily according to Auschwitz principles. From the fact that the Holocaust is modern, it does not follow that modernity is a Holocaust. The Holocaust is a by-product of the modern drive to a fully designed, fully controlled world, once the drive is getting out of control and running wild. Most of the time, modernity is prevented from doing so. Its ambitions clash with the pluralism of the human world; they stop short of their fulfilment for the lack of an absolute power absolute enough and a monopolistic agency monopolistic enough to be able to disregard, shrug off, or overwhelm all autonomous, and thus countervailing and mitigating, forces.

NOTES

1. Raul Hilberg, 'Significance of the Holocaust', in *The Holocaust: Ideology, Bureaucracy, and Genocide*, ed. Henry Friedlander & Sybil Milton (Millwood, NY: Kraus International Publications, 1980), pp. 101–2.
2. John P. Sabini & Mary Silver, 'Destroying the Innocent with a Clear Conscience: A Sociopsychology of the Holocaust', in *Survivors, Victims, and Perpetrators: Essays in the Nazi Holocaust*, ed. Joel E. Dinsdale (Washington: Hemisphere Publishing Corporation, 1980), pp. 329–30.

9

'THE EUROPEAN IMAGINATION IN THE AGE OF TOTAL WAR'

Omer Bartov

[...]

One of the most striking aspects of battlefield descriptions in Great War literature is the extent to which they resemble accounts of the Holocaust. The similarity is rooted in the sense of existing in an unimaginable environment, one that no human mind, not even the most perverse, could have conjured in fiction. The only fictive universe that can claim affinity to these worlds is that of Hell [...]. Yet Hell enjoys the advantage of accommodating only sinners, and is ruled by strict laws and divine logic. The landscapes of World War One and the Holocaust, on the other hand, are the domain of the innocent, inhabited by souls who never expected to end up in them, and conforming to no rational plan or logic decipherable by their victims (although precisely because they are real, their inhabitants and survivors are often obsessed with figuring out both the responsibility for and the purpose of their ordeal). Indeed, the major difference between a subterranean Hell and these earthly environs is that while the former is, by definition, either a product of the imagination or the creation of super-human forces, the latter are man-made, and defy any attempt at fictionalization. Neither before, nor during, nor indeed after the event, has any fictive imagination been able to fully capture the reality of the Western Front or of Auschwitz [...]. And yet that unimaginable reality was itself to a large extent the product of human imagination, even if the ultimate outcome greatly surpassed it, meta-morphosing itself into a wholly new and indescribable entity, just like the

From Omer Bartov (1996) 'The European Imagination in the Age of Total War', in *Murder in Our Midst: The Holocaust, Industrial Killing, and Representation*. New York: Oxford University Press.

Golem who had defied his creator's power and will. Moreover, once they came into being, these modern infernal regions have continued to haunt man's actions and phantasies, constantly hovering just under the surface, occasionally bursting out with all the ferocity of repressed, untreated passions and anxieties.

If Auschwitz could have neither been imagined nor come into being without the Great War, then by the same token the mechanical slaughter of the Great War could not have come about without that inescapable heritage of the Age of Rationalism and the French Revolution, namely, the 'armed nation,' made all the more formidable through the rapid industrialization of the Western world and emergence of the modern bureaucratic state. These common roots also shed some light on that other link between the Holocaust and 1914–18, namely, that in both cases the millions devoured by the event stubbornly perceived it for a long time as something quite different from what it actually was, which goes some way to explain not only their willingness to enter that universe from which so many did not return, but also our own difficulty in understanding their psychology, indeed our reluctance to 'empathize' with them, since they had been deceived while we already 'know' the 'truth' about their fate. Hence, even if few of us would put it so bluntly,[1] we perceive the victims as being complicit in their own destruction, the soldiers of the Great War by having marched so willingly into battle and conducted it for so long and with such untiring determination, the victims of the Holocaust by having put up so little resistance, reacting to Nazi genocide in traditional ways of seeking some arrangement with the persecutor and trying to maintain as much as possible the cohesion of their previous existence, actions that, as we know in retrospect, made the task of the perpetrators all the easier to accomplish.[2] And if the charge of complicity is on firmer ground (though rarely made) regarding the Great War, then its mere evocation in the case of the Holocaust is enough to unhinge some of our most basic assumptions about ourselves and the world we live in, not least because so many of the victims were children, that is, the *absolutely* innocent, as well as because the inmates of Hitler's camps hardly possessed the resources for fighting back and killing their murderers, whereas the soldiers of the Great War were, of course, themselves constantly engaged in killing, even if their targets were generally victims just like themselves.

In what follows I will argue that the evolution of a new image of war in Europe, originating in the French *levée en masse* of 1793 and closely related to the consequent progressively total material and psychological mobilization of whole nations for war, inevitably necessitated the articulation of concepts of wholesale destruction of armies, nations, and individuals, the latter both in the sense of killing people and discounting the individual importance of one's own citizens in favor of a 'higher' cause. Paradoxically, therefore, the Enlightenment and liberal concern with the individual, once translated to the realities of modern warfare, and practiced within the context of a rapidly industrializing society, reduced humanity to the role of only one component among many others in the machinery of war, on the one hand, and extended the definition of war to include the non-combatant population, on the other. Consequently, war gradually came to mean more than a strictly defined military confrontation between armies, or even nations, but rather spilled over to include both domestic struggles within the nation, race, or humanity at large, and to encompass peacetime as well, since the demarcation between war and peace became increasingly blurred. This metamorphosis in man's stature, this process of removing the individual from the center of the universe and reducing him to merely a tool in its transformation, culminated in the Great War, and, gathering even greater energy in the wake of that first instance of industrial killing, exploded with all the ferocity of vastly improved techniques and deeper, more disturbing anxieties, in the Holocaust.[3] It is the manner in which the European imagination grappled with (and redefined) the parameters of humanity in the nightmare of total war and destruction it had conjured up that will concern us here.

[...]

As the Great War ended, two opposite, but not wholly contradictory, and at times overlapping concepts of war emerged from the human and material devastation it had wrought.[4] Both views were deeply concerned with the experience of the war, whose most distinct feature was industrial killing; both attempted to offers ways of avoiding a repetition of this experience in the future. But the means differed. While the first view insisted on the need to escape industrial killing at any cost, that is, to prevent oneself, or one's class, or one's nation, from ever again being exposed to its horrors, the second was founded on the assumption that since industrial killing could no longer be avoided, the only means to escape its lethal consequences was to inflict it on others. Hence while the first view was passive, evasive, escapist, and justified indifference to the fate of others by stressing one's own interests, the second was active, confrontational, interventionist, and promoted involvement in the destruction of others as a means of preventing one's own annihilation.

[...]

In March 1936 one of the leaders of French pacifism, Félicien Challaye, in a response to Romain Rolland, pointed out that the ultimate evil was war, not Nazism. Hence he concluded that the destruction of war had to be avoided at all cost. Furthermore, Challaye insisted on the distinction between the 'struggle against internal Fascism . . . which we accept' and 'the struggle against external Fascism,' which 'takes on necessarily the aspect of war.' And on this point he saw no compromise: 'We want nothing to do with war, even that which is baptized antifascist and revolutionary. We are convinced, moreover, that one does not bring freedom on the tip of a sword, nor democracy in foreign troops carriers.'[5]

   This was an admirably steadfast position to take, and one that eventually led Challaye to claim that Pétain had 'saved the country in imposing the armistice,' and to insist on the 'duty to collaborate with Germany.'[6] Céline too had become convinced that France could not survive another war. Moreover, by 1937 he was certain that it was the Jews who were about to bring a second round of mass slaughter to the world, and concluded that the only way to prevent industrial killing was to commit it oneself: 'War, for us as we are, means the end of the show, the final tilt into the Jewish charnel house.' The seeds of Céline's rabidly antisemitic essays *Bagatelles pour un massacre* and *L'École des cadavres* were sown in 1914. Evasion of murder could come only through its perpetration, through the total elimination of all Jews, and, by extension it seems, of the rest of humanity along with them.[7] Céline, of course, was not alone in expressing such views, though his use of words was quite incomparable.[8] For on the other extreme of the political map, opposing pacifists like Challaye but about to join him in the collaborationist camp, were organizations such as the fascist league *La solidarité française*, whose leaflets warned the French of the 'Red Fascism' of 'social-communist Judeo-freemasons' conspiring 'against the freedom of thought, against the family, against the nation,' threatening to bring 'fire and bloodshed to France just as it had brought it to central Europe, Russia, and now Spain,' and about to incite 'sabotage against the national defense and a bloody revolution.'[9]

By this time the Nazi regime had already consolidated its power in Germany, had passed the Nuremberg laws, and was frantically preparing for another war. Less than five years after Céline had called for a general annihilation of the Jews, Hitler, who shared the French writer's general disgust with humanity, obsession with filth, and maniacal antisemitism, unleashed the 'Final Solution of the Jewish Question,' a program of industrial, bureaucratically organized genocide he believed would save the world from a repetition of the industrial killing of the Great War. As early as 1939, only two years after the publication of Céline's *Bagatelles*, Hitler proclaimed in a major speech to the Reichstag: 'Europe cannot find peace until the Jewish question has been solved. ... [I]f the international Jewish financiers in and outside Europe should succeed in plunging the nations once more into a world war, then the result will not be the Bolshevizing of the earth, and thus the victory of Jewry, but the annihilation of the Jewish race in Europe!'[10]

With the outbreak of the Second World War, escape from industrial killing by evasion became increasingly difficult; only a few people in Europe could safely remain pacifist, at least as long as they did not join the fascists. Nazi Germany had chosen the other path, escape by perpetration. This did not save Germany from being ultimately devastated, although not before it had destroyed large parts of Europe and brought about the death of even greater numbers of people than in 1914–18. But it did make for the creation in the most concrete form possible of the nightmare of industrial killing that had haunted the European imagination since the Great War. The killing was more efficient, the victims more varied in age and gender, and the cost for the killers miniscule in comparison. Had it not been for the war raging around this 'concentrationary universe,' it would have indeed been the ideal answer to the Western Front of 1914–18. It even resembled images of Hell more closely. George Steiner has suggested that 'The camp embodies … the images and chronicles of Hell in European art and thought from the twelfth to the eighteenth centuries,' and that 'these representations … gave the deranged horrors of Belsen a kind of "expected logic." ' Indeed, to his mind the death camps 'are *Hell made immanent*. They are the transference of Hell from below the earth to its surface. They are the deliberate enactment of a long, precise imagining.'[11] To be sure, images of Hell force themselves on us whenever we read descriptions of the Holocaust, and such images often also haunted the inmates and cheered the perpetrators. But this was a hell whose immediate origins were geographically and chronologically much closer, one which had already been seen on earth. For the Holocaust was far more directly the almost perfect reenactment of the Great War (and its own imagery of hell), with the important correction that all the perpetrators were on one side and all the victims on the other. Everything else was there: the barbed wire, the machine guns, the charred bodies, the gas, the uniforms, the military discipline, the barracks. But this reenactment had the great advantage that it was *totally* lethal for the inmates and *totally* safe for the guards. And the killing too, needless to say, was *total*.

Arriving at the camp, inmates were beset by a sense of unreality, disbelief, shock.[12] This did evoke in many a memory of hell, but their descriptions often resemble those of soldiers arriving at the front, who were similarly struck by its 'hellish,' nightmarish appearance: 'All around us were screams, death, smoking chimneys making the air black and heavy with soot and the smell of burning bodies. … It was just like a nightmare and it took weeks and weeks before I could believe it was really happening.'[13] If we recall the accounts of Great War soldiers […] we will realize where this universe of industrial killing, both its reality and the imagination that brought it into being, comes from. But it is, of course, immeasurably worse; the war is by now believable, since it happened, and is happening again (the Great War provides the image; the Second World War provides the context). *This* instance of industrial killing can still not be believed even by its victims; it is only after the fact that we accept it, and thereby also accept the possibility of its reenactment: 'Not far from us, flames were leaping up from a ditch, gigantic flames. They were burning something … little children. Babies! Yes, I saw it … Was I awake? I could not believe it … No, none of this could be true. It was a nightmare.'[14] This 'dream of Hell,'[15] now actualized, was so total, so close to images internalized over many centuries, that the victims had to force themselves to accept its reality: 'Many times I felt I must be dreaming, and I would call to myself: "Wake up! Wake up! You are having a nightmare!" I would look around me, trying to wake up, but alas, my eyes kept on seeing the same dismal picture.'[16] And what is the picture? It is hell, it is war, it is a death camp: 'Every chimney was disgorging flames. Smoke burst from the holes and ditches. … Sparks and cinders blinded us. Through the screened fence of the second crematory we could see figures with pitch forks moving against the background of flames. They were . . . turning the corpses in the pits . . . so that they would burn better.'[17]

It has been rightly noted that 'the drift of modern history domesticates the fantastic and normalizes the unspeakable. And the catastrophe that begins it is the Great War.'[18] Fiction has no business where such testimonies are heard: 'I stood in front of the pit quaking. For a fleeting moment I saw my companions in the pit. Some of them were still moving convulsively. I heard a loud rifle volley, then silence and darkness. . . . Is this death? . . . . I try to raise myself. . . . I cry out . . . "Are any of you alive?" . . . But in the pit . . . no one moves.'[19] Viewing this world of industrial killing from the inside, as seen by those on whom it was perpetrated – that is, those who made evasion, who made escape possible – is terrifying, numbing, shattering. And yet it evokes memories, memories of the Great War (novels, films, photographs, oral testimonies), and memories of hell, whose imagined reality, which informed the creators of these human worlds, fades in comparison to their achievement.

This is not a world of sacrifice, but of victimhood, and perhaps its most terrifying aspect is that it is based on the assumption that the victim is necessary. This victim is not a sinner; he does not go to hell for his actions, but in order to make it possible for others not to end up in the eternal flame. Therefore he is a modern figure, in a modern, man-made hell, where industrial murder is perpetrated by those who want to be saved from it. In this world, God is just as superfluous as fiction; but human imagination is omnipotent, for it both makes for this world's creation and its perpetuation. And from this perspective, this is anything but an unimaginable reality.

Yet there is much reluctance to associate the imagery of the Great War with the Holocaust. This has to do both with the discomfort of perceiving national wars as instances of industrial killing and with the general tendency to insist on the uniqueness of the Holocaust, or at least on the differences between genocide and war. But while there is clearly a distinction to be made between the mutual killing of soldiers and the wholesale massacre of defenseless populations, it is crucial to realize that total war and genocide are closely related. For modern war provides the occasion and the tools, the manpower and the organization, the mentality and the imagery necessary for the perpetration of genocide. With the introduction of industrial killing to the battlefield, the systematic murder of whole peoples became both practical and thinkable: those who had experienced the former could imagine and plan, organize, and perpetrate the latter. All that was needed was the will to act, and by the end of the Great War there were not a few men who believed that their only escape from the hell of modern war was to subject others to the industrial killing they had barely survived.

NOTES

1. And those who have, like Hannah Arendt, were heavily censured for doing so. See H. Arendt, *Eichmann in Jerusalem: A Report on the Banality of Evil*, rev. ed. (New York, 1977 [1963]).

2. These attitudes of numerous European Jewish communities are treated by R. Hilberg, *The Destruction of the European Jews*, 3 vols., rev. ed. (New York, 1985), 3: 1030–44.

3. I am well aware that another crucial instance of this process is the mass killings by Stalin's regime. See, e.g., R. Conquest, *The Great Terror: A Reassessment* (New York, 1990), idem., *The Harvest of Sorrow: Soviet Collectivization and the Terror-Famine* (New York, 1986).

4. For a vivid pictorial account of the Great War, see J. Winter, *The Experience of World War I* (New York, 1989).

5. N. Ingram, *The Politics of Dissent: Pacifism in France, 1919–1939* (Oxford, 1991), pp. 192–93.

6. Ibid., pp. 318–19.

7. See G. Steiner, 'Cat Man,' *The New Yorker* (August 24, 1992), pp. 81–84.

8. Nor did these essays create at the time the kind of scandal imputed to them after the war, because, as Michel Winock has pointed out, 'in 1930s France, antisemitism played a respectable role.' *Nationalisme, antisémitisme et fascisme en France* (Paris, 1990), pp. 374, 377–378.

9. See leaflets in Archives Nationales: F7 13233, 132335, 13239.

10. J. Noakes and G. Pridham (eds.), *Foreign Policy, War and Racial Extermination* (Exeter, 1988), vol. 3 of *Nazism, 1919–1945: A Documentary Reader*, 1049.

11. G. Steiner, *In Bluebeard's Castle* (New Haven, 1971), pp. 53–54, cited in T. Des Pres, *The Survivor: An Anatomy of Life in the Death Camps* (New York, 1976), p. 171.

12. Apart from the examples cited below, see the analysis of oral testimonies in L. L. Langer, *Holocaust Testimonies: The Ruins of Memory* (New Haven, 1991).

13. K. Hart, *I Am Alive* (London, 1962), pp. 92–93, cited in Des Pres, *The Survivor*, p. 83.

14. E. Wiesel, *Night* (New York, 1969), p. 42, cited in Des Pres, *The Survivor*, p. 84.

15. This is Des Pres' phrase. Ibid.

16. J. S. Newman, *In the Hell of Auschwitz* (New York, 1964), p. 20, cited in Des Pres, *The Survivor*, pp. 84–85.

17. K. Zywulska, *I Came Back* (London, 1951), p. 179, cited in Des Pres, *The Survivor*, pp. 172–173.

18. P. Fussell, *The Great War and Modern Memory* (Oxford, 1975), p. 74

19. R. Weiss, *Journey Through Hell* (London, 1961), pp. 74–75, cited in Des Pres, *The Survivor*, pp. 175–176.

10

THE ORIGINS OF THE NAZI GENOCIDE

Henry Friedlander

Every book has its history, and this one is no exception. I examined the euthanasia killings for the first time during my investigation of postwar German trials of Nazi criminals. In the immediate postwar years, during the late 1940s, the Allies did not permit German courts to judge German crimes against Allied nationals. Early German trials therefore dealt only with crimes committed against German nationals, and, with only one exception, these did not involve systematic mass murder. The euthanasia killings were that exception.

[...] I decided to use postwar trial records to construct a history of the Nazi euthanasia program. Although one of the first American war crimes trials in postwar Germany concerned Hadamar, the notorious euthanasia hospital, and the first Nuremberg successor trial, known as the Medical Trial, also dealt in part with the crime of euthanasia, the mass murder of hospital patients had never been adequately treated in histories of the Nazi period. I became convinced that these murders deserve study as a prologue to Nazi genocide.

I soon discovered that a massive documentary record substantiated the nature of these crimes. In addition to the Allied, German, and Austrian trials of the late 1940s, the German judiciary had conducted numerous detailed investigations and long trials during the 1960s and 1970s. I followed the paper trail, which led me to numerous offices of German state attorneys and through archives in the United States, Germany, and Austria.

From Henry Friedlander (1995) 'Preface', *The Origins of the Nazi Genocide: From Euthanasia to the Final Solution*. Chapel Hill, NC: University of North Carolina Press.

As I read through the evidence, I realized that the traditional description of the victims of euthanasia as 'mental patients [*Geisteskranke*]' was inaccurate. Of course, I had always known that the use of the term 'euthanasia' by the Nazi killers was a euphemism to camouflage their murder of human beings they had designated as 'life unworthy of life'; that their aim was not to shorten the lives of persons with painful terminal diseases but to kill human beings they considered inferior, who could otherwise have lived for many years. Although the victims were institutionalized in state hospitals and nursing homes, only some suffered from mental illness. Many were hospitalized only because they were retarded, blind, deaf, or epileptic or because they had a physical deformity. They were handicapped patients, persons who in the United States today are covered by the Act for Disabled Americans. Nor were these patients murdered to free hospital space or to save money; the killers were motivated by an ideological obsession to create a homogeneous and robust nation based on race. They wanted to purge the handicapped from the national gene pool.

[...] It was not my aim to write about German medicine; I wanted to understand the crimes of the Nazi regime. By the mid-1980s, my reading of the documents had convinced me that the euthanasia program had been intimately connected to Nazi genocide. I realized that the ideology, the decision-making process, the personnel, and the killing technique tied euthanasia to the 'final solution.' But I still thought of euthanasia as only a prologue to genocide. In 1984, the geneticist Benno Müller-Hill published an analysis of the involvement of scientists in Nazi crimes, and his arguments forced me to reevaluate my interpretation. I began to see that euthanasia was not simply a prologue but the first chapter of Nazi genocide.

I know, of course, that the term 'genocide' was coined to refer to the murder of national or ethnic groups. Nazi genocide, however, was not directed at national groups but at groups of human beings who supposedly shared racial characteristics. Heredity determined the selection of the victims. I was thus forced to define Nazi genocide – what is now commonly called the Holocaust – as the mass murder of human beings because they belonged to a biologically defined group.

Since the publication in the mid-1950s of Gerald Reitlinger's work on the so-called final solution, historians have categorized the Nazis' murder of the European Jews as totally different from their murder of other groups. Reitlinger's work showed that while the Nazis persecuted, incarcerated, and often killed men and women for their politics, nationality, religion, and behavior, they applied against the Jews a consistent and inclusive policy of extermination. In their drive against the Jews, they even killed infants and the very old, a policy they did not follow in their treatment of such enemies, for example, as communists, Poles, Jehovah's Witnesses, and homosexuals.

My research convinced me that this definition of Nazi genocide had to be slightly revised because Jews were not the only biologically selected target. Alongside Jews, the Nazis murdered the European Gypsies. Defined as a 'dark-skinned' racial group, Gypsy men, women, and children could not escape their fate as victims of Nazi genocide. Biology also determined the fate of the handicapped, who, just as Jews and Gypsies, could not change their condition to escape death. The Nazis killed handicapped infants in hospital wards as well as elderly men and women in nursing homes. I realized that the Nazi regime systematically murdered only three groups of human beings: the handicapped, Jews, and Gypsies.

This book is an attempt to explain how Nazi genocide developed. From the first, the regime excluded members of the three targeted groups from the national community. During the 1930s, the regime consistently escalated persecution, embracing ever more radical exclusionary policies, including compulsory sterilization for the handicapped, incarceration for Gypsies, and forced emigration for Jews. Eventually, the regime decided to implement a program of mass murder to eradicate these three targeted groups.

The chronology of Nazi mass murder unambiguously shows that the killing of the handicapped preceded the systematic murder of Jews and Gypsies. The record shows that Hitler made the decision and that government and party bureaucrats implemented it in January 1940. They devised a method to select the victims, created killing centers using gas, a unique German invention, and developed a technique that processed human beings on an assembly line through these centers.

The Chancellery of the Führer, with help from the Reich Ministry of Interior, directed this euthanasia program, working through a front organization known as T4 after its Berlin headquarters at Tiergarten Straße number 4. But all attempts at maintaining secrecy failed to prevent knowledge about the murders from becoming widespread, forcing Hitler in August 1941 to order the closing of killing centers on German soil. But the killings continued in other institutions and by other means.

As soon as conditions permitted, with the invasion of the Soviet Union in June 1941, the killings were extended to include Jews and Gypsies. Hitler commissioned Heinrich Himmler's SS and police to implement this final solution. After experimenting with mass shootings, which proved too public, too inefficient, and too demanding for the killers, Himmler's minions borrowed the tested T4 killing technique of gassing. They created killing centers and staffed them with experienced T4 killers. In any event, the T4 killings had shown that ordinary men and women were willing to become professional killers.

The euthanasia killing program occupies the largest portion of this book, partly because it is not as familiar as is the final solution and partly because it served as the model for all Nazi killing operations. In the remainder of the book, I have attempted to show the connection between the euthanasia killings and the final solution. I have provided a relatively detailed account of the murder of the Gypsies because their annihilation has until now received little attention. I have not covered the murder of the Jews, which has been the subject of much scrutiny and is relatively well known, in great detail but have discussed their persecution to make comparisons, show analogies, and point to connections. I have discussed the murder of handicapped Jews in detail, however, because their fate has not previously been recorded.

I have examined the ideological setting for genocide [. . .], attempting to show how belief in the inequality of man produced theories that pointed to the inferiority, degeneracy, and criminality of the handicapped and of members of different races. Antisemitism was one aspect of that ideology of inequality, but because its history is well known, I have not focused on the Judeophobia of the Nazi leaders. Nazi ideology was pervasive, and the T4 killers shared the common ideological outlook on race. Since their adherence to Nazi ideology is a given, I have concentrated on their party involvement, which reflected their commitment to that ideology, as well as on their nonideological motives for becoming killers.

Nazi genocide, the mass murder of entire biologically determined groups of human beings, cost the lives of millions of men, women, and children in the short period of four years and four months. The figure of 6 million dead is certainly not excessive if we are to account for all the Jews, Gypsies, and handicapped murdered by the Nazis.

PART III
NAZI CULTURE, FASCISM, AND ANTISEMITISM

NAZI CULTURE, FASCISM, AND ANTISEMITISM: INTRODUCTION

In the previous section we saw how the Holocaust forced historians to confront the limits of historical rationality. This part explores the limits of rationality from a different angle, by posing questions about phenomena frequently labeled 'irrational.' What inspired Hitler's followers to subordinate and sacrifice their own interests to the will of a charismatic demagogue? What drove their hatred and murder of European Jews? The notion of 'Nazi culture' in this part's title refers to the beliefs, attitudes, and practices that enabled and reproduced the subjection and violence endemic to Nazism.

Many of the authors in this part understand themselves to be working within the Marxist tradition, which faced its own crisis of reason in the 1920s and 1930s as conditions apparently ripe for international working-class revolution culminated instead in ultranationalist mobilization and war. To account for this contradiction these authors synthesize economic analysis with social-psychological speculation. These speculations draw from many different sources, including anthropological theory and the history of religion, the complex dynamics of social cohesion and modern temporality, as well as the problems of representation encountered in national identity formation and in comprehending abstract economic processes Some of the essays focus on the biological racism often seen as distinctive to German National Socialism; others interpret Nazism under the broader social-scientific rubric of fascism. A number of the texts were written before the war's end; two pre-date its beginning. We present these earlier texts because they have nevertheless remained important and provocative, if problematic, explorations of the questions at hand by some of the most influential European and American intellectuals of the twentieth century.

Kenneth Burke's 1939 review of the English translation of *Mein Kampf* provides a sharp rhetorical analysis of Hitler's polemical tract. Burke, an American literary critic, underlines both what is specific to Hitlerian ideology – most significantly, its radical antisemitism – and what it shares with other attempts to unify a people against a perceived enemy, such as its use of projection and scapegoating. Despite the early date of its appearance, Burke's too-little known essay already hints at the dangers to come, and its insights about the secular appropriation of religious motifs and the utopian dimensions of fascism remain remarkably relevant.

Writing in the years 1933 and 1934, French thinker Georges Bataille sees psychological factors as key to explaining the appeal of Hitler and Mussolini. Paralleling Burke, he tries to show how fascist dictatorships mobilize the psychic energy and symbolic authority traditionally cathected onto and exploited by religious and military leaders, the two of which merge in the figure of the 'royal sovereign.' Central to Bataille's essay is the distinction between the homogeneous and the heterogeneous. For Bataille, the homogeneous encompasses everything that fits into productive society and generalizable scientific models; the heterogeneous everything that stands outside of that society and those models. What is important to recognize in Bataille's notion of the heterogeneous is its fundamental ambivalence; it encompasses both the most authoritarian and the most subversive of social positions and energies. This ambivalence serves as the crux of Bataille's explanation of how fascism channels potentially revolutionary energies to its own ends.

In 'Elements of Antisemitism,' a chapter drawn from *Dialectic of Enlightenment*, Max Horkheimer and Theodor W. Adorno examine the role of religious, economic, political, and psychological factors in the rise of modern European antisemitism. Horkheimer and Adorno describe and critique the role of the Jews as scapegoats for capitalist domination For the most part, however, the selection presented here tells the story of the violent return of the repressed. The repressive agent is an increasingly instrumental civilization dominated by the homogenizing logic of capitalist exchange, but unlike Bataille's account, here it is not heterogeneity as such that is repressed, but mimesis. Horkheimer and Adorno's concept of mimesis is complex and deliberately difficult. It is often defined as the imitation of and assimilation into one's environment, and seems to be based on notions of primitive modes of surviving and finding pleasure in the natural world. Following Freud's *Civilization and its Discontents*, Horkheimer and Adorno claim that the pleasures of mimesis have been disavowed at great psychic cost as civilization 'progresses,' that is, becomes more rational and organized.

The Jews serve several functions in this story. As the first to reject the worship of images and idols, they are held responsible for the civilizing suppression of mimetic pleasure. At the same time, as objects of antisemitic fantasy, they are imagined to continue to enjoy the mimetic pleasures that have become taboo for others. As members of a minority that still struggles to assimilate, their behavior bears traces of mimesis, and these traces also serve as reminders of an outmoded form of economic life. The outmoded must be actively forgotten, and for this reason too the Jews are subject to violent repression.

Following Horkheimer and Adorno's argument, French philosopher Philippe Lacoue-Labarthe explains Nazi antisemitism as a response to the putatively Jewish contributions to civilization: the rejection of myth and idolatry and the institution of law. These contributions amount to a contradiction of the principles of form upon which Lacoue-Labarthe claims that the Nazi racial myth is based, and the Jews are therefore perceived as a fundamental threat to the Nazi construction of the German *Volk*'s identity. For Lacoue-Labarthe Jewishness thereby becomes the figure for 'endless mimesis': without a fixed form, 'the Jew' can take on many shapes and insinuate himself everywhere. Lacoue-Labarthe's argument employs a complex set of temporal coordinates. While Lacoue-Labarthe appeals, perhaps disturbingly, to a somewhat ahistorical notion of Jewishness, he also claims the Nazi myth of German identity emerges only in the era of Enlightenment secularization, after and in response to the perceived decline of Christianity and the crisis of liberal humanism.

Moishe Postone, an American political scientist, most directly takes up the challenge of reconciling Marxist theory with the problem of explaining the Holocaust, offering a solution that again ties Judaism to mimesis. The Nazi genocidal project, argues Postone, emerges out of a series of misunderstandings and projections typical of a certain strain of modern thought: Romantic anti-capitalism. Central to Postone's case are the uncanny similarities he finds between Marx's account of the realm of abstract value (the social relations that constitute commodities but are invisible in their physical appearance) and modern stereotypes of 'the Jew.' This connection is no coincidence: 'the Jew' is seen by the antisemite to *personify* the realm of abstract value, which otherwise has no concrete physical embodiment. Postone says that the Nazis, mistakenly perceiving the abstract dimension of capitalism projected onto the Jews as capitalism in its entirety, understood themselves in exterminating the Jews to be destroying capitalism and with it eliminating evil from the world.

Historian Christopher Browning's *Ordinary Men* emerges from a more empirically-oriented social scientific tradition. Basing his research on court interviews with the perpetrators, Browning provides a case study of a single police battalion's murder of thousands of Polish Jews. He is especially curious about the question of choice: it was made clear to this battalion that they would not be punished for their refusal to kill Jews, yet very few said no to killing. Browning examines the importance of factors such as antisemitic propaganda, wartime brutalization and demonization of 'enemy' groups, and psychological distancing. After giving all these elements their due, Browning emphasizes the influence of something rather 'banal': group conformity.

The stature of many of the figures in this part should not blind us to the problems of their arguments. Bataille's disturbingly ambivalent affective relationship to fascism is well-known; Horkheimer and Adorno often state that antisemitism concerns the pathology of the antisemite, not the sins of the Jews, yet 'Elements of Anti-Semitism' is not without moments in which the Jews seem to bear a portion of the blame for their plight. Postone's account of modern antisemitism is powerful, but the mechanisms by which antisemitism became murderous are not clear. Browning focuses on men and says nothing about masculinity; he finds antisemitism of limited explanatory value, and thereby raises all the more insistently the question of why the ordinary men he examines were so willing to perceive Jews as their enemy and slaughter them. Perhaps nowhere in this volume are the conceptual resources richer, and the call for further research more pressing.

OTHER WORKS IN HOLOCAUST STUDIES

Bloch, Ernst [1932] (1977) 'Non-Synchronism and the Obligation to Its Dialectics,' *New German Critique*, 11.

Herf, Jeffrey (1984) *Reactionary Modernism: Technology, Culture, and Politics in Weimar and the Third Reich*. New York: Cambridge University Press.

Mosse, George (1978) *Toward the Final Solution: A History of European Racism*. New York: H. Fertig.

Steiner, George (1971) *In Bluebeard's Castle: Some Notes Towards the Re-definition of Culture*. London and Boston: Faber & Faber.

RELEVANT THEORETICAL STUDIES

Balibar, Etienne and Immanuel Wallerstein (1991) *Race, Nation, Class: Ambiguous Identities*. New York: Verso.

Gilroy, Paul (2000) *Against Race: Imagining Political Culture Beyond the Color Line*. Cambridge, MA: Harvard University Press.

Goldberg, David Theo (ed.) (1990) *Anatomy of Racism*. Minneapolis, MN: University of Minnesota Press.

Memmi, Albert [1982, 1994] (2000) *Racism*. Minneapolis, MN: University of Minnesota Press.

I I

'THE RHETORIC OF HITLER'S "BATTLE" '

Kenneth Burke

The appearance of *Mein Kampf* in unexpurgated translation has called forth far too many vandalistic comments. There are other ways of burning books than on the pyre – and the favorite method of the hasty reviewer is to deprive himself and his readers by inattention. [...] Hitler's 'Battle' is exasperating, even nauseating. Yet the fact remains: If the reviewer but knocks off a few adverse attitudinizings and calls it a day, with a guaranty, in advance, that his article will have a favorable reception among the decent members of our population, he is contributing more to our gratification than to our enlightenment.

Here is the testament of a man who swung a great people into his wake. Let us watch it carefully; and let us watch it, not merely to discover some grounds for prophesying what political move is to follow Munich, and what move is to follow that move, etc.; let us try also to discover what kind of 'medicine' this medicine-man has concocted, that we may know, with greater accuracy, exactly what to guard against if we are to forestall the concocting of similar medicine in America.

[...]

Every movement that would recruit its followers from among many discordant and divergent bands, must have some spot towards which all roads lead. Each man may get there in his own way, but it must be the one unifying center of

From Kenneth Burke (1939–40) 'The Rhetoric of Hitler's "Battle" ', *Southern Review*, vol. 1, pp. 1–21.

reference for all. Hitler considered this matter carefully, and decided that this center must be not merely a centralizing hub of *ideas*, but a Mecca geographically located towards which all eyes could turn at the appointed hours of prayer (or, in this case, the appointed hours of prayer-in-reverse, the hours of vituperation). So he selected Munich, as the *materialization* of his unifying panacea. [...]

If a movement must have its Rome, it must also have its devil. For as Russell pointed out years ago, an important ingredient of unity in the Middle Ages. [...] was the symbol of a *common enemy*, the Prince of Evil himself. Men who can unite on nothing else can unite on the basis of a foe shared by all. [...]

As everyone knows, this policy was exemplified in his selection of an 'international' devil, the 'international Jew' (the Prince was international, universal, 'catholic'). This *materialization* of a religious pattern is, I think, one terrifically effective weapon of propaganda in a period where religion has been progressively weakened by many centuries of capitalist materialism. [...]

So, we have, as unifying step No. I, the international devil materialized, in the visible, point-to-able form of people with a certain kind of 'blood,' a burlesque of contemporary neo-positivism's ideal of meaning, which insists upon a *material* reference.

Once Hitler has thus essentialized his enemy, all 'proof' henceforth is automatic. If you point out the enormous amount of evidence to show that the Jewish worker is at odds with the 'international Jew stock exchange capitalist,' Hitler replies with 100 per cent regularity: That is one more indication of the cunning with which the 'Jewish plot' is being engineered. Or would you point to 'Aryans' who do the same as his conspiratorial Jews? Very well; it is proof that the 'Aryan' has been 'seduced' by the Jew.

The sexual symbolism that runs through Hitler's book, lying in wait to draw upon the responses of contemporary sexual values, is easily characterized: Germany in dispersion is the 'dehorned Siegfried.' The masses are 'feminine.' As such, they desire to be led by a dominating male. This male, as orator, woos them – and, when he has won them, he commands them. The rival male, the villainous Jew, would on the contrary 'seduce' them. If he succeeds, he poisons their blood by intermingling with them. Whereupon, by purely associative connections of ideas, we are moved into attacks upon syphilis, prostitution, incest, and other similar misfortunes, which are introduced as a kind of 'musical' argument when he is on the subject of 'blood-poisoning' by inter-marriage or, in its 'spiritual' equivalent, by the infection of 'Jewish' ideas, such as democracy.

The 'medicinal' appeal of the Jew as scapegoat operates from another angle. The middle class contains, within the mind of each member, a duality: its members simultaneously have a cult of money and a detestation of this cult. When capitalism is going well, this conflict is left more or less in abeyance. But when capitalism is balked, it comes to the fore. Hence, there is 'medicine' for the 'Aryan' members of the middle class in the projective device of the scapegoat, whereby the 'bad' features can be allocated to the 'devil,' and one can 'respect himself' by a distinction between 'good' capitalism and 'bad' capitalism, with those of a different lodge being the vessels of the 'bad' capitalism. It is doubtless the 'relief' of this solution that spared Hitler the necessity of explaining just how the 'Jewish plot' was to work out. Nowhere does this book, which is so full of war plans, make the slightest attempt to explain the steps whereby the triumph of 'Jewish Bolshevism,' which destroys *all* finance, will be the triumph of *'Jewish'* finance. Hitler well knows the point at which his 'elucidations' should rely upon the lurid alone.

[...]

His unification device, we may summarize, had the following important features:

(1) Inborn dignity. In both religious and humanistic patterns of thought, a 'natural born' dignity of man is stressed. And this categorical dignity is considered to be an attribute of *all men*, if they will but avail themselves of it, by right thinking and right living. But Hitler gives this ennobling attitude an ominous twist by his theories of race and nation, whereby the 'Aryan' is elevated above all others by the innate endowment of his blood, while other 'races,' in particular Jews and Negroes, are innately inferior. This sinister secularized revision of Christian theology thus puts the sense of dignity upon a fighting basis, requiring the conquest of 'inferior races.' After the defeat of Germany in the World War, there were especially strong emotional needs that this compensatory doctrine of an *inborn* superiority could gratify.

(2) *Projection* device. The 'curative' process that comes with the ability to hand over one's ills to a scapegoat, thereby getting purification by dissociation. This was especially medicinal, since the sense of frustration leads to a self-questioning. Hence if one can hand over his infirmities to a vessel, or 'cause,' outside the self, one can battle an external enemy instead of battling an enemy within. And the greater one's internal inadequacies, the greater the amount of evils one can load upon the back of 'the enemy.' [...] This was especially appealing to the middle class, who were encouraged to feel that they could conduct their businesses without any basic change whatever, once the businessmen of a different 'race' were eliminated.

(3) Symbolic rebirth. Another aspect of the two features already noted. The projective device of the scapegoat, coupled with the Hitlerite doctrine of inborn racial superiority, provides its followers with a 'positive' view of life. They can again get the feel of *moving forward*, towards a *goal* (a promissory feature of which Hitler makes much). In Hitler, as the group's prophet, such rebirth involved a symbolic change of lineage. Here, above all, we see Hitler giving a malign twist to a benign aspect of Christian thought. For whereas the Pope, in the familistic pattern of thought basic to the Church, stated that the Hebrew prophets were the *spiritual ancestors* of Christianity, Hitler uses this same mode of thinking in reverse. He renounces this 'ancestry' in a 'materialistic' way by

voting himself and the members of his lodge a different 'blood stream' from that of the Jews.

(4) Commercial use. Hitler obviously here had something to sell – and it was but a question of time until he sold it (i.e., got financial backers for his movement). For it provided a *noneconomic interpretation of economic ills*. As such, it served with maximum efficiency in deflecting the attention from the economic factors involved in modern conflict; hence by attacking 'Jew finance' instead of *finance*, it could stimulate an enthusiastic movement that left 'Aryan' finance in control.

Never once, throughout his book, does Hitler deviate from the above formula. Invariably, he ends his diatribes against contemporary economic ills by a shift into an insistence that we must get to the 'true' cause, which is centered in 'race.' The 'Aryan' is 'constructive'; the Jew is 'destructive'; and the 'Aryan,' to continue his *construction*, must *destroy* the Jewish *destruction*. The Aryan, as the vessel of *love*, must *hate* the Jewish *hate*.

Perhaps the most enterprising use of his method is in his chapter 'The Causes of the Collapse,' where he refuses to consider Germany's plight as in any basic way connected with the consequences of war. Economic factors, he insists, are 'only of second or even third importance,' but 'political, ethical-moral, as well as factors of blood and race, are of the first importance.' [...] This moral decay derived from 'a sin against the blood and the degradation of the race,' so its innerness was an outerness after all: the Jew, who thereupon gets saddled with a vast amalgamation of evils, among them being capitalism, democracy, pacifism, journalism, poor housing, modernism, big cities, loss of religion, half measures, ill health, and weakness of the monarch.

[...]

What are we to learn from Hitler's book? For one thing, I believe that he has shown, to a very disturbing degree, the power of repetition. Every circular advertising a Nazi meeting had, at the bottom, two slogans: 'Jews not admitted' and 'War victims free.' And the substance of Nazi propaganda was built about these two 'complementary' themes. He describes the power of spectacle; insists that mass meetings are the fundamental way of giving the individual the sense of being protectively surrounded by a movement, the sense of 'community.' [...]

But is it possible that an equally important feature of appeal was not so much in the repetitiousness *per se*, but in the fact that, by means of it, Hitler provided a 'world view' for people who had previously seen the world but piecemeal? Did not much of his lure derive, once more, from the *bad* filling of a *good* need? Are not those who insist upon a purely *planless* working of the market asking people to accept far too slovenly a scheme of human purpose, a slovenly scheme that can be accepted so long as it operates with a fair degree of satisfaction, but becomes abhorrent to the victims of its disarray? Are they not then psychologically ready for a rationale, *any* rationale, if it but offer them some specious 'universal' explanation? Hence, I doubt whether the appeal was in the sloganizing element alone [...]. And Hitler himself somewhat justifies my interpretation by laying so much stress upon the *half measures* of the middle-class politicians, and the contrasting *certainty* of his own methods. He was not offering people a *rival* world view; rather, he was offering a world view to people who had no other to pit against it.

As for the basic Nazi trick: the 'curative' unification by a fictitious devil-function, gradually made convincing by the sloganizing repetitiousness of standard advertising technique – the opposition must be as unwearying in the attack upon it. It may well be that people, in their human frailty, require an enemy as well as a goal. Very well: Hitlerism itself has provided us with such an enemy – and the clear example of its operation is guaranty that we have, in Hitler and all he stands for, no purely fictitious 'devil-function' made to look like a world menace by rhetorical blandishments, but a reality whose ominous-ness is clarified by the record of its conduct to date. In selecting his brand of doctrine as our 'scapegoat,' and in tracking down its equivalents in America, we shall be at the very center of accuracy. The Nazis themselves have made the task of clarification easier. Add to them Japan and Italy, and you have *case histories* of fascism for those who might find it more difficult to approach an under-standing of its imperialistic drives by a strictly economic explanation.

But above all, I believe, we must make it apparent that Hitler appeals by relying upon a bastardization of fundamentally religious patterns of thought. In this, if properly presented, there is no slight to religion. There is nothing in religion proper that requires a fascist state. There is much in religion, when misused, that does lead to a fascist state. There is a Latin proverb, '*Corruptio optimi pessima*,' the corruption of the best is the worst. And it is the corruptors of religion who are a major menace to the world today, in giving the profound patterns of religious thought a crude and sinister distortion.

Our job, then, our Anti-Hitler Battle, is to find all available ways of making the Hitlerite distortions of religion apparent, in order that politicians of his kind in America be unable to perform a similar swindle. The desire for unity is genuine and admirable. The desire for national unity, in the present state of the world, is genuine and admirable. But this unity, if attained on a deceptive basis, by emotional trickeries that shift our criticism from the accurate locus of our troubles, is no unity at all. For, even if we are among those who happen to be 'Aryans,' we solve no problems even for ourselves by such solutions, since the factors pressing towards calamity remain. Thus, in Germany, after all the upheaval, we see nothing beyond a drive for ever more and more upheaval, precisely because the 'new way of life' was no new way, but the dismally oldest way of sheer deception – hence, after all the 'change,' the factors driving towards unrest are left intact, and even strengthened. True, the Germans had the resentment of a lost war to increase their susceptibility to Hitler's rhetoric. But in a wider sense, it has repeatedly been observed, the whole world lost the War – and the accumulating ills of the capitalist order were but accelerated in their movement towards confusion. Hence, here too there are the resentments that go with frustration of men's ability to work and earn. At that point, a certain kind of industrial or financial monopolist may, annoyed by the contrary views of parliament, wish for the momentary peace of one voice, amplified by social organization, with all the others not merely quieted, but given the quietus. So he might, under Nazi promptings, be tempted to back a group of gangsters who, on becoming the political rulers of the state, would protect him against the necessary demands of the workers. His gangsters, then, would be his insurance against his workers. But who would be his insurance against his gangsters?

12

'THE PSYCHOLOGICAL STRUCTURE OF FASCISM'

Georges Bataille

[...]

Heterogeneous Social Existence

The entire problem of social psychology rests precisely upon that fact that it must be brought to bear on a form that is not only difficult to study, but whose existence has not yet been the object of a precise definition.

The very term *heterogeneous* indicates that it concerns elements that are impossible to assimilate; this impossibility, which has a fundamental impact on social assimilation, likewise has an impact on scientific assimilation. These two types of assimilation have a single structure: the object of science is to establish the *homogeneity* of phenomena; that is, in a sense, one of the eminent functions of *homogeneity*. Thus, the *heterogeneous* elements excluded from the latter are excluded as well from the field of scientific considerations: as a rule, science cannot know *heterogeneous* elements as such. Compelled to note the existence of irreducible facts – of a nature as incompatible with its own homogeneity as are, for example, born criminals with the social order – science finds itself *deprived of any functional satisfaction* (exploited in the same manner as a laborer in a capitalist factory, used without sharing in the profits). Indeed, science is not an abstract entity: it is constantly reducible to a group of men living the aspirations inherent to the scientific process.

From Georges Bataille (1994) 'The Psychological Structure of Fascism', in *Visions of Excess: Selected Writings 1927–1939*, trans. Allan Stoeckl, with Carl R. Lovitt and Donald M. Leslie, Jr. Minneapolis, MN: University of Minnesota Press.

In such conditions, the *heterogeneous* elements, at least as such, find themselves subjected to a *de facto* censorship: each time that they could be the object of a methodical observation, the functional satisfaction is lacking; and without some exceptional circumstances – like the intrusion of a satisfaction with a completely different origin – they cannot be kept within the field of consideration.

The exclusion of *heterogeneous* elements from the *homogeneous* realm of consciousness formally recalls the exclusion of the elements, described (by psychoanalysis) as *unconscious*, which censorship excludes from the conscious ego. The difficulties opposing the revelation of *unconscious* forms of existence are of the same order as those opposing the knowledge of *heterogeneous* forms. As will subsequently be made clear, these two kinds of forms have certain properties in common and, without being able to elaborate immediately upon this point, it would seem that the *unconscious* must be considered as one of the aspects of the *heterogeneous*. If this conception is granted, given what we know about repression, it is that much easier to understand that the incursions occasionally made into the *heterogeneous* realm have not been sufficiently coordinated to yield even the simple revelation of its positive and clearly separate existence.

It is of secondary importance to indicate here that, in order to avoid the internal difficulties that have just been foreseen, it is necessary to posit the limits of science's inherent tendencies and to constitute a knowledge of the *nonexplainable difference*, which supposes the immediate access of the intellect to a body of material prior to any intellectual reduction. Tentatively, it is enough to present the facts according to their nature and, with a view to defining the term *heterogeneous*, to introduce the following considerations:

1. Just as, in religious sociology, *mana* and *taboo* designate forms restricted to the particular applications of a more general form, the *sacred*, so may the *sacred* itself be considered as a restricted form of the *heterogeneous*.

Mana designates the mysterious and impersonal force possessed by individuals such as kings and witch doctors. *Taboo* indicates the social prohibition of contact pertaining, for example, to cadavers and menstruating women. Given the precise and limited facts to which they refer, these aspects of *heterogeneous* life are easy to define. However, an explicit understanding of the *sacred*, whose field of application is relatively vast, presents considerable difficulties. [...] It is nevertheless possible to admit that the *sacred* is known positively, at least implicitly (since the word is commonly used in every language, that usage supposes a signification perceived by the whole of mankind). This implicit knowledge of a heterogeneous value permits a vague but positive character to be communicated to its description. Yet it can be said that the heterogeneous world is largely comprised of the sacred world, and that reactions analogous to those generated by sacred things are provoked by *heterogeneous* things that are not, strictly speaking, considered to be sacred. These reactions are such that the *heterogeneous* thing is assumed to be charged with an unknown and dangerous force (recalling the Polynesian *mana*) and that a certain social prohibition of contact (*taboo*) separates it from the *homogeneous* or ordinary world (which corresponds to the profane world in the strictly religious opposition);

2. Beyond the properly sacred things that constitute the common realm of religion or magic, the *heterogeneous* world includes everything resulting from *unproductive* expenditure[1] (sacred things themselves form part of this whole). This consists of everything rejected by *homogeneous* society as waste or as superior transcendent value. Included are the waste products of the human body and certain analogous matter (trash, vermin, etc.); the parts of the body; persons, words, or acts having a suggestive erotic value; the various unconscious processes such as dreams or neuroses; the numerous elements or social forms that *homogeneous* society is powerless to assimilate: mobs, the warrior, aristocratic and impoverished classes, different types of violent individuals or at least those who refuse the rule (madmen, leaders, poets, etc.);

3. Depending upon the person *heterogeneous* elements will provoke affective reactions of varying intensity, and it is possible to assume that the object of any affective reaction is necessarily *heterogeneous* (if not generally, at least with regard to the subject). There is sometimes attraction, sometimes repulsion, and in cerain circumstances, any object of repulsion can become an object of attraction and vice versa;

4. *Violence, excess, delirium, madness* characterize heterogeneous elements to varying degrees: active, as persons or mobs, they result from breaking the laws of social *homogeneity*. This characteristic does not appropriately apply to inert objects, yet the latter do present a certain conformity with extreme emotions (if it is possible to speak of the violent and excessive nature of a decomposing body);

5. The reality of *heterogeneous* elements is not of the same order as that of *homogeneous* elements. *Homogeneous* reality presents itself with the abstract and neutral aspect of strictly defined and identified objects (basically, it is the specific reality of solid objects). *Heterogeneous* reality is that of a force or shock. It presents itself as a charge, as a value, passing from one object to another in a more or less abstract fashion, almost as if the change were taking place not in the world of objects but only in the judgments of the subject. The preceding aspect nevertheless does not signify that the observed facts are to be considered as subjective: thus, the action of the objects of erotic activity is manifestly rooted in their objective nature. [...]

6. *In summary*, compared to everyday life, *heterogeneous* existence can be represented as something *other*, as *incommensurate*, by charging these words with the *positive* value they have in *affective* experience.

Examples of Heterogeneous Elements

If these suggestions are now brought to bear upon actual elements, the fascist leaders are incontestably part of heterogeneous existence. Opposed to democratic politicians, who represent in different countries the platitude inherent to *homogeneous* society, Mussolini and Hitler immediately stand out as something *other*. Whatever emotions their actual existence as political agents of evolution provokes, it is impossible to ignore the *force* that situates them above men, parties, and even laws: a *force* that disrupts the regular course of things, the peaceful but fastidious homogeneity powerless to maintain itself (the fact that laws are broken is only the most obvious sign of the transcendent, *heterogeneous* nature of fascist action). Considered not with regard to its external action but with regard to its source, the *force* of a leader is analogous to that exerted in hypnosis.[2] The affective flow that unites him with his followers – which takes the form of a moral identification[3] of the latter with the one they follow (and reciprocally) – is a function of the common consciousness of increasingly *violent* and excessive energies and powers that accumulate in the person of the leader and through him become widely available. (But this concentration in a single person intervenes as an element that sets the fascist formation apart within the *heterogeneous* realm: by the very fact that the affective effervescence leads to unity, it constitutes, as *authority*, an agency directed *against* men; this agency is an existence *for itself* before being useful; an existence *for itself* distinct from that of a formless uprising where *for itself* signifies 'for the men in revolt.') This *monarchy*, this absence of all democracy, of all fraternity in the exercise of power – forms that do not exist only in Italy or Germany – indicates that the immediate natural needs of men must be renounced, under constraint, in favor of a transcendent principle that cannot be the object of an exact explanation.

In a quite different sense, the lowest strata of society can equally be described as heterogeneous, those who generally provoke repulsion and can in no case be assimilated by the whole of mankind. [...] The nauseating forms of dejection provoke a feeling of disgust so unbearable that it is improper to express or even to make allusion to it. By all indications, in the psychological order of disfiguration, the material poverty of man has *excessive* consequences. And, in the event that *fortunate* men have not undergone *homogeneous* reduction (which opposes a legal justification to poverty), if we except those shameless attempts at evasion such as charitable pity, the hopeless violence of the reactions immediately takes on the form of a challenge to reason.

THE FUNDAMENTAL DUALISM OF THE HETEROGENEOUS WORLD

The two preceding examples, taken from the broader domain of *heterogeneity*, and not from the sacred domain proper, nevertheless do present the specific traits of the latter. This is readily apparent with reference to the leaders who are manifestly treated by their followers as sacred persons. It is much less evident with reference to forms of poverty that are not the object of any cult.

But the revelation that such vile forms are compatible with the sacred character precisely marks the decisive headway made in the knowledge of the sacred as well as in that of the *heterogeneous* realm. The notion of the duality of sacred forms is one of the conclusive findings of social anthropology: these forms must be distributed among two opposing classes: *pure and impure* [...] This opposition splits the whole of the *heterogeneous* world and joins the already defined characteristics of *heterogeneity* as a fundamental element. (Undifferentiated *heterogeneous* forms are, in fact, relatively rare – at least in developed societies – and the analysis of the internal *heterogeneous* social structure is almost entirely reduced to that of the opposition between two contrary terms.)

THE IMPERATIVE FORM OF HETEROGENEOUS EXISTENCE: SOVEREIGNTY

Heterogeneous fascist action belongs to the entire set of higher forms. It makes an appeal to sentiments traditionally defined as *exalted* and *noble* and tends to constitute authority as an unconditional principle, situated above any utilitarian judgment.

Obviously, the use of the words *higher, noble, exalted* does not imply endorsement. Here these qualities simply designate that something belongs to a category *historically* defined as *higher, noble*, or *exalted*: such particularized or novel conceptions can only be considered in relation to the traditional conceptions from which they derive; they are, furthermore, necessarily hybrid, without any far-reaching effect, and it is doubtless preferable, if possible, to abandon any representation of this order [...].

Having formulated this reservation, the meaning of higher values must be clarified with the help of traditional qualifiers. *Superiority* (imperative sovereignty)[4] designates the entire set of striking aspects – affectively determining attraction or repulsion – characteristic of different human situations in which it is possible to dominate and even to oppress one's fellows by reason of their age, physical weakness, legal status, or simply of their necessity to place themselves under the control of one person: specific situations correspond to diverse circumstances, that of the father with regard to his children, that of the military leader with regard to the army and the civilian population, that of the master with regard to the slave, that of the king with regard to his subjects. To these real situations must be added mythological situations whose exclusively fictitious nature facilitates a condensation of the aspects characteristic of superiority.

The simple fact of dominating one's fellows implies the *heterogeneity* of the master, insofar as he is the master: to the extent that he refers to his nature, to his personal quality, as the justification of his authority, he designates his nature as *something other*, without being able to account for it rationally. But not only as *something other* with regard to the rational domain of the common denominator and the equivalent: the *heterogeneity* of the master is no less opposed to that of the slave. If the heterogeneous nature of the slave is akin to that of the filth in which his material situation condemns him to live, that of the master is formed by an act excluding all filth: an act pure in direction but sadistic in form.

In human terms, the ultimate imperative value presents itself in the form of royal or imperial authority in which cruel tendencies and the need, characteristic of all domination, to realize and idealize order are manifest in the highest degree. This double character is no less present in fascist authority, but it is only one of the numerous forms of royal authority, the description of which constitutes the foundation of any coherent description of fascism.

[...]

In fact, as a rule, *homogeneous* society excludes every *heterogeneous* element, whether filthy or noble; the modalities of the operation vary as much as the nature of each excluded element. For homogeneous society, only the rejection of impoverished forms has a constant fundamental value (such that the least recourse to the reserves of energy represented by these forms requires an operation as dangerous as *subversion*); but, given that the act of excluding impoverished forms necessarily associates *homogeneous* forms with imperative forms, the latter can no longer be purely and simply rejected. To combat the elements most incompatible with it, *homogeneous* society uses free-floating imperative forces; and, when it must choose the very object of its activity (the existence *for itself* in the service of which it must necessarily place itself) from the domain that it has excluded, the choice inevitably falls on those forces that have already proved most effective.

The inability of *homogeneous* society to find in itself a reason for being and acting is what makes it dependent upon imperative forces, just as the sadistic hostility of sovereigns toward the impoverished population is what allies them with any formation seeking to maintain the latter in a state of oppression.

[...]

Posing itself as the principle for the association of innumerable elements, royal power develops spontaneously as an imperative and destructive force against every other imperative form that could be opposed to it. It thereby manifests, at the top, the fundamental tendency and principle of all authority: the reduction to a personal entity, the individualization of power. While impoverished existence is necessarily produced as a multitude and homogeneous society as a reduction to the common denominator, the imperative agency – the foundation of oppression – necessarily develops along the lines of a reduction to a unit in the form of a human being excluding the very possibility of a peer, in other words, as a radical form of exclusion requiring avidity.

[...]

In the first place, fascist power is characterized by a foundation that is both religious and military, in which these two habitually distinct elements cannot be separated: it thus presents itself from the outset as an accomplished concentration.

It is true, however, that the military aspect is the predominant one. The affective relations that closely associate (identify) the leader to the member of the party (as they have already been described) are generally analogous to those uniting a chief to his soldiers. The imperative presence of the leader amounts to a negation of the fundamental revolutionary effervescence that he taps; the revolution, which is affirmed as a foundation is, at the same time, fundamentally negated from the moment that internal domination is militarily exerted on the militia. [...] But the religious value of the chief is really the fundamental (if not formal) value of fascism, giving the activity of the militiamen its characteristic affective tonality, distinct from that of the soldier in general. The chief as such is in fact only the emanation of a principle that is none other than that of the glorious existence of a nation raised to the value of a divine force (which, superseding every other conceivable consideration, demands not only passion but ecstasy from its participants). Incarnated in the person of the chief (in Germany, the properly religious term, prophet, has sometimes been used), the nation thus plays the same role that Allah, incarnated in the person of Mahomet or the Khalif,[5] plays for Islam.

[...]

THE FASCIST STATE

Fascism's close ties with the impoverished classes profoundly distinguish this formation from classical royal society, which is characterized by a more or less decisive loss of contact with the lower classes. But, forming in opposition to the established royal unification (the forms of which dominate society from too far above), the fascist unification is not simply a uniting of powers from different origins and a symbolic uniting of classes: it is also the accomplished uniting of the *heterogeneous* elements with the *homogeneous* elements, of sovereignty in the strictest sense with the State.

As a uniting, fascism is actually opposed as much to Islam as it is to traditional monarchy. In fact Islam was created from nothing, and that is why a form such as the State, which can only be the result of a long historical process, played no role in its immediate constitution; on the contrary, the existing State served from the outset as a frame for the entire fascist process of organic organization. This characteristic aspect of fascism permitted Mussolini to write that 'everything is in the State,' that 'nothing human or spiritual exists nor *a fortiori* does it have any existence outside of the State.'[6] But this does not necessarily imply an identity of the State and the imperative force that dominates the whole of society. Mussolini himself, who leaned toward a kind of Hegelian divinization of the State, acknowledges in willfully obscure terms a distinct principle of sovereignty that he alternatively designates as *the people, the nation*, and *the superior personality*, but that must be identified with the Fascist formation itself and its leader: 'if the people ... signifies the idea ... that is incarnated in the people as the will of a few or even of a single person ... It has to do,' he writes, 'neither with race nor with a determined geographical region, but with a grouping that is historically perpetuated, of a multitude unified by an idea that is a will to existence and to power: it is a self-consciousness, a personality.'[7] The term *personality* must be understood as *individualization*, a process leading to Mussolini himself, and when he adds that 'this superior personality is the nation as State. It is not the nation that creates the State . . .,'[8] it must be understood that he has: 1) substituted the principle of the sovereignty of the individualized fascist formation for the old democratic principle of the sovereignty of the nation; 2) laid the groundwork for a conclusive interpretation of the sovereign agency and the State.

National Socialist Germany – which, unlike Italy (under the patronage of Gentile), has not officially adopted Hegelianism and the theory of the State as soul of the world – has not been afflicted with the theoretical difficulties resulting from the necessity of officially articulating a principle of authority: the mystical idea of race immediately affirmed itself as the imperative aim of the new fascist society; at the same time it appeared to be incarnated in the person of the Führer and his followers. Even though the conception of race lacks an objective base, it is nonetheless subjectively grounded, and the necessity of maintaining the racial value above all others obviated the need for a theory that made the State the principle of all value. The example of Germany thus demonstrates that the identity established by Mussolini between the State and the sovereign form of value is not necessary to a theory of fascism.

[. . .]

NOTES

1. Cf. G. Bataille, 'La notion de dépense,' in *La critique sociale* 7, January 1933, p. 302.
2. On the affective relations of the followers to the leader and on the analogy with hypnosis, cf. Freud, *Group Psychology and the Analysis of the 'Ego'*.
3. Cf. W. Robertson Smith, *Lectures on the religion of the Semites*, first series, *The Fundamental Institutions*, Edinburgh, 1889.
4. The word *sovereign* comes from the lower Latin adjective *superaneus* meaning *superior*.
5. *Khalif* etymologically signifies *lieutenant* (standing in for [tenant lieu]; the full title is 'lieutenant of the emissary of God.'
6. Mussolini, *Enciclopedia italiana*, article *Fascismo*.
7. Ibid.
8. Ibid.

13

'ELEMENTS OF ANTI-SEMITISM'

Max Horkheimer and Theodor W. Adorno

[...]

Bourgeois anti-Semitism has a specific economic reason: the concealment of domination in production. In earlier ages the rulers were directly repressive and not only left all the work to the lower classes but declared work to be a disgrace, as it always was under domination; and in a mercantile age, the industrial boss is an absolute monarch. Production attracts its own courtiers. The new rulers simply took off the bright garb of the nobility and donned civilian clothing. They declared that work was not degrading, so as to control the others more rationally. They claimed to be creative workers, but in reality they were still the grasping overlords of former times. The manufacturer took risks and acted like a banker or commercial wizard. He calculated, arranged, bought and sold. On the market he competed for the profit corresponding to his own capital. He seized all he could, not only on the market but at the very source: as a representative of his class he made sure that his workers did not sell him short with their labor. The workers had to supply the maximum amount of goods. Like Shylock, the bosses demand their pound of flesh. They owned the machines and materials, and therefore compelled others to produce for them. They called themselves producers, but secretly everyone knew the truth. The productive work of the capitalist, whether he justifies his profit by means of gross returns as under liberalism, or by his director's salary as today, is an ideology cloaking the real nature of the labor contract and the grasping character of the economic system.

From Max Horkheimer and Theodor W. Adorno (1990) 'Elements of Anti-Semitism', in *Dialectic of Enlightenment*, trans. John Cumming. New York: Herder & Herder.

And so people shout: Stop thief! – but point at the Jews. They are the scapegoats not only for individual maneuvers and machinations but in a broader sense, inasmuch as the economic injustice of the whole class is attributed to them. [. . .]

The Jews were not the sole owners of the circulation sector. But they had been active in it for so long that they mirrored in their own ways the hatred they had always borne. Unlike their Aryan colleagues, they were still largely denied access to the origins of surplus value. It was a long time before, with difficulty, they were allowed to own the means of production. Admittedly, in the history of Europe and even under the German emperors, baptized Jews were allowed high positions in industry and in the administration. But they had to justify themselves with twice the usual devotion, diligence, and stubborn self-denial. They were only allowed to retain their positions if by their behavior they tacitly accepted or confirmed the verdict pronounced on other Jews: that was the purpose of baptism. No matter how many great achievements the Jews were responsible for, they could not be absorbed into the European nations; they were not allowed to put down roots and so they were dismissed as rootless. At best the Jews were protected and dependent on emperors, princes or the absolute state. But the rulers themselves all had an economic advantage over the remainder of the population. To the extent that they could use the Jews as intermediaries, they protected them against the masses who had to pay the price of progress. The Jews were the colonizers for progress. From the time when, in their capacity as merchants, they helped to spread Roman civilization throughout Gentile Europe, they were the representatives – in harmony with their patriarchal religion – of municipal, bourgeois and, finally, industrial conditions. They carried capitalist ways of life to various countries and drew upon themselves the hatred of all who had to suffer under capitalism. For the sake of the economic progress which is now proving their downfall, the Jews were always a thorn in the side of the craftsmen and peasants who were declassed by capitalism. They are now experiencing to their own cost the exclusive, particularist character of capitalism. Those who always wanted to be first have been left far behind. Even the Jewish president of an American entertainment trust lives hopelessly on the defensive in his cocoon of cash. The kaftan was a relic of ancient middle-class costume. Today it indicates that its wearer has been cast onto the periphery of a society which, though completely enlightened, still wishes to lay the ghosts of its distant past. Those who proclaimed individualism, abstract justice, and the notion of the person are now degraded to the condition of a species. Those who are never allowed to enjoy freely the civil rights which should allow them human dignity are referred to, without distinction, as 'the Jew.' Even in the nineteenth century the Jews remained dependent on an alliance with the central power. General justice protected by the state was the pledge of their security, and the law of exception a specter held out before them. The Jews remained objects, at the mercy of others, even when they insisted on their rights. Commerce was not their vocation but their fate. The

Jews constituted the trauma of the knights of industry who had to pretend to be creative, while the claptrap of anti-Semitism announced a fact for which they secretly despised themselves; their anti-Semitism is self-hatred, the bad conscience of the parasite.

[. . .]

Civilization has replaced the organic adaptation to others and mimetic behavior proper, by organized control of mimesis, in the magical phase; and, finally, by rational practice, by work, in the historical phase. Uncontrolled mimesis is outlawed. The angel with the fiery sword who drove man out of paradise and onto the path of technical progress is the very symbol of that progress. For centuries, the severity with which the rulers prevented their own followers and the subjugated masses from reverting to mimetic modes of existence, starting with the religious prohibition on images, going on to the social banishment of actors and gypsies, and leading finally to the kind of teaching which does not allow children to behave as children, has been the condition for civilization. Social and individual education confirms men in the objectivizing behavior of workers and protects them from reincorporation into the variety of circumambient nature. All devotion and all deflection has a touch of mimicry about it. The ego has been formed in resistance to this mimicry. In the constitution of the ego reflective mimesis becomes controlled reflection. [. . .]

In the bourgeois mode of production, the indelible mimetic heritage of all practical experience is consigned to oblivion. The pitiless prohibition of regression becomes mere fate; the denial is now so complete that it is no longer conscious. Those blinded by civilization experience their own tabooed mimetic features only in certain gestures and behavior patterns which they encounter in others and which strike them as isolated remnants, as embarrassing rudimentary elements that survive in the rationalized environment. What seems repellently alien is in fact all too familiar:[1] the infectious gestures of direct contacts suppressed by civilization, for instance, touch, soothing, snuggling up, coaxing. We are put off by the old-fashioned nature of these impulses. They seem to translate long verified human relations back into individual power relations: in trying to influence the purchaser by flattery, the debtor by threats and the creditor by entreaty. Every non-manipulated expression seems to be the grimace which the manipulated expression always was – in the movies, in lynch law, or in speeches by Hitler. However, undisciplined mimicry is the brand of the old form of domination, engraved in the living substance of the dominated and passed down by a process of unconscious imitation in infancy from generation to generation, from the down-at-heel Jew to the rich banker. This mimicry arouses anger because, in the face of the new conditions of production, it displays the old fear which, in order to survive those conditions, must be forgotten. True, personal anger in the civilized man is roused by the constraining situation: by the anger of the tormentor and of the tormented, who are indistinguishable in their grimace. The impotent semblance is answered by deadly reality, the game by seriousness.

[…]

The howling voice of Fascist orators and camp commandants shows the other side of the same social condition. The yell is as cold as business. They both expropriate the sounds of natural complaint and make them elements of their technique. Their bellow has the same significance for the pogrom as the noise generator in the German flying bomb: the terrible cry which announces terror is simply turned on. […] Anyone who seeks refuge must be prevented from finding it; those who express ideas which all long for, peace, a home, freedom – the nomads and players – have always been refused a homeland. Whatever a man fears, that he suffers. Even the last resting place is emptied of peace. The destruction of cemeteries is not a mere excess of anti-Semitism – it is anti-Semitism in its essence. […]

There is no anti-Semite who does not basically want to imitate his mental image of a Jew, which is composed of mimetic cyphers: the argumentative movement of a hand, the musical voice painting a vivid picture of things and feelings irrespective of the real content of what is said, and the nose – the physiognomic *principium individuationis*, symbol of the specific character of an individual, described between the lines of his countenance. The multifarious nuances of the sense of smell embody the archetypal longing for the lower forms of existence, for direct unification with circumambient nature, with the earth and mud. Of all the senses, that of smell – which is attracted without objectifying – bears clearest witness to the urge to lose oneself in and become the 'other.' As perception and the perceived – both are united – smell is more expressive than the other senses. When we see we remain what we are; but when we smell we are taken over by otherness. Hence the sense of smell is considered a disgrace in civilization, the sign of lower social strata, lesser races and base animals. The civilized individual may only indulge in such pleasure if the prohibition is suspended by rationalization in the service of real or apparent practical ends. The prohibited impulse may be tolerated if there is no doubt that the final aim is its elimination – this is the case with jokes or fun, the miserable parody of fulfillment. As a despised and despising characteristic, the mimetic function is enjoyed craftily. Anyone who seeks out 'bad' smells, in order to destroy them, may imitate sniffing to his heart's content, taking unrationalized pleasure in the experience. The civilized man 'disinfects' the forbidden impulse by his unconditional identification with the authority which has prohibited it; in this way the action is made acceptable. If he goes beyond the permitted bounds, laughter ensues. This is the schema of the anti-Semitic reaction. Anti-Semites gather together to celebrate the moment when authority permits what is usually forbidden, and become a collective only in that common purpose. There rantings are organized laughter. The more terrible their accusations and threats and the greater their anger, the more compelling their scorn. Anger, scorn, and embittered imitation are actually the same thing. The purpose of the Fascist formula, the ritual discipline, the uniforms, and the whole apparatus, which is at first sight irrational, is to allow mimetic behavior. The carefully thought out symbols (which are proper to every counterrevolutionary movement), the skulls and disguises, the barbaric drum beats, the monotonous repetition of words and gestures, are simply the organized imitation of magic practices, the mimesis of mimesis. The leader with his contorted face and the charisma of approaching hysteria take command. The leader acts as a representative; he portrays what is forbidden to everyone else in actual life. Hitler can gesticulate like a clown, Mussolini strike false notes like a provincial tenor, Goebbels talk endlessly like a Jewish agent whom he wants murdered, and Coughlin preach love like the savior whose crucifixion he portrays – all for the sake of still more bloodshed. Fascism is also totalitarian in that it seeks to make the rebellion of suppressed nature against domination directly useful to domination.

This machinery needs the Jews. Their artificially heightened prominence acts on the legitimate son of the gentile civilization like a magnetic field. The gentile sees equality, humanity, in his difference from the Jew, but this induces a feeling of antagonism and alien being. And so impulses which are normally taboo and conflict with the requirements of the prevailing form of labor are transformed into conforming idiosyncrasies. The economic position of the Jews, the last defrauded frauds of liberalistic ideology, affords them no secure protection. Since they are so eminently fitted to generate these mental induction currents, they serve such functions involuntarily. They share the fate of the rebellious nature as which Fascism uses them: they are employed blindly yet perspicaciously. It matters little whether the Jews as individuals really do still have those mimetic features which awaken the dread malady, or whether such features are suppressed. Once the wielders of economic power have overcome their fear of the Fascist administrators, the Jews automatically stand out as the disturbing factor in the harmony of the national society. They are abandoned by domination when its progressive alienation from nature makes it revert to mere nature. The Jews as a whole are accused of participating in forbidden magic and bloody ritual. Disguised as accusation, the subconscious desire of the aboriginal inhabitants to return to the mimetic practice of sacrifice finds conscious fulfillment. When all the horror of prehistory which has been overlaid with civilization is rehabilitated as rational interest by projection onto the Jews, there is no restriction. The horror can be carried out in practice, and its practical implementation goes beyond the evil content of the projection. The fantasies of Jewish crimes, infanticide and sadistic excess, poisoning of the nation, and international conspiracy, accurately define the anti-Semitic dream, but remain far behind its actualization. Once things have reached this stage, the mere word 'Jew' appears as the bloody grimace reflected in the swastika flag with its combination of death's head and shattered cross. The mere fact that a person is called a Jew is an invitation forcibly to make him over into a physical semblance of that image of death and distortion.

Civilization is the victory of society over nature which changes everything into pure nature. The Jews themselves have taken part in this process for thousands of years – with enlightenment as with cynicism. The oldest surviving patriarchate, the incarnation of monotheism, they transformed taboos into civilizing maxims when others still clung to magic. The Jews seemed to have succeeded where Christianity failed: they defused magic by its own power – turned against itself as ritual service of God. They did not eliminate adaptation to nature, but converted it into a series of duties in the form of ritual. They have retained the aspect of expiation, but have avoided the reversion to mythology which symbolism implies. And so they are thought to lag behind advanced civilization and yet to be too far ahead of it: they are both clever and stupid, similar and dissimilar. They are declared guilty of something which they, as the first burghers, were the first to overcome: the lure of base instincts, reversion to animality and to the ground, the service of images. Because they invented the concept of kosher meat, they are persecuted as swine. The anti-Semites make themselves the executors of the Old Testament: they want the Jews who have eaten of the tree of knowledge to return unto dust.

Anti-Semitism is based on a false projection. It is the counterpart of true mimesis, and fundamentally related to the repressed form; in fact, it is probably the morbid expression of repressed mimesis. Mimesis imitates the environment, but false projection makes the environment like itself. For mimesis the outside world is a model which the inner world must try to conform to: the alien must become familiar; but false projection confuses the inner and outer world and defines the most intimate experiences as hostile. Impulses which the subject will not admit as his own even though they are most assuredly so, are attributed to the object – the prospective victim. The actual paranoiac has no choice but to obey the laws of his sickness. But in Fascism this behavior is made political; the object of the illness is deemed true to reality; and the mad system becomes the reasonable norm in the world and deviation from it a neurosis. [...]

NOTE

1. Cf. Freud, *Das Unheimliche*, *Gesammelte Werke*, Vol. II, pp. 254, 259 etc.

14

'THE FICTION OF THE POLITICAL'

Philippe Lacoue-Labarthe

[...]

I believe it is absolutely essential that I indicate – in order to clarify matters –
what it was that Heidegger was breaking with when he broke with Jünger. My
hypothesis is that it was with nothing less than the political fiction of the
German myth, i.e. with something which in spite of everything (in spite of the
huge gulf regarding the thinking of Being which separated the two) was very
close to what might be defined as the Nazi myth.

By 'Nazi myth', I do not mean the reactivation of any particular myth
(whether Germanic, Indo-European or other) which Nazism might be seen as
having incorporated into the programme of its ideology or its propaganda, nor
even the elevation of *mythos* (as against *logos* or *ratio*) which formed the basic
essentials of the 'thinking' of Krieck or Baümler. This reassertion of the value of
myth is not foreign to the construction of the Nazi myth (nor is it absent from
Heidegger's thinking); it is, however, only a consequence of it. That is to say
that it is only an effect of Nazism's desire to mythify, or, in other words, of the
desire, for Nazism (the movement and later the State), to present itself as myth
or as realization of a myth (setting myth to work and breathing life into it). In
this sense, as is perfectly clear from a reading of Rosenberg,[1] myth is in no way
'mythological'. It is a 'power' (*puissance*), the power that is in the gathering
together of the fundamental forces and orientations of an individual or a people,
that is to say the power of a deep, concrete, embodied identity. Rosenberg

From Philippe Lacoue-Labarthe (1990) 'The Fiction of the Political', in *Heidegger, Art and Politics:
the Fiction of the Political*, trans. Chris Turner. New York: Basil Blackwell.

interprets this power as that of the dream, as the projection of an image with which one identifies through a total and immediate commitment. Such an image is in no way a product of 'fabulation', to which myth is ordinarily reduced; it is the figuration of a *type* conceived both as a model of identity and as that identity formed and realized. And this type in its turn provides the myth with its truth in that it allows the dream to lay hold of 'the whole man'. When Rosenberg writes that today (in 1930) 'we (Germans) are beginning to dream again our original dreams', he is thinking neither of Wotan nor Odin (Odin is dead, he says), but of the essence of the Germanic soul (which is the resurrection of Odin) in so far as it, like the Greek soul which was itself also Aryan, dreams the political (honour and the State) as *Formwillen*, the desire to form and the desire for form or *Gestaltung*: *as work*.

Naturally, this onto-typological interpretation of myth fits in with a racism: the Germanic soul is here that of a race which is only as it is by virtue of its belonging to blood and soil, and nothing of the frenzied (and 'scientific') incorporation of the echo of Greek autochthony is left out, not even the dream of being begotten by the father alone. But racism is a consequence of the onto-typology, not its cause: 'The freedom of the soul', explains Rosenberg, 'is *Gestalt*. The *Gestalt* is always limited in its form. This limitation (which outlines the figure, traces the contours of the type) is conditioned by race. But this race is the external figure of a determinate soul.' In other words, race (and such is the content of the myth: myth is the myth of the race) is the identity of a formative power, of a type, or, in other words, of a bearer of myth. This perfect circularity, in which we can recognize that *tautegory* Schelling borrowed from Coleridge, means nothing less than this: the myth (of the race) is the myth of myth, or the myth of the formative power of myths. It is the myth of 'mythopoiesis' itself, of which the type, by the very logic of aesthetico-political immanentism, is both productive of and produced by fiction. Moreover, this is why myth, signifying nothing other than itself, is a product of pure self-formation and finds its truth or its verification as the self-foundation of the people (or the race: the translation of the word *völkisch* is, in fact, undecidable) in conformity with its type. Equally, in the onto-typology thus arrived at, it is the ontology of subjectivity (of the will to will) that finds its fulfillment. Nazism is the Nazi myth, i.e. the Aryan type, as absolute subject, pure will (of the self) willing itself.

Several consequences follow from this:

(1) Ideology can no more be seen as a means to an end – for example as a 'propaganda technique' – than can the various forms of performance that generate an experience of fusion. The self-production of the Aryan myth is an end in itself, the end as immanent, embodied and immediate (Rosenberg, who constantly uses the term *Erlebnis* calls it a 'lived') realization of the self-identity of the people or the race. The end here is pure commitment to and participation in the myth and the type: 'The life of a race', writes Rosenberg, ... is the

formation of a mystic synthesis'. It is wrong to reduce fascism, as is often done, to a mass manipulation technique. Fascism is, rather, the mobilization of the identificatory emotions of the masses.

(2) The awakening of the power of myth – the auto-poietic act – becomes a necessity once the inconsistency of the abstract universals of reason has been revealed and the beliefs of modern humanity (Christianity and belief in humanity itself), which were at bottom only bloodless myths, have collapsed. But here again we should be careful: Nazism is a humanism in so far as it rests upon a determination of *humanitas* which is, in its view, more powerful – i.e. more effective – than any other. The subject of absolute self-creation, even if, occupying an immediately natural position (the particularity of the race), it transcends all the determinations of the modern subject, brings together and concretizes these same determinations (as also does Stalinism with the subject of absolute self-production) and constitutes itself as *the* subject, in absolute terms. The fact that this subject lacks the universality which apparently defines the *humanitas* of humanism in the received sense, still does not make Nazism an anti-humanism. It simply situates it within the logic, of which there are many other examples, of the realization and the becoming-concrete of 'abstractions'.

(3) The Jews do not belong to *humanitas* thus defined because they have neither dreams nor myths. Maurice Blanchot is right when he says 'the Jews embody . . . the rejection of myths, the eschewing of idols, the recognition of an ethical order which manifests itself in respect for the law. What Hitler is attempting to annihilate in annihilating the Jew, and the "myth of the Jew", is precisely man liberated from myths.'[2] This 'rejection of myths' is precisely what explains why the Jews do not constitute a type: they have, says Rosenberg, no *Seelengestalt* – and therefore no *Rassengestalt*. They are a formless, unaesthetic 'people', which by definition cannot enter into the process of self-fictioning and cannot constitute a subject, or, in other words, a being-proper (*être-propre*). It is this unassignable (and formidable) im-properness of the Jews which makes them, says Rosenberg once again, not the direct opposite (a counter-type) of the Teuton, but his contradiction – the very absence of type. Hence their power – they who are neither *Kulturbegründer* nor *Kulturschöpfer*, but mere *Kulturträger*, bearers of civilization – to insert themselves into every culture and State and then to live a life that is parasitic upon these, constantly threatening them with bastardization. All in all, the Jews are infinitely mimetic beings, or, in other words, the site of an *endless mimesis*, which is both interminable and inorganic, producing no art and achieving no appropriation. They are destabilization itself.

This is just one example, summarized here rather cursorily, of Nazi onto-typology.

It is immediately easy to see the features which make it *absolutely* impossible to confuse this schema with Jünger's argument on the *Gestalt* of the Worker, and, *a fortiori*, with the arguments of Heidegger – who moreover never troubled to conceal his contempt for Rosenberg – concerning the work of art, *Dichtung*, the people and history. It becomes all the more impossible to do so when one takes into account that this presentation credits Rosenberg with a coherence and a philosophical logic which are, in fact, totally absent from his work. *The Myth of the Twentieth Century* is a repetitive, jargon-ridden, barely readable hotch-potch of a book which belongs to that vein of authoritarian, voluntaristic logorrhea that formed the 'style' of the period and consists merely in noisy, stereotyped assertions. By no stretch of the imagination could it be confused with the work of Jünger or Heidegger, and, in any case, its anti-semitism renders it absolutely incompatible with their writings.

It is none the less the case that from a certain elevated vantage point, the one which our positionless position in history today gives us and the fact that in May 1968 (which was a political experience of which we have yet to feel all the – more than merely political – consequences) there was a clear-sighted renunciation of the archaeo-politics which would inevitably reconstitute itself sooner or later (in its hard revolutionary form; and it seemed better in the end to allow the restoration of the only more or less liveable political reality – with all its banal and, no less inevitable, burden of compromise – that had stubbornly survived through the catastrophic fulfilments of the Western political project),[3] from this lofty vantage point, then, it is nonetheless the same thing that is basically seeking expression in various quarters. From an even loftier height, that 'same thing' is perhaps contained in the oft-cited and indeed memorable sentence Thucydides attributes to Pericles in his *Funeral Oration*:

φιλοχαλοῦμευ τε γὰρ μετ᾽ ευτελδιαζ χὰι φιλοσουμεν ανευ μαλαχίας

This sentence is generally considered untranslatable. [...]

I shall opt for a literal translation. 'We love the beautiful with frugality and knowledge without softness.' 'Frugality' here is an economic category:[4] *euteleia* has never signified rightness of judgement, political or otherwise, but simplicity of means deployed. It is the absence of luxury, of pomp – and, first and foremost, of expenditure. In other words, it is rigour, if not indeed austerity. On the other hand, *malakia* certainly does mean 'softness', which is in fact the supreme Barbarian vice, i.e. the Oriental vice. Pericles' (and Thucydides') utterance celebrates the heroism – the *bearing* – in the combined practice of art and thought, which he knew he had raised to unsurpassed heights, of that 'haughty little people' as Nietzsche would call them, in the face of an adversity they had to confront without resources. Exposed to distress (*Not*), as Heidegger would say in the 1930s, identifying Germany with Greece and calling upon it, with all the force of *technē* (art and knowledge) to rise up against the overpowering force of the concealment of the essent.

How then could we not see that in this utterance, which brings together art and philosophy to say what constitutes the specific quality and the heroic singularity of the Athenian *polis*, there is, not the founding charter of our 'democracies', but the programme of something which had an horrific fulfilment of which we are, so to speak, the definitively caesura-ed heirs?

NOTES

1. Philippe Lacoue-Labarthe and Jean-Luc Nancy, 'Le mythe nazi' in *Les mecanismes du fascisme* (Colloque de Schiltigheim, Strasbourg, 1980). What follows is based upon the analyses that appear there. The reading of Rosenberg's *Myth of the Twentieth Century* and Hitler's *Mein Kampf* is the work of Jean-Luc Nancy, whose analysis I follow here.
2. 'Les intellectuels en question', *Le Débat* (33, May 1984).
3. I also wish to express here my profound agreement with the pages Maurice Blanchot devoted to May 1968 in *La Communauté inavouable* (Paris, Minuit, 1983) and *Michel Foucault tel que je l'imagine* (Paris, Fata Morgana, 1986).
4. I am indebted to Suzanne Saïd for this piece of information.

15

'ANTI-SEMITISM AND NATIONAL SOCIALISM'

Moishe Postone

[...]

Auschwitz, Belzec, Chelmno, Maidenek, Sobibor and Treblinka should not be treated outside of the framework of an analysis of National Socialism. They represent one of its logical endpoints, not simply its most terrible epiphenomenon. *No analysis of National Socialism which cannot account for the extermination of European Jewry is fully adequate.*

[...]

The first step must be a specification of the Holocaust and of modern anti-Semitism. The lack of a serious and intensive consideration of modern anti-Semitism renders inadequate any attempt to understand the extermination of European Jewry. The problem should not be posed quantitatively, whether of numbers of people murdered or of degree of suffering. There are too many historical examples of mass murder and genocide. (Many more Russians than Jews, for example, were killed by the Nazis.) The question, is, rather, one of *qualitative specificity*. Particular aspects of the extermination of European Jewry by the Nazis remain inexplicable so long as anti-Semitism is treated as a specific example of prejudice, xenophobia and racism in general, as an example of a scapegoat strategy whose victims could very well have been members of any other group.

From Moishe Postone (1986) 'Anti-Semitism and National Socialism', *New German Critique* 19 (Winter 1980), pp. 97–115, reprinted in Anson Rabinbach and Jack Zipes (eds), *Germans and Jews since the Holocaust: The Changing Situation in West Germany*. New York and London: Holmes & Meier.

The Holocaust was characterized by the sense of mission, the relative lack of emotion and immediate hate (as opposed to pogroms, for example) and, most importantly, its apparent lack of functionality. The extermination of the Jews was not a means to another end. They were not exterminated for military reasons, or in order to violently acquire land [...], or in order to wipe out those segments of the population around whom resistance could most easily crystallize [...] (as was Nazi policy towards the Poles and Russians), or for any other 'extrinsic' goal. *The extermination of the Jews not only was to have been total, but was its own goal* [...].

[...] Once this *qualitative specificity* of the extermination of European Jewry is recognized, it becomes clear that attempts at an explanation which deal with capitalism, racism, bureaucracy, sexual repression or the authoritarian personality, remain far too general. The specificity of the Holocaust requires a much more concretized mediation in order to even approach its understanding.

The extermination of European Jewry is, of course, related to anti-Semitism. The specificity of the former must be related to that of the latter. Moreover, *modern* anti-Semitism must be understood with reference to Nazism as a movement – a movement which, in terms of its own self-understanding, represented a revolt.

Modern anti-Semitism, which should not be confused with everday anti-Jewish prejudice, is an ideology, a form of thought, which emerged in Europe in the late 19th century. Its emergence presupposed centuries of earlier forms of anti-Semitism, which has almost always been an integral part of Christian western civilization. What is common to all forms of anti-Semitism is the degree of power attributed to the Jews: the power to kill God, unleash the Bubonic Plague and, more recently, introduce capitalism and socialism. In other words, anti-Semitic thought is strongly Manichean, with the Jews playing the role of the children of darkness.

It is not only the degree, but also the quality of power attributed to the Jews which distinguishes anti-Semitism from other forms of racism. Probably all forms of racism attribute potential power to the other. This power, however, is usually concrete – material or sexual – the power of the oppressed (as repressed), of the 'Untermenschen.' The power attributed to the Jews is not only much greater and 'real,' as opposed to potential, it is different. In *modern* anti-Semitism it is mysteriously intangible, abstract and universal. This power does not usually appear as such, but must find a concrete vessel, a carrier, a mode of expression. Because this power is not bound concretely, is not 'rooted,' it is of staggering immensity and is extremely difficult to check. It stands behind phenomena, but is not identical with them. Its source is therefore hidden – conspiratorial. The Jews represent an immensely powerful, intangible, international conspiracy.

[...] It is characteristic of modern anti-Semitism that the Jews are considered to be the force behind those 'apparent' opposites: plutocratic capitalism and socialism. 'International Jewry' is, moreover, perceived to be centered in the 'asphalt jungles' of the newly emergent urban megalopoli, to be behind 'vulgar, materialist, modern culture' and, in general, all forces contributing to the decline of traditional social groupings, values and institutions. The Jews represent a foreign, dangerous, destructive force undermining the social 'health' of the nation. Modern anti-Semitism, then, is characterized not only by its secular content, but also by its systematic character. Its claim is to explain the world – a world which had rapidly become too complex and threatening for many people.

[...]

[...] A careful examination of the modern anti-Semitic worldview reveals that it is a form of thought in which the rapid development of industrial capitalism with all of its social ramifications is personified and identified as the Jew. It is not that the Jews merely were considered to be the owners of money, as in traditional anti-Semitism, but that they were held responsible for economic crises and identified with the range of social restructuring and dislocation resulting from rapid industrialization: explosive urbanization, the decline of traditional social classes and strata, the emergence of a large, increasingly organized industrial proletariat, etc. In other words, the abstract domination of capital, which – particularly with rapid industrialization – caught people up in a web of dynamic forces they could not understand, became perceived as the domination of International Jewry. This was particularly true in countries such as Germany, in which the development of industrial capitalism was not only very rapid, but occurred in the absence of a previous bourgeois revolution and its consequent hegemonic liberal values and political culture.

This, however, is no more than a first approach. The personification has been described, not yet explained. It has not been grounded epistemologically. There have been many attempts at an explanation. The problem with those theories, like that of Max Horkheimer,[1] which concentrate on the identification of the Jews with money and the sphere of circulation, is that they cannot account for the notion that the Jews constitute the power behind social democracy and communism. At first glance, those theories, such as that of George Mosse,[2] which interpret modern anti-Semitism as a revolt against modernity, appear more satisfying. The problem, however, with that approach is that 'the modern' would certainly include industrial capital which, as is well known, was precisely *not* an object of anti-Semitic attacks, even in a period of rapid industrialization. What is required, then, is an approach which allows for a distinction between what modern capitalism is and the way it appears, between its essence and appearance. The concept 'modern' does not allow for such a distinction.

These considerations lead us to Marx's concept of the fetish, the strategic intent of which was to provide a social and historical theory of knowledge grounded in the difference between the essence of capitalist social relations and their manifest form.[3] When one examines the specific characteristics of the power attributed to the Jews by modern anti-Semitism – abstractness, intangibility, universality, mobility – it is striking that they are all characteristics of the value dimension of the social forms analyzed by Marx. Moreover, this dimension – like the supposed power of the Jews – does not appear as such, rather always in the form of a material carrier, such as the commodity. The carrier thus has a 'double character' – value and use-value.

[...]

[...] The dialectical tension between value and use-value in the commodity requires that this 'double character' be materially externalized in the value form, where it appears 'doubled' as money (the manifest form of value) and the commodity (the manifest form of use-value). The effect of this externalization is that the commodity, although it is a social form expressing both value and use-value, appears to contain only the latter, i.e., appears as purely material and 'thingly'; money, on the other hand, then appears to be the sole repository of value, i.e., as the manifestation of the purely abstract, rather than as the externalized manifest form of the value dimension of the commodity itself. The form of materialized social relations specific to capitalism appears – on this level of the analysis – as the opposition between money, as abstract, as the 'root of all evil,' and 'thingly' nature. Capitalist social relations appear to find their expression only in the abstract dimension – for example as money and as externalized, abstract, universal 'laws.'[4]

One aspect of the fetish, then, is that capitalist social relations do not appear as such and, moreover, present themselves antinomically, as the opposition of the abstract and concrete. Because, additionally, both sides of the antinomy are objectified, each appears to be quasi-natural: the abstract dimension appears in the form of 'objective,' 'natural' laws; the concrete dimension appears as pure 'thingly' nature. *The structure of alienated social relations which characterize capitalism has the form of a quasi-natural antinomy in which the social and historical do not appear.* This antinomy is recapitulated as the opposition between positivist and romantic forms of thought. Most critical analyses of fetishized thought have concentrated on that strand of the antinomy which hypostatizes the abstract as transhistorical – so-called positive bourgeois thought – and thereby disguises the social and historical character of existing relations. In this essay, the other strand will be emphasized – that of forms of romanticism and revolt which, in terms of their own self-understandings, are anti-bourgeois, but which in fact hypostatize the concrete and thereby remain bound within the antinomy of capitalist social relations.

Forms of anti-capitalist thought which remain bound within the immediacy of this antinomy tend to perceive capitalism, and that which is specific to that social formation, only in terms of the manifestations of the abstract dimension of the antinomy. The existent concrete dimension is then positively opposed to it as the 'natural' or ontologically human, which stands outside of the specificity of capitalist society. Thus, as with Proudhon, for example, concrete labor is understood as the non-capitalist moment which is opposed to the abstractness of money. That concrete labor itself incorporates and is materially formed by capitalist social relations is not understood.

With the further development of capitalism, of the capital form and its associated fetish, the naturalization immanent to the commodity fetish becomes increasingly biologized. The mechanical world view of the 17th and 18th centuries begins to give way; organic process begins to supplant mechanical stasis as the form of the fetish. The proliferation of racial theories and the rise of Social Darwinism in the late 19th century are cases in point. [...] For our purposes what must be noted is the implications for how capital can be perceived. As indicated above, on the logical level of the analysis of the commodity, the 'double character' allows the commodity to appear as a purely material entity rather than as the objectification of mediated social relations. Relatedly, it allows concrete labor to appear as a purely material, creative process, separable from capitalist social relations. On the logical level of capital, the 'double character' (labor proceeds valorization process) allows industrial production to appear as a purely material creative process, separable from capital. *Industrial capital then appears as the linear descendent of 'natural' artisanal labor, in opposition to 'parasitic' finance capital.* Whereas the former appears 'organically rooted,' the latter does not. Capital itself – or what is understood as the negative aspect of capitalism – is understood only in terms of the manifest form of its abstract dimension: finance and interest capital. In this sense, the biological interpretation, which opposes the concrete dimension (of capitalism) as 'natural' and 'healthy' to 'capitalism' (as perceived), does *not* stand in contradiction to a glorification of industrial capital and technology. Both are on the 'thingly' side of the antinomy.

[...] The positive emphasis on 'nature,' on blood, the soil, concrete labor, and *Gemeinschaft*, can easily go hand in hand with a glorification of technology and industrial capital.[5] This form of thought, then is not to be understood as anachronistic, as the expression of historical nonsynchronism (*Ungleichzeitigkeit*), any more than the rise of racial theories in the late 19th century should be thought of as atavistic. They are historically *new* forms of thought and in no way represent the reemergence of an older form. It is because of the emphasis on biological nature that they *appear* to be atavistic or anachronistic. However, this is itself a part of the fetish which presents the 'natural' as more 'essential' and closer to origins, and the course of history as one of increasing artificiality. Such forms of thought become prevalent *with* the development of industrial capitalism. They are *expressions* of that antinomic fetish, which gives rise to the notion that the concrete is 'natural,' and which increasingly presents the socially 'natural' in such a way that it is perceived in biological terms. [...]

This form of 'anti-capitalism,' then, is based on a one-sided attack on the abstract. The abstract and concrete are not seen as constituting an antinomy where the real overcoming of the abstract – of the value dimension – involves the historical overcoming of the antinomy itself as well as *each* of its terms. Instead there is the one-sided attack on abstract Reason, abstract law or, on another level, money and finance capital. [...] The 'anti-capitalist' attack, however, does not remain limited to the attack against abstraction. Even the abstract dimension also appears materially. On the level of the capital fetish, it is not only the concrete side of the antimony which is naturalized and biologized. The manifest abstract dimension is also biologized – as the Jews. The opposition of the concrete material and the abstract becomes the racial opposition of the Arians and the Jews. Modern anti-Semitism involves a biologization of capitalism – which itself is only understood in terms of its manifest abstract dimension – as International Jewry.

According to this interpretation, the Jews were not merely identified with money, with the sphere of circulation, but with capitalism itself. However, because of its fetishized form, this did not appear to include industry and technology. Capitalism appeared to be only its manifest abstract dimension which, in turn, was responsible for the whole range of concrete social and cultural changes associated with the rapid development of modern industrial capitalism. The Jews were not seen merely as *representatives* of capital (in which case anti-Semitic attacks would have been much more class-specific). They became the *personifications* of the intangible, destructive, immensely powerful, and international domination of capital as a social form. Certain forms of anti-capitalist discontent became directed against the manifest abstract dimension of capital, in the form of the Jews, because, given the antinomy of the abstract and concrete dimensions, capitalism appeared that way – not because the Jews were consciously identified with the value dimension. The 'anti-capitalist' revolt was, consequently, also the revolt against the Jews. The overcoming of capitalism and its negative social effects became associated with the overcoming of the Jews.

[...] The question remains why the biological interpretation of the abstract dimension of capitalism found its focus in the Jews. This 'choice' was, within the European context, by no means fortuitous. The Jews could not have been replaced by any other group. The reasons for this are manifold. The long history of anti-Semitism in Europe, and the related association of Jews with money are well known. The period of the rapid expansion of industrial capital in the last third of the 19th century coincided with the political and civil emancipation of the Jews in central Europe. [...]

[...] The nation was not only a political entity, it was also concrete, determined by a common language, history, traditions and religion. In this sense, the only group in Europe which fulfilled the determination of citizenship as a pure political abstraction, were the Jews following their political emancipation. They were German or French citizens, but not really Germans or Frenchmen. They were of the nation abstractly, but rarely concretely. They were, in addition, citizens of most European countries. The quality of abstractness, characteristic not only of the value dimension in its immediacy, but also, mediately, of the bourgeois state and law, became closely identified with the

Jews. In a period when the concrete became glorified against the abstract, against 'capitalism' and the bourgeois state, this became a fatal association. The Jews were rootless, international and abstract.

Modern anti-Semitism, then, is a particularly pernicious fetish form. Its power and danger is that it provides a comprehensive worldview which explains and gives form to certain modes of anti-capitalist discontent in a manner which leaves capitalism intact, by attacking the personifications of that social form. Anti-Semitism so understood allows one to grasp an essential moment of Nazism as a foreshortened anti-capitalist movement, one characterized by a hatred of the abstract, a hypostatization of the existing concrete and by a single-minded, ruthless – but not necessarily hate-filled – mission: to rid the world of the source of all evil.

[...]

A capitalist factory is a place where value is produced, which 'unfortunately' has to take the form of the production of goods. The concrete is produced as the necessary carrier of the abstract. The extermination camps were *not* a terrible version of such a factory but, rather, should be seen as its grotesque, Arian, 'anti-capitalist' *negation*. Auschwitz was a factory to 'destroy value,' i.e., to destroy the personifications of the abstract. Its organization was that of a fiendish industrial process, the aim of which was to 'liberate' the concrete from the abstract. The first step was to dehumanize, that is, to rip the 'mask' of humanity away and reveal the Jews for what 'they really are' – 'Muselmänner,' shadows, ciphers, abstractions. The second step was then to eradicate that abstractness, to transform it into smoke, trying in the process to wrest away the last remnants of the concrete material 'use-value': clothes, gold, hair, soap.

Auschwitz, not 1933, was the real 'German Revolution' – the real 'over-throw' of the existing social formation. By this one deed the world was to be made safe from the tyranny of the abstract. In the process, the Nazis 'liberated' themselves from humanity.

[...]

NOTES

1. Horkheimer, *Die Juden und Europa*, 1939.
2. George Mosse, *The Crisis of German Ideology*, New York, 1964.
3. The epistemological dimension of Marx's critique is immanent to all of *Capital* but was explicated only within the context of his analysis of the commodity. What underlies the concept of the fetish is Marx's analysis of the commodity, money, capital as social forms and *not* merely as economic concepts. In his analysis, capitalist forms of social relations do not appear as such, but are expressed in material form. As expressions of alienation, these materialized forms of social relations acquire a life of their own and reflexively form social action as well as social thought. The commodity as a form, for example, represents a duality of social dimensions (value and use-value) which interact such that the category simultaneously expresses particular 'reified' social relations and forms of thought. This is

any of this material could have deprived the men of Reserve Police Battalion 101 of the capacity for independent thought. Influenced and conditioned in a general way, imbued in particular with a sense of their own superiority and racial kinship as well as Jewish inferiority and otherness, many of them undoubtedly were; explicitly prepared for the task of killing Jews they most certainly were not.

Along with ideological indoctrination, a vital factor touched upon but not fully explored in Milgram's experiments was conformity to the group. The battalion had orders to kill Jews, but each individual did not. Yet 80 to 90 percent of the men proceeded to kill, though almost all of them – at least initially – were horrified and disgusted by what they were doing. To break ranks and step out, to adopt overtly nonconformist behavior, was simply beyond most of the men. It was easier for them to shoot.

Why? First of all, by breaking ranks, nonshooters were leaving the 'dirty work' to their comrades. Since the battalion had to shoot even if individuals did not, refusing to shoot constituted refusing one's share of an unpleasant collective obligation. It was in effect an asocial act vis-à-vis one's comrades. Those who did not shoot risked isolation, rejection, and ostracism – a very uncomfortable prospect within the framework of a tight-knit unit stationed abroad among a hostile population, so that the individual had virtually nowhere else to turn for support and social contact.

This threat of isolation was intensified by the fact that stepping out could also have been seen as a form of moral reproach of one's comrades: the nonshooter was potentially indicating that he was 'too good' to do such things. Most, though not all, nonshooters intuitively tried to diffuse the criticism of their comrades that was inherent in their actions. They pleaded not that they were 'too good' but rather that they were 'too weak' to kill.

Such a stance presented no challenge to the esteem of one's comrades; on the contrary, it legitimized and upheld 'toughness' as a superior quality. For the anxious individual, it had the added advantage of posing no moral challenge to the murderous policies of the regime, though it did pose another problem, since the difference between being 'weak' and being a 'coward' was not great. Hence the distinction made by one policeman who did not dare to step out at Józefów for fear of being considered a coward, but who subsequently dropped out of his firing squad. It was one thing to be too cowardly even to try to kill; it was another, after resolutely trying to do one's share, to be too weak to continue.[1]

Insidiously, therefore, most of those who did not shoot only reaffirmed the 'macho' values of the majority – according to which it was a positive quality to be 'tough' enough to kill unarmed, noncombatant men, women, and children – and tried not to rupture the bonds of comradeship that constituted their social world. Coping with the contradictions imposed by the demands of conscience on the one hand and the norms of the battalion on the other led to many tortured attempts at compromise: not shooting infants on the spot but taking them to the assembly point; not shooting on patrol if no 'go-getter' was along who might report such squeamishness; bringing Jews to the shooting site and firing but intentionally missing. Only the very exceptional remained indifferent to taunts of 'weakling' from their comrades and could live with the fact that they were considered to be 'no man.'[2]

Here we come full circle to the mutually intensifying effects of war and racism noted by John Dower, in conjunction with the insidious effects of constant propaganda and indoctrination. Pervasive racism and the resulting exclusion of the Jewish victims from any common ground with the perpetrators made it all the easier for the majority of the policemen to conform to the norms of their immediate community (the battalion) and their society at large (Nazi Germany). Here the years of anti-Semitic propaganda (and prior to the Nazi dictatorship, decades of shrill German nationalism) dovetailed with the polarizing effects of war. The dichotomy of racially superior Germans and racially inferior Jews, central to Nazi ideology, could easily merge with the image of a beleaguered Germany surrounded by warring enemies. If it is doubtful that most of the policemen understood or embraced the theoretical aspects of Nazi ideology as contained in SS indoctrination pamphlets, it is also doubtful that they were immune to 'the influence of the times' (to use Lieutenant Drucker's phrase once again), to the incessant proclamation of German superiority and incitement of contempt and hatred for the Jewish enemy. Nothing helped the Nazis to wage a race war so much as the war itself. In wartime, when it was all too usual to exclude the enemy from the community of human obligation, it was also all too easy to subsume the Jews into the 'image of the enemy,' or *Feindbild*.

In his last book, *The Drowned and the Saved*, Primo Levi included an essay entitled 'The Gray Zone,' perhaps his most profound and deeply disturbing reflection on the Holocaust.[3] He maintained that in spite of our natural desire for clear-cut distinctions, the history of the camps 'could not be reduced to the two blocs of victims and persecutors.' He argued passionately, 'It is naive, absurd, and historically false to believe that an infernal system such as National Socialism sanctifies its victims; on the contrary, it degrades them, it makes them resemble itself.' The time had come to examine the inhabitants of the 'gray zone' between the simplified Manichean images of perpetrator and victim. Levi concentrated on the 'gray zone of *protekcya* [corruption] and collaboration' that flourished in the camps among a spectrum of victims: from the 'picturesque fauna' of low-ranking functionaries husbanding their minuscule advantages over other prisoners; through the truly privileged network of Kapos, who were free 'to commit the worst atrocities' at whim; to the terrible fate of the Sonderkommandos, who prolonged their lives by manning the gas chambers and crematoria. (Conceiving and organizing the Sonderkommandos was in Levi's opinion National Socialism's 'most demonic crime.')

While Levi focused on the spectrum of victim behavior within the gray zone, he dared to suggest that this zone encompassed perpetrators as well. Even the SS man Muhsfeld of the Birkenau crematoria – whose 'daily ration of slaughter was studded with arbitrary and capricious acts, marked by his inventions of cruelty' – was not a 'monolith.' Faced with the miraculous survival of a sixteen-year-old girl discovered while the gas chambers were being cleared, the disconcerted Muhsfeld briefly hesitated. In the end he ordered the girl's death but quickly left before his orders were carried out. One 'instant of pity' was not enough to 'absolve' Muhsfeld, who was deservedly hanged in 1947. Yet it did 'place him too, although at its extreme boundary, within the gray band, that zone of ambiguity which radiates out from regimes based on terror and obsequiousness.'

Levi's notion of the gray zone encompassing both perpetrators and victims must be approached with a cautious qualification. The perpetrators and victims in the gray zone were not mirror images of one another. Perpetrators did not become fellow victims (as many of them later claimed to be) in the way some victims became accomplices of the perpetrators. The relationship between perpetrator and victim was not symmetrical. The range of choice each faced was totally different.

Nonetheless, the spectrum of Levi's gray zone seems quite applicable to Reserve Police Battalion 101. The battalion certainly had its quota of men who neared the 'extreme boundary' of the gray zone. Lieutenant Gnade, who initially rushed his men back from Minsk to avoid being involved in killing but who later learned to enjoy it, leaps to mind. So do the many reserve policemen who were horrified in the woods outside Józefów but subsequently became casual volunteers for numerous firing squads and 'Jew hunts.' They, like Muhsfeld, seem to have experienced that brief 'instant of pity' but cannot be absolved by it. At the other boundary of the gray zone, even Lieutenant Buchmann, the most conspicuous and outspoken critic of the battalion's murderous actions, faltered at least once. Absent his protector, Major Trapp, and facing orders from the local Security Police in Łuków, he too led his men to the killing fields shortly before his transfer back to Hamburg. And at the very center of the perpetrators' gray zone stood the pathetic figure of Trapp himself, who sent his men to slaughter Jews 'weeping like a child,' and the bedridden Captain Hoffmann, whose body rebelled against the terrible deeds his mind willed.

The behavior of any human being is, of course, a very complex phenomenon, and the historian who attempts to 'explain' it is indulging in a certain arrogance. When nearly 500 men are involved, to undertake any general explanation of their collective behavior is even more hazardous. What, then, is one to conclude? Most of all, one comes away from the story of Reserve Police Battalion 101 with great unease. This story of ordinary men is not the story of all men. The reserve policemen faced choices, and most of them committed terrible deeds. But those who killed cannot be absolved by the notion that anyone in the same situation would have done as they did. For even among them, some refused to kill and others stopped killing. Human responsibility is ultimately an individual matter.

At the same time, however, the collective behavior of Reserve Police Battalion 101 has deeply disturbing implications. There are many societies afflicted by traditions of racism and caught in the siege mentality of war or threat of war. Everywhere society conditions people to respect and defer to authority, and indeed could scarcely function otherwise. Everywhere people seek career advancement. In every modern society, the complexity of life and the resulting bureaucratization and specialization attenuate the sense of personal responsibility of those implementing official policy. Within virtually every social collective, the peer group exerts tremendous pressures on behavior and sets moral norms. If the men of Reserve Police Battalion 101 could become killers under such circumstances, what group of men cannot?

NOTES

1. Bruno, D., *Investigation and trial of Hoffmann, Wohlauf, and others*, Office of the State Prosecutor, Hamburg, 141 Js 1957/62, 2992.
2. Gustav, M., *Investigation of G. and others*, Office of the State Prosecutor, Hamburg, 141 Js 128/65, 169.
3. Primo Levi, *The Drowned and the Saved*, Vintage edition (New York, 1989), 36–69.

PART IV
RACE, GENDER, AND GENOCIDE

RACE, GENDER, AND GENOCIDE: INTRODUCTION

The category of gender has not always been considered central to study of the Nazi genocide. Although, with some notable exceptions, most work from the first decades of Holocaust studies was produced by men and relied heavily on primary sources written by men (both perpetrators and victims), the perspectives of men were considered to provide a neutral, 'universal' portrait of the events. Since the 1980s, however, scholars working across the disciplines have attempted to integrate the histories and perspectives of women into general knowledge of the Nazi period and the 'Final Solution.' Despite this valuable work controversy persists about the usefulness of gender as a category for analysis of the Holocaust. Some of the reasons for this are clear. Since the genocide targeted Jews according to a pseudo-scientific notion of 'race,' many people fear that attention to gender will distract from the primacy of anti-semitism in Nazi ideology and practice. Furthermore, a prominent feature of the Holocaust was the way the Nazis attempted radically to strip away all cultural attributes from the victims, including the characteristics (such as hair and clothes) that helped define them as men and women.

If such features seem to suggest the non-relevance of gender or feminist analysis for Holocaust studies, it is also possible to argue the opposite. Because the Holocaust was a genocide it necessarily targeted the reproductive capacities of Jews (as the Nazis did to others considered 'unworthy of life'). Such a radical negation of gender and sexuality would have had a differentiated impact on those who had been brought up as men or women in traditional European societies. In Myrna Goldenberg's evocative phrase, men and women shared the 'same hell,' but experienced 'different horrors,' horrors inflected by gender. It also seems clear, as Pascale Bos argues in her contribution, that even if the Nazis treated men and women similarly, women and men might have experienced that treatment according to a diverse pre-Holocaust socialization and might later recall and represent that experience differently as well.

During the same years that the topic of women and the Holocaust has emerged in the field of Holocaust studies, feminist scholars, and especially feminists of color, have been working through the problems posed by inter-secting axes of oppression. Contemporary feminist theory may thus help to address the challenges of treating gender in a multidimensional context cru-cially determined by the importance of race. Even when the histories at stake are very different from each other, students of the Holocaust have much to gain from considerations of, say, the long-term effects of slavery on the African American family (see Spillers, 1987). At the same time, the specificity of the Holocaust's extremity might challenge feminists to rearticulate the limits of gendered analysis from the perspective of a radically racist regime.

The question of race, gender, and genocide does not only concern Jewish men and women, as our first two entries clarify. The excerpt from *Male Fantasies*, Klaus Theweleit's radically innovative 1977 study of proto-Nazi masculinity, demands some introduction. Theweleit's work is first of all a study of writings by men of the *Freikorps*, irregular armies that emerged in Germany after World War I to fight revolutionary working-class movements at home and abroad and that ultimately fed into the ranks of National Socialism. More crucially for our purposes here, *Male Fantasies* is a work that puts gender at the center of theories of fascism and genocidal violence. Drawing on the heterodox psychoanalytic theory of Gilles Deleuze and Félix Guattari's *Anti-Oedipus*, Theweleit's work argues that fascist masculinity derives from a particular organization of the psyche in which the subject's own desire is repressed and instead projected onto various threatening others, especially Jews, women, and communists. This excerpt suggests how the Nazis tamed the 'floods' and 'streams' of desire associated with such dangerously 'fascinating' others through rituals meant to convert 'the flowing "feminine" into a rigid "masculine."'

Gisela Bock's carefully documented historical work could not be more different from Theweleit's speculative provocations, but, like him, she is concerned with the intersection of race and gender in a German context whose significance resonates beyond the specificities of Holocaust history. We have chosen an excerpt from Bock's important essay on reproductive politics in Nazi Germany that highlights the theoretical apparatus of her empirical research. Bock's focus on the eugenic dimension of Nazi policy – that is, on its concern with proper 'breeding' – allows her to synthesize histories of 'privileged' and socially stigmatized women to show how both groups are impacted by sexism and racism. Even if Bock has in more recent writings recognized racism as the dominant category in discussions of the Holocaust (see her contribution in Ofer and Weitzman, 1998), this essay is suggestive in its conceptualization of 'racist sexism' and 'sexist racism' as complex forms of oppression that are not the product of 'mere addition.'

The final two selections focus specifically on Jewish women in the Holocaust. The philosopher Joan Ringelheim was one of the first scholars to address the gendered experiences of Nazi victims. While she, too, later renounced some of her findings in the essay excerpted here as tainted by an essentialist understanding of women's culture, 'The Unethical and the Unspeakable' remains a path-breaking text that helped open up a new approach to the Shoah. Especially important is her critical analysis of influential works by such figures as the psychologist Bruno Bettelheim and the literary critic Lawrence Langer, in which she convincingly reveals the limits of gender-blind accounts of the camps.

Pascale Bos begins with a review of the early literature on women and the Holocaust, focusing especially on the contributions and limits of Ringelheim's project. She then draws on her training as a literary critic to provide a complex retheorization of the place of gender in studies of Holocaust victims and survivors. Bos calls for a more critical approach to the evidence of gender difference in Holocaust narratives and, applying insights from poststructuralist theory, emphasizes the discursive construction of the experience, memory, and representation of the past. The Nazis may not have treated Jewish men and women differently on the whole, Bos concludes, but that does not mean gender is not a significant issue; rather, we need to look elsewhere, to narrative and discourse, to understand the complex interaction between gender, experience, and history. Bos's essay begins to sketch the preconditions for future studies of race, gender, and genocide.

OTHER WORKS IN HOLOCAUST STUDIES

Goldenberg, Myrna (1990) 'Different Horrors, Same Hell: Women Remembering the Holocaust,' in Roger Gottlieb (ed.), *Thinking the Unthinkable: Meanings of the Holocaust*. Mahwah, NJ: Paulist Press.

Hirsch, Marianne and Leo Spitzer (1993) 'Gendered Translations: Claude Lanzmann's *Shoah*,' in Miriam Cooke and Angela Woollacott (eds), *Gendering War Talk*. Princeton, NJ: Princeton University Press, 1993, pp. 3–19.

Horowitz, Sara R. (1994) 'Memory and Testimony of Women Survivors of Nazi Genocide,' in Judith R. Baskin (ed.), *Women of the Word: Jewish Women and Jewish writing*. Detroit, MI: Wayne State University Press.

Kaplan, Marion A. (1998) *Between Dignity and Despair: Jewish Life in Nazi Germany*. New York: Oxford University Press.

Koonz, Claudia (1987) *Mothers in the Fatherland: Women, the Family and Nazi Politics*. New York: St. Martin's Press.

Ofer, Dalia and Lenore J. Weitzman (eds) (1998) *Women in the Holocaust*. New Haven, CT: Yale University Press.

Rittner, Carol and John Roth (eds) (1993) *Different Voices: Women and the Holocaust*. New York: Paragon House.

RELEVANT THEORETICAL STUDIES

Anzaldúa, Gloria (ed.) (1990) *Making Face, Making Soul: Haciendo Caras: Creative and Critical Perspectives by Feminists of Color*. San Francisco: Aunt Lute Books.

Bulkin, Elly, Minnie Bruce Pratt, and Barbara Smith (1984). *Yours in Struggle: Three Feminist Perspectives on Anti-Semitism and Racism.* Brooklyn, NY: Long Haul Press.

Butler, Judith (1993) *Bodies that Matter: On the Discursive Limits of 'Sex'.* New York: Routledge.

Spillers, Hortense (1987) 'Mama's Baby, Papa's Maybe: An American Grammar Book,' *Diacritics*, 17.2, 65–81.

Williams, Patricia (1991) *The Alchemy of Race and Rights*, Cambridge, MA: Harvard University Press.

17

'FLOODS, BODIES, HISTORY'

Klaus Theweleit

[...]

The Red Flood
    The raging stream is called violent
    But the riverbed that hems it in
    No one calls violent.[1]

(Brecht)

'The wave of Bolshevism surged onward, threatening not only to swallow up
the republics of Estonia and Latvia, neither of which had yet awakened to a life
of its own, but also to inundate the eastern border of Germany.'[2] F. von
Oertzen on the Baltic situation at the end of 1918.

Bolshevism seems to be a kind of ocean that surges onward in waves,
inundating and engulfing. Wherever the 'Red flood' – also the title of a novel
by Wilhelm Weigand, about the Munich socialist republic – was sighted, the cry
of 'Land under!' pierced the air. 'The Reds inundated the land';[3] so says a
certain Hartmann, volunteer in the Baltic Army, which 'for a time was the only
one to stand up to the Red wave' in the Baltic region.[4] 'In the east, coming from
the Baltic, the Red wave surged onward' (Walter Frank).[5] The Freikorps have
rescued Germany 'from the Bolshevistic flood ... and ruination.' (Wiemers-
Borchelshof)[6] In Upper Silesia, Germans troops struggle to dam up 'the raging
Polish torrent' (von Osten).[7] [...] The Freikorps were in the Baltic area[8] 'in

From Klaus Theweleit (1987) 'Floods, Bodies, History', in *Male Fantasies, 1. Women, Floods,
Bodies, History*. Minneapolis, MN: University of Minnesota Press.

order to stem the all-destroying flood that was slowly advancing toward the west'[9] (Wagener, a captain in the Iron Division). The Freikorps soldiers, volunteer dockworkers of the nation, were racing from every quarter to the border areas. 'The side of the ship of state that faced east was in the greatest danger. This was where the water gushed through its ribs and plates' (Rudolf Mann).[10]

A knee-jerk interpretative reflex would lead us immediately to say that political events are being described here as natural processes, and that everyone knows this is what reactionaries always do. Yet we would be saying no more or less than that the phrases quoted above were 'false'; were we to be asked why, our answer would be, 'in an attempt at disguise.' In other words, this inter-pretative reflex reacts to sentences of that kind simply by proclaiming them 'lies' or 'nonsense,' adding perhaps, as a corrective, that politics are not nature, and those fascists should be ashamed of themselves.

Yet do these words truly 'lie'? The powerful metaphor of the flood engenders a clearly ambivalent state of excitement. It is threatening, but also attractive: the flood approaches! Strong emotions are in play, and those don't lie. [...]

What are they really talking about? And why floods, torrents, raging water; why do they not say, for instance, 'the Bolshevists advanced like the fourth Ice Age,' or like a 'hurricane,' or an 'Asiatic sandstorm'? None of these would sound convincing. But why not? And why do the Bolshevists in particular flood in so terrifyingly, but not the Imperial German Army in its invasion of Belgium, or the Freikorps in the Baltic region? The latter march in dry and solid, an army of dam-builders with a song on their lips.[11]

It is not so much the metaphors of flood that are important here, as the specific use to which they are put. This particular use of language causes many things to flow: every brook and stream, 'après nous le Déluge,' still waters; floods of papers, political, literary, intellectual currents, influences. Everything is in flow, swimming upon this wave or that, with or against the current, in the mainstream or in tributaries. Drifting along ... scum ...

Our soldiers, conversely, want to avoid swimming at all costs, no matter what the stream. They want to stand with both feet and every root firmly anchored in the soil. They want whatever floods may come to rebound against them; they want to stop, and dam up, those floods. [...] Nothing is to be permitted to flow, least of all 'Red floods.' If anything is to move, it should be the *movement* (i.e., oneself) – but as *one* man; in formation; on command as a line, a column, a block; as a wedge, a tight unit. Death to all that flows.

But what is the source of that flowing, and of the peculiar attraction exerted by the flood on the soldiers? [...]

Salomon says that even as a cadet under the monarchy, he sensed that 'within the old order, the new flood was rising before every dam, threatening to pulverize its petrified forms of life.'[12] The expected flood was 'threatening,' all right, but it was also invested with positive traits. Salomon is no unquestion-ing defender of 'petrified forms of life.'

We find a similar ambivalence in Lutz Rossin: 'The grave-diggers of Germany had wielded their spades for the last time, piercing through the ancient dam of traditional state authority: an artificially created tumult flowed in a broad stream through Germany.'[13] While Rossin condemns this development, he nevertheless causes the flood to flow powerfully, 'in a broad stream.' What got to him most was the act of piercing through. The movement it triggers is reiterated in the sentence; it is carried across, and beyond, the colon. [...]

What Rossin does find repugnant is *the thing* that flows. 'The Red flood brought all of the worse instincts to the surface, washing them up on the land.'[14] The flood can be localized more specifically. It seems to flow from the inside of those from whom the constraint of the old order has been removed. Something comes to light that has hitherto been forbidden, buried beneath the surface; the 'worst instincts,' true enough, but *powerful* and exciting to watch. For a moment at least, one is *powerless* and hypnotized in the face of those floods – as if *defenseless*. [...]

The dam had broken in the West:

> The whole world poured out over Germany: Americans and New Zealanders, Australians and Englishmen, Portuguese and French. The bitterest pill to swallow was the stationing of blacks everywhere by the French: Moroccans and Senegalese negroes, Indochinese and Turks.[15] (Dwinger)

The notion of external invasions combined with internal dam ruptures seems to make it possible to subsume Germany's defeat in the war, and the revolutionary changes in and around Germany, under the image of the flood. Drives liberated by these invasions and ruptures abandon the riverbed to which they had been forcibly consigned by Wilhelmine society, to flow freely over their banks. [...]

[...]

DAM AND FLOOD: THE RITUAL OF PARADING IN MASS

After seizing power, the Nazis tamed the floods and let them flow inside their rituals. Streams became dams, and much more. Consider the 'parade of political leaders' (*Appell der politischen Leiter*). The participants: all party members with leadership roles. For a description, we turn to the *Niederelbischer Tageblatt* (Lower-Elbe Daily) of September 12, 1937:

> Dr. Ley announced the 'Entry March of the Banners.' For a moment, one could see nothing. But then they emerged from the blackness of the night, over on the south side. In seven columns, they poured into the spaces between the formations. You couldn't see the people, couldn't recognize the standard-bearers. All you saw was a broad, red, surging stream, its surface sparkling gold and silver, advancing slowly like fiery lava. Feeling the dynamism of that slow advance, you got some small impression of what those sacred symbols meant.[16]

The flood had a name now: 'Entry March of the Banners' (encoded stream). The threat of inundation had been eradicated. But even without the danger of sinking within it, the flood remained exciting, fascinating. Its ominous aspect had been removed by those formations, by transforming streams into 'columns,' by converting the flowing 'feminine' into a rigid 'masculine.' Where did the excitement come from, then? What made that 'broad, red, surging stream ... sacred'?

In *Moses and Monotheism*, Freud identified the link between the sacred and prohibition:

> What is sacred is obviously something that may not be touched. A sacred prohibition has a very strong emotional tone but has in fact no rational basis.[17]

With a characteristic (irresistible) twist, he concluded that sacredness was the hallmark of the incest taboo, which existed solely because of paternal authority and solely in order to perpetuate that authority. *Sacer*, he added, meant not only 'sacred' (*heilig*), but 'wicked' (*verrucht*), 'detestable' (*verabscheuenswert*).[18] Sacred rituals allowed 'wickedness' to be represented; that was the whole purpose of such rituals.

Seen in that light, a ritual such as the 'Entry March of the Banners' becomes a public staging of the forbidden – not only of incest, but also, if we strip off the Freudian encoding, of flowing desire in general. In the ritual, desiring-production is allowed to surface symbolically, as a representation of itself. Drives are given an outlet: 'But then they emerged from the blackness of the night ... poured into the spaces between the formations.'

That explains the enormous attraction of fascist celebrations and their overwhelming impact on participants: 'I can't believe my eyes ... what in the world are they doing?' – and then the liberating thought, 'But everybody's doing it ... my God, they're actually *doing* it!' (in the name of the law, too). This symbolic liberation of desires, this staged affirmation of drives (in the form of a monumental ornament, a model for the repression of drives), was fascism's way of depicting the dawn of freedom, a freedom in which the fascist precisely does *not* dissolve himself. In this ritual, the Nazis symbolically suspended the primary double bind by allowing access to its normally unattainable aspect: to incest at the very least, but also to the state of noncastration, nondismemberment; to power; and to flowing that did not signify death. Deleuze and Guattari are probably right when they suggest in passing that Hitler enabled fascists to have an erection.[19] 'At last, not to be castrated for once!' In a ritual that allowed the penis itself (the penis no one had) to be represented in abstract form (the seven columns), the individual, for once, was no longer castrated; he became part of the transcendantal phallus that gave meaning to everything (the emphasis on 'You couldn't see the people, couldn't recognize the standard-bearers' is revealing). For the moment at least, he felt privileged to be a stream himself, one small part of an enormous, tamed flood; for that one moment, he was lifted out of every double bind. The scenario of the parade abolished the contradiction between the desiring-production of the individual and the demands of social power. In the course of the ritual, the fascist came to represent both his own liberated drives and the principle that suppressed them. This inherent contradiction never manifested itself because, during the staging of the ritual, the individual participated in power. Benjamin's assertion that fascism built its monuments 'primarily [with] so-called human material' is based on this truth: the substance of those monuments was the flow of desire.[20] But even Benjamin seems to show traces of the Weimar Left's rationalist reflex when he says that the 'execution' of fascist mass art (he rightly includes parades in this category) put the masses 'into a trance that made them see themselves as monumental, that is, incapable of deliberate, autonomous actions.'[21] Revolutionary acts certainly don't need to be 'deliberate'; and it is almost impossible for them to be 'autonomous' in Benjamin's sense, since the type of 'ego' on which that notion of 'autonomy' is based rarely surfaces in oppressed classes. When the emphasis is put on the production of 'trances' or incapacitation, what is left out of account is precisely the side of things that fascists have never neglected. It is far more important to stress the sense of relief, the Utopia of deliverance, which participants in such rituals find: 'At last I don't have to hide anymore . . . At last, I can see and sense that other people feel the same way I do.'

That is how fascism translates internal states into massive, external monuments or ornaments as a canalization system, which large numbers of people flow into; where their desire can flow, at least within (monumentally enlarged) preordained channels; where they can discover that they are not split off and isolated, but that they are sharing the violation of prohibitions with so many others (preferably with all others). That's why these masses can't stand to see one man marching alone alongside their great blocks. Such a man isn't participating in their forbidden games. Worse yet, he is observing them. And how can you let yourself be observed when you are in the process of turning into a stream and becoming god?

Fine, except for one thing: All of that affirmation is theatrical; it never gets beyond representation, the illusion of production. Benjamin is right in saying that fascism may help the masses to express themselves, but that it certainly doesn't help them to gain their rights.[22] We need to go one step further, though, and specify *what* is being expressed. For fascism does not allow the masses to express their interests (class interests, economic interests) – communists, when they come to power, are the ones who tend to let those interests be *expressed*, though not satisfied. No, what fascism allows the masses to express are suppressed drives, imprisoned desires. Fascist masses may portray their desire for deliverance from the social double bind, for lives that are not inevitably entrapping, but not their desire for full stomachs. The success of fascism demonstrates that masses who become fascist suffer more from their internal states of being than from hunger or unemployment. Fascism teaches us that under certain circumstances, human beings imprisoned within themselves, within body armor and social constraints, would rather break out than fill their stomachs; and that their politics may consist in organizing that escape, rather than an economic order that promises future generations full stomachs for life. The utopia of fascism is an edenic freedom from responsibility. That in itself, I think, is a source of 'beauty in the most profound distortion.' Meanwhile, communists and the left in general still stubbornly refuse to accept fascism's horrifying proof that the materialism they preach and practice only goes halfway. The desiring-production of the unconscious, as molecular driving-force of history, has never entered their materialism – an omission that has had (and still has) tragic consequences.

In patriarchy, where the work of domination has consisted in subjugating, damming in, and transforming the 'natural energy' in society, that desiring-production of the unconscious has been encoded as the subjugated gender, or femaleness; and it has been affirmed and confirmed, over and over again, in the successive forms of female oppression. Luce Irigaray: 'To an extent, the unconscious is historically censored femaleness.'[23] In the course of the repression carried out against women, those two things – the unconscious and femaleness – were so closely coupled together that they came to be seen as nearly identical. It was almost inevitable, as Frieda Grafe says, that Freud 'would use the pathology of hysterical women as a basis' for constructing his science (that is, as a basis for his subsequent male scientific system).[24] In its denial of this coupling, male-rationalist thinking repeatedly renews its demand for the oppression of women each time it calls for the subjugation of 'nature.' When Kracauer writes that 'the mass ornamental display represents silent nature without anything built upon it,'[25] he fails to recognize what kind of 'nature' is involved here. This allows him to conclude, in Goethian fashion, that the process of humanization can 'forge ahead only if thought can curb nature and create man on rational lines.'[26] We do have to forge ahead, don't we? And we already know who will get left behind. Here, Kracauer was on the right track in beginning his reflections on the mass ornamental displays with the Tiller-girls,[27] those 'indissoluble formations of young women whose movements are mathematical demonstrations',[28] and on the mass displays of 'physical culture' which took place in stadiums, and whose ornamental configurations were carried far and wide by the newsreels. Thanks to Lippe and Elias, we know that the process in question here was nothing new: Ornaments made of human beings have helped the European ego adjust to new forms of the human body ever since the Renaissance. In fact, Kracauer's description of ornamental displays in stadiums closely resembles Beaujoyeulx's account of the ballet at the court of Henry III:

> They consist of angles and circles, the kind one finds in textbooks on euclidean geometry. They also make use of the fundamental shapes of physics, waves, and spirals. What they reject are the exuberance of organic forms and the emanations of spiritual life. (Kracauer)[29]

What had changed? Well, the ornamental displays were no longer carried out by the 'white' women of the court, or by any other women, but by 'the masses.' And the displays had become more elaborate in accordance with technological progress. Kracauer completely misreads the situation, though, when he says that organic and 'spiritual' elements were simply 'rejected.' Those elements were the very *substance* of the ornamental displays. The purpose of the displays, in fact, was to transform organic 'exuberance' into spirals; the purpose of the fascist mass ritual was to channel streams into a monumental system of dams. Benjamin writes:

> Under the gaze of the fascist rulers (which, as we've seen, sweeps across millennia), the distinctions between the slaves who built the pyramids out of blocks, and the proletarian masses who formed themselves into blocks before the Führer on exercise grounds and in open squares, begin to disappear.[30]

The 'rulers' gaze' – the fascists weren't the first to have it, but they did see something new. Their public rituals no longer depicted the subjugation of 'nature' (the desiring-production of the unconscious) directly as the subjugation of women, but instead as the subjugation of the masses, masses of men. In attempting to fend off the very real possibility of socialism, fascists found that women's bodies were no longer adequate for public stagings of the subjugation of 'nature.' Fascist rituals went directly inside men, taking their material from the male unconscious.

Men themselves were now split into a (female) interior and a (male) exterior – the body armor. And as we know, the interior and exterior were mortal enemies. What we see being portrayed in the rituals are the armor's separation from, and superiority over the interior: the interior was allowed to flow, but only within the masculine boundaries of the mass formations. Before any of this could happen, the body had to be split apart thoroughly enough to create an interior and exterior that could be opposed to each other as enemies. Only then could the two parts re-form 'in peace' in the ritual. What fascism promised men was the reintegration of their hostile components under tolerable conditions, dominance of the hostile 'female' element within themselves. This explains why the word 'boundaries,' in fascist parlance, refers primarily to the boundaries of the body (as we have seen).

As a matter of course, fascism excluded women from the public arena and the realms of male production. But fascism added a further oppression to the oppression of women. When a fascist male went into combat against erotic, 'flowing,' nonsubjugated women, he was also fighting his own unconscious, his own desiring-production. In this process, the wife of the ruler lost all function as a representative subjugated woman. This is clear from the fact that whereas in World War I, the Hohenzollern women had posed as nurses, Hitler concealed his 'beloved' from the public. Not only was she useless for the rituals that maintained Hitler's rule, she would have gotten in the way. For the Führer's 'wife,') in that fascist ritual, was the unconscious of the masses who were pouring into block formations.

> And now the screams of 'Heil!' erupt, becoming overwhelming, like some all-fulfilling wave that rips everything along with it. Fifty thousand voices merge into a single cry of 'Heil Hitler!' Fifty thousand arms shoot out in salutes. Fifty thousand hearts beat for this man who is now striding, bareheaded, through the narrow passage formed by all those thousands.[31]

[...]

NOTES

1. Bertolt Brecht, 'Über die Gewalt,' *Gesammelte Werke*, vol. 9 (Frankfurt, 1967), 602.
2. Friedrich von Oertzen, *Baltenland* (Munich, 1933), 300.
3. Georg Heinrich Hartmann, 'Erinnerungen aus den Kämpfen der Baltischen Landeswehr,' in Ernst Jünger, ed., *Der Kampf um das Reich* (Essen, 1929), 141.
4. Ibid., 145.
5. Walter Frank, *Franz Ritter von Epp* (Hamburg, 1934), 76.
6. Franz Wiemers-Borchelshof, 'Freikorps-Arbeitsdienst-Siedlung,' in Ernst Salomon, ed., *Das Buch vom deutschen Freikorpskämpfer* (Berlin, 1938), 407.
7. Edmund Osten, 'Der Kampf um Oberschlesien,' in Jünger, 263.
8. They had remained there since August 1919, defying the German government's order to withdraw. In other words, they were freebooters. The commander of the 'Iron Division,' Major Bischoff, had personally opposed the order to return to Germany. As the Iron Division and the 'German Legion,' his troops allied themselves with the White Russian army of Prince von Avaloff-Bermondt. See Robert G. L. Waite, *Vanguard of Nazism* (Cambridge, Mass., 1952), 122ff; Josef Bischoff, *Die letzte Front* (Berlin, 1919), 189.
9. Wilhelm Wagener, *Von der Heimat geächtet* (Stuttgart, 1920), 8.
10. Rudolf Mann, *Mit Erhardt durch Deutschland* (Berlin, 1921), 11.
11. True within limits to be discussed in volume 2 ('The Militant Body in Battle').
12. Ernst Salomon, *Die Geächteten* (Berlin, 1930), 347.
13. Lutz Rossin, *Aus dem roten Sumpf* (Berlin, 1923), 3.
14. Ibid., foreword.
15. Edwin Dwinger, 'Die Armee hinter Stacheldraht,' in *Deutsches Schicksal*, vol. 1 (Jena, 1929), 76. See Karl Buschbecker, *Wie unser Gesetz es befahl* (Berlin, 1936), 12.
16. Cited in Klaus Vondung, *Magie und Manipulation: Ideologischer Kult und politische Religion des Nationalsozialismus* (Göttingen, 1971), 190. The book is useful as an anthology of primary sources; as its title suggests, its theoretical framework is inadequate.
17. Sigmund Freud, *Moses and Monotheism*, vol. 23 of *The Standard Edition of the Complete Psychological Works of Sigmund Freud*, tr. James Strachey (London, 1953–74), 120.
18. Ibid., 121.
19. Gilles Deleuze and Félix Guattari, *Anti-Oedipus*, tr. Robert Hurley, et al. (Minneapolis, 1983), 293ff. (Also 104.)
20. Walter Benjamin, 'Pariser Brief,' *Angelus Novus* (Frankfurt, 1966). 503ff. (Quote, 510.)
21. Ibid., 510.
22. Walter Benjamin, 'The Work of Art in the Age of Mechanical Reproduction,' *Illuminations* (New York, 1969).

23. Luce Irigaray, cited in Frieda Grafe, 'Ein anderer Eindruck vom Begriff meines Körpers,' *Filmkritik* (March 1976), 125.
24. Grafe, 'Ein anderer Eindruck,' 120.
25. Siegfried Kracauer, *Das Ornament der Masse* (Frankfurt, 1963), 63.
26. Ibid.
27. The 'Tillergirls' were a precision female dancing troupe, popular in Germany in the 1920s and 1930s. The Hitler era, in particular, featured mass performances of calisthenics (and other physical exercises) in stadiums, – Trans.
28. Ibid., 50.
29. Ibid., 53.
30. Benjamin, 'Pariser Brief,' 510.
31. Thor Goote, *Die Fahne hoch* (Berlin, 1933), 413. See Ludwig Freiwald, *Der Weg der braunen Kämpfer* (Munich, 1934), 284, where the shouts of *Heil!* are described as a surge.

18

'RACISM AND SEXISM IN NAZI GERMANY'

Gisela Bock

'ALIEN RACES' AND THE 'OTHER SEX'

By presenting some largely unexplored features of women's lives under National Socialism in Germany, this essay considers larger questions about the complex connections between racism and sexism. It does not presume to exhaust the issue, or even touch on all its aspects. Instead, it approaches it through the perspective of one part of women's lives affected by state policy: reproduction or, as I prefer to call it, the reproductive aspect of women's unwaged housework. It can be no more than a contribution for two reasons. First, dealing with racism in Germany during this period involves considering an unparalleled mass murder of millions of women and men, an undertaking beyond the scope of any single essay. Second, this analysis is a first approach, for neither race nor gender, racism nor sexism – and even less their connection – has been a central theme in German social historiography.[1] When historians deal with women in modern Germany, they generally do not consider racism or racial discrimination against women,[2] while the literature dealing with anti-Jewish racism and the Holocaust generally does not consider either women's specific situation or the added factor of sexism.

The extent to which the racist tradition was concerned with those activities that then and now are considered 'women's sphere' – that is, bearing and rearing children – has also not been recognized. Perhaps we might argue even

From Gisela Bock (1993) 'Racism and Sexism in Nazi Germany: Motherhood, Compulsory Sterilization, and the State', in C. Rittner and J. K. Roth (eds), *Different Voices: Women and the Holocaust*. New York: Paragon House.

further that a large part of this racist tradition remained invisible precisely because the history of women and of their work in the family was not an issue for (mostly male) historians and theoreticians.[3]

To make the issue of motherhood and compulsory sterilization the center of discussion places the focus not so much on anti-Jewish racism, on which we have an extended literature, as on another form of racism: eugenics, or, as it was called before and during the Nazi regime and sometimes also in Anglo-Saxon literature, race hygiene.[4] It comprises a vast field of more or less popular, more or less scientific, traditions, which became the core of population policies throughout the Nazi regime.

Beyond the plain yet unexplored fact that at least half of those persecuted on racial grounds were women, there are more subtle reasons for women's historians' interest in the 'scientific' or eugenic form of racism. The race hygiene discourse since the end of the nineteenth century deals with women much more than do most other social or political theories, since women have been hailed as 'mothers of the race,' or, in stark contrast, vilified as the ones guilty of 'racial degeneration.' Then, too, definitions of race hygiene made at the time show some conscious links between this field and women's history, describing it, for instance, as 'procreation hygiene' (*Fortpflanzungshygiene*).[5] In fact, we might consider that most of the scientific and pseudoscientific superstructure of eugenic racism, especially its mythology of hereditary character traits, is concerned with the supposedly 'natural' or 'biological' domains in which women are prominent – body, sexuality, procreation, education – the heretofore 'private' sphere.[6]

For a third reason, eugenics and racism in general are significant to women's history. After a long hiatus, the result in part of Nazism, interest in the history of women in Germany has seen a revival during the past half decade or more. However, this interest has focused almost exclusively on the historical reconstruction and critique of those norms and traditions that underlined women's 'natural' destiny as wives, mothers, and homemakers whose work was not paid. Those with this perspective see National Socialism as either a culmination of, or a reactionary return to, belief in women's 'traditional' role as mothers and housewives; motherhood and housework become essential factors in a backward, premodern, or precapitalist 'role' assigned to women.[7]

Thus most historians seem to agree that under the Nazi regime women counted merely as mothers who should bear and rear as many children as possible, and that Nazi antifeminism tended to promote, protect, and even finance women as childbearers, housewives, and mothers. It seems necessary to challenge various aspects of this widely held opinion, but particularly its neglect of racism.[8] Printed and archival sources on Nazi policies, passages from Hitler's writings, other often-quoted sources like the Minister of Agriculture Walter Darré's breeding concepts, and documents from the lower echelons of the state and party hierarchy[9] show quite clearly that the Nazis were by no means simply interested in raising the number of childbearing women. They were just as bent on excluding many women from bearing and rearing children – and men from begetting them – with sterilization as their principal deterrent. It is true that the available literature does not altogether lose sight of these latter women. However, they are at best briefly hinted at, between quotation marks and parentheses, as mere negations of the 'Aryan,' the 'racially and hereditarily pure'; the general conclusions on 'women in Nazi society' usually neglect them further.[10]

Although the desirability of a new perspective seems clear, the historical singularity of the Holocaust and the need for more research before models can be constructed qualify the extent to which we may compare the interaction of racism and sexism under Nazism and under other historical conditions.[11] Yet specific comparative approaches seem possible and necessary: first, to compare the eugenics movements internationally in the first half of this century both with international population policy today and with the new sociobiological 'biocrats';[12] and second, in accord with new approaches in the United States, stimulated largely by women of color, to conceptualize the connection between racism and sexism not as the mere addition of two forms of exploitation – as a double oppression – but as a manifold and complex relationship.[13]

'KAISERSCHNITT' AND 'HITLERSCHNITT': NAZI BODY POLITICS

Along with discrimination and segregation of Jewish women and men, Nazi sterilization policies were the main strategy of 'gene and race care,' as eugenics or race hygiene was now called, from 1933 to 1939. Sterilization policy was one form of comprehensive Nazi racism. Jews, those eligible for sterilization, were defined as inferior. Along with the Jews, National Socialism had a second scapegoat held responsible for the degeneration of the race: millions of non-Jewish, inferior women and men, who supposedly were a 'burden' to the state. Like Jews, they were seen as 'ballast' and 'parasites' to the 'body' of *Volk* and race, though Jews were seen as threatening this body from the outside, and other inferior beings were seen as threatening it from the inside. For Jewish as for non-Jewish inferior people, one decree or law followed the other from 1933 on. Among other things, they served to identify them. Thus, having a Jewish grandmother defined a Jew or a Jew of 'mixed blood,' and a schizophrenic episode – one's own or that of one's grandmother – served to define a sterilization candidate. The identification of human beings as valuable, worthless, or of inferior value in supposedly hereditary terms was the common denominator of all forms of Nazi racism. Birth strategy was one of these forms.

Nazi pronatalism for desirable births and its antinatalism for undesirable ones were tightly connected. On May 26, 1933, two pieces of penal legislation preceding the 1926 reforms were reintroduced, prohibiting the availability of abortion facilities and services. More important was the stricter handling of the old antiabortion law, resulting in a 65 percent increase in yearly convictions between 1932 and 1938, when their number reached almost 7,000.[14] From 1935 on, doctors and midwives were obliged to notify the regional State Health Office of every miscarriage. Women's names and addresses were then handed over to the police, who investigated the cases suspected of actually being abortions.[15] In 1936 Heinrich Himmler, head of all police forces and the SS, established the Reich's Central Agency for the Struggle Against Homosexuality and Abortion, and in 1943, after three years of preparation by the Ministries of the Interior and of Justice, the law entitled Protection of Marriage, Family, and Motherhood called for the death penalty in 'extreme cases.'[16]

The corollary measure was race hygiene sterilization. Along with the new antiabortion legislation, a law was introduced on May 26, 1933, to legalize eugenic sterilization and prohibit voluntary sterilization.[17] Beyond this, the Cabinet, headed by Hitler, passed a law on July 14, 1933, against propagation of 'lives unworthy of life' (*lebensunwertes Leben*), called the Law for the Prevention of Hereditarily Diseased Offspring. It ordered sterilization for certain categories of people, its notorious Paragraph 12 allowing the use of force against those who did not submit freely.[18] Earlier, on June 28, the Minister of the Interior Wilhelm Frick had announced: 'We must have the courage again to grade our people according to its genetic values.'[19]

[. . .]

Popular vernacular expressed the situation pungently. Eugenic sterilization was called *Hitlerschnitt* (Hitler's cut), thereby linking it to an antiabortion policy that refused abortions even to women who had gone through two previous *Kaiserschnitte* (caesarean operations). Only after three caesareans did a woman have the right to an abortion, and then only on the condition that she also accept the sterilization.[20] Transcending older political partnerships, prohibition of abortion and compulsory sterilization, compulsory motherhood and prohibition of motherhood – far from contradicting each other – had now become two sides of a coherent policy combining sexism and racism.

[. . .]

CONCLUSION: SEXISM AND RACISM

One should not assume, as is often done, that Nazi sexism concerned only superior women and Nazi racism concerned only inferior women. Both Nazi racism and sexism concerned all women, the inferior as well as the superior. The 'birth achievement' demanded of acceptable women was calculated carefully according to the numbers of those who were not to give birth.[21] And the strongest pressure on such acceptable women to procreate, to create an orderly household for husband and children, and to accept dependency on the breadwinner perhaps came not so much from the continuous positive propaganda about 'valuable motherhood,' but precisely from its opposite: the negative propaganda and policy that barred unwelcome, poor, and deviant women from procreation and marriage and labeled either disorderly women or single women with too many children inferior. Thus, racism could be used, and was used, to impose sexism in the form of increased unwaged housework on superior women.

On the other hand, women who became or were to become targets of negative race hygiene tended also to be those who did not accept, could not accept, or were not supposed to accept the Nazi view of female housework, whose main features can be traced back to the late eighteenth century. Sexism, which imposed economic dependency on superior married women, could be used, and was used, to implement racism by excluding many women from the relative benefits granted to desirable mothers and children and forcing them to accept the lowest jobs in the labor-market hierarchy in order to survive. In fact, modern sexism has established, below the ideological surface of theories on 'women's nature' and the 'cult of true womanhood,' two different though connected norms for women. The demand was made of some women to administer orderly households and produce well-educated children, the whole enterprise supported by their husbands' money; others, overburdened and without support, were obliged to adopt menial jobs that paid little or nothing, while their children, like themselves, were treated as ballast. Racist-sexist discourses of various kinds have portrayed socially, sexually, or ethnically alien women as non-women, and thus as threatening to the norms for all other women: thus a racist view of Jewish or Gypsy women as prostitutes, the eugenic sexologists' view of lesbians as pseudo-men, the race hygienic view of prostitutes as asocial and infectious to the 'racial body,'[22] the fantasy of Polish or feeble-minded women 'breeding like animals.' But of course, much more is involved here than (predominantly male) images and symbols,[23] influential though they may be in determining women's very real treatment and self-image. Women's history needs to concentrate on the lives of those 'non'-women without marginalizing them as (male) history has done.

Precisely because of the complex links between sexism and racism and, therefore, because of the relevance of reproductive racism to all women, we should be careful not to term simply 'sexism' the demand placed on ethnically or socially superior women to have children they may not want, and not to term simply 'racism' the ban against ethnically or socially inferior women having children, even though they may want them. More strictly speaking, we might call the imposition on the first group of women *racist sexism*, since their procreation is urged not just because they are women, but because they are women *of a specific ethnicity or social position declared superior*. Accordingly, we might call the imposition on the second group of women *sexist racism*, since their procreation is prohibited not just on grounds of their genes and race, but on grounds of their real or supposed deviation, *as women, from social or ethnic standards for superior women*. Establishing in such terms the dual connection between racism and sexism does not (as may be evident from the context) give different weights to the experiences of racism and sexism, or suggest that racism is primary in one case and sexism primary in the other. Precisely the opposite is true: where sexism and racism exist, particularly with Nazi features, all women are equally involved in both, but with different experiences. They are subjected to one coherent and double-edged policy of *sexist racism* or *racist sexism* (a nuance only of perspective), but they are segregated as they live through the dual sides of this policy, a division that also works to segregate their forms of resistance to sexism as well as to racism.

Attempting to look at the situation of all women from the perspective of 'non'-women may help to analyze and break down the boundaries of such segregation. As far as the struggle for our reproductive rights – for our sexuality, our children, and the money we want and need – is concerned, the Nazi experience may teach us that a successful struggle must aim at achieving both the rights and the economic means to allow women to choose between having or not having children without becoming economically dependent on other people or on unwanted second and third jobs. Cutbacks in welfare for single mothers, sterilization abuse, and the attacks on free abortion are just different sides of an attack that serves to divide women. Present population and family policy in the United States and the Third World make the German experience under National Socialism particularly relevant. In Germany, new attacks on free abortion, the establishment of a university department of 'population science,' sterilization experiments on women and sterilization of welfare mothers without their knowledge, pressure on Gypsy women (especially those on welfare) not to have children, xenophobic outcries against immigrants 'breeding like animals' and sometimes asking for their castration or sterilization, all-too-easy abortions and sterilization on Turkish women, the reduction of state money connected to human reproduction, both private and public, have all occurred during the last two years.[24] It is an open question what will follow from these – still seemingly unconnected – events in the course of the present economic crisis.

NOTES

This is a revised version of the essay that appeared in *Signs: Journal of Women in Culture and Society* 8, no. 3 (1983).

1. The more progressive new generation of social historians in Germany since the 1960s has tended to present racism as a mere ideology, its application as more or less economically/politically 'rational' or 'irrational,' often as merely instrumental, and mostly as an appendage to more important developments, 'political' or 'economic.' See, for example, Peter M. Kaiser, 'Monopolprofit und Massenmord im Faschismus: Zur ökonomischen Funktion der Konzentrationslager im faschistischen Deutschland,' *Blätter für deutsche und internationale Politik* 5 (1975): 552–77.
2. A rare exception is Marion A. Kaplan, *The Jewish Feminist Movement in Germany: The Campaigns of the Jüdischer Frauenbund, 1904–1938* (Westport, Conn.: Greenwood Press, 1979).
3. However, three conferences of women historians on women's history have taken place: 'Women in the Weimar Republic and under National Socialism,' Berlin, 1979; 'Muttersein und Mutterideologie in der bürgerlichen Gesellschaft,' Bremen, 1980; and 'Frauengeschichte,' Bielefeld, 1981. Some of the workshops of the latter are documented in *Beiträge zur feministischen Theorie und Praxis* 5 (April 1981). Thus, women's history has been exploring this and similar themes in recent years, but much work still needs to be done, and many questions cannot yet be answered in a consistent way.

4. A good overview of the American and international eugenics movement is Allan Chase, *The Legacy of Malthus: The Social Costs of the New Scientific Racism* (New York: Knopf, 1977). Although there had been, at the beginning of this century, a debate among experts on distinctions between 'eugenics' and 'race hygiene,' I use these terms interchangeably, as does Chase, for I believe the issue dealt with in this article requires my doing so. On this debate see Georg Lilienthal, 'Rassenhygiene im Dritten Reich: Krise und Wende,' *Medizinhistorisches Journal* 14 (1979): 114–34.

5. See Alfred Grotjahn, *Geburten-Rückgang und Geburten-Regelung im Lichte der individuellen und der sozialen Hygiene* (Berlin and Coblenz, 1914; 2d ed., 1921), p. 153, and the chapter 'Birth Regulation Serving Eugenics and Race Hygiene'; and Agnes Bluhm, *Die rassenhygienischen Aufgaben des weiblichen Arztes: Schriften zur Erblehre und Rassenhygiene* (Berlin: Metzner, 1936), esp. the chapter 'Woman's Role in the Racial Process in Its Largest Sense.'

6. Good examples are the classic and influential books by Grotjahn, *Geburten Rückgang* (1914) and *Die Hygiene der menschlichen Fortpflanzung* (Berlin and Vienna: Urban and Schwarzenburg, 1926); Erwin Baur, Eugen Fischer, and Fritz Lenz, *Grundriss der menschlichen Erblichkeitslehre und Rassenhygiene*, Vol. 2, *Menschliche Auslese und Rassenhygiene* (Munich: Lehmann, 1921). These volumes had many interestingly divergent editions. I have used Vol. 1 (1936) and Vol. 2 (1931). For a scientific critique of the pseudoscientific theory of character traits see, e.g., Chase, chap. 8.

7. For a preliminary critique of this view, analyzing housework as no less modern and no less capitalist than employment outside the house, see Gisela Bock and Barbara Duden, 'Arbeit aus Liebe – Liebe als Arbeit: Zur Entstehung der Hausarbeit im Kapitalismus,' in *Frauen und Wissenschaft: Beiträge zur Berliner Sommeruniversität für Frauen, Juli 1976* (Berlin: Courage Verlag, 1977), pp. 118–99. Parts of it have been translated as 'Labor of Love – Love as Labor,' in *From Feminism to Liberation*, ed. Edith Hoshino Altbach, 2d ed. (Cambridge, Mass.: Schenkman, 1980), 153–92.

8. Dörte Winkler, *Frauenarbeit im 'Dritten Reich'* (Hamburg, Hoffmann und Campe, 1977), esp. pp. 42–65, revised this picture by showing that under Nazism, employment of lower- and middle-class women was not reduced. This is confirmed by various authors in the anthology edited by Frauengruppe Faschismusforschung, *Mutterkreuz und Arbeitsbuch: Zur Geschichte der Frauen in der Weimarer Republik und im Nationalsozialismus* (Frankfurt a.M.: Fischer, 1981). Leila J. Rupp, *Mobilizing Women for War: German and American Propaganda, 1939–1945* (Princeton: Princeton University Press, 1978), esp. pp. 11–50, revised the current view of the Nazi image of women. It was more diversified than usually assumed and did not simply stress home and housework, but any 'woman's sacrifice' for the state and 'the race,' including employment. See also Leila J. Rupp, 'Mothers of the *Volk*: The Image of Women in Nazi Ideology,' *Signs: Journal of Women in Culture and Society* 3, No. 2 (Winter 1977): 362–79. In relation to racism, I have tried to revise the picture in 'Frauen und ihre Arbeit im Nationalsozialismus,' in *Frauen in der Geschichte*, ed. Annette Kuhn and Gerhard Schneider (Düsseldorf: Schwann Verlag, 1979), pp. 113–49; and '"Zum Wohle des Volkskörpers": Abtreibung und Sterilisation unterm Nationalsozialismus,' *Journal für Geschichte* 2 (November 1980): 58–65.

9. Clifford R. Lovin, '*Blut und Boden*: The Ideological Basis of the Nazi Agricultural Program,' *Journal of the History of Ideas* 28 (1967): 279–88, esp. 286.

10. Cf. Hans Peter Bleuel, *Das saubere Reich: Theorie und Praxis des sittlichen Lebens im Dritten Reich* (Bern-Munich-Vienna: Scherz, 1972), p. 273; Jill Stephenson, *Women in Nazi Society* (London: Croom Helm, 1975), pp. 64, 69, 197.

11. Obviously, approaches exclusively or mainly based on ethnic women's labor-force participation are not useful to the issue of reproduction: e.g., Diane K. Lewis, 'A Response to Inequality: Black Women, Racism and Sexism,' *Signs* 3, No. 2 (Winter 1977): 339–61.

12. For a critique of the new sociobiology, see Ruth Hubbard, Mary Sue Henifin, and Barbara Fried, eds., *Women Look at Biology Looking at Women: A Collection of Feminist Critiques* (Cambridge, Mass.: Schenkman, 1979); Chandler Davis, 'La sociobiologie et son explication de l'humanité,' *Annales*, E.S.C. 36 (July–August 1981): 531–71. For the international dimension of older eugenics, see Chase, *Legacy of Malthus*; Loren R. Graham, 'Science and Values: The Eugenics Movement in Germany and Russia in the 1920's,' *American Historical Review* 82 (1977): 1133–64; G. R. Searle, *Eugenics and Politics in Britain, 1900–1914* (Leyden: Nordhoff International, 1976); and Anna Davin, 'Imperialism and Motherhood,' *History Workshop* (1978): 10–65. It is important to note that in fascist Italy, race hygiene did not take hold. Of course, present policies in the United States and women's campaigns for reproductive rights are immediately relevant to the issue and approach of this essay: Committee for Abortion Rights and Against Sterilization Abuse, *Women under Attack: Abortion, Sterilization Abuse, and Reproductive Freedom* (New York: CARASA, 1979).

13. Such new approaches have been presented at the Third National Women's Studies Association Conference, 'Women Respond to Racism,' Storrs, Connecticut, May 31–June 6, 1981. Of particular significance seemed to me the presentations by Vicky Spelman, Arlene Aviakin, and Mary Ruth Warner on 'Feminist Theory and the Invisibility of Black Culture.' See also Bonnie Thornton Dill, 'The Dialectics of Black Womanhood,' *Signs* 4, Vol. 3 (Spring 1979): 543–55, and Cherríe Moraga and Gloria Anzaldúa, eds., *This Bridge Called My Back: Writings of Radical Women of Color* (Watertown, Mass.: Persephone Press, 1981). For a different version of the double-oppression approach, see Gerda Lerner, 'Black Women in the United States: A Problem in Historiography and Interpretation' (1973), in *The Majority Finds Its Past: Placing Women in History* (New York and Oxford: Oxford University Press, 1979), pp. 63–82; and *Teaching Women's History* (Washington, D.C.: American Historical Association, 1981), pp. 60–65.

14. *Reichsgesetzblatt* 1933/I, p. 296 (hereafter RGB); *Wirtschaft und Statistik* 15 (1935): 737, and 19 (1939): 534.

15. RGB, 1935/I, p. 1035; Stephenson, *Women in Nazi Society*, p. 68.

16. Bundesarchiv Koblenz, R 18/5517, pp. 251–52 (hereafter BAK); RGB, 1943/I, p. 140.

17. RGB, 1933/I, p. 296; Eberhardt Schmidt, 'Das Sterilisationsproblem nach dem in der Bundesrepublik geltenden Strafrecht,' *Juristenzeitung* 3 (February 5, 1951): 65–70.

18. RGB, 1933/I, p. 529; Martin Broszat, *Der Staat Hitlers* (Munich: Deutscher Taschenbuch Verlag, 1969), p. 356; Kurt Nowak, *'Euthanasie' und Sterilisierung im 'Dritten Reich': Die Konfrontation der evangelischen und katholischen Kirche mit dem 'Gesetz zur Verhütung erbkranken Nachwuchses' und der 'Euthanasie'-Aktion* (Göttingen: Vanderhoeck & Ruprecht, 1980), esp. pp. 64–65.

19. Wilhelm Frick, *Ansprache auf der ersten Sitzung des Sachverständigenbeirates für Bevölkerungs- und Rassenpolitik* (Berlin: Schriftenreihe des Reichsausschusses für Volksgesundheitsdienst 1, 1933), p. 8.

20. Richard Grunberger, *The 12 Year Reich: A Social History of Nazi Germany, 1933–1945* (New York: Holt, Rinehart & Winston, 1972), p. 365; see also my article on sterilization and abortion, ' "Zum Wohle." '

21. E.g., Burgdörfer, *Geburtenschwund*, pp. 136–47; G. Pfotenhauer, 'Fortpflanzungspflicht – die andere Seite des Gesetzes zur Verhütung erbkranken Nachwuchses,' *Der öffentliche Gesundheitsdienst* 2 (1937): 604–08.

22. For lesbian women and their presentation as 'pseudo-men' by male psychiatrists since the last third of the nineteenth century, see Esther Newton and Carroll Smith-Rosenberg, 'Male Mythologies and their Internalization of Deviance from Krafft-Ebing to Radclyffe Hall,' and Gudrun Schwartz, 'The Creation of the *Mannweib*, 1860–1900' (papers presented at the Fifth Berkshire Conference on the History of

Women, Vassar College, June 16, 1981). For male views of prostitutes, see my article 'Prostituierte im Nazi-Staat' in *Wir sind Frauen wie andere auch*, ed. Pieke Biermann (Reinbek: Rowohlt, 1980), pp. 70–106; Judith Walkowitz, *Prostitution and Victorian Society: Women, Class and the State* (New York: Cambridge University Press, 1980), esp. chap. 10.

23. For an approach focusing on such symbols, see Elizabeth Janeway, 'Who is Sylvia? On the Loss of Sexual Paradigms,' *Signs 5*, No. 4 (Summer 1980): 573–89.

24. 'Population Science' has been established in Hamburg and Bielefeld, while women have been, in vain, trying to get women's studies recognized and financed: *Beiträge zur feministischen Theorie und Praxis 5* (April 1981): 119–27. For other information on immigrant women, sterilization, welfare, and state benefits, see the following issues of *Courage:* (March 1977): 16–29; 3 (April 1978): 14–29; 3 (September 1978): 11; 3 (October 1978): 44–47; 4 (June 1979): 39–40; 4 (September 1979): 27–29; 4 (October 1979): 12–17; 5 (April 1980): 12–13; 5 (May 1980): 12–13; 6 (March 1981): 5–8, 52; 6 (May 1981): 16–33; 6 (December 1981): 22–33; 7 (January 1982): 8–11. See also *Zu Hause in der Fremde*, ed. Christian Schaffernicht (Fischerhude: Verlag Atelier, 1981), pp. 74–75.

survivors and the evidence of certain scholars suggest that ways of resisting and surviving are, in fact, differentiated by gender; and that women's experiences of the Holocaust were different from those of men; and that women had different survival capabilities, different work, roles, and relationships. [...] Until now, we have been told only about token heroines; for example, Mala, Wanda, and Anne Frank. We must learn not only about them, but also about the clerks at Auschwitz, the couriers, the smugglers of weapons, the teachers, and the mothers.

[...]

Many writers, then, have hinted at the differences between the lives of women and those of men during the Holocaust. Yet these differences have not been investigated or explored in the written literature or affected its general conclusions on survival.[1] It does not seem possible to deny that the experiences and perceptions of women would have been different – perhaps significantly – from those of men during the Holocaust. While research on this subject is in the early phases, some things already seem clear. By ignoring the evidence of women's experience and providing a so-called 'universal framework,' we have misunderstood and mishandled questions dealing with resistance, survival, passivity, and compliance.

Women's history has 'disabused us of the notion that the history of women is the same as the history of men, and that the significant turning points in history have the same impact for one sex as for another.'[2] Literature in women's studies shows that women do not share with men the same ideas about self, family, heroism, character, power, sacrifice, and loyalty. Consequently, all generalizations and gender-neutral statements about survival, resistance, the maintenance or collapse of moral values, and the dysfunction of culture in the camps and ghettos must be reassessed from the perspective of women.

Gender-specific experiences are overlooked in Holocaust literature, especially that written by men. The stories told seem to erase or obscure women. In the instance of erasure, the fact that the main person in the story is a woman seems irrelevant to the teller. Women's lives are neutralized into a so-called 'human perspective,' which, on examination turns out to be a masculine one. Women are obscured (or mystified) when their perceptions, understanding, or actions are ignored in stories that are clearly about them (for example: rape, forced abortion, prostitution). It is as if stories about women were being used to tell about the men involved. Women are there, but they are in the background. Consequently, we are blinded to the fuller context – why something is happening and to whom. Just as those who write about the Holocaust from a 'universal perspective of evil' ignore Jews, those who write from a 'universal perspective of man' ignore women.[3]

Even stories about abortion, prostitution, and rape in the ghettos and camps obscure the perspective of women. Though these things happened to women, we hear only about the ways in which they affected men. [...]

The decision of the *Judenrat* of the Shavel ghetto to force abortions is cited in *Witness to the Holocaust*. It is a situation in which only women will be directly affected, yet women do not speak here; only men do. Not only do men make the decisions about nineteen abortions, they also decide that the nurse of one of the physicians will murder the fetus of a woman in her eighth month. The physician will induce premature birth but refuses to kill the newborn baby. The nurse, on the other hand, will not have a choice because she will not be told what she is doing. If the potential mothers refused the abortions, they would have sanctions placed against their families:

> ... deprive them of food cards, transfer their working members to worse jobs, deprive them of medical assistance, of firewood. If that doesn't work, then the woman must be called in and given an ultimatum – either an abortion or the committee will have to inform the security police. It was proposed that all physicians and midwives be forbidden to assist during childbirth.[4]

In this text, kinds of intimidation as strong as those used by the SS are employed by the *Judenrat* to force these abortions, yet the sense of this is somehow missing in the narration.

[...]

In Bettelheim's work we see a prime example of what I have called 'erasure.' The importance of including the perspective of women in our understanding about the Holocaust becomes even clearer when we look at his work. Bettelheim provides an inadequate explanation for what he calls 'the passive response':

> Psychologically speaking, most prisoners in the extermination camps committed suicide by submitting to death without resistance. ... (245) It may have been Jewish acceptance, without fight, of ever harsher discrimination and degradation that first gave the SS the idea that they could be gotten to the point where they would walk to the gas chambers on their own. (253) ... why did so few of millions of prisoners die like men, as did the men of only one of the Kommandos? (258)[5]

Aside from its historical inaccuracies, Bettelheim's interpretation is based on the immoral question of why the victim is a victim. He fails to see that the victim had few, if any, choices. He conceptualizes without taking into account the framework that surrounded all the victims, a world of torture, agony, terror, and ultimately death. Without this context, the issue of victimization is improperly analyzed; Bettelheim seems to suggest that something intrinsic to Jewish behavior made Jews victims. He does not clearly distinguish the overwhelming nature of Nazi occupation and persecution. He questions the values and behavior of the victims, without making the same inquiry regarding the oppressor and perpetrator. [...]

Bettelheim's generalizations about behavior under stress clearly do not apply to an extreme situation, i.e., Jewish response to the Nazi policy of deliberate extermination. Furthermore, what does Bettelheim mean by asking: 'Why did so few of millions of prisoners die like men?'[6] Why does he consider moral or physical courage an attribute of masculinity? Failing to differentiate between different types of force, he inappropriately blames the victim for succumbing.

Bettelheim's chapter on the response of prisoners contains a story or paradigm that serves as his analytical model of action; it illuminates his ideas about courage and honor: Naked prisoners moved towards the gas chambers. An SS officer, having learned that one prisoner was a dancer, ordered her to dance for him. As she danced 'she approached him, seized his gun and shot him. She too was immediately shot to death.'[7] Bettelheim comments:

> Isn't it probable that ... this dancing made her once again a person? No longer was she a number, a nameless, depersonalized prisoner, but the dancer she used to be. Transformed, however momentarily, she responded like her old self, destroying the enemy bent on destruction, even if she had to die in the process. ... this one example ... shows that in an instant the old personality can be regained, its destruction undone, once we decide on our own that we wish to cease being units in a system. Exercising the last freedom that not even the concentration camp could take away – to decide how one wishes to think and feel about the conditions of one's life – this dancer threw off her real prison. This she could do because she was willing to risk her life to achieve autonomy once more. If we do that, then if we cannot live, at least we die as men.[8]

Bettelheim criticizes the Jews for not acting like men, yet praises a *female* dancer for acting like a man and even makes her an example of 'manhood.' Perhaps we are expected to forget that she was a woman and ignore what actually happens to her in the story.

What actually happened was that she was molested, ogled, required to dance nude for the SS as she went to the gas. It sounds like a classic rape scene. Yet for Bettelheim what counts is 'dying like a man.' Once she can do this, he implies, she at last becomes a person. That this is a woman fighting off an SS officer does not even occur to Bettelheim, and he is unconscious that the phrase 'dying like a man' excludes women. He obviously intends to use it generically.

There is no aspect of the story, as told by Bettelheim, in which this woman's life *as a woman* counts. But the actions of the SS in this story were directed at a Jewish *woman* – not a Jewish *person*. Can we even suppose that this same sort of behaviour would be directed at male prisoners, Jewish or non-Jewish? Here is a legendary figure, yet she is not the most important part of the story. She is used, appropriated, not only by the SS but also by those who write about her. The *woman* in these stories is lost.

Honor and courage have more than one meaning. Are we to suppose that revenge or killing is the only action, and honor gained this way the only great value in the world? [...] Amongst Bettelheim's narrow concepts, the terms honor and courage emerge as universal constants, independent of gender, nationality, age, background, or circumstances. His concepts lack a context, the context of Nazi terror. In striving for a high degree of universalization and generalization, he overlooks significant differences and thus fails to understand the circumstances and people in that context. If resistance and survival do not mean the same thing for everyone, then expectations and analysis of resistance and survival must be more sophisticated and differentiated. As Lawrence Langer has said, we need to 'pluralize all efforts at analyzing survival.'[9]

In his article 'The Dilemma of Choice in the Death Camps' Langer writes of 'choiceless choices':

[...]

> In the absence of humanly significant alternatives ... alternatives enabling an individual to make a decision, act on it, and accept the consequences, all within a framework that supports personal integrity and self-esteem – one is plunged into a moral turmoil. ... The optionless anguish of the death camp could alienate dignity from choice ... reality in the death camps, where moral choice as we know it was superfluous, and inmates were left with the futile task of redefining decency in an atmosphere that could not support it.[10]

In addition to Bettelheim's example, there are other examples of such 'choiceless choices': the Greek mother who was told she could 'choose' which of her three children she could save; women who 'decided' not to let the newborn babies *and* their mothers die (as the Nazis wanted) – 'rather that ... we at least save the mothers (and kill the babies) ... so, the Germans succeeded in making murderers of even us.'[11]

Langer summarizes his analysis of 'choiceless choices' as follows:

> The real challenge before us is to invent a vocabulary of annihilation appropriate to the death camp experience; in its absence, we should at least be prepared to redefine the terminology of transcendence – 'dignity,' 'choice,' 'suffering,' and 'spirit' – so that it conforms more closely to the way of being in places like Auschwitz, where the situation that consumed so many millions imposed *impossible* decisions on victims not free to embrace the luxury of the heroic life.[12]

Langer is correct when he says we need to redefine the traditional language in ethics, if not transform it. Traditional constructs in ethics cannot be used to analyze the Holocaust because that language is applicable only to those situations of power in which there are real, concrete, morally significant alternatives and acts. He correctly points out that in the reality of the conditions of the Holocaust victims, these were lacking. Thus, Langer presents us with an important task not only for understanding the Holocaust, but also for the reconstruction of ethics.

[...]

However, Langer (perhaps understandably) is still confined to the paradigm of 'choice,' which is so central to traditional ethical theory. If he can ask, 'What could choice mean in the camps?' and his answer is, 'It's meaningless,' then we must also ask what the term 'choiceless choice' could mean. Is it not meaningless as well? It obfuscates the very material conditions Langer wants to illuminate. The situation constructed in the camps is one of oppression and domination; it is about the power and the lack of power to act meaningfully, not about choice or freedom.

Finally, Langer's way of speaking denies, however unintentionally, that the superfluousness of choice applies in any situations other than the Holocaust. This overlooks the fact that women and minorities, the working class and the poor, prior to and after the Holocaust, have often lived in conditions similar in kind (although not always in degree) to those in the Holocaust; namely, situations that present no significant alternatives – choosing which children will have food, staying with the family or leaving to try to get work, abandonment of children (even killing of babies) because of too little food or insufficient shelter, and abortion. This is a common situation for the oppressed, even if they are not necessarily presented with the organized force and terror experienced by the victims of the Holocaust. Thus, the responses during the Holocaust are not 'abnormal' as Langer would suggest; rather they reflect that 'choice' is not the real issue.[13]

Langer is correct in stating that we need a language that conforms more closely to the real experience of the Holocaust. However, I do not believe we have to invent a new vocabulary to do this. Rather, we must investigate those testimonies which have until now fallen on deaf ears – in this case, the vocabulary, concepts, lives, and deaths of women.

Charlotte Delbo's understanding of survival in terms of simple acts of relationship provides a useful framework.[14] Because of their different material conditions and social relations throughout life, women are able to create or recreate 'families' and so provide networks of survival. It is this set of responses (including variables of class, age, and nationality) that are crucial to understanding the moral dilemmas and decisions that arose. We must go outside traditional language and situations and begin to look at women's decisions for survival, for these have been at the heart of morality for women. A brief comparison and example will illuminate this claim.

Charlotte is ready to give up – she wants to 'surrender to death.' Viva slaps her back. She clings to Viva, who keeps her from falling into the snow. She listens to Viva who says, ' "Heads up. On your feet. ... Are you feeling better" and her voice is so reassuring in its tenderness that I answer, "Yes, Viva, I am feeling better." '[15] Another time she tells her friend Lulu that she cannot take it anymore. They change tools because Charlotte's is too heavy. Lulu asks Charlotte to get behind her:

> You can have a good cry. ... I cry. I did not want to cry, but the tears spill over, run down my cheeks. ... Sometimes (Lulu) turns around and with her sleeve, she gently wipes my face. ... Lulu tugs at me. 'That's all right now. Come work. There she is.' With so much kindness that I am not ashamed of having cried. It is as though I had cried on my mother's breast.[16]

This story is easily seen as part of the culture of women; it is not likely that a man would tell or indeed, for the most part, experience it. Keeping their humanity intact has always been a matter of different particulars for men and for women. Women's culture is different from men's culture; women's culture (not their biology) provides women with specific and different conditions in which to make moral choices and to act meaningfully. There must be further exploration of these differences between men and women; the assumption that 'human' responses are undifferentiable will not stand.

Alvin Rosenfeld, in *A Double Dying*, concludes his discussion of Styron's *Sophie's Choice* with this observation:

> ... one of the characteristics of Holocaust writings at their most authentic is that they are peculiarly and predominantly sexless.[17]

Anna Pawelczynska writes:

> Sexual distinctions ... were totally eliminated in camps; traces of these distinctions were reflected solely in the extra possibilities for tormenting and humiliating the prisoners.[18]

However I interpret these statements, I come to the same conclusion: they do not make sense of, or conform to, what was true in the experience of women.

At the very least, we must acknowledge the special abuse of women in sexual and parental roles, in gender-defined conditions and roles within the ghettos, in resistance groups, and in the camps. We need to define women's values and show how they helped shape their experiences. It is not so clear whether women's values were destroyed. The evidence, in its earliest stages, indicates that women's relationships with other women were significantly different from those of men with other men. Surely we cannot overlook this and simply proceed to talk in the usual way about the isolation of prisoners from one another or the destruction of values. In order to find out why or whether it might be true that women survived better, we must look at the ways in which women construct survival strategies and meaningful choices in varying conditions of powerlessness.

Since traditional philosophy and history are constructed by and apply to the lives of a particular group of men, it is obvious that there will be difficulties in using their theories and their language to speak of women's lives and choices.

Philosophical and historical assumptions about the primacy of reason notwithstanding, the history of our century has decisively undermined the traditional equation of rationality with civilization and morality. Indeed, it is not clear whether rationality was a restraining or a contributing force in the Holocaust. However that may be, assumptions about 'the rational' or 'the ethical' have been so narrowly conceived, yet so universally applied, as entirely to exclude the lives and experiences of Jews, women, and oppressed peoples. It has thus been impossible for historians and philosophers (among others) to consider such issues as relationships between parents and children, the home, childbearing and childrearing, friendship and bonding, beauty, marriage, and sexuality – major issues in a woman's life. They are clearly vital to any knowledge about and interpretation of the trauma caused by the Final Solution, to new conceptions of resistance and survival, and to the reconstruction of our understanding of moral theory and choice.

Historians, philosophers, and other scholars must reconsider the lives of women, not only to ask new questions about our language and theories of the Holocaust, but also simply to find out new information. Women's memoirs have too often been discounted as insignificant, rather than used to point to the inadequacy of existing research. To ask what happened to women, to use the perspectives of women in understanding the unspeakable, are important new processes in Holocaust study.[19] Then 'we can listen to a language' heretofore unspoken.[20] For it is these experiences that have been unspeakable in ethics, and they are part of what has until now been unspeakable in the literature about the Holocaust.

NOTES

1. Terrence Des Pres, *The Survivor* (New York, 1976); Dorothy Rabinowitz, *New Lives* (New York, 1976); Viktor E. Frankl, *Man's Search for Meaning* (Boston, 1967), and others have written books that in their own ways are powerful, perceptive, and important. However, they tend to use the category of 'persons' in a way that obscures. Compare Konnilyn G. Feig, *Hitler's Death Camps* (New York, 1981), 133–190.
2. Joan Kelly (Gadol), 'The Social Relations of the Sexes: Methodological Implications of Women's History,' *Signs* 1, no. 4 (Summer, 1976): 812.
3. See Alvin Rosenfeld, *A Double Dying: Reflections on Holocaust Literature* (Bloomington, Indiana, 1980), 164. See also Carol Gilligan's work on women and ethics, 'In A Different Voice: Women's Conception of the Self and Morality,' *Harvard Educational Review* 47, no. 4 (1977): 481–517; 'Are Women more Moral than Men?' interview with Gilligan by Martha Saxton in *Ms. Magazine* (December 1981): 63–66.
4. Azriel Eisenberg. ed., *Witness to the Holocaust* (New York, 1981), 153–54.
5. Bruno Bettelheim, *The Informed Heart* (New York, 1971), 245, 253, 258.
6. Bettelheim, *Informed Heart*, 258.
7. Ibid., 258–259. While there are different versions of this story, the point I am making does not hinge on Bettelheim's version, but rather on the interpretation. For other versions, see Borowski, *This Way to the Gas*, 143–146, and Sylvia Rothchild, ed., *Voices of the Holocaust* (New York, 1981), 162. A firsthand account can be found in Felix Muller, *Eyewitness Auschwitz* (New York, 1979), 87–89.

8. Bettelheim, *Informed Heart*, 259.
9. Lawrence Langer, early typescript version of 'The Dilemma of Choice in the Death Camps,' p. 41.
10. Lawrence Langer, 'The Dilemma of Choice in the Death Camps,' *Centerpoint: The Holocaust* 4, no. 1 (1980): 55.
11. Olga Lengyel, *Five Chimneys: The Story of Auschwitz* (New York, 1947), 99–100.
12. Langer, 'Dilemma of Choice,' 58.
13. I would like to thank Marion Kaplan, Renate Bridenthal, and Pamela Armstrong for their criticisms, insights, and ideas on 'choiceless choices.' See Nancy Hartsock, 'The Feminist Standpoint: Developing the Ground for a Specifically Feminist Historical Materialism,' in Sandra Harding and Merrill Hintikka, eds., *Discovering Reality: Feminist Perspectives on Epistemology, Metaphysics, Methodology, and Philosophy of Science* (Dordrecht, Holland, 1983), 283–310.
14. Charlotte Delbo, *None of Us Will Return* (Boston, 1968). Compare George Kren and Leon Rappoport, *The Holocaust and the Crisis of Human Behavior* (New York, 1980), 97–98.
15. Delbo, *None of Us Will Return*, 73–74.
16. Ibid., 116–117. Compare Primo Levi, *Survival at Auschwitz*, trans. Stuart Woolf (New York, 1969), 109–111. Primo Levi admits to having almost no relationships in the camps with the other prisoners. When he does speak of one, it is moving – still; it is a relationship with a civilian worker who came to the camp:

> The story of my relationship with Lorenzo . . . in concrete terms it amounts to little: an Italian civilian worker brought me a piece of bread and the remainder of his ration every day for six months; he gave me a vest of his, full of patches; he wrote a postcard on my behalf to Italy and brought me the reply. For all this he neither asked nor accepted any reward because he was good and simple and did not think that one did good for a reward. . . . I believe that it was really due to Lorenzo that I am alive today; and not so much for his material aid, as for his having constantly reminded me by his presence, by his natural and plain manner of being good, that there still existed a just world outside our own, something and someone still pure and whole, not corrupt, not savage, extraneous to hatred and terror; something difficult to define, a remote possibility of good, but for which it was worth surviving. . . . Thanks to Lorenzo, I managed not to forget that I myself was a man.

17. Rosenfeld, *A Double Dying*, 164. See William Styron, *Sophie's Choice* (New York, 1979).
18. Anna Pawelczynska, *Values and Violence in Auschwitz* (Berkeley, 1979), 53.
19. See Joan Miriam Ringelheim, 'Communities in Distress: Women and the Holocaust,' unpublished manuscript. See also *Proceedings of the Conference Women Surviving the Holocaust*, ed. Esther Katz and Joan Miriam Ringelheim (New York, 1983).
20. I thank Pamela Armstrong for this idea.

20

'WOMEN AND THE HOLOCAUST: ANALYZING GENDER DIFFERENCE'

Pascale Rachel Bos

Feminists have shown that as one introduces gender as an analytic tool, the culturally dominant and male ways of categorizing what is historically important and what is not are challenged. This challenge has led to unexpected and important new historical findings on women and the Holocaust, even as it has at times been considered controversial scholarship.

I support the underlying assumption of these studies (gender makes a difference) and believe that research on specifically gendered experiences is therefore relevant, important, and often sound. Nevertheless, it is important to take stock of what has been accomplished, and review our methods. In reevaluating the research thus far, it remains necessary to question critically *how* we study gender. Indeed, not all studies on women or gender and the Holocaust have been without methodological problems. Not all scholars agree on how we can or should study gender in such a historically charged arena, and not everyone takes gender to mean the same thing. It is also necessary to ask *how* we come to know what we know about gender and the Holocaust. For instance, when we come across gender differences in survivor narratives, we need to question how these are relevant. How do they come about? What do they mean? How should we interpret these narratives?

Finally, we need to ask ourselves what conclusions we mean to draw from these perceived differences. What do we mean when we say, for instance, that

From Pascale Rachel Bos (2003) 'Women and the Holocaust: Analyzing Gender Difference', in E. Baer and M. Goldenberg (eds), *Experience and Expression: Women and the Holocaust*. Detroit, MI: Wayne State University Press.

women had 'gender-specific coping skills'?[1] Or conversely, that we need to 'pay attention to the particularity of gendered wounding'?[2] By choosing to focus on women and gender, do we just 'enlarge our understanding of the impossible choices most Jews faced'?[3] Is this our (only) aim in looking at women or gender and the Holocaust, or are other issues at stake as well?

The way in which Holocaust history changes when gender is used as a category of analysis might be more complex than previously thought, and might be more ambiguous. Nevertheless, I argue that a careful analysis of gender is indispensable and should become an integral part of any Holocaust research.

To open this discussion, I first briefly consider some of the earlier research on women and the Holocaust and address some of the problems inherent in these studies. I then propose a conceptual framework for a different, *discursive* kind of gender analysis. This analysis seeks to bring to center stage questions about (gendered) subjectivity and autobiographical representation, the politics of memory and narrative, and the psychological function of testimony. The result, I hope, will be the start of a new dialogue on how we may (or may not) want to use gender as a category of analysis, and how to assess its importance in our reading of both Holocaust history and (autobiographical) Holocaust literature. Furthermore, I suggest that precisely in acknowledging (and high-lighting) the elements of choice and subversive power in the creation of (gendered) personal narratives we can conceive of survivors' agency in com-pelling new ways.

EARLY RESEARCH: WOMEN'S 'RESOURCES' AND 'VULNERABILITIES'

In order to pinpoint some of the problems in early feminist Holocaust research, I discuss briefly some of the work of Joan Ringelheim and that of a few other pioneers, as their research has long been central to the field. For Ringelheim and other feminist scholars the questions of women's particular *vulnerability* under the Nazis on the one hand, and their gendered *resourcefulness* on the other, were the main focus points.

What was of particular interest to Ringelheim was a comparison of the conditions to which Jewish women and Jewish men were subjected, since she wondered whether the misogyny of the Nazis might have led to 'dual' oppres-sion for Jewish women as *women*. Ringelheim determined that women were more vulnerable than men, even though some other feminist research had suggested that perhaps women were more resourceful.[4]

The problem with this research focus, however, is that the emphasis on Nazi sexism seems exaggerated or misplaced, as it has become clear that racism, always more than sexism, determined the Nazis' actions towards Jewish men and women. After all, in most cases, one's race determined whether gender even mattered, as what *kind* of woman or man one was constructed, and henceforth, what kind of treatment one received.[5] Furthermore, different sources provide conflicting numbers on whether more women were killed than men.[6] Once admitted into a camp, it seems unclear whether the odds for women were worse or better than for men, and other demographic factors such as physical strength and age[7] were certainly as influential as gender itself.[8]

The second research focus, the special or different *resources* of (Jewish) women under Nazi oppression, turned out to be problematic as well. Ringelheim and others searched for a specific 'women's culture,' a culture among women which made them share resources and depend on each other. Ringelheim concluded that women used their socialization as nurturers to create networks in the camps, and that these networks helped women survive.[9]

The first problem with this focus on women's specific strengths is that such an emphasis led in some cases to a rather generalized (and sometimes essentialized) analysis of gender difference which glorified women in general, instead of an attempt to catalogue the historical experiences of individual women.

From the start, such a generalizing interpretation was resisted by some scholars as well as by some survivors themselves, the 'subjects' under examination. Some survivors seemed to indicate that the feminist lens of the researchers, which reflected the newfound possibility to conceptualize one's identity and experiences as *gendered*, did not necessarily match their own self-perception at the time of the war. Nor were they willing or able to conceive retroactively of their experiences as affected by gender.

Another and more serious objection arose to this research which compared the 'strength' of women versus that of men; namely that it seems to suggest that the Nazis' extermination plan somehow created room for women's 'superior' survival skills to be developed and showcased. Ringelheim herself recognized this to be problematic. In later essays, Ringelheim acknowledged the problematic reliance in her own research on 'cultural feminism.' Her use of this framework changed respect for the stories of Jewish women into glorification, she concluded, and led her to suggest that women survivors transformed 'a world of death and inhumanity into one more act of human life.'[10] The problem with this approach, she now stated, is that 'to suggest that among those Jews who lived through the Holocaust, women rather than men survived better is to move toward an acceptance or valorization of oppression, even if one uses a cultural and not a biological argument.'[11] If we do find differences between men and women, she poses, we need to question how we interpret these differences.

With this essay, Ringelheim opened the discussion of the shortcomings of her own generation's scholarship: the tendency to research women's history with a set agenda; the risk of overgeneralizing male/female difference; and the tendency to glorify women's culture. The focus on women's strengths and vulnerabilities brought forth a certain methodological bias that today needs reviewing.

DECONSTRUCTING NARRATIVE

What is problematic furthermore in much first-generation research on the Holocaust and gender, is that there is no discussion of *how* Holocaust narratives (written or spoken) relate to lived experience. Instead, narratives are seen as trustworthy historical sources. Testimony is read or interpreted as if it were a reflection of an easily accessible truth. Literary critic Toril Moi dubs this tendency 'reflectionism.' A reflectionist reading fails to see narratives as a (re)construction of a confusing, multi-faceted experienced reality, but instead considers texts 'a more or less faithful reproduction of an external reality to which we all have equal and unbiased access.'[12] This kind of view fails 'to consider the proposition that the real is not only something we construct, but a controversial construct at that.'[13]

Understanding and analyzing experience along these lines means that survivor testimonies (by either women or men) do not allow us simple access to 'objective' history. For 'history never unfolds independently of the ways we have understood it.'[14] As scholars, we are thus engaged in performing historical analyses of these reconstructions, these representations. We perform an analysis of *discourse*.

Such an analysis suggests that it is possible to discern in Holocaust narratives several distinct ways in which survivors (both male and female) 'create meaning,' different levels on which a personal selection and narrative reconstruction comes into play. Selection takes place (consciously or unconsciously) on at least three separate (but not always easily *separable*) levels: first, survivors cannot tell us everything, so they select *certain* experiences to tell us about. Second, by necessity, there will be only certain events that they can remember or choose to remember, but not others. Third, survivors select a rhetorical strategy, a structure, a tone, a narrative order.

Moreover, I contend that the significance of their selection is almost always also linked to (and affected by) their self-perception as gendered, since belonging to a certain sex is at the heart of our self-image as human beings, and thus at the heart of the desire to 'normalize' life.

This active, subjective and constructive aspect of the testimonies tends to be overlooked in many earlier studies. Acknowledging this constructed nature of testimony, however, offers us an important window, not only on understanding gender difference but on conceptualizing survivors' agency. These (re)constructions suggest that they are able to renegotiate the past, and can produce meaning as subjects.

Overall, the events undergone by Jewish men and women caught in the Nazi nets were probably quite similar and comparable. Sometimes women and men were treated differently because of their sex, and these differences should be noted. The most striking differences brought forth in interviews and autobiographical narratives, however, are likely due to gender socialization of the subjects, growing up and living with certain discourses on gender. In other words, the *lens of gender* accounts for the fact that similar events and circumstances were sometimes experienced differently, were remembered differently, and are reconstructed differently in written or spoken testimony. That is, the socialization of those involved, the discourses in and through which one is constituted and understands one's self, affect what kinds of narratives one turns to to relate one's traumas.

This is not to deny the fact that ideas about sex differences also affected the events of the war itself: Jewish women, as a group, were sometimes treated differently from men, by both Nazis and their Jewish community, or a similar treatment was experienced differently, and thus led to different memories.[15] Moreover, although Gisela Bock and others have convincingly argued that for the Nazis 'racial hierarchy prevailed over gender hierarchy,' they did make a number of decisions based on gender which would indeed affect the experiences of men and women. These gender-based differences fall roughly into three categories.[16] First, the Nazis selected mostly men for the (relatively privileged) positions of Jewish leadership. Second, Jewish men were more often selected to work than women, thus women were more often killed immediately. Finally, as is to be expected, women were especially vulnerable in regard to their sexuality and reproductive function.[17]

Yet, even though sometimes gender did affect historical events and decisions in these ways, more often, men and women were treated similarly by the Nazis. Instead, most differences in their testimony can and need to be explained by the fact that men and women assign meaning differently. Men and women *experience*, *remember* and *recount* the same treatment or events differently.

The historical 'truth' of Holocaust survivors is thus necessarily tied up with various uses of narrative, which in turn are gendered. Therefore, even as we find noticeable gender differences in the interviews and the memoirs of survivors, we still need to analyze how and when these gender differences operate to be able to understand and appreciate them.

GENDERED EXPERIENCE, GENDERED MEMORY, GENDERED NARRATIVE

Did the Nazis treat men and women differently? (Did they for instance target women due to a sexist notion that they were less valuable labor?) Or, as I have suggested, was the treatment often similar but were the *effects* different for men and for women? Let us briefly consider the following example: the shaving off of inmates' hair. This was customary at a number of concentration camps and affected both women and men, but may have had a much greater emotional and psychological impact on women than on men, as comparisons of Auschwitz memoirs by male and female survivors suggest.[18] Concluding from these narratives that the Nazis targeted women (as they exploited their sense of modesty) is not correct. If men and women were subjected to the same treatment, how can we argue that women were 'targeted'? In fact, the Nazis generally did not distinguish in their treatment of Jewish men and women in concentration camps (apart from selection, at which women, due to frailty or motherhood, stood less of a chance), but the treatment itself was experienced differently.

What about gendered memory? Research on memory suggests that gender does in fact play a role in remembering.[19] Men and women do not differ in overall memory ability, but men and women do assume that there are distinct sex differences in memory, and this expectation of difference, the desire or need to conform to one's sense of what is gender-appropriate, affects their later recall. The selective *recall* of memories, the narratives used to form and share them, thus become gendered. Gender differences in memory are thus the effect of preference, a preference which in turn is caused by socialization.[20]

To acknowledge the potential importance of gendered recall for our understanding of the experiences of Jewish men and women under the Nazis, we should ideally compare narratives of men and women who lived under 'equivalent' circumstances. But there are too many factors to include to make any such comparison a useful one (besides gender, one would have to find a match between survivors' age, class, Jewish identity, nationality, education level, personality, and so on); it simply cannot be achieved.

These findings on gendered memory nevertheless have important consequences for our historical research. If we now know that the memories of men and women differ, we will need to consider how these differences have affected our perception of Holocaust history. Since testimony by male survivors has been examined much more than testimony by female survivors, is our image of 'what it was like' incorrect or incomplete? Have we only been reading historical experiences through the lens of (male) gendered recall? Work of the first generation of scholars does indeed suggest so, and our increased understanding of the gendered functioning of memory makes it more important to take women's testimony into account.

Finally, men and women might write differently about their experiences, not only because their experiences may have in fact differed and their memory of the events is gendered, but also because their style or mode of narration might differ. Feminist theories of autobiography consider the possibility that female authors are influenced by different literary and cultural models. Some theories even argue that women have different styles of writing than men, linked to their different psychological make-up. Although some of these claims risk essentializing gender difference once more, they are worth further inquiry.

Let me illustrate this with an example that relates back to an earlier feminist research focus: the existence of gendered support systems in camps. As men were (and are) generally socialized to value independence and autonomy greatly, these qualities are often what they will strive for and choose to emphasize in their narratives. Thus, one finds these traits both in their memories and in the narrative recollection of these memories. I would not wish to conclude on the basis of these statements, however, that unlike women, men did not have important relationships ('dyads') with other men in the camps. What the discovery of such a pattern in Holocaust narratives does suggest to me is that most men born in the first decades of this century, perhaps unconsciously, tend to underemphasize these bonds while placing more importance on recollections that contain instances of individual strength, heroism, or autonomy. Women, on the other hand, had been generally socialized to value relationships and interdependence, and they therefore tend to remember these friendships and connections more fondly and choose to emphasize them in a narrative, even to the point of personal effacement. In turn, the women's tendency to foreground these gendered memories in their narratives might strike us readers as particularly significant, but should be understood as 'normalizing' strategies, and not necessarily as reliable testimony on which to base historical conclusions about differences between male and female behavior.

Conforming to (sometimes competing) medical, biological, and bourgeois discourses on gender is thus at the heart of one's self image, and in turn will inform one's memories and narratives. Such socialization remains relevant in a situation as extreme as the Holocaust. Indeed, it might become strengthened, even exaggerated, as a survivor seeks to hold on to the last vestiges of decency and normalcy, to a normative (properly gendered) bourgeois discourse, to create some kind of narrative logic out of traumatic experiences. In the narrative recollection of these events, one can expect gendered patterns to become emphasized, especially when an individual tries to justify certain decisions and make sense of the inherently senseless. This form of subjectivity does not make survivors' testimony less valuable, though. It is in fact precisely here that we can localize survivors' agency: in the opportunity to renegotiate their histories and produce (narrate and emplot) their own stories. One needs to take these strategies and the process of producing testimony into consideration in a historical analysis, however, and resist neutralizing them by treating survivors as objective and disinterested observers.

Gender must thus certainly remain a relevant factor in current research on the Holocaust, but in a more complex way than has been suggested thus far. The danger of the particular approach much early feminist research used is of taking the statements about gender differences made by both men and women in memoirs and interviews at face value, and deriving rather general conclusions from them about men and women. What I am suggesting instead is that the answers as to why experiences between men and women as written about in memoirs and recounted in interviews differ at times are not that simple and clear-cut. They are not all located in Nazi policies aimed specifically at women (women's 'particular vulnerability'). Nor can they be attributed so easily to certain gendered coping mechanisms (women's 'particular resourcefulness'). Instead, we first need to look more carefully into the effects of men's and women's different prewar socialization. For as James Young suggests, 'each victim "saw" – i.e. understood and witnessed – his predicament differently, depending on his own historical past, religious paradigms, and ideological explanations.'[21] Secondly, the survivors' present-day location vis-à-vis the competing discourses of gender, class, Jewishness and their ensuing ways of acting in, looking at, describing and experiencing the world need to be considered as central to the narratives they will produce.

No longer can we approach oral testimony or autobiographical texts as transparent documents that represent the past 'as it was.' We will need to see them instead as gendered discourses which serve to construct, reshape and contest the memory of the past for various present purposes (personal and social) as much as they serve to preserve that past itself. For this very reason, these testimonies and texts will not be able to give us a quick and unequivocal answer to why the Holocaust meant different things to men and women, but they do suggest a locus of agency for survivors.

Notes

1. Dalia Ofer and Lenore J. Weitzman, 'Introduction: The Role of Gender in the Holocaust,' *Women in the Holocaust* (New Haven, CT: Yale University Press, 1998), 11.
2. Ofer and Weitzman, 16.
3. Ofer and Weitzman, 15.
4. See Myrna Goldenberg, 'Different Horrors, Same Hell', in Roger Gottlieb, ed., *Thinking the Unthinkable* (Mahwah, NJ: Paulist Press, 1990) and Sybil Milton, 'Issues and Resources' in Esther Katz and Joan Ringelheim, eds., *Proceedings of the Conference, Women Surviving: The Holocaust* (New York: Institute for Research in History, 1983), 17–19.
5. In addition, the presence of a greater number of female victims does not necessarily indicate a desire on the part of the Nazis to 'target' (Jewish) women, but may be indicative of other historical circumstances, as I discuss later. Nonetheless, as Atina Grossman points out, this does not mean that gender did not matter altogether. Atina Grossman, 'Feminist Debates about Women and National Socialism,' *Gender and History*, 3.3 (Autumn 1991): 356.
6. See the addendum to a reprint of Ringelheim's essay 'Women and the Holocaust: A Reconsideration of Research' in *Different Voices: Women and the Holocaust*, (edited by Carol Rittner and John K. Roth (New York: Paragon House, 1993) in which she provides numbers on comparative survival rates among men and women. The problem is that the greater women's death toll is attributed to the Nazis' intent to kill 'Jewish women ... as Jewish women not simply as Jews' (392), and not to a combination of factors, which includes the sexism within the Jewish community itself. In contrast, Goldenberg has argued that women had better chances for surviving than men (because of certain gendered skills) and suggests that there are several sources that report lower mortality rates for women inmates than for men, but she does not provide those sources. Goldenberg, 'Different Horrors,' 153.
7. Anna Pawelczynska does not use gender as an analytical category and suggests that: 'Any form of physical weakness reduced the chances of surviving the camp nearly to zero. In most cases it cancelled the chance to be admitted into the camp, and instead formed the basis of the decision for immediate, assembly-line-style death.' Anna Pawelczynska, *Values and Violence in Auschwitz: A Sociological Analysis* (Berkeley: University of California Press, 1978, 53.
8. In several camps, women and men under the age of 16 and over the age of 40–45, and any women with young children or who were visibly pregnant would be killed on arrival. Physical frailty is mentioned as risk factors in all studies. Other *personal* factors that proved beneficial to one's chance of survival: being accustomed to the harsh climate in Poland, understanding German, special work skills, political or other ties which connected one to a group of inmates in the camp. *General* factors that affected survival: the degree of German control in a region, the attitude of the local government, the availability of escape routes, and the logistics of the deportations (when and to where one was deported obviously played a great role in one's chance to survive).

9. Ringelheim, 'Women and the Holocaust' (in *Different Voices*), 378–379. Ringelheim does point out, however, that ultimately, survival was dependent on luck (381). But such an analysis is not particularly satisfying to her. For luck, she suggests, 'tells us very little if we want to find out about their maintenance strategies and how these strategies relate to their survival' (381).
10. Ringelheim, 'Women and the Holocaust' (in *Different Voices*), 387.
11. Ringelheim, 'Women and the Holocaust' (in *Different Voices*), 387.
12. Toril Moi, *Sexual/Textual Politics: Feminist Literary Theory* (London: Routledge, 1985), 45.
13. Moi, 45.
14. James Young, *Writing and Rewriting the Holocaust: Narrative and the Consequences of Interpretation* (Bloomington: Indiana University Press, 1988), 5.
15. For instance, Marion Kaplan argues that within the Jewish community decisions were made on the basis of gender that would affect Jewish women's experiences during the Holocaust: Jewish men more often than women were encouraged to flee occupied Europe, since they were believed to be in more serious danger; women more often than men were left to take care of elderly parents, as caretaking was expected of them more so than of sons. As a result of these two factors alone, more women than men were left in Europe when deportations started, and more women were rounded up and taken to ghettoes and camps. Marion Kaplan, 'Keeping Calm and Weathering the Storm: Jewish Women's Responses to Daily Life in Nazi Germany, 1933–1939,' Ofer and Weitzman, 45–51.
16. Gisela Bock, 'Ordinary Women in Nazi Germany: Perpetrators, Victims, Followers, and Bystanders,' Ofer and Weitzman, 95.
17. In some camps, entering while pregnant, or while being accompanied by young children, meant an automatic death sentence. Women's sexuality, on the other hand, could work both to the advantage and disadvantage of women; one ran the risk of being assaulted, but sometimes women were also in a position to barter sex for food rations.
18. Compare, for instance, the depictions of the shaving in Primo Levi, *Survival in Auschwitz* (New York: Collier, 1986), 23 and Judith Magyar-Isaacson, *Seed of Sarah: Memoir of a Survivor* (Urbana: University of Illinois Press, 1990), 66–67.
19. See Elizabeth Loftus, et al., 'Who Remembers What? Gender Differences in Memory,' *Michigan Quarterly Review*, 26.1 (1987): 64–85. This research suggests that males and females do not differ in overall memory ability, but motivation and training (i.e., socialization) does affect the *content* of what is remembered.
20. Marlene Heinemann hints at this problem of locating gender difference as she argues that survivors' *memories* of relationships in the camps are tied to socially and psychologically determined roles, which are in turn gender-based. See Heinemann, *Gender and Destiny: Women Writers and the Holocaust* (New York: Greenwood Press, 1986), 82.
21. Young, 26.

PART V

PSYCHOANALYSIS, TRAUMA, AND MEMORY

PSYCHOANALYSIS, TRAUMA, AND MEMORY: INTRODUCTION

Describing the Nazi genocide as a traumatic event is not simply another way of evoking its horror. Contemporary theories of trauma, which build on insights of Freud, Lacan, and others, provide new lenses for thinking about the nature of violence and its aftermath. As characterized by critic Cathy Caruth in her influential introduction to *Trauma: Explorations in Memory*, excerpted here, trauma is not simply the product of a particular type of event, but rather of 'the *structure of its experience* or reception.' Events become traumatic by virtue of the shock experienced by a subject who was not prepared for the event and was thus unable to assimilate it to an established framework of understanding. The overwhelming nature of the experience leads to the return of the event in flashbacks that haunt or 'possess' the traumatized person. Trauma's repetitions are different from those associated with 'the return of the repressed,' another key psychoanalytic concept, because, according to Caruth, the traumatic experience was never present in consciousness to begin with.

Because of trauma's disruptive force, confrontation with it demands a rethinking of taken for granted notions of subjectivity, history, truth, and cure. The partial disengagement of trauma from particular types of events has allowed contemporary trauma studies to flourish in multiple academic disciplines and has made the concept of trauma a key to understanding a range of individual and collective histories (including slavery, war, and sexual assault). The very breadth of trauma's applicability has led some critics to wonder about the intellectual and political implications of such a focus on woundedness (see Leys, Seltzer, and Yaeger's contribution to Miller and Tougaw, 2002). While the general category has proven useful for thinking comparatively about histories of violence, it is also necessary to make distinctions between kinds of traumatic experiences. Dominick LaCapra's 'Trauma, Absence, Loss' posits a crucial distinction between structural and historical trauma. Historical trauma derives from specific and generally human-made phenomena, such as genocide or systematic racism, and entails losses that can be enumerated and addressed socially and psychologically (even if they can never be fully overcome). Structural trauma, on the other hand, is LaCapra's term for humans' confrontation with originary, transhistorical absences. Entry into language, separation from the mother, the inability to found or take part in a fully unified community – all of these experiences can be traumatic, but they are so in a much different way than are historical events. Unlike historical losses, which can in principle be avoided and are thus subject to considerations of justice and reparations, structural absences are unavoidable and can only be lived with. LaCapra's distinction should provoke both a rethinking of the relationship between trauma and victimization and a new approach to critical and historical methodology.

Writing against the background of the German Historians' Debate, during which some German intellectuals explicitly attempted to minimize and excuse the violence of Germany's recent past, both Saul Friedlander and Eric Santner seek ways of incorporating victims' traumatic memories into historical consciousness. Unlike the majority of historians (but like LaCapra), Friedlander pays close attention to the psychological dynamics involved in all approaches to the past – especially those that consider histories that remain 'unmastered.' Focusing on German and Jewish intellectuals who were contemporaries of the Nazi period, Friedlander notes various methods of avoidance of the trauma of genocide in their historical research. He draws on Freud's notion of 'working through' to propose a means of addressing the traumatic nature of the Holocaust without giving up on the project of a scientific historical methodology. Incorporating self-reflexive commentary into historical narrative would allow the understanding of history to proceed without leading to a premature closure that denies the continued presence of the open wounds of the past. Santner is similarly concerned about the avoidance of trauma and the desire for premature closure, and he finds both of these not only among historians, but in a broad range of cultural discourses in contemporary Germany. Also inspired by Freud, Santner's notion of 'narrative fetishism' – the production of a narrative that seeks to erase the trauma that called it into being in the first place – is an enormously useful category for critical analysis of post-traumatic cultures. He finds evidence of such fetishism not only in the writings of participants in the Historians' Debate, but also in such popular German films as *Heimat*.

The entry by Dori Laub, who is both a Holocaust survivor and a psychoanalyst who works with trauma victims, brings the question of trauma back to the immediacy of the encounter between victims and those who listen to them in therapeutic or scholarly contexts. Because of the unassimilated nature of traumatic experience, narratives by victims are a necessary part of a process of reclaiming selfhood and healing from the wounds of violence. Such narratives also demand a listener who can serve as co-witness and help the victim reconstruct trust in the world. The importance of Laub's argument concerns not only the therapeutic dimensions of narrative, but also opens onto questions of historical truth, as his famous example of the chimneys of Auschwitz illustrates. It is precisely this concern with the nexus of narrative, identity, history, and suffering that makes trauma studies such a crucial component of the contemporary theoretical landscape.

OTHER WORKS IN HOLOCAUST STUDIES

Avni, Ora (1995) 'Beyond Psychoanalysis: Elie Wiesel's *Night* in Historical Perspective,' in Lawrence Kritzman (ed.), *Auschwitz and After*, New York: Routledge, pp. 203–18.

Bellamy, Elizabeth J. (1997) *Affective Genealogies: Psychoanalysis, Postmodernism, and the 'Jewish Question' after Auschwitz*. Lincoln, NE: University of Nebraska Press.

LaCapra, Dominick (1994). *Representing the Holocaust: History, Theory, Trauma*. Ithaca, NY: Cornell University Press.

Santner, Eric (1990) *Stranded Objects: Mourning, Memory, and Film in Postwar Germany*. Ithaca, NY: Cornell University Press.

OTHER RELEVANT THEORETICAL STUDIES

Brison, Susan J. (2002) *Aftermath: Violence and the Remaking of a Self*. Princeton, NJ: Princeton University Press.

Caruth, Cathy (1996) *Unclaimed Experience: Trauma, Narrative, and History*. Baltimore, MD: Johns Hopkins University Press.

Foster, Hal (1996) *The Return of the Real: The Avant-Garde at the End of the Century*. Cambridge, MA: MIT Press.

Freud, Sigmund (1955) *Beyond the Pleasure Principle*, in *The Standard Edition of the Complete Psychological Works of Sigmund Freud*, trans. James Strachey. London: Hogarth.

Hartman, Geoffrey (1995) 'On Traumatic Knowledge and Literary Studies,' *New Literary History*, 26, pp. 537–63.

Lacan, Jacques (1981) *The Four Fundamental Concepts of Psycho-Analysis*, trans. Alan Sheridan. New York: Norton.

Leys, Ruth (2000) *Trauma: A Genealogy*. Chicago: University of Chicago Press.

Miller, Nancy K. and Jason Tougaw (eds) (2002) *Extremities: Trauma, Testimony, and Community*. Urbana, IL: University of Illinois Press.

Morgenstern, Naomi (1996) 'Mother's Milk and Sister's Blood: Trauma and the Neoslave Narrative,' *differences: A Journal of Feminist Cultural Studies*, 8.2, pp. 101–26

Seltzer, Mark (1997) 'Wound Culture: Trauma in the Pathological Public Sphere,' *October*, 80, pp. 3–26.

21

'TRAUMA AND EXPERIENCE'

Cathy Caruth

In the years since Vietnam, the fields of psychiatry, psychoanalysis, and sociology have taken a renewed interest in the problem of trauma. In 1980, the American Psychiatric Association finally officially acknowledged the long-recognized but frequently ignored phenomenon under the title 'Post-Traumatic Stress Disorder' (PTSD), which included the symptoms of what had previously been called shell shock, combat stress, delayed stress syndrome, and traumatic neurosis, and referred to responses to both human and natural catastrophes. On the one hand, this classification and its attendant official acknowledgment of a pathology has provided a category of diagnosis so powerful that it has seemed to engulf everything around it: suddenly responses not only to combat and to natural catastrophes but also to rape, child abuse, and a number of other violent occurrences have been understood in terms of PTSD, and diagnoses of some dissociative disorders have also been switched to that of trauma. On the other hand, this powerful new tool has provided anything but a solid explanation of disease: indeed, the impact of trauma as a concept and a category, if it has helped diagnosis, has done so only at the cost of a fundamental disruption in our received modes of understanding and of cure, and a challenge to our very comprehension of what constitutes pathology. This can be seen in the debates that surround 'category A' of the American Psychiatric Association's definition of PTSD (a response to an event 'outside the range of usual human experience'), concerning how closely PTSD must be tied to specific kinds of events;[1] or in the

From Cathy Caruth (ed.) (1995) 'Trauma and Experience: Introduction', *Trauma: Explorations in Memory*. Baltimore, MD: Johns Hopkins University Press.

psychoanalytic problem of whether trauma is indeed pathological in the usual sense, in relation to distortions caused by desires, wishes, and repressions. Indeed, the more we satisfactorily locate and classify the symptoms of PTSD, the more we seem to have dislocated the boundaries of our modes of understanding – so that psychoanalysis and medically oriented psychiatry, sociology, history, and even literature all seem to be called upon to explain, to cure, or to show why it is that we can no longer simply explain or simply cure. The phenomenon of trauma has seemed to become all-inclusive, but it has done so precisely because it brings us to the limits of our understanding: if psychoanalysis, psychiatry, sociology, and even literature are beginning to hear each other anew in the study of trauma, it is because they are listening through the radical disruption and gaps of traumatic experience.

[...]

While the precise definition of post-traumatic stress disorder is contested, most descriptions generally agree that there is a response, sometimes delayed, to an overwhelming event or events, which takes the form of repeated, intrusive hallucinations, dreams, thoughts or behaviors stemming from the event, along with numbing that may have begun during or after the experience, and possibly also increased arousal to (and avoidance of) stimuli recalling the event.[2] This simple definition belies a very peculiar fact: the pathology cannot be defined either by the event itself – which may or may not be catastrophic, and may not traumatize everyone equally – nor can it be defined in terms of a *distortion* of the event, achieving its haunting power as a result of distorting personal significances attached to it. The pathology consists, rather, solely in the *structure of its experience* or reception: the event is not assimilated or experienced fully at the time, but only belatedly, in its repeated *possession* of the one who experiences it. To be traumatized is precisely to be possessed by an image or event. And thus the traumatic symptom cannot be interpreted, simply, as a distortion of reality, nor as the lending of unconscious meaning to a reality it wishes to ignore, nor as the repression of what once was wished. Indeed, in 1920, faced with the onset of 'war neuroses' from World War I, Freud was astonished at their resistance to the whole field of wish and unconscious meaning, comparing them to another long-resistant phenomenon he had dealt with, the accident neurosis:

> Dreams occurring in traumatic neuroses have the characteristic of repeatedly bringing the patient back into the situation of his accident, a situation from which he wakes up in another fright. This astonishes people far too little. ... Anyone who accepts it as something self-evident that dreams should put them back at night into the situation that caused them to fall ill has misunderstood the nature of dreams. (*SE*18:13)

The returning traumatic dream startles Freud because it cannot be understood in terms of any wish or unconscious meaning, but is, purely and inexplicably, the literal return of the event against the will of the one it inhabits. Indeed, modern analysts as well have remarked on the surprising *literality* and non-symbolic nature of traumatic dreams and flashbacks, which resist cure to the extent that they remain, precisely, literal. It is this literality and its insistent return which thus constitutes trauma and points toward its enigmatic core: the delay or incompletion in knowing, or even in seeing, an overwhelming occurrence that then remains, in its insistent return, absolutely *true* to the event. It is indeed this truth of traumatic experience that forms the center of its pathology or symptoms; it is not a pathology, that is, of falsehood or displacement of meaning, but of history itself. If PTSD must be understood as a pathological symptom, then it is not so much a symptom of the unconscious, as it is a symptom of history. The traumatized, we might say, carry an impossible history within them, or they become themselves the symptom of a history that they cannot entirely possess.

Yet what can it mean that history occurs as a symptom? It is indeed this curious phenomenon that makes trauma, or PTSD, in its definition, and in the impact it has on the lives of those who live it, intimately bound up with a question of truth. The problem arises not only in regard to those who listen to the traumatized, not knowing how to establish the reality of their hallucinations and dreams; it occurs rather and most disturbingly often within the very knowledge and experience of the traumatized themselves. For on the one hand, the dreams, hallucinations and thoughts are absolutely literal, unassimilable to associative chains of meaning. It is this literality as we have said that possesses the receiver and resists psychoanalytic interpretation and cure.[3] Yet the fact that this scene or thought is not a possessed knowledge, but itself possesses, at will, the one it inhabits, often produces a deep uncertainty as to its very truth:

> A child survivor of the Holocaust who had been at Theresienstadt continually had flashbacks of trains, and didn't know where they came from; she thought she was going crazy. Until one day, in a group survivor meeting, a man says, 'Yes, at Theresienstadt you could see the trains through the bars of the children's barracks.' She was relieved to discover she was not mad. (Kinsler, 1990)

The survivors' uncertainty is not a simple amnesia; for the event returns, as Freud points out, insistently and against their will. Nor is it a matter of indirect access to an event, since the hallucinations are generally of events all too accessible in their horrible truth. It is not, that is, having too little or indirect access to an experience that places its truth in question, in this case, but paradoxically enough, its very overwhelming immediacy, that produces its belated uncertainty. Indeed, behind these local experiences of uncertainty, I would propose, is a larger question raised by the fact of trauma, what Shoshana Felman [...] calls the 'larger, more profound, less definable crisis of truth ... proceeding from contemporary trauma.' Such a crisis of truth extends beyond the question of individual cure and asks how we in this era can have access to our own historical experience, to a history that is in its immediacy a crisis to whose truth there is no simple access.

I would suggest that it is this crisis of truth, the historical enigma betrayed by trauma, that poses the greatest challenge to psychoanalysis, and is being felt more broadly at the center of trauma research today. For the attempt to understand trauma brings one repeatedly to this peculiar paradox: that in trauma the greatest confrontation with reality may also occur as an absolute numbing to it, that immediacy, paradoxically enough, may take the form of belatedness. [...] Dori Laub has suggested that massive psychic trauma 'precludes its registration'; it is 'a record that has yet to be made' (Laub, 1991). [...] Central to the very immediacy of this experience, that is, is a gap that carries the force of the event and does so precisely at the expense of simple knowledge and memory. The force of this experience would appear to arise precisely, in other words, in the collapse of its understanding.

It is indeed the link between this inexplicable traumatic void and the nature of historical experience that is the focus of Freud's great study of Jewish history, *Moses and Monotheism*, in which he compares the history of the Jews with the structure of a trauma. What is striking, for Freud, is the return of the event after a period of delay:

> It may happen that someone gets away, apparently unharmed, from the spot where he has suffered a shocking accident, for instance a train collision. In the course of the following weeks, however, he develops a series of grave psychical and motor symptoms, which can be ascribed only to his shock or whatever else happened at the time of the accident. He has developed a 'traumatic neurosis.' This appears quite incomprehensible and is therefore a novel fact. The time that elapsed between the accident and the first appearance of the symptoms is called the 'incubation period,' a transparent allusion to the pathology of infectious disease. ... It is the feature one might term *latency*. (Freud, 1939, 84)

In the term 'latency,' the period during which the effects of the experience are not apparent, Freud seems to describe the trauma as the successive movement from an event to its repression to its return. Yet what is truly striking about the accident victim's experience of the event and what in fact constitutes the central enigma of Freud's example, is not so much the period of forgetting that occurs after the accident, but rather the fact that the victim of the crash was never fully conscious during the accident itself: the person gets away, Freud says, 'apparently unharmed.' The experience of trauma, the fact of latency, would thus seem to consist, not in the forgetting of a reality that can hence never be fully known, but in an inherent latency within the experience itself. The historical power of the trauma is not just that the experience is repeated after its forgetting, but that it is only in and through its inherent forgetting that it is first experienced at all. And it is this inherent latency of the event that paradoxically explains the peculiar, temporal structure, the belatedness, of historical experience: since the traumatic event is not experienced as it occurs, it is fully evident only in connection with another place, and in another time. If repression, in trauma, is replaced by latency, this is significant in so far as its blankness – the space of unconsciousness – is paradoxically what precisely preserves the event in its literality. For history to be a history of trauma means that it is referential precisely to the extent that it is not fully perceived as it occurs; or to put it somewhat differently, that a history can be grasped only in the very inaccessibility of its occurrence.[4]

Freud's late insight into this inextricable and paradoxical relation between history and trauma can tell us something about the challenge it presently poses for psychoanalysis; for it suggests that what trauma has to tell us – the historical and personal truth it transmits – is intricately bound up with its refusal of historical boundaries; that its truth is bound up with its crisis of truth. This is why, I would suggest, psychoanalysis has been beset by problems surrounding, precisely, the historical truth it accords to trauma, or whether it locates its ultimate origin inside or outside the psyche. On the one hand, many have noted in the debate surrounding the historical reality of trauma for Freud, that he was, from the beginning, always concerned with the relation between the occurrence of real traumatic events and the experience of pathology [...]. On the other hand, many have suggested that Freud's apparent 'giving up' of the reality of childhood seduction served – for Freud's followers, if not entirely for Freud himself – to relocate the origins of trauma entirely inside the psyche, in the individual's fantasy life, and hence to disavow the historical reality of violence (see, for example, Masson, 1984). While the insistence on the reality of violence is a necessary and important task, particularly as a corrective to analytic therapies that would reduce trauma to fantasy life or adult trauma to the events of childhood, nonetheless the debate concerning the location of the origins of traumatic experience as inside or outside the psyche may also miss the central Freudian insight into trauma, that the impact of the traumatic event lies precisely in its belatedness, in its refusal to be simply located, in its insistent appearance outside the boundaries of any single place or time. From his early claims, in the *Project for a Scientific Psychology*, that a trauma consists of two scenes – the earlier (in childhood) having sexual content but no meaning, the later (after puberty) having no sexual content but sexual meaning[5] – to his later claims, in *Moses and Monotheism*, that the trauma occurs only after a latency period, Freud seems to have been concerned, as we have suggested, with the way in which trauma is not a simple or single experience of events but that events, insofar as they are traumatic, assume their force precisely in their temporal delay. The apparent split between external and internal trauma in psycho-analytic theory, and related problems in other psychiatric definitions of trauma – whether to define it in terms of events or of symptomatic responses to events, or the relative contribution of previous traumas to the present one – would all be a function, in Freud's definition, of the split within immediate experience that characterizes the traumatic occurrence itself. It is the fundamental dislocation implied by all traumatic experience that is both its testimony to the event and to the impossibility of its direct access. [...]

This historical conception of trauma can also be understood as conveying the urgent centrality for psychoanalytic thinking of the relation between crisis and survival. [...] Freud's difficult thought provides a deeply disturbing insight into the enigmatic relation between trauma and survival: the fact that, for those who undergo trauma, it is not only the moment of the event, but of the passing out of it that is traumatic; that *survival itself*, in other words, *can be a crisis*.

[...]

[...] The trauma is a repeated suffering of the event, but it is also a continual leaving of its site. The traumatic reexperiencing of the event thus *carries with it* what Dori Laub calls the 'collapse of witnessing,' the impossibility of knowing that first constituted it. And by carrying that impossibility of knowing out of the empirical event itself, trauma opens up and challenges us to a new kind of listening, the witnessing, precisely, *of impossibility*.

[...]

The final import of the psychoanalytic and historical analysis of trauma is to suggest that the inherent departure, within trauma, from the moment of its first occurrence, is also a means of passing out of the isolation imposed by the event: that the history of a trauma, in its inherent belatedness, can only take place through the listening of another. The meaning of the trauma's address beyond itself concerns, indeed, not only individual isolation but a wider historical isolation that, in our time, is communicated on the level of our cultures. Such an address can be located, for example, in Freud's insisting, from his exile in England, on having his final book on trauma – *Moses and Monotheism* – translated into English before he died; or in the survivors of Hiroshima first communicating their stories to the United States through the narrative written by John Hersey, or more generally in the survivors of the catastrophes of one culture addressing the survivors of another.[6] This speaking and this listening – a speaking and a listening *from the site of trauma* – does not rely, I would suggest, on what we simply know of each other, but on what we don't yet know of our own traumatic pasts. In a catastrophic age, that is, trauma itself may provide the very link between cultures: not as a simple understanding of the pasts of others but rather, within the traumas of contemporary history, as our ability to listen through the departures we have all taken from ourselves

NOTES

1. This definition was used through DSM III-R. The phrase was eliminated from category A in the DSM IV definition, which appeared in 1994 (after the original publication of this introduction). The debate concerning what kinds of events may be considered potentially traumatizing nonetheless continues.
2. See for example the definition of PTSD in American Psychiatric Association (1987) and the discussion of PTSD in the introduction to van der Kolk (1984).

3. See Cohen, 1990a, 1990b.
4. See Caruth, 1991.
5. See Laplanche, 1970.
6. *Moses and Monotheism* tells not only about the ancient trauma of the Jews but about Freud's own unsettling departure from Vienna in 1938. On the circumstances of the book's translation, see Gay (1988), 637, 638, and 643. With regard to the Hiroshima survivors, the publication of Hersey's *Hiroshima* (1985), written in the third person but based on directly received first-person accounts, produced the first widespread reaction in the United States to the human effects of the bombing.

REFERENCES

American Psychiatric Association. 1987. *Diagnostic and Statistical Manual of Mental Disorders.* 3d ed., rev. Washington, D.C.: APA.

Caruth, Cathy. 1991. 'Unclaimed Experience: Trauma and the Possibility of History.' *Yale French Studies* 79 (1991).

Cohen, Jonathan. 1990a. 'The Role of Interpretation in the Psychoanalytic Therapy of Traumatized Patients.' Paper prepared for the Sixth Annual Meeting of the International Society for Traumatic Stress Studies, New Orleans.

————. 1990b. 'The Trauma Paradigm in Psychoanalysis.' Paper prepared for the Sixth Annual Meeting of the International Society for Traumatic Stress Studies, New Orleans.

Freud, Sigmund. 1939. *Moses and Monotheism.* Trans. Katherine Jones. New York: Vintage.

————. 1920 (1955). *The Standard Edition of the Complete Psychological Works of Sigmund Freud.* Vol. 18. Translated under the editorship of James Strachey in collaboration with Anna Freud, assisted by Alex Strachey and Alan Tyson. 24 vols. (1953–74). London: Hogarth.

Gay, Peter. 1988. *Freud: A Life for Our Time.* New York: Norton.

Hersey, John. 1985. *Hiroshima.* New York: Bantam.

Kinsler, Florabel. 1990. 'The Dynamics of Brief Group Therapy in Homogeneous Populations: Child Survivors of the Holocaust.' Paper prepared for the Sixth Annual Meeting of the International Society for Traumatic Stress Studies, New Orleans.

Laplanche, Jean. 1970. *Life and Death in Psychoanalysis.* Trans. Jeffrey Mehlman. Baltimore: Johns Hopkins University Press.

Laub, Dori. 1991. 'No One Bears Witness to the Witness.' In *Testimony: Crises of Witnessing in Literature, Psychoanalysis, and History.* ed. Shoshana Felman and Dori Laub. New York: Routledge.

Masson, Jeffrey. 1984. *The Assault on Truth: Freud's Suppression of the Seduction Theory.* New York: Penguin.

Terr, Lenore. 1988. 'Remembered Images and Trauma: A Psychology of the Supernatural.' *The Psychoanalytic Study of the Child.* New Haven: Yale University Press.

van der Kolk, Bessel A., ed. 1984. *Post-Traumatic Stress Disorder: Psychological and Biological Sequelae.* Washington, D.C.: American Psychiatric Press.

22

'TRAUMA, ABSENCE, LOSS'

Dominick LaCapra

[...]

[...] One may argue that structural trauma is related to (even correlated with) transhistorical absence (absence of/at the origin) and appears in different ways in all societies and all lives. As I indicated earlier, it may be evoked or addressed in various fashions – in terms of the separation from the (m)other, the passage from nature to culture, the eruption of the pre-oedipal or presymbolic in the symbolic, the entry into language, the encounter with the 'real,' alienation from species-being, the anxiety-ridden thrownness of *Dasein*, the inevitable genera-tion of the aporia, the constitutive nature of originary melancholic loss in relation to subjectivity, and so forth. I would reiterate that one difficulty in these scenarios is the frequent conversion of absence into loss or lack, notably through the notion of a fall from a putative state of grace, at-homeness, unity, or community. One can nonetheless postulate, hypothesize, or affirm absence as absence and recognize the role of something like untranscendable structural trauma without rashly rendering its role in hyperbolic terms or immediately equating it with loss or lack. By not conflating absence and loss, one would historicize and problematize certain forms of desire, such as the desire for redemption and totality or, in Sartre's words, the desire to be in-itself-for-itself or God.[1] One would also help prevent the indiscriminate generalization of historical trauma into the idea of a wound culture or the notion that everyone is somehow a victim (or, for that matter, a survivor).

From Dominick LaCapra (2001) 'Trauma, Absence, Loss', *Critical Inquiry* (Summer 1990) reprinted in *Writing History, Writing Trauma*. Baltimore, MD and London: Johns Hopkins University Press.

As distinguished analytically from structural trauma, historical trauma is specific, and not everyone is subject to it or entitled to the subject position associated with it. It is dubious to identify with the victim to the point of making oneself a surrogate victim who has a right to the victim's voice or subject position.[2] The role of empathy and empathic unsettlement in the attentive secondary witness does not entail this identity; it involves a kind of virtual experience through which one puts oneself in the other's position while recognizing the difference of that position and hence not taking the other's place. Opening oneself to empathic unsettlement is, as I intimated, a desirable affective dimension of inquiry which complements and supplements empirical research and analysis. Empathy is important in attempting to understand traumatic events and victims, and it may (I think, should) have stylistic effects in the way one discusses or addresses certain problems. It places in jeopardy fetishized and totalizing narratives that deny the trauma that called them into existence by prematurely (re)turning to the pleasure principle, harmonizing events, and often recuperating the past in terms of uplifting messages or optimistic, self-serving scenarios. (To some extent the film *Schindler's List* relies on such a fetishistic narrative.)

Empathic unsettlement also raises in pointed form the problem of how to address traumatic events involving victimization, including the problem of composing narratives that neither confuse one's own voice or position with the victim's nor seek facile uplift, harmonization, or closure but allow the unsettlement that they address to affect the narrative's own movement in terms of both acting out and working through. Without discounting all forms of critical distance (even numbing 'objectivity') that may be necessary for research, judgment, and self-preservation, one may also appeal to the role of empathy in raising doubts about positivistic or formalistic accounts that both deny one's transferential implication in the problems one treats and attempt to create maximal distance from them – and those involved in them – through extreme objectification.[3] But empathy that resists full identification with, and appropriation of, the experience of the other would depend both on one's own potential for traumatization (related to absence and structural trauma) and on one's recognition that another's loss is not identical to one's own loss.[4]

Everyone is subject to structural trauma. But, with respect to historical trauma and its representation, the distinction between victims, perpetrators, and bystanders is crucial. 'Victim' is not a psychological category. It is, in variable ways, a social, political, and ethical category. Victims of certain events will in all likelihood be traumatized by them, and not being traumatized would itself call for explanation. But not everyone traumatized by events is a victim. There is the possibility of perpetrator trauma which must itself be acknowledged and in some sense worked through if perpetrators are to distance themselves from an earlier implication in deadly ideologies and practices. Such trauma does not, however, entail the equation or identification of the perpetrator and the victim. The fact that Himmler suffered from chronic stomach

cramps or that his associate Erich von dem Bach-Zelewski experienced nocturnal fits of screaming does not make them victims of the Holocaust. There
may, of course, be ambiguous cases in what Primo Levi called the gray zone, but
these cases were often caused by the Nazi policy of trying to make accomplices
of victims, for example, the Jewish Councils or kapos in the camps. The gray
zone serves to raise the question of the existence and extent of problematic – at
times more or less dubiously hybridized – cases, but it does not imply the rashly
generalized blurring or simple collapse of all distinctions, including that
between perpetrator and victim. The more general point is that historical
trauma has a differentiated specificity that poses a barrier to its amalgamation
with structural trauma and which poses particular questions for historical
understanding and ethicopolitical judgment.[5]

Structural trauma is often figured as deeply ambivalent, as both shattering or
painful and the occasion for *jouissance*, ecstatic elation, or the sublime.
Although one may contend that structural trauma is in some problematic sense
its precondition, I would reiterate the basic point that historical trauma is
related to particular events that do indeed involve losses, such as the Shoah or
the dropping of the atom bomb on Japanese cities. The strong temptation with
respect to such limit events is to collapse the distinction and to arrive at a
conception of the event's absolute uniqueness or even epiphanous, sublime, or
sacral quality.[6] Perhaps this is the tangled region of thought and affect where
one should situate the founding trauma – the trauma that paradoxically
becomes the basis for collective or personal identity, or both. The Holocaust,
slavery, or apartheid – even suffering the effects of the atom bomb in Hiroshima
or Nagasaki – can become a founding trauma. Such a trauma is typical of myths
of origin and may perhaps be located in the more or less mythologized history of
every people. But one may both recognize the need for and question the function
of the founding trauma that typically plays a tendentious ideological role, for
example, in terms of the concept of a chosen people or a belief in one's
privileged status as victim. As historical events that are indeed crucial in the
history of peoples, traumas might instead be seen as posing the problematic
question of identity and as calling for more critical ways of coming to terms
with both their legacy and problems such as absence and loss.

A prominent motivation for the conflation of structural and historical trauma
is the elusiveness of the traumatic experience in both cases. In historical trauma,
it is possible (at least theoretically) to locate traumatizing events. But it may not
be possible to locate or localize the experience of trauma that is not dated or, in
a sense, punctual.[7] The belated temporality of trauma makes of it an elusive
experience related to repetition involving a period of latency. At least in Freud's
widely shared view, the trauma as experience is 'in' the repetition of an early
event in a later event – an early event for which one was not prepared to feel
anxiety and a later event that somehow recalls the early one and triggers a
traumatic response. The belated temporality of trauma and the elusive nature of
the shattering experience related to it render the distinction between structural

and historical trauma problematic but do not make it irrelevant. The traumatizing events in historical trauma can be determined (for example, the events of the Shoah), while structural trauma (like absence) is not an event but an anxiety-producing condition of possibility related to the potential for historical traumatization. When structural trauma is reduced to, or figured as, an event, one has the genesis of myth wherein trauma is enacted in a story or narrative from which later traumas seem to derive (as in Freud's primal crime or in the case of original sin attendant upon the Fall from Eden).

One may well argue that the Holocaust represents losses of such magnitude that, while not absolutely unique, it may serve to raise the question of absence, for example, with respect to divinity. Still, despite the extremely strong temptation, one may question the tendency to reduce, or confusingly transfer the qualities of, one dimension of trauma to the other – to generalize structural trauma so that it absorbs or subordinates the significance of historical trauma, thereby rendering all references to the latter merely illustrative, homogeneous, allusive, and perhaps equivocal, or, on the contrary, to explain all post-traumatic, extreme, uncanny phenomena and responses as exclusively caused by particular events or contexts. The latter move, what one might term *reductive contextualism*, is typical of historians and sociologists who attempt to explain, without significant residue, all anxiety or unsettlement – as well as attendant forms of creativity – through specific contexts or events, for example, deriving anxiety in Heidegger's thought exclusively from conditions in interwar Germany or explaining structuralism and the turn to the history of the *longue durée* in France solely in terms of the postwar avoidance of Vichy and the loss of national prestige and power.[8] The former tendency, deriving historical from structural trauma, is a great temptation for theoretically inclined analysts who tend to see history simply as illustrating or instantiating more basic processes. It should go without saying that the critique of reductive contextualism and theoreticism does not obviate the importance of specific contexts or of theory that addresses them and both informs and raises questions for research.

In *Telling the Truth about History*, the noted historians Joyce Appleby, Lynn Hunt, and Margaret Jacob write that 'once there was a single narrative of national history that most Americans accepted as part of their heritage. Now there is an increasing emphasis on the diversity of ethnic, racial, and gender experience and a deep skepticism about whether the narrative of America's achievements comprises anything more than a self-congratulatory masking the power of elites. History has been shaken down to its scientific and cultural foundations at the very time that those foundations themselves are being contested.'[9]

In this passage, one is close to reductive contextualism involving a variant of a golden age mythology, a variant in which the proverbial past-we-have-lost becomes the metanarrative we have lost. The purpose of the authors' own narrative is to explain current forms of multiculturalism and skepticism, and the contrast between past and present serves to frame or even validate that explanation. Yet we are never told precisely when 'there was a single narrative of national history that most Americans accepted as part of their heritage.' Nor are we told from what perspective that putative narrative was recounted. How, one might well ask, could one ever have fully reconciled narratives from the perspectives of Plymouth Rock, Santa Fe, and the Alamo? What about the perspective of American Indians in relation to the open frontier and manifest destiny? Where does one place the Civil War and the narratives related to it? I think one might argue that there never was a single narrative and that most Americans never accepted only one story about the past. The rhetorical attempt both to get one's own narrative off the ground and to account for current conflicts or discontents by means of a questionable opposition between the lost, unified past and the skeptical, conflictual present runs the risk of inviting underspecified, if not distorted, views of the past and oversimplified interpretations of the present.

Specificity is also in jeopardy when Žižek, who tends to be preoccupied with structural trauma (often construed as constitutive loss or lack), complements his convincing indictment of reductive contextualism with this comparably reductive assertion: 'All the different attempts to attach this phenomenon [concentration camps] to a concrete image ('Holocaust,' 'Gulag' . . .), to reduce it to a product of a concrete social order (Fascism, Stalinism . . .) – what are they if not so many attempts to elude the fact that we are dealing here with the 'real' of our civilization which returns as the same traumatic kernel in all social systems?'[10] Here, in an extreme and extremely dubious theoreticist gesture, concentration camps are brought alongside castration anxiety as mere manifestations or instantiations of the Lacanian 'real' or 'traumatic kernel.'

One way to formulate the problem of specificity in analysis and criticism is in terms of the need to explore the problematic relations between absence and loss (or lack) as well as between structural and historical trauma without simply collapsing the two or reducing one to the other. One may well argue that structural trauma related to absence or a gap in existence – with the anxiety, ambivalence, and elation it evokes – may not be cured but only lived with in various ways. Nor may it be reduced to a dated historical event or derived from one; its status is more like that of a condition of possibility of historicity (without being identical to history, some of whose processes – for example, certain ritual and institutional processes – may mitigate or counteract it). One may even argue that it is ethically and politically dubious to believe that one can overcome or transcend structural trauma or constitutive absence to achieve full intactness, wholeness, or communal identity and that attempts at transcendence or salvation may lead to the demonization and scapegoating of those on whom unavoidable anxiety is projected. But historical traumas and losses may conceivably be avoided and their legacies to some viable extent worked through both in order to allow a less self-deceptive confrontation with transhistorical, structural trauma and in order to further historical, social, and political specificity, including the elaboration of more desirable social and political institutions and practices.

NOTES

1. At least in one movement of his argument in *Being and Nothingness: An Essay on Phenomenological Ontology*, trans. Hazel E. Barnes (1943; New York: Washington Square Press 1953), Sartre did historicize this desire.
2. I find this tendency toward surrogate victim status in Claude Lanzmann as interviewer in his film *Shoah*. See my discussion in 'Lanzmann's *Shoah*: "Here There Is No Why," ' *Critical Inquiry* 23 (1997): 231–69; reprinted in *History and Memory after Auschwitz*, chap. 4.
3. Compare the formulation in Saul Friedlander, *Memory, History, and the Extermination of the Jews of Europe* (Bloomington: University of Indiana Press, 1993), 130–34.
4. As noted in Chapter 1, the type of empathy I am defending is discussed by Kaja Silverman in terms of heteropathic identification. See her *The Threshold of the Visible World* (New York: Routledge, 1996).
5. Here the cases of Blanchot and de Man pose a similar problem in judgment: whether early, direct, dubious, at times vehement writings receive an adequate critical response in later, indirect, allegorical, at times elusive writings that may indiscriminately mingle historical and structural trauma.
6. I discuss this problem from various perspectives both in *Representing the Holocaust* and in *History and Memory after Auschwitz*, esp. chap. 4. Inaugurating a form of what later came to be called 'nuclear criticism,' Georges Bataille, in an essay first published in 1947, denies the uniqueness of the bombing of Hiroshima in terms that threaten to go to the opposite extreme of leveling or hypostatizing the suffering and losses related to it by maintaining that 'horror is everywere the same' and appealing indiscriminately to 'misfortune's profound nonsense.' For Bataille, 'the tens of thousands of victims of the atom bomb are on the same level as the tens of millions whom nature yearly hands over to death. ... The point that, in principle, the one horror is preventable while the other is not is, in the last analysis, a matter of indifference' ('Residents of Hiroshima,' in *Trauma: Explorations in Memory*, ed. Cathy Caruth [Baltimore: Johns Hopkins University Press, 1995], 229). Going beyond even the initiative of Horkheimer and Adorno in *The Dialectic of Enlightenment*, he makes a mind-boggling attempt to show that the bombing of Hiroshima jeopardizes the pursuit of projects (or means-ends rationality) and attests instead to the 'sovereignty' of excessive expenditure and 'a boundless suffering that is joy, or a joy that is infinite suffering' (232).

    Comparable to Lyotard's construction of 'the jews' and Auschwitz as tropes or Trojan horses for his conception of postmodernism in terms of nomadism, un(re)-presentability, and the sublime, Bataille's questionable initiative includes the following assertions (which might most generously be read as an overreaction to his own tangled prewar relation to the charismatic appeal of fascism): 'The sensibility that goes to the furthest limits moves away from politics and, as is the case for the suffering animal, the world has at a certain point nothing more to it than an immense absurdity, closed in on itself. But the sensibility that looks for a way out and enters along the path of politics is always of cheap quality. It cheats, and it is clear that *in serving* political ends it is not more than a *servile*, or at least a subordinated[,] sensibility' (228). [...] See Lyotard's *Heidegger and 'the jews*,' trans. Andreas Michel and Mark T. Roberts, foreword by David Carroll (1988; Minneapolis: University of Minnesota Press, 1990), as well as my comments in *History and Reading: Tocqueville, Foucault, French Studies* (Toronto: University of Toronto Press, 2000), 206–9.
7. Bessel A. van der Kolk makes the questionable attempt to localize in a portion of the brain the trace or imprint of the experience of trauma. See Bessel A. van der Kolk and Onno van der Hart, 'The Intrusive Past: The Flexibility of Memory and the Engraving of Trauma,' in Caruth, *Trauma: Explorations in Memory*, 158–82.

Curiously, Caruth, despite her subtle analyses and stress on the elusiveness and belated temporality of the experience of trauma, accepts van der Kolk's literalizing view. Along with her contributions to *Trauma: Explorations in Memory*, see her *Unclaimed Experience: Trauma, Narrative, and History* (Baltimore: Johns Hopkins University Press, 1996).

8. The important and influential work of Pierre Bourdieu is sometimes prone to contextual reductionism or at least to a limited understanding of differential responses to contextual (or 'field') forces. See, for example, his *L'Ontologie politique de Martin Heidegger* (Paris: Editions de Minuit, 1988) and *The Rules of Art: Genesis and Structure of the Literary Field*, trans. Susan Emanuel (1992; Stanford: Stanford University Press, 1995).

9. Joyce Appleby, Lynn Hunt, and Margaret Jacob, *Telling the Truth about History* (New York: W. W. Norton, 1994), 1.

10. Slavoj Žižek, *The Sublime Object of Ideology* (London: Verso, 1989), 50.

23

'TRAUMA AND TRANSFERENCE'

Saul Friedlander

[...]

DEFENSES

If one accepts the suggestion that for the community of the victims, and for others as well, the Nazi epoch and the Holocaust remain an unmastered past – a 'past that refuses to go away,' as a notorious saying has it – then both the extreme character of the events and the indeterminacy surrounding their historical significance create even for the professional historian a field of projections, of unconscious shapings and reshapings, of an authentic transferential situation. As Dominick LaCapra has noted:

> The Holocaust presents the historian with transference in the most traumatic form conceivable – but in a form that will vary with the difference in subject position of the analyst. Whether the historian or analyst is a survivor, a relative of survivors, a former Nazi, a former collaborator, a relative of former Nazis or collaborators, a younger Jew or German distanced from more immediate contact with survival, participation, or collaboration, or a relative 'outsider' to these problems will make a difference even in the meaning of statements that may be formally identical.[1]

No doubt, any generalizing statement in such matters can have only the barest indicative function. There are any number of possible psychological aspects

From Saul Friedlander (1993) 'Trauma and Transference', in *Memory, History, and the Extermination of the Jews of Europe*. Bloomington and Indianapolis, IN: Indiana University Press.

linked to each of the subject positions previously mentioned by LaC;
suffices to recall shame, guilt, self-hatred, and all the shades of amb'
among the surviving victims in order to perceive the difference in n
produced from an apparently well-defined single vantage point. For Germa.
contemporaries of the Nazi epoch, particularly those who were adolescents or
young adults at the end of the war, the whole range of internal conflicts may be
as daunting in the variety of its results as it is for the victims. Moreover, complex
personal circumstances must often be taken into account. [...]

If, for the sake of simplicity, we consider both German and Jewish contemporaries of the Nazi period – contemporary adults, adolescents, or children,
even the children of these groups – what was traumatic for the one group was
obviously not traumatic for the other. For Jews of whatever age, the fundamental traumatic situation was and is the Shoah and its sequels; for Germans, it
was national defeat (including flight from the Russians and loss of sovereignty)
following upon national exhilaration. To that, however, a sequel must be
added, regardless of its psychological definition: the information growing over
time about Nazi crimes, especially the genocide. The victims of Nazism cope
with a fundamentally traumatic situation, whereas many Germans have to cope
with a widening stain, with potential shame or guilt.

Studies abound concerning the repression of the Nazi epoch in the German
public sphere, including the early phases of history writing.[2] Massive denial was
blatant in the historical work of the late forties and fifties. In the early sixties
signs of a transformation appeared, and that new approach dominated the late
sixties and the seventies. From then on various forms of denial and defensive
reactions surfaced in a new guise. The Historians' Controversy of the late
eighties became an unusual case of acting out. But how could one not mention
the German student movement of the late sixties? In clashing with their parents'
generation, they were fighting Nazism itself; 'fascism' as an overall tag, along
with the new awareness it created, shielded many of them from the specificity of
the Nazi past, and such ideological generalizations became deeply embedded in
subsequent historical discourse about Nazism. In short, the burden of the past,
at both the individual and the generational level, weighed and weighs as much
on the historical discourse in Germany as among the community of the victims.

Straight denial has not disappeared, although it is not massive. Until the late
1970s, for instance, the accepted mythology established a clear distinction
between the behavior of the Wehrmacht and that of the SS units on the eastern
front. To this day, this topic remains an area of repression, even within the most
painstaking historiography.

[...]

Far more widespread is a defense that could be termed 'splitting off.' It recently
found expression in the debate about 'the historicization of National Socialism.'[3] Early discussions of this issue left the place of 'Auschwitz' unmentioned.
In the debate that ensued, the centrality of Auschwitz was first relegated to the

domain of the victims' specific memory [. . .]; then it was suggested that the quasimythical dimension of Auschwitz in the victims' memory had to be taken into account alongside the more-nuanced approach to the history of the epoch. In short, facts perfectly well known – too well known in a sense – were split off from the main argument, as they were bound to create problems for the new approach to the history of Germany under Nazism. No clear way of integrating them was suggested.[4]

Various forms of avoidance, and particularly the splitting-off mechanism, have led to a growing fragmentation in the representation of the Nazi epoch.[5] The study of Nazism disintegrates into discrete, specialized, and unrelated domains and so understates the 'already well-known' facts of mass extermination and atrocity. There is ever-more minute research into various aspects of everyday life and social change during the Nazi era, without any compelling overall interpretive framework.[6] [. . .]

Turning to the historical and testimonial discourse of the victims, one encounters defenses that are not always outwardly different from what is perceptible on the German historical scene. However, such similarity covers totally different positions.

The fifteen or twenty years of 'latency' that followed the war in regard to talking or writing about the Shoah, particularly in the United States, should not be equated with massive repression exclusively, in contradistinction to the German scene. The silence did not exist within the survivor community. It was maintained in relation to the outside world and was often imposed by shame, the shame of telling a story that must appear unbelievable and was, in any case, entirely out of tune with surrounding society. This silence was breached, especially in Israel, by the debates from 1951 on concerning the reparations agreement with Germany, the Kastner trial, and finally the Eichmann capture and trial. These provided intense moments of emotional upheaval in a context dominated by the contrary currents of vulnerable awareness and of steadfast avoidance in both the national and the private domain.

Against this background, the more sustained silence of the intellectuals must be mentioned. None of the most renowned Jewish historians of the postwar period elected to pursue the Shoah as a subject of their research. This was true during the 1940s and 1950s, and with few exceptions, it did not change at any time later on. [. . .]

'Auschwitz' as such – not other facets of Nazism – seemed out of bounds. In their references to the Shoah, Theodor Adorno, Hannah Arendt, and Salo Baron were obvious exceptions within the wider Jewish intellectual landscape, as were the specialists at Yivo in New York, those working in Israel, or self-taught historians such as Léon Poliakov in France and Gerald Reitlinger in England. As for some of the best interpreters of modern German history, their silence or casual reference to the Holocaust is a chapter in itself.

The fragmentation of the historical field that characterizes much of current German historical writing on the Nazi epoch appears, though somewhat differently, in Jewish historiography. Jewish historians too seem to be at a loss to produce an overall history of the extermination of the Jews in Europe that is not a mere textbook presentation, an analysis of the internal cogs and wheels of the destruction machinery or a compendium of separate monographs. The 'Final Solution' in its epoch has not yet found its historian; and the problem cannot be reduced to a mere technical issue.

A closer look indicates that after the initial period of silence, and with the exclusion of ideologically dominated historiography, most historians approaching the subject have dealt either with descriptions of the background or with narrations of the Shoah, never, to my knowledge, with an integrated approach to both. There may be several unconscious motivations for this division of historical labor, chiefly among historians who were contemporaries of the Nazi epoch. Their emotional and intellectual life was marked by largely unbridged ruptures, whether in terms of direct experience or of sudden awareness; these ruptures (we could use the concept of deep memory in an attenuated sense) reappear in various facets of their work, in more ways than can be dealt with here. As for the following generation, its work seems to stay close to the patterns set by its predecessors. In short, notwithstanding the immense effort of documentary and monographic research and straightforward textbook presentation, historical interpretation by Jewish historians is still caught between hasty ideological closure (such as the 'catastrophe and redemption' theme) and a paralysis of attempts at global interpretation. For almost fifty years now, despite so much additional factual knowledge, we have faced surplus meaning or blankness with little interpretive or representational advance. This evaluation applies also to my own work.

On Working Through

In *Beyond the Pleasure Principle*, Freud defines as traumatic

> any excitations from outside which are powerful enough to break through the protective shield *[Reizschutz]*. It seems to me that the concept of trauma necessarily implies a connection of this kind with a breach in an otherwise efficacious barrier against stimuli. Such an event as an external trauma is bound to provoke a disturbance on a large scale in the functioning of the organism's energy and to set in motion every possible defense measure.[7]

Aside from being aware and trying to overcome the defenses already mentioned, the major difficulty of historians of the Shoah, when confronted with echoes of the traumatic past, is to keep some measure of balance between the emotion recurrently breaking through the 'protective shield' and numbness that protects this very shield. In fact, the numbing or distancing effect of intellectual work on the Shoah is unavoidable and necessary; the recurrence of strong emotional impact is also often unforeseeable and necessary.

'Working through' means, first, being aware of both tendencies, allowing for a measure of balance between the two whenever possible. But neither the protective numbing nor the disruptive emotion is entirely accessible to consciousness. A telling example is Raul Hilberg's magisterial work.[8] More than most of us, he has succeeded in balancing the necessary distancing or 'numbness' with elements of intense emotion. But the full impact of this emotion has on occasion been deflected toward overcritical comments on the behavior of the victims.

A main aspect of working through lies elsewhere: it entails, for the historian, the imperative of rendering as truthful an account as documents and testimonials will allow, without giving in to the temptation of closure. Closure in this case would represent an obvious avoidance of what remains indeterminate, elusive, and opaque. Put differently, working through means for the historian to face the dilemma which, according to Jean-François Lyotard, we try to escape in the face of 'Auschwitz': 'The silence that surrounds the phrase "Auschwitz was the extermination camp" is not a state of mind [*état d'âme*], it is a sign that something remains to be phrased which is not, something which is not determined.'[9]

Some of the remarks presented in the last two sections (the avoidance of closure, the ever-questioning commentary, and the 'excess' carried by the Shoah, which will be referred to below) could appear as an oblique reference to a deconstructionist approach to the history of this event.[10] Such a possibility demands a very brief clarification.

Any deconstructionist approach would necessarily demand a primacy of the rhetorical dimension in the analysis of the historical text and the impossibility of establishing any direct reference to some aspects at least of the concrete reality that we call the Shoah.[11] Moreover, it would exclude any ongoing quest for a stable historical representation. Obviously, the achievement of a total stability of this history and of some totalizing interpretation is neither possible nor desirable. However, coming closer to significant historical linkage seems to me to be necessary; it is the corollary of my previous remarks about the growing fragmentation of the history of the Nazi period as a defensive mechanism or as the result of some paralysis on the side of the victims. In a sense, what is suggested here is the simultaneous acceptance of two contradictory moves: the search for ever-closer historical linkages and the avoidance of a naive historical positivism leading to simplistic and self-assured historical narrations and closures.

THE PRESENCE OF COMMENTARY

The self-awareness of the historian of the Nazi epoch or the Shoah is essential. Such self-awareness itself should be accessible to critical reading. It seems therefore that this difficult historical quest imposes the sporadic but forceful presence of commentary. Whether this commentary is built into the narrative structure of a history or developed as a separate, superimposed text is a matter of choice, but the voice of the commentator must be clearly heard. The commentary should disrupt the facile linear progression of the narration, introduce alternative interpretations, question any partial conclusion, withstand the need for closure. Because of the necessity of some form of narrative sequence in the writing of history, such commentary may introduce splintered or constantly recurring refractions of a traumatic past by using any number of different vantage points.

The dimension added by the commentary may allow for an integration of the so-called mythic memory of the victims within the overall representation of this past without its becoming an obstacle to rational historiography. For instance, whereas the historical narrative may have to stress the ordinary aspects of everyday life during most of the twelve years of the Nazi epoch, the 'voice-over' of the victims' memories may puncture such normality, at least at the level of commentary.

The reintroduction of individual memory into the overall representation of the epoch implies the use of the contemporaries' direct or indirect expressions of their experience. Working through means confronting the individual voice in a field dominated by political decisions and administrative decrees which neutralize the concreteness of despair and death. The *Alltagsgeschichte* of German society has its necessary shadow: the *Alltagsgeschichte* of the victims. In a letter of June 1939, Walter Benjamin noted the following item: the Viennese gas company had stopped supplying its Jewish clients, since precisely the most important consumers were using gas to commit suicide and consequently leaving their bills unpaid.[12]

Commentary does not lead in any way to 'the use of fact and fiction, document and imaginative reconstruction, to ponder how history is made.'[13] But, working through does mean a confrontation with the starkest factual information, which loses its historical weight when merely taken as data. Raul Hilberg mentions a report sent by the German military headquarters in the Black Sea port of Mariupol in 1941. In only a single line it stated that '8,000 Jews were executed by the Security Service.'[14] Working through ultimately means testing the limits of necessary and ever-defeated imagination.

TENTATIVE SUMMATION

Whether one considers the Shoah as an exceptional event or as belonging to a wider historical category does not affect the possibility of drawing from it a universally valid significance. The difficulty appears when this statement is reversed. No universal lesson seems to require reference to the Shoah to be fully comprehended. The Shoah carries an excess, and this excess is the 'something [that] remains to be phrased which is not, something which is not determined.'

At the individual level, a redemptive closure (comforting and healing in effect), desirable as it would be, seems largely impossible. At the collective level, however, regardless of the present salience of these events, there can hardly be any doubt that the passage of time will erase the 'excess.' Such erasure will, most probably, characterize the work of the majority of historians as well, perhaps because of what has been aptly called the 'de-sublimation' of the discipline.[15] Thus, if we make allowance for some sort of ritualized form of commemoration, already in place, we may foresee, in the public domain, a tendency toward closure without resolution, but closure nonetheless.

There are two potential exceptions to this rather bleak forecast: notwithstanding present patterns of historiography, an extension of historical awareness may be attempted, possibly along some of the lines previously suggested. In that sense, the traumatic past would lead to what Caruth considered a 'possibility of history,' 'a point of departure.'[16]

And there is a growing sensitivity in literature and art. The voices of a second generation are as powerful as the best work produced by contemporaries of the Nazi epoch. This sensitization is not limited to the community of the victims. Sometimes it appears in unexpected cultural contexts, as in the case of an Indian novelist who related to me that at this very time he is addressing himself to the Shoah. It may well be that for some the trauma, the insuperable moral outrage, the riddle whose decoding never seems to surrender a fully comprehensible text, may present an ongoing emotional and intellectual challenge. However, I would venture to suggest that even if new forms of historical narrative were to develop, or new modes of representation, and even if literature and art were to probe the past from unexpected vantage points, the opaqueness of some 'deep memory' would probably not be dispelled. 'Working through' may ultimately signify, in Maurice Blanchot's words, 'to keep watch over absent meaning.'[17]

NOTES

1. Dominick LaCapra, 'Representing the Holocaust: Reflections on the Historians' Debate,' in Saul Friedlander, ed., *Probing the Limits of Representation: National-Socialism and the 'Final Solution'* (Cambridge: Harvard University Press, 1992), p. 110. On a related issue, see LaCapra, 'The Personal, the Political and the Textual: Paul de Man as Object of Transference,' *History & Memory* 4/2 (1992).
2. See, for instance, Alexander and Margarete Mitscherlich, *The Inability to Mourn: Principles of Collective Behavior* (New York: Grove Press, 1975); Eric L. Santner, *Stranded Objects: Mourning, Memory, and Film in Postwar Germany* (Ithaca: Cornell University Press, 1990).
3. For an English translation of Martin Broszat's 'Plea for a Historicization of National Socialism' and for the subsequent exchange of letters between Broszat and myself, see Peter Baldwin, ed., *Reworking the Past*, (Boston: Beacon Press, 1990) pp. 102–34.
4. Ibid.
5. As early as the 1960s Jean Améry spoke of a growing 'entropy' in the writing of this history. See his *Radical Humanism: Selected Essays* (Bloomington: Indiana University Press, 1984), p. 65. Such 'entropy' has considerably increased during the last few years.
6. See, for instance, Rainer Zitelman and Michael Prinz, eds., *Nationalsozialismus und Modernisierung* (Darmstadt: Wissenschaftliche Buchgesellschaft, 1991). This is not always the case, but sometimes the framework is no less problematic than the lack of it. See Götz Aly and Susanne Heim, *Vordenker der Vernichtung: Auschwitz und die deutschen Pläne für eine neue europäische Ordnung* (Hamburg: Hoffmann and Campe, 1991).

7. Sigmund Freud, *Beyond the Pleasure Principle*, in *The Standard Edition of the Complete Psychological Works*, ed. and trans. James Strachey (London: Hogarth Press, 1953–74), 18:29.
8. Raul Hilberg, *The Destruction of the European Jews* (Chicago: Quadrangle Books, 1961).
9. Jean-François Lyotard, *The Differend: Phrases in Dispute* (Minneapolis: University of Minnesota Press, 1988), 56–57.
10. This is how my remarks were understood in a seminar held at Berkeley on 15 April 1992. I am grateful for the comments made on this occasion.
11. I have stated my position on this issue in somewhat different terms but with similar intent in my introduction to *Probing the Limits of Representation*.
12. [...] Walter Benjamin, *Briefe* 2, ed. Gershom Scholem and Theodor W. Adorno (Frankfurt/Main: Suhrkamp, 1978), p. 820.
13. From the dust jacket of Simon Schama, *Dead Certainties (Unwarranted Speculations)* (New York: Knopf, 1991).
14. Hilberg, 'I Was Not There,' in Berel Lang, ed., *Writing and the Holocaust* (New York: Holmes and Meier, 1988), p. 18.
15. Hayden White, 'The Politics of Historical Interpretation: Discipline and De-Sublimation,' *The Content of the Form: Narrative Discourse and Historical Representation* (Baltimore and London: Johns Hopkins University Press, 1987), pp. 58–82.
16. Caruth, 'Unclaimed Experience,' *Yale French Studies* 79 (1991): 192.
17. Maurice Blanchot, *The Writing of the Disaster* (Lincoln: University of Nebraska Press, 1986), p. 42.

24

'HISTORY BEYOND THE PLEASURE PRINCIPLE: SOME THOUGHTS ON THE REPRESENTATION OF TRAUMA'

Eric L. Santner

[...]

By narrative fetishism I mean the construction and deployment of a narrative consciously or unconsciously designed to expunge the traces of the trauma or loss that called that narrative into being in the first place. The use of narrative as fetish may be contrasted with that rather different mode of symbolic behavior that Freud called *Trauerarbeit* or the 'work of mourning.' Both narrative fetishism and mourning are responses to loss, to a past that refuses to go away due to its traumatic impact. The work of mourning is a process of elaborating and integrating the reality of loss or traumatic shock by remembering and repeating it in symbolically and dialogically mediated doses; it is a process of translating, troping, and figuring loss [...]. Narrative fetishism, by contrast, is the way an inability or refusal to mourn emplots traumatic events; it is a strategy of undoing, in fantasy, the need for mourning by simulating a condition of intactness, typically by situating the site and origin of loss elsewhere. Narrative fetishism releases one from the burden of having to reconstitute one's self-identity under 'posttraumatic' conditions; in narrative fetishism, the 'post' is indefinitely postponed.

Here, of course, it might be said that it is unrealistic and may perhaps even represent a sort of category mistake to expect that historiography could or should perform *Trauerarbeit*. Historians, after all, strive for intellectual and not

From Eric L. Santner (1992) 'History beyond the Pleasure Principle: Some Thoughts on the Representation of Trauma', in S. Friedlander (ed.), *Probing the Limits of Representation: Nazism and the 'FInal Solution'*. Cambridge, MA: Harvard University Press.

psychic mastery of events. In this context I would recall LaCapra's deconstruction of this opposition between intellectual and psychic mastery, cognitive and affective dimensions of representation, 'scientific' and 'mythic' or 'ritualized' approaches to the past.[1] As LaCapra's reading of the historians' debate suggests, one might argue that because of the kinds and intensities of transferential dynamics it calls forth, a traumatic event is by definition one that implicates the historian in labors of psychic mastery. Any historical account of such an event will, in other words, include, explicitly or implicitly, an elaboration of what might be called the historian's own context of survivorship. [...] Central to any elaboration of survivorship is, I would argue, the work of mourning. As should be clear by now, my primary concern in the present context is with the tasks and burdens of mourning that continue to afflict and, as it were, interrupt processes of identity formation in postwar Germany. In other words, I am concerned here with the project and *dilemma* of elaborating a post-Holocaust German national and cultural identity. Germans are faced with the paradoxical task of having to constitute their 'Germanness' in the awareness of the horrors generated by a previous production of national and cultural identity.[2]

Perhaps Freud's most compelling characterization of the work of mourning is his discussion, in *Beyond the Pleasure Principle*, of the *fort/da* game that he had observed in the behavior of his one-and-a-half-year-old grandson. In this game the child is seen to master his grief over separation from the mother by staging his own performance of disappearance and return with props that D. W. Winnicott would call transitional objects. Bereft by the mother's absence, [...] he reenacts the opening of that abysmal interval within the controlled space of a primitive ritual. The child is translating, as it were, his fragmented narcissism [...] into the formalized rhythms of symbolic behavior; thanks to this procedure, he is able to administer in controlled doses the absence he is mourning. The capacity to dose out and to represent absence by means of substitutive figures at a remove from what one might call their 'transcendental signifier,' is what allows the child to avoid psychotic breakdown and transform his lost sense of omnipotence into a chastened form of empowerment. [...]

The dosing out of a certain negative – thanatotic – element as a strategy of mastering a real and traumatic loss is a fundamentally homeopathic procedure. In a homeopathic procedure the controlled introduction of a negative element – a symbolic or, in medical contexts, real poison – helps to heal a system infected by a similar poisonous substance. [...] In the *fort/da* game it is the rhythmic manipulation of signifiers and figures, objects and syllables instituting an absence, that serves as the poison that cures. These signifiers are controlled symbolic doses of absence and renunciation that help the child to survive and (ideally) be empowered by the negativity of the mother's absence.

To put these matters in a somewhat different light, one might say that the work of mourning is the way human beings restore the regime of the pleasure principle in the wake of trauma or loss. I call your attention to Freud's remarks in *Beyond the Pleasure Principle*, shortly following his discussion of the *fort/da* game, regarding the behavior of *Unfallsneurotiker*, individuals who have experienced and then repressed some trauma but return to it over and over again in their dreams. Concerning this oneiric repetition compulsion, Freud says the following:

> We may assume . . . that dreams are here helping to carry out another task, which must be accomplished before the dominance of the pleasure principle can even begin. These dreams are endeavouring to master the stimulus retrospectively, by developing the anxiety whose omission was the cause of the traumatic neurosis. They thus afford us a view of a function of the mental apparatus which, though it does not contradict the pleasure principle, is nevertheless independent of it and seems to be more primitive than the purpose of gaining pleasure and avoiding unpleasure.[3]

Given the homologies Freud underlined between the symptoms of the trauma victim and the symbolic behavior of the child at play, one may conclude that these other, more primitive psychic tasks are the tasks of mourning that serve to constitute the self and that must, at some level, be reiterated with all later experiences of loss or traumatic shock [. . .]. Both the child trying to master his separateness from the mother and the trauma victim returning, in dream, to the site of shock are locked in a repetition compulsion: an effort to recuperate, in the controlled context of symbolic behavior, the *Angstbereitschaft* or readiness to feel anxiety, absent during the initial shock or loss. It was Freud's thought that the absence of appropriate affect – anxiety – rather than loss per se is what leads to traumatization. Until such anxiety has been recuperated and worked through, the loss will continue to represent a past that refuses to go away. At the end of this process of psychic mastery, the ego becomes, as Freud says elsewhere, 'free and uninhibited' and open to new libidinal investments, that is, open to object relations under the regime of the pleasure principle. Fetishism, as I am using the term here, is, by contrast, a strategy whereby one seeks voluntaristically to reinstate the pleasure principle without addressing and working through those other tasks which, as Freud insists, 'must be accomplished before the dominance of the pleasure principle can even begin.' Far from providing a symbolic space for the recuperation of anxiety, narrative fetishism directly or indirectly offers reassurances that there was no need for anxiety in the first place.

When Ernst Nolte asks – to return now to the context of the historians' debate – whether it is 'not likely that the Nazis and Hitler committed this "Asiatic" deed [the "Final Solution"] because they saw themselves and others like them as potential or real victims of an "Asiatic" deed [the gulag],'[4] he is, so to speak, inviting his readers to locate themselves in a place – call it simply somewhere to the west of Asia – where they can feel morally and psychologically unthreatened by the traumas and losses – what I am calling the psychotic risk – signified by

Nazism and the 'Final Solution.' According to Nolte, in this magical zone to the west of Asia, the regime of the pleasure principle was never in any danger.

[...]

Arguing his case several years ago for more vigorous, plastic, and richly colored narrative strategies of historicizing National Socialism, Martin Broszat bemoaned the fact that when historians turn to this period of history their capacity for empathic interpretation and what he called the 'pleasure in historical narration' [*die Lust am geschichtlichen Erzählen*] appears to be blocked.[5] Broszat's plea for historicization was thus, among other things, a plea for a certain primacy of the pleasure principle in historical narration even, paradoxically, when it comes to narrating events the traumatic impact of which would seem to call the normal functioning of that principle into question.[...]

Finally, I would like to discuss very briefly the dynamics of narrative fetishism as it functions in a realm of cultural production where narrative and visual pleasure freely intermingle, namely film.[6] I take my example from Edgar Reitz's hugely successful film *Heimat*, which was first broadcast on German television in the fall of 1984. [...] In the present context, [...] it is especially interesting to note that one of the effects of the film [...] has been to make the word 'Heimat' newly available for libidinal investment in Germany, if only as the elegiac token of something lost. [...] The word Heimat becomes, in and through Reitz's film, a site of competing narratives. A word – one might say a 'mytheme' – that has figured prominently in the story of the social marginalization and eventual destruction of European Jewry, is, as it were, reoccupied within a new ideological and narrative ensemble in which Germans can see and cathect themselves as bereft victim, as the dispossessed.

This reoccupation of 'Heimat' takes on further resonance when one recalls that Reitz made his as a kind of counterfilm to the American television production *Holocaust*. His own film was intended, in large part, as a strategy of reclaiming memories – and, perhaps more important, the pleasure in their narration – that Germans have been forced to renounce under the sway of the American culture industry in general and media events like *Holocaust* in particular. (Reitz polemically refers to the aesthetics embodied by *Holocaust* as the 'real terror' of the twentieth century.)[7] Germans have, Reitz claims, abandoned their unique, regionally inflected experiences and memories, because they have been morally terrorized by spectacles like *Holocaust*.[8] Reitz's own work of resistance to this 'terror' therefore lies in the salvaging of local experience, local history, local memories:

> There are thousands of stories among our people that are worth being filmed, that are based on irritatingly detailed experiences which apparently do not contribute to judging or explaining history, but whose sum total would actually fill this gap. We mustn't let ourselves be prevented

from taking our personal lives seriously [...] The most serious act of expropriation occurs when a person is deprived of his or her own history. With *Holocaust*, the Americans have taken away our history.[9]

With *Heimat*, the pleasure in the historical narration of twentieth-century German history is taken back and reinstated with a vengeance. But as numerous critics have noted, Reitz's restoration of narrative and visual pleasure would seem to proceed along the route of the fetish, that is, at the price of disavowing the trauma signified by the 'Final Solution.' Here it is important to keep in mind that one can acknowledge the *fact* of an event, that is, that it happened, and yet continue to disavow the traumatizing impact of the same event.

The scene that perhaps best illustrates the fetishistic aspect of Reitz's particular deployment of narrative and visual pleasure comes in the first episode of the film. [...] It is 1923; Eduard and Pauline make an afternoon excursion to Simmern, the largest town near Schabbach. Pauline wanders off alone and finds herself looking at the window display of the town watchmaker and jeweler. Suddenly a group of young men run up behind her – including Eduard, armed as usual with camera and tripod – and begin throwing rocks at the window of the apartment above the watchmaker's shop where, as we learn, a Jew – in this case also branded as a separatist – resides. They are chased off by police, but the shards of fallen glass have cut Pauline's hand. Robert Kröber, the watchmaker, signals her to come into the shop where he cleans her wound, thereby initiating the love story of Pauline and Robert. Later on in the film – it is 1933 – we hear that the now married Pauline and Robert are buying the Jew's apartment. As Robert remarks, 'The house belongs to him and now he wants to sell it ... The Jews don't have it so easy anymore.'

This small Kristallnacht sequence shows how the shards of the Jew's shattered existence – we never see him in the flesh – are immediately absorbed into a sentimental story of love and courtship in the provinces. Though it is the filmmaker who alerts us to the ways in which experience (and narrative) construct themselves around such blind spots, Reitz refuses to allow such potentially traumatic moments to disrupt the economy of narrative and visual pleasure maintained throughout his fifteen and a half hours of film. This consistency is surely one of the reasons for the incredible success of the film. *Heimat* offers its viewers the opportunity to witness a chronicle of twentieth-century German history in which *die Lust am geschichtlichen Erzählen* is never in any serious danger.

I have argued in these pages that Nazism and the 'Final Solution' need to be theorized under the sign of massive trauma, meaning that these events must be confronted and analyzed in their capacity to endanger and overwhelm the composition and coherence of individual and collective identities that enter into their deadly field of force. To use, once more, metaphors suggested by Freud's discussion of traumatic neurosis, the events in question may represent for those whose lives have been touched by them, even across

25

'BEARING WITNESS OR THE VICISSITUDES OF LISTENING'

Dori Laub

A RECORD THAT HAS YET TO BE MADE

The listener to the narrative of extreme human pain, of massive psychic trauma, faces a unique situation. In spite of the presence of ample documents, of searing artifacts and of fragmentary memoirs of anguish, he comes to look for something that is in fact nonexistent; a record that has yet to be made. Massive trauma precludes its registration; the observing and recording mechanisms of the human mind are temporarily knocked out, malfunction. The victim's narrative – the very process of bearing witness to massive trauma – does indeed begin with someone who testifies to an absence, to an event that has not yet come into existence, in spite of the overwhelming and compelling nature of the reality of its occurrence. While historical evidence to the event which constitutes the trauma may be abundant and documents in vast supply, the trauma – as a known event and not simply as an overwhelming shock – has not been truly witnessed yet, not been taken cognizance of. The emergence of the narrative which is being listened to – and heard – is, therefore, the process and the place wherein the cognizance, the 'knowing' of the event is given birth to. The listener, therefore, is a party to the creation of knowledge *de novo*. The testimony to the trauma thus includes its hearer, who is, so to speak, the blank screen on which the event comes to be inscribed for the first time.

From Dori Laub (1992) 'Bearing Witness or the Vicissitudes of Listening', in S. Felman and D. Laub (eds), *Testimony: Crises of Witnessing in Literature, Psychoanalysis, and History*. New York and London: Routledge.

By extension, the listener to trauma comes to be a participant and a co-owner of the traumatic event: through his very listening, he comes to partially experience trauma in himself. The relation of the victim to the event of the trauma, therefore, impacts on the relation of the listener to it, and the latter comes to feel the bewilderment, injury, confusion, dread and conflicts that the trauma victim feels. He has to address all these, if he is to carry out his function as a listener, and if trauma is to emerge, so that its henceforth impossible witnessing can indeed take place. The listener, therefore, by definition partakes of the struggle of the victim with the memories and residues of his or her traumatic past. The listener has to feel the victim's victories, defeats and silences, know them from within, so that they can assume the form of testimony.

The listener, however, is also a separate human being and will experience hazards and struggles of his own, while carrying out his function of a witness to the trauma witness. While overlapping, to a degree, with the experience of the victim, he nonetheless does not become the victim – he preserves his own separate place, position and perspective; a battleground for forces raging in himself, to which he has to pay attention and respect if he is to properly carry out his task.

The listener, therefore, has to be at the same time a witness to the trauma witness and a witness to himself. It is only in this way, through his simultaneous awareness of the continuous flow of those inner hazards both in the trauma witness and in himself, that he can become the enabler of the testimony – the one who triggers its initiation, as well as the guardian of its process and of its momentum.

The listener to trauma, therefore, needs to know 'the lay of the land' – the landmarks, the undercurrents, and the pitfalls in the witness and in himself. He needs to know that the trauma survivor who is bearing witness has no prior knowledge, no comprehension and no memory of what happened. That he or she profoundly fears such knowledge, shrinks away from it and is apt to close off at any moment, when facing it. He needs to know that such knowledge dissolves all barriers, breaks all boundaries of time and place, of self and subjectivity. That the speakers about trauma on some level prefer silence so as to protect themselves from the fear of being listened to – and of listening to themselves. That while silence is defeat, it serves them both as a sanctuary and as a place of bondage. Silence is for them a fated exile, yet also a home, a destination, and a binding oath. To *not* return from this silence is rule rather than exception.

The listener must know all this and more. He or she must *listen to and hear the silence*, speaking mutely both in silence and in speech, both from behind and from within the speech. He or she must recognize, acknowledge and address that silence, even if this simply means respect – and knowing how to wait. The listener to trauma needs to know all this, so as to be a guide and an explorer, a companion in a journey onto an uncharted land, a journey the survivor cannot traverse or return from alone.

TESTIMONY AND HISTORICAL TRUTH

A woman in her late sixties was narrating her Auschwitz experience to interviewers from the Video Archive for Holocaust Testimonies at Yale. She was slight, self-effacing, almost talking in whispers, mostly to herself. Her presence was indeed barely noteworthy in spite of the overwhelming magnitude of the catastrophe she was addressing. She tread lightly, leaving hardly a trace.

She was relating her memories as an eyewitness of the Auschwitz uprising; a sudden intensity, passion and color were infused into the narrative. She was fully there. 'All of sudden,' she said, 'we saw four chimneys going up in flames, exploding. The flames shot into the sky, people were running. It was unbelievable.' There was a silence in the room, a fixed silence against which the woman's words reverberated loudly, as though carrying along an echo of the jubilant sounds exploding from behind barbed wires, a stampede of people breaking loose, screams, shots, battle cries, explosions. It was no longer the deadly timelessness of Auschwitz. A dazzling, brilliant moment from the past swept through the frozen stillness of the muted, grave-like landscape with dashing meteoric speed, exploding it into a shower of sights and sounds. Yet the meteor from the past kept moving on. The woman fell silent and the tumults of the moment faded. She became subdued again and her voice resumed the uneventful, almost monotonous and lamenting tone. The gates of Auschwitz closed and the veil of obliteration and of silence, at once oppressive and repressive, descended once again. The comet of intensity and of aliveness, the explosion of vitality and of resistance faded and receeded into the distance.

Many months later, a conference of historians, psychoanalysts, and artists, gathered to reflect on the relation of education to the Holocaust, watched the videotaped testimony of the woman, in an attempt to better understand the era. A lively debate ensued. The testimony was not accurate, historians claimed. The number of chimneys was misrepresented. Historically, only one chimney was blown up, not all four. Since the memory of the testifying woman turned out to be, in this way, fallible, one could not accept – nor give credence to – her whole account of the events. It was utterly important to remain accurate, lest the revisionists in history discredit everything.

A psychoanalyst who had been one of the interviewers of this woman, profoundly disagreed. 'The woman was testifying,' he insisted, 'not to the number of the chimneys blown up, but to something else, more radical, more crucial: the reality of an unimaginable occurrence. One chimney blown up in Auschwitz was as incredible as four. The number mattered less than the fact of the occurrence. The event itself was almost inconceivable. The woman testified to an event that broke the all compelling frame of Auschwitz, where Jewish armed revolts just did not happen, and had no place. She testified to the breakage of a framework. That was historical truth.'

The psychoanalyst who had interviewed that woman happened to have been myself, and though my attitude vis-à-vis her testimony was different than the attitude of the historians, I had myself the opportunity of encountering – during the very process of the interviewing – questions similar in nature to those that the historians were now raising. And yet I had to deal with those objections and those questions in a different manner.

I figured from the woman's testimony that in Auschwitz she had been a member of what is known as 'the Canada commando,' a group of inmates chosen to sort out the belongings of those who had been gassed, so that those belongings could be recuperated by the Nazis and sent back to Germany. The testifying woman spoke indeed at length of her work in a commando that would leave each morning, separately from the others, and return every night with various items of clothes and shoes in excellent condition. She emphasized with pride the way in which, upon returning, she would supply these items to her fellow inmates, thus saving the lives of some of them who literally had no shoes to walk in and no clothes to protect them from the frost. She was perking up again as she described these almost breathtaking exploits of rescue. I asked her if she knew of the name of the commando she was serving on. She did not. Does the term 'Canada commando' mean anything to her? I followed up. 'No,' she said, taken aback, as though startled by my question. I asked nothing more about her work. I had probed the limits of her knowledge and decided to back off; to respect, that is, the silence out of which this testimony spoke. We did not talk of the sorting out of the belongings of the dead. She did not think of them as the remainings of the thousands who were gassed. She did not ask herself where they had come from. The presents she brought back to her fellow inmates, the better, newer clothes and shoes, had for her no origin.

My attempt as interviewer and as listener was precisely to respect – not to upset, not to trespass – the subtle balance between what the woman *knew* and what she *did not*, or *could not, know*. It was only at the price of this respect, I felt, this respect of the constraints and of the boundaries of silence, that what the woman *did know* in a way that none of us did – what she came to testify about – could come forth and could receive, indeed, a hearing. The historians' stance, however, differed from my way of listening, in their firm conviction that the limits of the woman's knowledge in effect called into question the validity of her whole testimony.

'Don't you see,' one historian passionately exclaimed, 'that the woman's eyewitness account of the uprising that took place at Auschwitz is hopelessly misleading in its incompleteness? She had no idea what was going on. She ascribes importance to an attempt that, historically, made no difference. Not only was the revolt put down and all the inmates executed; the Jewish underground was, furthermore, betrayed by the Polish resistance, which had promised to assist in the rebellion, but failed to do so. When the attempt to break out of the camps began, the Jewish inmates found themselves completely alone. No one joined their ranks. They flung themselves into their death, alone and in desperation.'

When I interviewed the woman, I knew, of course, that the Auschwitz uprising was put down, but I myself did not know the specific contribution of the Polish underground to the defeat: I did not know of the extent of the betrayal.

Had I known, however, would I have questioned her about it? Probably not, since such questions might have in effect suppressed her message, suppressed what she was there to tell me.

Had I known, moreover, I might have had an agenda of my own that might have interferred with my ability to listen, and to hear. I might have felt driven to confirm my knowledge, by asking questions that could have derailed the testimony, and by proceeding to hear everything she had to say in light of what I knew already. And whether my agenda would have been historical or psychoanalytical, it might unwittingly have interfered with the process of the testimony. In this respect, it might be useful, sometimes, not to know too much.

Of course, it is by no means ignorance that I espouse. The listener must be quite well informed if he is to be able to hear – to be able to pick up the cues. Yet knowledge should not hinder or obstruct the listening with foregone conclusions and preconceived dismissals, should not be an obstacle or a foreclosure to new, diverging, unexpected information.

In the process of the testimony to a trauma, as in psychoanalytic practice, in effect, you often do not want to know anything except what the patient tells you, because what is important is the situation of *discovery* of knowledge – its evolution, and its very *happening*. Knowledge in the testimony is, in other words, not simply a factual given that is reproduced and replicated by the testifier, but a genuine advent, an event in its own right. In a case such as this witness, for example, I had to be particularly careful that what I knew would not affect – would not obstruct, coerce, or overshadow – what she was there to tell me. I had, in fact, to be all the more cautious because this testifying woman did not simply come to convey knowledge that was already safely, and exhaustively, in her possession. On the contrary, it was her very talk to me, the very process of her bearing witness to the trauma she had lived through, that helped her now to come to know of the event. And it was through my listening to her that I in turn came to understand not merely her subjective truth, but the very historicity of the event, in an entirely new dimension.

She was testifying not simply to empirical historical facts, but to the very secret of survival and of resistance to extermination. The historians could not hear, I thought, the way in which her silence was itself part of her testimony, an essential part of the historical truth she was precisely bearing witness to. She saw four chimneys blowing up in Auschwitz: she saw, in other words, the unimaginable taking place right in front of her own eyes. And she came to testify to the unbelievability, precisely, of what she had eyewitnessed – this bursting open of the very frame of Auschwitz. The historians' testifying to the fact that only one chimney was blown up in Auschwitz, as well as to the fact of the betrayal of the Polish underground, does not break the frame. The woman's testimony, on the other hand, is breaking the frame of the concentration camp by and through her very testimony: she is breaking out of Auschwitz even by her very talking. She had come, indeed, to testify, not to the empirical number of the chimneys, but to resistance, to the affirmation of survival, to the breakage of the frame of death; in the same way, she had come to testify not to betrayal, nor to her actual removal of the belongings of the dead, but to her vital memory of helping people, to her effective rescuing of lives. This was her way of being, of surviving, of resisting. It is not merely her speech, but the very boundaries of silence which surround it, which attest, today as well as in the past, to this assertion of resistance.

There is thus a subtle dialectic between what the survivor did not know and what she knew; between what I as interviewer did not know and what I knew; between what the historians knew and what they did not know. Because the testifier did not know the number of the chimneys that blew up; because she did not know of the betrayal of the Polish underground and of the violent and desperate defeat of the rebellion of the Auschwitz inmates, the historians said that she knew nothing. I thought that she knew more, since she knew about the breakage of the frame, that her very testimony was now reenacting.

PART VI
QUESTIONS OF RELIGION, ETHICS, AND JUSTICE

QUESTIONS OF RELIGION, ETHICS, AND JUSTICE: INTRODUCTION

The questions of ethics and justice that the Holocaust poses are notoriously easy to ask and difficult to answer: How could this happen? How can it be prevented from ever happening again? Such questions are implicit in various texts throughout this book, but they are confronted most directly in this section, where authors inquire into the nature of western moral traditions and why these traditions could not prevent industrialized murder, and into the ethical and political consequences to be drawn from the very occurrence of the Nazi genocide. The entries also reveal different positions on the relationship between the terms ethics and justice themselves, and their relative importance in developing a response to Auschwitz. Arguments about the state of Israel and the value of war crimes trials compete for precedence with reflections on the nature of human subjectivity and the complicity of the western philosophical tradition.

Given the deep mutual implication of religious thought and moral philosophy in the West, it was inevitable that theology too would grapple with such issues. Admittedly, thinkers such as Amos Funkenstein have questioned the very validity of theological inquiry into the Holocaust, since Auschwitz was made by men, not God. We nevertheless begin this chapter with selections that address broadly religious questions, not only because such work belongs to the tradition of post-Holocaust theoretical reflection as we understand it, but also because the confrontation with radical human evil is actually at the center of much theology since the war. Drawing from the concept of the divine tremendum, which describes the awe-ful, terrified encounter of humans with the divine, theologian Arthur A. Cohen develops the notion of a human tremendum to describe the collapse of structures of meaning and understanding in the face of the Holocaust. The philosopher Emil L. Fackenheim formulates a new commandment for the Jewish people: not to grant Hitler any posthumous victories. The new commandment serves, among other things, as a basis for Fackenheim's commitment to the Jewish state. It should also be noted that the very idea of writing a new commandment (itself widely disputed) demonstrates Fackenheim's sense of the incompletion of the commandments as handed down to Moses, and thus his sense of the need for Judaism to expose itself to modification, even possible refutation, by historical events.

For Fackenheim, then, the Holocaust raises questions for Jewish belief and practice; for other thinkers, western, European, or even simply German traditions of ethical and political thought must come under the closest scrutiny after Auschwitz. Central to this line of inquiry has been the work of the Jewish philosopher Emmanuel Levinas, who devoted his career to developing a philosophy explicitly conceived as an alternative to western philosophy since Plato. The Lithuanian-born Levinas, whose family was murdered by the Nazis, claims that the western philosophical tradition has always begun its inquiries with questions about the nature of being and knowledge, and that such questions are essentially egocentric and complicit with violence toward 'the other.' He proposes that philosophy should begin instead with the ethical relation, with the subject's necessary response to and responsibility for the other, a relation predicated not on knowledge and active mastery but ignorance and open passivity. Levinas thus aims to reverse the western philosophical tradition's privileging of 'the same' against the other. 'Ethics and Spirit' is typical of Levinas's thought in many ways, not least in that it does not directly refer to the Holocaust. For many interpreters, however, such essays clearly critique the logic of Nazism, which took the celebration of the same and violence towards the other to its most radical conclusion.

Our selection from the German-Jewish political philosopher Hannah Arendt focuses directly on the question of justice. In *Eichmann in Jerusalem*, which she based on her report on the 1961 trial in Israel of Adolf Eichmann, Arendt examines the novel politico-juridical challenges raised by the Nazi regime's crimes. Severely criticizing the manner in which the Israelis conducted the trial, she claims that the main issue the trial *should* have raised is how to render justice (rather than avenge or give voice to the victims) in the face of an unprecedented crime. Arendt is convinced that once something new enters the world, its reappearance is more likely; her reflections, then, are meant to outline the needs of a global legal order that may well face further genocidal projects.

The Italian philosopher Giorgio Agamben also focuses on a conspicuous feature of the Nazi regime that he sees repeated throughout the modern world. His essay, 'What is a Camp?', takes Carl Schmitt's concept of the 'state of exception' as its point of departure. In the state of exception sovereign power declares a suspension of the law, purportedly in order to preserve the legal order. Agamben argues that a camp is not simply one of a series of proper names including Auschwitz and Buchenwald, but a set of conditions that obtain wherever the state of exception is spatialized, be it surrounded by barbed wire, or in an airport or a soccer stadium. Those subject to the state of exception in the camp constitute 'bare' or 'naked' life, a condition which Agamben explains in a later work (*Homo Sacer*) means that they can be killed with impunity. Agamben's project shares with Zygmunt Bauman's (see Part II) the desire to locate political and legal conditions essential to the Holocaust and expose and criticize their continuing role.

Like Agamben, the English philosopher-sociologist Gillian Rose views Auschwitz as of a piece with a larger analysis of modernity. She sees the definitive crisis of modern society to lie in the separation of the realms of law and ethics. In her complex, often obscure magnum opus, *The Broken Middle*, Rose critiques a series of attempts in philosophy, theology, and sociology (including those by Levinas, Fackenheim, and Bauman) to respond to Auschwitz. Rose sees these authors as locating the Holocaust in a failure of either ethics or law. They then offer utopian solutions based on a fetishization of the other, privileged term: thus Bauman critiques modern institutions and calls for an ahistorical return to ethics, while Fackenheim rejects disengaged religious community and calls for Jews to found state institutions. Rose believes that in practice these strategies tend to reproduce the very violence they are meant to prevent. She insists instead on 'the equivocation of the ethical,' which seems to mean that we learn to live with, rather than find Manichean 'final' solutions to, the constitutive anxieties and ambivalences of modern life.

The French philosopher Jean-François Lyotard's reflections on Auschwitz are located at the intersection of the ethical and the legal. Like Hannah Arendt, Lyotard wants to prevent entrenched forms of thinking and judging from stifling recognition of and response to new situations. He too sees Auschwitz as that event which most acutely challenges established forms of thought and requires their reformulation if not outright abandonment. The 'differend' describes situations where an act or condition of oppression is articulated and yet is refused recognition, as, for example, when a Holocaust denier rejects the testimony of a survivor of the camps as inappropriate evidence for the existence of the gas chambers. There is a juridical component to Lyotard's work insofar as the very notion of the differend presupposes situations of conflict in need of resolution through judgment, where there is no shared ground or language from which the judgment can be made. The ethical demand Lyotard hears in the differend is a constant readiness to bear witness to and find a language for wrongs that have not yet been recognized and articulated as such. Lyotard thereby continues Levinas's identification of post-Holocaust ethics with a turn away from established knowledge and towards an openness to alterity.

The world has not changed enough since 1945 for these issues to have lost their urgency. Programs to wipe groups of people from the face of the earth in the name of 'ethnic cleansing' and historical retribution have continued in recent years with horrifying results, giving the lie to post-Holocaust promises of 'never again.' The measures taken by many western nations in the wake of the current war on terrorism have transformed Agamben's reflections from somewhat hyperbolic speculation to common sense. The rise of the truth and reconciliation commission model in Africa and Latin America offers an optimistic reworking of Arendt's ideas about justice after genocide, but how effective this model will be remains to be seen.

OTHER WORKS IN HOLOCAUST STUDIES

Agamben, Giorgio (1999) *Remnants of Auschwitz: The Witness and the Archive*, trans. Daniel Heller-Roazen. New York: Zone Books.
Douglas, Lawrence (2001) *The Memory of Judgment: Making Law and History in the Trials of the Holocaust*. New Haven, CT: Yale University Press.
Felman, Shoshana (2001) 'Theaters of Justice: Arendt in Jerusalem, the Eichmann Trial, and the Redefinition of Legal Meaning in the Wake of the Holocaust,' *Critical Inquiry*, 27.2.
Geras, Norman (1998) *The Contract of Mutual Indifference: Political Philosophy after the Holocaust*. New York: Verso.
Rose, Gillian (1993) *Judaism and Modernity: Philosophical Essays*. New York: Basil Blackwell.
Todorov, Tzvetan (1997) *Facing the Extreme: Moral Life in the Concentration Camps*, trans. Arthur Denner and Abigail Pollack. New York: Henry Holt.
Wyschogrod, Edith (1985) *Spirit in Ashes: Hegel, Heidegger, and Man-Made Mass Death*. New Haven, CT: Yale University Press.

RELEVANT THEORETICAL STUDIES

Agamben, Giorgio (1998) *Homo Sacer: Sovereign Power and Bare Life*, trans. Daniel Heller-Roazen. Stanford, CA: Stanford University Press.
Badiou, Alain (2001) *Ethics: An Essay on the Understanding of Evil*, trans. Peter Hallward. New York: Verso.
Bernstein, J. M. (2001) *Adorno: Disenchantment and Ethics*, New York: Cambridge University Press.
Derrida, Jacques (2002) *Acts of Religion*, ed. Gil Anidjar. New York: Routledge.
Funkenstein, Amos (1993) *Perceptions of Jewish History*. Berkeley and Los Angeles, CA:.University of California Press.
Nussbaum, Martha C. (1995) *Poetic Justice: The Literary Imagination and Public Life*. Boston: Beacon Press.

26

'THINKING THE TREMENDUM'

Arthur A. Cohen

[...]

Whatever we may learn from history, moral philosophy, psychopathology, or political science about the conditions which preceded and promoted the death camps, or the behavior of oppressors and victims which obtained within the death camps, is unavailing. All analysis holds us within the normative kingdom of reason, and however the palpable irrationality of the events, the employment of rational analysis is inappropriate. I do not feel the calm of reason to be obscene as some critics of the rational inquiry into the *tremendum* have described it. It is not obscene for human beings to try to retain their sanity before an event which disorders sanity. It is a decent and plausible undertaking. It is simply inappropriate and unavailing. Probative inquiry and dispassionate reason have no place in the consideration of the death camps, precisely because reason possesses a moral vector. To reason, that is to estimate and evaluate, is to employ discernment and discrimination before a moral ambiguity. The *tremendum* is beyond the discourse of morality and rational condemnation. It is not that the death camps were absolutely evil. Such judgments do not help. It is not enough to pronounce them absolutely evil. Absolute evil is a paradigm. There is nothing to which we can point in the history of men and nations which is absolutely evil, although the criterion of that abstraction has helped moralists to pronounce upon the relative evils of history.

From Arthur A. Cohen (1993) 'Thinking the Tremendum', in *The Tremendum: A Theological Interpretation of the Holocaust*. New York: Continuum.

Absolute evil – even if it designated something real – would be an inept formulation, for what does it mean, in fact, to say of some thing or event that it is absolutely evil? It means only that we can conceive of no greater evil, whereas in truth we can: we can conceive of a system that can murder all life (assuming, of course, that abundant life is an absolute good), but clearly this adds nothing to our absolute but exaggeration. We look for qualitative enrichment of our moral sensibility, a texturing and refinement, while all our language before the event presses us to grosser and more extreme formulations.

The relativity of evil in the deliberations of moralists rarely entails the exposition of the relative good. Relative evils do not complete themselves by the description of relative goods. Relative evil is measured in the mind against absolute evil. Of course, such a logic of moral experience has an ultimate reckoning. If it is commonplace for human beings to free themselves from the paradigm of the absolute, it becomes ever easier to ignore or to excuse transgression. Human beings learn to rationalize and justify so artfully and so well that the right time passes unobserved, when they should have shouted 'no, not this, not this.' But, of course, it is hard in a shouting and busy world, continuously assaulted by interests and needs, for any single human being to be heard warning against evil. During such times, the recognition that there are indeed absolute evils (even though abstractly described) has not prevented us from accumulating a mountain of small evils which, like the bricks of the Tower of Babel, might one day reach up and pierce the heavens. The point of this is to suggest that moral convention, a pragmatic regimen of norms and *regulae* of behavior retain their authority only so long as the absolute evil of which they are special and modest *exempla* remains abstract and unrealized. When absolute evil ceases, however, to be the abstract warning of the impending and possible and comes to be, how shall the descriptive domains of the moral and immoral retain their authority? Can one doubt the relevance of this to the politics of the twentieth century? Until the end of the eighteenth century the political theory of Europe centered about philosophies of law, right, duty, and freedom. It was understood that the relation of citizen and state was somehow a moral relation, that the citizen was a person educated to freedoms and informed by respon-sibilities. In our time such language has virtually disappeared from public inquiry and debate. The language of politics is not that of moral interaction and representation, but the calibration and weighting of power, influence, need, control in such fashion as to guarantee for one's own constituency a larger and measurably greater security both for and against uncontested aggression. Questions of right and law, of justice and equity have virtually disappeared as moral criteria for social and political action. The consequence of all this – the process of the demoralization of the political – is the consequent irrelevance of the 'absolute' and the 'utter' as the adjectival thunder of the putatively relative. What civilization once called murder or barbarism or cruelty or sadism has in our day become a useless rhetoric. Not one of us can summon these words with the authority with which John Milton or Voltaire might have spoken them, and few can hear the English rendering of the Hebrew prophets with little more than a recognition of their immense eloquence. Words no longer command us, precisely because they no longer reflect concepts and convictions which directly govern and thereby agitate conscience.

If this analysis is correct, it will be readily understood why I have come to regard the death camps as a new event, one severed from connection with the traditional presuppositions of history, psychology, politics, and morality. Anything which we might have known before the *tremendum* of this event is rendered conditional by its utterness and extremity. Note that I have not referred to Auschwitz as the name by which to concretize and transmit the reality of the *tremendum*. Auschwitz was only one among many sites of death. It was not even the largest death camp, although it may well have claimed the largest number of victims. Auschwitz is a particularity, a name, a specific. Auschwitz is the German name for a Polish name. It is a name which belongs to *them*. It is not a name which commemorates. It is both specific and other. And, if my perception is correct, what occurred then, from the time of the conception of the 'Final Solution' until the time that surreal 'idealism' was interrupted, is the transmutation of chosen persons into chosen people, of the scandal of Jewish particularity and doggedness into the scandal of Jewish universality. What might have been, until the time of the Final Solution, a controversy about the particularism and insularity of Judaism in contradistinction to the dogma of nationalist anti-Semites who wanted a Jewry divested of Judaism and Jewish identity, or a Jewish theological reform which wanted Jews rehabilitated by Western humanism and *Kultur*, or a Zionism which wanted Jews tied both to self-determination and socialist class consciousness in the struggle against Jewish temerity and timorousness, became in the death camps the brute factuality of the universal. Not the individual Jew, not the martyred Jew, not the survived Jew – not a Jew by any name or fortune – not such a Jew of particularity was chosen. Jew, simple Jew, nominative universal describing and containing all mankind that bears that racial lineament until the third generation of ancestry, became chosen and was universalized. The death camps ended forever one argument of history – whether the Jews are a chosen people. They are chosen, unmistakably, extremely, utterly.

[. . .]

[. . .] Is it not the case that in such a civilization all that was once permitted to the infinite power of God and denied to the finite and constrained power of men is now denied to the forgotten God and given over to the potency of infinitized man? Caution: I am not proposing in this yet another gloss to the familiar discussion of Faustian man compacted to the devil, with all its attendant critique of technology, machine-culture dehumanization. The argument here is different. It is the proposal of a counter to the *mysterium tremendum*. It is the human *tremendum*, the enormity of an infinitized man, who no longer seems to fear death or, perhaps more to the point, fears it so completely, denies death so mightily, that the only patent of his refutation and denial is to build a mountain of corpses to the divinity of the dead, to placate death by the magic of endless murder.

I call the death camps the *tremendum*, for it is the monument of a meaningless inversion of life to an orgiastic celebration of death, to a psychosexual and pathological degeneracy unparalleled and unfathomable to any person bonded to life. [...]

[...] We must return again and again to break our head upon the *tremendum* of the abyss, a phenomenon without analogue, discontinuous from all that has been, new beginning for the human race that knew not of what it was capable, willing to destroy and to be destroyed. We must create a new language in which to speak of this in order to destroy the old language which, in its decrepitude and decline, made facile and easy the demonic descent. When the preparations are completed, then the new beginning of the race which started in that quintessential perfection of the abyss must be thought (lest it be considered unthinkable) and redescribed (lest it be considered indescribable) and reconnected to the whole of the past (lest the abyss never be closed) and projected into the future (lest the future imagine it has no share in that past). In that way, first by separating the *tremendum* from all things and descending into the abyss, then by rejoining the *tremendum* to the whole experience of mankind as endpoint of the abyss and new beginning of the race, it is possible to link again the death camps, the *tremendum* of the abyss, to the *mysterium tremendum* of God who is sometimes in love with creation and its creatures and sometimes, it must initially be thought, indifferent to their fate.

27

'TO MEND THE WORLD'

Emil L. Fackenheim

[...]

A Jew thinking of Hitler remembers Pharaoh, Amalek, Haman: closest is Haman. Pharoah enslaved the Israelites. Amalek attacked the weakest. It was Haman who planned to kill all the Jews. However, Haman failed, and Jews celebrate. They celebrate on Purim.

Christians, too, celebrate. Their greatest celebration is Easter. But just this Christian celebration has unhappy memories for Jews – and, after Auschwitz, for conscientious Christians also. Of these, one, a German pastor, once felt compelled to go so far as to begin his Easter sermon as follows: 'This is the day on which we take vengence on the Jews for killing Christ.'

In 1967 Purim and Easter fell on the same day. It also so happened that for this Purim-Easter there was scheduled in New York a symposium, 'Jewish Values in the Post-Holocaust Future' [...]. I, too, was asked to participate. All my instincts wished to refuse, but how could I? I accepted. It would be the first time for me to speak on the Holocaust [...].

[...]

[...] In all the preceding years, why had I avoided the painful subject? As I struggled with the now accepted task, this became all too clear. A stumbling block for the historian, what if the Holocaust were a stumbling block also for Judaism? The historian stumbles only on the 'big' question: what if a Jew confronting the catastrophe had the Jewish faith destroyed – ever after? For two

From Emil L. Fackenheim (1989) 'Preface to the Second Edition', *To Mend the World: Foundations of Post-Holocaust Thought*, 2nd edn. New York: Schocken Books.

decades one part of my thought – the other had been philosophy – had been preoccupied with Judaism, the theological renewal of it and return to it: what if I had been whistling in the dark? Jewish thinkers still widely view the Holocaust as but another in the history of Jewish destructions, and Hitler as but another Pharaoh, Amalek or – most appropriate – Haman. They are respected, and I respect them myself, for I had done much the same thing for so long. But, in my struggle for Purim-Easter 1967, I could do it no more. Haman had failed; the new Haman had not. For the one, the death-meriting offense had been an act of one Jew; for the other, the birth of all. And as for viewing the murder of Jews as more important than the very survival of Persia, such an 'insane' idea never entered the biblical villain's mind. Nor did it enter the minds of the great and numerous Jewish commentators who, though bearing the burden of the many destroyers who had succeeded where Haman had failed, elaborated on the wickedness of Pharaoh, Amalek and, of course, Haman himself.

In preparation for the now unavoidable task, I desired two things. If unable to stay–stay exclusively – with biblical prototypes – Pharaoh, Amalek, Haman – I wished to stay at least with precedents of past destructions, such as those of the two temples, the expulsion from Spain, the seventeenth-century Chmelnitski massacres, for these, long absorbed as they were by the Jewish faith were, so to speak, safely past. Still more did I desire to keep the name of Hitler out. The rabbis add 'may his name be wiped out' if and when they do mention Titus and Hadrian, the one a Roman who destroyed the Jewish state, the other another Roman who some six decades later sought to destroy Judaism itself. But could Hitler's name be mentioned at all? When Hadrian forbade the practice of Judaism on pain of death, Rabbi Akiba and the rest of the 'ten martyrs' defied his edict, were caught and tortured, and died with the *Sh'ma Yisrael* on their lips: their martyrdom can be remembered even on Yom Kippur, the most solemn of Jewish festivals, for it has renewed the Jewish faith – and administered Hadrian a posthumous defeat. In the most painful possible contrast, Hitler's name could not be mentioned without the specter of posthumous victories for him. Hadrian's edict gave the ten martyrs the choice between life and the risk of death. But the new Jewish crime was not an act – the practice of *mitzvot*, the study of Torah, the ordination of new rabbis – but birth; and with Teutonic consistency the Holocaust was engineered so as to give few would-be Akibas the choice of how to die, and none at all that between life and the risk of death. For Judaism, then, the Holocaust is a destruction without adequate precedent: it is new.

Enough is recognized of this newness for Jews to have refused to mingle the commemoration of the Holocaust with that of other destructions: Yom ha-Shoah is set aside for the Holocaust alone. But how to observe it? A Jew may still fall back on past resources in memory of those left with the choice of how to die, the new martyrs with the *Sh'ma Yisrael* on their lips, the new heroes with guns in their hands. With birth being the new Jewish crime, however, the most characteristic new victims were those robbed of choice altogether: the children too young to choose, and the *Muselmänner* unable to choose any longer. Of the first, a Polish guard has testified that they were thrown into the Auschwitz flames without being killed first, that their screams could be heard at the camp. Of the second, Primo Levi has written: 'One hesitates to call them living; one hesitates to call their death death.' [...] *Muselmänner* were those near-skeletons who, their feelings, thought and even speech already murdered by hunger and torture, still walked for a while till they dropped to the ground.

Has Hitler, then, succeeded where Hadrian failed? Jewish faith is renewed by the ten martyrs: is it destroyed by the screams of the children and the no less terrible silence of the *Muselmänner*? [...]

What emerged at length and was presented at the symposium was the [...] '614th commandment,' forbidding Jews to give Hitler posthumous victories. According to the classical sources, 613 commandments were revealed to Moses on Mount Sinai. [...] Yet to stay with the 613 now proved impossible. As honesty with the facts and fidelity to the victims was making something new – the naming of Hitler – unavoidable, along with it emerged a new necessity. It was forbidden to allow the posthumous destruction of the Jewish faith in Man, God and – this even for the most secularist of Jews – that hope without which a Jew cannot live, the hope which is the gift of Judaism to all humanity. To deny Hitler the posthumous victory of destroying this faith was a moral-religious commandment. I no longer hesitated to call it the 614th commandment: for post-Holocaust Judaism it would be as binding as if it had been revealed to Moses at Mount Sinai. The long-avoided but now accepted task, then, did not destroy my Jewish thought but revolutionized it. [...] The necessity to deny Hitler posthumous victories is moral and religious, but is it an ontological possibility? If the Holocaust is 'not human nature'; if the 'humanly impossible' became real in the crimes of the criminals and the sufferings of the victims, how can the denial to Hitler of posthumous victories be a 'possibility' that lies within 'human nature'? When all is said and done, must not the Holocaust either cease to be a stumbling block for the Jewish faith, after all, in which case the 614th commandment is unnecessary, or else be and remain a stumbling block, in which to obey that commandment is 'humanly impossible'? Must not Judaism either survive the Holocaust fundamentally as it was, or else, if not destroyed, at least be altered beyond recognition?

[...]

The 614th commandment failed to address this Jewish question. It was inadequate also in responding to a Jewish question and to this alone.

> The martyrs, resistance fighters and most of all the victims are all viewed in a false perspective if the focus is on them and not the criminals.

I have made this assertion relative to history. It also applies to Jewish thought. Bar Kochba's fighters against Hadrian were inspired by hope; the ghetto-fighters against Hitler, by despair. When Hadrian had won, Akiba chose to risk death; when Hitler was winning, nameless Akibas could not choose whether but only how to die. Even these heroes and martyrs, then, are made different by the new crime. As thought – any thought – turns to the children and the *Muselmänner*, to avoid a shift to the crime and its newness becomes altogether impossible. How did the 'humanly impossible' become a real 'world' at Auschwitz, thus ceasing to be humanly impossible? If Auschwitz is 'not human nature,' what must be said of a world [. . .] in which the most 'unnatural' crimes were the norms of daily behavior, and any show of ordinary decency, itself unnatural? These questions are not for Jews alone. They are not about storm troopers and kapos alone. They concern the whole human condition – and are for philosophers. Can philosophers carry on with their traditional business – the part of it in which human nature is involved – as though the Holocaust had not occurred? [. . .]

28

'ETHICS AND SPIRIT'

Emmanuel Levinas

[...]

SPIRIT AND VIOLENCE[1]

Nothing is more ambiguous than the term 'spiritual life'. Could we not make it more precise by excluding from it any relation to violence? But violence is not to be found only in the collision of one billiard ball with another, or the storm that destroys a harvest, or the master who mistreats his slave, or a totalitarian State that vilifies its citizens, or the conquest and subjection of men in war. Violence is to be found in any action in which one acts as if one were alone to act: as if the rest of the universe were there only to *receive* the action; violence is consequently also any action which we endure without at every point collaborating in it.

Nearly every causality is in this sense violent: the fabrication of a thing, the satisfaction of a need, the desire and even the knowledge of an object. Struggle and war are also violent, for the only element sought out in the Other is the weakness that betrays his person. But violence can also lie, in large part, in the poetic delirium and enthusiasm displayed when we merely offer our mouths to the muse who speaks through us; in our fear and trembling when the Sacred wrenches us out of ourselves; in the passion – call it love – that wounds our side with a perfidious arrow.

But is a cause without violence possible? Who welcomes without being shocked? Let mystics be reassured: nothing can shock reason. It collaborates with what it hears. Language acts without being subdued, even when it is the

From Emmanuel Levinas (1990) 'Ethics and Spirit', in *Difficult Freedom: Essays on Judaism*, trans. Seán Hand. Baltimore, MD: Johns Hopkins University Press.

vehicle for an order. Reason and language are external to violence. They *are* the spiritual order. If morality must truly exclude violence, a profound link must join reason, language and morality. If religion is to coincide with spiritual life, it must be essentially ethical. Inevitably, a spiritualism of the Irrational is a contradiction. Adhering to the Sacred is infinitely more materialist than proclaiming the incontestable value of bread and meat in the lives of ordinary people.

The Jewish moralism of the nineteenth century based its negations on reason [*avait raison dans ses négations*]. In its naive respect for the scientism of the day, it excellently refused to confer any spiritual dignity on relations whose origins lay in magic and violence. For example, it perhaps threw suspicion on the idea of miracles solely in the name of scientific teaching. It is still the case that a miracle entails a degree of irrationality – not because it shocks reason, but because it makes no appeal to it. Spiritualizing a religion does not consist in judging one's experiences in the light of the scientific results of the day, but in understanding these very experiences as *links between intelligences*, links situated in the full light of consciousness and discourse. The intervention of the unconscious and, consequently, the horrors and ecstasies which it feeds – recourse to the magical action of the sacraments – all this is linked ultimately to violence.

SPIRIT AND THE FACE

The banal fact of conversation, in one sense, quits the order of violence. This banal fact is the marvel of marvels.

To speak, at the same time as knowing the Other, is making oneself known to him. The Other is not only known, he is *greeted* [*salué*]. He is not only named, but also invoked. To put it in grammatical terms, the Other does not appear in the nominative, but in the vocative. I not only think of what he is for me, but also and simultaneously, and even before, I *am* for him. In applying a concept to him, in calling him this or that, I am already appealing to him. I do not only *know* something, I am also part of society. This *commerce* which the word implies is precisely action without violence: the agent, at the very moment of its action, has renounced all claims to domination or sovereignty, and is already exposed to the action of the Other in the way it waits for a response. Speaking and hearing become one rather than succeed one another. Speaking therefore institutes the moral relationship of equality and consequently recognizes justice. Even when one speaks to a slave, one speaks to an equal. What one says, the content communicated, is possible only thanks to this face-to-face relationship in which the Other counts as an interlocutor prior even to being known. One looks at a look. To look at a look is to look at something which cannot be abandoned or freed, but something which *aims* [*vise*] at you: it involves looking at the *face* [*visage*].

The face is not the mere assemblage of a nose, a forehead, eyes, etc.; it is all that, of course, but takes on the meaning of a face through the new dimension it opens up in the perception of a being. Through the face, the being is not only enclosed in its form and offered to the hand, it is also open, establishing itself in depth and, in this opening, presenting itself somehow in a personal way. The face is an irreducible mode in which being can present itself in its identity. A thing can never be presented personally and ultimately has no identity. Violence is applied to the thing, it seizes and disposes of the thing. Things *give*, they do not offer a face. They are beings without a face. Perhaps art seeks to give a face to things, and in this its greatness and its deceit simultaneously reside.

'YOU SHALL NOT KILL'

Knowledge reveals, names and consequently classifies. Speech addresses itself to a face. Knowledge seizes hold of its object. It possesses it. Possession denies the independence of being, without destroying that being – it denies and maintains. The face, for its part, is inviolable; those eyes, which are absolutely without protection, the most naked part of the human body, none the less offer an absolute resistance to possession, an absolute resistance in which the temptation to murder is inscribed: the temptation of absolute negation. The Other is the only being that one can be tempted to kill. This temptation to murder and this impossibility of murder constitute the very vision of the face. To see a face is already to hear 'You shall not kill', and to hear 'You shall not kill' is to hear 'Social justice'. And everything I can hear [*entendre*] coming from God or going to God, Who is invisible, must have come to me via the one, unique voice.

'You shall not kill' is therefore not just a simple rule of conduct; it appears as the principle of discourse itself and of spiritual life. Henceforth, language is not only a system of signs in the service of a pre-existing system. Speech belongs to the order of morality before belonging to that of theory. Is it not therefore the condition for conscious thought?

Nothing, in fact, is more opposed to a relation with the face than 'contact' with the Irrational and mystery. The presence of the face is precisely the very possibility of understanding one another [*s'entendre*]. Inner life is defined, moves towards the single voice of the contract, and frees itself from the arbitrariness of our bad faith. The psychic fact receives from speech the power to be what it is. It is amputated from its unconscious prolongations which once transformed it into a mask and rendered its sincerity impossible. No more will thought be overrun by obscure and unconscious forces that subject it to a protean fate! We have entered the age of logic and reason!

In this way – and it, is after all, extraordinary – universality is established: a *self* [*moi*] can exist which is not a *myself* [*moi-même*]. This self, viewed face-on, is consciousness, existing by virtue of the fact that a sovereign self, invading the world naively – like 'a moving force', to use Victor Hugo's expression – perceives a face and the impossibility of killing. Consciousness is the impossibility of invading reality like a wild vegetation that absorbs or breaks or pushes back everything around it. The turning back on oneself of consciousness is the equivalent not of self-contemplation but of the fact of not existing violently and naturally, of speaking to the Other. Morality accomplishes human society. Can we ever gauge its miracle? It is something other than a coexistence of a multitude of humans, or a participation in new and complex laws imposed by the masses. Society is the miracle of moving out of oneself.

The violent man does not move out of himself. He takes, he possesses. Possession denies independent existence. To have is to refuse to be. Violence is a sovereignty, but also a solitude. To endure violence in enthusiasm and ecstasy and delirium is to be *possessed*. To know is to perceive, to seize an object – be it a man or a group of men – to *seize* a thing. Every experience of the world is at the same time an experience of self, possession and enjoyment of self [*jouissance de soi*]: it forms and nourishes me. The knowledge that makes us move out of ourselves is also like our slow absorption and digestion of reality. Reality's resistance to our acts itself turns into the *experience* of this resistance; as such, it is already absorbed by knowledge and leaves us alone with ourselves.

If 'know thyself' has become the fundamental precept of all Western philosophy, this is because ultimately the West discovers the universe within itself. As with Ulysses, its journey is merely the accident of a return. The *Odyssey*, in this sense, dominates literature. When a Gide recommends fullness of life and variety of experience as the fulfilment of freedom, he searches in freedom for the *experience* of freedom, not for the movement itself by which one moves out of oneself. It has to do with taking delight, experiencing oneself as a miraculous centre of radiance, and not with radiating.

Only the vision of the face in which the 'You shall not kill' is articulated does not allow itself to fall back into an ensuing complacency or become the experience of an insuperable obstacle, offering itself up to our power. For in reality, murder is possible, but it is possible only when one has not looked the Other in the face. The impossibility of killing is not real, but moral. The fact that the vision of the face is not an *experience*, but a moving out of oneself, a contact with another being and not simply a sensation of self, is attested to by the 'purely moral' character of this impossibility. A moral view [*regard*] measures, in the face, the uncrossable infinite in which all murderous intent is immersed and submerged. This is precisely why it leads us away from any experience or view [*regard*]. The infinite is given only to the moral view [*regard*]: it is not *known*, but is in *society* with us. The commerce with beings which begins with 'You shall not kill' does not conform to the scheme of our normal relations with the words, in which the subject knows or absorbs its object like a nourishment, the satisfaction of a need. It does not return to its point of departure to become self-contentment, self-enjoyment, or self-knowledge. It inaugurates the spiritual journey of man. A religion, for us, can follow no other path.

NOTE

1. We owe to Eric Weil's great thesis – whose philosophical importance and tenacity of logic will become crucial – the systematic and vigorous use of the term violence as the opposite of discourse (see *Logique de la philosophie* [Paris, Vrin, 1951]). We, however, give it a different meaning, as we have already shown in our article in *Revue de métaphysique et de morale*, February–March 1951, where we used the term.

29

EICHMANN IN JERUSALEM

Hannah Arendt

[...] The purpose of a trial is to render justice, and nothing else; even the noblest of ulterior purposes – 'the making of a record of the Hitler regime which would withstand the test of history,' as Robert G. Storey, executive trial counsel at Nuremberg, formulated the supposed higher aims of the Nuremberg Trials – can only detract from the law's main business: to weigh the charges brought against the accused, to render judgment, and to mete out due punishment.

The judgment in the Eichmann case, whose first two sections were written in reply to the higher-purpose theory as it was expounded both inside and outside the courtroom, could not have been clearer in this respect and more to the point: All attempts to widen the range of the trial had to be resisted, because the court could not 'allow itself to be enticed into provinces which are outside its sphere ... the judicial process has ways of its own, which are laid down by law, and which do not change, whatever the subject of the trial may be.' The court, moreover, could not overstep these limits without ending 'in complete failure.' Not only does it not have at its disposal 'the tools required for the investigation of general questions,' it speaks with an authority whose very weight depends upon its limitation. 'No one has made us judges' of matters outside the realm of law, and 'no greater weight is to be attached to our opinion on them than to that of any person devoting study and thought' to them. Hence, to the question most commonly asked about the Eichmann trial: What good does it do?, there is but one possible answer: It will do justice.

From Hannah Arendt (1963) 'Epilogue', in *Eichmann in Jerusalem: A Report on the Banality of Evil*. New York: Viking Press.

[...]

Had the court in Jerusalem understood that there were distinctions between discrimination, expulsion, and genocide, it would immediately have become clear that the supreme crime it was confronted with, the physical extermination of the Jewish people, was a crime against humanity, perpetrated upon the body of the Jewish people, and that only the choice of victims, not the nature of the crime, could be derived from the long history of Jew-hatred and anti-Semitism. Insofar as the victims were Jews, it was right and proper that a Jewish court should sit in judgment; but insofar as the crime was a crime against humanity, it needed an international tribunal to do justice to it. [...]

[...] The argument that the crime against the Jewish people was first of all a crime against mankind, upon which the valid proposals for an international tribunal rested, stood in flagrant contradiction to the law under which Eichmann was tried. Hence, those who proposed that Israel give up her prisoner should have gone one step further and declared: The Nazis and Nazi Collaborators (Punishment) Law of 1950 is wrong, it is in contradiction to what actually happened, it does not cover the facts. And this would indeed have been quite true. For just as a murderer is prosecuted because he has violated the law of the community, and not because he has deprived the Smith family of its husband, father, and breadwinner, so these modern, state-employed mass murderers must be prosecuted because they violated the order of mankind, and not because they killed millions of people. Nothing is more pernicious to an understanding of these new crimes, or stands more in the way of the emergence of an international penal code that could take care of them, than the common illusion that the crime of murder and the crime of genocide are essentially the same. The point of the latter is that an altogether different order is broken and an altogether different community is violated. [...]

[...] It is in the very nature of things human that every act that has once made its appearance and has been recorded in the history of mankind stays with mankind as a potentiality long after its actuality has become a thing of the past. No punishment has ever possessed enough power of deterrence to prevent the commission of crimes. On the contrary, whatever the punishment, once a specific crime has appeared for the first time, its reappearance is more likely than its initial emergence could ever have been. The particular reasons that speak for the possibility of a repetition of the crimes committed by the Nazis are even more plausible. The frightening coincidence of the modern population explosion with the discovery of technical devices that, through automation, will make large sections of the population 'superfluous' even in terms of labor, and that, through nuclear energy, make it possible to deal with this twofold threat by the use of instruments beside which Hitler's gassing installations look like an evil child's fumbling toys, should be enough to make us tremble.

It is essentially for this reason: that the unprecedented, once it has appeared, may become a precedent for the future, that all trials touching upon 'crimes against humanity' must be judged according to a standard that is today still an

'ideal.' If genocide is an actual possibility of the future, then no people on earth –
least of all, of course, the Jewish people, in Israel or elsewhere – can feel
reasonably sure of its continued existence without the help and the protection of
international law. Success or failure in dealing with the hitherto unprecedented
can lie only in the extent to which this dealing may serve as a valid precedent on
the road to international penal law. [...]

In sum, the failure of the Jerusalem court consisted in its not coming to grips
with three fundamental issues, all of which have been sufficiently well known
and widely discussed since the establishment of the Nuremberg Tribunal: the
problem of impaired justice in the court of the victors; a valid definition of the
'crime against humanity'; and a clear recognition of the new criminal who
commits this crime.

As to the first of these, justice was more seriously impaired in Jerusalem than
it was at Nuremberg, because the court did not admit witnesses for the defense.
In terms of the traditional requirements for fair and due process of law, this was
the most serious flaw in the Jerusalem proceedings. Moreover, while judgment
in the court of the victors was perhaps inevitable at the close of the war (to
Justice Jackson's argument in Nuremberg: 'Either the victors must judge the
vanquished or we must leave the defeated to judge themselves,' should be added
the understandable feeling on the part of the Allies that they 'who had risked
everything could not admit neutrals' [Vabres]), it was not the same sixteen years
later, and under circumstances in which the argument against the admission of
neutral countries did not make sense.

As to the second issue, the findings of the Jerusalem court were incomparably
better than those at Nuremberg. I have mentioned before the Nuremberg
Charter's definition of 'crimes against humanity' as 'inhuman acts,' which
were translated into German as *Verbrechen gegen die Menschlichkeit* – as
though the Nazis had simply been lacking in human kindness, certainly the
understatement of the century. To be sure, had the conduct of the Jerusalem
trial depended entirely upon the prosecution, the basic misunderstanding would
have been even worse than at Nuremberg. But the judgment refused to let the
basic character of the crime be swallowed up in a flood of atrocities, and it did
not fall into the trap of equating this crime with ordinary war crimes. What had
been mentioned at Nuremberg only occasionally and, as it were, marginally –
that 'the evidence shows that ... the mass murders and cruelties were not
committed solely for the purpose of stamping out opposition' but were 'part of a
plan to get rid of whole native populations' – was in the center of the Jerusalem
proceedings, for the obvious reason that Eichmann stood accused of a crime
against the Jewish people, a crime that could not be explained by any utilitarian
purpose; Jews had been murdered all over Europe, not only in the East, and their
annihilation was not due to any desire to gain territory that 'could be used for
colonization by Germans.' It was the great advantage of a trial centered on the
crime against the Jewish people that not only did the difference between war
crimes, such as shooting of partisans and killing of hostages, and 'inhuman

acts,' such as 'expulsion and annihilation' of native populations to permit colonization by an invader, emerge with sufficient clarity to become part of a future international penal code, but also that the difference between 'inhuman acts' (which were undertaken for some known, though criminal, purpose, such as expansion through colonization) and the 'crime against humanity,' whose intent and purpose were unprecedented, was clarified. At no point, however, either in the proceedings or in the judgment, did the Jerusalem trial ever mention even the possibility that extermination of whole ethnic groups – the Jews, or the Poles, or the Gypsies – might be more than a crime against the Jewish or the Polish or the Gypsy people, that the international order, and mankind in its entirety, might have been grievously hurt and endangered.

Closely connected with this failure was the conspicuous helplessness the judges experienced when they were confronted with the task they could least escape, the task of understanding the criminal whom they had come to judge. Clearly, it was not enough that they did not follow the prosecution in its obviously mistaken description of the accused as a 'perverted sadist,' nor would it have been enough if they had gone one step further and shown the inconsistency of the case for the prosecution, in which Mr. Hausner wanted to try the most abnormal monster the world had ever seen and, at the same time, try in him 'many like him,' even the 'whole Nazi movement and anti-Semitism at large.' They knew, of course, that it would have been very comforting indeed to believe that Eichmann was a monster, even though if he had been Israel's case against him would have collapsed or, at the very least, lost all interest. Surely, one can hardly call upon the whole world and gather correspondents from the four corners of the earth in order to display Bluebeard in the dock. The trouble with Eichmann was precisely that so many were like him, and that the many were neither perverted nor sadistic, that they were, and still are, terribly and terrifyingly normal. From the viewpoint of our legal institutions and of our moral standards of judgment, this normality was much more terrifying than all the atrocities put together, for it implied – as had been said at Nuremberg over and over again by the defendants and their counsels – that this new type of criminal, who is in actual fact *hostis generis humani*, commits his crimes under circumstances that make it well-nigh impossible for him to know or to feel that he is doing wrong. In this respect, the evidence in the Eichmann case was even more convincing than the evidence presented in the trial of the major war criminals, whose pleas of a clear conscience could be dismissed more easily because they combined with the argument of obedience to 'superior orders' various boasts about occasional disobedience. But although the bad faith of the defendants was manifest, the only ground on which guilty conscience could actually be proved was the fact that the Nazis, and especially the criminal organizations to which Eichmann belonged, had been so very busy destroying the evidence of their crimes during the last months of the war. And this ground was rather shaky. It proved no more than recognition that the law of mass murder, because of its novelty, was not yet accepted by other nations; or, in the language of the Nazis, that they had lost their fight to 'liberate' mankind from the 'rule of subhumans,' especially from the domination of the Elders of Zion; or, in ordinary language, it proved no more than the admission of defeat. Would any one of them have suffered from a guilty conscience if they had won?

Foremost among the larger issues at stake in the Eichmann trial was the assumption current in all modern legal systems that intent to do wrong is necessary for the commission of a crime. On nothing, perhaps, has civilized jurisprudence prided itself more than on this taking into account of the subjective factor. Where this intent is absent, where, for whatever reasons, even reasons of moral insanity, the ability to distinguish between right and wrong is impaired, we feel no crime has been committed. We refuse, and consider as barbaric, the propositions 'that a great crime offends nature, so that the very earth cries out for vengeance; that evil violates a natural harmony which only retribution can restore; that a wronged collectivity owes a duty to the moral order to punish the criminal' (Yosal Rogat). And yet I think it is undeniable that it was precisely on the ground of these long-forgotten propositions that Eichmann was brought to justice to begin with, and that they were, in fact, the supreme justification for the death penalty. Because he had been implicated and had played a central role in an enterprise whose open purpose was to eliminate forever certain 'races' from the surface of the earth, he had to be eliminated. And if it is true that 'justice must not only be done but must be seen to be done,' then the justice of what was done in Jerusalem would have emerged to be seen by all if the judges had dared to address their defendant in something like the following terms:

'You admitted that the crime committed against the Jewish people during the war was the greatest crime in recorded history, and you admitted your role in it. But you said you had never acted from base motives, that you had never had any inclination to kill anybody, that you had never hated Jews, and still that you could not have acted otherwise and that you did not feel guilty. We find this difficult, though not altogether impossible, to believe; there is some, though not very much, evidence against you in this matter of motivation and conscience that could be proved beyond reasonable doubt. You also said that your role in the Final Solution was an accident and that almost anybody could have taken your place, so that potentially almost all Germans are equally guilty. What you meant to say was that where all, or almost all, are guilty, nobody is. This is an indeed quite common conclusion, but one we are not willing to grant you. And if you don't understand our objection, we would recommend to your attention the story of Sodom and Gomorrah, two neighboring cities in the Bible, which were destroyed by fire from Heaven because all the people in them had become equally guilty. This, incidentally, has nothing to do with the newfangled notion of 'collective guilt,' according to which people supposedly are guilty of, or feel guilty about, things done in their name but not by them – things in which they did not participate and from which they did not profit. In other words, guilt and innocence before the law are of an objective nature, and even if eighty million Germans had done as you did, this would not have been an excuse for you.

'Luckily, we don't have to go that far. You yourself claimed not the actuality but only the potentiality of equal guilt on the part of all who lived in a state whose main political purpose had become the commission of unheard-of crimes. And no matter through what accidents of exterior or interior circumstances you were pushed onto the road of becoming a criminal, there is an abyss between the actuality of what you did and the potentiality of what others might have done. We are concerned here only with what you did, and not with the possible noncriminal nature of your inner life and of your motives or with the criminal potentialities of those around you. You told your story in terms of a hard-luck story, and, knowing the circumstances, we are, up to a point, willing to grant you that under more favorable circumstances it is highly unlikely that you would ever have come before us or before any other criminal court. Let us assume, for the sake of argument, that it was nothing more than misfortune that made you a willing instrument in the organization of mass murder; there still remains the fact that you have carried out, and therefore actively supported, a policy of mass murder. For politics is not like the nursery; in politics obedience and support are the same. And just as you supported and carried out a policy of not wanting to share the earth with the Jewish people and the people of a number of other nations – as though you and your superiors had any right to determine who should and who should not inhabit the world – we find that no one, that is, no member of the human race, can be expected to want to share the earth with you. This is the reason, and the only reason, you must hang.'

30

'WHAT IS A CAMP?'

Giorgio Agamben

What happened in the camps exceeds the juridical concept of crime to such an extent that the specific political-juridical structure within which those events took place has often been left simply unexamined. The camp is the place in which the most absolute *conditio inhumana* ever to appear on Earth was realized: this is ultimately all that counts for the victims as well as for posterity. Here I will deliberately set out in the opposite direction. Rather than deducing the definition of camp from the events that took place there, I will ask instead: *What is a camp? What is its political-juridical structure? How could such events have taken place there?* This will lead us to look at the camp not as a historical fact and an anomaly that – though admittedly still with us – belongs nonetheless to the past, but rather in some sense as the hidden matrix and *nomos* of the political space in which we still live.

Historians debate whether the first appearance of camps ought to be identified with the *campos de concentraciones* that were created in 1896 by the Spaniards in Cuba in order to repress the insurrection of that colony's population, or rather with the *concentration camps* into which the English herded the Boers at the beginning of the twentieth century. What matters here is that in both cases one is dealing with the extension to an entire civilian population of a state of exception linked to a colonial war. The camps, in other words, were not born out of ordinary law, and even less were they the product – as one might have believed – of a transformation and a development

From Giorgio Agamben (2000) 'What is a Camp?', in *Means without End: Notes on Politics*, trans. Vincenzo Binetti and Cesare Casarino. Minneapolis, MN: University of Minnesota Press.

of prison law; rather, they were born out of the state of exception and martial law. This is even more evident in the case of the Nazi *Lager*, whose origin and juridical regime is well documented. It is well known that the juridical foundation of internment was not ordinary law but rather the *Schutzhaft* (literally, protective custody), which was a juridical institution of Prussian derivation that Nazi jurists sometimes considered a measure of preventive policing inasmuch as it enabled the 'taking into custody' of individuals regardless of any relevant criminal behavior and exclusively in order to avoid threats to the security of the state. The origin of the *Schutzhaft*, however, resides in the Prussian law on the state of siege that was passed on June 4, 1851, and that was extended to the whole of Germany (with the exception of Bavaria) in 1871, as well as in the earlier Prussian law on the 'protection of personal freedom' (*Schutz der persönlichen Freiheit*) that was passed on February 12, 1850. Both these laws were applied widely during World War I.

One cannot overestimate the importance of this constitutive nexus between state of exception and concentration camp for a correct understanding of the nature of the camp. Ironically, the 'protection' of freedom that is in question in the *Schutzhaft* is a protection against the suspension of the law that characterizes the state of emergency. What is new here is that this institution is dissolved by the state of exception on which it was founded and is allowed to continue to be in force under normal circumstances. *The camp is the space that opens up when the state of exception starts to become the rule.* In it, the state of exception, which was essentially a temporal suspension of the state of law, acquires a permanent spatial arrangement that, as such, remains constantly outside the normal state of law. When Himmler decided, in March 1933, on the occasion of the celebrations of Hitler's election to the chancellorship of the Reich, to create a 'concentration camp for political prisoners' at Dachau, this camp was immediately entrusted to the SS and, thanks to the *Schutzhaft*, was placed outside the jurisdiction of criminal law as well as prison law, with which it neither then nor later ever had anything to do. Dachau, as well as the other camps that were soon added to it (Sachsenhausen, Buchenwald, Lichtenberg), remained virtually always operative: the number of inmates varied and during certain periods (in particular, between 1935 and 1937, before the deportation of the Jews began) it decreased to 7,500 people; the camp as such, however, had become a permanent reality in Germany.

One ought to reflect on the paradoxical status of the camp as space of exception: the camp is a piece of territory that is placed outside the normal juridical order; for all that, however, it is not simply an external space. According to the etymological meaning of the term *exception* (*ex-capere*), what is being excluded in the camp is *captured outside*, that is, it is included by virtue of its very exclusion. Thus, what is being captured under the rule of law is first of all the very state of exception. In other words, if sovereign power is founded on the ability to decide on the state of exception, the camp is the structure in which the state of exception is permanently realized. Hannah Arendt observed once that what comes to light in the camps is the principle that supports totalitarian domination and that common sense stubbornly refuses to admit to, namely, the principle according to which anything is possible. It is only because the camps constitute a space of exception – a space in which the law is completely suspended – that everything is truly possible in them. If one does not understand this particular political-juridical structure of the camps, whose vocation is precisely to realize permanently the exception, the incredible events that took place in them remain entirely unintelligible. The people who entered the camp moved about in a zone of indistinction between the outside and the inside, the exception and the rule, the licit and the illicit, in which every juridical protection had disappeared; moreover, if they were Jews, they had already been deprived of citizenship rights by the Nuremberg Laws and were later completely denationalized at the moment of the 'final solution.' *Inasmuch as its inhabitants have been stripped of every political status and reduced completely to naked life, the camp is also the most absolute biopolitical space that has ever been realized – a space in which power confronts nothing other than pure biological life without any mediation.* The camp is the paradigm itself of political space at the point in which politics becomes biopolitics and the *homo sacer* becomes indistinguishable from the citizen. The correct question regarding the horrors committed in the camps, therefore, is not the question that asks hypocritically how it could have been possible to commit such atrocious horrors against other human beings; it would be more honest, and above all more useful, to investigate carefully how – that is, thanks to what juridical procedures and political devices – human beings could have been so completely deprived of their rights and prerogatives to the point that committing any act toward them would no longer appear as a crime (at this point, in fact, truly anything had become possible).

If this is the case, if the essence of the camp consists in the materialization of the state of exception and in the consequent creation of a space for naked life as such, we will then have to admit to be facing a camp virtually every time that such a structure is created, regardless of the nature of the crimes committed in it and regardless of the denomination and specific topography it might have. The soccer stadium in Bari in which the Italian police temporarily herded Albanian illegal immigrants in 1991 before sending them back to their country, the cycle-racing track in which the Vichy authorities rounded up the Jews before handing them over to the Germans, the refugee camp near the Spanish border where Antonio Machado died in 1939, as well as the *zones d'attente* in French international airports in which foreigners requesting refugee status are detained will all have to be considered camps. In all these cases, an apparently anodyne place (such as the Hotel Arcade near the Paris airport) delimits instead a space in which, for all intents and purposes, the normal rule of law is suspended and in which the fact that atrocities may or may not be committed does not depend on the law but rather on the civility and ethical sense of the police that act temporarily as sovereign. This is the case, for example, during the four days foreigners may be kept in the *zone d'attente* before the intervention of French judicial authorities. In this sense, even certain outskirts of the great postindustrial cities as well as the gated communities of the United States are beginning today to look like camps, in which naked life and political life, at least in determinate moments, enter a zone of absolute indeterminacy.

From this perspective, the birth of the camp in our time appears to be an event that marks in a decisive way the political space itself of modernity. This birth takes place when the political system of the modern nation-state – founded on the functional nexus between a determinate localization (territory) and a determinate order (the state), which was mediated by automatic regulations for the inscription of life (birth or nation) – enters a period of permanent crisis and the state decides to undertake the management of the biological life of the nation directly as its own task. In other words, if the structure of the nation-state is defined by three elements – *territory, order*, and *birth* – the rupture of the old *nomos* does not take place in the two aspects that, according to Carl Schmitt, used to constitute it (that is, localization, *Ortung*, and order, *Ordnung*), but rather at the site in which naked life is inscribed in them (that is, there where inscription turns *birth* into *nation*). There is something that no longer functions in the traditional mechanisms that used to regulate this inscription, and the camp is the new hidden regulator of the inscription of life in the order – or, rather, it is the sign of the system's inability to function without transforming itself into a lethal machine. It is important to note that the camps appeared at the same time that the new laws on citizenship and on the denationalization of citizens were issued (not only the Nuremberg Laws on citizenship in the Reich but also the laws on the denationalization of citizens that were issued by almost all the European states, including France, between 1915 and 1933). The state of exception, which used to be essentially a temporary suspension of the order, becomes now a new and stable spatial arrangement inhabited by that naked life that increasingly cannot be inscribed into the order. *The increasingly widening gap between birth (naked life) and nation-state is the new fact of the politics of our time and what we are calling 'camp' is this disparity.* To an order without localization (that is, the state of exception during which the law is suspended) corresponds now a localization without order (that is, the camp as permanent space of exception). The political system no longer orders forms of life and juridical norms in a determinate space; rather, it contains within itself a *dislocating localization* that exceeds it and in which virtually every form of life and every norm can be captured. The camp intended as a dislocating localization is the hidden matrix of the politics in which we still live, and we must learn to recognize it in all of its metamorphoses. The camp is the fourth and inseparable element that has been added to and has broken up the old trinity of nation (birth), state, and territory.

It is from this perspective that we need to see the reappearance of camps in a form that is, in a certain sense, even more extreme in the territories of the former Yugoslavia. What is happening there is not at all, as some interested observers rushed to declare, a redefinition of the old political system according to new ethnic and territorial arrangements, that is, a simple repetition of the processes that culminated in the constitution of the European nation-states. Rather, we note there an irreparable rupture of the old *nomos* as well as a dislocation of populations and human lives according to entirely new lines of flight. That is why the camps of ethnic rape are so crucially important. If the Nazis never thought of carrying out the 'final solution' by impregnating Jewish women, that is because the principle of birth, which ensured the inscription of life in the order of the nation-state, was in some way still functioning, even though it was profoundly transformed. This principle is now adrift: it has entered a process of dislocation in which its functioning is becoming patently impossible and in which we can expect not only new camps but also always new and more delirious normative definitions of the inscription of life in the city. The camp, which is now firmly settled inside it, is the new biopolitical *nomos* of the planet.

(1994)

31

THE DIFFEREND

Jean François Lyotard

1. You are informed that human beings endowed with language were placed in a situation such that none of them is now able to tell about it. Most of them disappeared then, and the survivors rarely speak about it. When they do speak about it, their testimony bears only upon a minute part of this situation. How can you know that the situation itself existed? That it is not the fruit of your informant's imagination? Either the situation did not exist as such. Or else it did exist, in which case your informant's testimony is false, either because he or she should have disappeared, or else because he or she should remain silent, or else because, if he or she does speak, he or she can bear witness only to the particular experience he had, it remaining to be established whether this experience was a component of the situation in question.

2. 'I have analyzed thousands of documents. I have tirelessly pursued specialists and historians with my questions. I have tried in vain to find a single former deportee capable of proving to me that he had really seen, with his own eyes, a gas chamber' (Faurisson in Pierre Vidal-Naquet, 1981: 81). To have 'really seen with his own eyes' a gas chamber would be the condition which gives one the authority to say that it exists and to persuade the unbeliever. Yet it is still necessary to prove that the gas chamber was used to kill at the time it was seen. The only acceptable proof that it was used to kill is that one died from it. But if one is dead, one cannot testify that it is on account of the gas chamber. – The plaintiff complains that he has been fooled about the existence of gas

From Jean-François Lyotard (1988) *The Differend: Phrases in Dispute*, trans. Georges Van Den Abbeele. Minneapolis, MN: University of Minnesota Press.

chambers, fooled that is, about the so-called Final Solution. His argument is: in order for a place to be identified as a gas chamber, the only eyewitness I will accept would be a victim of this gas chamber; now, according to my opponent, there is no victim that is not dead; otherwise, this gas chamber would not be what he or she claims it to be. There is, therefore, no gas chamber.

[...]

7. This is what a wrong [*tort*] would be: a damage [*dommage*] accompanied by the loss of the means to prove the damage. This is the case if the victim is deprived of life, or of all his or her liberties, or of the freedom to make his or her ideas or opinions public, or simply of the right to testify to the damage, or even more simply if the testifying phrase is itself deprived of authority (Nos. 24–27). In all of these cases, to the privation constituted by the damage there is added the impossibility of bringing it to the knowledge of others, and in particular to the knowledge of a tribunal. Should the victim seek to bypass this impossibility and testify anyway to the wrong done to him or to her, he or she comes up against the following argumentation: either the damages you complain about never took place, and your testimony is false; or else they took place, and since you are able to testify to them, it is not a wrong that has been done to you, but merely a damage, and your testimony is still false.

[...]

9. It is in the nature of a victim not to be able to prove that one has been done a wrong. A plaintiff is someone who has incurred damages and who disposes of the means to prove it. One becomes a victim if one loses these means. One loses them, for example, if the author of the damages turns out directly or indirectly to be one's judge. The latter has the authority to reject one's testimony as false or the ability to impede its publication. But this is only a particular case. In general, the plaintiff becomes a victim when no presentation is possible of the wrong he or she says he or she has suffered. Reciprocally, the 'perfect crime' does not consist in killing the victim or the witnesses (that adds new crimes to the first one and aggravates the difficulty of effacing everything), but rather in obtaining the silence of the witnesses, the deafness of the judges, and the inconsistency (insanity) of the testimony. You neutralize the addressor, the addressee, and the sense of the testimony; then everything is as if there were no referent (no damages). If there is nobody to adduce the proof, nobody to admit it, and/or if the argument which upholds it is judged to be absurd, then the plaintiff is dismissed, the wrong he or she complains of cannot be attested. He or she becomes a victim. If he or she persists in invoking this wrong as if it existed, the others (addressor, addressee, expert commentator on the testimony) will easily be able to make him or her pass for mad. Doesn't paranoia confuse the *As if it were the case* with the *it is the case*?

10. But aren't the others acting for their part as if this were not the case, when it is perhaps the case? Why should there be less paranoia in denying the

existence of gas chambers than in affirming it? Because, writes Leibniz, 'nothing is simpler and easier than something' (Leibniz, 1714: § 7). The one who says there is something is the plaintiff, it is up to him or her to bring forth a demonstration, by means of well-formed phrases and of procedures for establishing the existence of their referent. [. . .] That is why it is up to the victims of extermination camps to prove that extermination. This is our way of thinking that reality is not a given, but an occasion to require that establishment procedures be effectuated in regard to it.

[. . .]

12. The plaintiff lodges his or her complaint before the tribunal, the accused argues in such a way as to show the inanity of the accusation. Litigation takes place. I would like to call a *differend* [*différend*] the case where the plaintiff is divested of the means to argue and becomes for that reason a victim. If the addressor, the addressee, and the sense of the testimony are neutralized, everything takes place as if there were no damages (No. 9). [. . .]

14. 'The survivors rarely speak' (no. 1). But isn't there an entire literature of testimonies . . .? – That's not it, though. Not to speak is part of the ability to speak, since ability is a possibility and a possibility implies something and its opposite. [. . .] To be able not to speak is not the same as not to be able to speak. The latter is a deprivation, the former a negation. (Aristotle, *De Interpretatione* 21 b 12–17; *Metaphysics* IV 1022 b 22 ff.). If the survivors do not speak, is it because they cannot speak, or because they avail themselves of the possibility of not speaking that is given them by the ability to speak? [. . .]

22. The differend is the unstable state and instant of language wherein something which must be able to be put into phrases cannot yet be. This state includes silence, which is a negative phrase, but it also calls upon phrases which are in principle possible. This state is signaled by what one ordinarily calls a feeling: 'One cannot find the words,' etc. A lot of searching must be done to find new rules for forming and linking phrases that are able to express the differend disclosed by the feeling, unless one wants this differend to be smothered right away in a litigation and for the alarm sounded by the feeling to have been useless. What is at stake in a literature, in a philosophy, in a politics perhaps, is to bear witness to differends by finding idioms for them.

23. In the differend, something 'asks' to be put into phrases, and suffers from the wrong of not being able to be put into phrases right away. This is when the human beings who thought they could use language as an instrument of communication learn through the feeling of pain which accompanies silence (and of pleasure which accompanies the invention of a new idiom), that they are summoned by language, not to augment to their profit the quantity of information communicable through existing idioms, but to recognize that what remains to be phrased exceeds what they can presently phrase, and that they must be allowed to institute idioms which do not yet exist.

[. . .]

26. [. . .] The survivors remain silent, and it can be understood 1) that the situation in question (the case) is not the addressee's business (he or she lacks the competence, or he or she is not worthy of being spoken to about it, etc.); or 2) that it never took place (this is what Faurisson understands); or 3) that there is nothing to say about it (the situation is senseless, inexpressible); or 4) that it is not the survivors' business to be talking about it (they are not worthy, etc.). Or, several of these negations together.

27. The silence of the survivors does not necessarily testify in favor of the nonexistence of gas chambers, as Faurisson believes or pretends to believe. It can just as well testify against the addressee's authority (we are not answerable to Faurisson), against the authority of the witness him- or herself (we, the rescued, do not have the authority to speak about it), finally against language's ability to signify gas chambers (an inexpressible absurdity). If one wishes to establish the existence of gas chambers, the four silent negations must be withdrawn: There were no gas chambers, were there? Yes, there were. – But even if there were, that cannot be formulated, can it? Yes, it can. – But even if it can be formulated, there is no one, at least, who has the authority to formulate it, and no one with the authority to hear it (it is not communicable), is there? Yes, there is.

[. . .]

93. 'It's not for nothing that Auschwitz is called the "extermination camp".' (Kremer in Vidal-Naquet, 1981: 85). Millions of human beings were extermi-nated there. Many of the means to prove the crime or its quantity were also exterminated. And even the authority of the tribunal that was supposed to establish the crime and its quantity was exterminated, because the constitution of the Nuremburg tribunal required an Allied victory in the Second World War, and since this war was a kind of civil war (Descombes, 1981b: 741 [. . .]) resulting from a lack of consensus over legitimacy in international relations, the criminal was able to see in his judge merely a criminal more fortunate than he in the conflict of arms. The differend attached to Nazi names, to *Hitler*, to *Auschwitz*, to *Eichmann*, could not be transformed into a litigation and regulated by a verdict. The shades of those to whom had been refused not only life but also the expression of the wrong done them by the Final Solution continue to wander in their indeterminacy. By forming the State of Israel, the survivors transformed the wrong into damages and the differend into a litiga-tion. By beginning to speak in the common idiom of public international law and of authorized politics, they put an end to the silence to which they had been condemned. But the reality of the wrong suffered at Auschwitz before the foundation of this state remained and remains to be established, and it cannot be established because it is in the nature of a wrong not to be established by consensus (Nos. 7, 9). What could be established by historical inquiry would be

the quantity of the crime. But the documents necessary for the validation were themselves destroyed in quantity. That at least can be established. The result is that one cannot adduce the numerical proof of the massacre and that a historian pleading for the trial's revision will be able to object at great length that the crime has not been established in its quantity. – But the silence imposed on knowledge does not impose the silence of forgetting, it imposes a feeling (No. 22). Suppose that an earthquake destroys not only lives, buildings, and objects but also the instruments used to measure earthquakes directly and indirectly. The impossibility of quantitatively measuring it does not prohibit, but rather inspires in the minds of the survivors the idea of a very great seismic force. The scholar claims to know nothing about it, but the common person has a complex feeling, the one aroused by the negative presentation of the indeterminate. *Mutatis mutandis*, the silence that the crime of Auschwitz imposes upon the historian is a sign for the common person. Signs [...] are not referents to which are attached significations validatable under the cognitive regimen, they indicate that something which should be able to be put into phrases cannot be phrased in the accepted idioms (No. 23). That, in a phrase universe, the referent be situated as a sign has as a corollary that in this same universe the addressee is situated like someone who is affected, and that the sense is situated like an unresolved problem, an enigma perhaps, a mystery, or a paradox. – This feeling does not arise from an experience felt by a subject. It can, moreover, not be felt. In any case, how can it be established that it is or is not felt? One comes up against the difficulties raised by idiolects [...]. The silence that surrounds the phrase, *Auschwitz was the extermination camp* is not a state of the mind [*état d'âme*], it is the sign that something remains to be phrased which is not, something which is not determined. This sign affects a linking of phrases. The indetermination of meanings left in abeyance [*en souffrance*], the extermination of what would allow them to be determined, the shadow of negation hollowing out reality to the point of making it dissipate, in a word, the wrong done to the victims that condemns them to silence – it is this, and not a state of mind, which calls upon unknown phrases to link onto the name of Auschwitz. – The 'revisionist' historians understand as applicable to this name only the cognitive rules for the establishment of historical reality and for the validation of its sense. If justice consisted solely in respecting these rules, and if history gave rise only to historical inquiry, they could not be accused of a denial of justice. In fact, they administer a justice in conformity with the rules and exert a positively instituted right. Having placed themselves, moreover, in the position of plain tiffs, who need not establish anything (Nos. 10, 11), they plead for the negative, they reject proofs, and that is certainly their right as the defense. But that they are not worried by the scope of the very silence they use as an argument in their plea, by this does one recognize a wrong done to the sign that is this silence and to the phrases it invokes. They will say that history is not made of feelings, and that it is necessary to establish the facts. But, with Auschwitz, something new has happened in history (which can only be a sign and not a fact), which is that the facts, the testimonies which bore the traces of *here*'s and *now*'s, the documents which indicated the sense or senses of the facts, and the names, finally the possibility of various kinds of phrases whose conjunction makes reality, all this has been destroyed as much as possible. Is it up to the historian to take into account not only the damages, but also the wrong? Not only the reality, but also the meta-reality that is the destruction of reality? Not only the testimony, but also what is left of the testimony when it is destroyed (by dilemma), namely, the feeling? Not only the litigation, but also the differend? Yes, of course, if it is true that there would be no history without a differend, that a differend is born from a wrong and is signaled by a silence, that the silence indicates that phrases are in abeyance of their becoming event [*en souffrance de leur événement*], that the feeling is the suffering of this abeyance [*cette souffrance*]. But then, the historian must break with the monopoly over history granted to the cognitive regimen of phrases, and he or she must venture forth by lending his or her ear to what is not presentable under the rules of knowledge. Every reality entails this exigency insofar as it entails possible unknown senses. Auschwitz is the most real of realities in this respect. Its name marks the confines wherein historical knowledge sees its competence impugned. It does not follow from that that one falls into non-sense. The alternative is not: either the signification that learning [*science*] establishes, or absurdity, be it of the mystical kind (White, 1982; Fackenheim, 1970).

BIBLIOGRAPHY

Aristotle, 'De Interpretatione' (tr. J. L. Ackrill), in *The Complete Works of Aristotle*, ed. J. Barnes, Oxford, 1984.

Aristotle, *Metaphysics* (tr. W. D. Ross), in *Complete Works*. Vincent Descombes 1981b, 'La guerre prochaine,' *Critique* 411–12.

Emil Fackenheim 1970, *God's Presence in History: Jewish Affirmations and Philosophical Reflections*, New York.

Gottfried W. Leibniz 1714, 'The Principle of Nature and of Grace, Based on Reason,' in *Philosophical Papers and Letters* (tr. and ed. L. Loemker), vol. 2, Dordrecht, 1969.

Pierre Vidal-Naquet 1981, 'A Paper Eichmann' (tr. M. Jolas), *Democracy* I, 2.

Hayden White 1982, 'The Politics of Historical Interpretation: Discipline and De-Sublimation,' *Critical Inquiry* 9 (September 1982).

32

'NEW POLITICAL THEOLOGY – OUT OF HOLOCAUST AND LIBERATION'

Gillian Rose

[...]

This rediscovery of Judaism *at the end of the end of philosophy*, at the *tertium quid*, the middle of ethics, occurs at the deepest difficulty of both philosophy and Judaism, where they are equally cast into crisis over the conceiving of law and ethics, ethics and *halacha*. This convergence on ethics turns out to be a mutual aspiration *without* a third, a middle, on which to converge. Yet the converging proceeds apace in the form of holy middle, loveful polity – beyond nature and freedom, freedom and unfreedom – but also without law and therefore without grace. This converging by philosophy and Judaism corrupts. For, in spite of the inversion of their previous meliorist intentions into contrary configuration, they introduce no reflection on that repetition; but, claiming such unconstrued inversion to be the 'totalized' and 'totalizing' domination of Western metaphysics, and its cognates, they would enthrone the equally 'total' expiation of holy jurisprudence, refusing any recognition of their own implication in the *rearticulation* of domination.

There are two kinds of proclaimed 'end' to philosophy: the end of 'metaphysics' from Kant to Nietzsche, Rosenzweig and Heidegger, which may well found a *new thinking*; and the end of 'philosophy' from Hegel and Marx to Lukács and Adorno, which raises the question of the *realization* of philosophy. By 'the end of' the end of philosophy, I mean the discovery in the long debate between Judaism and philosophy – understood in relation to the Greek quest for

From Gillian Rose (1992) 'New Political Theology – Out of Holocaust and Liberation', in *The Broken Middle: Out of Our Ancient Society*. Cambridge, MA: Blackwell.

the beginning – principles, causes – of the missing middle, the *tertium quid* – ethics, which finds itself always within the imperative, the commandment, and hence always already begun.

If Heidegger celebrates 'The End of Philosophy',[1] Levinas celebrates the end of the end of philosophy as ethics, presented in philosophical as well as in Judaic form – *lectures talmudiques*. Yet this is a distinction with much less difference than Levinas claims. For Levinas' 'overcoming' of ontology depends on characterizing ontology as the non-ethical other; while Heidegger's ethical impulse depends on the characterization of Western metaphysics, his other, as 'onto-theology'. To be sure, Levinas denies the ethics in the 'other' of his authorship, while Heidegger makes no claims for the ethics in his authorship. Yet *Ereignis*, 'the Event of appropriation', presented as playing and interplaying of the fourfold dimensions of time – 'pure space and ecstatic time' – or as the four-beinged 'round dance of appropriating' by 'earth and sky, divinities and mortals',[2] this ethical paganism, shares with its 'Judaic' counterpart of responsibility, initially domesticated and subsequently traumatized, the reintroduction of Revelation into philosophy, the incursion of unique alterity, divine singularity. Furthermore, they share this reintroduction of Revelation *without raising the question of realization*; and hence without critique of the metaphysics of nature and freedom which would make the specific history of modern freedom and unfreedom reconstructable. The current Heidegger controversy therefore remains far too close to its quarry.[3] For the production of holy middles, where Revelation is opposed to a totalized history of 'Western metaphysics' – 'metaphysics' unified, thereby, since the Greeks – continues to be licensed by the inventions of his late thinking. We are ourselves the test-case which we would project back to 1933–4: called by post-modern theology to the Kingdom – pagan, Judaic, Christian – beyond 'Western' metaphysics, we are blandished away from the very modern anxiety of polity: the opposition between morality and legality. Instead of heeding the anxiety of beginning in the equivocation of the ethical, we respond to new repetition in the feast – the promise of unending angelic conviviality – new but ancient political theology. [. . .]

[. . .]

This rediscovery of the holy city, pagan, nomadic, Judaic, these mended middles over broken middle, at the end of the end of philosophy, may be witnessed as the post-modern convergent aspiration which, in effect, disqualifies the third, the middle, on which they would converge. This very converging corrupts – for in figuring and consecrating its city, this holiness will itself be reconfigured by the resource and articulation of modern domination, knowable to these post-modern ministers only as mute and monolithic sedimentation.

Post-modernism is submodern: these holy middles of round-dance, ecstatic divine milieu, irenic other city, holy community – face to face or *halachic* – bear the marks of their unexplored precondition: the diremption between the moral discourse of rights and the systematic actuality of power, within and between modern states; and therefore they will destroy what they would propagate, for once substance is presented, even if it is not 'represented', however continuous with practice, it becomes procedural, formal, and its meaning will be configured and corrupted within the prevailing diremptions of morality and legality, autonomy and heteronomy, civil society and state. Mended middles betray their broken middle: antinomian yet dependent on renounced law; holy yet having renounced 'ideals'; yearning for nomadic freedom, yet having renounced nature and freedom. This thinking concurs in representing its tradition – reason and institutions – as monolithic domination, as 'totalitarian', while overlooking the *pre*-dominance of form – abstract legal form – as the unfreedom *and* freedom of modern states, thereby falling into the trap, not of positing another 'totalitarian' ideal, but of presenting a holy middle which arises out of and will be reconfigured in the all-pervasive broken middle.

This holiness corrupts because it would sling us between ecstasy and eschatology, between a promise of touching our ownmost singularity and the irenic holy city, precisely without any disturbing middle. But this 'sensual holiness' arises out of and falls back into *a triune structure* in which we suffer and act as singular, individual and universal; or, as *particular*, as represented in institutions of the *middle*, and as the *state* – where we are singular, individual and universal *in each position*. These institutions of the middle represent and configure the relation between particular and the state: they stage the agon between the three in one, one in three of singular, individual, universal; they represent the middle, broken between morality and legality, autonomy and heteronomy, cognition and norm, activity and passivity. Yet they stand and move between the individual and the state. It has become easy to describe trade unions, local government, civil service, the learned professions: the arts, law, education, the universities, architecture and medicine as 'powers'. And then renouncing knowledge as power, too, to demand total expiation for domination, without investigation into the dynamics of configuration, of the triune relation which is our predicament – and which, either resolutely or unwittingly, we fix in some form, or with which we struggle, to know, and still to misknow and yet to grow ... Because the middle is broken – because these institutions are systematically flawed – does not mean they should be eliminated or mended.

The holy middle corrupts because it colludes in the elimination of this broken middle – drawing attention away from the reconfiguration of singular, individual and universal at stake. Away from the ways in which under the promise of enhanced autonomy – whether for individuals or for communities – the middle is being radically undermined in a process of *Gleichschaltung* which, unlike the Nazi version, is quite compatible with the proclamation and actuality of civil society, with the proclamation and actuality of plurality, with the proclamation and actuality of post-modernity.

[...]

Walter Benjamin wrote [...] in 1939–40, before 'Auschwitz', in order to shock even those historians and politicians opposed to Fascism out of their progressivist conceptions of history: '*even the dead* will not be safe from the enemy if he wins. And this enemy has not ceased to be victorious.'[4] After 'Auschwitz', this strategic Messianism has also been literalized, and has come to found political theologies, Catholic and Jewish, based on a proleptic soteriology of the dead. Political theology out of the perspective of Resurrection proclaims: all 'future' thinking must do justice to (Fackenheim), or be conducted in the darkness of (Metz) the redemption of those who have died.[5] Out of this 'source', Fackenheim's holocaust theology, *To Mend the World* (1982), and Metz's political theology, *The Emergent Church* (1980), major Jewish and Catholic works, respectively, mend the middle with holy cities, crowning Love the principle of the ethical state – yet they thereby fall further into the reconfiguration of the law, of the middle, which they render unknowable. Knowing death but not diremption, political theologies out of holocaust and liberation converge yet again towards that middle which they undermine by consecration as holy elevation.

[...] The agon of authorship discernible in these works may be systematically compared and contrasted, as lamentation and threefold response: religious or anthropological; methodological or philosophical and political or social. The lamentation of 'Auschwitz' effects a 'disruption' to Metz, a 'rupture' to Fackenheim; it calls for a turning – *Metanoia*, Greek for 'repentance' – to Metz; a turning or being turned – *Teshiva*, Hebrew for 'repentance' – to Fackenheim. To both, 'Auschwitz' is a *Novum* in temporal and in divine history: God is powerless in the world (Metz); God is absent or has retreated from the world (Fackenheim).[6] The primary response in each case is 'religious', and based on the same criterion. 'We can pray *after* "Auschwitz" because people prayed *in* "Auschwitz"' (Metz); to hear and obey the commanding voice of 'Auschwitz' is an ontological possibility because the hearing and obeying was already an ontic reality then and there (Fackenheim).[7] In sum, we may resist to the extent and in the way they resisted (Fackenheim); 'We [Christians] are ... assigned to the victims of Auschwitz' (Metz).[8]

The divine and temporal *Novum* is to be met and matched by a methodological response which involves, first of all, renunciation of the whole intellectual tradition on the argument that any comprehension in itself amounts to reconciliation or assimilation (Metz); 'evasion-by-explanation' amounts to transcendence or supersession (Fackenheim).[9] For Metz, this entails apostasy from trinitarianism; for Fackenheim, from Hegelian mediation. In both cases, this renunciation of the third moment is presented as the rescinding of assured eschatological grace in contrast to the previous triumphalism of theology and philosophy. It involves opening up to the dangers of dialogue, to the relation to the other, the second not the third, which Metz calls 'narration' in the place of dogma, and which Fackenheim calls 'dialogue' where the outcome is not known in advance.[10] It involves opening up the broken middle, formerly closed and completed by trinitarianism as achieved eschatology and by philosophical comprehension of mediation.

Yet, the third historical and political response proceeds, uninhibitedly, to mend the middle: the basic community or emergent church (Metz); the Jewish nation state, 'return into history', as 'mending the world' – *Tikkun* – the Kabbalistic eschatological image of fallen light-splinters restored to their creator (Fackenheim).[11] Both authorships, unembarrassed by their arrogated authority, issue a call into history. Metz starts from modernity's philosophy of the formation of the subject, and issues a call to 'the people' to become the subject of their own history in the presence of God – to be 'liberated'.[12] Fackenheim starts from modernity's philosophical idea of Judaism as the disunion of union and disunion, evidence of the special qualification of the Jewish people to return to the land as the state of Israel, actualization of the Idea and equally of Revelation, a secular repentance.[13]

In both cases, the call, modernity's unrealized idea, subject or substance, rediscovers and defines the people – not the people the call; yet what is established is a community – not a polity, for there is no law and no contest; not a society, for there is no social organization; not a religion, for there is no liturgy and no theology. The collectivity imagined is soteriological and antinomian and yet it is to be temporal. It can only set off 'the people' as 'the nation', justified against others but with the internal cohesion of the community: 'solidarity' of community (Metz); or state, actualization of the Idea and of Revelation (Fackenheim).

From the death of others, dangerous memory (Metz), from the renewal of the command to remember, *Zakhor* (Fackenheim), to these political theologies for the future, the argument is structured by three movements: from the God of the living *and* the dead, to the future in the memory of suffering, by means of dialogue to foster the opening of the middle (Fackenheim), narration not dogma as mediation (Metz), theology of communicative action (Peukert).[14] Yet the middle emerges mended: figured as an ethical, communal, collective end-point, unspecified in terms of its history, its polity, its anthropology, its sociology. Named by its soteriology, 'anamnestic solidarity': 'The dead, after all, also belong equally to the universal community of all men in solidarity with each other.'[15]

This sacralizing of the dead, the dialogue and the deed, joining by divine fiat justice and sin, justice and knowledge, as well as what Levinas called for, 'justice and power', to force anthropology, ontology and *imperium* out of the city of death into the holy city, betrays the dirempted middle it would will away.

Fackenheim and Metz argue that the memory of the dead rectifies the triumphalism of the tradition.[16] This sanctimonious justification draws attention away from the lack of articulation in such obeisance to 'the dead'. The 'paradox of anamnestic solidarity', expatiated by Peukert, that 'the happiness of the living exists in the expropriation of the dead', refers explicitly to owing our 'solidarity', our 'happiness', to 'the conclusive irretrievable loss of the victims of the historical process',[17] to the inverse relation between future felicity and commemoration.[...]

Fackenheim and Metz concur that all previous thought, philosophical or theological, in both cases methodological, is fundamentally outmoded and discredited in the situation of historical and divine *Novum*. This negating position partakes of expiation; but it is not consistently maintained nor maintainable: for how could the uniqueness, the *Novum*, be recognized, and judged to be such, unless the universal and even absolute knowledge it insists on renouncing were available? The positive version that the renewed relation to Revelation and futurity renders the mediation of previous philosophy invalid, and renders the response of 'dialogue', of being open to the Other and to others, appropriate, rejoins Holocaust and Liberation Theology for all their 'modernity' to post-modern soteriologies that conjoin the singular and the divine in holy polity. [...] Without irony, this implicit philosophy can only be insinuation – not a new methodology, but an old, now familiar, aspirant authority.

[...]

If the broken middle is abandoned instead of thought systematically, then the resulting evasive theology, insinuated epistemology, sacralized polity, will import the features of the City of Death remorselessly. The community, mended world, response to the travail of history, emerges as the simple sociology at the end of this kind of Liberation and Holocaust Theology.

While Holocaust and Liberation Theology turn into unexamined sociology, Holocaust Sociology turns into its contrary – Levinas' overemployed theology.

[...]

Zygmunt Bauman's challenging argument in *Modernity and the Holocaust* follows the structure of Liberation and Holocaust Theology: prevalent intellectual methods and assumptions, in this case, sociological, are themselves implicated in and indicted for the failure to come to terms with 'the Holocaust'; 'the Holocaust' itself is not the breakdown but the test of modernity: not 'determined' by modernity, yet the basic features of modernity – instrumental rationality and its bureaucratic institutions – made 'the Holocaust' 'not only possible, but eminently reasonable'.[18] The City of Death is interpreted in this authorship as the rational outcome of a collective order based on the technical and bureaucratic institutions, not on 'moral standards'. Finally, borrowing from Levinas, Bauman argues that the social distancing produced by rational-technical means suppresses moral proximity; that socialization itself reduces moral capacity; that 'morality' is *pre-social*, not the product of society but manipulated by it.[19] Borrowing from Arendt, Bauman articulates and insists on the '*moral responsibility for resisting socialization*'.[20]

The crucial convergence Bauman seeks to establish is between modern bureaucracy and the culture of instrumental rationality which separates judgement of ends from organization of means and produces moral indifference, and the development of the sociological enterprise itself which is premised on the assumption that to socialize is to civilize: that normative social institutions control and gradually eliminate irrational and antisocial drives at the individual level and at the collective level; which, in the latter case, amounts to the concentration and specialization of violence simultaneous with the divesting of violence from daily life.[21] Bauman does not add, however, the parallel point that the elimination of antisocial drives in the individual may also lead to the internalization and specialization of violence in the psychic economy of the socialized ego: morality. Instead he will argue that the imposition of norms divests the individual of his/her 'presocial morality' or responsibility, 'the existential condition of 'being with others'.[22]

[...] The call to moral responsibility cannot prevail over instrumental rationality and bureaucracy for they share the same political history: correlated legitimacies of the inner and outer 'violence' that reproduces modernity.

Bauman's defence of personal 'morality' can only claim an existential sacrality; for he distrusts the risk of sociological authorship: that while no knowledge or politics may be *generally* available, or correspond to its insight, sociological reconstruction is still staked on comprehension and on practice. 'Violence' is thereby not translated into any oppositional holiness – moral, ecclesial or eschatological – but related to the history of the form of law as enabler and disabler. Classic sociological authorship is not ultimately nervous about its scientific credentials but about its circularity, its foundations: how to gain a perspective on, to criticize, the law which bestows its own form (legal-rationality or normative factuality) without collusion in that rationality (law) yet without ontologizing irrationality – violence; to acknowledge the limitations of representation, yet to avoid antinomianism.

The agon of authorship is to remain with anxiety of beginning and equivocation of the ethical: not to define the broken middle as 'violence', and to translate it into holiness – moral, ecclesial, eschatological. Because the middle cannot be mended, because no politics or knowledge may be available or employable, it does not mean that no comprehension or representation is possible, or that it is in any case avoidable. For as all these holy authorships, Arendt, Levinas, [...] Bauman, to name a few, reveal, to refuse the agon of comprehension or representation, to see only violence in the law,[23] involves the elevation of both Author and His or Her creation to love in the heavenly state – which is to ignore the violence perpetuated both in this divine fate and in its abandoned temporal mate.

NOTES

1. 'The End of Philosophy and the Task of Thinking,' *On Time and Being*, trans. Joan Stambaugh, New York, Harper & Row, 1972, pp. 55–78.
2. 'Time and Being,' *Zur Sache des Denkens*, Tübingen, Niemeyer, 1969 pp. 15–22, trans. pp. 15, 19, 21, and 'The End of Philosophy', p. 66, *On Time and Being*; 'The Thing', 1951 in *Vorträge und Aufsätze*, Pfullingen, Neske, (1954), 1978, pp. 172, 173, translation *Poetry, Language, Thought*, trans. Albert Hofstadter, New York,

Harper & Row, 1977, pp. 179, 180. See Rose, *Dialectic of Nihilism: Post-Structuralism and the Law*, Oxford: Blackwell, 1984, pp. 72–84.

3. For elaboration, see Rose, 'Diremption of Spirit: on Derrida's *De l'esprit*,' in *Judaism and Modernity*, Oxford, Blackwell Publishers (forthcoming).

4. 'Theses on the Philosophy of History', 1940, in *Gesammelte Schriften*, 1978 Frankfurt am Main, Suhrkamp, Bd VI, p. 695, translation *Illuminations*, trans. (1955) Harry Zohn, (ed.) Hannah Arendt, London, Collins, 1973, p. 257.

5. Emil Fackenheim, *To Mend the World: Foundations of Future Jewish Thought*, New York, Schocken, 1982, pp. 23, 133. Johann Baptist Metz, *The Emergent Church: The Future of Christianity in a Postbourgeois World*, 1980, trans. Peter Mann, London, SCM, 1981, pp. 18–19.

6. Metz, *The Emergent Church*, p. 2; Fackenheim, *To Mend the World*, pp. 250–2.

7. Metz, ibid., p. 19; Fackenheim, ibid., p. 25

8. Metz, ibid., p. 20; Fackenheim, ibid., p. 25

9. Metz, ibid., p. 19; Fackenheim, ibid., p. 26–8.

10. Metz, ibid., p. 4, *Faith in History and Society: Towards a Practical Fundamental Theology*, 1977, trans. David Smith, London, Burns & Oates, 1980, pp. 205f.; Fackenheim., ibid., pp. 128–30.

11. Metz, *The Emergent Church*, pp. 62–5; Fackenheim, ibid., pp. 250f.

12. Metz, *Faith in History and Society*, pp. 46–7.

13. Fackenheim, *To Mend the World*; compare pp. 127–30 with 144–6.

14. Helmut Peukert, *Science, Action and Fundamental Theology: Towards a Theology of Communicative Action*, 1976, trans. James Bohman, Cambridge, MIT, 1986.

15. Metz, *Faith in History and Society*, p. 75.

16. See Metz on 'dangerous memories', *Faith in History and Society*, pp. 109–15.

17. Peukert, *Science, Action and Fundamental Theology*, pp. 208, 209.

18. Bauman, *Modernity and the Holocaust*, Cambridge, Polity, 1989, p. 18

19. Ibid., p. 183.

20. Ibid., p. 177–8.

21. Ibid., p. 27–8.

22. Ibid., p. 182.

23. Where Arendt is concerned, this attribution of 'violence in the law' would seem to fly in the face of her argument in *On Violence*, where legitimate power is precisely the contrary of the violence of powerlessness. However, the condemnation of the modern as 'the social', and the affirmation of 'the political', with its ecclesial characteristics, means that Arendt, too, characterizes the modern as violent.

PART VII

LITERATURE AND CULTURE
AFTER AUSCHWITZ

LITERATURE AND CULTURE AFTER AUSCHWITZ: INTRODUCTION

The eminent critic Irving Howe once remarked that he could not 'think of another area of literary discourse in which a single writer has exerted so strong ... an influence as Theodor Adorno has on discussions of literature and the Holocaust.' Howe had in mind a particular phrase from an essay written by the German-Jewish philosopher Adorno in the late 1940s and published in the early 1950s. At the very end of 'Cultural Criticism and Society' – an essay which is not primarily about the Nazi genocide, but rather about the status of culture and cultural criticism in late capitalist society – Adorno provocatively claims that 'To write poetry after Auschwitz is barbaric.' Over the course of the next two decades Adorno would return several times to the question of 'poetry after Auschwitz' and to the more general question of culture and thought after the Holocaust. Each time he revisited the issue he modulated and refined his position, but it has been his original statement, frequently taken out of context and misquoted, that has exerted the influence of which Howe speaks (see Rothberg, 2000 for a complete account).

The entries in this part provide a range of Adorno's own writings, as well as a series of direct and indirect responses to Adorno's challenge. The first selection, however, comes from the important last text of Walter Benjamin, an associate of Adorno who did not manage to escape from the Nazis. With its reflections on the relationship between culture and barbarism and its radical critique of progressive notions of history, Benjamin's 'Theses on the Philosophy of History' (1940) can be seen as one of the sources of Adorno's later reflections. In her contribution, Sigrid Weigel even suggests that Benjamin's 'Theses,' although written *before* Auschwitz (albeit in the middle of the Nazi era), actually anticipates the demands of thought *after* Auschwitz, and does so decades before Adorno achieved similar insight.

Reading Adorno's successive conceptualizations of 'poetry after Auschwitz' does suggest that Weigel is correct in finding a significant break within Adorno's reflections on the Holocaust. Certainly, his evaluation of the role of literature in confronting atrocity seems to shift significantly from his early doubt about the efficacy of poetry to his self-critical assertions in the 1960s that literature must 'resist precisely this verdict' ('Commitment' 88) and that '[p]erennial suffering has as much right to expression as a tortured man has to scream' (*Negative Dialectics*). In 'Commitment' (which we have been unable to reproduce here), Adorno clarifies that suffering 'demands the continued existence of the very art it forbids; hardly anywhere else does suffering still find its own voice, a consolation that does not immediately betray it' (88).

But the shift between early and later Adorno takes another form as well. Between 'Cultural Criticism and Society' and *Negative Dialectics* (1966) Adorno has begun to measure the impact of the Nazi genocide on his own philosophical discourse. By the 1960s the certainty with which Adorno had earlier subsumed the Holocaust within a more general critique of capitalist modernity is tempered by a new understanding of how the fact of genocide challenges even the most radical thought. Thought must turn 'against itself' and explore its own limits in order to have a chance of participating in the construction of a genuinely post-Auschwitz world.

While the entries of Howe and Weigel provide a helpful close engagement with Adorno's difficult reflections, the other critics collected here provide more indirect responses to the challenge of writing after Auschwitz. Maurice Blanchot's *The Writing of the Disaster* does not engage directly with Adorno (although Blanchot does provide a suggestive rewriting of 'poetry after Auschwitz' in *Vicious Circles*). Blanchot's poetic-philosophical text is a highly mediated response to the Holocaust by a bystander who in the 1930s was involved with far-right, antisemitic French politics. *The Writing of the Disaster* can be read as a work of witness and mourning that is part of a long-term effort to work through that complicity. It is also an attempt to develop a form of writing and thinking adequate to 'the disaster' – a concept that cannot be reduced to the Holocaust, but which cannot be thought apart from it either.

The work of the Jewish poet Paul Celan has become a privileged locus in debates about poetry after Auschwitz. Celan, whose family was murdered by the Nazis and who himself was imprisoned in a Nazi labor camp, produced an elliptical, difficult oeuvre whose oblique reflection on the Holocaust is often seen to refute Adorno's dictum. Of particular interest and poignancy is the fact that Celan, who was born in Czernowitz, Romania, wrote in German, the very language of the perpetrators. In 'Shibboleth' the French philosopher Jacques Derrida meditates on how Celan's poetry commemorates singular, unnamed events and wounds. The essay circles around the paradox Derrida perceives in the concept of the date. For Derrida a date marks a unique event and yet, in order to be understood, it must be repeatable and thus must distinguish itself from that uniqueness. Derrida reads Celan's poetry as enacting and bearing witness to this paradox of the event's singularity.

Yale literary scholar Geoffrey Hartman's essay might also be understood as meditating on a paradox of post-Holocaust writing, in this case, one found in Derrida's own reflections on Celan. According to Hartman, Derrida, no less than Celan, develops an innovative, idiosyncratic style designed to interrogate and dismantle language and concepts complicit with the culture out of which genocide emerged. Yet Hartman is also troubled by Derrida's apparent refusal to directly address the events, even as he responds to them. Elsewhere, Derrida has said that Auschwitz is the 'sole theme' of 'Shibboleth'; one might well wonder with Hartman why he cannot say so within the essay itself.

Against the background of the debates sparked by Adorno, the Israeli critic Sidra Ezrahi concludes this section with an attempt to map out two dominant tendencies in artistic and theoretical representations of the Holocaust: the 'absolutist' tendency, which removes Auschwitz from any familiar geography and history, and the 'relativist' tendency, which believes in the possibility of 'an ongoing renegotiation' of the past. Ezrahi ends by suggesting that these tendencies are not as divergent as they seem, but that much is nevertheless at stake intellectually and politically in how one approaches Auschwitz.

As Ezrahi implies, reflection on the relationship between culture and catastrophe has become increasingly important in the last decades. The question of art's role in the face of extreme violence is being pursued not only in Holocaust studies but also in responses to various modern histories, from slavery and apartheid to war in the former Yugoslavia and now to terrorism and counter-terrorism. Does art only aestheticize violence, masking its harshness and superficially redeeming the losses associated with it? Or can art be a vital source of response to the disaster, a privileged locus for expressing suffering and for the construction of an ethically responsive and responsible community? To be sure, the answers to such questions will vary with the specificities of local histories and traditions, but much can be learned by reading across histories as well. The writing of poetry did not stop when Adorno declared it barbaric (quite the contrary); yet Adorno's dictum has had the salutary result of forcing artists and critics to become more self-conscious about just how closely related to each other the forces of creation and destruction can be.

OTHER WORKS IN HOLOCAUST STUDIES

Adorno, Theodor W. (1992) 'Commitment' [1962], in T. W. Adorno, *Notes to Literature, vol. II*, ed. R. Tiedemann, trans. S. W. Nicholsen. New York: Columbia University Press, pp. 76–94.

Felman, Shoshana and Dori Laub (1992) *Testimony: Crises of Witnessing in Literature, Psychoanalysis, and History*. New York: Routledge.

Friedlander, Saul (ed.) (1992) *Probing the Limits of Representation: Nazism and the 'Final Solution'*. Cambridge, MA: Harvard University Press.

Hartman, Geoffrey (1996) *The Longest Shadow: In the Aftermath of the Holocaust.* Bloomington, IN: Indiana University Press.

Kritzman, Lawrence (ed.) (1995) *Auschwitz and After: Race, Culture, and 'the Jewish Question' in France.* New York: Routledge.

Langer, Lawrence (1975) *The Holocaust and the Literary Imagination.* New Haven, CT: Yale University Press.

Rothberg, Michael (2000) *Traumatic Realism: The Demands of Holocaust Representation.* Minneapolis, MN: University of Minnesota Press, chapters 1 and 2.

Steiner, George (1967) *Language and Silence.* New York: Atheneum.

<h2 style="text-align:center">OTHER RELEVANT WORKS</h2>

Blanchot, Maurice (1985) *Vicious Circles*, trans. Paul Auster. Barrytown, NY: Station Hill Press.

Eagleton, Terry (1990) *The Ideology of the Aesthetic.* Oxford: Blackwell.

Forché, Carolyn (ed.) (1993) *Against Forgetting: Twentieth-Century Poetry of Witness.* New York: W. W. Norton.

Lyotard, Jean-François (1988) *The Differend: Phrases in Dispute*, trans. Georges Van Den Abbeele. Minneapolis, MN: University of Minnesota Press.

Sanders, Mark (2000) 'Truth, Telling, Questioning: The Truth and Reconciliation Commission, Antjie Krog's *Country of My Skull*, and Literature after Apartheid,' *Modern Fiction Studies*, 46.1: 13–41.

33

'THESES ON THE PHILOSOPHY OF HISTORY'

Walter Benjamin

VII

Consider the darkness and the great cold
In this vale which resounds with mysery.
— Brecht, *The Threepenny Opera*

To historians who wish to relive an era, Fustel de Coulanges recommends that they blot out everything they know about the later course of history. There is no better way of characterizing the method with which historical materialism has broken. It is a process of empathy whose origin is the indolence of the heart, *acedia*, which despairs of grasping and holding the genuine historical image as it flares up briefly. Among medieval theologians it was regarded as the root cause of sadness. Flaubert, who was familiar with it, wrote: '*Peu de gens devineront combien il a fallu être triste pour ressusciter Carthage.*'[1] The nature of this sadness stands out more clearly if one asks with whom the adherents of historicism actually empathize. The answer is inevitable: with the victor. And all rulers are the heirs of those who conquered before them. Hence, empathy with the victor invariably benefits the rulers. Historical materialists know what that means. Whoever has emerged victorious participates to this day in the triumphal procession in which the present rulers step over those who are lying prostrate. According to traditional practice, the spoils are carried along in the procession. They are called cultural treasures, and a historical materialist views

From Walter Benjamin (1968) 'Theses on the Philosophy of History', in *Illuminations*, ed. H. Arendt, trans. H. Zohn. New York: Schocken Books.

them with cautious detachment. For without exception the cultural treasures he surveys have an origin which he cannot contemplate without horror. They owe their existence not only to the efforts of the great minds and talents who have created them, but also to the anonymous toil of their contemporaries. There is no document of civilization which is not at the same time a document of barbarism. And just as such a document is not free of barbarism, barbarism taints also the manner in which it was transmitted from one owner to another. A historical materialist therefore dissociates himself from it as far as possible. He regards it as his task to brush history against the grain.

VIII

The tradition of the oppressed teaches us that the 'state of emergency' in which we live is not the exception but the rule. We must attain to a conception of history that is in keeping with this insight. Then we shall clearly realize that it is our task to bring about a real state of emergency, and this will improve our position in the struggle against Fascism. One reason why Fascism has a chance is that in the name of progress its opponents treat it as a historical norm. The current amazement that the things we are experiencing are 'still' possible in the twentieth century is *not* philosophical. This amazement is not the beginning of knowledge – unless it is the knowledge that the view of history which gives rise to it is untenable.

IX

> *Mein Flügel ist zum Schwung bereit,*
> *ich kehrte gern zurück,*
> *denn blieb ich auch lebendige Zeit,*
> *ich hätte wenig Glück.*
> – Gerhard Scholem, 'Gruss vom Angelus'[2]

A Klee painting named 'Angelus Novus' shows an angel looking as though he is about to move away from something he is fixedly contemplating. His eyes are staring, his mouth is open, his wings are spread. This is how one pictures the angel of history. His face is turned toward the past. Where we perceive a chain of events, he sees one single catastrophe which keeps piling wreckage upon wreckage and hurls it in front of his feet. The angel would like to stay, awaken the dead, and make whole what has been smashed. But a storm is blowing from Paradise; it has got caught in his wings with such violence that the angel can no longer close them. This storm irresistibly propels him into the future to which his back is turned, while the pile of debris before him grows skyward. This storm is what we call progress.

[...]

XIII

Every day our cause becomes clearer and people get smarter.
– Wilhelm Dietzgen, *Die Religion der Sozialdemokratie*

Social Democratic theory, and even more its practice, have been formed by a conception of progress which did not adhere to reality but made dogmatic claims. Progress as pictured in the minds of Social Democrats was, first of all, the progress of mankind itself (and not just advances in men's ability and knowledge). Secondly, it was something boundless, in keeping with the infinite perfectibility of mankind. Thirdly, progress was regarded as irresistible, something that automatically pursued a straight or spiral course. Each of these predicates is controversial and open to criticism. However, when the chips are down, criticism must penetrate beyond these predicates and focus on something that they have in common. The concept of the historical progress of mankind cannot be sundered from the concept of its progression through a homogeneous, empty time. A critique of the concept of such a progression must be the basis of any criticism of the concept of progress itself.

NOTES

1. 'Few will be able to guess how sad one had to be in order to resuscitate Carthage.'
2. *My wing is ready for flight,*
   I would like to turn back.
   If I stayed timeless time,
   I could have little luck.

34

'CULTURAL CRITICISM AND SOCIETY'

Theodor W. Adorno

[...]

The traditional transcendent critique of ideology is obsolete. In principle, the method succumbs to the very reification which is its critical theme. By transferring the notion of causality directly from the realm of physical nature to society, it falls back behind its own object. Nevertheless, the transcendent method can still appeal to the fact that it employs reified notions only in so far as society itself is reified. Through the crudity and severity of the notion of causality, it claims to hold up a mirror to society's own crudity and severity, to its debasement of the mind. But the sinister, integrated society of today no longer tolerates even those relatively independent, distinct moments to which the theory of the causal dependence of superstructure on base once referred. In the open-air prison which the world is becoming, it is no longer so important to know what depends on what, such is the extent to which everything is one. All phenomena rigidify, become insignias of the absolute rule of that which is. There are no more ideologies in the authentic sense of false consciousness, only advertisements for the world through its duplication and the provocative lie which does not seek belief but commands silence. Hence, the question of the causal dependence of culture, a question which seems to embody the voice of that on which culture is thought only to depend, takes on a backwoods ring. Of course, even the immanent method is eventually overtaken by this. It is dragged into the abyss by its object. The materialistic transparency of culture has not

From Theodor W. Adorno (1981) 'Cultural Criticism and Society', in *Prisms*, trans. S. and S. Weber. Cambridge, MA: MIT Press.

made it more honest, only more vulgar. By relinquishing its own particularity, culture has also relinquished the salt of truth, which once consisted in its opposition to other particularities. To call it to account before a responsibility which it denies is only to confirm cultural pomposity. Neutralized and ready-made, traditional culture has become worthless today. Through an irrevocable process its heritage, hypocritically reclaimed by the Russians, has become expendable to the highest degree, superfluous, trash. And the hucksters of mass culture can point to it with a grin, for they treat it as such. The more total society becomes, the greater the reification of the mind and the more paradoxical its effort to escape reification on its own. Even the most extreme consciousness of doom threatens to degenerate into idle chatter. Cultural criticism finds itself faced with the final stage of the dialectic of culture and barbarism. To write poetry after Auschwitz is barbaric. And this corrodes even the knowledge of why it has become impossible to write poetry today. Absolute reification, which presupposed intellectual progress as one of its elements, is now preparing to absorb the mind entirely. Critical intelligence cannot be equal to this challenge as long as it confines itself to self-satisfied contemplation.

35

'MEDITATIONS ON METAPHYSICS'

Theodor W. Adorno

1 AFTER AUSCHWITZ

We cannot say any more that the immutable is truth, and that the mobile, transitory is appearance. The mutual indifference of temporality and eternal ideas is no longer tenable even with the bold Hegelian explanation that temporal existence, by virtue of the destruction inherent in its concept, serves the eternal represented by the eternity of destruction. One of the mystical impulses secularized in dialectics was the doctrine that the intramundane and historic is relevant to what traditional metaphysics distinguished as transcendence – or at least, less gnostically and radically put, that it is relevant to the position taken by human consciousness on the questions which the canon of philosophy assigned to metaphysics. After Auschwitz, our feelings resist any claim of the positivity of existence as sanctimonious, as wronging the victims; they balk at squeezing any kind of sense, however bleached, out of the victims' fate. And these feelings do have an objective side after events that make a mockery of the construction of immanence as endowed with a meaning radiated by an affirmatively posited transcendence.

Such a construction would affirm absolute negativity and would assist its ideological survival – as in reality that negativity survives anyway, in the principle of society as it exists until its self-destruction. The earthquake of Lisbon sufficed to cure Voltaire of the theodicy of Leibniz, and the visible disaster of the first nature was insignificant in comparison with the second,

From Theodor W. Adorno (1973) 'Meditations on Metaphysics', in *Negative Dialectics*, trans. E. B. Ashton. New York: Seabury Press.

social one, which defies human imagination as it distills a real hell from human evil. Our metaphysical faculty is paralyzed because actual events have shattered the basis on which speculative metaphysical thought could be reconciled with experience. Once again, the dialectical motif of quantity recoiling into quality scores an unspeakable triumph. The administrative murder of millions made of death a thing one had never yet to fear in just this fashion. There is no chance any more for death to come into the individuals' empirical life as somehow conformable with the course of that life. The last, the poorest possession left to the individual is expropriated. That in the concentration camps it was no longer an individual who died, but a specimen – this is a fact bound to affect the dying of those who escaped the administrative measure.

Genocide is the absolute integration. It is on its way wherever men are leveled off – 'polished off,' as the German military called it – until one exterminates them literally, as deviations from the concept of their total nullity. Auschwitz confirmed the philosopheme of pure identity as death. The most far out dictum from Beckett's *End Game*, that there really is not so much to be feared any more, reacts to a practice whose first sample was given in the concentration camps, and in whose concept – venerable once upon a time – the destruction of nonidentity is ideologically lurking. Absolute negativity is in plain sight and has ceased to surprise anyone. Fear used to be tied to the *principium individuationis* of self-preservation, and that principle, by its own consistency, abolishes itself. What the sadists in the camps foretold their victims, 'Tomorrow you'll be wiggling skyward as smoke from this chimney,' bespeaks the indifference of each individual life that is the direction of history. Even in his formal freedom, the individual is as fungible and replaceable as he will be under the liquidators' boots.

But since, in a world whose law is universal individual profit, the individual has nothing but this self that has become indifferent, the performance of the old, familiar tendency is at the same time the most dreadful of things. There is no getting out of this, no more than out of the electrified barbed wire around the camps. Perennial suffering has as much right to expression as a tortured man has to scream; hence it may have been wrong to say that after Auschwitz you could no longer write poems. But it is not wrong to raise the less cultural question whether after Auschwitz you can go on living – especially whether one who escaped by accident, one who by rights should have been killed, may go on living. His mere survival calls for the coldness, the basic principle of bourgeois subjectivity, without which there could have been no Auschwitz; this is the drastic guilt of him who was spared. By way of atonement he will be plagued by dreams such as that he is no longer living at all, that he was sent to the ovens in 1944 and his whole existence since has been imaginary, an emanation of the insane wish of a man killed twenty years earlier.

Thinking men and artists have not infrequently described a sense of being not quite there, of not playing along, a feeling as if they were not themselves at all, but a kind of spectator. Others often find this repulsive; it was the basis of

Kierkegaard's polemic against what he called the esthetic sphere. A critique of philosophical personalism indicates, however, that this attitude toward immediacy, this disavowal of every existential posture, has a moment of objective truth that goes beyond the appearance of the self-preserving motive. 'What does it really matter?' is a line we like to associate with bourgeois callousness, but it is the line most likely to make the individual aware, without dread, of the insignificance of his existence. The inhuman part of it, the ability to keep one's distance as a spectator and to rise above things, is in the final analysis the human part, the very part resisted by its ideologists.

It is not altogether implausible that the immortal part is the one that acts in this fashion. The scene of Shaw on his way to the theater, showing a beggar his identification with the hurried remark, 'Press,' hides a sense of that beneath the cynicism. It would help to explain the fact that startled Schopenhauer: that affections in the face of death, not only other people's but our own, are frequently so feeble. People, of course, are spellbound without exception, and none of them are capable of love, which is why everyone feels loved too little. But the spectator's posture simultaneously expresses doubt that this could be all – when the individual, so relevant to himself in his delusion, still has nothing but that poor and emotionally animal-like ephemerality.

Spellbound, the living have a choice between involuntary ataraxy – an esthetic life due to weakness – and the bestiality of the involved. Both are wrong ways of living. But some of both would be required for the right *désinvolture* and sympathy. Once overcome, the culpable self-preservation urge has been confirmed, confirmed precisely, perhaps, by the threat that has come to be ceaselessly present. The only trouble with self-preservation is that we cannot help suspecting the life to which it attaches us of turning into something that makes us shudder: into a specter, a piece of the world of ghosts, which our waking consciousness perceives to be nonexistent. The guilt of a life which purely as a fact will strangle other life, according to statistics that eke out an overwhelming number of killed with a minimal number of rescued, as if this were provided in the theory of probabilities – this guilt is irreconcilable with living. And the guilt does not cease to reproduce itself, because not for an instant can it be made fully, presently conscious.

This, nothing else, is what compels us to philosophize. And in philosophy we experience a shock: the deeper, the more vigorous its penetration, the greater our suspicion that philosophy removes us from things as they are – that an unveiling of the essence might enable the most superficial and trivial views to prevail over the views that aim at the essence. This throws a glaring light on truth itself. In speculation we feel a certain duty to grant the position of a corrective to common sense, the opponent of speculation. Life feeds the horror of a premonition: what must come to be known may resemble the down-to-earth more than it resembles the sublime; it might be that this premonition will be confirmed even beyond the pedestrian realm, although the happiness of thought, the promise of its truth, lies in sublimity alone.

If the pedestrian had the last word, if it were the truth, truth would be degraded. The trivial consciousness, as it is theoretically expressed in positivism and unreflected nominalism, may be closer than the sublime consciousness to an *adaequatio rei atque cogitationis*; its sneering mockery of truth may be truer than a superior consciousness, unless the formation of a truth concept other than that of *adaequatio* should succeed. The innervation that metaphysics might win only by discarding itself applies to such other truth, and it is not the last among the motivations for the passage to materialism. We can trace the leaning to it from the Hegelian Marx to Benjamin's rescue of induction; Kafka's work may be the apotheosis of the trend. If negative dialectics calls for the self-reflection of thinking, the tangible implication is that if thinking is to be true – if it is to be true today, in any case – it must also be a thinking against itself. If thought is not measured by the extremity that eludes the concept, it is from the outset in the nature of the musical accompaniment with which the SS liked to drown out the screams of its victims.

2 METAPHYSICS AND CULTURE

A new categorical imperative has been imposed by Hitler upon unfree mankind: to arrange their thoughts and actions so that Auschwitz will not repeat itself, so that nothing similar will happen. When we want to find reasons for it, this imperative is as refractory as the given one of Kant was once upon a time. Dealing discursively with it would be an outrage, for the new imperative gives us a bodily sensation of the moral addendum – bodily, because it is now the practical abhorrence of the unbearable physical agony to which individuals are exposed even with individuality about to vanish as a form of mental reflection. It is in the unvarnished materialistic motive only that morality survives.

The course of history forces materialism upon metaphysics, traditionally the direct antithesis of materialism. What the mind once boasted of defining or construing as its like moves in the direction of what is unlike the mind, in the direction of that which eludes the rule of the mind and yet manifests that rule as absolute evil. The somatic, unmeaningful stratum of life is the stage of suffering, of the suffering which in the camps, without any consolation, burned every soothing feature out of the mind, and out of culture, the mind's objectification. The point of no return has been reached in the process which irresistibly forced metaphysics to join what it was once conceived against. Not since the youthful Hegel has philosophy – unless selling out for authorized cerebration – been able to repress how very much it slipped into material questions of existence.

Children sense some of this in the fascination that issues from the flayer's zone, from carcasses, from the repulsively sweet odor of putrefaction, and from the opprobrious terms used for that zone. The unconscious power of that realm may be as great as that of infantile sexuality; the two intermingle in the anal fixation, but they are scarcely the same. An unconscious knowledge whispers to the child what is repressed by civilized education; this is what matters, says the whispering voice. And the wretched physical existence strikes a spark in the supreme interest that is scarcely less repressed; it kindles a 'What is that?' and 'Where is it going?' The man who managed to recall what used to strike him in the words 'dung hill' and 'pig sty' might be closer to absolute knowledge than Hegel's chapter in which readers are promised such knowledge only to have it withheld with a superior mien. The integration of physical death into culture should be rescinded in theory – not, however, for the sake of an ontologically pure being named Death, but for the sake of that which the stench of cadavers expresses and we are fooled about by their transfiguration into 'remains.'

A child, fond of an innkeeper named Adam, watched him club the rats pouring out of holes in the courtyard; it was in his image that the child made its own image of the first man. That this has been forgotten, that we no longer know what we used to feel before the dogcatcher's van, is both the triumph of culture and its failure. Culture, which keeps emulating the old Adam, cannot bear to be reminded of that zone, and precisely this is not to be reconciled with the conception that culture has of itself. It abhors stench because it stinks – because, as Brecht put it in a magnificent line, its mansion is built of dogshit. Years after that line was written, Auschwitz demonstrated irrefutably that culture has failed.

That this could happen in the midst of the traditions of philosophy, of art, and of the enlightening sciences says more than that these traditions and their spirit lacked the power to take hold of men and work a change in them. There is untruth in those fields themselves, in the autarky that is emphatically claimed for them. All post-Auschwitz culture, including its urgent critique, is garbage. In restoring itself after the things that happened without resistance in its own countryside, culture has turned entirely into the ideology it had been potentially – had been ever since it presumed, in opposition to material existence, to inspire that existence with the light denied it by the separation of the mind from manual labor. Whoever pleads for the maintenance of this radically culpable and shabby culture becomes its accomplice, while the man who says no to culture is directly furthering the barbarism which our culture showed itself to be.

Not even silence gets us out of the circle. In silence we simply use the state of objective truth to rationalize our subjective incapacity, once more degrading truth into a lie. When countries of the East, for all their drivel to the contrary, abolished culture or transformed it into rubbish as a mere means of control, the culture that moans about it is getting what it deserves, and what on its part, in the name of people's democratic right to their own likeness, it is zealously heading for. The only difference is that when the apparatchiks over there acclaim their administrative barbarism as culture and guard its mischief as an inalienable heritage, they convict its reality, the infrastructure, of being as barbarian as the superstructure they are dismantling by taking it under their management. In the West, at least, one is allowed to say so.

The theology of the crisis registered the fact it was abstractly and therefore idly rebelling against: that metaphysics has merged with culture. The aureole of culture, the principle that the mind is absolute, was the same which tirelessly violated what it was pretending to express. After Auschwitz there is no word tinged from on high, not even a theological one, that has any right unless it underwent a transformation. The judgment passed on the ideas long before, by Nietzsche, was carried out on the victims, reiterating the challenge of the traditional words and the test whether God would permit this without intervening in his wrath.

A man whose admirable strength enabled him to survive Auschwitz and other camps said in an outburst against Beckett that if Beckett had been in Auschwitz he would be writing differently, more positively, with the front-line creed of the escapee. The escapee is right in a fashion other than he thinks. Beckett, and whoever else remained in control of himself, would have been broken in Auschwitz and probably forced to confess that front-line creed which the escapee clothed in the words 'Trying to give men courage' – as if this were up to any structure of the mind; as if the intent to address men, to adjust to them, did not rob them of what is their due even if they believe the contrary. That is what we have come to in metaphysics.

36

'WRITING AND THE HOLOCAUST'

Irving Howe

[...]

I cannot think of another area of literary discourse in which a single writer has exerted so strong, if diffused, an influence as Theodor Adorno has on discussions of literature and the Holocaust. What Adorno offered in the early 1950s was not a complete text or even a fully developed argument. Yet his few scattered remarks had an immediate impact, evidently because they brought out feelings held by many people.

'After Auschwitz,' wrote Adorno, 'to write a poem is barbaric.' It means to 'squeeze aesthetic pleasure out of artistic representation of the naked bodily pain of those who have been knocked down by rifle butts. ... Through aesthetic principles or stylization ... the unimaginable ordeal still appears as if it had some ulterior purpose. It is transfigured and stripped of some of its horror, and with this, injustice is already done to the victims.'

Adorno was by no means alone in expressing such sentiments, nor in recognizing that his sentiments, no matter how solemnly approved, were not likely to keep anyone from trying to represent through fictions or to evoke through poetic symbols the concentration and death camps. A Yiddish poet, Aaron Tsaytlin, wrote in a similar vein after the Holocaust: 'Were Jeremiah to sit by the ashes of Israel today, he would not cry out a lamentation. ... The Almighty Himself would be powerless to open his well of tears. He would maintain a deep silence. For even an outcry is now a lie, even tears are mere literature, even prayers are false.'

From Irving Howe (1988) 'Writing and the Holocaust', in B. Lang (ed.), *Writing and the Holocaust*. New York and London: Holmes & Meier.

37

'NON-PHILOSOPHICAL AMAZEMENT– WRITING IN AMAZEMENT: BENJAMIN'S POSITION IN THE AFTERMATH OF THE HOLOCAUST'

Sigrid Weigel

BENJAMIN'S AMAZEMENT AS AN HISTORICO-PHILOSOPHICAL BOUNDARY CASE
Walter Benjamin's remark on amazement in view of contemporary events as contained in his theses 'On the Concept of History',[1] written shortly before his unsuccessful attempt to flee France and his death, is one of the most frequently cited passages from his writings: 'The current amazement that the things we are experiencing are "still" possible in the twentieth century is *not* philosophical' (*GS* 1.2, 697; *Ill* 259).

This sentence is usually quoted in order to emphasize how normal and everyday violence, annihilation, and destruction have become in contemporary life – that is, in order to counter a stance of amazement, astonishment, or horror. In so doing, the intention is to give the numerous phenomena of man-made disasters a place in the logic of historical development, a logic that is always grasped in negatively charged concepts, even if they differ according to the commentator's particular attitude.[2] In other words, a negative course of history or a history of catastrophes is taken as the norm, and by this Benjamin's critique of the concept of progress is, in the final instance, re-forged in the shape of a negative teleology of history.

A more precise reading of the sentence on amazement clearly shows that Benjamin by no means attacked amazement *per se*, but instead rejected the philosophical status given it. He emphasizes two words in the sentence: by

From Sigrid Weigel (1996) 'Non-philosophical Amazement – Writing in Amazement: Benjamin's Position in the Aftermath of the Holocaust', in *Body- and Image-Space: Re-reading Walter Benjamin*, trans. G. Paul with R. McNicholl and J. Gaines. London and New York: Routledge.

placing the word 'still' in quotation marks he frames it as if it were a quoted commonplace, an *on dit* that becomes a sign of a 'notion of progress' which is the basis of and thus implicit to a specific form of amazement – namely, at that which is still possible. And by italicizing the word 'not', Benjamin strongly negates the philosophical status of amazement. This means that he does not reject amazement itself, but rather makes it the precondition for the sole form of cognition possible, as is shown by the very next sentence in Thesis VIII: 'This amazement is not at the beginning of a cognition – unless it is the cognition that the view of history which gives rise to it is untenable' (*GS* 1.2, 697; *Ill* 259, translation modified).[3]

Here, amazement stands at the possible beginning of a cognition of an untenable notion of the history that engendered it and at the same time marks the end of precisely that notion of history. Amazement is thus described as a boundary case (*Grenzfall*). Considered *not* philosophical, it pinpoints the caesura *vis-à-vis* a concept of history which describes contemporary events as inadequate or retrogressive parts of the course of history or the historical progression. And given that it is not philosophical, it is at the same time the condition of possibility for a different type of perception.

The meaning Benjamin gives amazement here, as a boundary case, corresponds to the way he uses the notion of a 'state of emergency' (*Ausnahmezustand*). At the beginning of Thesis VIII he states that the intention must be to arrive at a notion of history that corresponds to the doctrine 'that the "state of emergency" in which we live is not the exception but the rule' (*GS* I.2, 697; *Ill* 259). The words 'state of emergency' are again placed in quotation marks to show that they are a quotation of a widespread notion, from which Benjamin proceeds to set off his own concept of a 'real state of emergency' in what then follows.

If events which common sense must regard as constituting a state of emergency (such as those taking place under fascism) become the rule, then what Benjamin is interested in bringing about as a 'real state of emergency' is intended to break with this rule. This break does not involve a simple transformation of a progressive teleology of history into a negative variant; just as the well-known phrase from the *Passagen* project – namely, 'that things "just keep on going" *is* the catastrophe' (*GS* V.1, 592; *N* 64) – does not imply that the catastrophe is considered to be normal. For the opposite is true: here, it is the norm which is the catastrophe. This is the other side to the fact that all those phenomena which people like to term 'states of emergency' follow the rule or the order of things. 'Bringing about a real state of emergency' in Benjamin's sense thus requires a break with that concept of history which is based on a notion of progress as the rule and therefore regards everything that does not fit in with the rule as an exception, a relapse, barbarism, irrationality, or something similar.

[...]

With regard to the concept of history, this argumentation highlights two things: (1) a break with the synthesis of amazement and a philosophical discourse, and (2) a caesura with the traditional philosophy of history.

If amazement was at the root of all philosophy, then it was swiftly incorporated into *logos* by philosophy as a discipline and subjected to the rules of a rational and logical discourse. The need to find an explanation for enigmatic phenomena tended to strip these of any fear they might instil in the beholder. *To tambos* – that is to say amazement, fright, and horror – was incorporated in a discourse which in the interests of knowledge, explanation, and truth worked away at integrating the amazing into an order accessible to reason and thus, in the final instance, sublating its enigmatic elements. If, therefore, *after* the enlightenment of amazement, amazement occurs again, then it is a different type of amazement; namely, amazement at the deviation from reason that was assumed to be the rule or from the rule which was construed as reasonable. To this extent, amazement, having once been a stance that prompted philosophy, has now become a *non*-philosophical attitude that is an effect of and a residue after the history of philosophy. Only by then taking this latter form of amazement seriously and understanding it as marking the boundaries of traditional philosophy can a different form of conception emerge. This does not involve a return to some 'original', quasi pre-philosophical amazement, but instead a negation of philosophical amazement in order to make amazement the beginning of a different mode of cognition.

At the same time, Benjamin is thus suggesting that precisely that philosophy of history is untenable which is bound up with notions of totality, development, and meaningfulness.[4] Benjamin's phrase concerning the untenability of a specific 'view of history' not only pinpoints the limits of a concrete concept of history – for example, a concept of progress – but at the same time points up the limitations of any fundamental conception of 'history' as a meaningful process that unfolds over time, that is, a conception on which all such philosophies of history are based that construe the cognizability of reason in history as the precondition for finding a philosophical meaning in history – be it the Christian doctrine of salvation, or Kant, Hegel, Marx, or Löwith.[5] The critique of progress and of reason being innate to the course of history itself – that is, the critique of those phenomena which Horkheimer and Adorno, taking up Benjamin's theses, termed the 'dialectic of enlightenment' – involves reason in such contradictions, which can no longer be grasped in terms of an historico-philosophical discourse.

In Thesis XIII Benjamin explicitly states that he is not just interested in a critique of the 'conception of progress' (*Fortschritt*), but that such a critique must rest on a critique of the conception of historical progression, or going on (*Fortgang*) (*GS* I.2, 701; *Ill* 262–3). In other words, his theses focus on questions of how we construe history – that is, the 'concept of history' – which is why the title Adorno and Horkheimer gave the theses, namely *Geschichtsphilosophische Thesen* (literally, 'Historico-Philosophical Theses'), obscures the radical epistemological position the text contains. For Benjamin here precisely does not develop historico-philosophical theses as such, but rather theses *on* the philosophy of history (to this extent, the English title is more accurate) which expose its limits and constitute it as it were as a boundary case. Therefore the distorted title which affects the central argument is one of the preconditions for the lasting misrecognition of Benjamin's reflections on the concept of history.

In the passage that immediately precedes the thesis on non-philosophical amazement – namely, in the well-known Thesis IX about the 'angel of history' – Benjamin attempted to present this epistemological boundary case in terms of a thought-image (*Denkbild*). Neither the first angel from Gershom Scholem's poem, who formulates the desire for a return based in a negative teleology of history, nor the *Angelus Novus* frozen with its open mouth and wide-opened eyes – a mythical image that stresses the aspect of fear in amazement – engender a different notion of history. It is only with the figure of a counterstriving disposition (*gegenstrebige Fügung*) – in which the gaze of the frightened angel, who is being driven into the future by the storm of progress without being able to look the latter in the face, is positioned non-synchronously in relation to the chain of events we see – it is only with this constellation, then, that this different notion of history is presented. Wherever we see that 'things keep going on', the angel's gaze, and only his, sees a catastrophe. The catastrophe is therefore no exception, but rather is simply inaccessible to our gaze, which is trained only to see continual progression. It is the *other* gaze which is the condition of possibility for perceiving the catastrophe in history.

THE LIMITS OF PHILOSOPHY AFTER AUSCHWITZ: ADORNO

In part, the *Dialectic of Enlightenment*, which was written ensuing upon and taking up Benjamin's theses [...] is also shaped by the demands made by a different mode of cognition. However, the authors shy back from the radicality with which Benjamin breaks thought-images out of the continuum of philosophical discourse: 'It [our conception of history] is a critique of philosophy, and therefore refuses to abandon philosophy,' write Horkheimer and Adorno in the foreword to the 1969 edition of the book (Horkheimer and Adorno 1973: x). [...]

The 'final solution' as an objective historical caesura that, as far as historical data are concerned, comes between Benjamin's last text and the *Dialectic of Enlightenment*, to begin with at least left no obvious epistemological caesura in its wake. Conversely, Benjamin's text, which is characterized by a way of thinking that is closer to the danger (possibly owing to Benjamin's having written it in greater proximity to factual persecution), seems to reflect on an epistemological boundary case which, as a condition of possibility, provides the means for approaching the caesura in question retrospectively. Thought *after* Auschwitz will, at any rate, not be able to circumvent that amazement or horror to which Benjamin did full justice both as a boundary case and as the beginning of a new mode of cognition. This necessarily has consequences for the philosophical discourse after the Shoah.[6]

By contrast, Adorno's critical reflections on his own position and on the consequences which the name 'Auschwitz' had for thought for a long time take up the question of how we can speak when faced with the unspeakable, and discuss the paradigm of 'speaking after Auschwitz', frequently in relation to specific genres or disciplines. What strikes the eye is that Adorno did not extend the radical end he postulated for certain literary genres as such in the aftermath of Auschwitz – for poetry and satire, for example[7] – to philosophy. Now Adorno's sentence on poetry after Auschwitz, in contrast to the trivializing history of its reception, which has tended to take it out of context, is not a postulate, but describes a cultural-critical constellation which can clearly be read as a boundary case. The suggestion that 'it is barbaric to write a poem after Auschwitz' follows after a colon – thus earmarking a situation which cultural critique must address and which Adorno terms 'the final stage of the dialectic of culture and barbarism' ('Cultural Critique and Society' [1949]: Adorno 1981: 34). The latter, he says, even whittles away that 'knowledge, which expresses why it has become impossible to write poems today'.

Yet many years were to pass before he wrote a similarly radical sentence about philosophy. [. . .] It is not until 1966 that the 'final stage of the dialectic', as formulated in 'Cultural Critique and Society' in 1949, or rather the boundary case of cultural critique which he postulates there, becomes embedded in a central philosophical constellation and thus transformed into a 'negative dialectics'.

In the famous third chapter of Part Three, the figure of 'After Auschwitz' becomes one of the models of negative dialectics, even if the form of the text in question, its textual shape, keeps open the heterogeneity between philosophical discourse and the site named as 'after Auschwitz'. As a running head – not a title – 'After Auschwitz' seems to be a name that cannot be integrated into the philosophical text and therefore is strangely at loggerheads with the chapter title 'Meditations on Metaphysics'. Perhaps this constellation *literally* reflects the concept of thought thinking-versus-itself, as is postulated at the end of the first section.

Here, the motif of guilt which emerged fifteen years before in the dedication of *Minima Moralia* is taken up again and now positioned as the starting point of a *different* philosophy. It is the position of someone who has remained unscathed, who has managed to get away, of someone 'guilty solely by being alive': it is this that now becomes one of the necessary conditions of philosophy, indeed of a philosophy that is always already suspicious of itself.

> The guilt of life, which purely as a fact will strangle another life, according to statistics that eke out an overwhelming number of killed with a minimal number of rescued, as if this were provided in the theory of probabilities – this guilt is irreconcilable with living. And the guilt does not cease to

reproduce itself, because not for an instant can it be made fully, presently conscious [*weil sie dem Bewußtsein in keinem Augenblick ganz gegenwärtig sein kann*]. This, nothing else, is what compels us to philosophize. And in philosophy we experience a shock [*diese erfährt dabei den Schock*, literally 'philosophy experiences the shock']: the deeper, the more vigorous its penetration, the greater our [the] suspicion that philosophy removes us [*sie entferne sich*, literally that it, i.e. philosophy, is becoming removed] from things as they are.

(Adorno 1973: 364)

Even if in *Negative Dialectics* the figure of enlightenment's reflection on itself, a figure from the *Dialectic of Enlightenment*, is given a more radical form as the 'self-reflection of thinking', or a form of thought that 'must also be a thinking against itself' (1973: 365), there is still a residue left that is not conceptualized. If the only compulsion to engage in philosophy is the fact that the guilt cannot be completely present in consciousness at one single moment, then the question arises as to what form those elements of guilt which are *not present in our consciousness* take, what status they must be accorded, what form of knowledge they engender, how we can address them. Since the figure of a guilt which in no single moment can be fully present in consciousness precisely corresponds to the way in which Freud describes the trauma, these elements constitute the respective *Other* of consciousness; they are thus only readable in mnemic signs, symptoms, and other modes of the language of the unconscious. To justify the necessity of philosophy by referring to this guilt is at the same time to mark the limits of philosophy – that is, unless it incorporates theorems from psychoanalysis and other forms of reading the language of the unconscious. But that would bring a quite different form of philosophizing and quite different figures of thought into play. Adorno, by pointing to the non-presence of guilt as a whole, put his finger on a central problem, however. Yet it is also remarkable that he, in the very moment that he represses the cognition of the psychoanalytical structure of his own figure, displaces the shock from the survivors to philosophy: for in his words, it is philosophy that experiences the shock.

The various signs of a return of that guilt which is not integrated into consciousness strongly determined the shape that the further aftermath of National Socialism took, something that can be seen not least from the fact that as of the 1970s the paradigm of traumatization[8] has emerged ever further into the foreground of discussion. The *topos* of 'speaking after Auschwitz' for a long time informed cultural discourse in post-1945 Germany and clearly contributed to a more radical confrontation with the central problems of 'thought after Auschwitz' being skirted in the form of a figure of speech which, with its use of universal categories such as the ineffable (*das Unaussprechliche*), repeatedly diverted attention away from the specificities of the Shoah. It was not until the follow-up to the *Historikerstreit* that these central problems came

more clearly into focus. On the one hand, we have to do with the irreconcilability of the different positions in the aftermath of National Socialism, that is,
with the fact that the memories of the survivors and of the subsequent
descendants of the victims cannot be reconciled with the memories of the
descendants of the collective of perpetrators to create one coherent image of
history.[9] On the other, we are faced with attempts to present the politics of
extermination in an historical form, a project that constantly comes up against
an intractable contradiction that can no longer be described in terms of a
critique of instrumental reason or the dialectic of enlightenment – namely, the
simultaneity of the rationality with which the annihilation was perpetrated, on
the one side, and the irrationality and incomprehensibility of the motives and
justifications given for it, on the other. If the historico-philosophical 'connections among an assumption of rationality, ability to understand, and the
meaningful reconstruction' (Diner 1992: 142)[10] is fundamentally shattered
by the Shoah, then it is, in the final instance, the inability to 'think Auschwitz'
which prevents 'thought after Auschwitz' from ever coming to rest, an ability,
moreover, which cannot be overcome in any discourse, be it philosophical,
historiographical, or literary. [...]

Now, the problematics and reflective figures towards which 'thought after
Auschwitz' has been moving via all these detours are linked by the impossibility
of integrating the events into the existing notion of history with a stance that
could well be described in terms of Benjamin's negation of philosophical
amazement. In other words, they are moving towards the site of that boundary
case which he had already described in Thesis VIII.

NOTES

1. Benjamin's own title uses the term 'concept' (*Über den Begriff der Geschichte*) and
   not 'philosophy'. The title of the English translation, 'Theses on the Philosophy of
   History', follows the title *Geschichtsphilosophische Thesen* given by Adorno and
   Horkheimer.
2. Be it capitalism, patriarchy, destruction of nature, colonialism, or scientific revolution.
3. Benjamin's term '*Erkenntnis*' emphasizes the moment of cognition or realization,
   whilst the English translation 'knowledge' too much connotes already existing or
   established ideas. (Translator's note.)
4. 'As unity and totality, the time that begins and completes, i.e. the sphere of historical
   discourse, is full of sense: in a double sense of having direction and intelligibility'
   (Chatelet 1975: 205).
5. For example, Karl Löwith's description in his historico-philosophical *opus
   magnum*, in its analysis of the problems of eschatological thinking in modernity,
   is based on the paradigm of *crisis* instead of reflecting the limits of the philosophy of
   history.
6. For a thorough philosophical analysis of Adorno after Auschwitz, in relation to
   Heidegger's *Germanien*, see Garcia Düttmann (1991).
7. See 'Juvenal's error' in Adorno (1974).
8. See Bohleber's overview on this paradigm (Bohleber 1990).
9. See the Broszat–Friedländer debate. Concerning the *topos* of 'writing after Auschwitz', see the differentiation of the various forms of silence in Heller (1993).

10. Diner postulates a 'negative historics' cognition of history:

> Since historians must first become aware of the cancellation of assumptions of rationality in historical reconstruction before they can venture to engage in the enterprise of historicization. Or, to phrase it differently: due to the loss of its imaginability, it is necessary first to *think* Auschwitz before it can be written about historically.
>
> (1992: 142)

WORKS CITED

Adorno, Theodor (1973) *Negative Dialectics*, trans. E. B. Ashton. New York: Seabury Press.

———— (1981) *Prisms*, trans. S. and S. Weber. Cambridge, MA: MIT Press.

Benjamin, Walter (1973) *Illuminations*, ed. Hannah Arendt, trans. Harry Zohn. Glasgow: Fontana/Collins. [*Ill*]

———— (1980–89) *Gesammelte Schriften*, eds Rolf Tiedemann and Harmann Schweppenhäuser, 7 vols. Frankfurt am Main: Suhrkamp. [*GS*]

Bohleber, Werner (1990) 'Das Fortwirken des Nationalsozialismus in der zweiten und dritten Generation nach Auschwitz,' *Babylon* 7: 70–84.

Chatelet, François (1975) 'Die Geschichte,' *Geschichte der Philosophie*, vol. VII. Frankfurt am Main: Ullstein.

Diner, Dan (1992) 'Historical Understanding and Counterrationality: the *Judenrat* as Epistemological Vantage,' in S. Friedlander (ed.), *Probing the Limits of Representation: Nazism and the 'Final Solution'*. Cambridge, MA: Harvard University Press.

Garcia Düttmann, Alexander (1991) *Das Gedächtnis des Denkens: Versuch über Heidegger und Adorno*. Frankfurt am Main: Suhrkamp.

Heller, Agnes (1993) 'Die Weltzeituhr stand still: Schreiben nach Auschwitz? Schweigen nach Auschwitz? Philosophische Betrachtungen eines Tabus,' *Die Zeit*, 7 May 1993, p. 61.

Horkheimer, Max and Theodor W. Adorno (1973) *Dialectic of Enlightenment*, trans. John Cumming. London: Allen Lane.

38

THE WRITING OF THE DISASTER

Maurice Blanchot

◆ The disaster ruins everything, all the while leaving everything intact. It does not touch anyone in particular; 'I' am not threatened by it, but spared, left aside. It is in this way that I am threatened; it is in this way that the disaster threatens in me that which is exterior to me – an other than I who passively become other. There is no reaching the disaster. Out of reach is he whom it threatens, whether from afar or close up, it is impossible to say: the infiniteness of the threat has in some way broken every limit. We are on the edge of disaster without being able to situate it in the future: it is rather always already past, and yet we are on the edge or under the threat, all formulations which would imply the future – that which is yet to come – if the disaster were not that which does not come, that which has put a stop to every arrival. To think the disaster (if this is possible, and it is not possible inasmuch as we suspect that the disaster is thought) is to have no longer any future in which to think it.

The disaster is separate; that which is most separate.

When the disaster comes upon us, it does not come. The disaster is its imminence, but since the future, as we conceive of it in the order of lived time, belongs to the disaster, the disaster has always already withdrawn or dissuaded it; there is no future for the disaster, just as there is no time or space for its accomplishment.

◆ *He does not believe in the disaster. One cannot believe in it, whether one lives or dies. Commensurate with it there is no faith, and at the same time a sort*

From Maurice Blanchot (1995) 'The Writing of the Disaster', trans. Ann Smock. Lincoln, NE and London: University of Nebraska Press.

of disinterest, detached from the disaster. Night; white, sleepless night – such is the disaster: the night lacking darkness, but brightened by no light.

◆ The circle, uncurled along a straight line rigorously prolonged, reforms a circle eternally bereft of a center.

◆ 'False' unity, the simulacrum of unity, compromises it better than any direct challenge, which, in any case, is impossible.

◆ Would writing be to become, in the book, legible for everyone, and indecipherable for oneself? (Hasn't Jabès almost told us this?)

◆ If disaster means being separated from the star (if it means the decline which characterizes disorientation when the link with fortune from on high is cut), then it indicates a fall beneath disastrous necessity. Would law be the disaster? The supreme or extreme law, that is: the excessiveness of uncodifiable law – that to which we are destined without being party to it. The disaster is not our affair and has no regard for us; it is the heedless unlimited; it cannot be measured in terms of failure or as pure and simple loss.

Nothing suffices to the disaster; this means that just as it is foreign to the ruinous purity of destruction, so the idea of totality cannot delimit it. If all things were reached by it and destroyed – all gods and men returned to absence – and if nothing were substituted for everything, it would still be too much and too little. The disaster is not of capital importance. Perhaps it renders death vain. It does not superimpose itself upon dying's scope for withdrawal, filling in the void. Dying sometimes gives us (wrongly, no doubt), not the feeling of abandoning ourselves to the disaster, but the feeling that if we were to die, we would escape it. Whence the illusion that suicide liberates (but consciousness of the illusion does not dissipate it or allow us to avoid it). The disaster, whose blackness should be attenuated – through emphasis – exposes us to a certain idea of passivity. We are passive with respect to the disaster, but the disaster is perhaps passivity, and thus past, always past, even in the past, out of date.

◆ *The disaster takes care of everything.*

◆ The disaster: not thought gone mad; not even, perhaps, thought considered as the steady bearer of its madness.

◆ The disaster, depriving us of that refuge which is the thought of death, dissuading us from the catastrophic or the tragic, dissolving our interest in will and in all internal movement, does not allow us to entertain this question either: what have you done to gain knowledge of the disaster?

◆ The disaster is related to forgetfulness–forgetfulness without memory, the motionless retreat of what has not been treated – the immemorial, perhaps. To remember forgetfully: again, the outside.

◆ 'Have you suffered for knowledge's sake?' This is asked of us by Nietzsche, on the condition that we not misunderstand the word 'suffering': it means, not so much what we undergo, as that which goes under.[1] It denotes the *pas* ['not'] of the utterly passive, withdrawn from all sight, from all knowing. Unless it be the case that knowledge – because it is not knowledge of the disaster, but knowledge as disaster and knowledge disastrously – carries us, carries us off, deports us (whom it smites and nonetheless leaves untouched), straight to ignorance, and puts us face to face with ignorance of the unknown so that we forget, endlessly.

◆ The disaster: stress upon minutiae, sovereignty of the accidental. This causes us to acknowledge that forgetfulness is not negative or that the negative does not come after affirmation (affirmation negated), but exists in relation to the most ancient, to what would seem to come from furthest back in time immemorial without ever having been given.

◆ It is true that, with respect to the disaster, one dies too late. But this does not dissuade us from dying; it invites us – escaping the time where it is always too late – to endure inopportune death, with no relation to anything save the disaster as return.

◆ Never disappointed, not for lack of disappointment, but because of disappointment's always being insufficient.

◆ I will not say that the disaster is absolute; on the contrary, it disorients the absolute. It comes and goes, errant disarray, and yet with the imperceptible but intense suddenness of the outside, as an irresistible or unforeseen resolve which would come to us from beyond the confines of decision.

◆ To read, to write, the way one lives under the surveillance of the disaster: exposed to the passivity that is outside passion. The heightening of forgetfulness.

◆ It is not you who will speak; let the disaster speak in you, even if it be by your forgetfulness or silence.

◆ The disaster has already passed beyond danger, even when we are under the threat of ——. The mark of the disaster is that one is never at that mark except when one is under its threat and, being so, past danger.

◆ To think would be to name (to call) the disaster the way one reserves, in the back of one's mind, an unspoken thought.
    I do not know how I arrived at this, but it may be that in so doing I struck upon the thought which leads one to keep one's distance from thought; for it gives that: distance. But to go to the end of thought (in the form of this thought of the end, of the edge): is this not possible only by changing to another thought? Whence this injunction: do not change your thought, repeat it, if you can.

◆ The disaster is the gift; it gives disaster: as if it took no account of being or not-being. It is not advent (which is proper to what comes to pass): it does not happen. And thus I cannot ever happen upon this thought, except without knowing, without appropriating any knowledge. Or again, is it the advent of what does not happen, of what would come without arriving, outside being, and as though by drifting away? The posthumous disaster?

◆ Not to think: that, without restraint, excessively, in the panicky flight of thought.

◆ *He said to himself: you shall not kill yourself, your suicide precedes you. Or: he dies inept at dying.*

◆ Limitless space where a sun would attest not to the day, but to the night delivered of stars, multiple night.

◆ 'Know what rhythm holds men.' (Archilochus.) Rhythm or language. Prometheus: 'In this rhythm, I am caught.' Changing configuration. What is rhythm? The danger of rhythm's enigma.

◆ *'Unless there should exist, in the mind of whoever dreamed up humans, nothing except an exact count of the pure rhythmical motifs of being, which are its recognizable signs.'* (Mallarmé.)

◆ The disaster is not somber, it would liberate us from everything if it could just have a relation with someone; we would know it in light of language and at the twilight of a language with a *gai savoir*. But the disaster is unknown; it is the unknown name for that in thought itself which dissuades us from thinking of it, leaving us, but its proximity, alone. Alone, and thus exposed to the thought of the disaster which disrupts solitude and overflows every variety of thought, as the intense, silent and disastrous affirmation of the outside.

◆ A nonreligious repetition, neither mournful nor nostalgic, a return not desired. Wouldn't the disaster be, then, the repetition – the affirmation – of the singularity of the extreme? The disaster or the unverifiable, the improper.

◆ There is no solitude if it does not disrupt solitude, the better to expose the solitary to the multiple outside.

◆ Immobile forgetfulness (memory of the immemorable): so would the disaster without desolation be de-scribed, in the passivity of a letting-go which does not renounce, does not announce anything if not the undue return. Perhaps we know the disaster by other, perhaps joyful names, reciting all words one by one, as if there could be for words an all.

◆ *The calm, the burn of the holocaust, the annihilation of noon – the calm of the disaster.*

[…]

◆ The suffering of our time: '*A wasted man, bent head, bowed shoulders, unthinking, gaze extinguished.*' '*Our gaze was turned to the ground.*'

◆ Concentration camps, annihilation camps, emblems wherein the invisible has made itself visible forever. All the distinctive features of a civilization are revealed or laid bare ('Work liberates,' 'rehabilitation through work'). Work, in societies where, indeed, it is highly valued as the materialist process whereby the worker takes power, becomes the ultimate punishment: no longer is it just a matter of exploitation or of surplus-value; labor becomes the point at which all value comes to pieces and the 'producer,' far from reproducing at least his labor force, is no longer even the reproducer of his life. For work has ceased to be his way of living and has become his way of dying. Work, death: equivalents. And the workplace is everywhere; worktime is all the time. When oppression is absolute, there is no more leisure, no more 'free time.' Sleep is supervised. The meaning of work is then the destruction of work in and through work. But what if, as it has happened in certain commandos, labor consists of carrying stones at top speed from one spot and piling them up in another, and then in bringing them back at the run to the starting point (Langbein at Auschwitz; the same episode in the Gulag; Solzhenitsyn)? Then, no act of sabotage can cancel work, for its annulment is work's own very purpose. And yet labor retains a meaning: it tends not only to destroy the worker, but more immediately to occupy, to harness and control him and at the same time perhaps to give him an awareness that to produce and not to produce amount to the same – that the one and the other alike are work – yet thereby it also makes the worker, whom it reduces to naught, aware that the society expressed in the labor camp is what he must struggle against even as he dies, even as he survives (lives on despite everything, beneath everything, beyond everything). Such survival is (also) immediate death, immediate acceptance of death in the refusal to die (I will not kill myself, because that would please them; thus I kill myself opposing them, I remain alive despite them).

◆ Knowledge which goes so far as to accept horror in order to know it, reveals the horror of knowledge, its squalor, the discrete complicity which maintains it in a relation with the most insupportable aspects of power. I think of that young prisoner of Auschwitz (he had suffered the worst, led his family to the crematorium, hanged himself; after being saved at the last moment – how can one say that: *saved*? – he was exempted from contact with dead bodies, but when the SS shot someone, he was obliged to hold the victim's head so that the bullet could be more easily lodged in the neck). When asked how he could bear this, he is supposed to have answered that he 'observed the comportment of men before death.' I will not believe it. As Lewental, whose notes were found buried near a crematorium, wrote to us, 'The truth was always more atrocious, more tragic than what will be said about it.' Saved at the last minute, the young man of whom I speak was forced to live that last instant again and each time to live it once more, frustrated every time of his own death and made to exchange it every time for the death of all. His response ('I observed the comportment of men . . .') was not a response; he could not respond. What remains for us to recognize in this account is that when he was faced with an impossible question, he could find no other alibi than the search for knowledge, the so-called dignity of knowledge: that ultimate propriety which we believe will be accorded us by knowledge. And how, in fact, can one accept not to know? We read books on Auschwitz. The wish of all, in the camps, the last wish: know what has happened, do not forget, and at the same time never will you know.

◆ Can one say: horror reigns at Auschwitz, senselessness in the Gulag? Horror, because extermination in every form is the immediate horizon. Zombies, pariahs, infidels: such is the truth of life. However, a certain number resist; the word 'political' retains a meaning; there must be survivors to bear witness, perhaps to win. In the Gulag, until the death of Stalin and except for members of the political opposition about whom memorialists say little – too little (except Joseph Berger) – no one is political. No one knows why he is there. Resistance has no meaning, if not simply for oneself, or for the sake of friendship, which is rare. Only the religious have firm convictions capable of giving significance to life, and to death. Thus resistance is spiritual. Not until the revolts issuing from the depths, and then the dissidents and their clandestine writings, do perspectives open – do ruined words become audible rising from the ruins, traversing the silence.

Surely, senselessness is at Auschwitz, horror in the Gulag. Nonsense at its most derisory is best represented (perhaps) by the son of the Lagerführer Schwarzhuber. At ten years old, he sometimes came to fetch his father at the camp. One day, he couldn't be found, and right away his father thought: he's gotten swept up by mistake and thrown with the others into the gas chamber. But the child had only been hiding, and thereafter he was made to wear a placard for identification purposes. Another sign is Himmler's fainting at mass executions. And the consequence: fearing he'd shown weakness, he gave the order to multiply the executions, and gas chambers were invented: death humanized on the outside. Inside was horror at its most extreme. Or again, sometimes concerts were organized. The power of music seems, momentarily, to bring forgetfulness and dangerously causes the distance between murderers and victims to disappear. But, Langbein adds, for the pariahs there was neither sport nor music. There is a limit at which the practice of any art becomes an affront to affliction. Let us not forget this.

◆ We must still meditate (but is it possible?) upon this: in the camp, if (as Robert Antelme said while enduring it) need sustains everything, maintaining an infinite relation to life even if it be in the most abject manner (but here it is no longer a matter of high or low) – if need consecrates life through an egotism without ego – there is also the point at which need no longer helps one to live, but is an aggression against the entire person: a torment which denudes, an obsession of the whole being whereby the being is utterly destroyed. Dull, extinguished eyes burn suddenly with a savage gleam for a shred of bread, 'even if one is perfectly aware that death is a few minutes away' and that there is no longer any point in nourishment. This gleam, this brilliance does not illuminate anything living. However, with this gaze which is a last gaze, bread is given us as bread. This gift, outside all reason, and at the point where all values have been exterminated – in nihilist desolation and when all objective order has been given up – maintains life's fragile chance by the sanctification of hunger – nothing 'sacred,' let us understand, but something which is given without being broken or shared by him who is dying of it ('*Great is hungering*,' Levinas says, recalling a Jewish saying). But at the same time the fascination of the dying gaze, where the spark of life congeals, does not leave intact the need's demand, not even in a primitive form, for it no longer allows hunger (it no longer allows bread) to be related in any way to nourishment. In this ultimate moment when dying is exchanged for the life of bread, not, any longer, in order to satisfy a need and still less in order to make bread desirable, need – in need – also dies as simple need. And it exalts, it glorifies – by making it into something inhuman (withdrawn from all satisfaction) – the need of bread which has become an empty absolute where henceforth we can all only ever lose ourselves.

But the danger (here) of words in their theoretical insignificance is perhaps that they claim to evoke the annihilation where all sinks always, without hearing the 'be silent' addressed to those who have known only partially, or from a distance the interruption of history. And yet to watch and to wake, to keep the ceaseless vigil over the immeasurable absence is necessary, for what took up again from this end (Israel, all of us) is marked by this end, from which we cannot come to the end of waking again.

NOTE

1. 'Not so much what we undergo, as that which goes under' is my translation for *le subissement*, the word Blanchot supplies lest we misunderstand the word 'suffering' (*souffrance*), and which he forms from *subir* ('to undergo, to suffer'). Blanchot writes: ' "Est-ce que tu as souffert pour la connaissance?" Cela nous est demandé par Nietzsche, à condition que nous ne nous méprenions pas sur le mot souffrance: *le subissement*, le "pas" du tout à fait passif en retrait par rapport à toute vue, tout connaître.' – Tr.

39

'SHIBBOLETH'

Jacques Derrida

[...]

What is a date? Do we have the right to pose such a question, and in this form? The form of the question 'what is' has a provenance: it dates. That it is dated does not discredit it, but if we had the time, we could draw certain inferences from this fact.

[...]

As it reaches me, at least, the question 'what is a date?' presupposes two things. First of all, that the formulation 'what is ... etc.' has a history or provenance, in other words, that it is signed, engaged, or commanded by a date in relation to whose essence its power is limited, its claim finite, and its very pertinence contestable. [...] On the other hand, and this is a second presupposition, in the inscription of a date, in the phenomenon of dating, what is dated *must not be dated* [...]. The mark which one calls a date must be marked off in a particular manner, detached from that precisely which it dates – and in this very marking off or deportation it must become readable, readable as precisely a date, wresting or exempting itself from itself, freeing itself from what it nonetheless remains, a date. In it the *Unwiederholbar* must be repeated, that is to say, effaced, ciphered, or encrypted. [...]

[...]

From Jacques Derrida (1986) 'Shibboleth', trans. Joshua Wilner, in Geoffrey Hartman and Sanford Budick (eds), *Midrash and Literature*. New Haven, CT: Yale University Press.

The date effaces itself in its very readability; it must efface in itself some stigma of singularity in order to outlast, in the poem, what it commemorates; in this lies the chance of assuring its spectral return. And since this annulment in the annulation of return partakes of the very movement of dating, what must henceforth commemorate itself is the annihilation itself of the date, a kind of nothing – or ash.

[...]

A *Shibboleth*, the word *Shibboleth*, if it is one, names, in the broadest extension of its generality or its usage, any insignificant, arbitrary mark, for example the phonemic difference between *shi* and *si*, once it becomes discriminative and decisive, that is, divisive. This difference has no meaning in and of itself, and becomes what one must know how to mark or recognize if one is to *get* on, if, that is, one is to *get over* a border or the threshold of a poem, if one is to be granted asylum or the legitimate habitation of a language. And to inhabit a language, one must already have a *Shibboleth* at one's command: it is not enough simply to understand the meaning of the word, simply to *know* how it should be pronounced (*shi* and not *si*, this the Ephraimites knew). [...]

[...]

[...] The date (signature, moment, place, totality of singular marks) always functions as a *Shibboleth*. It marks the fact that there is ciphered singularity which is irreducible to any concept, to any knowledge, and even to a history or tradition, be it of a religious kind; a ciphered singularity in which a multiplicity gathers itself *in eins*, but through whose grill a poem remains readable: 'Aber das Gedicht spricht ja!' It reaches and leaves its mark on, and if it does not, at least it calls to, the other. It speaks to and addresses the other. In a language, in the poetic writing of a language, there is nothing but *Shibboleth*. And it permits, like every date, like a name, anniversaries, alliances, returns, commemorations, even if there should be no trace, scarcely an ash of what we thus date, celebrate, commemorate, or bless.

[...]

The turning-to-ash, the burning up or incineration of a date, is the infernal threat of an absolute crypt: non-recurrence, unreadability, amnesia with nothing left over. Such a risk is no more inessential to the date than the possibility of recurrence which may be a chance as well as a threat. And I will not speak here of the *holocaust*, except to say this: there is the date of a certain holocaust, the hell of our memory, but there is a holocaust for every date, somewhere in the world at every hour. Every hour is unique, whether it comes back or whether, the last, it comes no more, no more than the sister, the same, its other *revenant*, coming back:

Geh, deine Stunde	Go, your hour
hat keine Schwestern, du bist –	has no sisters, you are –
bist zuhause. Ein Rad, langsam,	are at home. A wheel, slow,
rollt aus sich selber / . . ./	rolls on its own / . . ./
die Nacht	the night
/ . . ./nirgends	/ . . ./ Nowhere
fragt es nach dir. / . . ./	any asking about you. / . . ./
Jahre.	Years.
Jahre, Jahre, ein Finger / . . . /	Years, years, a finger / . . . /
Asche.	Ash.
Asche. Asche.	Ash. Ash.
Nacht.	Night.
Nacht-und-Nacht.	Night-and-Night.
	(trans. Joachim Neugroschel)

If the date which is mentioned, commemorated, or blessed tends to merge with its recurrence in the mention, the commemoration, the blessing of it, one can in that case not distinguish in a poetic signature between the constative value of a certain truth and that other order of truth or of the non-truth of truth which would be associated with the poetic performative.

We should now go beyond that in language which classifies marks of dating according to the calendar or the clock. Radicalizing and generalizing, we may say, without artifice, that poetic writing is dating, through and through. It is all cipher of singularity, offering its place and recalling it, offering and recalling its time at the risk of losing them in the holocaustic generality of recurrence and the readability of the concept, in the anniversary and the repetition of the unrepeatable. Wherever a signature has entered into an idiom, leaving in language the trace of an incision which is *at once* both unique and iterable, cryptic and readable, there is date, there is the madness of 'when,' the *Wahnsinn* of 'Einmal,' 'once,' and the terrifying ambiguity of the *Shibboleth*, sign of membership and threat of discrimination.

This situation (a date is a *situation*) may give rise to calculations. But in the final analysis, it ceases to be calculable, the crypt ceases to be the result of a concealment on the part of a hermetic poet, one skilled at hiding and anxious to seduce with ciphers. A crypt occurs wherever a singular incision marks language, as one might engrave a date in a tree, burning the bark with figures of fire. The voice of the poem carries beyond the singular cut, it becomes readable for all those who had no part in the event or the constellation of events entered into it, for all those excluded from its partaking [*partage*]. Seen from the side of this generality or repeatable universality of meaning, a poem counts as a philosopheme; it may offer itself as the object of a hermeneutic labor which, for the purposes of its 'internal' reading, has no need of access to the singular secret once shared [*partagé*] by a few witnesses. Looking at it from the side of universal meaning which corresponds to the date as the possibility of a publicly commemorated recurrence, one may always speak, as in a panel title, of 'philosophical implications.' But seen from the other side, from the side of irreducibly singular dating and untranslatable incision, not only is there no philosophical implication as such, but the possibility of a philosophical reading encounters here, as does any hermeneutics, its limit. This limit, which would also be the symmetrical limit of a formal poetics, does not signify the failure of philosophical hermeneutics or formal analysis, and even less does it indicate the necessity of their renunciation. Rather it turns us back toward the effaced provenance, toward the *possibility* of both philosophical hermeneutics and of formal poetics. Both presuppose the date, that is to say the mark, incised in language, of a proper name or an idiomatic event. This is what I suggested in a somewhat elliptical way when I began by saying: the question 'what is?' dates. Philosophy, hermeneutics, and poetics can only be produced within idioms, within languages, within the body of events and dates, a metalinguistic overview of which I do not say is impossible but, on the contrary, that its possibility is guaranteed by the structure of marking off which pertains to the date's annulment. The effacement of the date, in its very recurrence – here is the origin and the possibility of philosophy, of hermeneutics, and of poetics. It is also the effacement of the proper name, of the signature, of language, in the necessity of knowledge and the transmission of meaning. Annulling it in its repetition, what is sent [*l'envoi*] presupposes and disavows the date, that is to say, the *Shibboleth*.

Formally, at least, the affirmation of Judaism has the same structure as that of the date. Is this only a formal analogy? When someone says, 'We Jews,' does he intend the reappropriation of some essence, the acknowledgment of a belonging, of a partaking [*partage*]? Yes and no. Celan recalls – for this is a common theme and also the title of a question – that there is no Jewish property. '/. . . you hear me, I'm the one, me, the one you hear, the one you think you hear, me and the other /. . ./ because the Jew, you know, what does he have, that really belongs to him, that isn't lent, borrowed, never given back . . .' ('Conversation in the Mountains'). The Jew is also the other, myself and the other; I am Jewish in saying: the Jew is the other who has no essence, who has nothing of his own or whose own essence is not to have one. Thus, at one and the same time, both the alleged universality of Jewish witness ('All the poets are Jews,' says Marina Tsvetayeva, cited in epigraph to 'Und mit dem Buch aus Tarussa') and the incommunicable secret of the Judaic idiom, the singularity of its 'unpronounceable name' ('Conversation in the Mountains'). The Jew's 'unpronounceable name' says so many things: it says *Shibboleth*, the word which is unpronounceable – which *can* not be pronounced – by one who does not partake of the covenant or alliance; it says the name of God which *must* not be pronounced; and it says also the name of the Jew which the non-Jew has *trouble* pronouncing and which he scorns or destroys for that very reason, which he expels as foreign and uncouth [comme 'un nom à coucher dehors,' i.e., a long, unpronounceable name – Trans.], or which he replaces with a derisory name which is easier to pronounce – as has sometimes happened on both sides of the Atlantic. Its unpronounceability keeps and destroys the name; it keeps it, like the name of God, or dooms it to annihilation. And these two possibilities are not simply different or contradictory. The Jew, the name Jew, is a *Shibboleth* prior even to any use of the *Shibboleth*, prior to any communal or discriminatory division [*partage*], whether he is master or proscript, Jew and *Shibboleth* partake of each other: witness to the universal, but by virtue of absolute singularity, dated, marked, incised by virtue of and in the name of the other. (And I will add as well, in parentheses, that in its terrifying political ambiguity, *Shibboleth* could today name the State of Israel, the state of the State of Israel.)

The impulse to designate the 'Judaic,' Jewishness, as yours and not only mine, as always something of the other's, inappropriable, may be read, for example, in the poem dated (this is its title) *Zürich, zum Storchen*, and dedicated, in the way that every date is dedicated, to Nelly Sachs. The semantics of I and you here appear to be as paradoxical as ever and this paradox is again that of the immeasurable relative to a measure of being, the disproportion or dissymmetry of too much or too little. The 'you,' the word *you*, may be addressed to the other as well as to oneself *as* other, and each time it overruns the economy of the discourse:

Vom Zuviel war die Rede, vom	The talk was of too much, of
Zuwenig. Von Du	too little. Of You
und Aber-Du, von	and Yet-You, of
der Trübung durch Helles, von	the dimming through light, of
Jüdischem, von	Jewishness, of
deinem Gott.	your God.
/.../	/.../
Von deinem Gott war die Rede, ich	The talk was of your God, I spoke
sprach gegen ihn ...	against him...

(trans. Joachim Neugroschel)

[...]

The *you*, the *yours*, may be addressed to the other as Jew but also to the self as other, as another Jew or as other *than* Jew. And this is no longer a true alternative. 'Die Schleuse' addresses you, and your mourning, to tell you that what has been lost, and lost beyond a trace, is the word which opens, like a *Shibboleth*, on what is most intimate; the word which was left me ('das mir verblieben war'), and, what is graver still, if this could be said, the word which opens the possibility of mourning what has been lost beyond a trace: not only the exterminated family, the incineration of the family name in the figure of the sister (for the word is a 'sister,' *Schwester*), at the moment of her death, and of the final hour which no longer has a sister ('deine Stunde / hat keine Schwester'), but the very word which grants me access to Jewish mourning: *Kaddish*. [...] The loss, when it extends to the death of the name, to the extinction of the proper name which a date, a bereaved commemoration, also is, cannot be worse than when we have crossed the boundary where what becomes denied us is mourning itself, the interiorization of death in memory, *Erinnerung*, the preserving of the other in a sepulcher or epitaph. The date is also a sepulcher which gives rise to [...] a work of mourning. Celan also names the incinerated beyond of the date, those words lost without sepulcher, 'wie unbestattete Worte' ('Und mit dem Buch aus Tarussa'), the errancy of spectral names, come back to roam (*streunend*) about the stelae.

There is an event, a rite of passage, which marks the legitimate entry of the Jew into his community and which takes place only once, on a specific date; this event is circumcision. One may translate this word as 'reading-wound,' as in the end of 'DEIN VOM WACHEN,' 'sie setzt / Wundgelesenes über.' I am not claiming that Celan is speaking here about circumcision, literally; I am translating what speaks about the translation or passing over ('sie setzt ... über') of that which is, if not, as the French translation says, a readable, ciphered, or decipherable wound [*blessure lisible*], at least read to the quick [*lu jusqu'au sang*] ('Wundgelesenes').

Circumcision, in the literality of its word (*Beschneidung*), is rarely mentioned, at least as far as I know. The example of which I am thinking and to which I will return in a moment concerns the circumcision of a word. But does one ever circumcise without circumcising a word, a name? And does one ever circumcise a name without something done to the body? If the word circumcision rarely appears, other than in connection with the circumcision of the word, by contrast the tropic of circumcision disposes cuts, caesurae, ciphered alliances, and rings throughout the text. The wound is also universal, a differential mark in language, precisely that which dates and sets turning the ring of recurrence. To say that 'all the poets are Jews,' is to state something which marks and annuls the mark of a circumcision. All those who deal or inhabit language as poets are Jews – but in a tropic sense.

[...]

Now among all these meanings, a certain tropic may displace the literality of membership in the Jewish community, if one could still speak of belonging to a community to which, we are reminded, nothing belongs as its own. In this case, those who have undergone the *experience* – a certain concise experience – of circumcision, circumcised and circumcisers, are, in all the senses of this word, Jews.

Anyone or no one may be Jewish. No one is (not) circumcised; it is no one's circumcision. If all the poets are Jews, they are all circumcised or circumcisers. This gives rise in Celan's text to a tropic of circumcision which turns from the *Wundgelesenes* toward all ciphered wounds, to all cut words [...]. And if I spoke a moment ago of 'no one's circumcision,' this was because the evocation of the exterminated race designates it both by a black erection in the sky, verge and testicle, *and* as the race and root of no one. [...]

Circumcise: the word appears once in the form of a verb, *beschneide*, a verb in the imperative mode, the mode of command, of appeal, or of prayer. And this word, this word of command, injunction, or supplication bears upon the word, this verb has the word as its object, this verb speaks about an operation to be performed on the *verbum*, on the word, its complement is the word, or rather the Word: 'beschneide das Wort.' It is a question of circumcising the Word and the interpellation apostrophizes a rabbi, a circumciser. Not any rabbi, but Rabbi Loew [...].

But here the knowledge and the power of Rabbi Loew, his knowledge and power to circumcise are annulled. They know how and are able to an infinite degree, but to an infinite degree also to annul themselves. For the writing of circumcision which the intercessor asks of him is a *writing of Nothing*. It performs its operation on Nothing, it consists in inscribing Nothing in the flesh, in the word, in the flesh of the circumcised word: 'Diesem / beschneide das Wort, diesem / schreib das lebendige / Nichts ins Gemüt.' [...]

No one's circumcision, the word's circumcision by the incision of Nothing in the circumcised heart of the other, of this one, you.

Circumcise the word for him, circumcise his word, what is meant by this demand? More than one can *mean-to-say*, more and less than this or that meaning. The circumcised word is *first of all* written, at once both incised and excised in a body, which may be the body of a language: the word which is entered into, wounded in order to be what it is, the poem's caesura, the word cut into. The circumcised word is, *next of all*, read, 'read-to-the-quick,' as was said in another place. *By the same token*, as it were, it grants access to the community, to the covenant or alliance, to the partaking [*partage*] of a language: of the Jewish language as poetic language, if all poetic language is, like all the poets according to the epigraph, Jewish in essence, but according to that expropriated disidentification, in the nothing of that non-essence, of which we have spoken. The Germanic language, like any other, but here with what privilege, must be circumcised by a Rabbi, and the Rabbi is in that case a poet. How can the German language receive circumcision at this poem's date, that is to say, following the holocaust? How may one bless these ashes in German? Finally, fourth and in consequence, the circumcised word, the word turned *Shibboleth*, at once both secret and readable, mark of membership and of exclusion, the shared wound of division [*blessure de partage*], reminds us also of what I will call the *double edge* of every *Shibboleth*. The mark of an alliance, it is also an index of exclusion, of discrimination, indeed of extermination. One may, thanks to the *Shibboleth*, recognize and be recognized by one's own, for better and for worse, for the sake of partaking [*partage*] and the ring of alliance *on the one hand*, but also, *on the other hand*, for the purpose of denying the other, of denying him passage or life. One may also, because of the *Shibboleth* and exactly to the extent that one may make use of it, see it turned against oneself: then it is the circumcised who are proscribed or held at the border, excluded from the community, put to death, or reduced to ashes merely on the sight of, or in the name of, the *Wundgelesenes*.

[...]

40

'LANGUAGE AND CULTURE AFTER THE HOLOCAUST'

Geoffrey H. Hartman

[...]

The assumption that a field of knowledge or the culture itself alters because of a macrohistorical event underlies most periodization. What is also evident, however, is a wishful quest for certainty, even the certainty of loss. With a death certificate, we can hope that a new era will commence. We declare one epoch over, that another has begun, and that the calendar itself should undergo a revision, at least in our internal reckonings. Thus 1997 could be redated as 52 After Auschwitz, or 55 After the Coordination of the Final Solution at the Wannsee Conference.[1] Let me consider further what is involved in proposing that the Holocaust's impact is strong enough to have created, in effect, a before and after.[2]

[...]

What does it matter, you may wonder, when exactly the evil started or took hold? Why should giving a date be important? Yet this is a major issue in cultural history because it diagnoses an illness or fixes blame. Is the Nazi period an exceptional moment in German history, or is it the outcome of a longer development, starting in 1813, 1848, 1870, or 1914? [...]

[...]

Dates are a duplicitous construct: on the one hand, a sublime rhetoric that arises from the sense that there exist transformative occasions, epochal events; on the

From Geoffrey H. Hartman (1997) 'Language and Culture after the Holocaust', in *The Fateful Question of Culture*. New York: Columbia University Press.

other hand, merely a statistic, a commonplace and even trivial way of organiz-ing the clutter and chaos of history. 'Era-tic' and erratic easily change places. This ambiguity surrounding dates, this potentiality they have for lapsing from sublime to trivial, affects verbal terms as well. (Words, that is, also approach the promissory or quasi-performative status of dates.) What the numerical date suggests, in its magic specificity, is a decisive event, a significant happening in a *histoire événementielle*. It is like birth or death, or the dawning of a new era, or even 'a date' in the colloquial sense: a rendezvous, though with destiny. Or is it like initiation rituals that actually require a physical mark, one that allows no identity ambiguity?

A date, then, branding the spirit, and though ambiguous in its own structure, potentially places us beyond ambivalence, embarrassment, perplexity, and verbal equivocation. Dates mark the intersection of being and time; while words, shadowed by dates, create a counterecstatic, temporizing temporality. It is not surprising that Derrida's *Schibboleth*, his book on Paul Celan, the poet most closely associated with the Holocaust, should open with: 'Une seule fois: la circoncision n'a lieu qu'une fois' ('One time only: circumcision takes place only once'), and that it quickly arrives at the subject of dates. [. . .]

By now we are privy to Derrida's style: we have heard that promissory 'Je parlerai' before; we note that the phrase 'the one-and-only time' is followed by the cliché 'in other words,' indicating that, as language, nothing is unique, unrepeatable; while 'revient' comes back as 'revenant' in the inaugural sentence of the later book on Heidegger. Here, moreover, the Holocaust is mentioned, quite deliberately. [. . .]

Dating subverts narrative time, even while making it possible. The result is an interlacing play with terms and texts that could be seen as an insidious universalizing of the Shoah, removing, that is, all historically specific coordi-nates, though not the agony. 'Each hour numbers its holocaust.' Derrida's title, *Schibboleth*, seems to announce an essay on particularism, or what defines national or racial identity, indeed *any* assumed or constructed – and potentially fatal – difference between self and other, nation and nation. Yet Derrida rarely proceeds by choosing one thematized focus; we cannot be sure that 'Jewishness' is central to the eccentric path of this discourse. What is clear is that he gives to Celan's 'unbestattete Worte' ('unburied words'), by means of their own sparseness and his wordy dissemination, more than 'a grave in the air': he gives them a universal, or at least repeatable presence. 'The poem raises its voice beyond the individualizing wound' ('Le poème porte sa voix au-delà de l'entaille singulière').[3]

Though Walter Benjamin is not named, the question of reproducibility, or whether the numinous quality of art he calls its aura can preserve itself in a technological and media-mediated age, joins this meditation from the outset. Emphasis shifts from the uniqueness ('Une seule fois . . .') of the historical Holocaust, or of Celan's elliptical testimony, to the analogous and familiar quest of bringing back – from the dead, from the past – what cannot be brought back and associating this orphic pursuit of the irrevocable ('Nach / dem Unwiederholbaren') with the fact that memories can only perpetuate themselves by entering a figurative space, an invented present different from the 'anterior present' they evoke. Because of the impossibility of 'presenting the present' and the paradox in 'representing the present,' there is always a virtual space – Maurice Blanchot identifies it with literature itself – in which such representation 'takes place.' Writing, in seeking to recapture the unique, or to image what is absent, hardens it, so that we are left with the consciousness of language as incorporating a void ('Ungeschriebenes, zu / Sprache verhärtet').[4] That void is at once very personal and quite impersonal: the loss of a sister, but also what language, as a condition of its possibility, passes over or sublimates (in Hegel's sense of *Aufhebung*). Thus literary space is marked by ellipsis, by conscious or unconscious 'avoidance,' even by lightness,[5] and the 'nothing' of this ellipsis makes discourse, despite its referential or memorial function, as spectral as the old moon holding the new in its arms.

The enigmatic opening of *De l'esprit* (the book on Heidegger) points to this at once numinous and ghostly status of writing, caught between *relève* (*Aufhebung*) and *revenant*. 'Je parlerai du revenant, de la flamme et des cendres' is close to a praeterition (cf. 'Comment ne pas parler')[6] in the form of its obverse: mock-epic invocation and enumeration. For Derrida's follow-up sentence, 'Et de ce que, pour Heidegger, *éviter* veut dire,' evokes not what is included but what is avoided or the meaning of that avoidance. Derrida's promissory opening turns on a periphrasis built around the voided/avoided referent 'holocaust' – which becomes, here, Derrida's avoidance too, not only Heidegger's.[7]

Yet does 'holocaust,' as the (a)voided word, resolve the periphrasis? The situation is more complex. Derrida is playing with fire, as he does explicitly in *Cinders* (*Feu la cendre*).[8] The word Heidegger would like to avoid, and uses only too often, turns out to be *Geist*, or 'spirit,' not 'holocaust.' Derrida, it is true, describes 'spirit' as 'cerné par le feu,' encircled by fire. He may be thinking implicitly about holocaustal fire, but explicitly he refers to all crimes committed in the name of the spirit and most literally to the book burning that was decreed for Helvetius's eighteenth-century book *L'esprit* or the larger, more vicious conflagration of May 1933 in Nazi Germany, shortly after Heidegger lauded a new order in his inaugural speech as rector of Freiburg.

[...]

If Derrida's first words in *De l'esprit* were only a way of skirting Heidegger's moral failure, the entire issue would be trivialized. But the avoidance alluded to is not just an *impensé*: it signals, I have suggested, a preoccupation with Heidegger's basic project of *Destruktion*, the project that also founded deconstruction. Heidegger's 'avoidance' subordinates everything to the deconstructive rescue of spirit speech from its unthinking (mechanical or now technological) unconscious and to the reconstruction of a more originary language possibility. This language, restored through a poetic as well as philosophical scrutiny, could recall us, in the words of Levinas, from modernity's mistaken attempt to turn the appropriation of being *by* knowledge (by deadly acts of domination and anaesthetic habits of classification) into something even worse: the identification of being *with* knowledge.

Yet who can ignore, after the event, the fatal convergence of *Geist* and Holocaust, the deep unease we feel that an ideal aspiration, a so-called spiritual revolution, backed up by institutionalized philosophy and cultural discourse, contributed to the tragedy? Derrida does not seek to determine *when* culture went wrong: this would only repeat the 'dating' error, which also affected Heidegger and is the residue of a sublime yet standard rhetoric. He lays bare the difficulty of escaping from a contaminating rhetoric. Heidegger, he shows, faces the 'Question of German Speech' and devises the linguistic and conceptual hygiene of *Destruktion*.[9]

[. . .]

Derrida, however, does not explicitly connect his insight to pressures on language after the Holocaust: to the extreme nature of that event or a crisis in the idea of culture that constitutes an absolute event, one to be dated by that fact. 'The circumcision of a word,' he writes, 'is not dated *in history*' (*Schibboleth*; my emphasis). Where is it dated then? Derrida's reserve includes an awareness that the word 'history' itself has become Hegelianized, that it always evokes a master narrative or metahistorical horizon. His refusal to historicize seems to accept one aspect of Heidegger's avoidance: his reluctance to locate the crisis in the epochal events of 1933–1945. He questions, at the same time, Heidegger's archaizing move, the logocentrism that seems to place the origin of the crisis *in illo tempore*, in a mysterious and historically developed schism that befell words long ago.

Derrida focuses on the pervasiveness of an identitarian, nationalistic, and decisionist rhetoric, which the language of philosophy has not escaped. That rhetoric tainted almost all discourse between the world wars and carried to the limit an older antinomy of nation and universality. Yet the full impact of the disaster related to this rhetoric hits consciousness, like a shock wave, only after the Holocaust.

The dilemma of the philosopher is that he cannot accept conditions that negate philosophy and its language, any more than Celan accepted those that negate poetry and his mother tongue. Style, therefore, in both Celan and Derrida, is the negation of a negation. The continuous solecism of Celan in poetry and of Derrida in philosophy gives an unexpected meaning to Adorno's 'To write poetry [or philosophy?] after Auschwitz is barbaric.' Writing – philosophy, fiction, poetry – is indeed ringed by fire but also by 'avoidances' that produce a silent scream. [. . .] Poetry and philosophy, even when they carry us beyond the datum, beyond a brute historical reality, remain inscribed – scarred – by it.

[...]

NOTES

1. The significance of the second date is not that it marks the beginning of the systematic extermination – which started before, with Hitler's Russian campaign – but that it reveals the all-important role of a bureaucratic machinery of destruction without which the Final Solution could not have taken place. It compels us, therefore, to reflect on the relation of bureaucracy and modernity: it points to an intellectual disclosure.

2. 'A new shape of knowing invades the mind,' is how Terrence Des Pres puts it in his 'Prolog' to *Praises and Dispraises: Poetry and Politics in the Twentieth Century* (New York: Penguin, 1989). 'Holocaust literature,' writes Alvin Rosenfeld, 'is an attempt to express a new order of consciousness, a recognizable shift in being. The human imagination after Auschwitz is simply not the same as it was before' (*A Double Dying: Reflections on Holocaust Literature* [Bloomington: Indiana University Press, 1980], 13).

3. Elsewhere Derrida is clearer in suggesting that uniqueness, understood strictly, is a form of closure that tries to contain or cordon off the Holocaust. Here too the issue of generational transmission of holocaust trauma can be raised. See, e.g., the issue of *Psyche* (49 [January 1995]) devoted to this matter.

4. In the case of Celan, this hidden and congealed element may include the seductive sublimity of Rilke's *Sonnets to Orpheus* or the *Duino Elegies*; in the case of Derrida, the *Chimères* of Nerval.

5. See Blanchot on the act of reading and communicating, in *L'espace littéraire* (Paris: Gallimard, 1955), 201 ff. Derrida, it seems to me, by what Blanchot would have called the 'errance' of his style – his refusal to sacralize the word 'holocaust,' for example, or a punning that moves between the demotic and the charged meaning of a word, or marked and unmarked semes ('revenant,' 'revient') – comes close to 'le risque de se livrer à l'inessentiel [qui] est lui-même essentiel' (the risk of abandoning oneself to the inessential, which is itself an essential act; *L'espace littéraire*, 177).

6. This essay is found in Derrida, *Psyché: Inventions de l'autre* (Paris: Galilée, 1987). It is translated by Ken Frieden as 'Denials,' in *Languages of the Unsayable: The Play of Negativity in Literature and Literary Theory*, ed. Sanford Budick and Wolfgang Iser (New York: Columbia University Press, 1989).

7. A further, symmetrically placed example occurs when he closes *Schibboleth* with the politeness formula 'permettez-moi de laisser tomber ceci' (allow me to pass this by), a rhetorical courtesy expressing his sense of the arbitrary character of closure. But translated as 'permit me to let this be entombed,' it speaks to his hope that Celan's 'unbestattete Worte' have been given a tomb, a *tombeau*.

8. *Feu la cendre* was published in 1982 and 1987. The English version, translated, edited, and with an introduction by Ned Lukacher, appeared in 1991 (Lincoln: Nebraska University Press). *De l'esprit* was also published in 1987.

9. In both Heidegger and Karl Mannheim '*Destruktion*' means a methodical destructuring – laying bare – of the unexamined social, epistemological, and ontological assumptions of Western concepts. Heidegger moreover thinks to create a language that has reformative as well as analytic-destructive vigor.

41

'REPRESENTING AUSCHWITZ'

Sidra DeKoven Ezrahi

There is a presumption in all the representations of the Holocaust and in all the discussions of the proprieties and limits of its representation that there is an Entity, an Event or a Place, to which the historical, artistic, cinematic or literary reflections do or do not correspond – an epicenter which is often imagined as a black hole, (re-)entered only at peril to the communicability of the act and the sanity of the actor. ('Was geschah?' asks the poet most identified with the impenetrability of the concentrationary universe; 'Der Stein trat aus dem Berge.' The mountain is unsayable; the echoes of the boulder that is the fragment of the place, the survivor's burden, resonate in language, toward the 'unsubsided' ('Sprache .../ Wohin gings? Gen Unverklungen').[1] I want to submit that the positioning of both the writer and the audience in relation to this mountain or this defiled center functions much as does the positioning of the pilgrim vis-à-vis the holy mountain or the sacred center; in what closely approximates a theological quest at the postmodern end of our millennium, a new aesthetics and ethics of representation are being forged with Auschwitz as the ultimate point of reference. Pronouncements on the poetics of (or after) Auschwitz tend to establish a symbolic geography in which the camp represents both center and periphery: it constitutes the very center of evil but is located in a realm just beyond the borders of civilized speech and behavior. That unspeakable place of extermination (dis)articulated by Jean-François Lyotard resembles the extra-territorial place designated earlier by T. W. Adorno as 'barbaric' – a place

From Sidra DeKoven Ezrahi (1996) 'Representing Auschwitz', in *History and Memory*, vol. 7, no. 1, pp. 121–54.

outside the community of selves. It both establishes the limits of what is human and threatens its annihilation. In what has become a *locus classicus* for the discussion of the license to speak, Lyotard invokes the murder not only of the subject and of language itself, but also of the means of assessing the loss; the analogy he draws is to an earthquake that destroys not only buildings and people but the very instruments for measuring the destruction. Nevertheless, 'the silence that surrounds the phrase "Auschwitz was the extermination camp" is . . . a sign that something remains to be phrased which is not, something which is not determined. . . .'[2]

The choice of metaphors is quite suggestive, particularly in the ongoing French dialogue with the *philosophes* of the late eighteenth century whose formative experience was the Lisbon earthquake of 1755. But it is a metaphor to beat all metaphors, since it insists that even the instruments of evaluation and comparison have been destroyed; commensurability, which is the premise of the metaphoric act and of all acts that establish a continuum in history, may then be what is most at stake in this discussion. It is a high stake, as metaphor is the first expression of consolation that the human mind can produce.[3]

My argument is that the discourse that has evolved in the pages of this and other journals and the cultural and intellectual enterprises of the last decades have generated two major clusters of attitudes with far-reaching implications. In the literature of testimony as well as of the imagination, in the theories of historiographical and of poetic representation, one can begin to discern a fundamental distinction between a static and a dynamic appropriation of history and its moral and social legacies. The static or absolutist approach locates a non-negotiable self in an unyielding place whose sign is Auschwitz; the dynamic or relativist position approaches the representation of the memory of that place as a construction of strategies for an ongoing *re*negotiation of that historical reality. For the latter, the immobility of the past is mitigated, at times undermined, by the very conventions mobilized to represent it; for the former, an invented language grounded in a sense of sustained 'duration' or unmastered trauma prevents convention and commensurability from relativizing the absolute reality of the place. In each case, the work of history or art is being performed in the aftermath, at a 'safe' distance – but again it is distance itself which is at stake. My purpose in referring here to a wide range of literature, film, critical and theoretical discussions is to try to demonstrate the diffusion of these two sensibilities in postwar culture at large, with allowances for the particular semantics of each interpretive community.

[. . .]

ALTERNATIVE HISTORIES

Whether located in the Jewish quarter in Amsterdam, the Umschlagplatz in Warsaw, Auschwitz I or Birkenau – or the oral testimony of survivors – the search for a geographical, verbal or symbolic locus of the crime signals a need to

the epicenter of the earthquake. The farther away from Auschwitz it is,
re likely that center is to furnish the opportunity for an alternative legacy.
gh [...] Primo Levi succeeds – just – in providing some distance between
f and Auschwitz, it requires an enormous effort not to be swallowed up
by the black hole when one is so close. [...]

Resistance [...] is based on some measure of distancing, repression or even
effacement, extending to the physical evidence itself. In a short statement on
'Revisiting the Camps,' which accompanied an exhibition of photographs of the
camps held in Milan in 1986, Levi acknowledged that the 'old trauma, the scar
of remembrance' still prevails, *hence the need for distance*. If, at the time of
liberation, we had been asked: "what would you like to do with these infected
barracks, these wire fences, these rows of toilets, these ovens, these gallows?" I
think that most of us would have answered: "get rid of everything, raze it to the
ground, along with Nazism and everything German."' He went on to say that
such a statement would have been wrong, because, as he realizes forty years
later, these 'are not mistakes to efface' but take on significance as 'a Warning
Monument.'[4]

A QUESTION OF LIMITS

What we have begun to identify are clusters of attitudes that can be reduced to a
fairly simple but far-reaching dichotomy between absolutist and relativist
positions; between disruption and continuity in reconstructing the traumatic
past; and between incommensurability and commensurability as aesthetic
principles. History is appropriated either as a set of documents frozen in time
and providing the locus that articulates the Event Itself or as yielding to ongoing
interpretive and narrative enterprises. Ethics resides in the absolutizing or
relativizing of categories of good and evil. Artistic representation is an ongoing
search for languages bordering on the danger zones of 'transgression' and the
'barbaric.' Both the mythifying and the relativizing positions can lead, in their
extreme manifestations, to a suspension of the idea of historical verifiability or
reality – the one because of its focus on the metaphysical or demonic nature of
death under the sign of the Swastika and the place called Auschwitz, and the
other because of the profound skepticism that characterizes the most radical
versions of poststructuralism.

[...]

Arguments against setting 'limits' to representation arise from the principle of
desire and change as a counterforce to the rituals and myths that freeze memory.
[...] It is the static encounters with Auschwitz, or centripetal movement drawn
toward the stasis of an unspeakable place, that preclude the dynamic of a fore-
and after-life; such encounters are encapsulated in certain rituals of space and
time. To the extent that rituals are mythic representations of the past experienced in a suspended present,[5] and that myths represent the unchanging and
fictions the changing patterns of memory, 'limits' can be perceived as the

collective enforcement of propriety over the past. Hans Kellner defines the 'desire to represent the Holocaust' not as

> the desire to repeat it as an event, nor necessarily the desire to repeat the form-giving pleasure of representation itself; rather, it is a desire to repeat the Holocaust in a suitably altered form to meet complex, often contradictory, sets of present needs.[6]

Desire as a counter-force to frozen time, fiction as the dynamic answer to myth, alternative history as the future's answer to the past, carry the obvious dangers that inhere in any act of revisionism. It is only within the critical and ongoing self-examination of specific interpretive communities that such acts are both disciplined and incorporated selectively into the open-ended argument of 'life' with history.

[...]

TERMINUS OR POINT OF DEPARTURE?

The centripetal thrust toward a *terminus* is, then, contemporaneous with a centrifugal thrust that establishes the physical and symbolic center as *point of departure*. As clusters of radically divergent sensibilities, the 'mythifiers' and the 'relativizers' generate alternative languages of history, art and ethics, exemplifying not only the problematics inherent in any attempt to enforce limits, decorum or standards of propriety in cultural activity but the consensus that one cannot ignore Auschwitz without destroying the moral foundations of culture. In this sense the Holocaust, like revelation, becomes the event whose interpretation controls the meaning of the present and the future. However, unlike the original chaos that preceded all Creation, Auschwitz-as-Dis-order must take account of the order that preceded it; as the chasm that terminates one world and constitutes the point of departure for another, it establishes the relative status of each. Auschwitz becomes, then, the ultimate link between the new post-Enlightenment languages of truth and morality. The affirmation that Auschwitz was a fact, a real place or a real event becomes the constitutive base of late twentieth-century ethical discourse; claiming to fully or exhaustively represent Auschwitz is a form of arrogation of authority as arbiter of moral conflict. The more 'The Event' is deemed critical to everything that follows, the more the exclusive claim to know, define or represent it is mobilized to privilege one's own interpretation or evaluation of the world.

What I have presented as two divergent orientations are actually part of the same dialectic which posits the wholly transcendent as wholly unrepresentable. For the mythifiers, it is inherently unsayable, elusive, inscrutable and immutable, the sole determinant and ultimate extinguisher of meaning. For the relativizers, it is precisely in its ineffability that it is infinitely and diversely representable; the urgency of representation, then, unfolds in continual tension between desire and its limits. When it gives license to pluralistic interpretations and shifting sites of memory, Auschwitz 'authorizes' the open horizons of a post-Holocaust world.

<h2 style="text-align:center">NOTES</h2>

1. Paul Celan, *Poems of Paul Celan*, bilingual ed., trans. Michael Hamburger (New York, 1988), 204–5.
2. Jean-François Lyotard, *The Differend: Phrases in Dispute* (Minneapolis, 1988), 57, 56.
3. 'To what shall I compare thee ... *that I may comfort thee?*' asks the elegist in the book of Lamentations (2:13), the original canonic text of consolation.
4. Primo Levi, 'Revisiting the Camps,' reprinted in James E. Young, ed., *The Art of Memory: Holocaust Memorials in History* (Prestel, 1994), 185 (my emphasis). [...]
5. See Paul Connerton, *How Societies Remember* (Cambridge, 1989), 41–71; Hans Kellner, ' "Never Again" is Now,' *History and Theory* 33, no. 2 (1994), 129; Robert Braun, 'The Holocaust and Problems of Historical Representation,' *History and Theory* 33, no. 2 (1994), 179.
6. Kellner, ' "Never Again" is Now,' 128. The reference of course is to the volume in which the question of limits is embedded in the very title and to which members of different intellectual disciplines, including history, philosophy, literature and film, contributed: *Probing the Limits of Representation*. See especially Saul Friedlander's introduction. See also Jean Améry (Hans Meyer), who was one of the first to contemplate the 'limits' of the intellectual inquiry into the Holocaust: *At the Mind's Limits*, trans. Sidney Rosenfeld and Stella P. Rosenfeld (Bloomington, 1980).

PART VIII
MODES OF NARRATION

MODES OF NARRATION: INTRODUCTION

As a field of Holocaust representation, narrative is distinguished from poetry and visual culture by the questions it raises about the status of *fictions* about the Holocaust and about the cognitive, ethical, and political implications of specific narrative forms. (The question of the *authority* to narrate is also an underlying, persistent concern here, but it is explored more extensively in this volume's Parts I and X on 'Theory and Experience' and 'Latecomers.')

While Adorno's suspicions about the place of the aesthetic (see Parts VII and IX 'Literature and Culture after Auschwitz' and 'Rethinking Visual Culture') are often invoked in discussions of the legitimacy of Holocaust fiction, it is arguably the figure of Elie Wiesel, who has famously pronounced that a novel about Auschwitz is either not a novel or not about Auschwitz, that casts the longest shadow in this context. The American philosopher Berel Lang might be seen as attempting to offer a sustained philosophical rationale for such a claim, one based on firm distinctions between history and fiction, the literal and the figural. Unlike Wiesel, Lang does not completely reject the possibility of literary renderings of the Holocaust, but he does insist that all fiction about the Holocaust inevitably imposes the artifice of style, point of view, and personification upon its subject matter. This artifice, Lang claims, distorts the Holocaust's singular features, such as the collective agency of its perpetration and the depersonalized, objectified condition of its victims.

Many contemporary scholars, however, are less interested in hierarchically distinguishing history and fiction than in exploring their interactions and their shared problems. Thus James E. Young emphasizes the ways in which the Holocaust itself is *constituted* by the interpretations and narratives of those whose lives were caught up in it: thus, the meaning various actors ascribe to each other and to what was happening around them is not an 'addition,' but an essential part of the events.

Young's work thereby introduces to Holocaust studies the humanities and social sciences' recent turn to narrative as a transdisciplinary master category of human cultural practice and cognition. For philosophers of a broadly hermeneutic inclination such as Richard Rorty, Charles Taylor, Alasdair MacIntyre, Arthur Danto, and Paul Ricoeur narrative is a means of understanding action and constructing personal and communal identities. Meanwhile, the work of such scholars as political scientist Benedict Anderson and literary theorist Homi K. Bhabha has focused attention on how national identities in particular are imagined, constituted, and reinforced by certain narrative forms – especially the novel, but, as the case of the German Historians' Debate indicates, not exclusively so.

If narrative is a way of understanding selfhood, action and agency, as these thinkers claim, what narratives can be produced about events in which the victims were left unable to act and were reduced to a collective, fantasmatic identity with the most terrible of real consequences? And if stories are how we make sense of ourselves and the world, what kinds of stories can be told about an event that to many observers makes no sense at all? Historian Hayden White's work on Holocaust narrative offers one direct response to such questions. In literary modernism – exemplified by the radical new narrative forms developed by Joyce, Woolf, Stein and others in the early part of the twentieth century – White sees a response to the modern world, a world of global conflict and industrial-scale killing, none of which he thinks can be represented adequately in older forms such as the nineteenth-century realist novel. It is also important to note that White's essays on Holocaust representation form a kind of defense of his early work against charges of relativism. His 1973 *Metahistory* argued that all historical writing conformed to one narrative genre or another, and that any historical event could be narrated within any genre. His Holocaust essays therefore attempt to show that, while any genre of Holocaust narrative is *possible*, some Holocaust narratives are more adequate than others.

Like White and Young, Michael André Bernstein is more interested in the similarities than the differences between fictional and historical narratives, and like White, he prefers certain forms to others. But where White wants to identify innovative, impersonal narrative forms as the most mimetically appropriate to mass-scale modern catastrophe, Bernstein would turn Lang's charge that fictional narrative inevitably personifies into a virtue: individual human action is just what should be at issue. Bernstein rejects narratives that represent the Holocaust as inevitable because they diminish the everyday concerns and behavior of European Jews who did not foresee it. Such narratives are thereby guilty of what he calls *backshadowing*. Bernstein rejects backshadowing in favor of narratives that *sideshadow*; these narratives display an awareness of the contingency of history, of the possibility of events turning out otherwise. He sees a sideshadowing Holocaust narrative as morally preferable because it knows that the past was once someone's unforeseen future, and thus recognizes and mourns (rather than condemns) the situated agency of its subjects. Side-shadowing is a notion that bears on broader concerns about narration, nation, and identity in several ways: it critiques the construction of Israeli national ideology, for a long time predicated on self-differentiation from the supposed blindness and passivity of European Jewry, and it elaborates the question of how to narrate and transmit collective cultural identities when much of the collective has been wiped out, much of the culture destroyed.

Like Bernstein and White, Lawrence L. Langer and Shoshana Felman reflect upon formally innovative Holocaust narratives. Their focus, however, is not written texts but the words and gestures of Holocaust survivors as they appear in video testimony (Langer) and Claude Lanzmann's remarkable epic film *Shoah* (Felman). The still-living victim of Nazism has *not* survived the event, says Langer, but has experienced (and continues in 'deep memory' to experience) her or his own death. In this sense, Langer explicitly opposes the damaged, diminished selves revealed in these testimonies to Charles Taylor's affirmation of the relationship between narrative and self-making. For Langer, oral testimony provides better access to this truth of Holocaust experience because of its immediacy and its freedom from the literary traditions and conventions that shape written memoirs of the Holocaust. Curiously enough then, for Langer the new media enable a seemingly less *mediated* mode of Holocaust narration.

Felman (like Gertrud Koch in Part IX) argues that *Shoah* is not simply a Holocaust documentary, but also a major work of art that self-consciously reflects upon the nature of testimony and memory. Implicit in her essay's title, 'The Return of the Voice,' are not only the momentous events of the film: the return of witnesses to the sites and situations of their past and their resumption of speech about what happened after years of silence. Felman's essay also represents the return of the voice as an object of theoretical reflection. In early American deconstruction, of which she was an exponent, the human voice is subject to tremendous suspicion as the locus of 'metaphysical presence.' In *Shoah*, however, the human voice itself is meant to testify to the historical crisis of witnessing, to the 'impossibility' of witnessing the Holocaust – by which Felman means principally the Nazi plan to eliminate all witnesses to the genocide as well as the victims' own incomprehension of the events they experienced. In the wake of both new atrocities throughout the world and recent attempts to work through old ones by means of Truth and Reconciliation Commissions, especially in Africa and Latin America, the 'age of testimony' cannot be considered over, and the Holocaust should remain a pertinent point of reference for scholarship on testimony and narrative.

OTHER WORKS IN HOLOCAUST STUDIES

Ezrahi, Sidra DeKoven (1980) *By Words Alone: The Holocaust in Literature*. Chicago: University of Chicago Press.

Horowitz, Sara (1997) *Voicing the Void: Muteness and Memory in Holocaust Fiction.* Albany, NY: State University of New York Press.

Vice, Sue (1999) *Holocaust Fiction.* New York: Routledge.

RELEVANT THEORETICAL STUDIES

Anderson, Benedict (1991) *Imagined Communities: Reflections on the Origin and Spread of Nationalism.* New York: Verso.

Bhabha, Homi K. (ed.) (1990) *Nation and Narration.* London and New York: Routledge.

Danto, Arthur C. (1985) *Narration and Knowledge: including the integral text of Analytical Philosophy of History.* New York: Columbia University Press.

Gugelberger, Georg (ed.) (1996) *The Real Thing: Testimonial Discourse and Latin America.* Durham, NC: Duke University Press.

MacIntyre, Alasdair (1981) *After Virtue: A Study in Moral Theory.* Notre Dame, IN: University of Notre Dame Press.

Ricoeur, Paul (1984–88) *Time and Narrative.* Chicago: University of Chicago Press.

Rorty, Richard (1989) *Contingency, Irony, and Solidarity.* Cambridge and New York: Cambridge University Press.

Taylor, Charles (1989) *Sources of the Self: the Making of Modern Identity.* Cambridge, MA: Harvard University Press.

42

'THE MORAL SPACE OF FIGURATIVE DISCOURSE'

Berel Lang

Even if the claim of an unusual role for historical strategies in imaginative writing about the Nazi genocide were accepted, this would not entail the second part of the thesis posed here: that documentary and historical writings about the genocide have been more adequate and more compelling – in sum, more *valuable* – than the imaginative writings about that subject. Indeed, it could be argued that by adopting the strategies of historiography, imaginative writing would combine the strengths of those two forms of discourse. But the second claim here argues the contrary: that the historical emphasis in imaginative writings about the Nazi genocide is symptomatic and confessional – at once reflecting the challenge for literary representation in the moral enormity of that event and conceding the inadequacy for such representation of the means available in figurative discourse. Imaginative writing about the Nazi genocide, in other words, attempts to enlarge on its usual means because, for *that* subject, its conventional resources fail. In this sense, imaginative writing 'knows itself' – testifying to this by the impossible ideal it adopts of a form of writing that attempts at one time to be both literary and historical.

[...]

[...] If [...] the act of genocide is directed against individuals who do not motivate that act *as* individuals, and if the evil represented by genocide also

From Berel Lang (1990) *Act and Idea in the Nazi Genocide*. Chicago and London: University of Chicago Press.

reflects a deliberate intent for evil in principle – in conceptualizing the group and in deciding to annihilate it – then, the intrinsic limitations of figurative discourse for the representation of genocide come into view. [. . .] Imaginative representation would personalize even events that are impersonal and corporate; it would dehistorcize and generalize events that occur specifically and contingently. And the unavoidable dissonance here is evident. For a subject which historically combines the features of impersonality with a challenge to the conception of moral boundaries, the attempt to personalize it – or, for that matter, only to *add* to it – appears at once gratuitous and inconsistent, gratuitous because it individualizes where the subject by its nature is corporate; inconsistent because it sets limits when the subject itself has denied them. The effect of the addition is then to misrepresent the subject and thus – where the aspects misrepresented are essential – to diminish it. In asserting the possibility of alternative figurative perspectives, furthermore, the writer asserts the process of representation and his own persona as elements of the representation – a further diminution of what, for a subject such as the Nazi genocide, is its essential core; beside it, an individual 'perspective' is at most irrelevant. For certain subjects, it seems, their significance may be too broad or deep to be chanced by an individual point of view, morally more compelling – and actual – than the concept of possibility can sustain. Under this pressure, the presumption of illumination usually conceded to the act of writing (*any* writing) begins to lose its force.

These moral consequences appear concretely in the figurative process itself. As figuration imposes a particularized point of view, not only what is seen by way of the latter but its status *as* a point of view constitutes a theme. The discourse, in other words, is personalized; the writer obtrudes. And whatever the writer's motives, certain consequences of this obtrusion are unavoidable. The features of the literary subject, then, are heard, filtered through the writer's voice, with the personalization of perspective and the emphasis on the *means* of expression that this involves. When a literary subject is open to articulation of this sort – as in lyric poetry, where the subject is characteristically personal and emotive – then to shape it perspectivally by means of an authorial point of view may disclose features visible only by that means. But where impersonality and abstractness are essential features of the subject, as in the subject of the Nazi genocide, then a literary focus on individuation and agency 'contradicts' the subject itself – a literary equivalent to logical inconsistency revealed through a disproportion in the moral correlatives mentioned earlier. Sentimentality or bathos, it has often been pointed out, are persistent failings in many of the novels and poems on the subject of the Nazi genocide. And understandable as the causes may be for the occurrence of such disproportions between feeling and fact where that subject is concerned, the failings are nonetheless accountable, both morally and literarily.

[. . .] The author's obtrusion, moreover, brings to a point the other effects of figuration that have been mentioned. Since by that obtrusion the subject is personalized, stylized – *figured* – the implication is unavoidable of a subject that could be represented in many different ways and that thus has no necessary and perhaps not even an actual basis. The figurative assertion of alternative possibilities, in other words, suggests a denial of limitation: *no* possibilities are excluded. And although for some literary subjects openness of this sort may be warranted or even desirable, for others it represents a falsification, morally *and* conceptually.

Another version of these same objections derives more immediately from 'literary abstraction' – the process of generalization set in motion by the act of figuration. Where the specific historical character of a subject is crucial, the consequence of abstracting from that particularity – in the example at issue here, by representing the Nazi genocide as an instance of evil in general – is to distort the subject [...]. To be sure, each individual or group in the nonliterary origins of a literary subject will in some sense be singular. But not every individual or group is assigned a role or fate historically *because* of that specification. This is, again, a distinctive mark of the process and then of the representation of genocide. Thus, the means of literary representation which can for some subjects generalize from specific cases without distortion are for other subjects open to exactly that charge.

To be sure, any representation of evil may understandably evoke general reflections on its nature. Certain figurative representations of individual evil-doing, moreover, are aesthetically as well as morally compelling ([...] Iago or Satan). But in these generalized representations, too, evil appears as the purpose and idea of an individual imagination or will; and rare as the evidence is for willed evil of this sort, it is still more difficult to find literary representations of evil for which a *collective* will is responsible. Literary agency is characteristically individual; thus, where what is crucial in the literary subject is the impersonality of its causes and reasons, to aestheticize or individualize those sources is to falsify or misrepresent the subject. For the reasons given, in respect to the relation between figurative discourse and its subject, the representation of a particular historical event in literary or figurative terms is intrinsically open to moral judgment; the impulse to overcome or at least to extend history in figurative discourse requires a warrant. And if this is a general condition to be met by the process of literary representation, imaginative writing about the events of the Nazi genocide faces the added difficulty of the 'antirepresentational' features of those events themselves.

These antirepresentational features include a number of elements in the historical character of that literary subject. One important such element appears in the agency that shapes literary plot in narrative fiction and drama. The movement of narrative form is sustained by the motivation of the agents who appear within it – not only for what they do in the text, but for their 'prehistory,' what they have been or done at the point where the text begins. Thus, fictional narratives are judged at least minimally by criteria of plausibility and consistency – both of these criteria based on extraliterary evidence of human motives and conduct. Narrative representation thus presupposes individual agency prior to as well as within the representation. The importance of such agency is evident in the scarcity of texts from which it is absent. [...]

This requirement of human agency cannot be met in writings about the Nazi genocide [...]. The Jews were the victims in that process not because of anything they did individually, nor was it in their power, in terms of the act of genocide, to affect the future prescribed for them. To sublimate *this* basis into the individual agency required for narrative plot and character is to introduce a fundamental distortion: it is not the presumptive knowledge on which literary representation can base a narrative. Admittedly, in historical terms, as the victims of the genocide were faced by its imminence they could (and did) respond individually; it can be argued that at *that* point, they became agents who then, in historical fact and potentially in literary representation, could motivate narrative structures. In one sense, moreover, writing always starts in medias res: something will always have happened before a literary narrative begins. Thus, it could be held that the fact of the genocide may appear as a 'given' in the development of literary plot [...].

The literary subject in this case, however, is closely tied to – depends on – the historical subject, and this relation holds also for what 'happens' before the literary plot begins. Here, too, then, writing about the Nazi genocide confronts the events of the genocide itself, in which individual agency, on one side at least, had no essential role. The Jews did not become victims as a consequence of their own decisions or choices. They were the objects – not the subjects – of genocide, and this means that in narrative fiction about the Nazi genocide, no literary basis is available for that one principal source of the discourse. In this respect, imaginative writing about the Nazi genocide is intrinsically arbitrary – since its starting point has no basis in even a marginally free definition of self by its main protagonists and only as much to do even with the Nazis as the choice of 'principled' and impersonal evil can provide in the way of specific motivation. [...]

To find agency in the role of the perpetrator in imaginative narratives of the Nazi genocide, moreover, is hardly a lesser problem than to find it in the role of the victim. To be sure, the motives historically of individual Nazis varied, and such differences might reappear literarily in their translation into imaginative characters. But if [...] the Nazi genocide involves a knowing commitment to evil in principle beyond the psychological motives of its individual agents, the difficulties of literary representation will also be encountered there. Few literary characters choose evil for its own sake, and those few invariably have a mythological aura about them (again, as in Milton's Satan). The reasons for this are historical even more fundamentally than they are literary. What stories *could* be told of a person whose identity, whether in the representation or before it, was so constant as to suggest that no choice or decision had motivated them? And then, also historically, even the most infamous villains have tried to see themselves as acting on the basis of justified reason and purpose that by their own standards account for their actions. When the commitment to evil in principle is set in a network of bureaucratic and technological causality which further diffuses the role of individual agency, the options of literary representation are proportionately limited. One of the few and still among the most compelling representations of the Nazi as malefactor is that of Hannah Arendt's Eichmann – in what is an historical rather than a fictional work, and in which the claim is made for the 'banal,' not the radical or deliberate nature of his evil. Here, again, historical representation, which is not dependent on a role of subjective agency, is at once better able than figurative discourse – and more likely to try – to convey the features of the Nazi genocide.

Outlined in these theoretical terms, the failings ascribed to figurative discourse may seem a priori, oblivious to individual instances, actual or possible, of imaginative writing about the Nazi genocide. Furthermore, the differences in quality evident among various writings on the Nazi genocide indicate that the limitations that have been asserted here affect some of those writings less than others: here, too, the differences are quite real. But the evaluative thesis that has been posed does not deny the *possibility* of literary (and now moral) value in such works. It argues on grounds at once of practice and principle (in any event, not a priori) that the emphasis on historical authenticity among writings on the Nazi genocide has a basis in literary structure itself; thus, that for such writing, the risks – conceptual, moral, literary – increase in proportion to the distance the writing moves from that ideal. The logical implication of this view is that *no* imaginative representation of the Nazi genocide escapes these risks or the likelihood of failure, no matter how original or compelling it otherwise is. That there are valuable literary works on that subject does not mean that they are counterexamples; an alternative conclusion would view them as standing at one end of a continuum, with the shadow of moral liability cast over them as well; part of what they disclose is the contingency, even the arbitrariness of their achievement.

[...]

[...] It can be argued that what turns out to be at issue here is, as Plato had asserted, the moral justification for literature or art as such, not for imaginative writings about a single subject, even one as morally charged as the Nazi genocide. Undoubtedly, this more general issue is affected by the thesis that has been posed, but the immediate implications of this relation bear on the consideration of writing about the Nazi genocide more than on the general issue. The implication recurs here, too, that the analysis of this morally extreme situation, far from leading to anomalous conclusions, discloses significant aspects of common experience and understanding. If genocide is distinctive among acts that are open to moral judgment – that is, with conditions of impersonality in the object and the will for evil in principle on the part of the agent – then [...] figurative representation of that event will diminish the moral understanding of those events, not as it happens or for certain representations, but intrinsically. This same balance (more precisely, imbalance) may not affect every such instance of literary representation; still more evidently, it may not affect them all equally. On the other hand, the constraints on figurative discourse that have been alleged have at least one more inclusive implication: that in the relation between representation and its subject, the question of the moral status of literary form becomes unavoidable. As literary representation mediates between a subject and its reader, the process of representation becomes morally accountable in its consequences for each of them – and the imaginative writings of the Nazi genocide provide an unusual view of what is at stake in those relations.

43

'WRITING THE HOLOCAUST'

James E. Young

To a great extent, Holocaust studies have always been interdisciplinary: historical inquiry provokes political and sociological questions, while philosophical and religious inquiry inevitably entail larger literary issues. With the rise of contemporary literary and historical theory, scholars of the Holocaust have come increasingly to recognize that interpretations of both the texts and events of the Holocaust are intertwined. For both events and their representations are ultimately beholden to the forms, language, and critical methodology through which they are grasped. Religious meaning and significance, historical causes and effects, are simultaneously reflected and generated in Holocaust narrative – as well as in the names, periodization, genres, and icons we assign this era. What is remembered of the Holocaust depends on how it is remembered, and how events are remembered depends in turn on the texts now giving them form.

Instead of isolating events from their representations, this approach recognizes that literary and historical truths of the Holocaust may not be entirely separable. That is, the truths of the Holocaust – both the factual and the interpretive – can no longer be said to lie beyond our understanding, but must now be seen to inhere in the ways we understand, interpret, and write its history. Indeed, since the facts of the Holocaust eventually obtain only in their narrative and cultural reconstructions, the interrelated problems of literary and historical interpretation might now be seen as conjoining in the study of 'literary

From James E. Young (1990) *Writing and Rewriting the Holocaust: Narrative and the Consequences of Interpretation*. Bloomington and Indianapolis, IN: Indiana University Press.

historiography.' This is not to question the ultimate veracity in any given account, but it is to propose a search for the truth in the interpretation intrinsic to all versions of the Holocaust: both that interpretation which the writer consciously effects and that which his narrative necessarily accomplishes for him.

[...]

While previous studies of Holocaust literature have begun to raise some of these hermeneutical issues, there has also been an unmistakable resistance to overly theoretical readings of this literature. Much of this opposition is well founded and stems from the fear that too much attention to critical method or to the literary construction of texts threatens to supplant not only the literature but the horrible events at the heart of our inquiry. That is, if Holocaust narrative is nothing but a system of signs merely referring to other signs, then where are the events themselves? To concentrate on the poetics of a witness's testimony, for example, over the substance of testimony seems to risk displacing the events under discussion altogether. By seeming to emphasize the ways we know the Holocaust to the apparent exclusion of the realities themselves, critics threaten to make the mere form of study their content as well. Instead of drawing closer to events, in this view, critics would impose an even greater distance between readers and events. Other potential and equally unacceptable consequences of an unlimited deconstruction of the Holocaust include the hypothetical possibility that events and texts never existed outside each other and that all meanings of events created in different representations are only relative.

Because we are now dependent on mediating texts for our knowledge, however, does not make these texts alone the object of our study, or make the meanings generated in these mediated versions less valuable. For the significance and meaning of events created in these texts often reflect the kind of understanding of events by victims at the time; and as these 'mere' interpretations led to their responses, the interpreted versions of the Holocaust in its texts now lead us to our actions in the world in light of the Holocaust. That is, by sustaining the notion of these interpretations' agency in events, the contemporary critic can assert both the historicity of events and the crucial role interpretation played in the events themselves. This is not to deny the historical facts of the Holocaust outside of their narrative framing, but only to emphasize the difficulty of interpreting, expressing, and acting on these facts outside of the ways we frame them.

Applied carelessly, however, contemporary theory and its often all-consuming vocabulary can obscure as much as it seeks to illuminate in this literature. [...] But other qualities of critical analysis encouraged in contemporary inquiry, such as sensitivity to hermeneutical activity within the production of texts, hold much value in this study. For these aspects seem ideal for understanding more deeply the cause and effect relationship – the reciprocal exchange – between events and their interpretations as they unfolded, as well as the ways Holocaust narrative reflects, creates, and leads us toward particular meanings in events afterwards.

One may indeed wonder, after Robert Alter, whether the 'larger social and cultural purposes of scholarship are better served by pondering the literary refractions of mass murder or by undertaking . . . a critical biography of Sholem Aleichem.'[1] But by suggesting that these two academic pursuits are mutually exclusive somehow, we overlook the ways in which 'the literary refractions of mass murder' and Sholem Aleichem's view of the universe may, in fact, have everything to do with each other. As should become clear, in fact, the purely literary and the purely historical worlds were never really pure of each other, but were often all too tragically interdependent.[2] Contrary to those who see the world and its representations operating independently of one another, 'life' and 'life-in-writing' – catastrophe and our responses to it – have always interpenetrated; in this way, literature remembers past destructions even as it shapes our practical responses to current crisis.

For, as Hayden White has suggested, 'contemporary critical theory permits us to believe more confidently than ever before that "poetizing" is not an activity that hovers over, transcends, or otherwise remains alienated from life or reality, but represents a mode of praxis which serves as the immediate base of all cultural activity . . .'[3] If we recognize this 'poetizing' activity also as one of the bases of worldly praxis, then the issue here becomes not just 'the facts' of the Holocaust, but also their 'poetic' – i.e., narrative – configuration, and how particular representations may have guided writers in both their interpretations of events and their worldly responses to them. As becomes painfully clear, it was not 'the facts' in and of themselves that determined actions taken by the victims of the Holocaust – or by the killers themselves; but it was the structural, mythological, and figurative apprehension of these facts that led to action taken on their behalf.

The case for a critical literary historiography of the Holocaust is thus justified neither by finding new meanings in the Holocaust, nor by rendering ingenious interpretations of its texts, but rather by considering the possible *consequences* of interpretation – for both the victims at the time and for the survivors in their understanding of a post-Holocaust world. The critical aim of such a reading must therefore never be merely to deconstruct Holocaust narrative into so many columns of inert myths, grammars, and figures. Instead of engaging in a sterile pursuit of deep mythological, religious, and linguistic structures constituting only the literary texts of the Holocaust, the aim here is to explore both the plurality of meanings in the Holocaust these texts generate *and* the actions that issue from these meanings outside of the texts. Rather than merely deconstructing this narrative or its criticism, or de-historicizing it altogether, I attempt here to re-historicize it by looking beyond interpretation to its consequences in history.

Until now the historians' concern with Holocaust narrative has often been to unravel its myths and tropes in order to excavate the 'historical actuality' of events. While literary scholars have also attempted to penetrate narrative for its underlying facts, they have tended more often to focus on the narrative strategies by which writers represent the Holocaust. In addition, like many of the traditional exegetes before them, some critics have viewed themselves as much the guardians of these texts as their interpreters. In this view, the critical task has included protecting – even privileging – texts like the Holy Scriptures and survivors' testimony from 'heretical' readings that undermine these texts' authority. As a consequence, even the most insightful and theoretically informed Holocaust literary scholars have often preferred to excavate previously unknown works, collecting them into literary histories, where they can be subjected to either historical or new critical analysis. The aim here, however, is to understand the manner in which historical actuality and the forms in which it is delivered to us may be intertwined: it is to know what happened in how it is represented.

This is to suggest that the events of the Holocaust are not only shaped *post factum* in their narration, but that they were initially determined as they unfolded by the schematic ways in which they were apprehended, expressed, and then acted upon. In this way, what might once have been considered merely a matter of cultural, religious, or national perspective of the Holocaust assumes the force of agency in these events: world views may have both generated the catastrophe and narrated it afterward. Thus perceived, history never unfolds independently of the ways we have understood it; and in the case of the Holocaust, the interpretation and structural organization of historical events as they occurred may ultimately have determined the horrific course they eventually took.

This is to move beyond the question of whether or not literary and historical accounts of the Holocaust are 'perspective ridden' to understand how various literary forms, cultural and religious traditions, and precedent experiences have indeed shaped the Holocaust. In this way, the critical reader can begin to assess the manner in which these 'versions of the Holocaust' may have determined both the historical responses taken on their behalf – actions comprising the ultimate index to the kind of knowledge we possess – and the understanding subsequent generations infer from these versions. If pursued with care and tact, a sensitivity to these issues might add significantly to our understanding of both the Holocaust as it happened and of its history-as-it-is-written in literature.

NOTES

1. Robert Alter, 'Deformations of the Holocaust,' *Commentary*, February 1981, p. 49.
2. For insight into the ways Sholem Aleichem's literary and historical worlds interpenetrated, see David Roskies, 'Laughing Off the Trauma of History,' in *Against the Apocalypse: Responses to Catastrophe in Modern Jewish Culture* (Cambridge, Mass., and London: Harvard University Press, 1984), pp. 163–95.
3. Hayden White, *Tropics of Discourse: Essays in Cultural Criticism* (Baltimore and London: Johns Hopkins University Press, 1978), p. 126.

44

'THE MODERNIST EVENT'

Hayden White

[...]

It is a commonplace of contemporary criticism that modernist literature and, by extension, modernist art in general dissolves the trinity of event, character, and plot which still provided the staple both of the nineteenth-century realist novel and of that historiography from which nineteenth-century literature derived its model of realism. But the tendency of modernist literature to dissolve the event has especially important implications for understanding the ways in which contemporary Western culture construes the relationship between literature and history. Modern historical research and writing could get by without the notions of character and plot, as the invention of a subjectless and plotless historiography in the twentieth century has amply demonstrated.[1] But the dissolution of the event as a basic unit of temporal occurrence and building block of history undermines the very concept of factuality and threatens therewith the distinction between realistic and merely imaginary discourse. The dissolution of the event undermines a founding presupposition of Western realism: the opposition between fact and fiction. Modernism resolves the problems posed by traditional realism, namely, how to represent reality realistically, by simply abandoning the ground on which realism is construed in terms of an opposition between fact and fiction. The denial of the reality of the event undermines the very notion of fact informing traditional realism. Therewith, the taboo against mixing fact with fiction except in manifestly

From Hayden White (1999) 'The Modernist Event', in *Figural Realism: Studies in the Mimesis Effect*. Baltimore, MD and London: Johns Hopkins University Press.

imaginative discourse is abolished. And, as current critical opinion suggests, the very notion of fiction is set aside in the conceptualization of literature as a mode of writing which abandons both the referential and poetic functions of language use.

It is this aspect of modernism that informs the creation of the new genres of postmodernist parahistorical representation, in both written and visual form, called variously *docudrama, faction, infotainment, the fiction of fact, historical metafiction*, and the like.[2] [...]

What happens in the postmodernist docudrama or historical metafiction is [...] the placing in abeyance of the distinction between the real and the imaginary. Everything is presented as if it were of the same ontological order, both real and imaginary – realistically imaginary or imaginarily real, with the result that the referential function of the images of events is etiolated. Thus, the contract that originally mediated the relationship between the nineteenth-century (bourgeois?) reader and the author of the historical novel has been dissolved. [...]

[...]

Issues such as these arise within the context of the experience, memory, or awareness of events that not only could not possibly have occurred before the twentieth century but whose nature, scope, and implications no prior age could even have imagined. Some of these events – such as the two world wars, a growth in world population hitherto unimaginable, poverty and hunger on a scale never before experienced, pollution of the ecosphere by nuclear explosions and the indiscriminate disposal of contaminants, programs of genocide undertaken by societies utilizing scientific technology and rationalized procedures of governance and warfare (of which the German genocide of six million European Jews is paradigmatic) – function in the consciousness of certain social groups exactly as infantile traumas are conceived to function in the psyche of neurotic individuals. This means that they cannot be simply forgotten and put out of mind or, conversely, adequately remembered, which is to say, clearly and unambiguously identified as to their meaning and contextualized in the group memory in such a way as to reduce the shadow they cast over the group's capacities to go into its present and envision a future free of their debilitating effects.[3]

The suggestion that, for the groups most immediately affected by or fixated upon these events, their meanings remain ambiguous and their consignment to the past difficult to effectuate should not be taken to imply in any way that such events never happened. On the contrary, not only are their occurrences amply attested, but also, their continuing effects on current societies and generations that had no direct experience of them are readily documentable. But among those effects must be listed the difficulty felt by present generations of arriving at some agreement as to their meaning – by which I mean what the facts established about such events can possibly tell us about the nature of our own current social and cultural endowment and what attitude we ought to take with respect to them as we make plans for our own future. In other words, what is at issue here is not the facts of the matter regarding such events but the different possible meanings that such facts can be construed as bearing.

The distinction between facts and meanings is usually taken to be a basis of historical relativism. This is because, in conventional historical inquiry, the facts established about a specific event are taken to *be* the meaning of that event. Facts are supposed to provide the basis for arbitrating among the variety of different meanings that different groups can assign to an event for different ideological or political reasons. But the facts are a function of the meaning assigned to events, not some primitive data that determine what meanings an event can have. It is the anomalous nature of modernist events – their resistance to inherited categories and conventions for assigning meanings to events – that undermine not only the status of facts in relation to events but also the status of the event in general.

But to consider the issue of historical objectivity in terms of an opposition of real to imaginary events, on which the opposition of fact to fiction is in turn based, obscures an important development in Western culture which distinguishes modernism in the arts from all previous forms of realism. Indeed, it seems as difficult to conceive of a treatment of historical reality that would not use fictional techniques in the representation of events as it is to conceive of a serious fiction that did not in some way or at some level make claims about the nature and meaning of history.[4] And this for a number of quite obvious reasons. First, the twentieth century is marked by the occurrence of certain 'holocaustal' events (two world wars, the Great Depression, nuclear weapons and communications technology, the population explosion, the mutilation of the zoosphere, famine, genocide as a policy consciously undertaken by 'modernized' regimes, etc.) that bear little similarity to what earlier historians conventionally took as their objects of study and do not, therefore, lend themselves to understanding by the commonsensical techniques utilized in conventional historical inquiry nor even to representation by the techniques of writing typically favored by historians from Herodotus to Arthur Schlesinger. Nor does any of several varieties of quantitative analysis, of the kind practiced in the social sciences, capture the novelty of such events.[5] Moreover, these kinds of event do not lend themselves to explanation in terms of the categories underwritten by traditional humanistic historiography, which features the activity of human agents conceived to be in some way fully conscious and morally responsible for their actions and capable of discriminating clearly between the causes of historical events and their effects over the long as well as the short run in relatively commonsensical ways – in other words, agents who are presumed to understand history in much the same way as professional historians do.

[. . .]

[...] The notion of the historical event has undergone radical transformation as a result of the occurrence in our century of events of a scope, scale, and depth unimaginable by earlier historians and the dismantling of the concept of the event as an object of a specifically scientific kind of knowledge. So too, however, for the notion of the story; it has suffered tremendous fraying and at least potential dissolution as a result of that revolution in representational practices known as cultural modernism[6] and the technologies of representation made possible by the electronic revolution.

[...]

[...] After modernism, when it comes to the task of storytelling, whether in historical or in literary writing, the traditional techniques of narration become unusable – except in parody.[7] Modernist literary practice effectively explodes the notion of those characters who had formerly served as the subjects of stories or at least as representatives of possible perspectives on the events of the story; and it resists the temptation to emplot events and the actions of the characters so as to produce the meaning-effect derived by demonstrating how one's end may be contained in one's beginning. Modernism thereby effects what Fredric Jameson calls the derealization of the event itself. And it does this by consistently voiding the event of its traditional narrativistic function of indexing the irruption of fate, destiny, grace, fortune, providence, and even of history itself into a life (or at least into some lives) 'in order to pull the sting of novelty' and give the life thus affected at worst a semblance of pattern and at best an actual, transocial, and transhistorical significance.[8]

[...]

Contemporary discussions of the ethics and aesthetics of representing the Holocaust of the European Jews – what I take to be the paradigmatic modernist event in Western European history – provide insights into the modernist view of the relationship between history and fiction. With respect to the question of how most responsibly to represent the Holocaust, the most extreme position is *not* that of the so-called revisionists, who deny that this event ever happened;[9] but, rather, that of those who hold that this event is of such a kind as to escape the grasp of *any* language even to describe it and of *any* medium – verbal, visual, oral, or gestural – to represent it, much less of any merely historical account adequately to explain it. [...]

The historian Christopher R. Browning addresses questions and assertions such as these in a remarkably subtle reflection on the difficulties he had to face in his efforts to reconstruct, represent, and explain a massacre of some 1,500 Jews – women, children, elders, and young men – by German Army Reserve Battalion 101 on 13 July 1942 in the woods outside the Polish village of Jozefów. [...] Browning's aim was to write the history of one day in the life of the 'little men' who were the perpetrators of specific crimes against specific people at a specific time and place in a past that is rapidly receding from living memory and passing into history. And in his report on his research, Browning asks:

> Can the history of such men ever be written? Not just the social, organizational, and institutional history of the units they belonged to. And not just the ideological and decision-making history of the policies they carried out. Can one recapture the experiential history of these killers – the choices they faced, the emotions they felt, the coping mechanisms they employed, the changes they underwent?[10]

He concludes that such an 'experiential history' of this event, all too typical of all too many events of the Holocaust, is virtually impossible to conceive. The Holocaust, he reminds us, 'was not an abstraction. It was a real event in which more than five million Jews were murdered, most in a manner so violent and on a scale so vast that historians and others trying to write about these events have experienced nothing in their personal lives that remotely compares.' And he goes on to assert that 'historians of the Holocaust, in short, know nothing – in an experiential sense – about their subject.' This kind of 'experiential shortcoming,' Browning points out, 'is quite different from their not having experienced, for example, the Constitutional Convention in Philadelphia or Caesar's conquest of Gaul. Indeed, a recurring theme of witnesses [to the Holocaust] is how "unbelievable" [that event] was to them even as they lived through it.'[11]

The shortcoming in question pertains to the nature of the events under scrutiny; these events seem to resist the traditional historian's effort at the kind of empathy which would permit one to see them, as it were, from the inside, in this case, from the perpetrators' perspective. And the difficulty, Browning argues, is not methodological. It is a question not of establishing the facts of the matter but of representing the events established as facts in such a way as to make those events believable to readers who have no more experience of such events than the historian himself.

Browning, in short, draws back from suggesting what appears to me to be the obvious conclusion one might derive from this problem. Which is that the problem is indeed not one of method but, rather, one of representation and that this problem, that of representing the events of the Holocaust, requires the full exploitation of modernist as well as premodernist artistic techniques for its resolution. He draws back from this possibility because, like Saul Friedlander and other experts in the study of representations of the Holocaust, [...] he fears the effects of any aestheticization of this event. And especially by making it into the subject matter of a narrative, a story that, by its possible 'humanization' of the perpetrators, might enfable the event – render it fit therefore for investment by fantasies of intactness, wholeness, and health which the very occurrence of the event denies.

According to Eric Santner, the danger of yielding to the impulse to tell the story of the Holocaust – and, by extension, any other traumatic event – opens the investigator of it to the danger of 'narrative fetishism,' which is, on his view, a 'strategy of undoing, in fantasy, the need for mourning by simulating a condition of intactness, typically by situating the site and origin of loss else-where.'[12] In short, the threat posed by the representation of such events as the Holocaust, the Nazi Final Solution, the assassination of a charismatic leader such as Kennedy or Martin Luther King or Gandhi, an event, such as the destruction of the *Challenger*, which had been symbolically orchestrated to represent the aspirations of a whole community, this threat is nothing other than that of turning them into the subject matter of a narrative. Telling a story, however truthful, about such traumatic events might very well provide a kind of intellectual mastery of the anxiety that memory of their occurrence may incite in an individual or a community. But precisely insofar as the story is identifiable as a story, it can provide no lasting psychic mastery of such events.

And this is why it seems to me that the kinds of antinarrative nonstories produced by literary modernism offer the only prospect for adequate representations of the kind of 'unnatural' events – including the Holocaust – that mark our era and distinguish it absolutely from all of the history that has come before it. In other words, what Jameson calls the psychopathologies of modernist writings and film, which he lists as 'their artificial closures, the blockage of narrative, [their] deformation and formal compensations, the dissociation or splitting of narrative functions, including the repression of certain of them, and so forth,'[13] – it is these very psychopathological techniques, which explode the conventions of the traditional tale (the passing of which was lamented and at the same time justified by Benjamin in his famous essay 'The Storyteller'), that offer the possibility of representing such traumatic events as those produced by the monstrous growth and expansion of techno-logical modernity (of which Nazism and the Holocaust are manifestations) in a manner less fetishizing than any traditional representation of them would necessarily be.

What I am suggesting is that the stylistic innovations of modernism, born as they were of an effort to come to terms with the anticipated loss of the peculiar sense of history which modernism is ritually criticized for not possessing, may provide better instruments for representing modernist events (and premodernist events in which we have a typically modernist interest) than the storytelling techniques traditionally utilized by historians for the representation of the events of the past that are supposed to be crucial to the development of their communities' identity. Modernist techniques of representation provide the possibility of defetishizing both events and the fantasy accounts of them which deny the threat they pose in the very process of pretending to represent them realistically and clear the way for that process of mourning which alone can relieve the burden of history and make a more if not totally realistic perception of current problems possible.

[...]

Notes

1. Fredric Jameson, 'Metacommentary [1971],' in *The Ideologies of Theory: Essays, 1971–86* (Minneapolis: University of Minnesota Press, 1988), chap. 1.
2. Linda Hutcheon, *A Poetics of Postmodernism: History, Theory, Fiction* (New York: Routledge, 1988), 76. [...]
3. The inclusion of the Holocaust in this list may be questioned by scholars of that event who insist on its uniqueness, if not in all of history, then at least in the history of genocides. In my view, all historical events are by definition unique, one of a kind, but still comparable with other events of the same species. [...] My point is that the events in this list are all uniquely twentieth-century events [...].
4. Cf. Sidney Monas, 'Introduction: Contemporary Historiography: Some Kicks in the Old Coffin,' in *Developments in Modern Historiography*, ed. H. Kozicki (New York: St. Martin's Press, 1992), 1–16.
5. See Zygmunt Bauman, *Modernity and the Holocaust* (Ithaca: Cornell University Press, 1989), 122.
6. Thus, Jameson defines literary modernism as a product of a double crisis, on the one hand, a 'social crisis of narratable experiences,' and, on the other, a 'semiotic crisis of narrative paradigms.' Fredric Jameson, *Sartre: The Origins of a Style* (New York: Columbia University Press, 1984), 211. I want to make clear that by the term *modernism* I am not referring to that program of dominating nature through reason, science, and technology supposedly inaugurated by the Enlightenment; I refer, rather, to the literary and artistic movements launched in the late nineteenth and early twentieth centuries against this very program of modernization and its social and cultural effects, the movement represented by writers such as Pound, Eliot, Stein, Joyce, Proust, Woolf, and so on.
7. [...]. See Craig Owen, 'The Allegorical Impulse: Toward a New Theory of Postmodernism,' in *Beyond Recognition: Representation, Power, and Culture* (Berkeley: University of California Press, 1992), 52 ff.
8. Jameson, 'The Nature of Events,' in *Sartre*, chap. 2.
9. I want to stress the difference between the modernist problematization of the event and the effort on the part of a group of parahistorians known as Revisionists to deny that the event known as the Holocaust ever happened. It should be noted that the revisionists have a very traditional notion of both historical events and evidence. What they wish to establish on the basis of a very literalist interpretation of the evidence is that the occurrence of the Holocaust cannot be proven. They are rather like fundamentalist Christians interpreting the evidence for evolutionism.
10. Christopher R. Browning, 'German Memory, Judicial Interrogation, Historical Reconstruction,' in *Probing the Limits of Representation: Nazism and the Final Solution*, ed. Saul Friedlander (Cambridge: Harvard University Press, 1992), 27.
11. Ibid., 25. Cf. Martin Jay, 'Experience without a Subject: Walter Benjamin and the Novel,' *New Formations* no. 20 (Summer 1993): 145–55.
12. Eric Santner, 'History beyond the Pleasure Principle,' in Friedlander, *Probing the Limits*, 146.
13. Jameson, *Sartre*, 210.

45

'AGAINST FORESHADOWING'

Michael André Bernstein

A: What is the great world-historical event of 1875?
B: Vladimir Ilych Lenin turned five!
              A characteristic Russian joke during the Brezhnev era

[...] In the heavily forestructured universe of *The Brothers Karamazov*, Dostoevsky points to the radical freedom of human beings from any kind of determinism, and his technical, literary way of showing this is to throw into doubt the time-honored device of foreshadowing. Smerdyakov may grow up to be his father's killer – indeed, without that resolution there would be no story to tell – but he is not *predestined* for that deed, and the man he does murder may, in fact, not even have been his biological father. Such a strategy can be defined as a kind of *sideshadowing*: a gesturing to the side, to a present dense with multiple, and mutually exclusive, possibilities for what is to come.[1] In narrative terms, sideshadowing is best understood in opposition to the familiar technique of foreshadowing, a technique whose enactment can vary tremendously in its degree of intricacy, but whose logic must always value the present, not for itself, but as the harbinger of an already determined future. The Russian joke quoted above is a fine jibe at the remarkably crude foreshadowing that habitually characterizes any global and monolithic way of thinking, and it is probably salutary to insist that *all* foreshadowing is vulnerable to the kind of irony that

From Michael André Bernstein (1994) *Foregone Conclusions: Against Apocalyptic History*. Berkeley and Los Angeles, CA: University of California Press.

the Russians learned over the decades to direct at their own institutionalized version of the *topos*.

[...]

At its extreme, foreshadowing implies a closed universe in which all choices have already been made, in which human free will can exist only in the paradoxical sense of choosing to accept or willfully – and vainly – rebelling against what is inevitable. [...]

Sideshadowing's attention to the unfulfilled or unrealized possibilities of the past is a way of disrupting the affirmations of a triumphalist, unidirectional view of history in which whatever has perished is condemned because it has been found wanting by some irresistible historico-logical dynamic. Against foreshadowing, sideshadowing champions the incommensurability of the concrete moment and refuses the tyranny of all synthetic master-schemes; it rejects the conviction that a particular code, law, or pattern exists, waiting to be uncovered beneath the heterogeneity of human existence. [...]

[...] Especially in the face of a catastrophe, there is an urge to surrender to the most extreme foreshadowing imaginable, thereby resisting sideshadowing altogether. We try to make sense of a historical disaster by interpreting it, according to the strictest teleological model, as the climax of a bitter trajectory whose inevitable outcome it must be. [...] When an event is so destructive for a whole people, so hideous in its motivation, enactment, and consequences as was the Shoah, there is an almost irresistible pressure to interpret it as one would a tragedy, to regard it as the simultaneously inconceivable and yet foreordained culmination of the entire brutal history of European anti-Semitism. [...]

[...] The Shoah as a whole, moreover, can never be represented plausibly as a tragedy because the killings happened as part of an ongoing political and bureaucratic process. In the domain of history, unlike in the world 'seen with the eyes of the [tragic] genre,' there are always multiple paths and sideshadows, always moment-by-moment events, each of which is potentially significant in determining an individual's life, and each of which is a conjunction, unplottable and unpredictable in advance of its occurrence, of specific choices and accidents. Indeed, every survivor's narrative I have read emphasizes the multiple contingencies, the intersection of fortuitous events too wildly improbable for any fiction, that made survival possible. Primo Levi's account, *Se questo è un uomo*, is, of course, the classic instance of such a survivor's narrative, stressing, as it does, how many separate and unforeseeable incidents had to combine for Levi to live through his time in Auschwitz. [...]

[...] Every interpretation of the Shoah that is grounded in a sense of historical inevitability resonates with both implicit and often explicit ideological implications, not so much about the world of the perpetrators of the genocide, or about those bystanders who did so little to halt the mass murder, but about the lives of the victims themselves. The bitterness of inevitability, whether seen as tragic or pathetic, endows an event with a meaning, one that can be used both to make an ideationally 'rich' sense of the horror and to begin a process of coming to terms with the pain by enfolding it within some larger pattern of signification. And for the Shoah, especially in its uncannily delayed representation in Zionist writing, that pattern has been primarily one of proving the untenability of the Diaspora, and the self-destructive absurdity of the attempts by European and, more specifically, by Austro-German Jewry to assimilate to a society that only waited for its chance to exterminate them.[2] [...]

[...]

The realization that we ourselves are often still deeply implicated in historical conflicts and debates whose terms we have not so much shaped as inherited, leads to the most pervasive, but also the most pernicious, variant of foreshadowing, a variant that I have called 'backshadowing.' Backshadowing is a kind of retroactive foreshadowing in which the shared knowledge of the outcome of a series of events by narrator and listener is used to judge the participants in those events *as though they too should have known what was to come.* Thus, our knowledge of the Shoah is used to condemn the 'blindness' and 'self-deception' of Austro-German Jewry for their unwillingness to save themselves from a doom that supposedly was clear to see. [...]

[...] The discretion required, a discretion that sideshadowing is particularly concerned to teach us, is (1) not to see the future as pre-ordained; and, as a direct corollary, (2) not to use our knowledge of the future as a means of judging the decisions of those living before that (still only possible) future became actual event. [...]

[...]

[...] In the corpus of works on the Shoah, I think there is a powerful but largely unrecognized connection that links together a set of contradictions which are so persistent that they have become constitutive of the whole discourse. On a historical level, there is the contradiction between conceiving of the Shoah as simultaneously unimaginable *and* inevitable. On an ethical level, the contradiction is between saying no one could have foreseen the triumph of genocidal anti-Semitism, while also claiming that those who stayed in Europe are in part responsible for their fate because they failed to anticipate the danger. On a narrative level, the contradiction is between insisting on the unprecedented and singular nature of the Shoah as an event and yet still using the most lurid formal tropes and commonplace literary conventions to narrate it.

[...]

No writer on the Shoah has been more aware of the risks of representing the ultimate viciousness of the Shoah, or more careful to avoid feeding an appetitive fascination with evil, than Aharon Appelfeld. A child of wealthy, thoroughly assimilated Bukovina Jews who were murdered in the Shoah, the nine-year-old Appelfeld survived by escaping alone from the Transnistria camp. [...] He ended up in a refugee camp on the Italian coast, from which he was taken to Palestine by the Zionist youth rescue movement. Appelfeld, beyond any other prose writer, is credited in Israel with having made the Shoah into a legitimate theme for novelists. [...]

[...]

Appelfeld's importance is centrally grounded in the fact that he is not only writing about the genocide as such, but rather, attempting to narrate the relationship between that catastrophe and the world it obliterated. But if the very act of representing European Jewry in its final months before the Shoah constituted both a thematic breakthrough and a polemical assertion of resistance in Israeli letters, the perspective from which Appelfeld treats his characters betrays an unconscious but thorough complicity with the sabras' contemptuous dismissal of the values and dignity of those Jews. There is a deeply troubling failure of historical and moral comprehension at the core of some of Appelfeld's most celebrated novels, and this failure is all the more disturbing since it is so strikingly at odds with the potential imaginative richness of Appelfeld's project as a whole. It is as though Appelfeld could only transgress the Israeli taboo against chronicling the unheroic lives of ordinary, assimilated Austro-German Jews, as well as the larger prohibition against any representation of the Shoah, by treating his characters as marionettes whose futile gestures on an absurd stage we watch, half in horror, half in anxiously bemused melancholy at their foolishness. We know they are doomed; they stubbornly refuse to know it, and in the interaction between our knowledge and their ignorance a fable of willed self-delusion unfolds whose motifs would have satisfied the strictest of Appelfeld's Zionist instructors in the youth movements.

[...]

The best way to illustrate the cost of Appelfeld's technique is to look closely at *Badenheim 1939*, the first and critically most acclaimed of his novels to have appeared in English. [...] Badenheim is a typical Austrian spa town, where prosperous, thoroughly secularized Jews spend their vacations enjoying the restorative mineral baths, the rich hotel food, and the cultural life of an annual music and theatrical summer festival. In the novel, the town becomes a microcosm of the world of Austro-German Jewry with its cultural pretensions, its rejection of any overt signs of Jewishness, especially as embodied by the 'vulgar *Ostjuden*' (Jews from Eastern Europe, whose style of dress, language, and religious observance exacerbated the unease of westernized Jews),[3] and its hallucinatory refusal to confront the danger that was literally enclosing it from every side.[4] [...] Even at the end, although the Jews of Badenheim have been deprived of their freedom, their jobs, and their contact with the outside world, and have been ordered about like so much chattel (but without any overt physical coercion, which would violate the book's fable-like tone), they retain their by now clearly absurd optimism. Dr. Pappenheim, a renowned impresario and musical connoisseur, and the most fully described character in the book, ends *Badenheim 1939* with the cheerfully encouraging comment, 'If the coaches are so dirty it must mean that we have not far to go'.[5]

But every reader of the novel knows the names of the stations where the train will disgorge its passengers, and if Appelfeld can avoid mentioning Theresienstadt, Auschwitz, or Mauthausen, it is only because of his certainty that the reader will do so in his place. The reader hears the desperate will to lie to oneself in Pappenheim's final words and understands how soon and how methodically that Panglossian confidence will be silenced. And what is of crucial importance, the reader understands this precisely from a deep familiarity with the kinds of Shoah texts and images Appelfeld is applauded for having excluded, so that in a sense everything that Appelfeld formally bars from his fictional world he invites back in by virtually compelling his readers to stage the horrific set-pieces in their own imaginations. Ultimately, there is less difference than either Appelfeld or his admirers would like to claim between a concluding sentence like 'If the coaches are so dirty it must mean that we have not far to go' and Pawel's 'in the not too distant Austrian town of Braunau, one Clara née Plözl, wife of the customs inspector Aloïs Hitler, had given birth to ... a sickly infant whose survival seemed doubtful. He survived.'[...]

[...]

The expected, or, more accurately, the *necessary* importation of our knowledge about the Shoah is a particularly manipulative example of backshadowing because it seems so unemphatic and 'natural.' Moreover, it harmonizes perfectly with the tone of distant and aloof mockery used to describe the characters and their determinedly blinkered concentration on the quotidian banalities of resort life. But such an account of European Jewry only makes sense as a kind of *reductio ad absurdum* of the Zionist interpretation of Austro-Hungarian Jews stumbling blindly to their doom, willfully ignoring ever-clearer warning signs of the untenability of their position, and concerned only to distance themselves as much as possible from any acknowledgment of a common Jewish identity. (Leo Strauss used to call such rhetoric *reductio ad Hitlerum*.) Nothing can break through the triviality of the vacationers' narrow egotism, and when they leave for the railway station and its 'four filthy freight cars,' it is not a real existence that has been terminated, but only a sham construct with no more substance than the elaborate pastries of the Badenheim *Konditorei*. Appelfeld's fable, for all its seeming lightness of touch, is as moralistic and judgmental as the sternest critic of Austro-German Jewry, and, just as with all backshadowing perspectives, its termination in the abyss of the Shoah is adduced to 'prove' the meaninglessness of Jewish life in Aryan Europe.

[...]

One way to crystallize the general implications of Appelfeld's practice in terms of my earlier discussion is to see how the 'overdetermination' of signification forecloses any chance at sideshadowing. Since the relentless glare of the Shoah is ever present, not merely at the book's end but throughout its unfolding, it floods the various scenes with its overpowering significance so that none of them can have a consequence independent of that all-dominant one. Appelfeld himself clearly recognized the aesthetic and moral problem raised by backshadowing: his determination to avoid directly representing the Shoah by ending the novel before the killings actually began is part of this recognition. But since he never tries to voice an alternative and less monolithic vision of history, his novel incorporates none of the openness of sideshadowing, and his decision remains an isolated scruple unrelated to achieving a more complete understanding of the world of the victims.

[...] There is a crucial and often unacknowledged distinction between the 'inevitability' of an anticipated climax in classical epic and tragedy, or in densely 'realistic' novels like those of the *Comédie humaine*, and the retrospective, backshadowing historico-moral judgments of a book like *Badenheim 1939*. In works like *The Iliad, King Lear*, or *Splendeurs et misères des courtisanes*, the grim ending is not used retroactively to constitute the primary source of judgment on the characters. What the characters in these works do is seen as good or bad, evil or virtuous, at the moment their actions are committed. Lear is manifestly wrong and morally at fault right from his first speech – even if Goneril and Regan had kept their pledges and even if Cordelia were to have lived happily ever after in France, Lear's tyrannical self-indulgence would be palpably reprehensible. But if there had been no Shoah, the assimilationists vacationing in Badenheim might be considered, from certain perspectives, as weak or lacking in ethnic self-dignity, but from many other points of view, which probably included those of the majority of European Jewry, their self-definition as 'Austrian citizens of Jewish origin' (21) would be entirely reasonable. To focus on one's private family ties, love affairs, careers, or artistic longings, is completely unobjectionable by normal, quotidian standards; only in the light of the genocide awaiting all of the characters can these kinds of priorities be found inadequate. In other words, the Shoah looming at the novel's end is used throughout the text, instant by instant and scene by scene, to judge everyone's behavior, and it forces us to interpret that behavior as escapist, futile, and ultimately self-destructive. This is not the case in a text, whether epic, tragedy, or novel, whose ending, once it has occurred, may seem retrospectively to have been predetermined but in which the episode-by-episode, moment-by-moment behavior of the characters is significant in its own right. [..]

[...]

Of course my examples here are from works that we do not necessarily read for their historical specificity or analysis, but [...] the ethical implications of backshadowing are registered as powerfully in historical as in fictional writing. As we have seen, in a sense it is clear that without a knowledge of what followed them, it is impossible to grasp the significance and implications of decisive past events (e.g., the first anti-Semitic laws passed by the Nazis). But it is not the course of a particular historical unfolding that is at issue here; rather, it is a respect for people living at a time *before* that unfolding was complete who could not, and should not, be expected to have any knowledge of the future. Sideshadowing is not concerned to deny to either the historian or the novelist a retrospective awareness of important events; but it *is* concerned (1) not to regard the future from which the writers speak as the inevitable outcome of the past, and (2) not to let retrospection impose a hierarchy of significant/insignificant, fertile/futile, etc., judgments on the actions and thoughts of the characters in their narratives when the terms of that hierarchy are entirely determined by the story's ending.

[...] Even if some Austrian Jews did refuse to acknowledge their perilous situation, the question of sideshadowing only indirectly concerns their likelihood of survival, which often was entirely out of their own hands; instead, sideshadowing seeks only to draw attention to the diversity of the stances they took toward their predicament and the particular ways they sought to maintain their existence and identity within their catastrophic new circumstances. It is crucial to recognize that the likelihood of success of any action is not the criterion by which a multiplicity of possibilities can be determined. Even if none of the available options has a very strong chance of succeeding, there are still differences among them (and since the issue here is one of saving individual human lives, surely even a small percentage is of enormous significance), and peoples' characters can be judged partially by which option they in fact attempt. [...]

I am claiming here that to acknowledge the validity of sideshadowing is not merely to reject historical inevitability as a theoretical model. Far more important, it means learning to value the contingencies and multiple paths leading from each concrete moment of lived experience, and recognizing the importance of those moments not for their place in an already determined larger pattern but as significant in their own right. This is what I have called a prosaics of the quotidian, and it is fundamentally linked to the historical logic of sideshadowing. [...]

What may seem like merely formal decisions about how much knowledge of the future to include in a narrative set in an earlier epoch, or about how much to let the narrative glance sideways and project forward to events that never happened, is already thematically charged and thereby morally significant. If it is absurd to see the 'great world-historical event' of 1875 as Lenin's fifth birthday, and if we can smile at the idea of a secular angel arriving in Langres in 1713 to tell Mme. Diderot that she would soon give birth to a great encyclopedist, then we also have to learn to absolve from any blame those Jews who attended the summer festivals of Salzburg or Badenheim and went about dressed in *Trachten* rather than in the paramilitary gear of the *Haganah* or the *tephillin* of the orthodox. There is ample reason to find preposterous that it is now time to forgive the murderers. Recognizing the contingencies and uncertainties in human events can prevent us from blaming the victims for their disastrous choices, but it in no way mitigates the decisions and choices of their murderers. The consequences of evil actions may be unpredictable and continue long into the future, but they are committed by particular people at specific moments and can be recognized as evil as soon as they are performed. The murderers became such at the instant they participated in murder, and sideshadowing in no way minimizes – in fact, it only emphasizes – their moral culpability.[6] [...]

NOTES

1. [...] The term *sideshadowing* was originally coined by Gary Saul Morson [...]. I then coined the corollary concept of *backshadowing*, and at one time Morson and I thought of publishing our work together as a single, two-part study. [...]
2. I say uncannily delayed because one of the more surprising aspects of Hebrew literature is that, in Alan Mintz's description, 'between World War II and the Eichmann trial in the early sixties there are no significant works of Hebrew literature which directly engage the Holocaust, with the major exception of [the poet] Uri Zvi Greenberg.' Mintz, *Hurban: Responses to Catastrophe in Hebrew Literature* (New York: Columbia University Press, 1984), 158 [...].
3. On this theme, see Steven E. Aschheim, *Brothers and Strangers: The East European Jew in German and German Jewish Consciousness, 1800–1923* (Madison: University of Wisconsin Press, 1983).
4. Austrian Jews had long been in the habit of vacationing at resorts that were *Judenfreundlich* [hospitable to Jews], less out of any particular 'clannishness' or desire to remain exclusively among their own kind, than as a consequence of being barred from numerous other spas.[...]
5. Aharon Appelfeld, *Badenheim 1939*, trans. Dalya Bilu (Boston: David R. Godine, 1980), 148. Future references are to this edition and are acknowledged in the body of the text.
6. One of the strengths of recent studies like Christopher Browning's *Ordinary Men: Reserve Police Battalion 101 and the Final Solution in Poland* (New York: Harper Collins, 1992) and *The Path to Genocide: Essays on Launching the Final Solution* (New York: Cambridge University Press, 1992) is how clearly they show the crucial role of individual decisions and choices in carrying out the genocide.

46

'DEEP MEMORY: THE BURIED SELF'

Lawrence L. Langer

[...]

[...] Literate readers can eventually work their way through the pages of a book, no matter what the theme, because the form and style of the narrative are designed to make us complicit with the text. But literacy has little to do with the problem of entering into meaningful intellectual or emotional dialogue with the contents of [...] videotaped testimonies. As viewers, we have difficulty doing this because the testimonies are not based on common experience or an imaginable past, real or literary. Though eager to participate with sympathetic understanding, we are driven by the nature of the material to the periphery of comprehension. Odd as it may sound, we need to search for the inner principles of *in*coherence that make these testimonies accessible to us.

A written narrative is finished when we begin to read it, its opening, middle, and end already established between the covers of the book. This *appearance* of form is reassuring (even though the experience of reading may prove an unsettling challenge). Oral testimony steers a less certain course, like a fragile craft veering through turbulent waters unsure where a safe harbor lies – or whether one exists at all! The following illustration offers dramatic evidence of the difference between the two forms of presentation, because the witness also has written an autobiographical historical novel about her camp experience. We thus have an opportunity to observe both forms of narrative at work on an identical theme.

From Lawrence L. Langer (1991) *Holocaust Testimonies: The Ruins of Memory*. New Haven, CT: Yale University Press.

In her testimony, Barbara T. draws on the memory of her camp experience *as well as* on the book she has written about it. We become, as it were, auditors and readers simultaneously, forced to pay attention to the disjunction between the two approaches. Asked by the interviewer to describe her arrival at Auschwitz, Barbara T. begins: 'It was night, but it was light because there were flames and there were powerful searchlights in the square. The air stank. Some people in the cars had died of thirst, of hunger, of madness. I felt a tremendous thirst. We had no water. And as the doors opened, I breathed in air as if it would be water, and I choked. It stank. And eventually we saw these strange-looking creatures, striped pajamas, who got us into a marching line.' Then an odd thing happens. The witness pauses, half-hypnotized by her own narrative, as if returning from a strange place, and apologizes for what she calls her 'absence': 'I'm sorry, OK, I ... I ... forgive me ... all right ... I'm going to ... I kind of was back there.' Intensely aware of the exclusive *and* inclusive privacy of that moment, which she inhabits simultaneously alone and in the presence of the interviewer (to say nothing of a potentially larger audience of viewers), the witness struggles to resume her narrative, to plunge back into the present, as it were, but succeeds only for an instant: 'Inmates whipped us out of the cattle cars,' she says, 'and they got us into rows of five.'

At this point Barbara T. pauses and asks, 'Do you want me to talk about that?' 'Yes,' the interviewer replies, 'I think so.' 'I would like to read it,' the witness responds. 'It's easier.'[1] She then reaches for her book, which is lying on the table beside her, and begins to read on camera: 'we are dragged out of cattle cars, vomited into an impenetrable black night. Suddenly torches brighten up a black sky and i clearly see the night: it engulfs a square drenched in searing brilliance by powerful floodlights.' She hesitates an instant, skips a paragraph, and resumes her reading: 'screams knife the air and i cover my ears with my hands. torches keep licking the sky like rainbows, flaming rainbows, and i quickly close my eyes but i still see the flames through my closed lids and the screams slash through my hands, into my ears, then a horrible stench hits my nostrils, i gasp for air but i choke. i am terrified. i don't know what to do.'[2] Certainly this passage is vivid. But it also is transparently literary, alien to the speech rhythms of the oral narrative. Of the many dozens of testimonies I have viewed about arrival at Auschwitz, not one has mentioned anything remotely resembling being 'vomited into an impenetrable black night.' When one compares this self-conscious striving for stylistic impact with Barbara T.'s *spoken* testimony – 'inmates whipped us out of the cattle cars,' for example – one cannot escape the uncomfortable feeling that the *book's* idiom may be intrusive on and distracting from the more unencumbered flow of the oral testimony.

Written accounts of victim experience prod the imagination in ways that speech cannot, striving for analogies to initiate the reader into the particularities of their grim world. This literature faces a special challenge, since it must give most readers access to a totally unfamiliar subject. When searchlights at

Auschwitz are said to lick the sky like 'flaming rainbows,' we are invited to use this simile as a ticket of entry to the bizarre deathcamp landscape. The singular *in*appropriateness of an image of natural beauty, symbolizing good fortune and joy, to describe one's arrival at Auschwitz underlines the difficulty of finding a vocabulary of comparison for such an incomparable atrocity. Indeed, the unexpected juxtaposition of literary and oral versions of the same moment of camp experience raises some vital questions about interpreting such testimonies that until now few commentators have sought to confront.

When the witness in an oral testimony leans forward toward the camera (as happens frequently in these tapes), apparently addressing the interviewer(s) but also speaking to the potential audience of the future – asking: 'Do you understand what I'm trying to tell you?' – that witness confirms the vast imaginative space separating what he or she has endured from our capacity to absorb it. Written memoirs, by the very strategies available to their authors – style, chronology, analogy, imagery, dialogue, a sense of character, a coherent moral vision – strive to narrow this space, easing us into their unfamiliar world through familiar (and hence comforting?) literary devices. The impulse to *portray* (and thus refine) reality when we write about it seems irresistible. Describing the SS man who greeted her and her mother on the ramp at Auschwitz, Barbara T. writes: 'his pale blue eyes dart from side to side like a metronome,'[3] and once again one has the uneasy feeling of the literary *transforming* the real in a way that obscures even as it seeks to enlighten. [. . .] Videotaped oral testimonies provide us with an unexplored archive of 'texts' that solicit from us original forms of interpretation. Reading a book that tries to carry us 'back there' is an order of experience entirely different from witnessing someone like Barbara T. vanishing from contact with us even as she speaks, momentarily returning to the world she is trying to evoke instead of recreating it for us in the present. Yet her presence before us dramatically illustrates the merging of time senses (so often revealed by witnesses in oral testimony) that *creates* meaning through the very manner of her narrative.[4] A complex kind of 'reversible continuity' seems to establish itself in many of these testimonies, one foreign to the straight chronology that governs most written memoirs.

A further distinction may be necessary here. Normal oral discourse – the speech, the lecture, the political address – assumes that the audience is no mystery and that competent presentation and substantial content will rouse and hold an audience's interest. And that is generally true. But the first effect of many of these testimonies is just the opposite, no matter how vivid the presentation: they induce fear, confusion, shame, horror, skepticism, even disbelief. The more painful, dramatic, and overwhelming the narrative, the more tense, wary, and self-protective is the audience, the quicker the instinct to withdraw. Unlike the writer, the witness here lacks inclination and strategies to establish and maintain a viable bond between the participants in this encounter.

To reverse the direction of that initial estrangement, a viewer must find some entry into the realm of disrupted lives and become sensitized to the implications of such disruption. In other words, we should not come to the encounter unprepared – yet we do. We have little choice. It is virtually useless, as we soon discover, to approach the experience from the reservoir of normal values, armed with questions like 'Why didn't they resist?' and 'Why didn't they help one another?' The first answer is that they did; the second is that sometimes it made no difference; and the third is that, under those circumstances, more often than not they couldn't. All are true, just as each testimony is true, even when the testimonies contradict one another. They impose on us a role not only of passive listener but also of active *hearer*. This requires us to suspend our sense of the normal and to accept the complex immediacy of a voice reaching us simultaneously from the secure present and the devastating past. That complexity, by forcing us to redefine our role as audience *throughout* the encounter, distinguishes these testimonies from regular oral discourse as well as from written texts.

Confrontation with these videotaped testimonies begins in separate narrative and ends in collective memory, though one hardly feels any satisfaction from mastering the 'text.' Listening to accounts of Holocaust experience, we unearth a mosaic of evidence that constantly vanishes, like Thomas Mann's well of the past, into bottomless layers of incompletion. There is no closure, because the victims who have *not* survived – in many ways, the most important 'characters' in these narratives – have left no personal voice behind. They can only be evoked, spoken *about*. We wrestle with the beginnings of a permanently unfinished tale, full of incomplete intervals, faced by the spectacle of a faltering witness often reduced to a distressed silence by the overwhelming solicitations of deep memory.

Witnesses' chronic frustration and skepticism about the audience's ability to understand their testimony is almost a premise of these encounters. Written texts, on the other hand, whether memoirs, fiction, or poetry, are *designed* to avert this possibility – otherwise, one assumes, they would not be published. Indeed, the initial problem surfacing in these oral testimonies with sufficient regularity to call it a 'theme' is exactly the opposite: whether *anything* can be meaningfully conveyed. One former member of the Polish underground reports: 'If you were not there, it is difficult to describe and say how it was. It sounds very, very, very … I don't know if there is [a] word to describe the nightmare one go through … how men function under such a stress is one thing, and then how you communicate and express [to] somebody who never knew that such a degree of brutality [is] existing seems like a fantasy.' This witness adds that if he tried to sit with his daughter today to explain what his life was like between 1939 and 1946, she would say to him: 'Daddy, you're making all that up.'[5] For us as audience, the summons is to induce an involuntary suspension of disbelief, because there is little chance of inspiring a willing one.

How best to do this? How to do it at all? We turn to former victims for insight. One reports that when he was first brought into a crematorium area with a work detail, he did not flinch at the piles of bodies because every day in the Lodz ghetto, from which he had been deported to the deathcamp, he had seen dozens of corpses strewn about the streets. What might seem like fantasy to us became a sign of 'ordinary' reality for him, so he could make the adjustment enabling him to accept this 'abnormality' as part of his normal daily routine. A similar imaginative transition is required of us, if we are to 'hear' the implications of these testimonies, but in the absence of a moral authority, not to mention experiential precedent, to sanction such unions of the normal with the abnormal, we flounder at the point of intersection. Only a collaborative effort can validate the testimony, a transvaluation requiring us to assent to the 'normality' of piles of corpses destined for the crematorium. The perplexity of witnesses today at their own moral distance from those moments does little to simplify our task.

One of the most powerful themes on these tapes is thus the difficulty of narrating, from the context of normality *now*, the nature of the abnormality *then*, an abnormality that still surges into the present to remind us of its potent influence. Two time frames converge and then coalesce in the following narrative moment from the testimony of Baruch G., as he tries to explain why, during family celebrations of weddings and bar mitzvahs, he has a sense of being utterly alone, because absolutely no one is there from 'his side':

> Loneliness has various aspects to it. I remember after liberation, I suffered probably more from the loneliness and the isolation, more than during the Holocaust period. . . . I suppose it has to do with the fact that after, the life around you seems to be normal but *you* are abnormal. Well, why? . . . In concentration camps and labor camps, there was a preoccupation with survival. . . . But then after what was called liberation – actually, the realization of liberation was not vivid to me, was not real with me for a long time, but I remember during the years '45, '46, '47, and even up to '48, I would find myself crying, and quite frequently . . . [experiencing] a feeling of 'Yes, I'm alive, but that's it, the rest doesn't matter.'[6]

How can one be alone amid friends and family? The internalized dual existence of witnesses like this one requires of us a responsive and reciprocal duality of vision that might grasp what another former victim meant when she said of her Auschwitz past: 'I don't live with it. It lives with me.' One of the paradoxes emerging from these testimonies is that, although nothing could be more final than the deaths recorded there, nothing could be *less* final either. As a result, the concrete meanings of words like 'survival' and 'liberation' blur, because they cannot be separated from the doom of those whose 'preoccupation with survival' failed. Individual 'successes' are invariably tainted by this conjunction; 'I'm alive,' to use Baruch G.'s terms, simply lacks the moral resonance of 'I survived.'

The tension between imposed isolation and the impulse to community, between the revelations of deep memory and the consolations of common memory, remains unresolved. When Baruch G. speaks drearily of 'what was called liberation,' when he fails to infuse an expression like 'preoccupation with survival' with the moral exhilaration that commentators often attribute to it, when he defines it by implication merely as the tenacity for staying alive one more day, a definition that he knows may appear abnormal from the vantage point of the present – then we are invited to consider the possibility of some words and gestures being welcome and misplaced at the same time. Distinctions between commitment to life and surrender to death dim, while the sharp-edged demarcations separating liberation from confinement grow blunt. A familiar face [...] can be a source of awed surprise that mingles with but does not replace one's private pain. Oral testimony repeatedly dramatizes the immediacy of such confusions.

Notes

1. Fortunoff Video Archive for Holocaust Testimonies, Yale University (hereafter FVA), tape T-780. Testimony of Barbara T.
2. Barbara Fischman Traub, *The Matrushka Doll* (New York: Richard Marek, 1979), pp. 27–28.
3. Ibid., p. 28.
4. For a similar effect with an artfully contrived (and controlled) narrative voice in fiction, see Jorge Semprun's *The Long Voyage* and *What a Beautiful Sunday*!
5. FVA tape T-49. Testimony of Stanley M.
6. Tape T-295. Testimony of Baruch G.

47

'THE RETURN OF THE VOICE: CLAUDE LANZMANN'S *SHOAH*'

Shoshana Felman

The Impossibility of Testimony

Shoah is a film about testimony [. . .] in an infinitely more abysmal, paradoxical and problematic way than it first seems: the *necessity of testimony* it affirms in reality derives, paradoxically enough, from the *impossibility of testimony* that the film at the same time dramatizes. I would suggest that this impossibility of testimony by which the film is traversed, with which it struggles and against which it precisely builds itself is, in effect, the most profound and most crucial subject of the film. In its enactment of the Holocaust as the *event-without-a-witness*, as the traumatic impact of a historically ungraspable *primal scene* which erases both its witness and its witnessing, *Shoah* explores the very boundaries of testimony by exploring, at the same time, the historical impossibility of witnessing and the historical impossibility of *escaping* the predicament of being – and of having to become – a witness. At the edge of the universe of testimony which is the universe of our era, at the frontiers of the necessity of speech, *Shoah* is a film about silence: the paradoxical articulation of a *loss of voice* – and of a loss of mind. The film is the product of a relentless struggle for remembrance, but for the self-negating, contradictory, conflictual remembrance of – precisely – an *amnesia*. The testimony stumbles on, and at the same time tells about, the impossibility of telling.

From Shoshana Felman (1992) 'The Return of the Voice: Claude Lanzmann's *Shoah*', in Shoshana Felman and Dori Laub (eds), *Testimonies: Crises of Witnessing in Literature, Psychoanalysis, and History*. New York: Routledge.

No one can describe it. No one can recreate what happened here. Impossible? And no one can understand it. Even I, here, now ... I can't believe I'm here. No, I just can't believe it. It was always this peaceful here. Always. When they burned two thousand people – Jews – every day, it was just as peaceful. No one shouted. Everyone went about his work. It was silent. Peaceful. Just as it is now.[1]

What cannot be grasped in the event-without-a-witness, and what the witness nonetheless must now (impossibly) bear witness to, is not merely the murder but, specifically, the autobiographical moment of the witness's death, the historical occurrence of the *dying* of the subject of witnessing as such.

> *What died in him in Chelmno?*
> Everything died. But he's only human, and he wants to live. So he must forget. He thanks God ... that he can forget. And let's not talk about that.
> *Does he think it's good to talk about it?*
> For me it's not good.
> *Then why is he talking about it?*
> Because you're insisting on it. He was sent books on Eichmann's trial. He was a witness, and he didn't even read them. [7]

Podchlebnik, in whom 'everything died' as a witness, retrospectively gives testimony in the Eichmann trial, but he still would rather keep the witness dead, keep the witness as a (dead) secret from his own eyes by *not reading* anything about his own role in the trial. The desire not to read, and not to talk, stems from the fear of hearing, or of witnessing, oneself. The *will-to-silence* is the will to *bury* the dead witness inside oneself.

But the film is 'insisting,' here again, that the 'Jewish cemetery' (to return to the dialogue with Mrs. Pietyra) cannot be once and for all 'closed' (18), that the witness must himself precisely now reopen his own burial as witness, even if this burial is experienced by him, paradoxically enough, as the very condition of his survival.

THE MATTER OF THE WITNESS, OR THE MISSING BODY

What would it mean, however, for the witness to reopen his own grave – to testify precisely from inside the very cemetery which is not yet closed? And what would it mean, alternatively, to bear witness from inside the witness's *empty grave* – empty both because the witness in effect did not die, but only died unto himself, and because the witness who did die was, consequent to his mass burial, dug up from his grave and burned to ashes – because the dead witness did not even leave behind a corpse or a dead body? One of the most striking and surprising aspects of *Shoah* as a film about genocide and war atrocities is the absence of dead bodies on the screen. But it is the *missing* corpses which *Shoah* remarkably gives us to witness, in its 'travelings' throughout the graveyard with no bodies, and in its persistent exploration of the empty grave which is both haunted and yet *uninhabited* by the dead witness.

[...]

'No one was supposed to be left to bear witness,' testifies in turn Richard Glazar (50). The Nazi plan is in effect to *leave no trace* not only of the crime itself of the historical mass murder, but of all those who materially witnessed that crime, to eliminate without trace any possible eyewitness. Indeed, even the corpses of the now dead witnesses or the *Figuren* are still material evidence by which the Nazis might, ironically, be *figured out*. The corpses still continue to materially *witness* their own murderers. The scheme of the erasure of the witnesses must therefore be completed by the literal erasure – by the very burning – of the bodies. [...]

Testifying from Inside

Is it possible to literally *speak from inside the Holocaust* – to bear witness from inside the very *burning* of the witness? I would suggest that it is by raising, by experiencing and by articulating such a question that the film takes us on its oneiric and yet materially historic trip, and that it carries out its cinematic exploration – and its philosophical incorporation – of the radical *impossibility of testimony*. To put it differently, the very testimony of the film (insofar precisely as it is a groundbreaking testimony) actively confronts us with the question: in what ways, by what creative means (and at what price) would it become possible *for us* to witness the-event-without-a-witness? A question which translates into the following terms of the film: Is it possible to witness *Shoah* (the Holocaust and/or the film) from inside?[2] Or are we necessarily outside (outside the blazes of the Holocaust, outside the burning of the witness, outside the fire that consumes the film) and witnessing it from outside? What would it mean to witness *Shoah* from inside?

It is the implications of this rigorous, tormented question that guide, I would suggest, the topographical investigation of the film and specifically, the inquiry addressed by Lanzmann to Jan Piwonski, the Polish pointsman who directed the death trains from the outside world into the concrete inside of the extermination camp:

> *Exactly where did the camp begin?*
> ...Here there was a fence that ran to those trees you see there...
> *So I'm standing inside the camp perimeter, right?*
> That's right.
> *Where I am now is fifty feet from the station, and I'm already* outside *the camp. This is the Polish part, and over there was death.*
> Yes. On German orders, Polish railmen split up the trains. So the locomotive took twenty cars, and headed toward Chelm ... Unlike Treblinka, the station here is part of the camp. And at this point we are *inside* the camp. [39, my emphasis]

I would suggest that this precision, this minute investigation and concretization of the film's cinematic space, derives not simply from a geographical or topographical attempt at definition, but from the quest of the whole film to get to witnessing precisely this *inside* of the death camp. In contrast to the Nazi teacher's wife, who insists on having seen the gas vans only from outside [...] the crucial task and the concrete endeavor that separates *Shoah* from all its filmic predecessors is, precisely, the attempt to witness from inside.

What does it mean, however, once again, to witness from inside a death camp? And supposing such a witnessing could in itself be (or become, thanks to the film,) possible, what would the consequent necessity of *testifying out of that inside* precisely mean? One after the other, Lanzmann explores the philosophical challenges and the concrete impossibilities/necessities that such a testimony from inside the death camp would entail:

1. It would mean *testifying from inside the death, the deadness and the very suicide of the witness*. There are two suicides in the film, of two (unrelated) Jewish leaders.[3] Both suicides are elected as the desperate solutions to the impossibility of witnessing, whose double bind and dead end they materialize. To kill oneself is, in effect, at once to *kill the witness* and to remain, by means of one's own death, *outside the witnessing*. Both suicides are thus motivated by the *desire not to be inside*.[4] How then to bear witness *from inside the desire not to be inside?*

2. Testifying from inside a death camp would mean, at the same time, equally impossibly, the necessity of *testifying from inside the absolute constraint of a fatal secret*, a secret that is felt to be so binding, so compelling and so terrible that it often is kept secret even from oneself.[5] For many reasons, the transgression of such secrecy does not seem possible to those who feel both bound and bonded by it. 'For we were "the bearers of the secret,"' says Philip Müller, an ex-Sonderkommando member: 'we were reprieved dead men. We weren't allowed to talk to anyone, or contact any prisoner, or even the SS. Only those in charge of the Aktion' (68). Victims as well as executioners[6] come to believe in their elected fate to join a tongue-tied cult of muteness, to be the destined *bearers of the silence*. Because the secret is at once a bondage and a bond, the breach of silence sometimes is no longer at the disposal of a conscious choice, or of a simple (rational) decision of the will. So that concentration camps' survivors will historically maintain the secret, and the silence, even years after the war.
   Since the testimony, like the oath of silence, is in turn a speech act, but a speech act that, both in its utterance and in its stakes, is specifically the opposite act to the pledge of secrecy, how would it be possible to testify not just in spite of, but precisely *from inside the very binding of the secret?*

3. In the sequence of concrete and philosophical impossibilities, bearing witness *from inside a death camp* would equally entail the paradoxical necessity of *testifying from inside a radical deception*, a deception that is, moreover, doubled and enhanced by *self-deception*:

(Philip Müller)

All eyes converged on the flat roof of the crematorium. . . . Aumeyer addressed the crowd: 'You're here to work for our soldiers . . . Those who can work will be all right.'

It was clear that hope flared in those people . . . The executioners have gotten past the first obstacle . . . Then he questioned a woman: 'What's your trade?' 'Nurse,' she replied. 'Splendid! We need nurses in our hospitals . . . We need all of you. But first, undress. You must be disinfected. We want you healthy.' I could see the people were calmer, reassured by what they've heard, and they began to undress. [69]

(Franz Suchomel)

We kept on insisting: 'You're going to live!' We almost believed it ourselves. If you lie enough, you believe your own lies. [147]

How to attest to the way things were *from within the very situation of delusion and illusion* – from inside the utter blindness to what in reality things were? How to bear witness to historic truth *from inside the radical deception* (amplified by self-deception) by which one was separated from historic truth at the very moment one was most involved in it?

4. Finally, the necessity of testifying *from inside* (the topographical determination to bear witness from inside the death camp) amounts to the film's most demanding, most uncompromising and most crucial question: *How to testify from inside Otherness?*

When the Jews talked to each other . . . the Ukrainians wanted things quiet, and they asked . . . yes, they asked them to shut up. So the Jews shut up and the guard moved off. Then the Jews started talking again, in their language . . .: *ra-ra-ra*, and so on. [30]

Lanzmann, who is listening to the Polish peasant Czeslaw Borowi in the company of his interpreter, knows, as soon as his attentive ears pick up the 'ra-ra-ra,' that the foreign language he is listening to is no longer simply Polish. He interrupts the Pole and, addressing him through the interpreter without waiting for her complete translation, asks:

What's he mean, la-la-la? *What's he trying to imitate?*

Their language–

answers the interpreter by way of explanation, or translation, not of Borowi's sounds but of his intention. But this is one moment in which Lanzmann *does not want translation*. In response to the translator's explanation, the inquirer insists:

No, ask him. Was the Jews' noise something special?
They spoke Jew–
Borowi replies, misnaming Yiddish but finally returning to the scene of discourse, and gracefully offering a *meaning* to explain the strangeness of his previous sounds and to dispel their unintelligibility.
Does Mr. Borowi understand 'Jew'?
No. [30–31]
To testify *from inside Otherness* is thus to be prepared, perhaps, to bear witness from within a 'ra-ra-ra,' to be prepared to testify not merely in a foreign language but *from inside the very language of the Other*: to speak from within the Other's tongue insofar precisely as the *tongue of the Other* is by definition the very tongue *we* do not speak, the tongue that, by its very nature and position, one by definition *does not understand*. To testify from inside Otherness is thus to bear witness from inside the living pathos of a tongue which nonetheless is bound to be heard as mere noise.

INSIDERS AND OUTSIDERS

It is therefore in reality impossible to testify from inside otherness, or from inside the keeping of a secret, from inside amnesia or from inside deception and the delusion of coercive self-deception, in much the same way as it is impossible to testify, precisely, from inside death. It is impossible to testify from the inside because *the inside has no voice*, and this is what the film is attempting to convey and to communicate to us. From within, the inside is unintelligible, it is *not present to itself*. Philip Müller, who spent years working in the management of the dead bodies in the Auschwitz crematorium, testifies:

> I couldn't understand any of it. It was like a blow on the head, as if I'd been stunned. I didn't even know where I was ... I was in shock, as if I'd been hypnotized, ready to do whatever I was told. I was so mindless, so horrified...[59]

In its absence to itself, the inside is *inconceivable* even to the ones who are already in. 'Still I couldn't believe what had happened there on the other side of the gate, where the people went in,' says Bomba: 'Everything disappeared, and everything got quiet' (47). As the locus of a silence and as the vanishing point of the voice, the inside is *untransmittable*. 'It was pointless,' says Müller, 'to tell the truth to anyone who crossed the threshold of the crematorium' (125). The film is about the relation between truth and threshold: about the impossibility of telling the truth, and about the consequent historical necessity of recovering the truth, precisely past a certain threshold. And it is this threshold that now needs to be historically and philosophically recrossed. Inside the crematorium, 'on the other side of the gate' where 'everything disappeared and everything got quiet,' there is loss: of voice, of life, of knowledge, of awareness, of truth, of the capacity to feel, of the capacity to speak. The truth of this loss constitutes precisely what it means to be inside the Holocaust. But the loss also defines an impossibility of testifying from inside to the truth of that inside.

Who would be in a position, then, to tell? The truth of the inside is even less accessible to an outsider. If it is indeed impossible to bear witness to the Holocaust from inside, it is even more impossible to testify to it from the outside. From without, the inside is entirely *ungraspable*, even when it is not simply what escapes perception altogether and remains invisible as such (as for the Nazi teacher's wife), nor even simply (as in Borowi's case) what is witnessed as pure noise and perceived as mere acoustic interference. To Jan Karski, the most honest, generous and sympathetic outside witness, the wartime messenger who politically accepted, in his mission as an underground Polish courier, to see the Jewish ghetto with his own eyes so as to report on it to the Western allies, his own testimony makes *no sense*. The *inside of the ghetto* in effect remains to him as utterly *impenetrable* as a bad dream, and his bewildered, grieving memory retains the image of this wretched inside only as what makes of him, forever, an *outsider*.

> It was a nightmare for me ...
> *Did it look like a completely strange world? Another world, I mean?*
> It was not a world. There was not humanity ... It wasn't humanity. It was some ... some hell ... They are not human ... We left the ghetto. Frankly, I couldn't take it any more ... I was sick. Even now I don't want ... I understand your role. I am here. I don't go back in my memory. I couldn't tell any more.
>
> [...]
>
> [167, 173–174]

Since for the outsider, even in the very grief of his full empathy and sympathy, the truth of the inside remains the truth of an *exclusion* – 'It was not a world, there was not humanity' – it is not really possible to *tell the truth*, to testify, from the outside. Neither is it possible, as we have seen, to testify from the inside. I would suggest that the impossible position and the testimonial effort of the film as a whole is to be, precisely, neither simply inside nor simply outside, but paradoxically, *both inside and outside*: to create a *connection* that did not exist during the war and does not exist today *between the inside and the outside* – to set them both in motion and in dialogue with one another.

NOTES

1. *Shoah*, the complete text of the film by Claude Lanzmann, New York, Pantheon Books, 1985, p. 6. Quotations from the text of the film will refer to this edition and will be indicated henceforth only by page number (in the parentheses following the citation).
2. I owe the formulation of this last point to Peter Canning.
3. One by Czerniakow, the Jewish leader of the Warsaw ghetto, who attempts at first to negotiate with the Germans, but commits suicide when he understands that his negotiations failed, the day after the first transport of the Jews of Warsaw to

Treblinka takes place (188–190); the other is by Freddy Hirsch, one of the Jewish leaders of the Czech family camp and specifically the protector of the (hundred) children, who commits suicide when he is urged to participate in the camp's armed resistance, a participation which necessitates his abandonment of the children to their likely death (157, 159–162).

4. The same is true of the self-blazing of the Warsaw ghetto, which might be seen as yet another suicide, and as yet another materialization of the desire not to be inside (not to be inside the ghetto).

5. Cf. Podchlebnik's way of refusing to read books about the Eichmann trial, thus keeping his own witness, his own testimony in the trial as a sort of secret from himself (7).

6. On the German side, see Franz Schalling's narrative:

> *You weren't in the SS, you were...*
> Police.
> *Which police?*
> Security guards ... An SS man immediately told us: 'This is a top-secret mission!'
> *Secret?*
> 'A top-secret mission.' 'Sign this!' We each had to sign. There was a form ready for each of us, a pledge of secrecy. We never even got to read it through.
> *You had to take an oath?*
> No, just sign, promising to shut up about whatever we'd see. Not say a word. After we'd signed, we were told: 'Final solution of the Jewish question.'
> [74]

PART IX
RETHINKING VISUAL CULTURE

RETHINKING VISUAL CULTURE:
INTRODUCTION

Encounters with photographs or film footage of the camps provide many people with their initial (often traumatic) awareness of the Holocaust. Despite, or perhaps precisely because of, the widespread dissemination and disturbing power of such images, nowhere does Adorno's dictum against representation after Auschwitz resonate more deeply than in the heterogeneous field of visual culture, which includes painting, sculpture, photography, film and television, and the new media. Indeed, many observers have questioned the need for any visual depictions whatsoever of the Holocaust.

Behind Adorno's proscription stands the second commandment's prohibition of images (*Bilderverbot*), the ancient Jewish taboo on visual depictions of the divine and human form. Adorno and others, arguably seeing in its origins a certain symbolic appropriateness, transpose the *Bilderverbot* into a modern taboo on representing unimaginable crimes of which the Jews were chief victims. This taboo on images also emerges from more contemporary concerns: the danger of deriving pleasure from the visual depiction of extreme suffering, and the risk that Holocaust art would create a falsely redemptive metaphysics, making beauty and meaning out of events that had neither, and thus offering consolation where there should be none.

Yet the question of whether to represent the Holocaust visually has always been raised in the face of already-existing images of the events and has often been a way of posing the question of *how* to represent the Holocaust with an especial rigor. Indeed, as both Gertrud Koch and Liliane Weissberg point out, Adorno himself later acknowledged that despite his proscriptions against representation, suffering nevertheless deserves artistic *expression*.

Koch draws on this idea to argue that Claude Lanzmann's film *Shoah* (1985) be seen as part of a tradition of authentic, largely modernist art that explores what of the Nazi genocide can and cannot be imagined. Weissberg offers a wide-ranging exploration of the relationship between the suffering of Holocaust victims and aesthetics in philosophy, museum architecture, and photography in order to critique contemporary attempts by critics such as Elaine Scarry to resurrect the classical notion that the contemplation of beauty fosters justice. How, asks Weissberg, can beauty be seen to promulgate justice in such a manifestly unjust world?

Koch and Weissberg are both predominantly concerned that visual representations do justice to victims. But the Holocaust not only raises questions about images of the victims; theorists have long been troubled by an awareness of the importance of visual culture to Nazism itself. Mass spectacles of the kind celebrated in Leni Riefenstahl's 1935 film of the Nazis' Nuremberg Party Rally, *Triumph of the Will*, exemplify how, as Walter Benjamin famously put it, fascism aestheticizes politics. Nazi racial ideology also had a crucial visual component. The healthy/degenerate distinction, so crucial both to Nazi cultural policy, especially in the visual arts (see Levi, 1998 on the Nazi exhibition of 'Degenerate Art'), and to the pseudo-science the Nazis used to justify their racial theories, relied heavily on claims which they voluminously 'documented' in photography and film. Here the Nazi visual aesthetic converged with and became integral to the genocide.

In *Reflections of Nazism* Saul Friedlander explores the *contemporary* return of aspects of Nazi visual culture. Beginning in the 1970s, in works including the films of Fassbinder, Hans Jürgen Syberberg, and Liliana Cavani, Friedlander sees the emergence of a 'new discourse.' Whereas earlier postwar literature and film had clearly designated Nazism as evil, the new discourse strikes Friedlander as succumbing to what Susan Sontag calls the *fascination* of fascism. Nazism itself becomes, as it were, sexier, and the strange, simultaneous longing for harmony and destruction (kitsch and death) that Friedlander sees as unique to Nazism resurfaces, with intellectually interesting but psychologically and politically unsettling results.

Whereas Friedlander's work is ultimately meant to warn against reviving Nazi imagery, Andreas Huyssen's exploration of paintings and photographs by contemporary German artist Anselm Kiefer argues against too strict a taboo on it. Huyssen rejects views of Kiefer's art, which draws heavily on iconography directly or indirectly associated with Nazism, as either a regressive neofascist revival (the left-wing German response) or as proof of a successful German 'overcoming' of the Nazi past (the American response). He insists that, when properly understood as contributing to the dialogue about German culture and identity after Auschwitz, Kiefer's work offers risky challenges to *work through*, rather than repress, the alluring power of Nazism that is the source of these problems in the first place.

In the late 1970s the success of the American mini-series *Holocaust* led French sociologist Jean Baudrillard to declare it part of the Nazi machinery of extermination. Yet Baudrillard's argument does not address the exclusion of certain historical facts or even the inappropriateness of melodrama to mass murder. He hones in, rather, on the medium of television. Drawing on media theorist Marshall McLuhan's distinction between hot and cold media, Baudrillard asserts that, like the events of the Holocaust itself, television is 'cold.' Rather than issuing a *Bilderverbot*, Baudrillard claims that, as a 'cold' medium, television exterminates memory precisely because it does not present proper images, which would possess 'an imaginary' and thereby *enable* memory.

The connections between these inquiries and broader issues of visual culture are manifold. Debates surrounding movies such as *Shoah* and *Schindler's List* resonate with continuing discussions in cultural studies about commodification, consumption, popular and mass culture, and political economy. Reflections on Nazi visual culture can clearly inform study of the highly aestheticized violence that is a staple of Hollywood films. The connections Baudrillard, Weissberg, and others make between visual technology and death have, since the Gulf War of 1991, shifted from theoretical speculation to commonplaces, which nevertheless makes those connections all the more urgently in need of exposure and critique. Finally, questions about the power and meaning of photographic images of the camps have arisen again in recent years as pictures of emaciated prisoners behind barbed wire in Serbian concentration camps appeared in newspapers around the world. What do such historical resonances, and the political uses to which they can and have been put, tell us about the relationship between images, knowledge, and action?

OTHER WORKS IN HOLOCAUST STUDIES

Hirsch, Marianne (1997) *Family Frames: Photography, Narrative, and Postmemory.* Cambridge, MA: Harvard University Press.

Insdorf, Annette (1989) *Indelible Shadows: Film and the Holocaust.* New York: Cambridge University Press.

Levi, Neil (1998) ' "Judge For Yourselves!" The "Degenerate Art" Exhibition as Political Spectacle,' *October* (Summer 1998) 85: 41–64.

Liss, Andrea (1998) *Trespassing through Shadows: Memory, Photography, and the Holocaust.* Minneapolis, MN: University of Minnesota Press.

Sontag, Susan (1980) 'Fascinating Fascism,' *Under the Sign of Saturn.* New York: Farrar, Straus, & Giroux.

Van Alphen, Ernst (1997) *Caught by History: Holocaust Effects in Contemporary Art, Literature, and Theory.* Stanford, CA: Stanford University Press.

Zelizer, Barbie (1998) *Remembering to Forget: Holocaust Memory Through the Camera's Eye.* Chicago: University of Chicago Press.

Zelizer, Barbie (ed.) (2001) *Visual Culture and the Holocaust.* New Brunswick, NJ: Rutgers University Press.

RELEVANT THEORETICAL STUDIES

Benjamin, Walter [1936] (1973) 'The Work of Art in the Age of Mechanical Reproduction,' trans. Harry Zohn, in *Illuminations*, ed. Hannah Arendt. New York: Schocken.

Crary, Jonathan (1990) *Techniques of the Observer: On Vision and Modernity in the Nineteenth Century*. Cambridge, MA: MIT Press.

Hansen, Miriam Bratu (1994), '*Schindler's List* is not *Shoah*: The Second Commandment, Popular Modernism, and Public Memory,' *Critical Inquiry* 22 (Winter), 292–312.

Huyssen, Andreas (1986) *After the Great Divide: Modernism, Mass Culture, Postmodernism*. Bloomington and Indianapolis, IN: Indiana University Press.

Jay, Martin (1993) *Downcast Eyes: The Denigration of Vision in Twentieth-Century French Thought*. Berkeley, CA: University of California Press.

Kracauer, Siegfried (1947) *From Caligari to Hitler: A Psychological History of the German Film*. Princeton, NJ: Princeton University Press.

Scarry, Elaine (1999) *On Beauty and Being Just*. Princeton, NJ: Princeton University Press.

Silverman, Kaja (1996) *Threshold of the Visible World*. New York: Routledge.

Gilman, Sander (1991) *The Jew's Body*. New York: Routledge.

48

REFLECTIONS OF NAZISM

Saul Friedlander

[...]

At the end of the war, Nazism was the damned part of Western civilization, the symbol of evil. Everything the Nazis had done was condemned, whatever they touched defiled; a seemingly indelible stain darkened the German past, while preceding centuries were scrutinized for the origins of this monstrous development. A sizable portion of the European elites, who two or three years before the German defeat had made no secret of their sympathy for the new order, were struck dumb and suffered total amnesia. Evidence of adherence, of enthusiasms shared, the written and oral record of four years of coexistence with it, and indeed of collaboration, often vanished. From one day to the next, the past was swept away, and it remained gone for the next twenty five years.

By the end of the Sixties, however, the Nazi image in the West had begun to change. Not radically or across the board, but here and there, and on the right as well as the left, perceptibly and revealingly enough to allow one to speak of the existence of a new kind of discourse. In France, for example, at the same time that the film *The Sorrow and the Pity* marked a further stage in a more authentic perception of collaboration and of the Resistance, Michel Tournier's novel *The Ogre* appeared as one of the first major manifestations of this new discourse.

This book is [...] an attempt to grasp these manifestations and understand the logic of this transformation, this reelaboration. For a minority of little interest here, the transformation of the past is deliberate; for others, it is a free

From Saul Friedlander (1984) 'Introduction', in *Reflections of Nazism: An Essay on Kitsch and Death*, trans. Thomas Weyr. New York: Harper & Row.

game of phantasms. [...] For still others – for those who perhaps matter the most – it is a desire to understand, or, perhaps, a form of exorcism. 'Do we ever free ourselves from the oppressing evil of guilt if we do not penetrate to the core of the disease that wastes us?' Hans-Jürgen Syberberg asks in the introduction to the published text of *Hitler, a Film from Germany*. Although the intentions are varied, a structure common to the whole of this new discourse is apparent. By and large, the works selected here – from various countries, mostly Germany, Italy, and France – as illustrations of this reinterpretation have enjoyed great popularity, a measure of their true significance and the reason for analyzing them. Despite differences of national, political, or social background, the profound logic of the changes they expound allows for numerous points of contact among them.

Such an amalgam of nationalities might be acceptable, but what about the ideological and social one? There is a new discourse about Nazism on the right as well as on the left. There is also an aesthetic reelaboration that goes beyond ideology. Can these varied approaches be considered as a whole? At one and the same time, can one move from political pamphlet to film, from film to novel, from novel to historical work, without changing tone and register? In short, can one deal with Michel Tournier, Hans-Jürgen Syberberg, and Albert Speer all at once?

One can, but not without explanation, and so a brief detour is needed. My point of departure is simple: It seems to me that any analysis of Nazism based only on political, economic, and social interpretations will not suffice. [...]

[...] Only a synthesis of diverse interpretations appears satisfactory: Nazism can thus be seen as a product of a social and economic evolution whose internal dynamic Marxism has perhaps illuminated; of a political transformation in part independent of the socioeconomic 'infrastructure'; and, finally, of a psychological process, responsive to its own logic, that is intertwined with the economics and the politics. Today the socioeconomic conditions needed for the appearance of a Nazi-type phenomenon do not exist, and the political evolution of the West does not resemble in the least that of Europe between the two world wars.

That leaves the psychological dimension, which, being autonomous, followed its own course. It did not rest on complex arguments nor sometimes on very clear ideological positions. These evidently existed, but they hid something else – an activity of the imagination that cannot be reduced to the usual distinctions between right and left. Nazism's attraction lay less in any explicit ideology than in the power of emotions, images, and phantasms. Both left and right were susceptible to them – at least during that crucial period from around 1930 until the German defeats midway through the war.

It seems logical, therefore, to suppose, a priori, that a new discourse on Nazism will develop at the same level of phantasms, images, and emotions. More than ideological categories, it is a matter of rediscovering the durability of these deep-seated images, the structure of these phantasms common to both right and left. At that level, the works to be discussed lead independent lives in our imaginations as readers and viewers. Thus it does not matter whether Rainer Werner Fassbinder was a leftist, Joachim Fest is a right-wing liberal, and that Albert Speer may have altered his political convictions. What does matter, in Speer's memoirs, is the evocation of the night of August 23, 1939, when nature seemed to be in relationship to historical events; in *Lili Marleen*, the Führer symbolized as intense light; and in Fest's book, the meditation on Hitler's grandeur.

One can argue that the scene Speer describes is only one among many and should be put in its proper context; that the intense light in *Lili Marleen* is designed to enhance the film's irony; and that Fest's meditation on Hitler's grandeur is framed in the form of a question. It is equally arguable that Michel Tournier's fascinating portrait of Kaltenborn's SS prytaneum can be understood only within the general architecture of a work where the notion of 'malignant inversion' plays a central role. Such objections would be valid if it were a matter of a test of intentions, a critique of attitudes, or the rendering of judgments. But my purpose, let me repeat, is different: [...] I shall trace associations of imagery, because I believe that these works, among others, carry within them a latent discourse ruled by a profound logic that needs to be clarified.

[...]

[...] An analysis of the new discourse clearly shows that it is precisely this reevocation and reinterpretation of the past that helps us better to understand the past itself, especially in its psychological dimensions. Thus theme and aesthetics of *The Damned* and *Hitler, a Film from Germany*, for example, allow us to perceive something of the psychological hold Nazism had in its day. Thanks to their reflections in the present, some elements that a direct approach has not clarified up to now are revealed, *not so much by what this or that writer or director has intended to say, but by what they say unwittingly, even what is said despite them.* In effect, by granting a certain freedom to what is imagined, by accentuating the selection that is exercised by memory, a contemporary reelaboration presents the reality of the past in a way that sometimes reveals previously unsuspected aspects. It may help us to understand a fascination thus re-created, the elements of which seem to repeat themselves from one work to another. As a result of this kind of analysis, themes become visible, roads open up. The focus shifts from the new discourse about Nazism toward Nazism itself, and from Nazism back to the new discourse, allowing us to grasp some hidden forms of past and present imagination.

More precisely, beneath the visible themes one will discover the beginning of a frisson, the presence of a desire, the workings of an exorcism.

At the heart of each of the zones of meanings, profound contradictions emerge: an aesthetic frisson, created by the opposition between the harmony of kitsch [...] and the constant evocation of themes of death and destruction; a desire aroused by the eroticization of the Leader as Everyman, close to everyone's heart and of a total power of destruction flung into nothingness; an exorcism, finally, whose total endeavor, in the past and in the present, is – in the face of Nazi criminality and extermination policies – to maintain distance by means of language, to affirm the existence of another reality by inverting the signs of this one, and finally to appease by showing that all the chaos and horror is, after all, coherent and explainable.

In fact, an analysis of the new discourse, in revealing a deep structure based on the coexistence of the adoration of power with a dream of final explosion – the annulment of all power – puts us on the track of certain foundations of the psychological hold of Nazism itself, of a particular kind of bondage nourished by the simultaneous desires for absolute submission and total freedom.

Nazism has disappeared, but the obsession it represents for the contemporary imagination – as well as the birth of a new discourse that ceaselessly elaborates and reinterprets it – necessarily confronts us with this ultimate question: Is such attention fixed on the past only a gratuitous reverie, the attraction of spectacle, exorcism, or the result of a need to understand; or is it, again and still, an expression of profound fears and, on the part of some, mute yearnings as well?

[…]

Attention has gradually shifted from the reevocation of Nazism as such, from the horror and the pain – even if muted by time and transformed into subdued grief and endless meditation – to voluptuous anguish and ravishing images, images one would like to see going on forever. It may result in a masterpiece, but a masterpiece that, one may feel, is tuned to the wrong key; in the midst of meditation rises a suspicion of complacency. Some kind of limit has been overstepped and uneasiness appears: It is a sign of the new discourse.[1]

[…]

No doubt Nazism in its singularity, as in its general aspects, is the result of a large number of social, economic, and political factors, of the coming to a head of frequently analyzed ideological currents, and of the meeting of the most archaic myths and the most modern means of terror. [...] Moreover, it is evident that the reappearance of movements similar to Nazism – whatever the precise form – depends above all on social and political conditions, at once multiple and convergent, that one does not perceive on the horizon, but that leaves unanswered the question of the context of the imponderable elements, the fusion of opposites that I have tried to illuminate.

Now, this fusion is only the expression of a kind of malaise in civilization, linked to the acceptance of civilization, but also to its fundamental rejection. *Modern society and the bourgeois order are perceived both as an accomplishment and as an unbearable yoke. Hence this constant coming and going between the need for submission and the reveries of total destruction, between love of harmony and the phantasms of apocalypse, between the enchantment of Good Friday and the twilight of the gods.* Submission nourishes fury, fury clears its conscience in the submission. To these opposing needs, Nazism – in the constant duality of its representations – offers an outlet; in fact, Nazism found itself to be the expression of these opposing needs. Today these aspirations are still there, and their reflections in the imaginary as well.

[...]

NOTE

1. Puzzlement sometimes replaces uneasiness, as when one discovers, for instance, the nature of a key idea that explains the main structure of Syberberg's film. Answering the question 'Why make a seven-hour film on Hitler?' Syberberg states: 'And – because Hitler was the greatest film maker of all times. He made the Second World War, like Nuremberg for Leni Riefensthal, in order to view the rushes privately every evening for himself, like King Ludwig attending a Wagner opera alone' (Steve Wasserman, 'Interview with Hans-Jürgen Syberberg,' *The Threepenny Review*, Summer 1980, p. 4). [...] In fact, in its more complex examples, the new discourse about Nazism is almost always a mixture of the three following levels of discourse: the language of images and the fascination it creates; strange statements – implicit in the works, explicit in interviews with the authors and directors – about history, modern civilization, the Nazis, the Jews, etc.; and an extremely sophisticated super-structure referring to metaphysics, theories of myth, the function of art and literature today, and so on. [...]

49

'HOLOCAUST'

Jean Baudrillard

Forgetting extermination is part of extermination, because it is also the extermination of memory, of history, of the social, etc. This forgetting is as essential as the event, in any case unlocatable by us, inaccessible to us in its truth. This forgetting is still too dangerous, it must be effaced by an artificial memory (today, everywhere, it is artificial memories that efface the memory of man, that efface man in his own memory). This artificial memory will be the restaging of extermination – but late, much too late for it to be able to make real waves and profoundly disturb something, and especially, especially through a medium that is itself cold, radiating forgetfulness, deterrence, and extermination in a still more systematic way, if that is possible, than the camps themselves. One no longer makes the Jews pass through the crematorium or the gas chamber, but through the sound track and image track, through the universal screen and the microprocessor. Forgetting, annihilation, finally achieves its aesthetic dimension in this way – it is achieved in retro, finally elevated here to a mass level.

Even the type of sociohistorical dimension that still remained forgotten in the form of guilt, of shameful latency, of the not-said, no longer exists, because now 'everyone knows,' everybody has trembled and bawled in the face of extermination – a sure sign that 'that' will never again occur. But what one exorcises in this way at little cost, and for the price of a few tears, will never in effect be

From Jean Baudrillard (1994) 'Holocaust', in *Simulacra and Simulation*, trans. Shiela Faria Glaser. Ann Arbor, MI: University of Michigan Press.

reproduced, because it has always been in the midst of currently reproducing itself, and precisely in the very form in which one pretends to denounce it, in the medium itself of this supposed exorcism: television. Same process of forgetting, of liquidation, of extermination, same annihilation of memories and of history, same inverse, implosive radiation, same absorption without an echo, same black hole as Auschwitz. And one would like to have us believe that TV will lift the weight of Auschwitz by making a collective awareness radiate, whereas television is its perpetuation in another guise, this time no longer under the auspices of a *site* of annihilation, but of a *medium* of deterrence.

What no one wants to understand is that *Holocaust* is *primarily* (and exclusively) an event, or, rather, a *televised* object (fundamental rule of McLuhan's, which must not be forgotten), that is to say, that one attempts to rekindle a *cold* historical event, tragic but cold, the first major event of cold systems, of cooling systems, of systems of deterrence and extermination that will then be deployed in other forms (including the cold war, etc.) and in regard to cold masses (the Jews no longer even concerned with their own death, and the eventually self-managed masses no longer even in revolt: deterred until death, deterred from their very own death) to rekindle this cold event through a cold medium, television, and for the masses who are themselves cold, who will only have the opportunity for a tactile thrill and a posthumous emotion, a deterrent thrill as well, which will make them spill into forgetting with a kind of good aesthetic conscience of the catastrophe.

In order to rekindle all that, the whole political and pedagogical orchestration that came from every direction to attempt to give meaning to the event (the televised event this time) was not at all excessive. Panicked blackmailing around the possible consequence of this broadcast on the imagination of children and others. All the pedagogues and social workers mobilized to filter the thing, as if there were some danger of infection in this artificial resurrection! The danger was really rather the opposite: from the cold to the cold, the social inertia of cold systems, of TV in particular. It was thus necessary that the whole world mobilize itself to remake the social, a hot social, heated discussion, hence communication, from the cold monster of extermination. One lacks stakes, investment, history, speech. That is the fundamental problem. The objective is thus to produce them at all cost, and this broadcast served this purpose: to capture the artificial heat of a dead event to warm the dead body of the social. Whence the addition of the supplementary medium to expand on the effect through feedback: immediate polls sanctioning the massive effect of the broadcast, the collective impact of the message – whereas it is well understood that the polls only verify the televisual success of the medium itself. But this confusion will never be lifted.

From there, it is necessary to speak of the cold light of television, why it is harmless to the imagination (including that of children) because it no longer carries any imaginary and this for the simple reason that *it is no longer an image*. By contrast with the cinema, which is still blessed (but less and less so because more and more contaminated by TV) with an intense imaginary – because the cinema is an image. That is to say not only a screen and a visual form, but a *myth*, something that still retains something of the double, of the phantasm, of the mirror, of the dream, etc. Nothing of any of this in the 'TV' image, which suggests nothing, which mesmerizes, which itself is nothing but a screen, not even that: a miniaturized terminal that, in fact, is immediately located in your head – you are the screen, and the TV watches you – it transistorizes all the neurons and passes through like a magnetic tape – a tape, not an image.

multiple ironies begin to appear. In almost all of the photos the Sieg Heil figure is miniscule, dwarfed by the surroundings; the shots are taken from afar. In one of the photos the figure stands in a bathtub and is seen against a backlit window. There are no jubilant masses, marching soldiers, nor any other emblems of power and imperialism that we know from historical footage from the Nazi era. The artist does not identify with the gesture of Nazi occupation, he ridicules it, satirizes it. He is properly critical. But even this consideration does not lay to rest our fundamental uneasiness. Are irony and satire really the appropriate mode for dealing with fascist terror? Doesn't this series of photographs belittle the very real terror which the Sieg Heil gesture conjures up for a historically informed memory? There just seems no way out of the deeply problematic nature of Kiefer's 'occupations,' this one as well as those that were to follow in the 1970s, paintings that occupied the equally shunned icons and spaces of German national history and myth.

There is another dimension, however, to this work, a dimension of self-conscious mise-en-scène that is at its conceptual core. Rather than seeing this series of photos only as representing the artist occupying Europe with the fascist gesture of conquest, we may, in another register, see the artist occupying various framed image-spaces: landscapes, historical buildings, interiors, precisely the image-spaces of most of Kiefer's later paintings. But why then the Sieg Heil gesture? I would suggest that it be read as a conceptual gesture reminding us that indeed Nazi culture had most effectively occupied, exploited, and abused the power of the visual, especially the power of massive monumentalism and of a confining, even disciplining, central-point perspective. Fascism had furthermore perverted, abused, and sucked up whole territories of a German image-world, turning national iconic and literary traditions into mere ornaments of power and thereby leaving post-1945 culture with a tabula rasa that was bound to cause a smoldering crisis of identity. After twelve years of an image orgy without precedent in the modern world, which included everything from torch marches to political mass spectacles, from the mammoth staging of the 1936 Olympics to the ceaseless productions of the Nazi film industry deep into the war years, from Albert Speer's floodlight operas in the night sky to the fireworks of antiaircraft flak over burning cities, the country's need for images seemed exhausted. Apart from imported American films and the cult of foreign royalty in illustrated magazines, postwar Germany was a country without images, a landscape of rubble and ruins that quickly and efficiently turned itself into the gray of concrete reconstruction, lightened up only by the iconography of commercial advertising and the fake imagery of the *Heimatfilm*. The country that had produced the Weimar cinema and a wealth of avant-garde art in the 1920s and that would produce the new German cinema beginning in the late 1960s was by and large image-dead for about twenty years: hardly any new departures in film, no painting worth talking about, a kind of enforced minimalism, ground zero of a visual amnesia.

[...]

While Kiefer's material and aesthetic employment of figuration does not give me ideological headaches, I think it is legitimate to ask whether Kiefer indulges the contemporary fascination with fascism, with terror, and with death. [...] Such questions are all the more urgent because, I would argue, Kiefer's own treatment of fascist icons seems to go from satire and irony in the 1970s to melancholy devoid of irony in the early 1980s.

Central for a discussion of fascinating fascism in Kiefer are three series of paintings from the early 1980s: the paintings of fascist architecture; the March Heath works, which hover between landscape painting, history painting, and an allegorization of art and artist in German history; and the Margarete/ Shulamite series, which contains Kiefer's highly abstract and mediated treatment of the holocaust. Together with the Meistersinger/Nuremberg series, this trilogy of works best embodies those aspects of his art that I am addressing in this essay.

Let me first turn to the watercolors and oil paintings of fascist architectural structures: the two watercolors entitled *To the Unknown Painter* (1980, 1982) and the two large oil paintings of fascist architectural structures entitled *The Stairs* (1982–83) and *Interior* (1981). These works exude an overwhelming statism, a monumental melancholy, and an intense aesthetic appeal of color, texture, and layering of painterly materials that can induce a deeply meditative, if not paralyzing state in the viewer. I would like to describe my own very conflicting reactions to them, with the caveat that what I will sketch as a sequence of three stages of response and reflection was much more blurred in my mind when I first saw the Kiefer retrospective at the Museum of Modern Art in New York.

Stage one was fascination – fascination with the visual pleasure Kiefer brings to the subject matter of fascist architecture. If seen in photographs, such buildings will most likely provoke only the Pavlovian reaction of condemnation: everybody knows what fascist architecture is and what it represents. Being confronted with Kiefer's rendering of the interior of Albert Speer's Reichschancellery was therefore like seeing it for the first time, precisely because 'it' was neither Speer's famous building nor a 'realistic' representation of it. And what I saw was ruins, images of ruins, the ruins of fascism in the mode of allegory that seemed to hold the promise of a beyond, to suggest an as yet absent reconciliation. True, there is the almost overbearing monumentalism of size and subject matter of these paintings, with central point perspective driven to its most insidious extreme. But then this monumentalism of central perspective itself seems to be undermined by the claims the multiply layered surfaces make on the viewer, by the fragility and transitoriness of the materials Kiefer uses in his compositions, by the eerie effects he achieves in his use of photography overlaid by thick oil paint, emulsion, shellac, and straw. Dark and somber as they are, these paintings assume a ghostlike luminosity and immateriality that belies their monumentality. They appear like dream images, architectural structures that seem intact, but are intriguingly made to appear as ruins: the resurrected ruin of fascism as simulacrum, as the painterly realization of a contemporary state of mind.

At this point I became skeptical of my own first reaction. Stage two was a pervasive feeling of having been had, having been lured into that fascinating fascism, having fallen for an aestheticization of fascism which today complements fascism's own strategies, so eloquently analyzed by Walter Benjamin some fifty years ago, of turning politics into aesthetic spectacle. I remembered the romantic appeal of ruins and the inherent ambivalence of the ruin as celebration of the past, of nostalgia and feelings of loss. And I recalled the real ruins left by fascism, the ruins of bombed-out cities and the destruction left in the wake of fascist invasion and retreat. Where, I asked myself, do these paintings reflect on this historical reality? Even as images of fascist ruins, they are still monuments to the demagogic representation of power, and they affirm, in their overwhelming monumentalism and relentless use of central-point perspective, the power of representation that modernism has done so much to question and to reflect critically. The question became: Is this fascist painting at one remove? And if it is, how do I save myself from being sucked into these gigantic spacial voids, from being paralyzed by melancholy, from becoming complicit in a vision that seems to prevent mourning and stifle political reflection?

Finally, my initial thoughts about Kiefer's 'occupations' asserted themselves again. What if Kiefer, here too, intended to confront us with our own repressions of the fascist image-sphere? Perhaps his project was precisely to counter the by now often hollow litany about the fascist aestheticization of politics, to counter the merely rational explanations of fascist terror by recreating the aesthetic lure of fascism for the present and thus forcing us to confront the possibility that we ourselves are not immune to what we so rationally condemn and dismiss. Steeped in a melancholy fascination with the past, Kiefer's work makes visible a psychic disposition dominant in postwar Germany that has been described as the inability to mourn. If mourning implies an active working through of a loss, then melancholy is characterized by an inability to overcome that loss and in some instances even a continuing identification with the lost object of love. This is the cultural context in which Kiefer's reworking of a regressive, even reactionary painterly vocabulary assumes its politically and aesthetically meaningful dimension. How else but through obsessive quotation could he conjure up the lure of what once enthralled Germany and has not been acknowledged, let alone properly worked through? How else but through painterly melancholy and nightmarish evocation could he confront the blockages in the contemporary German psyche? At the same time, the risk of confronting contemporary German culture with representations of a collective lost object of love is equally evident: it may strengthen the static and melancholy disposition toward fascism rather than overcome it.

Here, then, is the dilemma: whether to read these paintings as a melancholy fixation on the dreamlike ruins of fascism that locks the viewer into complicity, or, instead, as a critique of the spectator, who is caught up in a complex web of melancholy, fascination, and repression.

[...]

[...] A negative reading of the architecture paintings is contradicted by the Margarete/Shulamite series, a series of paintings based on Paul Celan's famous 'Death Fugue,' a poem that captures the horror of Auschwitz in a sequence of highly structured mythic images. In these paintings, where Kiefer turns to the victims of fascism, the melancholy gaze at the past, dominant in the architecture paintings, is transformed into a genuine sense of mourning. [...]

[...]

[...] Perhaps the most powerful painting in the series inspired by Paul Celan is the one entitled *Shulamite*, in which Kiefer transforms Wilhelm Kreis's fascist design for the Funeral Hall for the Great German Soldiers in the Berlin Hall of Soldiers (c. 1939) into a haunting memorial to the victims of the holocaust. The cavernous space, blackened by the fires of cremation, clearly reminds us of a gigantic brick oven, threatening in its very proportions, which are exacerbated by Kiefer's use of an extremely low-level perspective. No crude representation of gassing or cremation, only the residues of human suffering are shown. Almost hidden in the depth of this huge empty space we see the seven tiny flames of a memorial candelabra dwarfed by the horror of this murderous space. Kiefer succeeds here in avoiding all the ambiguity that haunted his other paintings of fascist architecture. And he is successful because he evokes the terror perpetrated by Germans on their victims, thus opening a space for mourning, a dimension that is absent from the paintings I discussed earlier. By transforming a fascist architectural space, dedicated to the death cult of the Nazis, into a memorial for Nazism's victims, he creates an effect of genuine critical *Umfunktionierung*, as Brecht would have called it, an effect that reveals fascism's genocidal telos in its own celebratory memorial spaces.

[...] The potential for rebirth and renewal that fire, mythic fire, may hold for the earth does not extend to human life. Kiefer's fires are the fires of history, and they light a vision that is indeed apocalyptic, but one that raises the hope of redemption only to foreclose it.

NOTE

1. Mark Rosenthal, *Anselm Kiefer*, Chicago and Philadelphia, Art Institute of Chicago and the Philadelphia Museum of Art, 1987, p. 7.

51

'THE AESTHETIC TRANSFORMATION OF THE IMAGE OF THE UNIMAGINABLE: NOTES ON CLAUDE LANZMANN'S *SHOAH*'

Gertrud Koch

[...]

If we recall the debates that have revolved for several decades, with greater or lesser intensity, around the question of an aesthetics after Auschwitz, we find that they divide along the lines of a moral and a material question. The moral question would be whether, after all hope for the stability of the human foundation of civilization had been destroyed, the utopia of the beautiful illusion of art had not finally dissolved into false metaphysics – whether, generally, art is still possible at all. The second, material question concerns whether and how Auschwitz can and has been inscribed in aesthetic representation and the imagination. In his 'Meditations on Metaphysics,' which conclude his *Negative Dialectics*, Theodor W. Adorno provides a succinct response to those who tried to construct a normative moral taboo upon his earlier aperçu that, after Auschwitz, poetry could no longer be written. 'Perennial suffering has as much right to expression as a tortured man has to scream; hence it may have been wrong to say that after Auschwitz you could no longer write poems.'[1]

But, Adorno continues, the question that arises after Auschwitz is not only that of the survival of art, but also the survival of those marked by the guilt of having survived: '[Their] mere survival calls for the coldness, the basic principle of bourgeois subjectivity, without which there could have been no Auschwitz; this is the drastic guilt of him who was spared.'[2] The moral question cannot be

From Gertrud Koch (1989) 'The Aesthetic Transformation of the Image of the Unimaginable: Notes on Claude Lanzmann's *Shoah*', trans. Jamie Owen Daniel and Miriam Hansen, *October*, vol. 48, Spring, pp. 15–24.

isolated as an aesthetic one, but we can determine where aesthetics degenerates into bad metaphysics: wherever the aesthetic imagination extorts metaphysical meaning from the mass annihilations. This tendency manifests itself early on, in the first literary testimonies dealing with mass annihilation, in theological or metaphysically oriented, existentialist interpretations. [...] Attempts to find confirmation of the moral substance of the human in the very hell organized by human beings, as if the perspective of survival could thereby be brought into a meaningful context free of the universal feeling of guilt, have not diminished. Thus Sami Nair, in his essay on Claude Lanzmann's film *Shoah* in *Les Temps Modernes*, can still allow himself to get carried away by metaphysical tropes when he writes that Lanzmann 'rehabilitates the survivors from the Jewish work commandos who assisted the Nazis in murdering their [Jewish] brothers and sisters ... and transfigures them here into saints by revealing their inner *innocence* ...'[3]

What makes Nair's argument so unfortunate is its implied assumption of an *inner* margin of moral choice within the framework of which someone could become guilty or remain innocent. To be sure, the moral dimension of human action is based on the capacity to decide and on the decision to do what one considers right. Yet, where the possibility of making a decision is destroyed to the extreme degree that it is within the terroristic confines of a concentration camp, the celebration of minimalized processes of consciousness can only appear as metaphysical. [...] This is not to deny that there were actual differences in behavior; but the individual's 'inner' potential for resistance cannot be used to infer that everyone conducts him- or herself morally in situations which eliminate every human measure of freedom. No doubt Nair owes this implicit idea of an intact 'inner' freedom to the premises of a one-sided, dogmatically construed existentialism, which has its foundations in Sartre's fatal paradigm that freedom of choice exists even under torture – a paradigm that accompanied the above mentioned debates.

[...]

At this point I would like to suggest that Nair's comments may apply to the general tone of the 1950s and to the topos of the limit situation in particular, but not to the aesthetic construction of Lanzmann's film. The film takes up neither the constricted situational context nor the theological variation of those literary treatments of the death camps which attribute affirmative meaning to them. [...] Besides, the various patterns of meaning inscribed in the representations of the death camps cannot be distinguished according to literary forms or genres. Just as purely autobiographical, documentary literature is not free of the compulsion to search for meaning, aesthetically wrought works like Paul Celan's do not necessarily lapse into affirmative idealization because of their aesthetic stylization. [...]

Authenticity as a criterion indeed encompasses many forms and genres. Yet it unmistakably opts for a modernist aesthetic which aims at expression rather than communication. If the affirmative aspects of the metaphysical and/or theological imputation of patterns of meaning to mass annihilation can be linked to a premodern aesthetic, there are, on the other side of the scale, the unresolved aporias of autonomous art. The latter obtains its power from the theory of the imagination, the notion of art as idea or image (*Vorstellung*) rather than representation (*Darstellung*), expression rather than illustration. The imagination claims its own autonomy; it can project, annihilate social existence, transcend it to become radically other, while allowing the speechless, hidden substratum of nature in the mute body to reappear. At first glance, the autonomous freedom of the imagination, which does not allow itself to be confined by any concept of meaning, seems far less burdened with the tendency to suffocate, through affirmation, the claims to expression made by the oppressed and tormented.

The autonomy of art, however, is itself not unlimited. In a certain sense it finds its limits in the capacity of the human imagination. It is therefore appropriate that Langer places a quotation from Samuel Beckett at the beginning of the first chapter of his book: 'I use words you taught me. If they don't mean anything anymore, teach me others. Or let me be silent.'[4] The increasing silence, the hermetic character of modern art is itself already a reflection on this limit. The following passage from Adorno's 'Meditations on Metaphysics I: After Auschwitz,' cited earlier, also touches on this aesthetic nerve of the imagination: 'The earthquake of Lisbon sufficed to cure Voltaire of the theodicy of Leibniz, and the visible disaster of the first nature was insignificant in comparison with the second, social one, which defies human imagination as it distills a real [*reale*] hell from human evil.'[5]

The limits of the imagination of a human evil are those of society, which allows what can still be conceived of by the imagination as human evil to become a *real* hell. This accounts for the difficult and tenacious struggle for 'inner innocence,' the desire to push the outer limits of the imagination back within. Alas, in the face of this historical dimension of an insurmountable difference between what can be humanly imagined and what has been proven to be socially possible, even the attempt to posit evil as an absolute category, at least within aesthetics, as Karl Heinz Bohrer has recently attempted to do, seems almost touchingly antiquated. The satanic evil of the imagination is just as incapable as the Beelzebub of theology or the negative absolute of metaphysics of surpassing real hell through aesthetic illusion. In order to be able to maintain his theory, Bohrer must conjure up the 'disquieting step into the namelessness of an unlimited power of imagination which can no longer be controlled by any familiar discourse,'[6] whereas historically the limits of imaginative power have long since been delineated, and not in terms that are defined by aesthetic content, but rather socially.

But the argument – itself not entirely free of false pathos – that the attempt to imagine the annihilation aesthetically should therefore be discontinued altogether is even more misguided, directed as it is against legitimate claims to expression. The desire to establish a normative aesthetics of content from an objective social limit is an authoritarian longing; rather – and above all – we should investigate how this limit is reflected and re-marked in art itself. What nonetheless constitutes the *skandalon*, as the irreducible condition of the aesthetic, is the pleasure contained even in the most resistant work of art – a pleasure culled from the transformation into the imaginary that enables distance, the coldness of contemplation.

In the following I would like to show how a radical aesthetic transformation of this problematic is achieved in Claude Lanzmann's film *Shoah*. The debate about this film, especially in West Germany, has in most cases refrained from aesthetic criticism and instead presented the film as a 'stirring document' from which we can extract various historical, political, and moral dynamics. The fact that it is also a work of art is acknowledged only in passing and almost with embarrassment. Purists of the documentary form came closest to acknowledging the problem, since they were struck by the fact that long stretches of the film are not 'documentary' at all.

Lanzmann himself has left no doubt that his conception of the film extends far beyond the portrayal of eyewitnesses. He would argue that the people in his film are acting; they are playing out what they have lived through, *le veçu*. But, this implies something other than 'remembering.' To remember can mean, 'Oh, yes, I remember, it was a hot day, I found myself in such and such a situation,' etc. Such a statement of memory need not contain anything of how I experience this situation. For this reason Lanzmann must insist that the people in his film do not narrate memories but rather reexperience situations. What this entails can be illustrated by a crass example. In a long sequence of the film, the exiled Polish politician Jan Karski says that he has never spoken about his experience of the Warsaw Ghetto. As a memory this is questionable – historians know that Karski reported on his visit to the ghetto immediately afterward, that he even published such a report. But what is expressed in his formulation is the feeling of being able to speak only with difficulty about what he had experienced – the shock he felt in the ghetto that rendered him speechless when he saw what was to be seen there.

It is crucial to Lanzmann's strategy that he encourage a certain margin for play. He allows entire scenarios to be played out in a borrowed railroad car, challenging his protagonists to reenact particular gestures and actions. This strategy is no doubt indebted to the concept, central to Sartrean existential psychoanalysis, that there is a physical materiality even prior to the symbolizing process of language – an impudent laugh, the barely repressed sadistic glee over a threatening gesture. Such materiality breaks through only when gestures, physical movements, are repeated. In playing these everyone again becomes who he is – that is *Shoah*'s criterion for authenticity, that is the immense visual power of this film, which so clearly sets it apart from other 'interview' films. The smiling mask that covers the petrified inner world of the former *Musulmann*, who could only survive in the concentration camp by adopting an expression that anticipated rigor mortis, is no less an authentic expression than a dramatic breakdown. It is precisely this transformation into play which determines the seriousness of the representation (*Darstellung*). Indeed, Lanzmann seduces, lures, and cajoles the protagonists into doing and saying things which would otherwise have remained silenced and hidden. This strategy has made Lanzmann the target of a moral criticism which reveals much of the old resentment against everything aesthetic, that the stolen image entrapped the soul of whatever it portrayed. To some extent, every aesthetic image contains the spoils wrested from social existence, but it is therefore no less legitimate. This is in no sense an example of aesthetic coquetry or the vain presumption of a director who does not want to give up control over his production. What Lanzmann is aiming at here is precisely the problem of the imagination – whenever something is narrated, an image (*Vorstellung*) is presented, the image of something which is absent. The image, the imaginary – and here Lanzmann is a loyal Sartrean – is the presence of an absence which is located outside the spatiotemporal continuum of the image.

Lanzmann remains strictly within the limits of what can be imagined: for that which cannot be imagined, the concrete industrial slaughter of millions, he suspends the concrete pictorial representation. There are no images of the annihilation itself; its representability is never once suggested by using the existing documentary photographs that haunt every other film on this subject. In this elision, Lanzmann marks the boundary between what is aesthetically and humanly imaginable and the unimaginable dimension of the annihilation. Thus the film itself creates a dialectical constellation: in the elision, it offers an image of the unimaginable.

But the film also approaches the problem from another angle: it begins quite literally with the aesthetic transformation of the statement that the annihilation 'took *place*,' in that it projects this statement into spatial visibility. It travels to the locations of the annihilation. The spatialization occurs in the present; what remains absent is what is temporally removed, the annihilation itself. The latter is narrated (often from off-screen) only fragmentarily from the imaginations of the protagonists. The length of the film may have obscured, for many viewers, its complex montage structure, which plays on multiple levels with real and filmic time. The juxtapositions, on the same temporal plane, of real events separated by very distant locations – such as, for example, the voice of the narrator from Israel on the soundtrack and a walk through the forested terrain of a death camp – are designed to irritate our realistic sense of spatiotemporal certainty; the presence of an absence in the imagination of the past is bound up with the concreteness of images of present-day locations. Past and present intertwine; the past is made present, and the present is drawn into the spell of the past. The long pans that realize the real time of the gaze remain trapped in historical space. What many of these shots convey is a sense of not being able to run away, of being closed in. Whenever the camera does not assume the subjective gaze, it may, for instance, move in such a way that, as in one particularly extreme longshot, a group of people approaching us from a distant edge of the woods are never really able to come closer, but are again and again kept at a distance in the field by the camera. The camera's movement is aesthetically autonomous; it is not used in a documentary fashion, but imaginatively.

This method is at its most radical when Lanzmann uses camera movement for fictive scenarios of reenactment into which he manipulates not only the protagonists, but himself and the viewers as well. As the railroad car enters Treblinka, it does so in a subjective shot. The viewer is driven along with the train: this is also an insidious seduction. First Lanzmann has the former engineer of the train reenact his run once again, then it is Lanzmann himself who is doing so, and, after a delayed second of horror, the viewer finally realizes that he or she, too, is sitting in the train that unremittingly follows the tracks into the enclosure of the death camp. Yet the subjective camera never exceeds the limit; it takes us just far enough to allow us to sense, on the edge of the imagination, the reality of the annihilation, the frictionless matter-of-factness of its implementation – without lapsing into the embarrassments of gruesome shock effects.

In the montage of space and time described above, Lanzmann aesthetically organizes the experience of the most extreme discrepancy between what there is to see and the imagination (*Vorstellung*) triggered by that seen. It is the experience of the discrepancy between the indifference of the first and the horrors of the second. Thus Lanzmann resumes representational strategies which appear early on in literary treatments of the annihilation. I am reminded here above all of the stories of Tadeusz Borowski, in particular the following passage from a story entitled 'This Way to the Gas, Ladies and Gentlemen':

> A small square; ruins surrounded by the green of tall trees. In former times, this was a tiny little train station somewhere in the provinces. Somewhat off to the side, close to the road, there is a tumble-down shack, smaller and uglier than the smallest, ugliest shack I've ever seen. A little farther on, behind the wooden shack, entire hillsides of railroad ties are piling up, mountains of tracks, enormous piles of splintered boards, bricks, stones, and well rings. This is the loading dock for everything destined for Birkenau. Materials for building the camp and human material for the gas ovens. It was a working day like any other: trucks drive by and load up with boards, cement, and people.[7]

If we substitute 'today' for 'former times' and read what follows in the past tense, Lanzmann's scenario emerges. This effect is even more pronounced in other passages of the same story:

> We pass by all the sections of Camp II B, the uninhabited Section C, the Czech camp, the quarantine, and then we plunge into the green of the apple and pear trees that surround the troop infirmary. This green, which has burst forth in these few hot days, seems to us like an unfamiliar landscape on the moon.[8]

And even the church, to which Lanzmann cuts from the Jewish cemetery, is present in Borowski:

> Idle and indifferent, their eyes followed the majestic figures in the green uniforms, drifting to the near and yet unattainable green of the trees, to the church steeple, from which a late Angelus rang out.[9]

This is not to say that Lanzmann has filmed Borowski's story. Rather, the comparison is meant to emphasize that there is an aesthetic transformation of the experience of the annihilation that does not permit itself to become ensnared in the pitfalls of the usual indictments and paradigms. Claude Lanzmann's *Shoah*, I would argue, is part of this tradition of the aesthetic transformation of the image of the unimaginable. Without question, the film also contributes significant material to the necessary political and historical debates. But the fascination it exerts, its melancholy beauty, is an aesthetic quality that we cannot afford to suppress or displace onto subliminal resentment against the character of its author.

NOTES

1. Theodor Adorno, *Negative Dialectics*, trans. E. B. Ashton, New York, Seabury, 1973, p. 362.
2. *Ibid.*, p. 363.
3. Sami Nair, '*Shoah*, une leçon d'humanité,' *Les Temps Modernes*, no. 470 (September 1985), p. 436.
4. Lawrence L. Langer, *Versions of Survival*, New York, 1982, p. 1.
5. Adorno, *Negative Dialectics*, p. 361 (translation modified).
6. Karl Heinz Bohrer, 'Das Böse – eine ästhetische Kategorie?' *Merkur*, vol. 39, no. 6 (June 1985), p. 472.
7. Tadeusz Borowski, 'Die Herrschaften werden zum Gas gebeten,' in Marcel Reich-Ranicki, ed., *16 polnische Erzähler*, Reinbek, 1964, p. 111. (An English translation appeared in the collection *This Way for the Gas, Ladies and Gentlemen*, trans. Barbara Vedder, New York, Penguin Books, 1967; since this English translation deviates radically from the German version quoted in this article, however, the translations here and following are our own. – Translators.)
8. *Ibid.*, pp. 110–111.
9. *Ibid.*, p. 113.

52

'IN PLAIN SIGHT'

Liliane Weissberg

BEAUTY AND SUFFERING

[...]

Adorno was not concerned with the viewer's imagination, but with the object represented. For him, the search for a language of art after the Holocaust, the ultimate event of suffering, could only lead to one of two results. The first still insisted on a bond between art and beauty, and denied art after the Holocaust any legitimacy. The post-Holocaust world needed to be encountered with artistic silence and an insistence on the void and gap that had marked (and in some way continues) the 'break with civilization.' The second option was to deny the link of art with beauty and to define art as a mode of expression instead. Thus, art had to be made to render the scream, to give words and images to a suffering that denied any listener or viewer the experience of pleasure. Perhaps art had to express suffering rather than try to depict it. It is interesting to note that this option mainly coincided with a postwar development in modern art, where forms of abstraction often replaced figurative representation, and, more radically perhaps, representational art was replaced by performance art that redrew the boundaries between art and life, time and experience. [...]

[...] The bond between pain and beauty, suffering and pleasure, which gave birth to aesthetics in the first place, was seemingly broken by an event whose

From Liliane Weissberg (2002) 'In Plain Sight', in Barbie Zelizer (ed.), *Visual Culture and the Holocaust*. New Brunswick, NJ: Rutgers University Press.

'completion' exceeded human imagination. Art lost its innocence, and artists began to reject or question traditional modes of 'representation.' Adorno's problem of conceiving of an art after the Holocaust seemed intensified by any artistic endeavor to deal with the event directly. Holocaust memorials that represented the past by reproducing contorted human figures [...] seemed hopelessly naïve, too comforting even in their limitedness [...] New attempts were made to search for a different language and other forms of expression. And, like the return of the repressed, the danger of beauty continues to haunt art, even in those works that question representation, insist on the void, counter the tradition of art. Is it possible at all to create a work of art that does not offer some sense of pleasure? And is one permitted to feel this aesthetic satisfaction in viewing a work of art about the Holocaust?

EXHIBITING THE HOLOCAUST

The question of the relationship of the Holocaust to art not only emerges with each work dedicated to this event and historical period, but also with the museums that are built to display the Holocaust's residue: photographs, clothing, objects gathered from concentration camps. 'The Holocaust in its enormity defies language and art, and yet both must be used to tell the tale, the tale that must be told,' wrote Elie Wiesel.[1] Again, a relationship between art and narrative was forged, and a tradition of aesthetics both denied and insisted upon.

Wiesel was a driving force behind the construction of the U.S. Holocaust Memorial Museum, and the occasion for his statement was the announcement of the selection of the museum's architect, James Ingo Freed, in 1986. The museum opened in 1993. Much has been written on the museum's design, and Freed has been widely celebrated for his building. Quite obviously, Wiesel wrote only of the 'use' of art, but the difference between the use of art for the documentation of the Holocaust and the artistic expression of the Holocaust is a subtle one. [...] The museum offers an overwhelming visual experience, even if the objects displayed tell a horrible tale. In the U.S. Holocaust Memorial Museum, names of places that have lost all or most of their Jewish population are engraved in alphabetical order in straight lines on the glass walls of a corridor; the first names of victims are engraved into the glass wall of another. These corridors evoke the Vietnam memorial with its seemingly endless row of victims' names. Rendered in glass, however, the museum's inscriptions do not bear the heaviness of any gravestone. Like smoke from chimneys, these names seem to dance in air and, at the same time, diffuse the light and provide an oblique view of the floor below. Bridges evoke those built to connect parts of the Warsaw ghetto, but they are crafted in perfectly rendered steel. The building itself offers multiple angles, and the glass panels refract light. Thus, the architecture alludes not only to the architectural models of the ghetto and concentration camp, but also to the refraction in which we are now forced to view the historical events.

The *Architectural Record* lauded the design as a challenge to 'literal architectural interpretations of history.' For this journal's critic, however, another separation could be made. The Holocaust Museum could function without its objects:

> At first glance, the U.S. Holocaust Memorial Museum ... appears to mirror the built symbols of American democracy that surround it. PCF design partner James Ingo Freed, however, organizes these elements into a cathartic evocation, even without exhibits, of the physically and psychically disturbed world.[2]

Freed's building, praised for a design that would allow multiple point of views and interpretations, wanted to tell the story of the Holocaust already, as well as the ambiguity of the symbols of American democracy that surround it and that it transforms. The museum structure itself may suffice as a memorial, without offering any of the 'authentic' objects of the Holocaust that its rooms want to display, and it can become such a memorial because of its artistic success. A brochure about the museum, published by Freed's architectural firm, is distributed at the museum's entrance. It gives minute details of the museum's plan and the story of its construction, and is a description of an object fully mastered by its creators. It is longer, and more extensive, than any descriptions of the displayed exhibits. New museum buildings have been praised elsewhere for their appropriateness, innovative design, and visual gratification. But Freed's building attempted an unusual effort. Its steel and glass construction of corridors not only tells the story of ghetto bridges and railroad tracks, but turns them into an object praised for its aesthetic satisfaction, even pleasure.

In his book on the Holocaust Museum, its first director, Jeshajahu Weinberg, was eager to describe it as a 'living museum.'[3] What keeps a museum that offers objects of death alive? While the U.S. Holocaust Memorial Museum was opened to exhibit an already established and growing collection of images and objects relating to the Holocaust, the Jewish Museum in Berlin has not been conceived of as a Holocaust museum at all. It was planned as an 'Extension to the Berlin Museum,' and to house Berlin's small collection of Jewish artifacts. Initially, at least, the Berlin Museum's theater collection should be added there as well. Daniel Libeskind's design of 1989 coincided with a new period in German history: the fall of the Berlin Wall and the move for German reunification.

Libeskind created the building in the shape of a broken Star of David that extends the older, classical structure of the Berlin Museum. It came to signify German Jewish history and Berlin history after the Holocaust. Like Freed's building, Libeskind's museum's design was guided by a list of victims' names. Freed etched them in glass on the walls of his corridors, Libeskind used them as a builder's alphabet. While Freed tried to reimagine elements of concentration camp architecture, Libeskind's structure lived by abstraction. He described it thus:

[T]he first aspect is the invisible and irrationally connected star which shines with absent light of individual address. The second one is the cut of Act Two of [Arnold Schönberg's opera] *Moses and Aaron*, which has to do with the non-musical fulfilment of the word. The third aspect is that of the deported or missing Berliners, and the fourth aspect is Walter Benjamin's urban apocalypse along the One Way Street. . . . Out of the terminus of history, which is nothing other than the Holocaust with its concentrated space of annihilation and complete burn-out of meaningful redevelopment of the city, and of humanity – out of this event which shatters this place comes that which cannot really be given by architecture. The past fatality of the German Jewish cultural relation in Berlin is enacted now in the realm of the Invisible. (It is this remoteness which I have tried to bring to consciousness.)[4]

Libeskind's building – a building which relates to the invisible, which 'enacts' the impossibility of architecture rather than architecture itself – has become a landmark nevertheless. Like Freed, Libeskind received multiple awards for his museum, and it has indeed become a tourist site even before its completion. Tour guides lead visitors through the empty building. [. . .] Thus, it is Libeskind's building which has realized precisely what the *Architectural Record*'s reviewer had imagined: it is a museum that could exist without any exhibitions. Planned to house a collection that should give evidence of the Jewish life in Berlin, it has, perhaps unavoidably, turned into the only Holocaust museum in Germany. One may suspect that it is not only the 'cathartic effect' of its dramatic performance that pleases the museum's many visitors. This is not a building for the blind. Like Freed's structure, although more by symbolic abstraction than by visual citations, it can offer aesthetic pleasure.

It is difficult to separate Freed's building from the plans of the exhibition designers who use the building's features and the objects displayed to forge a bond between the visitor and the victim.[5] Libeskind's deconstructionist building, on the other hand, offers a challenge for exhibitors. In Libeskind's writings, it is interesting to note how the notion of the void and the invisible shifts from the impossibility of the depiction of the Holocaust to the invisibility of a higher power in which faith may rest: '[It is a] conception, rather, which reintegrates Jewish Berlin history through the unhealable wound of faith, which, in the words of Thomas Aquinas, is the "substance of things hoped for; proof of things invisible"' (87). Lessing's imagination that tries to complete the sculpture's narrative is here replaced by the unhealable wound of faith and the paradoxical projection of hope.

If Libeskind's museum is able to turn recent history into a work of art, has art become just that, an 'unhealable wound of faith'? The Greek term for wound is, of course, trauma. Libeskind's architecture seems to be inherently informed by psychoanalytic theory – the trauma not only of the Holocaust, but of architecture itself: 'It's not a collage or a collision or a dialectic simply, but a new type of organization which really is organized around a center which is not, the void, around what is not visible. And what is not visible is the collection of this Jewish Museum, which is reducible to archival and archeological material since its physicality has disappeared' (87).

THE ORIGIN OF THE WORK OF ART

Human beings give testimony. Testimonies are also given by objects. In Freed's Holocaust museum, hundreds of photographs of the prewar Lithuanian shtetl Ejszyszki near Vilnius and its inhabitants, placed in a tower-like structure, are made to tell the story of a destroyed community. Another room offers not photographs, but objects, hundreds of shoes of the victims of the Majdanek concentration camp near Lublin, Poland. Metonymically, they give evidence for people about whom little more is known today.

Miles Lerman, national campaign chairman for the museum, recalled the transfer of artifacts from Poland in one of his fund-raising letters, and the moment when he was asked to pose for a photograph with a child's shoe:

> I was asked to pose for a photograph with one of these items – a child's shoe.
> Let me tell you, when this little shoe was handed to me, I froze.
> Bear in mind that I am a former partisan. I was hardened in battle and I deal with this Holocaust story almost on a daily basis. But when I held in my hand that shoe – the shoe of a little girl who could have been my own granddaughter – it just devastated me.[6]

An object like a shoe should aid identification and bridge time. But Lerman did not speak about any shoe, but the shoe of a child whose innocence was made palpable by the object. Innocence and victimhood came within one's grasp. The museum wanted to repeat this experience, even if the objects exhibited were beyond the visitor's reach.

In the museum's exhibition, however, this child's shoe is not singled out. It is the mere number of shoes, a fraction of the surviving pairs found in a concentration camp, that gives evidence of the enormity of the crime. These were shoes sorted out by prisoners once their owners had been selected for the gas chambers, but they were not used again: sandals, walking shoes, children's slippers. In the photograph published in Weinberg and Elieli's publication, the shoes are depicted as a sea of leather and canvas, discolored by time into a uniform gray.[7] The museum installation itself does not show an endless horizontal cover; instead, the shoes are piled high in an otherwise empty room.

[...]

The shoes in the Holocaust museum speak less about the sufferings of their bearers, than of their lives cut short by suffering and death. The story of why they were purchased or received and worn is rivaled by that of their forced removal and of their owners' disappearance. They become useless objects; and their owners' real sufferings take place after they were left behind. Faded to a uniform color that masks their individual shapes, they are unable to tell any stories of their bearers. [. . .] Once worn by living human beings, these shoes are now evidence of their death, and of the anonymity of their owners, the anonymity they found in death. Homogenized as one group, these shoes speak as a mass and exemplify mass murder.

[. . .] The installation of a mountain of shoes translates into the experience of the vastness of a crime; it is a peculiar form of the sublime.

STILL LIVES

In the winter of 1993, the Magnum photographer Erich Hartmann returned to Germany to take pictures of concentration camps that were later gathered in a volume entitled *In the Camps*. Hartmann had left Germany with his family in the summer of 1938 for America, and his journey back was emotionally charged. [. . .]

[. . .] Hartmann's pictures show barracks, rooms, railroad tracks, barbed wire – some of it already replaced by a maintenance crew that preserves these sites. The photographs are taken in black and white, and a cold light and melancholic air pervade them. Architectural structures and signs appear as geometrical shapes. The property of the victims is featured as well. One picture of Auschwitz offers a pile of suitcases, placed in a showcase. It is reflected through the camera lens, taken through the glass of the showcase, and the image reflects the backlit windows of the room. The suitcases, like gravestones, bear the names of their owners, their birthdays, their places of origin; the dates of death are absent. Another picture shows an already familiar sight. In another glass case that reflects those backlit windows, Hartmann reproduces another of Auschwitz's current exhibits: a pile of shoes. Like many others in this book, this photograph is printed in a black frame that resembles a death notice. The text that accompanies the picture could have been taken from a history book:

> A top-secret document of February 6, 1943, from the Reich Ministry of Economics listed among almost three million kilograms of clothing from Auschwitz and Majdanek 31,000 men's, 11,000 women's, and 22,000 children's shoes to be redistributed to 'ethnic Germans.'[8]

Visible here are obviously not only the remains of the victims' possessions, but also a residue of another kind: shoes that failed to reach their new owners. The photograph documents a war effort that was stopped, quite literally, in its tracks. While Hartmann emphasizes the mass of shoes, one shoe stands out in the window light's reflection.

The reflection of the showcase produces the simulacrum of a double exposure; the picture is a document of imprisonment that hints toward a world outside. But Hartmann renders an image that has already become a marker for the suffering of the camp's inhabitants. The museum's shoes were a 'gift' from the Majdanek camp; these are photographed in Auschwitz. Both the museum installation and photograph remind the viewer that images can easily turn into repeatable motives; the pile of shoes is similar as well to the images of countless bones, corpses, and victims' objects discovered shortly after the liberation of the camps, and published by the international press.[9]

There is a certain similarity between Hartmann's black-and-white photographs and those by Ira Nowinski, for example, published in Sybil Milton's book, *In Fitting Memory*, in 1991.[10] Nowinski's photographs, which documented memorial sights, communicate a melancholy mood, work with oblique lighting, and search for new and unconventional vantage points. 'His documentary style discloses the unexpected and the haunting natural beauty that exists even at sites of humanity's evil' (271), Milton wrote. For her, these were images that 'enable the reader to access the visual heritage of the Holocaust' (271). But what would the 'visual heritage' of the Holocaust be? Certainly, this 'heritage' did not only pertain to the concentration camp sites, but to a vocabulary of images that has become a common language (see the citations in Freed's museum architecture). In Nowinski's photographs as well, no human beings were visible; the landscapes were transformed into still lifes. Trees appeared as weeping willows; in Hartmann's photographs, they are bare of leaves. In the work of both photographers, objects take on the feel of ruins, and the difference between nature and machine is blurred. Bush and shoe and wire become monuments of sorts. The perspectival geometry has a modernist feel, but the decaying structures and the wintery gloom conform to the Romantic tradition of infinite spaces and nature's grandeur, as well as its preference for ruins. These are images of mourning. The camera completes, paradoxically, the work of a technology that had death as its primary imperative, turning human beings into objects in the first place. These are not images of trauma, but of belatedness.

HOLOCAUST AESTHETICS

[...] Auschwitz has been a preoccupation for many visual artists, just as there has been the repeated challenge to translate these recent historical events into a visual display for museums and exhibitions. The demand to articulate the limits of representation has not resulted in the end of artistic productivity. It has resulted in its own language of mourning, absence, and trauma. [...] The Holocaust aesthetics no longer centers on the scream, but on its absence.

[...] It has also produced criteria of judgment: Holocaust memorials and museum buildings, as well as individual artworks, selected through competitions whose judges ask not only for historical message or educational impact, but also for 'good' art. '[B]eautiful things give rise to the notion of distribution, to a lifesaving reciprocity, to fairness not just in the sense of loveliness of aspect but in the sense of "a symmetry of everyone's relation to one another," ' wrote Scarry.[11] Can beauty exist when the relationships are broken, and no lifesaving reciprocity exists? Do we as artists or audience carry any ethical responsibility if we derive pleasure from 'unfairness'? These questions will remain, even as the new academic interest in beauty continues.

NOTES

1. Herbert Muschamp, 'Shaping a Monument to Memory,' *New York Times* (April 11, 1993), sec. 2; 1, 32; here 1.
2. 'U.S. Holocaust Museum Challenges Literal Architectural Interpretations of History,' 'Design News,' *Architectural Record* (May 1993): 27. Freed is a member of the architectural firm Pei Cobb Freed.
3. Jeshajahu Weinberg and Rina Elieli, *The Holocaust Museum in Washington* (New York: Rizzoli, 1995), 17.
4. Daniel Libeskind, *Countersign* (New York: Rizzoli, 1992), 86–87.
5. For a more extensive discussion, see Liliane Weissberg, 'Memory Confined,' *documents* 4–5 (1994): 81–98; reprinted in *Cultural Memory and the Construction of Identity*, ed. Dan BenAmos and Liliane Weissberg (Detroit: Wayne State University Press, 1999), 45–76.
6. Miles Lerman, undated letter mailed to potential donors, spring 1993.
7. Weinberg and Elieli, 14.
8. Erich Hartmann, 'Afterword,' *In the Camps* (New York: W. W. Norton & Co., 1995), 28.
9. See Barbie Zelizer, *Remembering to Forget: Holocaust Memory Through the Camera's Eye* (Chicago: University of Chicago Press, 1998).
10. Sybil Milton, *In Fitting Memory: The Art and Politics of Holocaust Memorials*, photographs by Ira Nowinski (Detroit: Wayne State University Press, 1991).
11. Elaine Scarry, *On Beauty* (Princeton: Princeton University Press, 1999).

PART X
LATECOMERS: NEGATIVE SYMBIOSIS, POSTMEMORY, AND COUNTERMEMORY

LATECOMERS: NEGATIVE SYMBIOSIS, POSTMEMORY, AND COUNTERMEMORY: INTRODUCTION

Trauma, as we have seen, is defined in part by its belated effects on the individual – by the insistent return of an event that was not experienced fully at the time of its occurrence. The belatedness of the traumatic effects of the Holocaust is not just an individual matter, however. Much creative, critical, and historical work of recent years has demonstrated that the impact of the Nazi genocide is collective and may, under certain circumstances, be transmitted to generations born after the war. The intergenerational transmission of trauma to children and grandchildren of survivors is a concept that has been contested by some scholars (for instance, by Peter Novick in *The Holocaust in American Life*, 1999), but it is also a phenomenon found in the aftermath of other traumatic histories. The novels of Toni Morrison, for example, are not primarily historical reconstructions of slavery, but are rather attempts to come to terms with the legacy of slavery in the lives of African Americans born after emancipation. Characters such as Milkman in *Song of Solomon* (1977) and Denver in *Beloved* (1988) take part in the 'working through' of a history that is not directly theirs, but which haunts them nonetheless. Their task is not fundamentally different from that of descendants of Holocaust survivors, such as Artie in Art Spiegelman's *Maus* (1986, 1991) or Mathieu Litvak in Henri Raczymow's *Writing the Book of Esther* (1995).

The apparent paradox of being haunted by a memory that is not one's own is at the core of all of the essays in this part. Henri Raczymow considers the situation of children of Holocaust survivors in France, although the implications of his reflections can be taken beyond that particular national context. Raczymow, an important contemporary French writer, is concerned with the holes in the memory of contemporary French Jews, but he refuses to ascribe them only to the impact of the Holocaust. Rather, he traces the origins of absent memory back to the effects of the Jewish Enlightenment or *Haskalah*, a social and intellectual movement that began a process of secularization that led many Jews to distance themselves from religious tradition and community. Yet, despite recognizing the effects of this long-term history on modern Jewish identity, Raczymow is quite aware of the qualitatively different and decisively destructive impact of the Holocaust on Jewish life in Europe (especially the Eastern Europe of his ancestors). This essay, as well as his fiction, is an attempt to measure his distance from and proximity to the European Jewish history that preceded him.

Taking inspiration from Nadine Fresco, Raczymow, Spiegelman, and others, the critic Marianne Hirsch has coined the useful term 'postmemory' to describe the dilemmas of memory and identity experienced by children of survivors of trauma. In an important essay on *Maus*, included in her book *Family Frames*, Hirsch suggests that 'postmemory is distinguished from memory by genera-tional distance and from history by deep personal connection.' For Hirsch, postmemory has become a crucial influence on contemporary art, with photo-graphy being an especially vital site for its articulation and exploration, since 'in their enduring "umbilical" connection to life [photographs] are precisely the medium connecting first- and second-generation remembrance.' Here she considers the use of photography in Spiegelman's comic-book memoir *Maus*, one of the most well known American texts of postmemory.

Our last two essays take up the question of the Holocaust's aftermath in a specifically German context. With his concept of 'negative symbiosis,' Dan Diner brings out a painful irony of postwar life: while it is now impossible to talk of German-Jewish symbiosis (or cultural cooperation) in the years preced-ing the Holocaust, today the identities of both Germans and Jews are inevitably constructed around the negative core of Auschwitz. Even in their attempts to forget or distance themselves from the past, Diner suggests, Germans and Jews demonstrate, in disparate ways, the continuing hold that the traumatic events of the genocide have on them. The postwar artists who are the subject of James Young's essay are fully aware of the complexities of post-Holocaust identity and memory. They attempt to transmute the absence or negativity of genocidal history into an aesthetic form that is critical of the urge either to forget or redeem the German past. In the excerpt here from his pathbreaking book *The Texture of Memory*, Young focuses on the work of Jochen and Esther Gerz, whose Hamburg 'countermonument' turns memorialization against itself – as Adorno sought to turn thought against itself – in order to attempt a provocative anti-fascist art.

As the catastrophic twentieth century gives way to the uncertainties of the twenty-first, responding to the long-term effects of violence remains an intel-lectually as well as psychologically and politically significant task. Although the specificities of different histories surely demand a variety of responses, the literature, art, and criticism of the post-Holocaust generations provide essential resources for coming to terms with the past and attempting to construct a future less haunted by trauma.

OTHER WORKS IN HOLOCAUST STUDIES

Berger, Alan (1997) *Children of Job: American Second-Generation Witnesses to the Holocaust*. Albany, NY: SUNY Press.

Epstein, Julia and Lori Hope Lefkowitz (eds) (2001) *Shaping Losses: Cultural Memory and the Holocaust* Urbana, IL: University of Illinois Press.

Finkielkraut, Alain (1994) *The Imaginary Jew*, trans. Kevin O'Neill and David Suchoff. Lincoln, NE: University of Nebraska Press.

Fresco, Nadine (1984) 'Remembering the Unknown,' trans. Alan Sheridan, *The International Review of Psycho-Analysis*, 11.4, pp. 417–27.

Novick, Peter (1999) *The Holocaust in American Life*. New York: Houghton Mifflin.

Raczymow, Henri (1995) *Writing the Book of Esther*, trans. Dori Katz. New York: Holmes & Meier.

Spiegelman, Art (1986, 1991) *Maus: A Survivor's Tale*, 2 vols. New York: Pantheon.

OTHER RELEVANT WORKS

Abraham, Nicholas and Maria Torok (1994) *The Shell and the Kernel*. Chicago: University of Chicago Press.

Hirsch, Marianne (2002) 'Marked by Memory: Feminist Reflections on Trauma and Transmission,' in N. K. Miller and J. Tougaw (eds), *Extremities: Trauma, Testimony, and Community*. Urbana, IL: University of Illinois Press, pp. 71–91.

Miller, Nancy K. (2000) *Bequest and Betrayal: Memoirs of a Parent's Death*. Bloomington, IN: Indiana University Press.

Morrison, Toni (1988) *Beloved*. New York: Plume.

Morrison, Toni (1977) *Song of Solomon*. New York: Plume.

53

'MEMORY SHOT THROUGH WITH HOLES'

Henri Raczymow

This is the text of a presentation entitled, 'Exil, mémoire, transmission,' which was read at a colloquium of Jewish writers held at the Sorbonne on 12 January 1986.

My place here is somewhat paradoxical. I am supposed to speak, yet I have nothing to say. No lesson to teach, no advice to give, no message to deliver, no strategies to propose. I bear tidings neither of war nor of peace. Like everyone else, I have opinions about everything, but my opinions are no more interesting than anyone else's.

There is one thing of which I can speak: my work as a writer. I do not necessarily believe that a writer is best suited to speak of his work. A careful, somewhat impassioned critic can do just as well, perhaps even better. But I can shed some particular light on one aspect of my writing: the Jewish concerns that run throughout.

The paradox I mentioned – my speaking while not having anything to say – is not simply a more or less gratuitous rhetorical figure. The paradox becomes clear to me as I think of when I began to write, or rather, first decided to write. I had an overwhelming desire to write, which has never left me, yet at the same time I felt I had nothing to say. The theories of the 'new novelists' appealed to me. They took delight in repeating that they had nothing to say, that they needed to devise new forms of fiction. I thought I was attracted to such theories

From Henri Raczymow (1994) 'Memory Shot Through with Holes', *Yale French Studies*, vol. 85. *Discourses of Jewish Identity in Twentieth-Century France*, ed. and trans. Alan Astro. New Haven, CT: Yale University Press, pp. 98–105.

for purely ideological or esthetic reasons, but that was not at all true. Some years later I came to understand that I did *not* have *nothing to say*. Like many others I could have said, or written, just about anything. Rather, I had *to say nothing*, which is not the same thing. As the years went by, as I wrote more, I discovered that the nothing I had to say, to write, to explore – the nothing I turned into sentences, narratives, books – the nothing I could not escape saying as a positive nothing, was my Jewish identity.

My Jewish identity was not nothing, it was *nothingness*, a kind of entity in itself, with its own weight, value, stylistic possibilities, contours, colors, moorings. It might seem that my view is similar to the one expressed by Alain Finkielkraut in *Le Juif imaginaire*, but that is not the case.[1] Unlike Finkielkraut I would not say that Jewish identity is necessarily defined by absence, that it has to be an empty category, something imaginary. For some years now I have been teaching in an orthodox Jewish school, and my students, as becomes immediately apparent, are anything but imaginary Jews. I, however, am one, and I believe that the Holocaust has nothing to do with that. The figure of the imaginary Jew predates the Holocaust. It has been around for a while, having emerged in the *Haskalah*, the Jewish enlightenment, with the secularization of the Jews.[2] If Alex Derczansky were speaking instead of me, he could address the subject quite knowledgeably.[3] He might tell you about Bialik's poem, *On the Threshold of the Beit Hamidrash* [House of Prayer] which portrays the warmth within and the cold without.[4] The warmth within is the warmth of the *beit hamidrash*, and as a *maskil*, an 'enlightened' Jew, Bialik remains on the threshold:

> On my tortuous path
> I have known no sweetness
> My eternity is lost.[5]

The lost eternity of which the poet speaks is Judaism itself, at least traditional Judaism. For Ashkenazic Jewry, eternity was lost well before the Holocaust, well before emigration to the West. I could say, 'We are all German Jews,' as the student slogan had it in May 1968.[6] But here that would mean that we are all modern Jews, all orphaned Jews, bereft of Judaism. We would not have seen, in the last few years, such a forceful return to the Judaism, to the Talmud, to Jewish languages, if precisely all that had not been lost. To return implies having left. Nonetheless, some fragments had been transmitted. 'An I-don't-know what and a next-to-nothing,' as Vladimir Jankélévitch would say.[7] But a few words of Yiddish do not constitute a legacy, but merely a remnant, the 'next-to-nothing' that remains of what was lost. It is the proof or the mark of the loss – its trace. So a trace remains. In turn, we can lose the trace. Lose loss itself. Lose, if you will, the feeling of loss. And dissolve into nothing.

At the end of the 1970s, I made a voyage. I did not know then that I was not the only one. It was an imaginary voyage. I went to Poland, to the Jewish Poland that my grandparents had left. From this imaginary trip – I have never set foot in

Poland – I brought back a short book in which I attempted to explore the 'next-to-nothing' in my own memory.[8] A memory devoid of memory, without content, beyond exile, beyond the forgotten. What did I know about Jewish life in Poland? What had been told to me? Once again, nothing – or next to nothing. The unsaid, the untransmitted, the silence about the past were themselves eloquent.

Itzhok Niborski and Annette Wieviorka, in their work on *Les Livres du souvenir*, attempt to explain why immigrants from Poland could not or would not transmit their heritage.[9] They write: 'The *shtetl* generation possesses a treasure that they are unwilling or unable to share. They feel that those who did not know life in the *shtetl* cannot understand or identify with anything about it.'[10] After the Holocaust, for that generation and even more so for the second and third generations born in France, the prevailing feeling is one of nostalgia, something very ambiguous. Nostalgia is an ambiguous sentiment because it is rife with mythology about a lost paradise, an idyllic 'before,' summed up here in the word *shtetl*. But well before the Holocaust, the *shtetl* was a world already belonging to the past and falling apart.

You have to distinguish between two kinds of nostalgia. The nostalgia of the generations of Jews born in France is not the same as the nostalgia of the generation born in Poland. That generation, as Niborski and Wieviorka have shown, has to imagine their place of origin beyond death, beyond the extermination of their families, towards whom they feel a debt. The 'memorial books' they produced after the war to commemorate their towns take the place of graves for those who had no graves. Those works embellish the past simply because it was the past, the world before the Holocaust. In some way, the authors are lying to themselves, for they knew that world only too well. Roman Vishniac's photos of Jewish Poland, taken in 1938, hold no secrets for them.[11] How could they be nostalgic for the filth, the wretchedness, the poverty shown in those pictures? In turn, those born in France, especially the third generation looking back to the vanished world of their grandparents, also mythologize the past, but they do so unconsciously. We are submerged in mythology, and in their case even their nostalgia is mythical, for it is for something that they never knew, that no longer exists and that will never again exist. Their nostalgia is devoid of content, like the memory devoid of content I spoke of earlier; it is motivated by the very fact that the world they long for is no more, having been entirely reduced to ashes.

However, it is not the world Vishniac shows us that is missed, but rather the community, the 'warmth within' (to repeat Bialik's phrase), a world where Jews truly formed a people whose very language was Jewish. They were a people, not a lobby, or a fad, or a topic for cocktail party conversations, or learned symposia. Emigration has excluded us from that world, from that life, which themselves were wiped off the map.

It is only after something has taken place that we can measure its importance. After writing the slender volume in which I tried to recreate a Jewish Poland, I realized that my book formed a kind of parenthesis. I opened the parenthesis on a Poland that I knew led directly to Auschwitz or Treblinka, and I closed it on a portrayal of the place of immigration, the Parisian Jewish quarter of Belleville in the 1950s. In the center of this parenthesis stood a blank. Even later, quite recently in fact, I discovered that this blank had a name, but I could not bring myself to utter it. My first book, *La Saisie*, devoid of Jewish subject matter, had portrayed absence, emptiness.[12] A few years later, my first 'Jewish' book, *Contes d'exil et d'oubli*, reiterated this absence, this blank, but inscribed it in a Jewish space. A parenthesis was formed by the before and after, the prewar and postwar; it was a frame in whose center lay silence. For me at that time, only silence could evoke the horror. A taboo weighed upon it.

I could, though only in my imagination, conjure up life before, claim to remember a Poland unknown and engulfed, whose language I had heard but never spoken. I could also portray what happened afterwards, in the semblance of a *shtetl* that Belleville was in the postwar years, with its simulacrum of *Yiddishkeit*.[13] It was a *shtetl*, a *Yiddishkeit*, shot through with holes, with missing links: the names of the dead. But what happened between the before and the after, when the drama was played out, when all disappeared, was off limits to me. I had no right to speak of it. Unlike Elie Wiesel, I could not ask how to speak of it, how to find the words for it. For you can always figure out how to speak, you can always find the words, in accordance with your ethics. My question was not '*how* to speak' but '*by what right* could I speak,' I who was not a victim, survivor, or witness. To ask, 'By what right could I speak,' implies the answer, 'I have no right to speak.' However, as any psychoanalyst will tell you, the time comes when you have to speak of what is troubling you. That was the point of my last book, caught in the abyss between my imperious need to speak and the prohibition on speaking.[14] It is inscribed in what English-speaking psychoanalysts call a double bind.

What I name the 'pre-past' or prehistory, along with the Holocaust, was handed down to me precisely as something *not* handed down to me. That was my case, but I believe it was quite common. Writing was and still is the only way I could deal with the past, the whole past, the only way I could tell myself about the past – even if it is, by definition, a recreated past. It is a question of filling in gaps, of putting scraps together. In my opinion, or at least in my case, 'Abraham's memory' does not exist.[15] It is a myth. Abraham's memory is shot through with holes. The memory has burst, as a balloon bursts, but we spend out time sewing it back up. Sewing is an old tradition among us. In fact, sewing scraps together is every writer's task, a hypothetically endless task, an impossible task. That is why my work consists in presenting the scraps in all their diversity, in their disorder, in their dispersion, in a kind of diaspora – if I may use that well-worn metaphor.

In a remarkable essay, Nadine Fresco speaks of the 'diaspora of ashes.'[16] The hopeless attempt to trace down the ashes, to follow the trains [. . .] is the only thing that gives me roots. Mine are superficial roots, along the railroad tracks across Europe, through the paths of emigration and deportation. But I neither emigrated not was deported. The world that was destroyed was not mine. I never knew it. But I am, so many of us are the orphans of that world. Our roots are 'diasporic.' They do not go underground. They are not attached to any particular land or soil. [...] Rather they creep up along the many roads of dispersion that the Jewish writer explores, or discovers, as he puts his lines down on the paper. Such roads are endless.

[...] My books do not attempt to fill in empty memory. They are not simply part of the struggle against forgetfulness. Rather, I try to present memory *as* empty. I try to restore a non-memory, which by definition cannot be filled in or recovered. In everyone there is an unfillable symbolic void, but for the Ashkenazic Jew born in the diaspora after the war, the symbolic void is coupled with a real one. There is a void in our memory formed by a Poland unknown to us and entirely vanished, and a void in our remembrance of the Holocaust through which we did not live. We cannot even say that we were *almost* deported.

There are holes as well in our genealogy. We have no family trees. At the most, we can go back to our grandparents. There is no trace of anyone before. Whose graves can we go visit? What hall of records can we consult? Everything was burned. It seems that what was transmitted to a whole generation of Ashkenazic Jews was anything but a full body of knowledge. It was more like a cloud of neurosis in which the individual cannot orient himself. [...]

[...] Recapturing the past, trying to pursue it as we do the horizon, has been the purpose of my work as a writer. Of course, people will say to me (in fact, they have already said it, or I have read it here and there): 'Well, that's all quite disappointing. You're always looking back, caught up in nostalgia, brooding over the past, a past dead and buried that no longer interests anybody. Why don't you follow the example of the American Jewish writers who tell us about their day-to-day lives as American Jews in the here and now? They don't bore us with stories about Poland and exile.' To which I reply: 'The Jews who came from Eastern Europe are inextricably tied to the past. Their world has been destroyed and the Jewish blood that was shed pollutes the entire European continent, from north to south and east to west. America is free of such pollution. Even those of us who did not live through those times tread every day upon ground where trains rolled towards Auschwitz, every day...'

I spoke earlier of a cloud of neurosis, our only legacy. I believe it has to do with the feeling all of us have, deep down, of having missed a train. You know which train. [...] Out of the impossibility of recapturing the past, some forge the very meaning of their writing, well aware of how ridiculous the pursuit of the impossible is.

– Translated by Alan Astro

NOTES

1. Alain Finkielkraut, *Le Juif imaginaire* (Paris: Seuil, 1980). [*All footnotes to this piece are by the translator.*]

2. The *Haskalah* ('enlightenment' in Hebrew) was the movement of nineteenth-century Eastern European Jewish intellectuals, called *maskilim*, who disseminated Western ideas of progress among their coreligionists.
3. A well-known scholar in the field of Yiddish, Alex Derczansky has taught at the Institut National des Langues et Civilisations Orientales, Paris.
4. Chaim Nachman Bialik (1873–1934) is a foremost figure of modern Hebrew poetry. A clanking, rhyming translation of *On the Threshold of the House of Prayer* appears in *Selected Poems of Hayyim Nakman Bialik*, ed. Israel Efros (New York: Histadruth Ivrit of America, 1948), 29–33. The original, *Al Saf Beit-Hamidrash* can be found in Bialik, *Collected Poems 1890–1898*, ed. Dan Miron (Tel Aviv: Dvir and Katz Research Institute, 1983), 253–55.
5. Vv. 41–43. We translate from the French version that Raczymow quotes.
6. During the May 1968 student uprising in Paris, this slogan became a popular protest against the planned explusion of Danny Cohn-Bendit, a German Jewish student leader.
7. Vladimir Jankélévitch is a contemporary French philosopher whose works include *Le Je-ne-sais-quoi et le presque-rien* (Paris: Seuil, 1980).
8. Raczymow is referring here to his *Contes d'exil et d'oubli* ['Tales of Exile and Forgetfulness'], an excerpt of which is translated in this issue of *Yale French Studies*.
9. Annette Wieviorka and Itzhok Niborski, *Les Livres du souvenir: Mémoriaux juifs de Pologne* (Paris: Gallimard-Julliard, 1983). 'Livres du souvenir' and 'memorial books' translate *yisker-bikher*, the Yiddish term for the volumes of commemorative texts, maps, and photographs published by survivors of Eastern and Central European towns whose Jewish populations were decimated. For a presentation in English of such works, see Jack Kugelmass and Jonathan Boyarin, trans. and ed., *From a Ruined Garden: The Memorial Books of Polish Jewry* (New York: Schocken, 1983).
10. *Les Livres du souvenir*, 174. The term *shtetl*, a diminutive of the Yiddish word *shtot* ('town' or 'city'), is commonly used to designate the semirural localities in which many Jews lived in Eastern and Central Europe. Folklore on the *shtetl* has fostered a largely romanticized conception of Jewish history, exemplified by the musical *Fiddler on the Roof*. Actually, on the eve of World War II, great numbers of Jews lived in large cities such as Warsaw, Odessa, Kiev, Budapest.
11. Roman Vishniac's photographs of Polish Jews were republished in *A Vanished World* (New York: Farrar, Straus and Giroux, 1983).
12. Raczymow, *La Saisie* (Paris: Gallimard, 1973).
13. *Yiddishkeit* (literally, 'Jewishness') is a Yiddish word that can denote either Orthodox Judaism, or a Jewish way of life defined less in terms of religion than of culture. Raczymow is using the term in the second sense.
14. Raczymow, *Un Cri sans voix* (Paris: Gallimard, 1985). A translation by Dori Katz, *A Cry Without a Voice*, is to be published by Holmes & Meier. For a study of this and other novels by Raczymow, see Ellen S. Fine, 'The Absent Memory: The Act of Writing in Post-Holocaust French Literature' in Berel Lang. ed., *Writing and the Holocaust* (New York: Holmes & Meier, 1988), 41–57.
15. This is a reference to Marek Halter's *La Mémoire d'Abraham* (literally, 'Abraham's Memory') (Paris: Laffont, 1983), a best-selling romantic saga of Jewish history since its beginnings. It was translated by Lowell Bair as *The Book of Abraham* (New York: Holt, 1986).
16. Nadine Fresco, 'La Diaspora des cendres,' *Nouvelle Revue de Psychanalyse* (Fall 1981): 205–20.

54

'MOURNING AND POSTMEMORY'

Marianne Hirsch

[...]

I propose the term 'postmemory' with some hesitation, conscious that the prefix 'post' could imply that we are beyond memory and therefore perhaps, as Nora fears, purely in history. In my reading, postmemory is distinguished from memory by generational distance and from history by deep personal connection. Postmemory is a powerful and very particular form of memory precisely because its connection to its object or source is mediated not through recollection but through an imaginative investment and creation. This is not to say that memory itself is unmediated, but that it is more directly connected to the past. Postmemory characterizes the experience of those who grow up dominated by narratives that preceded their birth, whose own belated stories are evacuated by the stories of the previous generation shaped by traumatic events that can be neither understood nor recreated. I have developed this notion in relation to children of Holocaust survivors, but I believe it may usefully describe other second-generation memories of cultural or collective traumatic events and experiences.[1]

I prefer the term 'postmemory' to 'absent memory,' or 'hole of memory,' also derived in Nadine Fresco's illuminating work with children of survivors.[2] Postmemory – often obsessive and relentless – need not be absent or evacuated: it is as full and as empty, certainly as constructed, as memory itself. My notion of postmemory is certainly connected to Henri Raczymow's

From Marianne Hirsch (1997) 'Mourning and Postmemory', in *Family Frames: Photography, Narrative, and Postmemory*. Cambridge, MA: Harvard University Press.

'mémoire trouée,' his 'memory shot through with holes,' defining also the indirect and fragmentary nature of second-generation memory.[3] Photographs in their enduring 'umbilical' connection to life are precisely the medium connecting first- and second-generation remembrance, memory and post-memory. They are the leftovers, the fragmentary sources and building blocks, shot through with holes, of the work of postmemory. They affirm the past's existence and, in their flat two-dimensionality, they signal its unbridgeable distance.

Like all pictures, the photos in *Maus* represent what no longer is. But they also represent what has been and, in this case, what has been violently destroyed. And they represent the life that was no longer to be and that, against all odds, nevertheless continues to be. If anything throws this contradictory and ultimately unassimilable dimension of photography – perched between life and death – into full relief, it has to be the possibility, the reality, of survival in the face of the complete annihilation that is the Holocaust. Holocaust photographs, as much as their subjects, are themselves stubborn survivors of the intended destruction of an entire culture, its people as well as all their records, documents, and cultural artifacts.[4]

The photographs in *Maus* are indeed defined by their inclusion in Spiegelman's very particular imagetext, his provocative generic choice of an animal fable comic book to represent his father's story of survival and his own life as a child of survivors. If Holocaust representation has been determined by Theodor Adorno's suggestion in his 1949 essay 'After Auschwitz,' that 'after Auschwitz you could no longer write poems,' then what can we say of Spiegelman's comics and of the photographs embedded in them?

[...]

By placing three photographs into his graphic narrative, Art Spiegelman raises not only the question of how, forty years after Adorno's dictum, the Holocaust can be represented, but also the question of how different media – comics, photographs, narrative, testimony – can interact to produce a more permeable and multiple text that may recast the problematics of Holocaust representation and definitively eradicate any clear-cut distinction between documentary and aesthetic. In moving us from documentary photographs – perhaps the most referential representational medium – to cartoon drawings of mice and cats, Spiegelman lays bare the levels of mediation that underlie *all* visual representational forms. But confronting these visual media with his father's spoken testimony adds yet another axis to the oppositions between documentary and aesthetic, on the one hand, testimony and fiction, on the other. Considering these two axes in relation to each other may enable us to come back to the Holocaust photo – and, through it, to photography more generally – and to look at its particular articulation of life and death, representation and mourning.

[...]

Taken together, the three photographs in *Maus I* and *II* reassemble a family violently fractured and destroyed by the Shoah: they include, at different times, in different places, and in different guises, all the Spiegelmans – Art and his mother, Art's brother Richieu, and the father, Vladek. Sparsely distributed over the space of the two volumes, these three pictures tell their own narrative of loss, mourning and desire, one that inflects obliquely, that both supports and undercuts the story of *Maus*.[5]

But these three images are not equal. The first, the picture of mother and son [...] has a unique generative power in the son's text, a power that comes from the 'double dying' and the double survival in which it is embedded.[6] The photograph clarifies the importance of the mother's suicide twenty-three years after her liberation from Auschwitz in the story the father and son construct, reinforcing the work of memory and postmemory that generates their text.

The photograph of Artie and his mother, labeled 'Trojan Lake, N.Y. 1958' (*Maus*, 100) introduces 'The Prisoner on the Hell Planet,' the account of Anja Spiegelman's suicide. In the picture, the family is obviously vacationing – the 10-year-old Art is squatting in a field, smiling at the camera, and Anja is standing above him, wearing a bathing suit, one hand on his head, staring into space. Presumably the picture is taken by the invisible father, a conventional division of labor in 1950s family pictures. But the very next frame announces the destruction of this interconnected family group: 'In 1968, when I was 20, my mother killed herself. She left no note.' Poignantly, Spiegelman juxtaposes the archival photograph with the message of death which, through the presence of the photo's 'having-been-there,' is strengthened, made even more unbearable. This echoes an earlier moment in the text when Art, holding his mother's photograph, tries to engage his father in the project of testimony: 'Start with Mom' (*Maus*, 12).

[...]

But *Maus* is dominated by this absence of Anja's voice, the destruction of her diaries, her missing note. Anja is recollected by others; she remains a visual and not an aural presence. She speaks in sentences imagined by her son or recollected by her husband. In their memory she is mystified, objectified, shaped to the needs and desires of the one who remembers – whether it be Vladek or Art. Her actual voice could have been in the text, but it isn't: 'These notebooks, and other really nice things of mother,' Vladek explains to Art, '... One time I had a very bad day ... and all of these things I destroyed.' 'You what?' Art exclaims. And Vladek replies: 'After Anja died I had to make an order with everything ... these papers had too many memories, so I burned them' (*Maus*, 158–159). Vladek did not read the papers Anja left behind, he only knows that she said: 'I wish my son, when he grows up, he will be interested by this' (*Maus*, 159). Her legacy was destroyed and *Maus* itself can be seen as an attempt to reconstruct it, an attempt by father and son to provide the missing perspective of the mother. Much of the *Maus* text rests on her absence and the destruction of her papers, deriving from her silence its momentum and much of its energy. Through her picture and her missing voice Anja haunts the story told in both volumes, a ghostly presence shaping familial interaction – the personal and the collective story of death and survival.

[...]

While 'Prisoner on the Hell Planet' is the work of memory, *Maus* itself is the creation of postmemory. In fact, that is the status of the two photographs in *Maus II*. The second volume carries two dedications: 'For Richieu and for Nadja' [...] Richieu is the brother Art never knew because he died during the war, before Art's birth; Nadja is Spiegelman's daughter. The volume is dedicated to two children, one dead, the other alive, one who is the object of postmemory, the other who will herself carry on her father's postmemory. Whose picture, in fact, illustrates the dedication page? I have assumed that it is Richieu's: a serious child about three years old, hair parted, wearing knit overalls. But upon reflection the picture is quite indeterminate. Could it be Nadja? Could it be a childhood image of Vladek, I wonder, noting the resemblance between the two pictures which frame *Maus II*? Or could it be Art himself? A few pages into *Maus II*, Art alludes to a photograph of his 'ghost-brother,' wondering if they would have gotten along: 'He was mainly a large blurry photograph hanging in my parents' bedroom.' Françoise is surprised: 'I thought that was a picture of you, though it didn't look like you' (*Maus II*, 15). Based on appearance alone, the picture could be Art or Vladek or Nadja or Richieu, and Spiegelman does not specify. But in terms of function, the picture in the bedroom and the one on the dedication page clearly have to be Richieu: 'That's the point. They didn't need photos of me in their room, I was alive! The photo never threw tantrums or got in any kind of trouble ... It was an ideal kid, and I was a pain in the ass. I couldn't compete' (*Maus II*, 15). This photograph signifies death and loss, even while, as a kind of 'fetish object,' it disavows loss. The parents keep it in their bedroom to live with; Art competes with it; and we take it as the ultimately unassimilable fact that it was a child who died unnaturally, before he had the chance to live. The child who could not survive to live his own life – especially in his equivalence with Art and Nadja – becomes the emblem of the incomprehensibility of Holocaust destruction. [...] Because of its anonymity, this photograph, and many others like it, refers to the anonymity of the victims and corpses represented in photographs of concentration and extermination camps. At the end of the volume, Art becomes Richieu and Richieu takes on the role of listener and addressee of Vladek's testimony, a testimony addressed to the dead and the living. 'So,' Vladek says as he turns over in his bed, 'Let's stop, please, your tape recorder. I'm tired from talking, Richieu, and it's enough stories for now' (*Maus II*, 136). Richieu is both a visual presence and a listener – and, as he and Art merge to transmit the tale, he is neither. The child's photograph, visible in other frames portraying Vladek's bedroom, itself becomes the ultimate witness to the survivor's tale. In this role Richieu, or his photograph, confirms the interminable nature of the mourning in *Maus*, and the endlessness of Vladek's tale, a tale subtitled 'And here my troubles began.' This is a phrase Spiegelman takes from Vladek's narrative, an ironic aside about Auschwitz. Reading *Maus II* we realize not only that his troubles began long before, but that his troubles (and his son's) never end.

If the child's photograph at the beginning of this volume is the emblem of incomprehensible and unacceptable death, Vladek's photograph at the end works as a sign of life that reconnects Vladek and Anja after the liberation [. . .] 'Anja! guess what! A letter from your husband just came!' 'He's in Germany . . . He's had typhus! . . . And here's a picture of him! My God – Vladek is really alive!' (*Maus II*, 134). Reproduced in the next frame, but at a slant, jumping out of the frame, is a photograph of the young Vladek, serious but pleasant, standing in front of a curtain, wearing a starched, striped camp uniform and hat. He explains the picture: 'I passed once a photo place what had a camp uniform – a new and clean one – to make souvenir photos.' Just as Vladek keeps pictures of the deceased Anja on his desk, he asserts that 'Anja kept this picture always.' The photograph which signifies life and survival is as important, as cherished, as the one signaling loss and death. But this photograph is particularly disturbing in that it *stages, performs* the identity of the camp inmate. Vladek wears a uniform in a souvenir shop in front of what looks like a stage curtain; he is no longer in the camp but he reenacts his inmate self even as he is trying to prove – through his ability to pose – that he survived the inmate's usual fate.

In Anja's eyes the uniform would not call into question the picture's message: 'I am alive, I have survived.' She last saw Vladek in Auschwitz and would certainly have noticed the difference between this clean uniform and the one he actually must have worn. The uniform would signal to her their common past, their survival, perhaps their hope for a future. It is a picture Vladek could have sent only to *her* – someone else might have misunderstood its performative aspect. For readers of *Maus* this picture plays a different role: it situates itself on a continuum of representational choices, from the authenticity of the photos, to the drawings of humans in 'Hell Planet,' to the mice masks, to the drawings of mice themselves. This photograph both is documentary evidence (Vladek was in Auschwitz) and isn't (the picture was taken in a souvenir shop). This picture may look like a documentary photograph of the inmate – it may have the appearance of authenticity – but it is merely, and admittedly, a simulation, a dress-up game. The identity of Vladek, the camp survivor, with the man wearing the camp uniform in the picture is purely coincidental – anyone could have had this picture taken in the same souvenir shop – any of us could have, just as perhaps any of us could be wearing uniforms in our dreams, as Art is. [. . .]

Breaking the frame, looking intently at the viewer/reader, Vladek's picture dangerously relativizes the identity of the survivor. As listeners of his testimony, as viewers of Art's translation and transmission of that testimony, we are invited to imagine ourselves inside that picture. Like Frieda's picture, Vladek's photo, with all its incongruous elements, suggests a story and *Maus* is that story. With Art and with Vladek, but without Anja, the reader is in what Dori Laub calls 'the testimonial chain':

> Because trauma returns in disjointed fragments in the memory of the survivor, the listener has to let these trauma fragments make their impact both on him and on the witness. Testimony is the narrative's address to hearing ... As one comes to know the survivor, one really comes to know oneself; and that is no simple task ... In the center of this massive dedicated effort remains a danger, a nightmare, a fragility, a woundedness that defies all healing. (*Testimony*, 71–73)

Maus represents the aesthetic of the trauma fragment, the aesthetic of the testimonial chain – an aesthetic that is indistinguishable from the documentary. It is composed of individually framed fragments, each like a still picture imbricated in a border that is closed off from the others. These frames are nevertheless connected to one another in the very testimonial chain that relates the two separate chronological levels, the past and the present, that structure the narrative of *Maus* relating teller to listener. But, once in a while, something breaks out of the rows of frames, or out of the frames themselves, upsetting and disturbing the structure of the entire work. The fragments that break out of the frames are details functioning like Barthes's 'punctum'; they have the power of the 'fetish' to signal and to disavow an essential loss. Anja Spiegelman, because of her missing voice and her violently destroyed diary, is herself one such point of disturbance, made more so by the photograph that is included among the stylized drawings. And embedded in those fragments – in spite of the conventional fairy-tale ending of the second volume where Vladek and Anja are reunited and Vladek insists that 'we were both very happy and lived happy, happy ever after,' in spite of the tombstone that enshrines their togetherness in the book's last frame and establishes a seemingly normalized closure – the nightmare, the fragility, the woundedness remain. The power of the photographs Spiegelman includes in *Maus* lies not in their evocation of memory, the connection they can establish between present and past, but in their status as fragments of a history we cannot assimilate. Utterly familiar, especially in the context of the defamiliarizing images of mice and cat drawings, these photographs forge an affiliative look that enables identification: they could be any of ours. At the same time, this same context – both the story of the Holocaust and the cartoon drawings in which they are embedded – makes them strangely unfamiliar, opaque.

[...] The three photographs in *Maus*, and the complicated marginal narrative of unassimilable loss that they tell, perpetuate what remains in the two volumes as an incongruity appropriate to the aesthetic of the child of survivors, the aesthetic of postmemory [. . .]. They reinforce at once incomprehensibility and presence, a past that will neither fade away nor be integrated into the present.

NOTES

1. 'Postmemory' is usefully connected to Kaja Silverman's notion of 'heteropathic recollection' – her elaborate psychoanalytic theorization of the self's ability to take on the memory of others, even culturally devalued others, through a process of heteropathic identification. Silverman's argument also relies on the visual and considers the role of photography, though not the notion of family. See *The Threshold of the Visible World*, (New York: Routledge, 1996) esp. ch. 5.
2. Nadine Fresco, 'Remembering the Unknown,' *International Review of Psychoanalysis* 11 (1984): 417–427.
3. Henri Raczymow, 'Memory Shot Through with Holes,' *Yale French Studies 85* (1994): 98–106.
4. In conjunction with a 1996 photographic exhibit in Warsaw, 'And I Still See Their Faces,' one Zahava Bromberg writes: 'I carried this photograph of my mama through two selections by Dr. Mengele at Auschwitz. Once I held it in my mouth, the second time I had it taped with a bandage to the bottom of my foot. I was 14 years old.' *New York Times* (May 19, 1996): 1.
5. The CD-Rom edition of *Maus* features a number of additional photographs in the appendix that outlines the Spiegelmans's and the Zylberbergs's family trees. We can click on some of the names to make the photographs appear. As in the book edition, the photographs function to reassemble what has been severed. Mostly the photographs feature pairs, Anja and Vladek, parents, siblings. They are formal pictures, such as wedding photos. Together, they help to rebuild the family tree of a fractured family. In this version, however, they do not intervene in the narrative, but stand apart. In addition, any of the pictures' ambiguity is removed since, in this medium, each image is clearly labeled.
6. I take this phrase from the title of Alvin K. Rosenfeld's book on the literature of the Holocaust, *A Double Dying: Reflections on Holocaust Literature* (Bloomington: Indiana University Press, 1980).

55

'NEGATIVE SYMBIOSIS: GERMANS AND JEWS AFTER AUSCHWITZ'

Dan Diner

Gerschom Scholem has correctly rejected as false the portrayal of German-Jewish relations before the Nazi Regime as a 'symbiosis.' The image of a German-Jewish symbiosis is a distortion because it suggests that the limited, idealized period between the emancipation of the Jews and National Socialist barbarism, which lasted only two generations, was the rule rather than the exception. This image of German-Jewish symbiosis becomes especially misleading when, in the wake of Auschwitz, it is stylized as a deplorable loss. Such heightened reverence toward the intellectual patchwork that was German-Jewish creativity disrupts our view – already clouded enough – of the monstrosity of the greatest crime in human history.

After Auschwitz it is actually possible – what a sad irony – to speak of a 'German-Jewish symbiosis,' albeit a negative one. For both Jews and Germans, whether they like it or not, the aftermath of mass murder has been the starting point for self-understanding – a kind of communality of opposites. Once again, Germans and Jews have been brought together. For generations to come, this negative symbiosis, created by the Nazis, will color the relationship between the two groups. The facile and optimistic hopes that distance from Auschwitz would soften the memory of its horror, would weaken the impressions of that nightmarish break with civilization, have proven to be unfounded. The memory of Auschwitz, the living presence of what is

From Dan Diner (1990) 'Negative Symbosis: Germans and Jews after Auschwitz', in P. Baldwin (ed.), *Reworking the Past: Hitler, the Holocaust, and the Historian's Debate*. Boston: Beacon Press.

euphemistically termed a 'past' event, has gained ever greater weight within contemporary consciousness.

Thus it appears that Auschwitz, that 'past' event, may make its most lasting impact on consciousness in the future. With increased distance, the view of this incomprehensible occurrence has become sharper; its outlines have emerged more distinctly in the aftermath of the disorienting shock that this break with civilization had upon the West. The effect of Auschwitz now goes beyond the creation of a common identity among its victims and survivors. The mind demands a rational response even to irrational events, to the actualization of senselessness.

To live in the shadow of Auschwitz? Not a very pleasant prospect, at least not for the communities of the perpetrators and the victims. The two groups necessarily live in different, even opposite, ways with the memory of what occurred, or try to avoid its memory altogether. Thus Jewish victims perceive German attempts to forget as plots against the collective memory. And such attempts can, in the face of continuous Jewish reminders of that horror, turn into blind rage – anti-Semitism as a result of Auschwitz? The failure to overcome the past because the monstrosity of the crime makes overcoming impossible, intense efforts that prove to be at best hopeless attempts to free oneself from the burden of the past – these are the fruits of a culture deeply marked by guilt over Auschwitz and constantly in search of relief. Yet these understandable attempts at avoidance are in vain. The omnipresence of the event leads those who seek to flee it Sisyphus-like back to memories saturated with Auschwitz. For Jews, the memory of Auschwitz produces a horror vacui of boundless helplessness – an incomprehensible emptiness best kept plugged with other memories and distractions if life is to go on.

Above and beyond the extermination of the Jews, Auschwitz was a practical refutation of Western civilization. An unfathomable act of purposeless destruction for destruction's sake repulses a consciousness steeped in the logic of instrumental rationality. An understanding formed by secular patterns of thought cannot integrate such an action – at least not without splitting apart. This impossibility makes the victims' failure to act in the face of the gas ovens understandable: the power of imagination needed for action is impossible in the case of the unimaginable.

In an article written many years ago, the Dutch historian Louis de Jong aptly described the conceptual trap represented by Auschwitz: understanding Auschwitz in the face of Auschwitz is comparable to staring with open eyes directly into the sun. The victims, individuals equipped with defensive mechanisms which protect them and permit them to survive and live on, must evade this dread-inspiring reality. 'It may sound paradoxical, but it is a fact that can be explained both historically and psychologically: the Nazi death camps only became a psychic reality for most people … when, and precisely because, they no longer existed.'[1] This accords with the recent and paradoxical discovery: coming to terms intellectually as well as emotionally with Auschwitz requires temporal distance. This coming to terms leads, for both Jews and Germans, to those necessarily opposing perceptions and patterns of reaction which have had such an enduring impact on the contemporary consciousness – above all of those born after 1945.

In a letter to Karl Jaspers in 1946, on the occasion of the Nuremberg Trials, Hannah Arendt addressed the basic idea of a 'negative symbiosis' of Germans and Jews after Auschwitz. She also touched on the problem of a guilt that would be commensurate with the crimes committed, yet could not be traced back to particular individuals. Describing the basis for an expanding, free-floating collective guilt that would affect above all the younger generation, she wrote:

> These crimes cannot be dealt with in the normal legal manner, and it is precisely that which makes them so monstrous. There are no fitting punishments for such crimes. To hang Göring is necessary, but it is by no means enough. Such a guilt, in contrast to all criminal guilt, goes well beyond, in fact shatters, any legal order. This is the reason why the Nazis at Nuremberg are so pleased: because of course they know this. And the innocence of the victims is equally inhuman. Human beings cannot be as innocent as those people were as they stood together before the gas ovens. ... One can do nothing either personally or politically about a guilt that lies beyond crime and an innocence that lies beyond good or virtue. ... For the Germans are burdened with thousands or tens of thousands or hundreds of thousands who can no longer be properly punished within a system of law; and we Jews are burdened with millions of innocents, because of whom each Jew today looks like innocence personified.[2]

The abstractness of the extermination, that is, the functional participation of German society as a whole in industrial mass murder organized through a division of labor, renders everyone, with the exception of active resistance fighters, a part of the killing process. The younger generation's feelings of guilt confirm this. Even though the actual criminals and those directly responsible have been punished, a critical mass of guilt remains which cannot be attributed to any particular person. This is a result of the abstract, depersonalized, and collective division of labor through which the extermination of the Jews was carried out. Attempts to reconstruct the genesis of Auschwitz historically also run up against the phenomenon of the Holocaust's abstractness. Can the extermination of the Jews be traced back to a clear intention, to a criminal aim present from the very beginning? Or was this an autonomous, functional process, rooted in a blind self-radicalization of the system, in which the atomized individuals who were part of an industrial division of labor became the unconscious executors of the Holocaust?

The crime is, in fact, too monstrous to be reduced to intention alone. Moreover, the reactions of the victims and witnesses alike are incomprehensible if one attributes the act only to a clear design that was present from the start. The road to Auschwitz was not straight; in retrospect, other possible routes can be constructed, at least hypothetically. In West Germany, however, the theory of an overpowering totalitarian system, of a directionless autonomous process ending in Auschwitz, encourages an exculpating approach that sees no actors, although the event took place.

However the debate among the historians develops – and the latest publications lead one to fear the worst – the abstract sense of responsibility that afflicts society as a whole culminates in a conceptualization that both refers to the deep collective cause of the Holocaust and is also helpful in characterizing the guilty feelings of the younger generation: Auschwitz has taken place. It has happened – *it* [*id*] in an emphatically psychoanalytic sense. Auschwitz is thus part of the unconscious in a double sense: as something unconscious that was *realized* in a collective act, and as a continuing, collective sense of guilt caused by the act.

It is possible to react in various ways to a sense of collective guilt. It may manifest itself as an archaic feeling of immanent punishment if there is no expiation for the horror of the Holocaust, an occurrence which was not part of the war, but was carried out in its shadow. Through identification with parents or grandparents – bound together through an intergenerational psychic wound – the fear of anticipated revenge, of anticipated expiation (in a word, a punishment anxiety) is passed on. In moments of real or imagined political crisis, the repressed or denied punishment anxiety over Auschwitz can burst forth in a productive manner – unless it is condemned to silence by a complicitous pact between the generations, in which case it may later lead to demands for exoneration from guilt.

[...]

The existence of an uncomprehended past in the present is not without its consequences. It can, for example, lead to a ritualized self-stylization as a victim, such as wearing a yellow star as a sign of political protest. This is presumably not just an instance of tasteless, false identification with the real victims of National Socialism. Rather, the past appears here as a subterranean fear, stemming from inherited feelings of guilt and anxiety which have been symbolically reversed and magically invoked. One presents oneself as a supposed victim in order to shake off the burden of guilt transmitted by one's parents. In so doing, however, the possibility of bringing this guilt to consciousness and dealing with it is lost.

In their book *The Inability to Mourn*, the Mitscherlichs have shown that, while history does not always repeat itself, the compulsion to repeat it is always realized in some way. No political event provides a better illustration of this claim than the German reaction to the Israeli invasion of Lebanon in 1982. It is important to remember, in this context, that Israel always possesses a double meaning in the Christian West: first as a reality (an aspect not to be discussed here) and second as a metaphor. It is a metaphor which stands in close relation to the Western image of the Jew and thus belongs to the historical context of anti-Semitism. If that is so, then it should be impossible in West Germany to judge Israel simply as the Israeli state, since the German consciousness in relation to the Jews has been darkened by a myth, in the face of which every attempt at enlightenment must look like magic. When Israel's behavior was characterized as 'genocide,' as a Holocaust, one could not help but feel that it was not the horrors of war, the helplessness of the Palestinians, or the suffering of the Lebanese victims that was really at issue here. Rather, it was as if the Jews were being spontaneously encouraged actually to commit genocide, so that the German sense of guilt could be excised through expiation and the fearful punishment anxiety finally lifted.

The Right has attempted to gain political capital from such reactions by ascribing them solely to the Left. But punishment anxiety, combined with fantasies of Jewish power connected with the state of Israel, are universally shared in Germany. In light of the reactions in 1982, the view that the pro-Israeli enthusiasm of 1967 in West German public opinion can be explained by an identification with the military successes of these 'Prussians of the Middle East' must be revised. If it is true that guilty feelings toward the Jews are universal in Germany, then the noisy manifestations of joy at the victories won by the former victims were actually expressions of relief that the awaited punishment had been meted out to others, to the Arabs, and that expiation – albeit via the wrong people – had finally occurred.

The threatening presence of Jews in the German collective consciousness after Auschwitz has brought forth strange means of dealing with the past, such as the phenomenon of 'covering memories' (*Deckerinnerung*). This term refers to a certain way of living with the past, one characterized by a new historical assiduity that brings one closer to the events of 1933–45, yet at the same time leaves out the source of one's own unease. Other victims of National Socialism are thus thrust into the foreground in order to avoid confronting the particularity of the extermination of the Jews, an act which is still felt to be exceptional. Let there be no misunderstanding: no hierarchy of victims is being advocated here. The point is not to rate Jewish victims higher than other groups that were also singled out by the Nazis for ethnic or biological reasons. The sacrifice of those exterminated because of anti-Semitism is no different in quality from that of those victims killed for reasons of socalled racial or social hygiene. It is only within the collective memory that a hierarchy of victims is first established. This may be a consequence of the fact that the fantasies linked to the different victims of Nazism touch various levels of historical memory. Thus anti-Judaism and anti-Semitism go far back into Western history and are, indeed, part of the founding myth of Christian civilization. Antagonism toward the Jews is older than racism. On the other hand, racism rests on deeper strata of the unconscious, evokes richer myths than either eugenics or so-called social hygiene. There thus exists an historically differentiated stratification of memories that pertain to the victims. This differential hierarchy of victims within the collective unconscious means that Auschwitz will be associated with the Nazis' principal victims for as long as historical memory lasts.

[...]

Negative symbiosis as a result of Auschwitz also means that Jewish encounters with this event are also accompanied by 'covering memories' – although, of course, for opposite reasons. In addition to the incomprehensibility, abstractness, and monstrosity of industrially organized mass murder, whose secular meaning becomes understandable even to the victims only with greater distance, there are also other reasons for the tenacity of 'covering memories,' reasons that are directly related to the extermination itself. The victims cannot bear the fact that at Auschwitz something senseless and purposeless occurred. To be sure, the genesis of the Holocaust is unimaginable without a historically latent anti-Semitism. But while traditional anti-Semitism was a requirement of the Shoah, the Holocaust did not of necessity flow from such anti-Semitism. Integrating industrial mass murder into the confines of an exclusively Jewish view of history removes it from its universal context and transfigures the Holocaust into a meaningful national martyrdom.

A further element in a misleading Jewish perception of the Shoah is shame: shame at the supposed failure to resist; shame at the fact that the Jews allowed themselves to be led away 'like lambs to the slaughter.' This is not the place to rehearse the historical and sociological conditions that might have made resistance possible. Suffice it to say that 'the Jews' as a coherent national group or a cohesive collectivity did not exist in Europe. The Nazis, especially in Germany, first had to define Jews in order to treat them accordingly. What level of social and political density would have been necessary within an atomized population, one which had been brought together in the first place only by the Nazis, in order to have made military resistance even thinkable? For such is the notion of resistance seemingly contained in the implicit reproach; the image of lambs being led away to the slaughter.

[...]

[...] The question that Jews ask themselves time and again, why there was no resistance – that shame-filled reproach, that as victims they acted dishonorably – is based on an insistent refusal to understand Auschwitz. This lasting ignorance leads one to suppose that, because of its secular monstrosity, this occurrence should not be understood.

A Jewish barrier to understanding Auschwitz is also created by attempting to derive an exclusively particularist interpretation from it. As mentioned above, as an expression of anti-Semitism the mass extermination would be comprehensible only in a narrowly Jewish view of history; understanding the Holocaust only as a giant pogrom would confirm the correctness and necessity of the classic reaction to European persecution of the Jews – a withdrawal from the world of the non-Jews. The Zionist answer to the anti-Semitism of persecution may on the whole be a perfectly consistent one. Yet such an answer is necessarily wrong and fruitless when the classic anti-Semitism of persecution becomes an anti-Semitism of extermination.

This was novel: the Nazis sought to deprive the Jews of life wherever they could get hold of them, even in Palestine. [...] The nagging feeling (a constant reminder of Auschwitz) that one survived because of pure chance, rather than because of Zionism, must be so unbearable that it is masked by a 'historiosophic' construction of reality: Israel as a reaction, an answer to the Holocaust that is once again integrated into a view of history shaped by traditional anti-Semitism. Because of the proto-Zionist consciousness of Jews after 1945, Israel has become a constituent part of the 'covering memory,' part of that plug of memory, of that psychic crutch, that is supposed to, and in the last analysis really does, give life after Auschwitz a meaning and a purpose. For the conflict in and over Palestine, the link between Nazi mass murder and traditional anti-Semitism is of course disastrous. On the one hand, the uniqueness of the Shoah is inadmissably extended; on the other hand, the confrontation between Jews and Arabs which is at the heart of this conflict is falsely turned into one between Jews and non-Jews – a reversal of the anti-Semitic world view. In this way, both the causes of the conflict and the possibilities of its solution are ignored. In such an interpretation, the confrontation between Jews and Arabs fits into the hopeless and apocalyptic opposition between Jews and non-Jews.

And what of Jews in Germany? For them, more than for anyone else, Israel represents a psychic support, a substitute identity, because they must explain over and again, both to themselves and to Jews elsewhere, why they, by living in the hangman's house, have helped give the impression that after Auschwitz normality has returned to German-Jewish relations – a normality that implies that nothing happened. This certainly corresponds to the interests of the West German state's representatives. The presence of Jews here was of great importance for the moral rehabilitation of the Germans; the existence of Jewish communities in the Federal Republic bolstered its international legitimacy. The current and increasingly marked reidentification of Germans with Germany continues to depend on the presence of Jews as a support for this German desire for normality.

[...]

What keeps the Jews in Germany today? Prosperity alone is not a sufficient explanation. Worldy considerations may have been important for many, but the real reasons probably lie deeper. It sounds overdrawn, even presumptuous: Jews in Germany, disparaged and ostracized by Jews in the rest of the world for their presence in that country, seem to stay there because by maintaining the closest possible proximity to the scene of the crime and to the collectivity of the perpetrators, they maintain the strongest ties to the past. It is as if in Germany they could make good the eternal loss, fill the void created by Auschwitz. There the memory is strongest, there their constant presence challenges the collectivity

DAN DINER

of the perpetrators to remember their deeds – as if in Germany, with the help of
the Germans, that which was lost could be found again.

Such a linkage renders the negative symbiosis, the relationship between
Germans and Jews after Auschwitz, even more difficult and conflict-ridden
as the distance from the events themselves increases. This is true especially as the
passive normality that has been characteristic of Germany since 1945 is
transformed into an active normalization of the Germans as Germans, a change
that is taking place because of a desire for reconciliation with the generation of
the parents, a phenomenon which is being expressed in German political culture
as the demand for a positive national identity.

[…]

NOTES

1. Louis de Jong, 'Die Niederlande und Auschwitz,' in *Vierteljahrshefte für Zeit-
geschichte* (1969): 16.
2. Hannah Arendt and Karl Jaspers, *Briefwechsel 1926–1969*, ed. Lotte Köhler and
Hans Janer (Munich, 1985), 90.

430

56

'THE COUNTERMONUMENT: MEMORY AGAINST ITSELF IN GERMANY'

James E. Young

Away with the monuments!
–Friedrich Nietzsche

For a new generation of artists in Germany today, the question is not whether to remember or to forget the Holocaust. Rather, given the tortuous complexity of their nation's relation to its past, they wonder whether the monument itself is more an impediment than an incitement to public memory. Perhaps the most stunning and inflammatory response to Germany's memorial conundrum is the rise of its countermonuments: brazen, painfully self-conscious memorial spaces conceived to challenge the very premises of their being.

Ethically certain of their duty to remember, but aesthetically skeptical of the assumptions underpinning traditional memorial forms, a new generation of contemporary artists and monument makers in Germany is probing the limits of both their artistic media and the very notion of a memorial. They are heirs to a double-edged postwar legacy: a deep distrust of monumental forms in light of their systematic exploitation by the Nazis, and a profound desire to distinguish their generation from that of the killers through memory.[1]

At home in an era of earthworks, conceptual and self-destructive art, these young artists explore both the necessity of memory and their incapacity to recall events they never experienced directly. To their minds, neither literal nor

From James E. Young (1990) 'The Countermonument: Memory against Itself in Germany', in *The Texture of Memory: Holocaust Memorials and Meaning*. New Haven, CT and London: Yale University Press.

figurative references suggesting anything more than their own abstract link to the Holocaust will suffice. Instead of seeking to capture the memory of events, therefore, they remember only their own relationship to events, the great gulf of time between themselves and the Holocaust.

For German artists and sculptors like Jochen Gerz, Norbert Radermacher, and Horst Hoheisel, the possibility that memory of events so grave might be reduced to exhibitions of public craftsmanship or cheap pathos remains intolerable. They contemptuously reject the traditional forms and reasons for public memorial art, those spaces that either console viewers or redeem such tragic events, or indulge in a facile kind of *Wiedergutmachung* or purport to mend the memory of a murdered people. Instead of searing memory into public consciousness, they fear, conventional memorials seal memory off from awareness altogether. For these artists, such an evasion would be the ultimate abuse of art, whose primary function to their minds is to jar viewers from complacency, to challenge and denaturalize the viewers' assumptions. In the following case studies of four contemporary countermonuments, we explore the process whereby artists renegotiate the tenets of their memory-work, whereby monuments are born resisting the very possibility of their birth.

THE GERZES' COUNTERMONUMENT

To some extent, this new generation of artists in Germany may only be enacting a critique of memory-places already formulated by cultural and art historians long skeptical of the memorial's traditional function. As if in response to the seemingly generic liabilities of monuments, conceptual artists Jochen and Esther Gerz have designed what they call a *Gegen-Denkmal* (countermonument). It was built at the city of Hamburg's invitation to create a 'Monument against Fascism, War, and Violence – and for Peace and Human Rights.' The artists' first concern was how to commemorate such worthy sentiments without ameliorating memory altogether. That is, how would their monument emplace such memory without usurping the community's will to remember? Their second concern was how to build an antifascist monument without resorting to what they regarded as the fascist tendencies in all monuments. 'What we did not want,' Jochen Gerz declared, 'was an enormous pedestal with something on it presuming to tell people what they ought to think.'[2]

To their minds, the didactic logic of monuments, their demagogical rigidity, recalled too closely traits they associated with fascism itself. Their monument against fascism, therefore, would amount to a monument against itself: against the traditionally didactic function of monuments, against their tendency to displace the past they would have us contemplate – and finally, against the authoritarian propensity in all art that reduces viewers to passive spectators.

The artists decided that theirs would be a self-abnegating monument, literally self-effacing. So when Hamburg offered them a sun-dappled park setting, they rejected it in favor of what they termed a 'normal, uglyish place.' Their countermonument would not be refuge in memory, tucked away from the hard edges of urban life, but one more eyesore among others on a blighted cityscape. They chose the commercial center of Harburg, a somewhat dingy suburb of Hamburg, located thirty minutes from the city center by subway across the river, just beyond a dioxin dump, populated with a mix of Turkish guest-workers and blue-collar German families. Set in a pedestrian shopping mall, their countermonument would rise sullenly amid red brick and glass shop windows: package-laden shoppers could like it or hate it, but they could not avoid it.

Unveiled in 1986, this twelve-meter-high, one-meter-square pillar is made of hollow aluminum, plated with a thin layer of soft, dark lead. A temporary inscription near its base reads – and thereby creates constituencies in – German, French, English, Russian, Hebrew, Arabic, and Turkish: 'We invite the citizens of Harburg, and visitors to the town, to add their names here to ours. In doing so, we commit ourselves to remain vigilant. As more and more names cover this 12 meter tall lead column, it will gradually be lowered into the ground. One day it will have disappeared completely, and the site of the Harburg monument against fascism will be empty. In the end, it is only we ourselves who can rise up against injustice.' A steel-pointed stylus, with which to score the soft lead, is attached at each corner by a length of cable. As one-and-a-half-metter sections are covered with memorial graffiti, the monument is lowered into the ground, into a chamber as deep as the column is high. The more actively visitors participate, the faster they cover each section with their names, the sooner the monument will disappear. After several lowerings over the course of four or five years, nothing will be left but the top surface of the monument, which will be covered with a burial stone inscribed to 'Harburg's Monument against Fascism.' In effect, the vanishing monument will have returned the burden of memory to visitors: one day, the only thing left standing here will be the memory-tourist, forced to rise and to remember for himself.

With audacious simplicity, the countermonument thus flouts any number of cherished memorial conventions: its aim is not to console but to provoke; not to remain fixed but to change; not to be everlasting but to disappear; not to be ignored by passersby but to demand interaction; not to remain pristine but to invite its own violation and desanctification; not to accept graciously the burden of memory but to throw it back at the town's feet. By defining itself in opposition to the traditional memorial's task, the countermonument illustrates concisely the possibilities and limitations of all memorials everywhere. In this way, it functions as a valuable 'counterindex' to the ways time, memory, and current history intersect at any memorial site.

How better to remember forever a vanished people than by the perpetually unfinished, ever-vanishing monument? As if in mocking homage to national forebears who planned the Holocaust as a self-consuming set of events – that is, intended to destroy all traces of itself, all memory of its victims – the Gerzes have designed a self-consuming memorial that leaves behind only the rememberer and the memory of a memorial. As the self-destroying sculpture of Jean

Tinguely and others challenged the very notion of sculpture, the vanishing monument similarly challenges the idea of monumentality and its implied corollary, permanence. But while self-effacing sculpture and monuments share a few of the same aesthetic and political motivations, each also has its own reasons for vanishing. Artists like Tinguely created self-destroying sculpture in order to preempt the work's automatic commodification by a voracious art market. They hoped such works would thereby remain purely public and, by vanishing, would leave the public in a position to examine itself as part of the piece's performance. 'The viewer, in effect, [becomes] the subject of the work,' as Douglas Crimp has observed. Or, in Michael North's elaboration of this principle, 'the public *becomes* the sculpture.'[3]

The Gerzes' countermonument takes this insight several steps further. 'Art, in its conspicuousness, in its recognizability, is an indication of failure,' Jochen Gerz has said. 'If it were truly consumed, no longer visible or conspicuous, if there were only a few manifestations of art left, it would actually be where it belongs – that is, within the people for whom it was created.'[4] The counter-monument is direct heir to Gerz's ambivalence toward art's objecthood. For him, it seems, once the art object stimulates in the viewer a particular complex of ideas, emotions, and responses which then come to exist in the viewer independently of further contact with the piece of art, it can wither away, its task accomplished. By extension, once the monument moves its viewers to memory, it also becomes unnecessary and so may disappear. As a result, Gerz suggests, 'we will one day reach the point where anti-Fascist memorials will no longer be necessary, when vigilance will be kept alive by the invisible pictures of remembrance' (p. 47). 'Invisible pictures,' in this case, would correspond to our internalized images of the memorial itself, now locked into the mind's eye as a source of perpetual memory. All that remains, then, is the memory of the monument, an afterimage projected onto the landscape by the rememberer. The best monument, in Gerz's view, may be no monument at all, but only the memory of an absent monument.

The Gerzes are highly regarded in Europe as poets and photographers, and as conceptual and performance artists. In fact, much of their conceptual art conflates photographs and poetry, overlaying image with word. In their performances, they aspire simultaneously to be 'the painter, medium, paint-brush, and not just witness to a work.'[5] In their countermonument, the artists have attempted a 'performative piece' that initiates a dynamic relationship between artists, work, and viewer, in which none emerges singularly dominant. In its egalitarian conception, the countermonument would not just commem-orate the antifascist impulse but enact it, breaking down the hierarchical relationship between art object and its audience. By inviting its own violation, the monument humbles itself in the eyes of beholders accustomed to maintain-ing a respectful, decorous distance. It forces viewers to desanctify the memorial, demystify it, and become its equal. The countermonument denaturalizes what the Gerzes feel is an artificial distance between artist and public generated by the holy glorification of art. Ultimately, such a monument undermines its own authority by inviting and then incorporating the *authori*ty of passersby.

In fact, in this exchange between artist, art object, and viewer, the sense of a single authority, a single signatory, dissolves altogether: that the work was never really self-possessing and autonomous is now made palpable to viewers. The artist provides the screen, passersby add their names and graffiti to it, which causes the artist to sink the monument into the ground and open up space for a fresh exchange. It is a progressive relationship, which eventually consumes itself, leaving only the unobjectified memory of such an exchange. In its abstract form, this monument claims not to prescribe – the artists might say, dictate – a specific object of memory. Rather, it more passively accommodates all memory and response, as the blank-sided obelisk always has. It remains the obligation of passersby to enter into the art: it makes artist-rememberers and self-memorializers out of every signatory. By inviting viewers to commemorate themselves, the countermonument reminds them that to some extent all any monument can do is provide a trace of its makers, not of the memory itself.

The Gerzes' monument is an intentional visual pun: as the monument would rise up symbolically against fascism before disappearing, it calls upon us to rise up literally in its stead. It reminds us that all monuments can ever do is rise up symbolically against injustice, that the practical outcome of any artist's hard work is dissipated in its symbolic gesture. The Gerzes suggest that it is precisely the impotence of this symbolic stand that they abhor in art, the invitation to vicarious resistance, the sublimation of response in a fossilized object. In contrast, they hope that the countermonument will incite viewers, move them beyond vicarious response to the actual, beyond symbolic gesture to action.

From the beginning, the artists had intended this monument to torment – not reassure – its neighbors. They have likened it, for example, to a great black knife in the back of Germany, slowly being plunged in, each thrust solemnly commemorated by the community, a self-mutilation, a kind of topographical harakiri.[6] The countermonument objectifies for the artists not only the Germans' secret desire that all these monuments just hurry up and disappear, but also the urge to strike back at such memory, to sever it from the national body like a wounded limb. In particular, the Gerzes take mischievous, gleeful delight in the spectacle of a German city's ritual burial of an antifascist monument on which it has spent $144,000 – enough, in the words of Hamburg's disgruntled mayor, to repave ninety-seven yards of autobahn. Indeed, the fanfare and celebration of its 1986 unveiling are repeated in all subsequent lowerings, each attended by eager city politicians, invited dignitaries, and local media. That so many Germans would turn out in such good faith to cheer the destruction of a monument against fascism exemplifies, in the artists' eyes, the essential paradox in any people's attempt to commemorate its own misdeeds.

At every sinking, the artists attempt to divine a little more of the local reaction. 'What kind of monument disappears?' some citizens demand to know. 'Is it art when we write all over it?' ask teenagers. At one point, the Gerzes went from shop to shop to gather impressions, which varied from satisfaction at the attention it had generated in the commercial district to less encouraging responses. 'They ought to blow it up,' said one person. Another chimed in, 'It's not so bad as far as chimneys go, but there ought to be some smoke coming out of it.'[7] The Gerzes found that even resentment is a form of memory.

In their original conception, the Gerzes had hoped for row upon row of neatly inscribed names, a visual echo of the war memorials of another age. This black column of self-inscribed names might thus remind all visitors of their own mortality, not to mention the monument's. Execution did not follow design, however, and even the artists were taken aback by what they found after a couple of months: an illegible scribble of names scratched over names, all covered over in a spaghetti scrawl, what Jochen likened to a painting by Mark Tobey. People had come at night to scrape over all the names, even to pry the lead plating off the base. There were hearts with 'Jurgen liebt Kirsten' written inside, stars of David, and funny faces daubed in paint and marker pen. Inevitably, swastikas also began to appear: how better to remember what happened than by the Nazis' own sign? After all, Jochen insists, 'a swastika is also a signature.' In fact, when city authorities warned of the possibility of vandalism, the Gerzes had replied, 'Why not give that phenomenon free rein and allow the monument to document the social temperament in that way?[8]

The town's citizens were not as philosophical, however, and began to condemn the monument as a trap for graffiti. It was almost as if the monument taunted visitors in its ugliness. But what repels critics is not clear. Is it the monument's unsightly form or the grotesque sentiments it captures and then reflects back to the community? As a social mirror, it becomes doubly troubling in that it reminds the community of what happened then and, even worse, how they now respond to the memory of this past. To those members of the community who deplore the ease with which this work is violated, the local newspaper answered succinctly: 'The filth brings us closer to the truth than would any list of well-meaning signatures. The inscriptions, a conglomerate of approval, hatred, anger and stupidity, are like a fingerprint of our city applied to the column.'[9] The countermonument accomplishes what all monuments must: it reflects back to the people – and thus codifies – their own memorial projections and preoccupations.

Its irreverence notwithstanding, the memorial quality to most graffiti is legendary: we know Kilroy was here, that he existed, by the inscribed trace he left behind. As wall and subway graffiti came to be valued as aesthetic expressions of protest, however, they were also appropriated commercially by galleries and museums, which absorbed them as a way of naturalizing – hence neutralizing – them. (How else does one violate a graffiti-covered wall? By cleaning it?) In its gestures to both graffiti artists and to the *Mauerkunst* of the Berlin Wall, the countermonument points guiltily at its own official appropriation of guerrilla art, even as it redeems itself in its eventual self-destruction.

In addition to demonstrating the impulse toward self-memorialization and the violation of public space, some of these graffiti also betray the more repressed xenophobia of current visitors. Inscriptions like 'Ausländer raus' (Foreigners, get out) echo an antipathy toward more recent national 'guests,' as well as the defiling of Jewish cemeteries and other memorials in Germany. By retaining these words, the countermonument acknowledges that all monuments ultimately make such emendations part of their memorial texts. That is, the monument records the response of today's visitors for the benefit of tomorrow's, thus reminding all of their shared responsibility in that the recorded responses of previous visitors at a memorial site become part of one's own memory.

Finally, part of the community's mixed reaction to the countermonument may also have been its discomfort with this monument's very liveliness. Like other forms of art, the monument is most benign when static: there when you face it, gone when you turn your back. But when it begins to come to life, to grow, shrink, or change form, the monument may become threatening. No longer at the mercy of the viewer's will, it seems to have a will of its own, to beckon us at inopportune moments. Such monuments become a little like Frankenstein's monster, a golem out of the maker's control.

NOTES

Epigraph: Friedrich Nietzsche, *The Use and Abuse of History*, trans. Adrian Collins (New York: Macmillan, 1985), 13.
1. For elaboration of this theme, see Matthias Winzen, 'The Need for Public Representation and the Burden of the German Past,' *Art Journal* 48 (Winter 1989): 309–14.
2. From Claude Gintz, '"L'Anti-Monument" de Jochen et Esther Gerz,' *Galeries Magazine* 19 (June–July 1987): 87.
3. See Michael North, 'The Public as Sculpture: From Heavenly City to Mass Ornament,' *Critical Inquiry* 16 (Summer 1990): 861. As North shows, such an impulse has a long history in its own right. For further discussion of these dimensions to contemporary sculpture, see Henry M. Sayre, *The Object of Performance: The American Avant-Garde since 1970* (Chicago, 1989), Lucy R. Lippard, *Changing: Essays in Art Criticism* (New York, 1971), 261–64; Douglas Crimp, 'Serra's Public Sculpture: Redefining Site Specificity,' in Rosalind Krauss, ed. *Richard Serra/Sculpture* (New York, 1986).
4. From Doris Von Drateln, 'Jochen Gerz's Visual Poetry,' *Contemporanea* (September 1989): 47.
5. Gintz, '"Anti-Monument,"' p. 80.
6. From a public presentation by the Gerzes on the *Gegen-Denkmal* at a conference on art and the Holocaust, Evangelischen Akademie Loccum, West Germany, 20 May 1989.
   Berlin-born and speaking in German to a German audience, Jochen Gerz was making an obvious, if ironic, allusion to the Nazis' own notoriously literal-minded reference to being 'stabbed in the back' by enemies internal, external, and imagined. Appropriating the Nazis' language in this way was clearly intended both as a provocation and as an ironic self-identification by the Gerzes as 'enemies of the Reich.' See *Kunst und Holocaust: Bildiche Zeugen von Ende der Westlichen Kultur*, ed. Detlef Hoffmann and Karl Ermert (Rehburg-Loccum, Germany, 1990).

7. Quoted in Michael Gibson, 'Hamburg: Sinking Feelings,' *ARTnews* 86 (Summer 1987): 106–7.
8. Ibid., p. 106.
9. Ibid., p. 107.

PART XI
UNIQUENESS, COMPARISON, AND
THE POLITICS OF MEMORY

UNIQUENESS, COMPARISON, AND THE POLITICS OF MEMORY: INTRODUCTION

As the Holocaust has become more central to the public memory of European and North American societies since the late 1970s it has brought with it a host of difficult questions about the politics of Holocaust commemoration and the relationship of the Nazi genocide to other histories of extreme violence. Many of these questions cluster around the alleged 'uniqueness' of the Holocaust, which has become a tenet of much Holocaust scholarship and public consciousness. Some scholars, including Yehuda Bauer and Steven Katz, find it important to single out the unprecedented features of the Nazi genocide in order to ensure that the events will not be repeated. Other scholars, including Peter Novick and Norman Finkelstein, point out that all historical events are unique and argue that it becomes offensive to assert the uniqueness of one group's suffering because it may distract from the suffering of others. Such claims take on different meanings in different contexts; for example, the assertion of the Holocaust's uniqueness has a different resonance in the land of the perpetrators, Germany, than it does in the United States, a nation that has its own, frequently disavowed, violent origins and history.

In making one's way through this historical and political minefield, it may be helpful to consider three different dimensions of the uniqueness claim. First, we can consider the uniqueness of the Holocaust in the context of Jewish history. Jewish history is filled with centuries of persecution – in what ways was the Holocaust continuous or discontinuous with that history? This question not only helps situate the Holocaust in modern history but it can also lead to a better understanding of the responses of victims during the Holocaust. If those victims understood their persecution as continuous with centuries of traditional antisemitism they would respond differently than if they had grasped the events as a novel form of violence – this is James Young's argument about the 'consequences of interpretation.' Second, we can consider the uniqueness of the Holocaust in relationship to Nazi crimes against other groups, such as the Roma (Gypsies), the handicapped, homosexuals, and Slavs. While most scholars understand the treatment of Jews as occupying a qualitatively different place in the history of National Socialism than that of the other groups, the relationship between these different histories remains a highly contested area of research (see the entry by Henry Friedlander in Part II and Bauer's *Rethinking the Holocaust* for opposing views). The question becomes even more fraught when we move to the third level of the uniqueness claim: that the Holocaust is unique in relationship to all other histories throughout time and across geographies. With so much at stake for our understanding of world history and contemporary politics, it is not surprising that at this level the discussions can become especially bitter.

In this part we focus on the conceptual dimensions of uniqueness and on the Holocaust's relationship to multiple histories of extreme violence and genocide. While the writers differ from each other dramatically in terms of methodology and ideology, all are committed to identifying the particularities of histories through a comparative approach.

Alan Milchman and Alan Rosenberg open the section with a philosophical reflection on the concept of uniqueness. They argue that uniqueness should not be conceived as opposed to historicization, as many scholars of various persuasions seem to believe. Rather, the specificity of the Holocaust emerges by locating it squarely within the history of the West, as the product of what Milchman and Rosenberg call 'planetary technics and the rage against alterity.' The Israeli historian Yehuda Bauer takes a very different approach to defining the unprecedented nature of the Holocaust. In this selection, Bauer considers the coining of the word 'genocide' and remarks on its ambiguity: it can refer either to the complete or partial destruction of a people. Bauer seeks to refine the concept by differentiating between complete destruction (what he terms a Holocaust) and partial destruction (genocide). He hopes that this distinction will not serve the end of invidious comparisons, but will help people to combat different forms of mass murder.

The next three entries move away from Holocaust history into adjacent realms of atrocity. While acknowledging the uniqueness of the Holocaust, the cultural studies scholar Paul Gilroy looks to the diasporic experiences of blacks and Jews as resources for a critique of modernity from below. Inspired by Benjamin and Adorno, as well as by African diaspora scholars and cultural producers, Gilroy points to important areas for future research: 'the relationship between rationalities and racisms,' the critique of progress, 'the similar patterns of social remembrance found among Jews and blacks and the effects of protracted familiarity with ineffable, sublime terror.' The Ugandan scholar Mahmood Mamdani moves forward and backward in history from the Holocaust, and contrasts the Nazi genocide to both the recent Rwandan genocide and the early twentieth-century extermination of the Herero by German colonialists in Southwest Africa. Writing in a more polemical vein, the German-Jewish-Native-American critic Lilian Friedberg asks us to 'dare to compare' and provides a thought-provoking account of the asymmetries between responses to the Nazi genocide and the genocide of the indigenous peoples of the Americas.

Finally, Peter Novick asks why fascination with the Holocaust has emerged belatedly in places with little direct connection to the events. While his focus is on the United States, the implications of his argument extend further. Drawing on the concept of collective memory developed by Maurice Halbwachs, Novick provocatively suggests that consciousness of the Holocaust can be linked to the contemporary interests of the American-Jewish community and he asks whether Holocaust memory is actually in the best interests of that community (or others). While we continue to believe in the importance of further reflection on the Nazi genocide, Novick's challenge ought to inspire a serious assessment of the stakes of contemporary Holocaust studies.

OTHER WORKS IN HOLOCAUST STUDIES

Boyarin, Jonathan (1992) *Storm from Paradise: The Politics of Jewish Memory*. Minneapolis, MN: University of Minnesota Press.

Finkelstein, Norman (2000) *The Holocaust Industry*. New York: Verso.

Katz, Steven (1994) *The Holocaust in Historical Context*. New York: Oxford University Press.

Kramer, Jane (1996) *The Politics of Memory: Looking for Germany in the New Germany*. New York: Random House.

Levy, Daniel and Natan Sznaider (2002) 'Memory Unbound: The Holocaust and the Formation of Cosmopolitan Memory,' *European Journal of Social Theory*, 5.1.

Linenthal, Edward T. (1995) *Preserving Memory: The Struggle to Create America's Holocaust Museum*. New York: Penguin.

Melson, Robert (1992) *Revolution and Genocide: On the Origins of the Armenian Genocide and the Holocaust*. Chicago: University of Chicago Press.

Rosenbaum, Alan (ed.) (2001) *Is the Holocaust Unique?* Boulder, CO: Westview Press.

Rothberg, Michael (2001) 'W. E. B. Du Bois in Warsaw: Holocaust Memory and the Color Line, 1949–1952,' *Yale Journal of Criticism*, 14.1.

Segev, Tom (1993) *The Seventh Million: The Israelis and the Holocaust*, trans. Haim Watzman. New York: Hill & Wang.

OTHER RELEVANT WORKS

Churchill, Ward (1997) *A Little Matter of Genocide: Holocaust and Denial in the Americas, 1492 to the Present*. San Francisco: City Lights Books.

Gourevitch, Philip (1998) *We Wish to Inform You That Tomorrow We Will Be Killed with Our Families: Stories from Rwanda*. New York: Farrar, Straus, & Giroux.

Huyssen, Andreas (2001) 'Pasts Present: Media, Politics, Amnesia,' in Arjun Appadurai (ed.), *Globalization*. Durham, NC: Duke University Press, pp. 57–77.

Nora, Pierre (1989) 'Between Memory and History: *Les Lieux de Mémoire*,' *Representations*, 26: 7–25.

Sturken, Marita (1997) *Tangled Memories: The Vietnam War, the AIDS Epidemic, and the Politics of Remembering*. Berkeley, CA: University of California Press.

Toker, Leona (2000) *Return from the Archipelago: Narratives of Gulag Survivors*. Bloomington, IN: Indiana University Press.

57

'TWO KINDS OF UNIQUENESS: THE UNIVERSAL ASPECTS OF THE HOLOCAUST'

Alan Milchman and Alan Rosenberg

Of all the dilemmas, paradoxes, and enigmas facing those who study the Holocaust, the question of its uniqueness or singularity is perhaps the most vexing and divisive, the one issue most likely to generate partisan debate, and to provoke emotional heat in discussion.[1] Quite apart from the intensity with which the question of the uniqueness of the Shoah is often propounded or rejected, those involved in this debate, with some notable exceptions, are in agreement on at least one fundamental point: the issue of the singularity of the Holocaust is embedded in a series of binary oppositions. Thus, the uniqueness of the Shoah is counterposed to its historicization, the one excluding the other. Similarly, the singularity of the Holocaust is counterposed to its universality – and once again, the one excludes the other.[2]

The historicization of the Holocaust, with its insistence on the need for contextualization and by its use of comparative methods to explore the similarities as well as differences between the Holocaust and other manifestations of human-made mass-death, seems to challenge any claims for its singularity. Thus Ernst Nolte's insistence that Stalin's Gulag is comparable to the Holocaust, and that the Extermination was itself provoked by Hitler's fear of the Gulag, to which it was a desperate reaction, points to the danger of the historicization of the Holocaust becoming the occasion for its relativization, and normalization, which can even – as it does in Nolte's hands – degenerate into apologetics.[3]

From Alan Milchman and Alan Rosenberg (1996) 'Two Kinds of Uniqueness: The Universal Aspects of the Holocaust', in R. Millen (ed.), *New Perspectives on the Holocaust: A Guide for Teachers and Scholars*. New York and London: New York University Press.

Though representing a very different political perspective than Nolte's, because it involves not even the least hint of apologetics but rather insists on the extreme horror of Auschwitz, André Glucksmann's writings manifest the same binary opposition between uniqueness and historicization in their treatment of the Holocaust. For Glucksmann, the singularity of the Holocaust is elided as it is submerged in a train of barbarism, and human-made mass-death, that have punctuated the history of the West, and of modernity in particular: 'at Buchenwald and Auschwitz the Germans did indeed act in the European way, exemplifying a European (even Western, modern, revolutionary) manner of imposing "final solutions," a manner which was illustrated equally well at Pulo-Condor in Vietnam, under French and then American occupation, and, through half a century, in the Soviet Union's Kolyma.'[4] What we want to highlight here is not Glucksmann's insistence that Auschwitz was a product of European or Western civilization, nor his use of comparisons with other cases of modern barbarism, both of which seem to us to be sound, but rather the ease with which the uniqueness of the Shoah simply vanishes in a discourse which historicizes.[5]

The recourse to binary oppositions is no less evident when the question of the singularity of the Holocaust encounters the claims for its universality. Thus, Elie Wiesel has passionately argued that the uniqueness of the Holocaust is such that it cannot even be designated an event in history: 'the universe of concentration camps, by its design, lies outside if not beyond history. Its vocabulary belongs to it alone.'[6] Such a view sees the Shoah as a transcendent event, unconnected to the trajectory of our techno-scientific civilization sprung from the sociocultural matrix of the West; its singularity is such that it exceeds the power of language to express it: the Holocaust is finally ineffable.

[...]

In this paper, we intend to argue for the uniqueness of the Shoah. However, our own conception of that uniqueness seeks to explode the binary oppositions in which this question has been entangled. For us, the very singularity of the Holocaust must be integrally linked to its historicization, and contextualization, which perforce will involve comparisons, aimed at elucidating similarities as well as distinctions between different manifestations of human-made mass-death. Contextualization, and the comparative method, far from eliminating the unique elements of the Holocaust, in our view can highlight its singularity, even as they focus our attention on its similarities to other exterminatory events. In much the same fashion, we will insist that the singularity of the Extermination is inextricably bound to its universality. The Holocaust world that emerged in all its singularity, albeit in an incipient form at Auschwitz, and the other Nazi death camps, has now become an objective-real possibility on the front of history.

[...]

We now want to turn to the complex of factors that lead us to insist on the uniqueness of the Holocaust, even as we argue for both its historicization and its universality. The claim of 'uniqueness' is intended to set apart from other historical events, to distinguish in the flow of history, just that singular event that has the potential of transforming a culture, or altering the course of history, in a profound or decisive way. We believe that the Holocaust was just such a transformational event. Indeed, following Phillipe Lacoue-Labarthe, we can best describe the Holocaust – or to use Lacoue-Labarthe's terminology, 'the Extermination' – as a caesura in global history.[7] For Lacoue-Labarthe, a 'caesura would be that which, within history, interrupts history and opens up another possibility of history, or else closes off all possibility of history.'[8] The German-Jewish historian and social theorist, Dan Diner, has expressed the transformational character of Auschwitz by his designation of it as a *Zivilisationsbruch*, or break or rupture in civilization.[9] Tropes such as a caesura, or *Zivilisationsbruch*, are intended to make manifest the starkness of the transformation wrought by the Extermination, to emphasize the uniqueness of the event, which rent the very fabric of civilization. The Holocaust, of which Auschwitz is emblematic, opened a door into a world in which human-made mass-death can become constitutive of the sociocultural matrix.

While constituting the novum that opened a door into a possible Holocaust world, Auschwitz also closed a door on another world, the world shaped by the dream of the imminent dawn of perpetual peace, and the idea of inevitable and continuous progress, that had been one strand of the Enlightenment project. [...]

Yet the caesura that was Auschwitz did not appear out of nowhere. As Claude Lanzmann has insisted,

> To say that the Holocaust is unique and incommensurable does not imply that it is an aberration that eludes all intellectual and conceptual comprehension, which falls outside history and is denied the dignity of being a historical event. On the contrary, we consider the Holocaust to be a completely historical event, the legitimate, albeit monstrous, product of the entire history of the Western world.[10]

Linking the Holocaust, and its uniqueness, to the history of the West, however, raises several crucial questions. It is important to avoid the trap of a teleological reading of the history of the West, in which the Holocaust becomes fate, the preordained outcome of the flow of history. While Lanzmann's formulation may be open to such a reading, Lacoue-Labarthe seems to us to have fallen clearly into just that trap when he asserts that 'in the Auschwitz apocalypse, it was nothing less than the West, in its essence, that revealed itself.'[11] History is not the revelation of essences; indeed, the whole vocabulary of essence, and its revelation, must be suspect. Teleology apart, Lanzmann's formulation is questionable because it totalizes, and demonizes, the history of the West. We too believe that the Holocaust is the outcome of profound tendencies integral to the project of the West, but that project, that history, cannot be reduced to an antechamber to Auschwitz.

In contextualizing the Holocaust firmly within the history of the West, we must be clear as to just which facets of its project could have produced the Shoah, and warrant its designation as unique. The Israeli historian, Otto Dov Kulka, expanding on the pathbreaking work of Shmuel Ettinger, has argued that the singularity of the Holocaust derives from the centrality of anti-Semitism to the Nazi project. However, in a bold move, Kulka links this anti-Semitism to the whole trajectory of the West, where it constitutes a leitmotiv of its cultural history. For Kulka, anti-Semitism is not merely an expression of conservative or reactionary trends which have opposed the project of modernity, which is where most historians locate the phenomenon, but of the very 'progressive' tendencies arising in the Enlightenment and providing the cultural dynamic for the project of modernity.[12] Far from making the anti-Semitism that he finds central to the Shoah the occasion for interpreting it as a transcendent event, Kulka's argument for the singularity of the Holocaust rests on its historicization; for Kulka, 'the "Jewish Question" was placed at the heart of an historical event [the Holocaust] that can be regarded as the gravest and most menacing crisis of Western civilization: an attempt to revolt against the roots of its very existence.'[13]

[...]

While the understanding of the role of anti-Semitism in the singularity of the Holocaust cannot be separated from its contextualization in the history of the West, we cannot reduce the uniqueness of the Extermination to its choice of victim. Hannah Arendt's strictures in this regard cannot be ignored: 'Anti-Semitism by itself has such a long and bloody history that the very fact that the death factories were chiefly fed with Jewish "material" has somewhat obliterated the uniqueness of this operation.'[14] It is not only that anti-Semitism has been a constant in the history of the West, whereas the exterminatory project, and its actualization in the death camps, was a novum, that led Arendt to look beyond the Jewish question for the bases of the uniqueness of the Holocaust. It was the 'nonutilitarian character' of the camps, their senselessness in terms of instrumental reason, that seemed to her one of the bases for distinguishing the death camps from earlier orgies of bloodletting, whatever the nature of their victims.[15]

Nonetheless, we want to insist on two other factors firmly ensconced within the project of modernity which seem to us to be integral to designating the Holocaust as unique: the reign of planetary technics and the rage against alterity.

In the Shoah, the practice of mass-murder and genocide, which had previously occurred in history, was inextricably linked to the very development of science and modern technology. One of the crucial distinctions between the death-world created by the Nazis, and orgies of mass-murder before and even after (as in Bosnia today), was the technical efficiency and organization of the Holocaust. The Shoah was made possible by the ruthless application of the prodigious creations of twentieth-century science and technology. This is not simply a matter of the actual instruments of death, for as Steven T. Katz has pointed out, 'death by gas was not a major technological advance as compared with, say, the jet engine, radar, and sonar, the Nazis' own V1 and V2 rockets, or, above all else as a qualitative breakthrough, the atomic bomb.'[16] Nonetheless, Zyklon B, and the crematoria, as instruments of death, were far more technically sophisticated than the guns of the Einsatzgruppen, or the deliberate torture, starvation, or working to death of millions in the Gulag. Indeed, they were the fruits of the same nexus of technological and scientific productivity that resulted in the atomic bomb, and upon which our late-twentieth-century civilization now rests. More pertinent, perhaps, is the fact that the direct instruments of death were themselves inserted into a matrix that was the culmination of the West's technological development – transport, record-keeping, surveillance – which made possible the industrialization of mass-death that was a unique characteristic of the Holocaust.

[...]

In the Holocaust, perhaps for the first time in human history, science and technology, together with their bases in planetary technics, were joined in the effort to totally exterminate the Other, alterity itself – in that instance in the form of the Jews. The more the inexorable 'progress' of techno-scientific civilization atomizes human beings, and shatters the bonds of communities, the more the modern state is compelled to fabricate a 'pseudo-community' based on a mass mobilization around populist-nationalist ideologies. Such 'pseudo-communities' are less an effort to return to a premodern world, than an adaptation of techno-scientific civilization to a situation that its basic conditions of existence may have rendered irreversible. Absolute rage at the Other, at alterity itself, is the counterpart to the effort to create 'pseudo-communities' within the shell of modernity. The Other is a nonperson in a 'pseudo-community' which demonizes him, victimizes her – and then erases them from its collective memory. In Hitler's Germany, the Jews were the embodiment of alterity, the Other, a scourge to be exterminated.

If the Holocaust was, to use Blanchot's words, 'the absolute event of history,'[17] then its uniqueness, we believe, lies in its unprecedented combination of the utilization of all the fruits of planetary technics, and its science and technology, in the service of the total elimination of the Other. It is precisely this singularity that confers universality on the Holocaust. The elements out of which the Holocaust emerged remain features integral to our modernity. Planetary technics and the rage against alterity await a political movement which can recombine them, perhaps with a lethality comparable to that of the Nazis. [...]

The universality of the Holocaust lies precisely in the fact that its constituent elements, those that stamped it with its singularity, are overripe in our techno-scientific civilization, and that the cry that arose from the ashes at Auschwitz, 'never again!', may prove to have been futile.

NOTES

1. For an overview of the intense debate over the singularity of the Holocaust and an annotated bibliography of some of the most important literature see Alan Rosenberg and Evelyn Silverman, 'The Issue of the Holocaust as a Unique Event' in Michael N. Dobkowski and Isidore Wallimann, *Genocide in Our Time: An Annotated Bibliography with Analytical Introductions* (Ann Arbor, Mich.: Pierian Press, 1992).

2. Though our own view is quite different from his, among scholars of the Holocaust, Steven T. Katz is one of the few who insists on viewing its uniqueness in a historical, and comparative, perspective. See the essays collected in his *Historicism, the Holocaust, and Zionism: Critical Studies in Modern Jewish Thought and History* (New York: New York University Press, 1992), as well as his *The Holocaust in Historical Context*, vol. 1 (Oxford: Oxford University Press, 1994), the first of three volumes.

3. See Ernst Nolte, 'Between Historical Legend and Revisionism? The Third Reich in the Perspective of 1980,' and 'The Past that Will Not Pass: A Speech that Could Be Written but Not Delivered,' both in James Knowlton and Truett Cates, trans., *Forever in the Shadow of Hitler? Original Documents of the Historikerstreit: The Controversy concerning the Singularity of the Holocaust* (Atlantic Highlands, N.J.: Humanities Press, 1993). It is important to note that Nolte, in contrast to Paul Rassinier or Robert Faurisson, is no 'denier' who controverts the existence of the death camps, but a relativizer, or 'trivializer,' for whom the Holocaust loses its uniqueness in the midst of the many other examples of human-made mass-death which have made the twentieth century so bloody.

4. André Glucksmann, *The Master Thinkers* (New York: Harper and Row, 1980), 44. In his most recent work, *Le XIe Commandement*, Glucksmann extends his analysis of 'final solutions' to include the butcheries perpetrated by Third World dictators such as Khomeini and Saddam Hussein, subsuming the human-made mass-death inflicted on its subjects by the state under a kind of 'fundamentalism' or ideological will-to-mastery that originated in European civilization, but which has now become global.

5. Two other examples of the binary opposition between singularity and historicization are apposite here. William V. Spanos has argued that insisting on the uniqueness of the Holocaust will make us insensitive to other cases of human-made mass-death that punctuate the history of the West to the present day, for example the horrors inflicted on the Vietnamese by the United States, 'a violence that was also racist and genocidal and thus in some fundamental sense commensurate in its horrible consequences for the Vietnamese people with the horror of the Nazi project to exterminate the Jews.' See William V. Spanos, *Heidegger and Criticism: Retrieving the Cultural Politics of Destruction* (Minneapolis: University of Minnesota Press, 1993), 220. Detlev J. K. Peukert has contended that the insistence on the singularity of the Shoah and its Jewish victims obscures the fate of other victims of the Nazi terror: 'The thesis of the "singularity" of the Holocaust is to be rejected because, consciously or not, it hierarchizes the victims of the National Socialist machinery of destruction.' See Detlev J. K. Peukert, 'Alltag and Barbarei: Zur Normalität des Dritten Reiches' in Dan Diner, *Ist der Nationalsozialismus Geschichte? Zur Historisierung und Historikerstreit* (Frankfurt am Main: Fischer Taschenbuch Verlag, 1987), 54. As long as singularity and historicization are viewed in terms of binary oppositions, either the specificity of the fate of the Jews or the agonizing cries of the other victims of mass-death are bound to be slighted.

6. Elie Wiesel, 'Now We Know' in Richard Arens, ed., *Genocide in Paraguay* (Philadelphia: Temple University Press, 1976), 165.

7. Lacoue-Labarthe speaks of the history of the West. In fact, the expansion of the West and its techno-scientific civilization, encompassing virtually the whole planet in the course of the twentieth century, is tending to create an effectively global history.

8. Philippe Lacoue-Labarthe, *Heidegger, Art, and Politics: The Fiction of the Political* (Oxford: Basil Blackwell, 1990), 45.

9. Dan Diner, 'Between Aporia and Apology: On the Limits of Historicizing National Socialism' in Peter Baldwin, ed., *Reworking the Past: Hitler, the Holocaust, and the Historians' Debate* (Boston: Beacon Press, 1990), 143, translation modified. For a collection of essays devoted to German-Jewish thinkers who viewed the Holocaust as a *Zivilisationsbruch*, including Theodor W. Adorno, Max Horkheimer, Leo Löwenthal, Hannah Arendt, Günther Anders, and Ernst Bloch, see Dan Diner, ed., *Zivilisationsbruch: Denken nach Auschwitz* (Frankfurt am Main: Fischer Taschenbuch Verlag, 1988).

10. Claude Lanzmann, 'From the Holocaust to the *Holocaust*' in *Telos*, no. 42 (Winter 1979–80): 137–38. [...]

11. Lacoue-Labarthe, *Heidegger, Art, and Politics*, 35.

12. Otto Dov Kulka, 'Critique of Judaism in European Thought: On the Historical Meaning of Modern Anti-Semitism' in *The Jerusalem Quarterly*, no. 52 (Fall 1989): 141–44.

13. Ibid., 141. [...]

14. Hannah Arendt, 'Social Science Techniques and the Study of Concentration Camps' in Alan Rosenberg and Gerald E. Myers, eds., *Echoes from the Holocaust: Philosophical Reflections on a Dark Time* (Philadelphia: Temple University Press, 1988), 367.

15. Ibid., 366. Dan Diner also points to the 'antirationality' and negation of instrumental reason as the conceptual key to the uniqueness of the Holocaust. See Diner, 'Between Aporia and Apology,' 143–44.

16. Steven T. Katz, 'Technology and Genocide: Technology as a "Form of Life"' in Katz, *Historicism, the Holocaust, and Zionism*, 195.

17. Maurice Blanchot, *The Writing of the Disaster* (Lincoln: University of Nebraska Press, 1986), 47.

58

'WHAT WAS THE HOLOCAUST?'

Yehuda Bauer

[...]

The term *genocide* was coined by Raphael Lemkin, a refugee Polish-Jewish lawyer in the United States, in late 1942 or early 1943. Lemkin's definition is contradictory. On the one hand, he defines *genocide* as the 'destruction of a nation or of an ethnic group ... Generally speaking, genocide does not necessarily mean the immediate destruction of a nation. It is intended rather to signify a coordinated plan of different actions aiming at the destruction of essential foundations of the life of national groups, with the aim of annihilating the groups themselves.'[1] (It seems that he intends to say 'the groups as such,' not necessarily all the individuals in them.) Yet in the preface of the same book he says that 'the practice of extermination of nations and ethnic groups ... is called by the author "genocide".' The destruction of the essential foundations of national life includes, according to Lemkin, the destruction of the national economic structure, its religious institutions, its moral fiber, its education system, and, always, selective mass killings of parts of the targeted population.[2] What he describes are two distinct alternatives: one, a radical and murderous denationalization accompanied by mass murder, which destroys the group as an entity but leaves many or most of the individuals composing it alive; the other, murder of every single individual of the targeted group. It may perhaps be argued that partial mass annihilation leads to total extermination.

From Yehuda Bauer (2001) 'What Was the Holocaust?', in *Rethinking the Holocaust*. New Haven, CT: Yale University Press.

But this is not what Lemkin says, though such a possibility certainly cannot be discounted.

The discussion here is not just academic. Lemkin's definitions were adopted, in large part, by the United Nations. In the Genocide Convention, approved on December 9, 1948, *genocide* is defined as 'any of the following acts committed with the intent to destroy, in whole or in part, a national, ethnical or religious group, as such.' Again, both meanings are included, and the phrase 'in whole or in part' indicates that what is meant is not the development of partial destruction into total murder but two variations that do not necessarily follow one upon the other.

The historical context for Lemkin's work in early 1943 consisted of the information he possessed as to what was happening to Poles, Czechs, Serbs, Russians, and others. Horrifying information had been received concerning the fate of the Jews, but decent human beings evinced an understandable reluctance to believe that the accounts were literally and completely true. What was happening to some of these people, mainly perhaps the Poles, fitted Lemkin's description of denationalization accompanied by selective mass murder. It seems that he made his definition fit real historical developments as he saw them; the vagueness with which he contemplates the possibility of murdering all Jews reflects the state of consciousness in America of the Jewish fate.

We then come to 1948. The United Nations is not a symposium of scholars – far from it. Documents emerging from that quarter are less than perfect, because they reflect political pressures and horse trading between states. Thus, unsuccessful pressure was exercised in 1948 to include, for instance, the destruction of political groups within the definition of genocide. The inclusion of religious groups – not a part of Lemkin's definition – was accepted after a long struggle. The lack of consistency in the U.N. convention is apparent the moment we continue the quotation: Genocide, it says, means any of the following acts: '(a) Killing members of the group; (b) Causing serious bodily or mental harm to members of the group; (c) Deliberately inflicting on the group conditions of life calculated to bring about its physical destruction in whole or in part; (d) Imposing measures intended to prevent births within the group; (e) Forcibly transferring children of the group to another group.'[3] We again see inclusion of both partial and total destruction.

The conclusion to draw is that one ought to differentiate between the intent to destroy a group in a context of selective mass murder and the intent to annihilate every person of that group. To make this as simple as possible, I would suggest retaining the term *genocide* for 'partial' murder and the term *Holocaust* for total destruction. I will argue that *Holocaust* can be used in two ways: to describe what happened to the Jews at Nazi hands and to describe what might happen to others if the Holocaust of the Jewish people becomes a precedent for similar actions. Whichever way *Holocaust* is used, it and *genocide* are clearly connected, they belong to the same species of human action, and the differences between them remain to be seen, beyond the obvious one of partial versus total destruction.

The next point to consider is crucial: which groups to describe when we talk about genocide. Lemkin talked only about national or ethnic groups, and he would probably have agreed to extend his category to include so-called racial groups. The U.N. convention adds religious groups. A number of scholars have added political groups as well.[4] Neither of these last two additions makes much sense. People persecuted because of their religious beliefs can, in principle if not always in practice, go over to the persecutors' religious faith and save themselves. [...]

The same applies to political persecutees. Even in Soviet Russia, joining the Communist Party was often – not always – a way of avoiding stigmatization as 'bourgeois.' [...] In Nazi Germany, millions of Communists became loyal Nazis.

For both religious and political groups, membership is a matter of choice – again, in principle, if not always in practice. One can change one's religion or one's political color. One cannot change one's ethnicity or nationality or 'race' – only the persecutor can do that, as the Germans did when they 'Germanized' Polish adults and children. Without such action, there is absolutely no way out for the member of a targeted ethnic or national group: that person is a Pole, or a Rom ('Gypsy'), or a Jew, or a Serb. Hence my conclusion that the term *genocide* should be used only for attacks on the groups specified by Lemkin.

Genocide, then, is the planned attempt to destroy a national, ethnic, or racial group using measures like those outlined by Lemkin and the U.N. convention, measures that accompany the selective mass murder of members of the targeted group. Holocaust is a radicalization of genocide: a planned attempt to physically annihilate every single member of a targeted ethnic, national, or racial group.

How important is such a definition? It may help us differentiate between different crimes against humanity, the ultimate purpose of such analyses being to help lessen, and in some future perhaps do away with, such horrors. In the end, as I have pointed out, reality is more complicated by far than our attempts to describe it. I would therefore suggest that these definitions be used to describe a continuum of human mass destruction. One could even use the term *self-destruction*, because by destroying other humans, the perpetrators very radically diminish their own humanity. Such an approach may well use the paradigms proposed by Rudolph J. Rummel in his books *Democide* and *Death by Government*.[5]

According to Rummel, between 1900 and 1987 close to 170 million civilians (and disarmed POWs) were killed by governments and quasi-governmental organizations (political parties, etc.), the overwhelming majority of them by nondemocratic regimes. He calls this phenomenon 'democide' (killing of people). He says that 38 million of the people killed were victims of genocide (he uses the definition of the U.N. convention), and close to 6 million of those were killed in the Holocaust. There is no reason not to expand Rummel's paradigm to include wars which are reciprocal mass murders committed by opposing groups of people, usually males, distinguished from one another by funny clothes called uniforms; such mass murders, too, are committed at the instigation of governments and quasi-governmental organizations. Adding wars gives us a continuum of human actions of deadly violence ranging from wars, via the murder of civilians for a vast variety of reasons, to genocide and Holocaust. This does not mean that wars are 'better' than genocides, nor that the mass murder of civilians is less reprehensible than genocide; it does mean that there are obvious connections between all these, and that occasionally one form merges into another.

No gradation of human suffering is possible. A soldier who lost a leg and a lung at Verdun suffered. How can one measure his suffering against the horrors that Japanese civilians endured at Hiroshima? How can one measure the suffering of a Rom woman at Auschwitz, who saw her husband and children die in front of her eyes, against the suffering of a Jewish woman at the same camp who underwent the same experience? Extreme forms of human suffering are not comparable, and one should never say that one form of mass murder is 'less terrible,' or even 'better,' than another. The difference between the Holocaust and less radical genocides lies not in the amount of sadism or the depth of hellish suffering, but elsewhere. [...]

NOTES

1. Raphael Lemkin, *Axis Rule in Occupied Europe*, Howard Fertig, New York, 1973, pp. 79 ff.
2. Lemkin, pp. xi–xii.
3. Yehuda Bauer, 'The Holocaust in Contemporary History,' *Studies in Contemporary Jewry*, no. 1, Jerusalem, 1984, p. 204.
4. As in Frank Chalk and Kurt Jonassohn, *The History and Sociology of Genocide*, Yale University Press, New Haven, 1990, p. 23; Frank Chalk, 'Definitions of Genocide and Their Implication for Prediction and Prevention,' *Holocaust and Genocide Studies*, vol. 4, no. 2, 1989, pp. 149–160; Kurt Jonassohn, 'Prevention Without Prediction,' *Holocaust and Genocide Studies*, vol. 7, no. 1, 1993, pp. 1–13.
5. Rudolph J. Rummel, *Democide*, Transaction Press, New Brunswick, N.J., 1992; Rummel, *Death by Government*, Transaction Press, New Brunswick, N.J., 1995. Rummel has been criticized for exaggerating the losses. Even if the criticisms were valid, a figure lower by 10 or 20 or even 30 percent would make absolutely no difference to the general conclusions that Rummel draws.

59

THE BLACK ATLANTIC

Paul Gilroy

[...]

It is often forgotten that the term 'diaspora' comes into the vocabulary of black studies and the practice of pan-Africanist politics from Jewish thought. It is used in the Bible[1] but begins to acquire something like its looser contemporary usage during the late nineteenth century – the period which saw the birth of modern Zionism and of the forms of black nationalist thought which share many of its aspirations and some of its rhetoric. The themes of escape and suffering, tradition, temporality, and the social organisation of memory have a special significance in the history of Jewish responses to modernity. From this source they flow into the work of several generations of Jewish cultural and religious historians, literary critics, and philosophers who have delved into the relationship between modernity and anti-Semitism and into the roles of rationalism and irrationalism in the development of European racist thought.[2] In these settings, the same themes are associated with the ideas of dispersal, exile, and slavery. They also help to frame the problem of simultaneous intra- and intercultural change which has engaged Jewish thinkers in Europe from the eighteenth century onwards.

Some of these discussions, particularly the contributions from writers whose relationship to Jewish lore and law was remote or ambivalent, have been a rich resource for me in thinking about the problems of identity and difference in the black Atlantic diaspora.[3] In the preparation of this book I have been repeatedly

From Paul Gilroy (1994) ' "Not a Story to Pass On": Living Memory and the Slave Sublime', in *The Black Atlantic: Modernity and Double Consciousness*. Cambridge, MA: Harvard University Press.

drawn to the work of Jewish thinkers in order to find both inspiration and resources with which to map the ambivalent experiences of blacks inside and outside modernity. [...]

[...]

It is important to emphasise that any correspondences that can be identified between the histories of blacks and Jews take on a radically different significance after the Holocaust. I want to resist the idea that the Holocaust is merely another instance of genocide. I accept arguments for its uniqueness. However, I do not want the recognition of that uniqueness to be an obstacle to better understanding of the complicity of rationality and ethnocidal terror to which this book is dedicated. This is a difficult line on which to balance but it should be possible, and enriching, to discuss these histories together. This can be done without the development of an absurd and dangerous competition and without lapsing into a relativising mode that would inevitably be perceived as an insult.[4] There are a number of issues raised by literature on the Holocaust which have helped me to focus my own inquiries into the uncomfortable location of blacks within modernity. However, it seems appropriate to ask at this point why many blacks and Jews have been reluctant about initiating such a conversation. I want to argue that its absence weakens all our understanding of what modern racism is and undermines arguments for its constitutive power as a factor of social division in the modern world. The way that the history of scientific racism and eugenics in the Americas has been overlooked as a factor in the development of German racial science provides a striking example of this failure.[5] Black and Jewish writers have missed untold opportunities to develop this critical dialogue. Zygmunt Bauman, for example, whose work offers a wealth of insights into the complicity of rationality with racial terror and the advantages of marginality as a hermeneutic standpoint, discusses the relationship between racism and anti-Semitism without even mentioning the Americas let alone exploring the significant connections between what he calls the gardening state and the plantation state and the colonial state. Whether born of ignorance or disregard, his view of the Jews as 'the *only* "non-national nation"'[6] (emphasis added) and the only group 'caught in the most ferocious of historical conflicts: that between the pre-modern world and advancing modernity'[7] typifies a Eurocentrism that detracts from the richness of his intellectual legacy. [...]

Bauman's indifference to or ignorance of the extent to which the Eurocentric conception of modernity forecloses on a sense of the relationship between anti-black racism in and after slavery and anti-Semitism in Europe supplies a depressing counterpart to the nullity and banality of similarly indifferent 'Africentric' thinking in which themes like the involvement of Jews in the slave trade are invoked as simple eloquent facts without the need of interpretation. Bauman's rather cursory discussion of racism in *Modernity and the Holocaust* fits very neatly with his attempts elsewhere to lodge the dynamic interplay between modernity and ethnic particularity into the overloaded encounter between friends, enemies, and strangers and a model of the cultural politics of assimilation derived from their interaction. [...] The slaves stood opposed to their masters and mistresses as neither simply enemies nor strangers. Their relationships with those who owned them were governed by shifting modes of ambivalence and antipathy, intimacy and loathing, which engage Bauman so much in other settings, but his analysis comes nowhere near touching the complex dynamics of the master-mistress-slave relationship. [...]

As in so many discussions of the scope and status of the concept of modernity, the issue of science becomes a pivotal matter, not least because it has such profound consequences for the final verdict upon rationality. Robert Proctor, Richard M. Lerner, and Benno Muller Hill[8] have been some of the very few voices prepared to speculate about the links between histories allocated to different academic specialisms and commanded by different political constituencies. Their work can be used to make a powerful case for showing that European eugenics developed closely in step with American racial science and received substantial encouragement from the development of colonial social relations.

It bears repetition that exploring these relationships need not in any way undermine the uniqueness of the Holocaust. It is therefore essential not to use that invocation of uniqueness to close down the possibility that a combined if not comparative discussion of its horrors and their patterns of legitimation might be fruitful in making sense of modern racisms. This may be an especially urgent task in Europe, where the lines of descent linking contemporary racisms with the Nazi movement are hard to overlook but have posed a series of insoluble questions for anti-racist political organisations. Perhaps amidst the forms of ethnic and racial jeopardy consequent upon the reactivation of European fascism it might be possible to ask whether that uniqueness might be more carefully specified? Primo Levi, whose thoughtful studies of the grey 'zone of ambiguity which irradiates around regimes based on terror and obsequiousness'[9] have deepened our understanding of what racial slavery must have meant, can contribute something here. Levi speaks from a position that exemplifies the strengths of an understanding of the uniqueness of the Holocaust that is not prescriptive because it exists in a dialectical relationship with a sense of the ubiquity and normality of similar events. For example, he draws attention to the fact that a system of slave labour was one of the three core purposes of the concentration camps along with 'the elimination of political adversaries and the extermination of the so-called inferior races.' He links the issue of slavery to what he calls the useless violence of the camp experience but also to an argument about the ambiguous insertion of the camps into the normal economic structures of German society.[10] Levi's work can be used to specify other elements of the camp experience that might be used in a preliminary way to locate the parameters of a new approach to the history of those modern terrors that exhaust the capacity of language. His arguments about the nature of the journey to the camp and the condition of namelessness into which new inmates were inducted have the most ready equivalents in the literature and history of racial slavery in the new world. The value of combining these histories or at least of placing them relative to one another in the same conceptual scheme is a better indictment of the bourgeois humanist ideology which is clearly implicated in the suffering of both groups.[11] This is no trifling matter for, as Martin Bernal has recently demonstrated, anti-Semitism and racism are closely associated in nineteenth-century historiography and remain largely unacknowledged factors in the history of the human sciences.

The small world of black cultural and intellectual history is similarly populated by those who fear that the integrity of black particularity could be compromised by attempts to open a complex dialogue with other con-sciousnesses of affliction. Political urgency apart, some of the pivotal themes which make such a dialogue possible are the relationship between rationalities and racisms, the repudiation of the ideology of progress by the racially subordinated who have lubricated its wheels with their unfree labour, the similar patterns of social remembrance found among Jews and blacks and the effects of protracted familiarity with ineffable, sublime terror on the devel-opment of a political (anti)aesthetics. There are dangers for both blacks and Jews in accepting their historic and unsought association with sublimity. One has only to recall Nietzsche's attempts in *Dawn* to invest his hopes for the regeneration of mankind in the Jews to see the ambiguities inherent in this legacy.

This idea of a special redemptive power produced through suffering has its ready counterparts in the writings of black thinkers who have, at various times, identified similar relationships between the history of modern racial slavery and the redemption of both Africa and America. The capacity of blacks to redeem and transform the modern world through the truth and clarity of perception that emerge from their pain is, for example, a familiar element in the theology of Martin Luther King, Jr.,[12] which argues not only that black suffering has a meaning but that its meaning could be externalised and amplified so that it could be of benefit to the moral status of the whole world. Equally ambiguous is the use which some black thinkers have made of models of cultural struggle derived from a reading of the role that Jewish intellectuals have played in developing the political interests of their community. In this approach, the Jews supply a strategy which some black intellectuals try to emulate. They seek to follow the precedent established by Jewish thinkers who are thought to have been able to make the suffering of their people part of the ethical agenda of the West as a whole:

> The Jew's suffering is recognized as part of the moral history of the world and the Jew is recognized as a contributor to the world's history: this is not true for blacks. Jewish history, whether or not one can say it is honoured, is certainly known: the black history has been blasted, maligned, and despised. The Jew is a white man, and when white men rise up against

oppression they are heroes: when black men rise they have reverted to their native savagery. The uprising in the Warsaw ghetto was not described as a riot, nor were the participants maligned as hoodlums: the boys and girls in Watts and Harlem are thoroughly aware of this, and it certainly contributes to their attitudes toward the Jews.[13]

These are James Baldwin's words. Baldwin is important to this aspect of black Atlantic political culture because he has been identified by both Harold Cruse[14] and Stanley Crouch as the progenitor of a strategy for black expression in which victims are first blessed and then required to play a special role in illuminating and transforming the world. Cruse deals harshly with Baldwin, but both of them end up enamoured of the role that Jewish intellectuals have played in consolidating the interests and self-consciousness of their communities through systematic cultural activism. Cruse sees this group as 'propagandists' capable of supplying the Zionist cause with an 'inner strength.' He suggests that their activities point towards a black 'cultural nationalism' equivalent to that which has made Jewish intellectuals a force to be reckoned with in America. Baldwin, on the other hand, sees 'a genuinely candid confrontation between American Negroes and American Jews' as 'of inestimable value'[15] – an essential pre-condition for the emancipation of American blacks. Baldwin's approach is doubly relevant here because he has also been identified by Crouch as the source of a political theory of black culture which has played a uniquely destructive role in the development of 'racial letters.' Crouch places Toni Morrison's novel *Beloved* in the shadow of this theory of art which is for him merely a theory of black martyrdom in which the downtrodden were canonised before their misery could be sifted for its special, moral magic. He attacks the novel as a list of atrocities rather than an explanation of 'the mystery of human motive and behaviour.'[16] His final, cruel charge against Morrison is that 'Beloved, above all else, is a blackface holocaust novel.' It is, he continues, a book that 'seems to have been written in order to enter American slavery in the big-time martyr ratings contest.' I do not accept that this is either Morrison's intention or the inevitable effect of her moving excursion into the relationship between terror and memory, sublimity and the impossible desire to forget the unforgettable. [...]

What would be the consequences if the book had tried to set the Holocaust of European Jews in a provocative relationship with the modern history of racial slavery and terror in the western hemisphere? Crouch dismisses without considering it the possibility that there might be something useful to be gained from setting these histories closer to each other not so as to compare them, but as precious resources from which we might learn something valuable about the way that modernity operates, about the scope and status of rational human conduct, about the claims of science, and perhaps most importantly about the ideologies of humanism with which these brutal histories can be shown to have been complicit.

[...]

NOTES

1. Deuteronomy 28: 25.
2. A. Hertzberg, *The French Enlightenment and the Jews* (New York: Columbia University Press, 1990); L. Poliakov, *The History of Anti-Semitism*, vol. 1 (Oxford: Oxford University Press, 1985); Zygmunt Bauman, *Modernity and the Holocaust* (Cambridge: Polity, 1988), and *Intimations of Postmodernity* (London: Routledge, 1991); Leon Poliakov, *The Aryan Myth* (London: Sussex University Press, 1974); Gershom Scholem, *From Berlin to Jerusalem: Memories of My Youth*, trans. Harry Zohn (New York: Schocken Books, 1980), and *The Messianic Idea in Judaism and Other Essays on Jewish Spirituality* (New York: Schocken, 1971); George Mosse, *Nationalism and Sexuality* (Madison: University of Wisconsin Press, 1985); Paul Lawrence Rose, *Revolutionary Anti-Semitism in Germany from Kant to Wagner* (Princeton, N.J.: Princeton University Press, 1990).
3. Robert Alter, *Necessary Angels: Tradition and Modernity in Kafka, Benjamin, and Scholem* (Cambridge, Mass.: Harvard University Press, 1991), ch. 2, 'On Not Knowing Hebrew.'
4. This charge is made by Michael Burleigh and Wolfgang Wippermann in *The Racial State: Germany, 1933–1945* (Cambridge: Cambridge University Press, 1991).
5. Robert Proctor's book *Racial Hygiene: Medicine under the Nazis* (Cambridge, Mass.: Harvard University Press, 1988) is a rare and valuable exception to this rule.
6. Zygmunt Bauman, *Intimations of Postmodernity* (London: Routledge, 1991), p. 225.
7. Zygmunt Bauman, *Modernity and the Holocaust* (Cambridge: Polity Press, 1989), p. 45.
8. Richard M. Lerner, *Final Solutions: Biology, Prejudice and Genocide* (University Park: Pennsylvania State University Press, 1992); Benno Muller Hill, *Murderous Science: Elimination by Scientific Selection of Jews, Gypsies and Others, Germany, 1933–1945* (Oxford: Oxford University Press, 1988). Bauman discusses this work and the work of Robert Proctor in ch. 1 of his *Modernity and Ambivalence* (Ithaca: Cornell University Press, 1991).
9. Primo Levi, *The Drowned and the Saved* (London: Abacus, 1988), p. 41.
10. Ibid., p. 100.
11. Jean-François Lyotard, *The Inhuman* (Cambridge: Polity, 1992).
12. Keith D. Miller, *Voice of Deliverance: The Language of Martin Luther King and Its Sources* (New York: Free Press, 1992); Cornel West, 'The Religious Foundations of the Thought of Martin Luther King, Jr.,' in Peter J. Albert and Ronald Hoffman, eds., *We Shall Overcome: Martin Luther King and the Black Freedom Struggle* (New York: Pantheon, 1990). See also James H. Cone, *For My People: Black Theology and the Black Church* (Braamfontein: Skotaville Publishers, 1985).
13. James Baldwin, 'Negroes Are Anti-Semitic Because They Are Anti-White,' in *The Price of the Ticket* (London: Michael Joseph, 1985), p. 428.
14. Harold Cruse, 'Negroes and Jews: The Two Nationalisms and the Bloc(ked) Plurality,' in *The Crisis of the Negro Intellectual* (New York: Quill, 1984).
15. Baldwin, *The Price*, p. 430.
16. Stanley Crouch, 'Aunt Medea,' in *Notes of a Hanging Judge* (New York: Oxford University Press, 1990), p. 205.

60

'THINKING ABOUT GENOCIDE'

Mahmood Mamdani

[…]

No one can say with certainty how many Tutsi were killed between March and July of 1994 in Rwanda. In the fateful one hundred days that followed the downing of the presidential plane – and the coup d'état thereafter – a section of the army and civilian leadership organized the Hutu majority to kill all Tutsi, even babies. In the process, they also killed not only the Hutu political opposition, but also many nonpolitical Hutu who showed reluctance to perform what was touted as a 'national' duty. The estimates of those killed vary: between ten and fifty thousand Hutu, and between 500,000 and a million Tutsi.[1] Whereas the Hutu were killed as individuals, the Tutsi were killed as a group, recalling German designs to extinguish the country's Jewish population. This explicit goal is why the killings of Tutsi between March and July of 1994 must be termed 'genocide.' This single fact underlines a crucial similarity between the Rwandan genocide and the Nazi Holocaust.[2]

In the history of genocide, however, the Rwandan genocide raises a difficult political question. Unlike the Nazi Holocaust, the Rwandan genocide was not carried out from a distance, in remote concentration camps beyond national borders, in industrial killing camps operated by agents who often did no more than drop Zyklon B crystals into gas chambers from above. The Rwandan genocide was executed with the slash of machetes rather than the drop of crystals, with all the gruesome detail of a street murder rather than the bureaucratic

From Mahmood Mamdani (2001) 'Introduction', in *When Victims Become Killers: Colonialism, Nativism, and the Genocide in Rwanda*. Princeton, NJ: Princeton University Press.

efficiency of a mass extermination. The difference in technology is indicative of a more significant social difference. The technology of the holocaust allowed a few to kill many, but the machete had to be wielded by a single pair of hands. It required not one but many hacks of a machete to kill even one person. With a machete, killing was hard work, that is why there were often several killers for every single victim. Whereas Nazis made every attempt to separate victims from perpetrators, the Rwandan genocide was very much an intimate affair. It was carried out by hundreds of thousands, perhaps even more, and witnessed by millions. In a private conversation in 1997, a minister in the Rwanda Patriotic Front-led government contrasted the two horrors: 'In Germany, the Jews were taken out of their residences, moved to distant far away locations, and killed there, almost anonymously. In Rwanda, the government did not kill. It prepared the population, enraged it and enticed it. Your neighbors killed you.' And then he added, 'In Germany, if the population participated in the killing, it was not directly but indirectly. If the neighbor's son killed, it is because he joined the army.'[3]

The Rwandan genocide unfolded in just a hundred days. 'It was not just a small group that killed and moved,' a political commissar in the police explained to me in Kigali in July 1995. 'Because genocide was so extensive, there were killers in every locality – from ministers to peasants – for it to happen in so short a time and on such a large scale.' Opening the international conference on Genocide, Impunity and Accountability in Kigali in late 1995, the country's president, Pasteur Bizimungu, spoke of 'hundreds of thousands of criminals' evenly spread across the land:

> Each village of this country has been affected by the tragedy, either because the whole population was mobilized to go and kill elsewhere, or because one section undertook or was pushed to hunt and kill their fellow villagers. The survey conducted in Kigali, Kibungo, Byumba, Gitarama and Butare Préfectures showed that genocide had been characterized by torture and utmost cruelty. About forty-eight methods of torture were used countrywide. They ranged from burying people alive in graves they had dug up themselves, to cutting and opening wombs of pregnant mothers. People were quartered, impaled or roasted to death.

On many occasions, death was the consequence of ablation of organs, such as the heart, from alive people. In some cases, victims had to pay fabulous amounts of money to the killers for a quick death. The brutality that characterised the genocide has been unprecedented.[4]

[...]

The violence of the genocide was the result of both planning and participation. The agenda imposed from above became a gruesome reality to the extent it resonated with perspectives from below. Rather than accent one or the other side of this relationship and thereby arrive at either a state-centered or a society-centered explanation, a complete picture of the genocide needs to take both sides into account. For this was neither just a conspiracy from above that only needed enough time and suitable circumstance to mature, nor was it a popular *jacquerie* gone berserk. If the violence from below could not have spread without cultivation and direction from above, it is equally true that the conspiracy of the tiny fragment of *génocidaires* could not have succeeded had it not found resonance from below. The design from above involved a tiny minority and is easier to understand. The response and initiative from below involved multitudes and presents the true moral dilemma of the Rwandan genocide.

In sum, the Rwandan genocide poses a set of deeply troubling questions. Why did hundreds of thousands, those who had never before killed, take part in mass slaughter? Why did such a disproportionate number of the educated – not just members of the political elite but, as we shall see, civic leaders such as doctors, nurses, judges, human rights activists, and so on – play a leading role in the genocide? Similarly, why did places of shelter where victims expected sanctuary – churches, hospitals, and schools – turn into slaughterhouses where innocents were murdered in the tens and hundreds, and sometimes even thousands?

THREE SILENCES: A STARTING POINT

Accounts of the genocide, whether academic or popular, suffer from three silences. The first concerns the *history* of genocide: many write as if genocide has no history and as if the Rwandan genocide had no precedent, even in this century replete with political violence. The Rwandan genocide thus appears as an anthropological oddity. For Africans, it turns into a Rwandan oddity; and for non-Africans, the aberration is Africa. For both, the temptation is to dismiss Rwanda as exceptional. The second silence concerns the *agency* of the genocide: academic writings, in particular, have highlighted the design from above in a one-sided manner. They hesitate to acknowledge, much less explain, the participation – even initiative – from below.[5] When political analysis presents the genocide as exclusively a state project and ignores its subaltern and 'popular' character, it tends to reduce the violence to a set of meaningless outbursts, ritualistic and bizarre, like some ancient primordial twitch come to life. The third silence concerns the *geography* of the genocide. Since the genocide happened within the boundaries of Rwanda, there is a widespread tendency to assume that it must also be an outcome of processes that unfolded within the same boundaries. A focus confined to Rwandan state boundaries inevitably translates into a silence about regional processes that fed the dynamic leading to the genocide.

We may agree that genocidal violence cannot be understood as rational; yet, we need to understand it as thinkable. Rather than run away from it, we need to realize that it is the 'popularity' of the genocide that is its uniquely troubling aspect. In its social aspect, Hutu/Tutsi violence in the Rwandan genocide invites comparison with Hindu/Muslim violence at the time of the partition of colonial

India. Neither can be explained as simply a state project. One shudders to put the words 'popular' and 'genocide' together, therefore I put 'popularity' in quotation marks. And yet, one needs to explain the large-scale civilian involvement in the genocide. To do so is to contextualize it, to understand the logic of its development. My *main* objective in writing this book is to make the popular agency in the Rwandan genocide thinkable. [...]

By taking seriously the historical backdrop to political events, I hope to historicize both political choices and those who made these choices. If it is true that the choices were made from a historically limited menu, it is also the case that the identity of agents who made these choices was also forged within historically specific institutions. To benefit from a historically informed insight is not the same as to lapse into a politically irresponsible historicism. To explore the relationship between history and politics is to problematize the relationship between the historical legacy of colonialism and postcolonial politics. [...]

COLONIALISM AND GENOCIDE

[...]

I argue that the Rwandan genocide needs to be thought through within the logic of colonialism. The horror of colonialism led to two types of genocidal impulses. The first was the genocide of the native by the settler. It became a reality where the violence of colonial pacification took on extreme proportions. The second was the native impulse to eliminate the settler. Whereas the former was obviously despicable, the latter was not. The very political character of native violence made it difficult to think of it as an impulse to genocide. Because it was derivative of settler violence, the natives' violence appeared less of an outright aggression and more a self-defense in the face of continuing aggression. Faced with the violent denial of his humanity by the settler, the native's violence began as a counter to violence. It even seemed more like the affirmation of the native's humanity than the brutal extinction of life that it came to be. When the native killed the settler, it was violence by yesterday's victims. More of a culmination of anticolonial resistance than a direct assault on life and freedom, this violence of victims-turned-perpetrators always provoked a greater moral ambiguity than did the settlers' violence.

Settlers' Genocide

[...]

Whereas the prototype of settler violence in the history of modern colonialism is the near-extermination of Amerindians in the New World, the prototype of settler violence in the African colonies was the German annihilation of over 80 percent of the Herero population in the colony of German South West Africa in a single year, 1904.[6] Its context was Herero resistance to land and cattle appropriation by German settlers and their *Schutztruppe* allies. Faced with continuing armed resistance by the Herero, German opinion divided between two points of views, one championed by General Theodor Leutwein, who commanded the army in the colony, and the other by General Lothar von Trotha, who took over the military command when General Leutwein failed to put down native resistance. The difference between them illuminates the range of political choice in a colonial context.

General Trotha explained the difference in a letter:

> Now I have to ask myself how to end the war with the Hereros. The views of the Governor and also a few old Africa hands [*alte Afrikaner*] on the one hand, and my views on the other, differ completely. The first wanted to negotiate for some time already and regard the Herero nation as necessary labour material for the future development of the country. I believe that the nation as such should be annihilated, or, if this was not possible by tactical measures, have to be expelled from the country by operative means and further detailed treatment. This will be possible if the water-holes from Grootfontein to Gobabis are occupied. The constant movement of our troops will enable us to find the small groups of the nation who have moved back westwards and destroy them gradually.

Equally illuminating is General Trotha's rationale for the annihilation policy: 'My intimate knowledge of many central African tribes (Bantu and others) has everywhere convinced me of the necessity that the Negro does not respect treaties but only brute force.'[7]

The plan Trotha laid out in the letter is more or less the fate he meted to the Herero on the ground. To begin with, the army exterminated as many Herero as possible.[8] For those who fled, all escape routes except the one southeast to the Omeheke, a waterless sandveld in the Kalahari Desert, were blocked. The fleeing Herero were forcibly separated from their cattle and denied access to water holes, leaving them with but one option: to cross the desert into Botswana, in reality a march to death. This, indeed, is how the majority of the Herero perished. [...]

The genocide of the Herero was the first genocide of the twentieth century. The links between it and the Holocaust go beyond the building of concentration camps and the execution of an annihilation policy and are worth exploring. It is surely of significance that when General Trotha wrote, as above, of destroying 'African tribes with streams of blood,' he saw this as some kind of a Social Darwinist 'cleansing' after which 'something new' would 'emerge.' It is also relevant that, when the general sought to distribute responsibility for the genocide, he accused the missions of inciting the Herero with images 'of the bloodcurdling Jewish history of the Old Testament.'[9] [...] It seems to me that Hannah Arendt erred when she presumed a relatively uncomplicated relationship between settlers' genocide in the colonies and the Nazi Holocaust at home: When Nazis set out to annihilate Jews, it is far more likely that they thought of themselves as natives, and Jews as settlers. Yet, there is a link that connects the genocide of the Herero and the Nazi Holocaust to the Rwandan genocide. That link is *race branding*, whereby it became possible not only to set a group apart as an enemy, but also to exterminate it with an easy conscience.

Natives' Genocide

[...]

The great crime of colonialism went beyond expropriating the native, the name it gave to the indigenous population. *The greater crime was to politicize indigeneity in the first place*: first negatively, as a settler libel of the native; but then positively, as a native response, as a self-assertion. The dialectic of the settler and the native did not end with colonialism and political independence. To understand the logic of genocide, I argue, it is necessary to think through the political world that colonialism set into motion. This was the world of the settler and the native, a world organized around a binary preoccupation that was as compelling as it was confining. It is in this context that Tutsi, a group with a privileged relationship to power before colonialism, got constructed as a privileged *alien settler* presence, first by the great nativist revolution of 1959, and then by Hutu Power propaganda after 1990.

In its motivation and construction, I argue that the Rwandan genocide needs to be understood as a natives' genocide. It was a genocide by those who saw themselves as sons – and daughters – of the soil, and their mission as one of clearing the soil of a threatening *alien* presence. This was not an 'ethnic' but a 'racial' cleansing, not a violence against one who is seen as a neighbor but against one who is seen as a foreigner; not a violence that targets a transgression across a boundary into home but one that seeks to eliminate a foreign presence from home soil, literally and physically. From this point of view, we need to distinguish between racial and ethnic violence: ethnic violence can result in massacres, but not genocide. Massacres are about transgressions, excess; genocide questions the very legitimacy of a presence as alien. For the Hutu who killed, the Tutsi was a settler, not a neighbor. Rather than take these identities as a given, as a starting point of analysis, I seek to ask: When and how was Hutu made into a native identity and Tutsi into a settler identity? The analytical challenge is to understand the historical dynamic through which Hutu and Tutsi came to be synonyms for native and settler. [...]

NOTES

1. The lower estimate comes from the UN Commission of Experts. The figure of a million is often heard of in the media and in RPF statements. Gérard Prunier gave the figure as 'between 800,000 and 850,000' or roughly 11 percent of the population in his 1995 book. The 1997 multinational, multidonor evaluation team scaled the numbers down, writing that 'an estimated five to eight hundred thousand' were killed 'as a result of civil war and genocide' over three months in 1994. The final estimate has come from the 1999 book jointly published by Human Rights Watch and Fédération Internationale des Ligues des Droits de l'Homme. The book opens with the lower estimate: 'In the 13 weeks after April 6, 1994, at least half a million

people perished in the Rwandan genocide.' However, it then goes on to cite the demographer William Seltzer's estimate of 657,000 dead, a figure extrapolated from 1991 census data, which in turn are accepted as problematic by some authorities. See 'UN Commission of Experts Established Pursuant to Security Council Resolution 935 (1994) on Rwanda,' *Final Report*, Geneva, 25 November 1994; Gérard Prunier, *The Rwanda Crisis: History of a Genocide, 1959–1994* (London: Hurst & Co., 1995), p. 265; Tor Sellstom and Lennart Wohlgemuth, *The International Response to Conflict and Genocide: Lessons from the Rwanda Experience*, Study 1, *Historical Perspective: Some Explanatory Factors* (Uppsala, Sweden: The Nordic Africa Institute, 1997), p. 1; Human Rights Watch and Fédération Internationale des Ligues des Droits de l'Homme, 'Leave None to Tell the Story: Genocide in Rwanda' (London and New York: Human Rights Watch; and Paris: Fédération Internationale des Ligues des Droits de l'Homme, 1999), pp. 1 and 15.

2. Many Jewish scholars here insisted that it was the Nazi intention to eliminate Jews as a people – and not the numbers of Jews killed – that marked the Holocaust as different from any other mass killing in history. As we shall see, others, like Hannah Arendt, disagreed and pointed out that genocide too has a history. Michael R. Marrus, *The Holocaust in History* (New York: Meridian Penguin, 1987), pp. 24–28.
3. Patrick Mazimpaka, Interview, Kigali, 11 July 1997.
4. Opening speech by H. E. Pasteur Bizimungu, president of the Republic of Rwanda, International Conference on Genocide, Impunity and Accountability, Kigali, 1–5 November, 1995, mimeo, pp. 1–2, 3.
5. See, for example, the articles submitted at the CODESRIA conference on the Rwandan genocide, held in Arusha in March 1995, and the articles in the special edition on the Rwandan genocide in the official magazine of the African Studies Association of USA, Issues 23/2 (1995).
6. For details, see Jan-Bart Gewald, *Herero Heroes: A Socio-Political History of the Herero of Namibia, 1890–1923* (Oxford: James Currey, 1999) chapters 5 and 6, pp. 141–230; Tilman Dedering, ' "A Certain Rigorous Treatment of all Parts of the Nation": The Annihilation of the Herero in German South West Africa, 1904,' in Mark Levene and Penny Roberts, *The Massacre in History* (New York: Berghahn Books, 1999), pp. 204–222; Regina Jere-Malanda, 'The Tribe Germany Wants to Forget,' *New African* (London), no. 383 (March 2000): 16–21; Horst Drechsler, '*Let Us Die Fighting': The Struggle of the Herero and the Nama against German Imperialism (1884–1915)* (London: Zed Press, 1980).
7. Cited in Jan-Bart Gewald, *Herero Heroes: A Socio-Political History of the Herero of Namibia, 1890–1923* (Oxford: James Currey, 1999), p. 173.
8. Jan Cloete, who had acted as a guide for the Germans, deposed the following oath: 'I was present when the Herero were defeated in a battle at Hamakiri in the vicinity of Waterberg. After the battle all men, women and children who fell into German hands, wounded or otherwise, were mercilessly put to death. Then the Germans set off in pursuit of the rest, and all those found by the wayside and in the sandveld were shot down and bayoneted to death. The mass of the Herero men were unarmed and thus unable to offer resistance. They were just trying to get away with their cattle.' Drechsler, '*Let Us Die Fighting*,' p. 157.
9. Dedering, ' "A Certain Rigorous Treatment," ' p. 213.

61

'DARE TO COMPARE: AMERICANIZING THE HOLOCAUST'

Lilian Friedberg

[...]

In the pathological dynamic of genocidal histories, the perpetrator culture invariably turns its gaze to the horrors registered in the archives and accounts of the 'other guys.'[1] This is why Holocaust studies in the United States focus almost exclusively on the atrocity of Auschwitz, not of Wounded Knee or Sand Creek. Norman Finkelstein, in his discussion of the way images of the Holocaust have been manufactured to reap moral and economic benefits for members of the Jewish elite, states that the presence of the Holocaust Museum in Washington is 'particularly incongruous in the absence of a museum commemorating crimes in the course of American history' and makes specific reference to the slave trade and genocide against the American Indians.[2] Peter Novick suggests that the Holocaust has become a sort of 'civil religion' for American Jews who have lost touch with their own ethnic and religious identity, and asserts that 'in the United States the Holocaust is explicitly used for the purpose of national self-congratulation: the Americanization of the Holocaust has involved using it to demonstrate the difference between the Old World and the New, and to celebrate, by showing its negation, the American way of life.'[3]

The *Historikerstreit* or 'Historians' Debate' in Germany during the mid-1980s disrupted the traditional historiographical narrative, which placed three groups of actors at the scene of the Nazi crime – perpetrators, bystanders, and victims. [...]

From Lilian Friedberg (2000) 'Dare to Compare: Americanizing the Holocaust', *American Indian Quarterly*, vol. 24, no. 3, pp. 353–80.

The Historians' Debate directed international attention to the issue of historical liability as it relates to public memory and national identity in territories known to have been host to genocidal campaigns. However, what got lost in translation when the debate migrated to America was the very real opportunity this controversy might have presented for an authentic 'working through' or 'mastery' of *this* country's traumatic genocidal past. Instead, the dispute conveniently constructed a site of transference upon which the melancholic drama of 'manifest manners' could be acted out.[4] American intellectuals, confronted with the quandary of whether to see or not to see, chose to look the other way. [...]

The same kinds of arguments attempting to 'historicize' America's past in the interest of 'normalizing' its present from the perspective of the perpetrator population do not unleash the same scandalous international controversy as do similar efforts on the part of historians negotiating a revision of German history. The genocide against the Jews is considered an ugly chapter in Germany's past and acknowledged internationally as one of the gravest crimes against humanity in the twentieth century. But while the whole fabric of German culture remains 'under the shadow of Hitler,' the genocide against indigenous populations in North America is still today denied or dismissed as the inevitable prelude to the rise of the greatest nation on Earth.

Reactionary historian James Axtell, in his 1992 study, *Beyond 1492: Encounters in Colonial North America*, writes:

> We make a hash of our historical judgments because we continue to feel guilty about the real or imagined sins of our fathers and forefathers ... [We] can stop flogging ourselves with our 'imperialistic' origins and tarring ourselves with the broad brush of 'genocide.' As a huge nation of law and order and increasingly refined sensibility, we are not guilty of murdering Indian women and babies, of branding slaves on the forehead, or of claiming any real estate in the world we happen to fancy.[5]

Statements like this, when proffered in defense of Germany's genocidal history, elicit vehement opposition from the academic and intellectual community, yet, with regard to America's tragic past, go virtually unchallenged and are integrated into the canon of acceptable discourse.

As the success of Daniel Jonah Goldhagen's indictment of the German people in *Hitler's Willing Executioners: Ordinary Germans and the Holocaust* illustrates, public flogging of the German people for their willing participation in the melee represents an acceptable and indeed lucrative form of public and academic discourse. [...] It is interesting to note, in this context, that Native American scholar Ward Churchill's stellar and seminal piece of scholarship on Holocaust and denial in the Americas, *A Little Matter of Genocide*, did not meet with the same degree of public success.

[...]

But even before the Historians' Debate, the relative singularity of the Nazi Holocaust had long been the center of international debate. Uniqueness proponents such as Deborah Lipstadt, Steven Katz, Saul Friedländer, Michael Marrus, Yehuda Bauer, Lucy Dawidowicz, and others share an insistence on the exclusivity of the Nazi Holocaust as an unparalleled event in the history of the twentieth century. This view has been challenged by survivors and scholars, among them a number of Jewish intellectuals such as Hannah Arendt, Irving Louis Horowitz, Israel Charny, Helen Fein, Simon Wiesenthal, Norman Finkelstein, Peter Novick, and others. Increasingly, Native American scholars and their allies have entered the conversation, pointing out that the historical archive of the *American* Holocaust has been compiled, collated, and indeed constructed to a large degree by perpetrators, their descendants, and beneficiaries writing from a subject position inflected with a vested interest in maintaining the illusion of innocence concerning the 'facts of the case.'

The exclusivists' most compelling argument against the comparability of the two acts of genocide has been that the decimation of the American Indian population, unlike the extermination of the Jews, was unintentional – 'caused by microbes, not militia ... that is, this depopulation happened unwittingly rather than by design.'[6] Preeminent uniqueness proponent Steven Katz, in *The Holocaust in Historical Context*, while documenting the fact that the American Holocaust far exceeded the Nazi Holocaust in scope, at the same time reduces the American travesty to a mere case of 'depopulation.'[7] These conclusions are drawn from comparisons not of a simple corpse count but rather of the *rate* of extermination experienced by each group. Recent studies demonstrate that precontact population estimates generated by historians and demographers from the subject position of the perpetrators have been egregiously low. It is today commonly assumed that precontact populations were far and above the one-million figure that has acted as a standard of measure for centuries. More recent and more honest studies estimate the precontact civilization to have been between nine and eighteen million. This standard of measure puts the rate of attrition of indigenous populations at between 98 and 99 percent – that is, near total extermination. The rate of attrition of Jewish populations in Europe is commonly calculated at between 60 and 65 percent. Put in terms of survival rates, this means that two-thirds of the global Jewish population and about one third of the European Jewish population survived the Nazi Holocaust, whereas a mere remnant population of 1 to 2 percent survived the American Holocaust. This seriously calls into question any notion of 'unparalleled' or 'total extermination' of the Jews in the Nazi Holocaust.

Katz argues that the Nazi Holocaust is 'phenomenologically' unique based on the 'merciless, exceptionless, biocentric intentionality of Hitler's "war against the Jews".'[8] Katz's argument centers on *documented* intentionality and governmental policy in the Nazi period. What Katz does not take into account is that a twelve-year period in a twentieth-century industrialized society lends itself more readily to documentation than a five-hundred-year period, most of which is historically and geographically situated in the midst of a preindustrial 'virgin wasteland,' nor does he significantly engage the discourse generated by Native American scholars in recent years. It does not, however, take a paragon of intellectual prowess to deduce an implied intent to 'destroy, in whole or in part, a national, ethnic, racial or religious group,' from the events that transpired in the process of 'depopulating' the New World – a slaughter that Katz patently refuses to define as 'genocide' even though it conforms precisely to the definition of the phenomenon as outlined by Raphael Lemkin, who coined the term in his 1944 *Axis Rule in Occupied Europe*.[9] The murder of 96 percent of any given population does not occur 'inadvertently,' especially when members of that group are viewed by their assassins as belonging to a separate (and inferior) national, ethnic, racial *and* religious order.

Furthermore, there is evidence to suggest that the introduction of diseases to the Native populations of North America was anything but an incidental byproduct of 'westward expansion.' In what is likely the world's first documented case of genocide accomplished by bacterial means, Lord Jeffrey Amherst suggested that smallpox-infected blankets be distributed to the Ottawa and Lenape peoples, stating in a 1763 letter to his subordinate, Colonel Henry Bouquet, 'You will do well to [infect] the Indians by means of blankets as well as to try every other method that can serve to extirpate this [execrable] race.'[10] This statement indicates that the annihilation of the Indian population by way of disease was neither arbitrary nor incidental to the aims of the European settler population and its government. Even as early as 1763, the settler population and its sovereign representatives acted in full cognizance of the impact their introduction of disease would have on the Native populations. [...] Survivor testimony and statistical records from the Nazi death camps reveal that the uncontrolled spread of disease among inmates was *also* a major factor contributing to the death toll during the Nazi Holocaust, but that argument has never been forwarded in favor of exonerating the perpetrators – at least not in serious scholarship on the subject.

If, as Yehuda Bauer contends, '[t]here was no governmental intention to exterminate the victim population' in the Americas, how else are we to understand the now well-known statement attributed to General Philip Henry Sheridan at Fort Cobb in January of 1889: 'The only good Indian is a dead Indian?'[11] While Bauer concedes that 'important figures in the U.S. administration expressed genocidal hopes and intentions,' he still insists that 'there was no clear governmental policy of total murder.'[12] It would seem redundant, in this context, to point to the innumerable studies that have been conducted since 1945 in the attempt to ascertain whether or not Adolf Hitler himself had issued the order for the Final Solution.

The introduction of diseases to indigenous populations was accompanied by a systematic destruction of 'the indigenous agricultural base [in order to] impose starvation conditions upon entire peoples, dramatically lowering their resistance to disease and increasing their susceptibility to epidemics.'[13] What is more, the ideology of Manifest Destiny is itself founded on an implied intent to kill – it is the 'central constituent ideology translated into action' that Bauer posits as the defining characteristic that sets the Nazi Holocaust apart from all other genocidal campaigns in the history of humanity.

[...]

Churchill speaks in terms of the need for a 'denazification ... a fundamental alteration in the consciousness of this country.'[14] I would suggest that 'de-manifestation' is a more apt designation for the paradigmatic shift requisite for decentering the hegemonistic reign of the 'master narratives' of Manifest Destiny and the master race that govern our understanding of history as it relates to national identity in the United States. Thinking in terms of 'de-manifestation' has the advantage of disaggregating the specific modalities of similar, but not identical, historical phenomena and of dislocating – geographically and intellectually – the source of the 'problem' from the site of European history to that of American history. What follows is an attendant shift in temporal focus that allows us to properly place the postulates of Manifest Destiny and the master race in historically correct chronological order with relation to the *subsequent* emergence of theories of *Lebensraumpolitik* and the assumed superiority of the Aryan race on the European continent. Whereas 'denazification' clearly connotes a 'thing of the past,' 'de-manifestation' implies a present, 'manifest' reality. From this vantage point, the German *Sonderweg* is rerouted and an already trammeled trail of rampant plundering, pillage, and mass murder is revealed to have been blazed in the forward wake of the historical caesura that the Nazi Holocaust represents.

NOTES

1. See also Henry R. Huttenbach, 'The Psychology and Politics of Genocide Denial: A Comparison of Four Case Studies,' in *Studies in Comparative Genocide*, eds. Levon Chorbajian and George Shirinian (New York: St. Martin's Press, 1999), 216: 'Denial has become an integral part of genocide; not to take this aspect into consideration is to fail to comprehend a major component of the dynamics of extermination.'
2. At the time of this writing, Finkelstein's most recent work *The Holocaust Industry: Reflections on the Exploitation of Jewish Suffering* was scheduled for publication by Verso in July 2000. Citations here are from an 11 June 2000 review by Bryan Appleyard published in the online version of *The Sunday Times* (http://www.Sunday-times.co.uk/ news/pages/sti/2000/06/11/stirevnws02006.html).
3. Peter Novick, *The Holocaust in American Life* (New York: Houghton Mifflin 1999), 13.
4. Gerald Vizenor, *Manifest Manners: Narrative on Postindian Survivance* (Lincoln: University of Nebraska Press, 1994), 4.
5. James Axtell, *Beyond 1492: Encounters in Colonial North America* (New York: Oxford University Press, 1992), 262–63.
6. Steven Katz, 'The Uniqueness of the Holocaust: The Historical Dimension,' in *Is the Holocaust Unique?: Perspectives on Comparative Genocide*, ed. Alan Rosenbaum (Boulder Co: Westview Press, 1996), 21.

7. See Katz's chapter on 'The Depopulation of the New World in the Sixteenth Century' in *The Holocaust in Historical Context: Volume I: The Holocaust and Mass Death before the Modern Age* (New York: Oxford University Press, 1994), 87–91.

8. Katz, *The Holocaust in Historical Context*, 59.

9. Raphael Lemkin, *Axis Rule in Occupied Europe* (Washington DC: Carnegie Endowment for International Peace, 1944), cited in Katz, *Holocaust in Historical Context*, 125. Lemkin's definition has been reprinted in most standard works on genocide. For the reader who may be unfamiliar with the text of Article 2 of the UN Convention on Genocide adopted by the General Assembly in November 1948, which was based on Lemkin's original delineation of the term and the crime's parameters, I reprint it here: 'In the present Convention, genocide means any of the following acts committed with intent to destroy, in whole or in part, a national, ethnical, racial or religious group, as such:

    1. Killing members of the group.
    2. Causing serious bodily or mental harm to members of the group.
    3. Deliberately inflicting on the group conditions of life calculated to bring about its physical destruction in whole or in part.
    4. Imposing measures intended to prevent births within the group.
    5. Forcibly transferring children of the group to another group, (Cited in Katz, *Holocaust in Historical Context*, 125)

Ward Churchill's *A Little Matter of Genocide: Holocaust and Denial in the Americas 1492 – Present* (San Francisco: City Lights Books, 1997) firmly establishes, point by point, the manner and degree to which policies and actions on the part of the U.S. government and its people conform to the definition of genocide as outlined by Lemkin and by the UN convention.

10. Lord Jeffrey Amherst, cited in Churchill, *Matter of Genocide*, 154.

11. While sources may disagree on the exact wording of Sheridan's now infamous statement, the sentiment, regardless of wording, is always the same. My source here is *The Oxford Dictionary of Quotations* (Oxford: Oxford University Press, 1955), 499. The examples cited here reflect but the tip of the iceberg in a documented litany of official and unofficial statements issued by governmental authorities and representatives of the people of the United States, which express clear and unequivocal intent to exterminate the entire indigenous population of North America.

12. Yehuda Bauer, 'Comparison of Genocides' in Chorbajian and Shirinian, *Studies in Comparative Genocide*, 38.

13. Lenore A. Stiffarm with Phil Lane, 'The Demography of Native North America,' in *The State of Native America: Genocide, Colonization, and Resistance*, ed. Annette Jaimes (Boston: South End Press, 1992), 33.

14. Ward Churchill, 'A Summary of Arguments Against the Naming of a University Residence Hall After Clinton M. Tyler' (report prepared at the request of the assistant vice chancellor for academic services, University of Colorado at Boulder, July 1981, cited in Annette Jaimes, ed., *The State of Native America*, 5).

62

THE HOLOCAUST IN AMERICAN LIFE

Peter Novick

[...]

Part of my puzzlement about how Americans became so 'Holocaust conscious' had to do with timing: why now? Generally speaking, historical events are most talked about shortly after their occurrence, then they gradually move to the margin of consciousness. It was in the 1920s and 1930s, not the 1950s and 1960s, that novels, films, and collective consciousness were obsessed with the carnage of Passchendaele and the Somme. By the fifties and sixties – forty years and more after the events of the Great War – they had fallen down a memory hole where only historians scurry around in the dark. The most-viewed films and the best-selling books about the Vietnam War almost all appeared within five or ten years of the end of that conflict, as did the Vietnam Veterans Memorial in Washington. With the Holocaust the rhythm has been very different: hardly talked about for the first twenty years or so after World War II; then, from the 1970s on, becoming ever more central in American public discourse – particularly, of course, among Jews, but also in the culture at large. What accounts for this unusual chronology?

The other part of my puzzlement was: why here? There is nothing surprising about the Holocaust's playing a central role in the consciousness of Germany, the country of the criminals and their descendants. The same might be said of Israel, a country whose population – or much of it – has a special relationship to the victims of the crime. To a somewhat lesser extent, this could be said of

From Peter Novick (1999) 'Introduction', in *The Holocaust in American Life*. New York: Houghton Mifflin.

nations occupied by Germany during the war which were the scene of the deportation to death (or the actual murder) of their Jewish citizens. In all of these countries the parents or grandparents of the present generation directly confronted – resisted, assisted, in any case witnessed – the crime; in all cases, a fairly close connection. In the case of the United States none of these connections are present. The Holocaust took place thousands of miles from America's shores. Holocaust survivors or their descendants are a small fraction of 1 percent of the American population, and a small fraction of American Jewry as well. Only a handful of perpetrators managed to make it to the United States after the war. Americans, including many American Jews, were largely unaware of what we now call the Holocaust while it was going on; the nation was preoccupied with defeating the Axis. The United States was simply not connected to the Holocaust in the ways in which these other countries are. So, in addition to 'why now?' we have to ask 'why here?'

Although these questions haven't been looked at systematically by scholars – perhaps because they haven't been looked at systematically – there is something of a tacit consensus on the answer. This answer – sometimes explicitly, always implicitly, Freudian – treats the current centrality of the Holocaust as an inevitable development. 'Trauma,' according to the standard dictionary of psychoanalysis, is 'an event in the subject's life defined by its intensity, by the subject's incapacity to respond adequately to it, and by the upheaval and long-lasting effects that it brings about in the psychical organization.' For a time the trauma can be repressed, but 'repressed material ... has a permanent tendency to re-emerge into consciousness.'[1] Indeed, in the Freudian canon, 'trauma' and 'repression' define each other. Trauma is that which is so unbearable that it has to be repressed; repression is the consequence of something too traumatic to be borne; together they inevitably give rise to 'the return of the repressed.' The Holocaust, according to this influential explanation, had been a traumatic event, certainly for American Jews, more diffusely for all Americans. Earlier silence was a manifestation of repression; the explosion of talk in recent years has been 'the return of the repressed.'

For all of its elegance, I don't find this schema persuasive in explaining the evolution of Holocaust consciousness in the United States. Its applicability to various European countries, and to Israel, has been treated by other writers, and won't much concern us here. In the United States, in the special case of Holocaust survivors, the succession of trauma, repression, and return of the repressed often seems plausible. (Even here, though, as we'll see, survivors in the late 1940s frequently wanted to talk about their Holocaust experiences and were discouraged from doing so.) And surely there were some American Jews – perhaps even some gentiles – for whom the Holocaust was a traumatic experience. But the available evidence doesn't suggest that, overall, American Jews (let alone American gentiles) were traumatized by the Holocaust, in any worthwhile sense of that term. They were often shocked, dismayed, saddened, but that's not the same thing, certainly not for purposes of setting in train the inexorable progression of repression and the return of the repressed. Characteristically, it is simply assumed that the Holocaust *must* have been traumatic. And if it wasn't talked about, this *must* have been repression.

There is another way to look at the evolution of Holocaust consciousness in the United States, one that doesn't involve conjuring up such dubious entities as a 'social unconscious.' In the 1920s the French sociologist Maurice Halbwachs began to study what he was one of the first to call 'collective memory.' Instead of viewing collective memory as the past working its will on the present, Halbwachs explored the ways in which present concerns determine what of the past we remember and how we remember it. [...]²

Collective memory, as Halbwachs used the phrase, is not just historical knowledge shared by a group. Indeed, collective memory is in crucial senses ahistorical, even anti-historical. To understand something historically is to be aware of its complexity, to have sufficient detachment to see it from multiple perspectives, to accept the ambiguities, including moral ambiguities, of protagonists' motives and behavior. Collective memory simplifies; sees events from a single, committed perspective; is impatient with ambiguities of any kind; reduces events to mythic archetypes. Historical consciousness, by its nature, focuses on the *historicity* of events – that they took place then and not now, that they grew out of circumstances different from those that now obtain. Memory, by contrast, has no sense of the passage of time; it denies the 'pastness' of its objects and insists on their continuing presence. Typically a collective memory, at least a significant collective memory, is understood to express some eternal or essential truth about the group – usually tragic. A memory, once established, comes to define that eternal truth, and, along with it, an eternal identity, for the members of the group. [...]

If in looking at Holocaust memory in the United States we take Halbwachs's approach, relating memory to current concerns, we're led to look at just what those concerns have been, how they've been defined, and who has defined them. We'll consider how those concerns have, in one period, made Holocaust memory seem inappropriate, useless, or even harmful; in another period, appropriate and desirable. As we examine the changing fortunes of Holocaust memory, we'll be struck by how they relate to changing circumstances and, particularly among American Jews, changing decisions about collective self-understanding and self-representation.

[...]

The growth of a 'victim culture' wasn't the cause of American Jewry's focusing on the Holocaust in recent decades, but it has been an important background condition. As we'll see, in the 1940s and 1950s American Jews believed they had more reason than others to shun a victim identity, and this resulted in conscious decisions to downplay the Holocaust. By the 1980s and 1990s many Jews, for various reasons, wanted to establish that they too were members of a 'victim community.' Their contemporary situation offered little in the way of

[...]

NOTES

1. J. Laplanche and J.-B. Pontalis, *The Language of Psychoanalysis* (New York, 1973), 465, 398.
2. A good introduction to Halbwachs's thought is Lewis A. Coser, ed., *Maurice Halbwachs on Collective Memory* (Chicago, 1992).
3. French Jewish filmmaker Marcel Ophuls observed that 'New York Jews who never got any closer than Rumpelmayer's to the Warsaw ghetto claim the uniqueness of their suffering.' (Joan Dupont, 'Marcel Ophuls: Seeking Truth in an Uneasy Present,' *International Herald Tribune*, 15 November 1994.)
4. Cynthia Ozick, 'All the World Wants the Jews Dead,' *Esquire* 82 (November 1974): 103ff.
5. Yosef Hayim Yerushalmi, *Zakhor: Jewish History and Jewish Memory* (Seattle, 1982), 5.
6. There are exceptions. See Raphael Patai, 'Memory in Religion,' *Midstream* 29 (December 1983).
7. As a secularist, I'm not entitled to object to all of this on religious grounds, but it grates on me all the same, just as, without observing the laws of *kashrut*, I'm put off by the idea of butter on a meat sandwich.

INDEX

Adorno, Theodor W., 5, 6, 8, 10, 12, 67, 104–5, 208, 263, 273–4, 275, 288, 289–90, 293, 294–6, 318, 325, 371, 389, 391, 396–7, 417, 442

Agamben, Giorgio, 11, 230–1, 232

Akiba, Rabbi, 238, 239–40

Aleichem, Sholem, 338n

Alter, Robert, 337

Améry, Jean, 5, 7, 11–12, 25, 26, 27

Amherst, Lord Jeffrey, 471

Anderson, Benedict, 326

Antelme, Robert, 304

Appelfeld, Aharon, 348–51

Appleby, Joyce, 202

Aquinas, Thomas, 399

Archilochus, 302

Arendt, Hannah, 5, 7, 8, 11, 36, 94n, 208, 230, 231, 232, 254, 268, 270n, 333, 425, 448, 465, 467n, 470

Aristotle, 259

Avaloff-Bermondt, Prince Paul von, 158

Axtell, James, 469

Bach-Zelewski, Erich von dem, 201

Badiou, Alain, 11

Bakhtin, Mikhail, 14

Baldwin, James, 459

Baron, Salo, 208

Barthes, Roland, 421

Bartov, Omer, 60–1

Bataille, Georges, 8, 104, 105, 204n

Baudrillard, Jean, 5, 13, 373

Bauer, Yehuda, 441, 442, 470, 471

Bauman, Zygmunt, 9–10, 11, 60, 61, 231, 268–9, 456–7

Beaujoyeulx, Balthazar, 156

Beckett, Samuel, 12, 283, 287, 391

Benjamin, Walter, 12, 64, 155, 157, 211, 266, 273, 285, 291–4, 297, 314, 344, 372, 387, 399, 442

Berger, Joseph, 304

Bernal, Martin, 458

Bernstein, Michael André, 14, 326–7

Bettelheim, Bruno, 149, 171–3

Bhabha, Homi K., 326

Bialik, Chaim Nachman, 411, 412

Bischoff, Josef, 158

Bizimungu, Pasteur, 462

Blanchot, Maurice, 2, 12, 129, 204n, 212, 274, 315, 448

Bock, Gisela, 9, 148–9, 182

Bohrer, Karl Heinz, 391

Borowski, Tadeusz, 394–5

Bos, Pascale, 9, 148, 149

Bouquet, Colonel Henry, 471

Brecht, Bertolt, 52, 151, 277, 286, 388

Bromberg, Zahava, 422n

Broszat, Martin, 75, 217

Brown, Wendy, 18

Browning, Christopher, 8, 9, 105, 106, 342–3, 353n

Burke, Kenneth, 8, 104

Butler, Judith, 4

Caruth, Cathy, 16, 189, 212

Celan, Paul, 12, 274–5, 309, 311, 314, 316, 317n, 388, 390

Céline, Louis-Ferdinand, 92

Challaye, Félicien, 91, 92

Charny, Israel, 470

Churchill, Ward, 469, 472

Cloete, Jan, 467n

Cohen, Arthur A., 10, 229

Cohn-Bendit, Daniel, 415n

Cole, Tim, 18
Coughlin, Charles, 125
Coulanges, Fustel de, 277
Crimp, Douglas, 434
Crouch, Stanley, 459
Cruse, Harold, 459
Culler, Jonathan, 4, 5
Czerniakow, Adam, 366n

Danto, Arthur, 326
Darré, Walter, 161
Dawidowicz, Lucy, 470
De-Nur, Yehiel, 7
Delbo, Charlotte, 5, 7, 25, 26, 27, 174–5
Deleuze, Gilles, 148, 154
Derczansky, Alex, 411
Derrida, Jacques, 5, 12, 274–5, 314,
    315–16, 317n
Dietzgen, Wilhelm, 279
Diner, Dan, 1, 16, 60, 297, 408, 446, 450n
Dostoevsky, Fyodor, 346
Dwinger, Edwin, 153

Eckhardt, A. Roy, 11
Eichmann, Adolf, 6–8, 10, 73, 208, 230,
    246–51, 333, 361
Elias, Norbert, 156
Enzensberger, Hans Magnus, 43
Ettinger, Shmuel, 447
Ezrahi, Sidra DeKoven, 275

Fackenheim, Emil L., 10–11, 230, 231,
    266–8
Fassbinder, Rainer Werner, 13, 377
Faurisson, Robert, 260, 449n
Fein, Helen, 470
Felman, Shoshana, 194, 327
Fest, Joachim, 67, 377
Fink, Ida, 25
Finkelstein, Norman, 18, 441, 468, 470
Finkielkraut, Alain, 411
Flaubert, Gustave, 277
Foscolo, Ugo, 34
Frank, Anne, 6, 12, 170
Frank, Walter, 151
Freed, James Ingo, 397–9, 400, 402
Fresco, Nadine, 17, 408, 413, 416

Freud, Sigmund, 14, 16, 73, 104, 154,
    156, 189, 190, 193, 194, 195–7, 201,
    202, 209, 214, 215–16, 218–19, 290,
    296
Freyer, Hans, 66
Frick, Wilhelm, 163
Friedberg, Lilian, 443
Friedlander, Henry, 60, 61, 442
Friedlander, Saul, 5, 9, 13, 20n, 25, 60, 75,
    190, 343, 372, 470
Funkenstein, Amos, 229

Garçon, Maurice, 42
Gerz, Esther, 408, 432–6
Gerz, Jochen, 408, 432–6, 437n
Gide, André, 244
Gilroy, Paul, 17, 442
Glucksmann, André, 445
Goebbels, Joseph, 125
Goethe, Johann Wolfgang von, 50
Goldenberg, Myrna, 147, 185n
Goldhagen, Daniel Jonah, 8, 469
Grafe, Frieda, 156
Green, Gerald, 289
Greenberg, Irving, 10
Greenberg, Uri Zvi, 353n
Grossman, Atina, 185n
Guattari, Félix, 148, 154

Habermas, Jürgen, 10, 59–60
Halbwachs, Maurice, 443, 476
Haman, 237, 238
Hartman, Geoffrey, 5, 15, 275
Hartmann, Eric, 401–2
Hartmann, Georg Heinrich, 151
Hausner, Gideon, 249
Hegel, Georg Wilhelm Friedrich, 11, 263,
    285, 286, 293, 315
Heidegger, Martin, 2, 16, 66, 127, 130,
    202, 263, 264, 314, 315–16, 317n
Heinemann, Marlene, 186n
Helvetius, Claude-Adrien, 315
Hersey, John, 197
Heydrich, Reinhard, 70
Hilberg, Raul, 82–3, 210, 211
Himmler, Heinrich, 9, 60, 69–71, 72, 73,
    98, 163, 200, 253, 304

Hirsch, Freddy, 367n
Hirsch, Marianne, 16, 408
Hitler, Adolf, 8, 19, 30, 39, 44, 49, 63, 67, 71, 72, 85, 87, 92, 98, 103, 104, 107–11, 116, 123, 125, 129, 154, 157–8, 161, 230, 238, 239–40, 247, 253, 285, 317n, 377, 379n, 383, 444, 448, 469, 471
Hoheisel, Horst, 432
Horkheimer, Max, 8, 10, 104–5, 134, 293, 294
Horowitz, Louis, 470
Horowitz, Sara, 9
Höss, Rudolph, 73
Howe, Irving, 273, 274
Hugo, Victor, 243
Hunt, Lynn, 202
Hussein, Saddam, 449
Huyssen, Andreas, 13, 15, 372

Irigaray, Luce, 156

Jabès, Edmond, 300
Jäckel, Eberhard, 67
Jackson, Robert H., 248
Jacob, Margaret, 202
Jacobson, Edith, 65
Jameson, Fredric, 342, 344, 345n
Jankélévitch, Vladimir, 411
Jaspers, Karl, 63, 64, 66, 425
Jentsch, Ernst, 73
Jong, Louis de, 424
Jünger, Ernst, 66, 127, 129, 130

Kafka, Franz, 37, 285
Kant, Immanuel, 64, 74n, 263, 285, 293
Kaplan, Marion, 9, 186n
Karski, Jan, 392
Kastner, Rudolph, 208
Katz, Steven, 441, 448, 470–1
Kellner, Hans, 321
Kempner, Robert M. W., 36
Khomeini, Ayatollah, 449
Kiefer, Anselm, 372, 383–8
Kierkegaard, Søren, 284
King, Jr., Martin Luther, 458
Klee, Paul, 278

Kluger, Ruth, 5, 7, 25, 26–7
Koch, Gertrud, 327, 371–2
Kocka, Jürgen, 67
Kracauer, Siegfried, 156
Kreis, Wilhelm, 388
Kulka, Otto Dov, 447

Lacan, Jacques, 189
LaCapra, Dominick, 16, 20n, 190, 206–7, 215
Lacoue-Labarthe, Philippe, 8, 105, 446
Lang, Berel, 325
Langbein, Hermann, 303, 304
Langer, Lawrence, 15, 20n, 26, 149, 173–4, 327, 391
Lanzmann, Claude, 53, 54, 59, 327, 360–6, 372, 390, 392–5, 446
Laub, Dori, 25, 190–1, 195, 197, 421
Leibniz, Gottfried Wilhelm von, 259, 282, 391
Lemkin, Raphael, 451–2, 453, 471
Lenin, Vladimir, 346
Lerman, Miles, 400
Lerner, Richard, 457
Leutwein, General Theodor, 465
Levi, Primo, 5, 7, 11–12, 25–6, 27, 142–3, 201, 239, 320, 347, 457
Levinas, Emmanuel, 5, 10, 11, 230, 231, 264, 267, 268, 305, 316
Lewental, Salmen, 303
Leys, Ruth, 16
Libeskind, Daniel, 398–400
Lippe, Rudolf zur, 156
Lipstadt, Deborah, 2, 470
Littell, Franklin, 11
Lowe, Judah, 312
Löwith, Karl, 293
Lukács, Georg, 263
Lyotard, Jean-François, 5, 204n, 210, 231, 318–19

MacIntyre, Alasdair, 326
McLuhan, Marshall, 373, 381
Mallarmé, Stephan, 302
Mamdani, Mahmood, 442
Man, Paul de, 2, 16, 204n
Mann, Rudolf, 152

Mann, Thomas, 44, 357
Mannheim, Karl, 317n
Marcel, Gabriel, 39
Marrus, Michael, 470
Marx, Karl, 64, 134–5, 138–9n, 263, 285, 293
Metz, Johann Baptist, 266–8
Milchman, Alan, 17, 441
Milgram, Stanley, 141
Milton, John, 332
Milton, Sybil, 402
Mitscherlich, Alexander, 426
Mitscherlich, Margerete, 426
Mohanty, Satya, 27
Moi, Toril, 181
Molo, Walter von, 44
Mommsen, Hans, 67
Montefiore, Alan, 74
Morrison, Toni, 17, 407, 459
Mosse, George, 134
Müller, Phillip, 363
Müller-Hill, Benno, 97, 457
Musil, Robert, 14
Mussolini, Benito, 104, 116, 119–20, 125

Nair, Sami, 390
Neher, André, 40
Niborski, Itzhok, 412
Nietzsche, Friedrich, 39–40, 130, 263, 301, 431
Nolte, Ernst, 68, 216–17, 444, 445
North, Michael, 434
Novick, Peter, 18, 407, 441, 443, 468, 470
Nowinski, Ira, 402

Oertzen, Friedrich von, 151
Ofer, Dalia, 9
Osten, Edmund von, 151
Ozick, Cynthia, 477

Pawelczynska, Anna, 175
Pétain, Henri, 91–2
Peukert, Detlev J. K., 449n
Peukert, Helmut, 267
Picart, Yvonne, 46
Piwonski, Jan, 362
Plato, 333

Podchlebnik, Mordechai, 367n
Poliakov, Léon, 208
Popper, Karl, 67
Postone, Moishe, 8, 105, 106
Proctor, Robert, 457
Proudhon, Pierre, 135, 139n
Prunier, Gérard, 466n

Raczymow, Henri, 16, 17, 407–8, 416–17
Radermacher, Norbert, 432
Rassinier, Paul, 449n
Rawicz, Piotr, 289
Reitlinger, Gerald, 36, 97, 208
Reitz, Edgar, 14, 217–18
Ricoeur, Paul, 326
Riefenstahl, Leni, 372, 379n
Ringelheim, Joan, 9, 149, 179–80
Rittner, Carol, 9
Rogat, Yosal, 250
Rolland, Romain, 91
Rorty, Richard, 326
Rose, Gillian, 11, 231
Rosenberg, Alan, 17, 442
Rosenberg, Alfred, 127–8, 129–30
Rosenfeld, Alvin, 175, 317n
Rosenzweig, Franz, 263
Rossin, Lutz, 153
Roth, John, 9
Roth, Philip, 14
Rousset, David, 25
Rubenstein, Richard, 10
Rummel, Rudolph, 453–4
Russell, Bertrand, 108
Rymkiewicz, Jaroslaw M., 14

Sachs, Nelly, 310
Said, Edward, 4
Salomon, Ernst, 152
Santner, Eric, 14, 16, 190, 343
Sartre, Jean-Paul, 199, 390, 392, 393
Scarry, Elaine, 372, 402
Schelling, Friedrich Wilhelm Joseph von, 128
Schmitt, Carl, 66, 230, 255
Scholem, Gershom (Gerhard), 278, 294, 423
Schönberg, Arnold, 399

Schwarzhuber, Lagerführer, 304
Scott, Joan, 27
Segev, Tom, 7
Seltzer, Mark, 16
Seltzer, William, 467n
Semprun, Jorge, 25, 359n
Shackle, George, 76, 77
Shaw, Bernard, 284
Sheridan, General Philip Henry, 471
Silverman, Kaja, 422n
Sontag, Susan, 13, 372
Spanos, William, 449n
Speer, Albert, 377, 383, 385, 386
Spiegelman, Anja, 418–19, 420, 421
Spiegelman, Art, 16, 407, 408, 417–22
Spiegelman, Nadja, 419
Spiegelman, Richieu, 418, 419–20
Spiegelman, Vladek, 418, 419–21
Spivak, Gayatri, 4
Stalin, Joseph, 71, 85, 87, 95n, 304, 444
Stangl, Franz, 31
Steiner, George, 93
Storey, Robert G., 246
Strauss, Leo, 350
Styron, William, 175
Syberberg, Hans-Jürgen, 13, 376, 379n

Tal, Uriel, 79
Taylor, Charles, 326
Theweleit, Klaus, 8, 148
Thucydides, 130
Tinguely, Jean, 433–4
Tobey, Mark, 436
Tolstoy, Leo, 289

Tournier, Michel, 375, 377
Traub, Barbara Fischman, 355, 356
Trotha, General Lothar von, 465
Trunk, Isaiah, 77
Tsaytlin, Aaron, 288–9
Tsvetayeva, Marina, 309

Vabres, Donnedieu de, 248
Vishniac, Roman, 412
Voltaire, François Marie Arouet de, 282, 391

Wagener, Wilhelm, 152
Wagner, Richard, 379n, 383
Weber, Max, 64
Weigand, Wilhelm, 151
Weigel, Sigrid, 273, 274
Weil, Eric, 245
Weinberg, Jeshajahu, 398
Weissberg, Liliane, 371–2
Weitzman, Lenore, 9
White, Hayden, 14, 326, 337
Wiemers-Borchelshof, Franz, 151
Wiesel, Elie, 25, 59, 325, 397, 413, 445, 478
Wiesenthal, Simon, 29, 470
Wieviorka, Annette, 412
Winnicott, D. W., 215

Yaeger, Patricia, 16
Yerushalmi, Yosef, 478
Young, James E., 184, 325–6, 408, 442

Žižek, Slavoj, 4, 203